w, Appendixes

DICTIONARY OF
COMPUTING AND
INFORMATION TECHNOLOGY

English–Swedish

DICTIONARY OF
COMPUTING
AND
INFORMATION
TECHNOLOGY

English–Swedish

S. M. H. Collin
Johan Hjelm
Jan Sandred
Bo Lindestam

PETER COLLIN PUBLISHING

First published in Great Britain 1990
by Peter Collin Publishing Ltd
8 The Causeway, Teddington, Middlesex, TW11 0HE

© S.M.H. Collin and Esselte Ordbok AB 1990

British Library Cataloguing in Publication Data

Collin, S.M.H., *1966–*
English – Swedish dictionary of computing and information
technology.
   1. Computer systems
   I. Title
   004

   ISBN 0-948549-16-5

Computer processing by Compulexis, Charlton-on-Otmoor, Oxford
Text computer typeset by Systemset, Stotfold, Hertfordshire

Förord

Esselte Ordboks fackordböcker har som grund en serie enspråkiga engelska fackordböcker utgivna av Peter Collin Publishing Ltd. Varje bok omfattar ca 5 000 – 8 000 uppslagsord med fraser som utgör ett brittiskt-amerikanskt basordförråd inom respektive fack, t. ex. Business, Law, Computing/Information Technology. I den svenska versionen har uppslagsord och definierade fraser försetts med översättningar. Definitionerna av uppslagsord och fraser på enkel engelska har behållits. Förutom de översatta fraserna innehåller böckerna ett rikt urval autentiska språkexempel som visar i vilket sammanhang uppslagsordet vanligen används. Användaren får också hjälp med enklare grammatik, t. ex. konstruktion eller oregelbunden böjning, olikheter i användning av brittisk och amerikansk engelska.

För att ytterligare anpassa serien till den svenska användarens behov har den svenska utgåvan försetts med uttal till uppslagsorden. Ett antal svenska uppslagsord finns insorterade i bokstavsordning bland de engelska. De fungerar som en typ av ingångsord tillbaka till engelskan:

Ex. datalagring ⇒ information

I artikeln **information** hittar man så *information storage* med översättningen datalagring. Man måste alltså slå upp den engelska artikeln för att få översättningen.

Området data och informationsteknologi befinner sig i snabb utveckling. I många fall finns ännu inga etablerade svenska ord och uttryck, varför de i boken presenterade översättningarna får betraktas som förslag till svenska termer.

Varje fackordbok innehåller ett supplement med olika mått, tabeller och dokumentuppställningar som rör respektive ämne.

Stockholm i juni 1990
Esselte Ordbok

Ordboken innehåller ett antal ord som har sitt ursprung i varumärken. Detta får inte feltolkas så, att ordens förekomst här och sättet att förklara dem skulle ändra varumärkenas karaktär av skyddade kännetecken eller kunna anföras som giltigt skäl att beröva innehavarna deras skyddade ensamrätt till de ifrågavarande beteckningarna.

Aa

A [eɪ] = AMPERE base SI unit of electrical current *Ampere (A);* defined as the current flowing through an impedance of one ohm which has a voltage of one volt across it *Ampere (A)*

A [eɪ] hexadecimal equivalent to decimal number 10 *talet tio skrivet med hexadecimal notation*

A1, A2, A3, A4, A5 [eɪ'wʌn eɪ'tuː eɪ'θriː eɪ'fɔː eɪ'faɪv] *subst.* ISO recommended international standard sizes of paper *or* sizes of screen *standardiserade storlekar på papper eller bildskärmar;* **you must photocopy the spreadsheet on A3 paper; we must order some more A4 headed notepaper; a standard 300 d.p.i. black and white A4 monitor**

abbreviation [ə,briːvɪ'eɪʃ(ə)n] *subst.* short form of a word *or* command *or* instruction *förkortning;* **within the text, the abbreviation proc is used instead of processor; abbreviated addressing** *or* **abb. add.** = use of a smaller computer address word than normal which provides faster address decoding operations *förkortad adressering*

abend ['æbənd] *subst.* = ABNORMAL END unexpected stoppage of a program being run, due to a fault *or* error *or* power failure *onormal avslutning, onormalt avbrott;* **an interrupt from a faulty printer caused an abend; abend recovery program** = software that will reload a program (or system software) and restart it at the point where the abend occurred *återstartprogram (vid onormal avslutning), återställnings-program;* **if a fault occurs, data loss will be minimized due to the improved abend recovery program**

aberration [,æbə'reɪʃ(ə)n] *subst.* **(a)** distortion of a light beam *or* image due to defects in the optical system *aberration, avbildningsfel* **(b)** distortion of a television picture caused by a corrupt signal *or* incorrect adjustment *aberration, bildstörning; see also* SPHERICAL

abnormal [æb'nɔːm(ə)l] *adj.* not normal *onormal;* **its abnormal for two consecutive disk drives to break down; abnormal error; abnormal end** *or* **abend** *or* **abnormal termination** = unexpected stoppage of a program being run, caused by a fault *or* error *or* power failure *onormal avslutning, onormalt avbrott*

abnormally [æb'nɔːməlɪ] *adv.* not as normal *or* not as usual *onormalt;* **the signal is abnormally weak; the error rate with this disk is abnormally high**

abort [ə'bɔːt] *vb.* to end a process (when a malfunction occurs), by switching the computer off manually *or* by an internal feature *avbryta;* **the program was aborted by pressing the red button; abort the program before it erases any more files;** *see also* RESET

above-the-line costs [ə'bʌv ðə laɪn 'ksts] *subst pl.* variable costs involved in making TV films (such as scriptwriters, actors, sets, etc.) as opposed to below-the-line costs (film crew, technicians, etc.) *"set-kostnader"*

absolute address ['æbs(ə)luːt ə'dres] *or* **actual address** ['æktʃuəl ə'dres] *or* **machine address** [mə'ʃiːn ə'dres] *subst.* **(a)** computer storage address that directly, without any modification, accesses a location *or* device *direktadress, absolutadress; compare* INDEXED ADDRESS; **program execution is slightly faster if you code only with absolute addresses (b)** computer storage address that can only access one location *absolutadress;* **absolute addressing** = locating a data word in memory by the use of its absolute address *absolutadressering;* **absolute assembler** = type of assembly language program designed to produce code which uses only absolute addresses and values *absolutassemblerare;* **absolute code** = binary code which directly operates the central processing unit, using only absolute addresses and values (this is the final form of a program after a compiler *or* assembler pass) *absolutkod; see also* OBJECT CODE; **absolute instruction** = instruction which completely describes the operation to be performed (no other data is required) *absolutinstruktion;* **absolute loader** = program that loads a section of code into main memory *absolutladdare;* **absolute maximum rating** = maximum values or limits of a system *maximalt nominellt värde;* **absolute program** = computer program written in absolute code *absolutprogram;* **absolute value** = size *or* value of a number, regardless of its sign *absolutvärde;* **the absolute value of -62.34 is 62.34; an absolute value of the input is generated**

absolutinstruktion ⇨ **instruction**

absolutkod ⇨ direct

absorb [əb'sɔːb] *vb.* to take in (light *or* liquid) *absorbera, suga upp*

absorptance [əb'sɔːpt(ə)ns] *subst.* percentage of light that is absorbed by a material instead of reflecting it *absorbtans* NOTE: the opposite is **reflectance**

absorption [əb'sɔːpʃ(ə)n] *subst.* power loss of a signal when travelling through a medium, due to its absorptance *absorbering, absorption, uppsugning;* **absorption filter** = filter that blocks certain colours of light *absorptionsfilter, färgfilter*

abstract ['æbstrækt] **1** *subst.* short version of a book *or* article *sammandrag;* **in our library, abstracts are gathered together in separate volumes allowing an easy and rapid search for a particular subject 2** *vb.* **(a)** to remove something from something *abstrahera* **(b)** to make a summary of an article *sammanfatta*

A-bus ['eɪ 'bʌs] *subst.* main internal bus in a microprocessor *huvudbuss*

AC ['eɪ'siː] = ALTERNATING CURRENT electric current whose value varies with time in a regular, sinusoidal way *växelström*

COMMENT: the mains electricity supply uses alternating current to minimize transmission power loss, with a frequency of 50Hz in U.K., 60Hz in the USA

ACC ['eɪsiː'siː] *subst.* = ACCUMULATOR most important internal CPU storage register, containing the data word that is to be processed *ackumulator*

acceleration time [ək,selə'reɪʃ(ə)n 'taɪm] *subst.* **(a)** time taken for a disk drive to spin a disk at the correct speed, from rest *accelerationstid;* **allow for acceleration time in the access time (b)** total time between an access instruction being issued (to a peripheral) and the data being is transferred *åtkomsttid*

accent ['æks(ə)nt] *subst.* small sign placed on *or* above a printed *or* written character to show that it is pronounced in a different way *accent;* **acute accent** = accent above a character, which slopes upwards to the right *akut accent;* **circumflex accent** = accent above a character, shaped like an upside down 'v' *cirkumflex;* **grave accent** = accent above a character, which slopes upwards to the left *grav accent; see also* CEDILLA, TILDE, UMLAUT

accented [æk'sentɪd] *adj.* (letter) with an accent on it *försedd med accent*

accept [ək'sept] *vb.* **(a)** to agree to do something *godta, acceptera;* **he accepted the quoted price for printing; she has accepted**

our terms; **he did not accept the programming job he was offered (b)** to take something which is being offered *acceptera, ta emot, motta;* **the laser printer will accept a card as small as a business card; the multi-disk reader will accept 3.5 inch disks as well as 5.25 inch formats; call accept signal** = signal sent by a device showing that it is willing to accept (caller's) data *redosignal (allmänt begrepp)*

acceptable [ək'septəbl] *adj.* which can be accepted *godtagbar;* **the error rate was very low, and is acceptable; for the price, the scratched case is acceptable**

acceptance [ək'sept(ə)ns] *subst.* action of accepting something *godkännande;* **acceptance angle** = angle of total field of view of a lens *or* optic fibres *acceptansvinkel, öppningsvinkel;* **a light beam at an angle greater than the acceptance angle of the lens will not be transmitted; acceptance sampling** = testing a small random part of a batch to see if the whole batch is up to standard *stickprovskontroll;* **acceptance test** *or* **testing** = method of checking that a piece of equipment will perform as required *or* will reach required standards *leveranskontroll, leveransprov*

access ['ækses] **1** *subst.* being allowed to use a computer and read *or* alter files stored in it (this is usually controlled by a security device such as a password) *åtkomst;* **to have access to something** = to be able to get *or* examine *or* reach something *ha tillgäng till något;* **to have access to a file of data; he has access to numerous sensitive files; to bar access to a system** = to prevent a person from using a system *neka tillgång till ett system;* **after he was discovered hacking, he was barred access to the system; access arm** = mechanical device in a disk drive used to position the read/write head over the correct track on a disk *sökarm;* **the access arm moves to the parking region during transport; access charge** = cost due when logging onto a system *or* viewing special pages on a bulletin board *anslutningskostnad, åtkomstkostnad;* **access code** = series of characters *or* symbols that must be entered to identify a user before access to a computer is permitted *lösenord, åtkomstkod; see also* PASSWORD; **access line** = permanently connected communications line between a terminal and a computer *terminalledning;* **access method** = means used for the internal transfer of data between memory and display *or* peripheral devices (differences in the methods used is often the cause of compatibility problems) *åtkomstmetod;* **access point** = test point on a circuit board *or* in software, allowing an engineer to check signals *or* data *testpunkt;* **direct access storage device (DASD)** =

storage medium whose memory locations can be directly read *or* written to *direktminne, (sekundär-)minne för direktåtkomst;* **disk access =** operations required to read from or write to a magnetic disk, including device selection, sector and track address, movement of read/write head to the correct location and access the location on disk *skivminnesåtkomst;* **disk access management =** regulating the users who can access stored data *åtkomsthantering;* **direct memory access (DMA) =** direct, rapid link between a peripheral and a computer's main memory which avoids the use of accessing routines for each item of data required *direktminnesåtkomst;* **public access terminal =** terminal which can be used by anyone to access a computer *allmän terminal;* **instantaneous access =** storage that has virtually no access time delay, such as access to RAM *direktåtkomst, omedelbar åtkomst;* **the instantaneous access of the RAM disk was welcome; parallel access =** data transfer between two devices with a number of bits (usually one byte wide) being sent simultaneously *parallellåtkomst;* **random access =** ability to access immediately memory locations in any order *slumpmässig åtkomst;* **sequential access =** method of retrieving data from a storage device by starting at the beginning of the medium (such as tape) and reading each record until the required data is found *sekventiell åtkomst;* **serial access =** one item of data accessed by reading through all the data in a list until the correct one is found *seriell åtkomst* **2** *vb.* to call up (data) which is stored in a computer *anropa, hämta;* to obtain data from a storage device *anropa, öppna fil;* **she accessed the employee's file stored on the computer**

access control ['ækses kən'trəʊl] *subst.* security device (such as a password) that only allows selected users to use a computer system *or* read files *behörighetskontroll, åtkomstkontroll*

COMMENT: a good access control system should allow valid users to gain access and operate the computer easily with the minimum of checks, whilst barring entry to hackers *or* unauthorized users

accessible [ək'sesəbl] *adj.* which can be reached *or* accessed *tillgänglig, åtkomlig;* **details of customers are easily accessible from the main computer files**

accessions [æk'seʃ(ə)nz] *subst pl.* new books which are added to a library *accessioner, nyförvärv (om de nyaste böckerna);* **accession number =** serial number used in a library indexing system *accessionsnummer*

accessory [ək'sesəri] *subst.* useful device which is attached to *or* used with another *tillbehör;* **the printer comes with several accessories, such as a soundproof hood; this popular home computer has a large range of accessories**

access time ['ækses taɪm] *subst.* **(a)** total time which a storage device takes between the moment the data is requested and the data being returned *åtkomsttid;* **the access time of this dynamic RAM chip is around 200nS - we have faster versions if your system clock is running faster (b)** length of time required to find a file *or* program, either in main memory *or* a secondary memory source *åtkomsttid*

accidental [,æksɪ'dentl] *adj.* which happens by accident *oavsiktlig;* **always keep backup copies in case of accidental damage to the master file**

accordion fold [ə'kɔːdjən fəʊld] *or* **fanfold** ['fænfəʊld] *subst.* method of folding continuous paper, one sheet in one direction, the next sheet in the opposite direction, allowing the paper to be fed into a printer continuously with no action on the part of the user *dragspelsvikning för papper i löpande bana*

accumulate [ə'kjuːmjʊleɪt] *vb.* to gather several things together over a period of time *samla, ackumulera;* **we have gradually accumulated a large databank of names and addresses**

accumulator [ə'kjuːmjʊleɪtə] *or* **ACC (register)** ['eɪsiːsiː: ('redʒɪstə)] *subst.* most important internal CPU storage register, containing the data word that is to be processed *ackumulator(-register);* **accumulator shift instruction =** command to shift the contents of an accumulator left *or* right by one bit *skiftinstruktion, ackumulatorskift*

accuracy ['ækjʊrəsɪ] *subst.* total number of bits used to define a number in a computer, the more bits allocated the more accurate the definition *noggrannhet, precision*

accurate ['ækjʊrət] *adj.* correct *riktig, noggrann;* without any errors *exakt;* **the printed bar code has to be accurate to within a thousandth of a micron**

COMMENT: most high level languages allow numbers to be represented in a more accurate form by using two or more words to store the number

accurately ['ækjʊrətlɪ] *adv.* correctly *or* with no errors *noggrant, riktigt, exakt;* **the OCR had difficulty in reading the new font accurately; the error was caused because the data had not been accurately keyed**

acetate ['æsɪteɪt] *subst.* sheet of transparent plastic used for making overlays *acetatfilm;* **the graphs were plotted on acetate, for use on an overhead projector**

achieve [əˈtʃiːv] *vb.* to succeed in doing something *uppnå;* **the hardware designers are trying to achieve compatibility between all the components of the system**

achromatic [ˌækrə(ʊ)ˈmætɪk] *adj.* (an optical device) that has been corrected for chromatic aberration *akromatisk*

ACIA [eɪsiːaɪˈeɪ] = ASYNCHRONOUS COMMUNICATIONS INTERFACE ADAPTER circuit that allows a computer to transmit and receive serial data using asynchronous access *asynkron kommunikationsenhet*

ACK [ækˈnɒlɪdʒ] = ACKNOWLEDGE signal that is sent from a receiver to indicate that a transmitted message has been received and that it is ready for the next one *kvittenssignal, ACK-signal;* **the printer generates an ACK signal when it has received data**

Ackerman's function ['ækəmənz 'fʌŋ(k)ʃ(ə)n] *subst.* recursive function used to test the ability of a compiler to cope with recursion *Ackermanfunktion*

acknowledge [əkˈnɒlɪdʒ] **1** *subst.* signal that is sent from a receiver to indicate that a transmitted message has been received and that it is ready for the next one *kvitteringssignal* **2** *vb.* (i) to tell a sender that a message *or* letter has been received *kvittera;* (ii) to send a signal from a receiver to show that a transmitted message has been received *kvittera;* **acknowledge character** = special code sent by a receiver to indicate to the transmitter that the message has been correctly received *kvittenstecken*

acknowledgements [əkˈnɒlɪdʒmənts] *subst.* text printed at the beginning of a book, where the author *or* publisher thanks people who have helped *erkännanden*

ackumulator ⇨ **ACC**

acoustic [əˈkuːstɪk] *adj.* referring to sound *akustisk, ljud-;* **acoustic hood** = soundproof hood placed over a printer to reduce the noise *ljudhuv;* **the acoustic hood allows us to speak and print in the same room; acoustic delay line** = original data storage method that delays data (in the form of sound pulses) as it travels across a medium *akustisk fördröjningsledning;* **acoustic store** *or* **acoustic memory** = (old) regenerative memory that uses an acoustic delay line *akustiskt minne*

acoustical feedback [əˈkuːstɪk(ə)l 'fiːdbæk] *subst.* distortion in an audio signal, due to a part of an amplified signal

being picked up by the microphone and amplified again until the amplifier is overloaded *(akustisk) återkoppling, rundgång*

acoustic coupler [əˈkuːstɪk ˈkʌplə] *subst.* device that connects to a telephone handset, converting binary computer data into sound signals to allow data to be transmitted down a telephone line *akustiskt modem;* **I use an acoustic coupler with my lap-top computer**

COMMENT: the acoustic coupler also converts back from sound signals to digital signals when receiving messages; it is basically the same as a modem but uses a loudspeaker on which a handset is placed to send the signals rather than direct connection to the phone line. It is portable, and clips over both ends of a normal telephone handset; it can be used even in a public phone booth

acoustics [əˈkuːstɪks] *subst.* study and science of sound waves *akustik*

acquisition [ˌækwɪˈzɪʃ(ə)n] *subst.* accepting *or* capturing *or* collecting information *insamling;* **data acquisition** = gathering data about a subject *datainsamling*

ACR ['eɪsiːˈɑː] = AUDIO CASSETTE RECORDER *kassettbandspelare, ljudbandspelare;* **ACR interface** = interface which allows a cassette recorder to be linked to a computer *gränssnitt mot kassettbandspelare, kassettbandspelaran-slutning*

acronym ['ækrə(ʊ)nɪm] *subst.* abbreviation, formed from various letters, which makes up a word which can be pronounced *akronym, initialförkortning (som uppfattas som ett namn eller ord);* **the acronym FORTRAN means Formula Translator; the acronym RAM means Random Access Memory**

actinic light [ækˈtɪnɪk laɪt] *subst.* light which is able to cause chemical change in a material, such as film *aktinisk, kemiskt verkande*

action ['ækʃ(ə)n] *subst.* **(a)** thing which has been done *handling, åtgärd;* **action has been taken to repair the fault; to take action** = to do something *åtgärda, handla;* **action cycle** = complete set of actions involved in one operation (including reading data, processing, storing results, etc.) *operationscykel, processcykel;* **action message** = prompt given to inform the user that an action *or* input is required *ledtext* **(b)** movement *rörelse;* **action field** = area to be photographed by a camera *spelyta;* **action frame** = camera field of view where the filmed action is taking place *kamerasynfält;* **action shot** = still photograph showing action taking place (such as a person running) *ögonblicksbild*

activate ['æktɪveɪt] *vb.* to start a process *or* to make a device start working *aktivera, starta;* **pressing CR activates the printer**

active ['æktɪv] *adj.* busy *or* working *or* being used *aktiv, verksam;* **active device** = electronic component that requires electrical power to operate and provides gain *or* a logical function; **active file** = file which is being worked on *aktiv fil;* **active star** = network consisting of a central point with nodes branching out, in which a central processor controls and routes all messages between devices *aktivt stjärnnät;* **active state** = electronic state in which an action occurs *aktivt tillstånd;* **active window** = area of display screen in which you are currently working *aktivt fönster, arbetsfönster; see also* WINDOW

activity [æk'tɪvətɪ] *subst.* **(a)** being active *or* busy *aktivitet;* **activity loading** = method of organizing disk contents so that the most often accessed files *or* programs can be loaded quickly *lagring efter frekvens;* **activity ratio** = number of files currently in use compared to the total stored *aktivitetsförhållande* **(b) activities** = jobs *or* tasks which are being performed on a computer *aktiviteter, uppgifter, jobb*

actual address ['æktʃʊəl ə'dres] *or* **absolute address** ['æbs(ə)luːt ə'dres] *subst.* computer storage address that directly, without any modification, accesses a location *or* device *absolut adress; compare with* INDEXED ADDRESS; **actual code** = binary code which directly operates the central processing unit, using only absolute addresses and values (this is the final form of a program after a compiler *or* assembler pass) *maskinkod;* **actual instruction** = the resulting instruction executed after the modification of an original instruction *faktisk instruktion*

actuator ['æktjʊ,eɪtə] *subst.* mechanical device that can be controlled by an external signal (such as the read/write head in a disk drive) *ställdon, verkställande mekanism*

ACU ['eɪsiː'juː] = AUTOMATIC CALLING UNIT device which allows a computer to call stations *or* dial telephone numbers automatically *automatuppringningsenhet*

acuity [ə'kjuːətɪ] *subst.* **(a)** ability of the eye to define between shades and shapes of an object *synskärpa* **(b)** ability of the ear to detect frequency *or* volume changes *hörselskärpa*

acutance [ə'kjuːt(ə)ns] *subst.* ability of a lens to produce clear edges *skärpa, inställningsskärpa*

acute [ə'kjuːt] *adj.* **(a)** very sharp *or* clear *spetsig, skarp, akut* **(b) acute accent** = accent above a character, which slopes upwards to the right *akut accent*

AD ['eɪ'diː] = ASSISTANT DIRECTOR, ASSOCIATE DIRECTOR

A/D ['eɪ'diː] *or* **A to D** ['eɪtə'diː] = ANALOG TO DIGITAL change a signal from an analog form to a digitally coded form *analog till digital*

ADA ['eɪdiː'eɪ] *subst.* high-level programming language that is used mainly in military, industrial and scientific fields of computing *programmeringsspråket Ada*

adapt [ə'dæpt] *vb.* to change to fit *anpassa;* **can this computer be adapted to take 5.25 inch disks?**

adaptation [,ædæp'teɪʃ(ə)n] *subst.* ability of a device to adjust its sensitivity range according to various situations *anpassning;* **the adaptation of the eye to respond to different levels of brightness**

adapter [ə'dæptə] *or* **adaptor** [ə'dæptə] *subst.* device that allows two *or* more incompatible devices to be connected together *anpassningsenhet, adapter;* **the cable adapter allows attachment of the scanner to the SCSI interface; the cable to connect the scanner to the adapter is included in the package; adapter card** = add-on interface board that allows incompatible devices to communicate *anpassningskort;* **adapter plug** = plug which allows devices with different plugs (two-pin, three-pin, etc.) to be fitted into the same socket *anpassningskontakt;* **data adapter unit** = device that interfaces a CPU to one *or* more communications channels *dataanpassningsenhet*

adaptiv ⇨ **adaptive channel allocation**

adaptive channel allocation [ə'dæptɪv 'tʃænl ,ælə(ʊ)'keɪʃ(ə)n] *subst.* providing communications channels according to demand rather than a fixed allocation *adaptiv kanaltilldelning;* **adaptive routing** = ability of a system to change its communications routes according to various events *or* situations such as line failure *adaptivt vägval;* **adaptive systems** = ability of a system to alter its responses and processes according to inputs *or* events *or* situations *adaptiva system*

adaptivt vägval ⇨ **distribute**

adaptor [ə'dæptə] *see* ADAPTER

ADB ⇨ **dp, EDP**

ADC ['eɪdiː'siː] *subst.* = ANALOG TO DIGITAL CONVERTER device used to convert analog input to a digital output form, that can be understood by a computer *analog-digitalomvandlare*

add [æd] *vb.* **(a)** to put figures together to make a total *addera;* **in the spreadsheet each column should be added to make a subtotal; add time** = period of time taken to perform one addition operation (either of a CPU *or* adder) *additionstid;* **add register** = register which is an adder *additionsregister* **(b)** to put things together to form a larger group *tillägga;* **the software house has added a new management package to its range of products; adding or deleting material from the text is easy using function keys**

added entry ['ædɪd 'entrɪ] *subst.* secondary file entry in a library catalogue *tilläggsbegrepp*

addend [æ'dend] *subst.* number added to the augend in an addition *addend*

adder ['ædə] *subst.* device *or* routine that provides the sum of two *or* more (digital *or* analog) inputs *adderare;* **adder-subtractor** = device that can either add or subtract *adderare-subtraherare;* **full adder** *or* **three input adder** = binary addition circuit which can produce the sum of two inputs, and can also accept a carry input, producing a carry output if necessary *heladderare;* **half adder** *or* **two input adder** = binary addition circuit which can produce the sum of two inputs and a carry output if necessary, but will not accept a carry input *halvadderare, tvåingångsadderare;* **parallel adder** = a number of full adders arranged in parallel to add two words at once *parallelladderare;* **serial adder** = one bit full adder used to add two words one bit at a time *serieadderare*

COMMENT: a parallel adder takes one clock cycle to add two words, a serial adder takes a time equal to the number of bits in a word to add

adderare ⇨ **adder**

add-in ['ædɪn] *subst. & adj.* (something) which is added *tillsats-, insticks-;* **the first method is to use a page description language, the second is to use an add-in processor card; can you explain the add-in card method? processing is much faster with add-in cards**

addition [ə'dɪʃ(ə)n] *adj.* arithmetic operation that produces the sum of an addend and augend *addition;* **addition record** = record with changes used to update a master record *or* file *uppdateringslista;* **addition time** = time an adder takes to carry out an add operation *additionstid;* **addition without carry** = addition operation without any carry bits *or* words *addition utan överföringssiffra; same as* EXOR FUNCTION; **destructive addition** = addition operation in which the result is

stored in the location of one of the operands used in the sum, so overwriting it *överskrivande addition*

additional [ə'dɪʃənl] *adj.* which is added *or* which is extra *extra, ytterligare;* **can we add three additional workstations to the network?**

additive colour mixing ['ædɪtɪv 'kʌlə 'mɪksɪŋ] *subst.* mixing different coloured lights to produce the colour which is wanted *additiv färgblandning*

add-on ['æd'ɒn] *subst. & adj.* piece of software *or* hardware that is added to a computer system to improve its performance *tilläggs-;* **the add-on hard disk will boost the computer's storage capabilities; the new add-on board allows colour graphics to be displayed**

address [ə'dres] **1** *subst.* **(a)** details of number, street and town where an office is or a person lives *adress;* **my business address and phone number are printed on the card; cable address** = short address for sending cables *telegramadress;* **home address** = address of a house or flat where someone lives *bostadsadress;* **please send the documents to my home address; address list** = list of addresses *adresslista, adressregister;* **we keep an address list of two thousand businesses in Europe (b)** number allowing a central processing unit to reference a physical location in a storage medium in a computer system *adress;* **each separate memory word has its own unique address; this is the address at which the data starts; absolute address** *or* **actual address** *or* **direct address** = (i) computer storage address (within a CPU's address range) that directly, without any modification, accesses a location *or* device *direktadress, absolutadress;* (ii) computer storage address that can only access one location *absolutadress;* **address access time** = total time which a storage device takes between the moment the data is requested and the data being returned *(adress)åtkomsttid;* **address bus** = physical connection that carries the address data in parallel form from the central processing unit to external devices *adressbuss;* **address computation** = operation on address data (in an instruction) *adressberäkning;* **address decoder** = logical circuit that will produce a signal when a certain address *or* range is placed on the address bus *adressavkodare;* **address field** *or* **operand field** = part of a computer instruction that contains the location of the operand *adressfält, operandfält;* **address format** = rules defining the way the operands, data and addresses are arranged in an instruction *adressformat;* **address mapping** = virtual address translated to an absolute real address *adressavbildning;* **address**

mark = special code on a disk that indicates the start of sector location data *adressmarkering;* **address modification** = changing the address field, so that it can refer to a different location *adressmodifiering, adress(för)ändring;* **address register** = register in a computer that is able to store all the bits that make up an address which can then be processed as a single unit (in small micros, the address register is usually made up of two data bytes) *adressregister; see also* MAR; **address space** = total number of possible locations that can be directly addressed by the program *or* CPU *adressutrymme;* **address strobe** = signal (pulse) that indicates that a valid address is on the address bus *adresspuls;* **address track** = track on a magnetic disk containing the addresses of files, etc., stored on other tracks *adresspår;* **address word** = computer word, usually made up, in a small micro, of two data words that contain the address data *adressord;* **base address** = initial address in a program used as a reference for others *basadress;* **initial address** = address at which the first location of a program is stored *startadress, grundadress;* **machine address** = storage address that directly, without any modification, accesses a location *or* device *maskinadress, absolutadress;* **relative address** = location specified in relation to a reference (address) *relativadress* **2** *vb.* **(a)** to write the details of an address on an envelope, etc. *adressera;* **to address a letter** *or* **a parcel; please address your reply to the manager; a letter addressed to the managing director; an incorrectly addressed package (b)** to put the location data onto an address bus to identify which word in memory *or* storage device is to be accessed *adresser;* **a larger address word increases the amount of memory a computer can address**

addressability ['æ,dresə'bɪlətɪ] *subst.* the control available over pixels on screen *adresserbarhet*

addressable [ə'dresəbl] *adj.* which can be addressed *adresserbar;* **all the 5Mb of RAM is addressable; addressable cursor** = cursor which can be programmed to be placed in a certain position *adresserbar markör;* **addressable terminal** = terminal that will only accept data if it has the correct address and identification number in the message header *adresserbar terminal*

addressee [,ædre'si:] *subst.* person to whom a letter *or* package *or* communication is addressed *adressat*

addressing [ə'dresɪŋ] *subst.* process of accessing a location in memory *adressering;* **absolute addressing** = locating a data word stored in memory, by the use of its absolute address *absolutadressering;*

abbreviated addressing = use of a smaller address word than normal, which provides faster address decoding operations *förkortad adressering;* **bit addressing** = selecting a register and examining one bit within it *bitadressering;* **deferred addressing** = indirect addressing where the location accessed contains the address of the operand to be processed *indirekt adressering;* **direct addressing** = method of addressing where the storage location address given in the instruction is the location to be used *direktadressering;* **immediate addressing** = accessing data immediately because it is held in the address field itself *omedelbar adressering;* **indexed addressing** = addressing mode, in which the storage location to be accessed is made up of a start (base) address and an offset (index) word, which is then added to it to give the address to be used *indexerad adressering;* **indirect addressing** = way of addressing data, where the first instruction refers to an address which contains a second address *indirekt adressering;* **addressing capacity** = largest location that a certain program *or* CPU can directly address, without special features (such as virtual memory *or* memory banks) *adresseringskapacitet;* **addressing level** = zero-level: operand is the address part of the instruction *(grund)adresseringsnivå;* first-level: operand stored at the address of the instruction *första adresseringsnivån;* second-level: operand stored at the address given in the instruction *andra adresseringsnivån;* **addressing method** = manner in which a section of memory is located *adresseringsmetod;* **addressing mode** = way in which a location is addressed, either sequential, indexed, direct, etc. *adresseringstillstånd*

addressing machine [ə'dresɪŋ mə'ʃi:n] *subst.* machine which puts addresses on envelopes automatically *adresseringsmaskin*

adjacent [ə'dʒeɪs(ə)nt] *adj.* which is near *or* next to something *närliggande;* **the address is stored adjacent to the customer name field**

adjust [ə'dʒʌst] *vb.* to change something to fit new conditions *or* so that it works better *justera, anpassa;* **you can adjust the brightness and contrast by turning a knob**

adjustment [ə'dʒʌs(t)mənt] *subst.* slight change made to something so that it works better *justering;* **the brightness needs adjustment; I think the joystick needs adjustment as it sometimes gets stuck**

administrationsprogram ⇨ **program**

administrationstillägg(skod) ⇨ **overhead**

administrator [əd'mɪnɪstreɪtə] *subst.* control *or* supervisor *or* executive software *or* person *administratör, övervakare;* **data administrator** = control section of a database management system *dataadministrationsprogram;* **database administrator (DBA)** = person in charge of running and maintaining a database system *databasadministratör*

ADP ['eɪdiː'piː] = AUTOMATIC DATA PROCESSING data processing done by a computer *ADB, automatisk databehandling*

adressanpassande program ⇨ self-

adressformat ⇨ format

adressfri operation ⇨ operation

adressfält ⇨ field

adresskanal ⇨ highway

adresskonvertering ⇨ float

adresslista ⇨ mailing

adresslutsignal ⇨ end

advance [əd'vɑːns] *vb.* to move forward *gå fram(åt);* to make something move forward *flytta fram(åt), stega fram;* **the paper is advanced by turning this knob; advance the cursor two spaces along the line**

advanced [əd'vɑːnst] *adj.* more complicated *or* more difficult to learn *avancerad;* **advanced version** = program with more complex features for use by an experienced user *avancerad version*

adventure game [əd'ventʃə geɪm] *subst.* game played on a computer, where the user pretends to be a hero in an imaginary land and has to get through various dangerous situations, fight monsters, etc. *äventyrsspel*

aerial ['eərɪəl] **1** *subst.* device for receiving *or* sending radio transmissions by converting electromagnetic impulses into electrical signals and vice-versa *antenn;* **aerial cable** = wire stretched between poles which acts as an aerial *antennkabel* **2** *adj.* in the air *luft-, i luften, flyg-;* **aerial image** = a view from high above a scene *flygbild, översiktsbild*

affect [ə'fekt] *vb.* to touch *or* to influence *or* to change something *påverkan, inverka på, ändra;* **changes in voltage will affect the way the computer functions**

affiliate [ə'fɪlɪeɪt] *vb.* to connect *or* join with *ansluta, uppta*

affiliated [ə'fɪlɪeɪtɪd] *adj.* connected with *or* owned by another company *ansluten, antagen, upptagen;* **one of our affiliated companies**

affirmative [ə'fɜːmətɪv] *adj.* meaning "yes" *jakande;* **the answer was in the affirmative** = the answer was "yes" *bekräftande;* **affirmative acknowledgement** = acknowledge signal from the receiver that it has accepted the message and is ready for the next one *bekräftande kvittens*

AFNOR ['æfnɔːr] *in France* Association Française de Normalisation (the French standards organization) *franska standardiseringsorganisationen*

afterglow ['ɑːftəgləʊ] *see* PERSISTENCE

AGC ['eɪdʒiː'siː] = AUTOMATIC GAIN CONTROL electronic device that provides a constant amplitude output signal from a varying input signal by changing its gain *AFK, automatisk förstärkningskontroll*

agenda [ə'dʒendə] *subst.* list of things to be discussed at a meeting *föredragningslista, dagordning;* **the conference agenda** *or* **the agenda of the conference; after two hours we were still discussing the first item on the agenda; the secretary put finance at the top of the agenda; the chairman wants two items removed from** *or* **taken off the agenda; agenda item** = topic on an agenda to be discussed *punkt på dagordningen*

aggregate ['ægrɪgət] *subst.* **data aggregate** = collection of items of data that are related *datamängd*

AI ['eɪ'aɪ] = ARTIFICIAL INTELLIGENCE the design and development of computer programs that attempt to imitate human intelligence and decision-making functions, providing basic reasoning and other human characteristics *AI, artificiell (konstgjord) intelligens; see also* EXPERT SYSTEM, IKBS

A & I ['eɪənd'aɪ] = ABSTRACTING AND INDEXING making summaries and indexes for articles and books *att sammanfatta artiklar och göra index för böcker*

aid [eɪd] **1** *subst.* help *hjälp;* **the computer is a great aid to rapid processing of large amounts of information; diagnostic aid** = hardware *or* software device that helps find faults *analyshjälpmedel, felsökningshjälpmedel* **2** *vb.* to help *hjälpa, bistå, understödja;* **industrial design is aided by computers;** *see also* COMPUTER-AIDED

air circuit breaker [eə 'sɜːkɪt 'breɪkə] *subst.* mechanical device that has an electrical *or* manual switched circuit isolator *luftbrytare*

air gap ['eə 'gæp] *subst.* narrow gap between a recording *or* playback head and the magnetic medium *luftgap*

aktivera ⇨ activate, arm

aktivera avbrott ⇨ **interrupt**

aktiveringssignal ⇨ **select**

aktiv reserv ⇨ **standby**

aktivt kort ⇨ **smart**

aktivt vänteläge ⇨ **warm standby**

aktualiseringsfil ⇨ **journal**

akustiskt modem ⇨ **acoustic coupler**

alarm [ə'lɑːm] *subst.* ringing or other sound which warns of a danger *alarm;* **all staff must leave the building if the alarm sounds; an alarm rings when the printer has run out of paper**

albumen plate ['ælbjumɪn pleɪt] *subst.* photographic plate, with a light-sensitive coating *albumenplatta*

ALC ['eɪel'siː] = AUTOMATIC LEVEL CONTROL *see* AGC

algebra ['ældʒɪbrə] *subst.* use of letters in certain mathematical operations to represent unknown numbers *or* a range of possible numbers *algebra;* **Boolean algebra** = rules set down to define, simplify and manipulate logical functions, based on statements that are true or false *Boolsk algebra*

ALGOL [ælgɒl] = ALGORITHMIC LANGUAGE high level programming language using algorithmic methods for mathematical and technical applications *programmeringsspråket ALGOL*

algorithm [ælgə'rɪðm] *subst.* rules used to define *or* perform a specific task *or* to solve a specific problem *algoritm*

QUOTE image processing algorithms are step by step procedures for performing image processing operations
Byte
QUOTE the steps are: acquiring a digitized image, developing an algorithm to process it, processing the image, modifying the algorithm until you are satisfied with the result
Byte
QUOTE the complex algorithms needed for geometrical calculations make heavy demands on the processor
PC Business World

---

algorithmic [ælgə'rɪðmɪk] *adj.* expressed using algorithms *algoritmisk;* **algorithmic language** = computer language designed to process and express algorithms, such as ALGOL *algoritmiskt språk*

alien ['eɪljən] *adj.* different *or* not fitting the usual system *främmande, okänd, avvikande;* **alien disk** = disk formatted on another system *or* containing data in a format which is in a form that cannot be read *or* understood *främmande diskett;* **alien disk reader** = add-on device which allows a computer to access data on disks

from other computers *or* systems *läsare för främmande diskett;* **when you have an alien disk select the multi-disk option to allow you to turn the disk drive into an alien disk reader**

align [ə'laɪn] *vb.* (a) to make sure that the characters to be printed are spaced and levelled correctly *inställa, ställa in på en linje* (b) to ensure that a read/write head is correctly positioned over the recording medium *inställa, centrera*

aligner [ə'laɪnə] *subst.* device used to make sure that the paper is straight in a printer *inställningsdon*

aligning edge [ə'laɪnɪŋedʒ] *subst.* edge of an optical character recognition system used to position a document *inställningskant*

alignment [ə'laɪnmənt] *subst.* correct spacing and levelling of printed characters *gruppering;* **in alignment** = correctly aligned *rätlinjig;* **out of alignment** = not aligned correctly *ej i linje;* **alignment pin** = peg that fits in a hole to ensure that two devices are correctly aligned *inställningsskift*

allmänna datakommunikationsnät och -tjänster ⇨ **data**

allmän variabel ⇨ **global**

allocate ['ælə(ʊ)keɪt] *vb.* to divide (a period of time *or* a piece of work) in various ways and share it out between users *tilldela, fördela, allokera;* **the operating system allocated most of main memory to the spreadsheet program**

allocation [ælə(ʊ)'keɪʃ(ə)n] *subst.* dividing something in various ways *tilldelning, fördelning, allokering;* **allocation of time** *or* **capital to a project; allocation routine** = short program that divides the memory resources of a system between the software and peripherals that use it *fördelningsrutin;* **dynamic allocation** = system where resources are allocated during a program run, rather than being determined in advance *dynamisk tilldelning;* **band allocation** = range of frequencies allocated to various users *or* for various purposes *frekvenstilldelning;* **the new band allocation means we will have more channels**

allokera ⇨ **allocate**

allophone ['æləfəʊn] *subst.* smallest unit of sound from which speech can be formed *allofon, fonemvariant*

alphabet ['ælfəbet] *subst.* the 26 letters used to make words *alfabet*

alpha beta technique ['ælfə 'biːtə tek'niːk] *subst.* (free structure) technique used in artificial intelligence for solving game and strategy problems *alfabetateknik*

alphabetically [ˌælfəˈbetɪk(ə)lɪ] *adv.* in alphabetical order *alfabetiskt;* **the files are arranged alphabetically under the customer's name**

alphabetical order [ˌælfəˈbetɪk(ə)l ˈɔːdə] *subst.* arrangement of records (such as files, index cards) in the order of the letters of the alphabet (A,B,C,D, etc.) *bokstavsordning, alfabetisk ordning*

alphabetic character (set) [ˌælfəˈbetɪk ˈkærəktə (set)] *subst.* characters (capitals and small letters) that make up the alphabet *alfabetiskt tecken, bokstav, alfabetisk teckenuppsättning;* **alphabetic string =** string that only contains alphabetic characters *alfabetisk teckensträng*

alphabetize [ˈælfəbəˌtaɪz] *vb.* to put into alphabetical order *sortera i bokstavsordning;* **enter the bibliographical information and alphabetize it**

alphageometric [ˌælfədʒɪə(ʊ)ˈmetrɪk] *adj.* (set of codes) that instruct a teletext terminal to display various graphics patterns *or* characters

alphameric [ˈælfəˈmerɪk] *US* = ALPHANUMERIC

alphamosaic [ˌælfəmə(ʊ)ˈzeɪk] *adj.* (character set) used in teletext to provide alphanumeric and graphics characters

alphanumeric [ˌælfənjuːˈmerɪk] *adj.* **alphanumeric characters** *or* **alphanumerics =** roman letters and arabic numerals (and other signs such as punctuation marks) *alfanumeriskt tecken;* **alphanumeric data =** data that represents the letters of the alphabet and the arabic numerals *alfanumeriska data;* **alphanumeric display =** display device able to show characters as well as numbers *alfanumerisk skärm;* **alphanumeric keyboard =** keyboard containing character keys as well as numerical keys *alfanumeriskt tangentbord;* **alphanumeric operand =** operand which can contain alphanumeric characters, such as a string *alfanumerisk operand;* **alphanumeric string =** series of alphanumeric characters that are manipulated and treated as a single unit *alfanumerisk sträng*

> QUOTE geometrical data takes up more storage space than alphanumeric data
> **PC Business World**

alphaphotographic [ˌælfəfəʊtəˈgræfɪk] *adj.* which represents pictures using predefined graphics characters, for teletext services *med fördefinierad grafik*

alpha radiation [ˈælfə ˌreɪdɪˈeɪʃ(ə)n] *subst.* naturally occurring radiation *alfastrålning;* **alpha-particle =** emitted alpha radiation particle *alfapartikel;* **alpha-particle sensitivity =** problem experienced by certain (MOS) memory devices exposed to alpha radiation, causing loss of stored charge (data) *alfapartikelkänslighet*

alphasort [ˈælfəˌsɔːt] *vb.* to sort data into alphabetical order *sortera i bokstavsordning*

alpha wrap [ˈælfə ræp] *subst.* method used for feeding tape into a helical scan video recorder to make sure the alignment is correct *alfamatning*

alter [ˈɔːltə] *vb.* to change *ändra, förändra;* **to alter the terms of a contract; the program specifications have just been altered**

alterable [ˈɔːlt(ə)rəbl] *adj.* which can be altered *ändringsbar, förändringsbar; see* EAPROM, EAROM

alteration [ˌɔːltəˈreɪʃ(ə)n] *subst.* change which has been made *ändring;* **the agreement was signed without any alterations; the new version of the software has many alterations and improvements**

alternate 1 [ˈɔːltəneɪt] *vb.* to change from one state to another and back, over and over again *växla* **2** [ˈɔːltənət] *adj.* which change from one to another *växel-, växlingsbar;* **alternate mode =** application for multi-user use, where two operators can access and share a single file at the same time *växeltillstånd, växeldrift;* **alternate route =** backup path in a communications system, used in case of a fault *or* breakdown *alternativväg*

alternately [ɔːlˈtɜːnətlɪ] *adv.* switching from one to the other *alternativt*

alternating current [ˈɔːltəneɪtɪŋ ˈkʌr(ə)nt] *or* **AC** *subst.* electric current whose value varies with time in a regular, sinusoidal way (changing direction of flow each half cycle) *växelström*

alternation [ˌɔːltəˈneɪʃ(ə)n] *subst.* logical function that produces a true output if any input is true *växling*

alternative [ɔːlˈtɜːnətɪv] **1** *subst.* thing which can be done instead of another *alternativ;* **what is the alternative to re-keying all the data?; we have no alternative =** there is nothing else we can do *vi har inget val* **2** *adj.* other *or* which can take the place of something *annan, alternativ;* **alternative denial =** logical function whose output is false if all inputs are true and true if any input is false *alternativ uteslutning (negerad konjunktion)*

alternativväg ⇨ **alternate**

alternator ['ɔːltəneɪtə] *subst.* device which produces an alternating current *omformare*

ALU ['eɪel'juː] = ARITHMETIC LOGIC UNIT section of the CPU that performs all arithmetic and logical functions *aritmetisklogisk enhet*

aluminiumpapper ▷ **electrosensitive**

AM ['eɪ'em] = AMPLITUDE MODULATION

A-MAC ['eɪ'mæk] low bandwidth variation of MAC *standardiserat TV-signalsformat med låg bandbredd*

ambient ['æmbɪənt] *adj.* normal background (conditions) *bakgrund, omgivning;* **ambient noise level** = normal background noise level *bakgrundsbrus;* **the ambient noise level in the office is greater than in the library; ambient temperature** = normal average temperature of the air around a device *omgivningstemperatur*

ambiguity [ˌæmbɪ'gjuːətɪ] *subst.* something which is not clearly defined *tvetydighet;* **ambiguity error** = error due to incorrect selection of ambiguous data *tvetydighetsfel*

ambiguous [æm'bɪgjuəs] *adj.* which has two possible meanings *tvetydig;* **ambiguous filename** = filename which is not unique to a single file, making it difficult to locate the file *tvetydigt filnamn*

ambisonics [ˌæmbɪ'sɒnɪks] *subst.* recording more than one audio signal to give the effect of being surrounded by sound *ambiotoni*

amendment record [ə'men(d)mənt 'rekɔːd] *subst.* record containing new information used to update a master record *or* file *ändringspost, kompletteringspost, uppdateringspost*

American National Standards Institute (ANSI) [ə'merɪkən 'næʃənl 'stændədz 'ɪnstɪtjuːt] organization which specifies computer and software standards including those of high-level programming languages *amerikanska standardiserings-organisationen*

American Standard Code for Information Interchange (ASCII) [ə'merɪkən 'stændəd 'kəʊd fə ˌɪnfə'meɪʃ(ə)n 'ɪntə'tʃeɪn(d)ʒ] code which represents alphanumeric characters as binary codes *amerikansk standardiserad teckenuppsättning för datorer*

AMM ['eɪem'em] = ANALOG MULTIMETER multimeter that uses a graduated scale and a moving needle as a readout for voltage, current and impedance levels *analogt universalinstrument; compare with* DMM

amount [ə'maʊnt] **1** *subst.* quantity of data *or* paper, etc. *mängd, storlek, summa;* **what is the largest amount of data which can be processed in one hour? 2** *vb.* **to amount to** = to make a total of *uppgå till;* **the total keyboarded characters amount to ten million**

amp [æmp] *or* **ampere (A)** ['æmpeə (eɪ)] *subst.* base SI unit of electrical current *ampere;* defined as the current flowing through an impedance of one ohm which has a voltage of one volt across it *ampere (A)*
NOTE: used with figures: **a 13-amp fuse**

ampersand ['æmpəsænd] *subst.* printing sign (&) which means "and" *och-tecken, et-tecken*

amplification [ˌæmplɪfɪ'keɪʃ(ə)n] *subst.* the output-to-input signal strength ratio *förstärkning;* **increase the amplification of the input signal; the amplification is so high, the signal is distorting**

amplifier ['æmplɪfaɪə] *subst.* electronic circuit that magnifies the power of a signal *förstärkare;* **audio amplifier** = domestic amplifier that handles frequencies in the human hearing range *ljudförstärkare;* **low noise amplifier** = high-quality amplifier placed very close to a receiving aerial to amplify the received signals before they are corrupted by noise *lågbrusförstärkare;* **amplifier class** = way of classifying the design of amplifiers meant for different jobs *förstärkarklass;* **amplified telephone** = system to allow hands-off telephone conversations *högtalande telefon*

amplify ['æmplɪfaɪ] *vb.* to magnify a signal power *or* amplitude *förstärka;* **the received signal needs to be amplified before it can be processed**

amplitude ['æmplɪtjuːd] *subst.* strength *or* size of a signal *amplitud;* **amplitude distortion** = distortion of a signal due to uneven (non-linear) amplification (high levels amplified less than low) *amplituddistortion;* **amplitude modulation (AM)** = system that varies the amplitude of a constant carrier according to an external signal *amplitudmodulering;* **amplitude quantization** = conversion of an analog signal to a numerical representation *amplitudkvantisering*

analog ['ænəlɒg] *or* **analogue** ['ænəlɒg] *subst.* representation and measurement of numerical data by continuously variable physical quantities, such as the size of electrical voltages *analog; compare with* DIGITAL; **analog channel** = communications line that carries analog signals such as speech *analog kanal;* **analog computer** = computer which processes data in analog form (that is, data which is represented by a continuously varying signal - as opposed to digital data) *analogdator;* **analog gate** = logic gate whose output is proportional to an input signal *analog grind;* **analog input card** = all circuitry on one PCB required for amplifying and converting analog input signals to a digital form *analogt ingångskort;* **analog multimeter** = multimeter that uses a graduated scale and a moving needle as a readout for voltage, current and impedance levels *analogt universalinstrument; compare with* DMM; **analog output card** = all circuitry on one PCB required to convert digital output data from a computer to an analog form *analogt utgångskort;* **analog recording** = storing signals in their natural form without conversion to digital form *analog inspelning;* **analog representation** = value *or* variable in analog form *analog representation;* **analog signal** = continuously varying signal *analog signal;* **analog to digital (A to D** *or* **A/D)** = change a signal from an analog form to a digitally coded form *analog till digital;* **analog to digital converter (ADC** *or* **A to D converter)** = device used to convert an analog input signal to a digital output form, that can be understood by a computer *analog-digitalomvandlare;* **digital to analog converter (DAC** *or* **D to A converter)** = circuit that outputs an analog signal that is proportional to the input digital number, and so converts a digital input to an analog form *digital-analogomvandlare*

COMMENT: a DAC allows the computer to work outside the computer's environment, controlling machines, producing sound *or* speech, etc.; an ADC allows real-world signals to be processed by a computer

analyse ['ænəlaız] *or* **analyze** ['ænəlaız] *vb.* to examine in detail *analysera;* **to analyse a computer printout; to analyse the market potential for a new computer**

analysis [ə'næləsɪs] *subst.* detailed examination and report *analys;* **market analysis; sales analysis; to carry out an analysis of the market potential; to write an analysis of the sales position; cost analysis** = examination in advance of the costs of a new product *kostnadsanalys;* **data analysis** = to extract information and results from data *dataanalys;* **systems analysis** = analysing a process *or* system to see if it could be more efficiently carried out by computer *systemanalys* NOTE: plural is **analyses**

analyst ['ænəlɪst] *subst.* person who carries out an analysis of a problem *analytiker;* **systems analyst** = person who specializes in systems analysis *systemanalytiker*

analyzer ['ænə,laɪzə] *subst.* electronic test equipment that displays various features of a signal *analysator;* **frequency analyzer** = test equipment that displays the amplitudes of the various frequency components of a signal *frekvensanalysator*

anamorphic image ['ænə'mɔːfɪk 'ɪmɪdʒ] *subst.* image which has been distorted in one direction *anamorfisk bild*

ANAPROP ['ænə'prɒp] = ANOMALOUS PROPAGATION distortion of transmitted television signals due to atmospheric conditions *onormal utbredning*

anastigmatic [,ænæstɪg'mætɪk] *subst.* lens *or* optical device that has been corrected for astigmatism *anastigmater*

ancestral file [æn'sestr(ə)l faɪl] *subst.* system of backing up files (son to father to grandfather file), where the son is the current working file *föräldrafil, 'ursprungsfil*

ancillary equipment [æn'sɪlərɪ ɪ'kwɪpmənt] *subst.* equipment which is used to make a task easier, but which is not absolutely necessary *tillbehör*

AND [ənd] *or* **coincidence function** [kəʊ'ɪnsɪd(ə)ns 'fʌn(k)ʃən] *subst.* logical function whose output is true if both its inputs are true *och-funktion;* **AND** *or* **coincidence gate** *or* **circuit** *or* **element** = electronic gate that performs a logical AND function on electrical signals *och-grind;* **AND** *or* **coincidence operation** = processing two or more input signals, outputting their AND function *och-operation*

COMMENT: if both inputs are 1, results of the AND will be 1; if one of the input digits is 0, then AND will produce a 0

anechoic [æn'kəʊɪk] *adj.* (room) that produces no echoes, used for testing audio equipment *ekofri*

angle ['æŋgl] *subst.* measure of the change in direction, usually as the distance turned from a reference line *vinkel;* **wide-angle lens** = lens which has a large acceptance angle *vidvinkelobjektiv*

angstrom ['æŋstrəm] *subst.* unit of measurement equal to one thousand millionth of a metre *Ångström*

anhålla ⇨ **request**

animate ['ænɪmeɪt] *vb.* to make a series of drawings which, when filmed, will create moving images *animera*

animation [,ænɪ'meɪʃ(ə)n] *subst.* drawing images on film, especially using a computer to create moving graphical images, such as cartoons *animation*

annotation [ˌænə(ʊ)ˈteɪʃ(ə)n] *subst.* comment *or* note in a program which explains how the program is to be used *kommentar;* **annotation symbol =** symbol used when making flowcharts, to allow comments to be added *kommentarsymbol*

annunciator [əˈnʌnʃɪeɪtə] *subst. & adj.* signal that can be heard *or* seen that is used to attract attention *uppmärksamhetssignal, uppmärksamhetstecken, alarmsignal*

anode [ˈænəʊd] *subst.* positive electrical terminal of a device *anod*

anomalistic period [əˌnɒməˈlɪstɪk ˈpɪərɪəd] *subst.* time taken for a satellite to travel between consecutive maximum points in its orbit *anomalistisk period*

anpassningsenhet ➭ **adapter**

anrop ➭ **calling**

anropa ➭ **access, call**

anropskvot ➭ **file**

ANSI [ˈænsɪ] *US* = AMERICAN NATIONAL STANDARDS INSTITUTE organization which specifies computer and software standards, including those of high-level programming languages *amerikanska standardiseringsorganisationen*

anslag ➭ **keystroke**

anslagsanhåll ➭ **key**

anslagsfri skrivare ➭ **non-impact printer**

anslagskraft ➭ **key**

anslagsskrivare ➭ **impact**

anslutning ➭ **interconnection, port**

answer [ˈɑːnsə] **1** *subst.* reply *or* letter *or* conversation coming after someone has written or spoken *svar;* **I am writing in answer to your letter of October 6th; my letter got no answer** *or* **there was no answer to my letter; I tried to phone his office but there was no answer; answer time =** time taken for a receiving device to respond to a signal *svarstid* **2** *vb.* **(a)** to speak *or* write after someone has spoken or written to you *svara;* **to answer a letter =** to write a letter in reply to a letter which you have received *svara på ett brev;* **to answer the telephone =** to lift the telephone when it rings and listen to what the caller is saying *svara i telefon* **(b)** to reply to a signal and set up a communications link *svara;* **the first modem originates the call and the second answers it; answer back =** signal sent by the receiving end of a communications system to identify itself *or* to transmit a message *svarssignal*

answering [ˈɑːnsərɪŋ] *subst.* **answering machine =** machine which answers the telephone automatically when someone is not in the office *telefonsvarare;* **answering service =** office which answers the telephone and takes messages for someone *or* for a company *ung. telefonsvararservice*

answerphone [ˈɑːnsəˌfəʊn] *subst.* cassette recorder attached to a telephone, which plays a prerecorded message and records messages from people dialling the number *telefonsvarare*

anteckningsblock ➭ **memory, scratchpad**

antenna [ænˈtenə] *subst.* aerial *or* device for receiving *or* sending radio transmissions by converting electromagnetic impulses into electrical signals and vice-versa *antenn;* **antenna array =** series of small transmitting *or* receiving elements connected in parallel, that make up a complex antenna *antenngrupp, antennuppsättning;* **antenna gain =** transmitted signal power increase due to using a certain type of antenna *antennförstärkning*

anti- [ˈæntɪ] *prefix* meaning against *anti-, icke-;* **anticoincidence circuit** *or* **function =** logical function whose output is true if either (of 2) inputs is true, and false if both inputs are the same *symmetriskt negerad disjunktion, antingen-eller-krets*

antingen-eller-grind (XOR) ➭ **exclusive, EXOR, gate**

antingen-grind ➭ **except**

anti-tinkle suppression [ˈæntɪ ˈtɪŋkl səˈpreʃ(ə)n] *subst. (in a modem)* switch which prevents other telephones on a line ringing when a modem dials out *ringsignalsundertryckning*

användardiagram ➭ **external**

användare ➭ **user, liveware**

användarfel ➭ **error**

användargränssnitt ➭ **man machine interface (MMI), user**

användarhandbok ➭ **manual, user**

användarhandledning ➭ **manual, user**

användarvänlig ➭ **user-friendly**

använd tid ➭ **elapsed time**

APD [ˈeɪpiːˈdiː] = AVALANCHE PHOTODIODE

aperture [ˈæpətjʊə] *subst.* opening in a device that allows a certain amount of light *or* a signal to pass through it *bländare, öppning;* **aperture card =** method of storing microfilmed information with a card surround, that can contain punched information *bländarkort, mikrofilm-strålkort;* **aperture illumination** = pattern generated from an aperture antenna *lobdiagram (för riktantenn);* **aperture mask** = mask used in colour televisions *or* monitors to keep the red, green and blue beams separate *avbländningsmask*

APL ['eɪpiː'el] = A PROGRAMMING LANGUAGE high-level programming language used in scientific and mathematical work *programmerings-språket APL*

apochromatic lens [ˌæpəkrəˈmætɪk ˈlenz] *subst.* optical lens that has been corrected for chromatic aberration *apokromat, apokromatisk lins*

apogee ['æpə(ʊ)dʒiː] *subst.* point in a satellite's orbit where it is at its maximum distance from the earth *apogeum, (satellits) maximala avstånd (högsta punkt)*

apostrophe [əˈpɒstrəfi] *subst.* printing sign ('), which generally indicates that a letter is missing *or* used in ('s), to indicate possession *apostrof*
NOTE: so **computer's** can mean 'belonging to a computer' *or* 'the computer is': **the computer's casing is blue; the computer's broken and has to be repaired.** Note that this is different from **it's** = 'it is' as opposed to **its** = "belonging to it": **it's easy to program; you cannot edit a disk when its write protect tag is closed**

apparat ⊳ **device**

apparatoberoende ⊳ **device**

append [əˈpend] *vb.* to add data to an existing file *or* record *tillägga, lägga till*

appendix [əˈpendiks] *subst.* section at the back of a book, containing additional information *appendix, bilaga;* **for further details see the appendices; a complete list is printed in the appendix**
NOTE: plural is **appendices**

appliance [əˈplaɪəns] *subst.* machine, especially one used in the home *maskin, hjälpmedel, hushållsmaskin;* **all electrical appliances should be properly earthed**

appliance computer [əˈplaɪəns kəmˈpjuːtə] *subst.* ready to run computer system that can be bought in a shop, taken home and used immediately for a particular purpose *nyckelfärdig dator, nyckelfärdigt system; see also* TURNKEY

application [ˌæplɪˈkeɪʃ(ə)n] *subst.* **(a)** asking for something, usually in writing *ansökan;* **application for an account on the system; application form** = form to be filled in when applying *ansökningsblankett;* **to fill in an application (form) for an account on the system (b)** task which a computer performs *or* problem which a computer solves (as opposed to an operating system which is the way in which a computer works) *tillämpning;* **application layer** = top layer in an ISO/OSI network, which requests a transmission (from a users program) *tillämpningsskikt;* **application orientated language** = programming language that provides functions that allow the user to solve certain application problems *tillämpningsorienterat språk;* **applications package** = set of computer programs and manuals that cover all aspects of a particular task (such as payroll, stock control, tax, etc.) *tillämpningspaket;* **applications software** *or* **applications program** = programs which are used by a user to make the computer do what is required, designed to allow a particular task to be performed *tillämpningsprogram;* **the multi-window editor is used to create and edit applications programs; applications specific integrated circuits (ASIC)** = specially designed ICs for one particular function *or* to special specifications *tillämpningsspecifika integrerade kretsar;* **applications terminal** = terminal (such as at a sales desk) which is specially configured to carry out certain tasks *användarterminal*

QUOTE they have announced a fourth generation application development tool which allows users of PCs and PC networks to exchange data with mainframe databases
Minicomputer News

---

apply [əˈplaɪ] *vb.* **(a)** to ask for something, usually in writing *ansöka* **(b)** to affect *or* to touch *beröra, gälla;* **this formula applies only to data received after the interrupt signal**

appoint [əˈpɔɪnt] *vb.* to choose for a job *utnämna, utse, tillsätta;* **to appoint James Smith (to the post of) manager; we have appointed a new computer services manager** NOTE: you appoint a person **to** a job

appointee [əpɔɪnˈtiː] *subst.* person who is appointed to a job *utnämnd (utsedd, tillsatt) person*

appointment [əˈpɔɪntmənt] *subst.* **(a)** arrangement to meet *möte;* **to make** *or* **to fix an appointment for two o'clock; to make an appointment with someone for two o'clock; he was late for his appointment; she had to cancel her appointment; appointments book** = desk diary in which appointments are noted *möteskalender* **(b)** being appointed to a job *utnämning;* **on his appointment as manager** = when he was made manager *när han utnämndes till chef;* **letter of appointment** = letter in which someone is appointed to a job *utnämningsbesked* **(c)** job *ämbete, befattning;* **staff appointment** = job on the staff *stabspost;* **computer appointments vacant** = list (in a newspaper) of jobs which are available in the computer industry *platsannonser för datorindustrin*

approval [ə'pruːv(ə)l] *subst.* **(a)** agreement that something can be used *godkännande (motsvaras t.ex. i Sverige av televerkets "T"-märkning);* **a BABT approval is needed for modems; certificate of approval** = document showing that an item has been approved officially *intyg, registreringsbevis* **(b) on approval** = sale where the buyer only pays for goods if they are satisfactory *till påseende;* **to buy a photocopier on approval** NOTE: no plural

approve [ə'pruːv] *vb.* **(a) to approve of** = to think something is good *godkänna, gilla;* **the new graphics monitor was approved by the safety council before being sold; I approve of the new editor - much easier to use (b)** to agree to something *godkänna, godta, bifalla;* **to approve the terms of a contract; the software has to be approved by the board; an approved modem should carry a label with a green circle and the words "Approved by ...."**

approximate [ə'prɒksɪmət] *adj.* not exact, but almost correct *ungefärlig, approximativ;* **we have made an approximate calculation of the time needed for keyboarding**

approximately [ə'prɒksɪmətlɪ] *adv.* almost correctly *ungefärligen, uppskattningsvis;* **processing time is approximately 10% lower than during the previous quarter**

approximating [ə'prɒksɪmeɪtɪŋ] *adj.* which is nearly correct *uppskattad, ungefärlig;* **using approximating A to D**

approximation [əˌprɒksɪ'meɪʃ(ə)n] *subst.* rough calculation *närmevärde, approximering, approximation;* **approximation of keyboarding time; the final figure is only an approximation ; approximation error** = error caused by rounding off a real number *uppskattningsfel*

A programming language (APL) ['eɪ 'prəʊɡræmɪŋ 'læŋɡwɪɡʒ] *subst.* high-level programming language used for scientific and mathematical work *programmeringsspråket APL*

APT [æpt] = AUTOMATICALLY PROGRAMMED TOOLS programming language used to control numerically controlled machines *programmeringsspråket APT*

Arabic ['ærəbɪk] *adj.* **Arabic numbers** or **figures** = figures such as 1, 2, 3, 4, etc. (as opposed to the Roman numerals I, II, III, IV, etc.) *arabiska siffror;* **the page numbers are written in Arabic figures**

arbetsfönster ⇨ **window**

arbetsstation ⇨ **workstation**

arbetssteg ⇨ **job**

arbitration [ˌɑːbɪ'treɪʃ(ə)n] *subst.* **bus arbitration** = protocol and control of transmission over a bus that ensures fair usage by several users *medling*

arcade game [ɑː'keɪd ɡeɪm] *subst.* computer game played on a machine in a public place *videospel (i spelhall)*

archetype ['ɑːkɪtaɪp] *subst.* document or book that illustrates the styles of a particular time and subject *förebild, original, arketyp*

architecture ['ɑːkɪtektʃə] *subst.* layout and interconnection of a computer's internal hardware and the logical relationships between CPU, memory and I/O devices *arkitektur;* **onion skin architecture** = design of a computer system in layers, according to function or priority *flerlagersarkitektur;* **the onion skin architecture of this computer is made up of a kernel at the centre, an operating system, a low-level language and then the user's programs**

archival quality [ɑː'kaɪv(ə)l 'kwɒlətɪ] *subst.* length of time that a copy can be stored before it becomes illegible *arkivkvalitet (att en handling duger att arkivera)*

archive ['ɑːkaɪv] **1** *subst.* storage of data over a long period *arkiv;* **archive file** = file containing data which is out of date, but which is kept for future reference *arkivfil* **2** *vb.* to put data in storage *arkivera;* **archived copy** = copy kept in storage *arkivkopia*

> QUOTE on-line archiving is also used to keep down the interruption needed for archiving to seconds
> **Computer News**

area ['eərɪə] *subst.* **(a)** measurement of the space taken up by something (calculated by multiplying the length by the width) *yta, area;* **the area of this office is 3,400 square feet; we are looking for a shop with a sales area of about 100 square metres; type area** = space on a page which is taken up by printed characters *textyta;* **area composition** = organizing and setting up pages before photocomposition *sammanställning, (sid)montering* **(b)** section of memory or code that is reserved for a certain purpose *minnesarea, programarea, yta;* **area search** = search for specific data within a certain section of memory or files *areasökning;* **image area** = region of a display screen in which characters can be displayed *bildyta;* **input area** = section of main memory that holds data transferred from backing store until it is processed *indataarea* **(c)** part of a country *or* town *region;* **his sales area is the centre of the town; he finds it difficult to cover all his area in a week; area code =** part of a telephone number that allows the exchange to identify the part of the country required *riktnummer;* **the area code for London is 01; area exchange =** central point in a part of a country where telephone calls are directed to their correct destination inside the area *or* to another exchange   *(publik) telefonstation, växelstation*

area manager ['eərɪə 'mænɪdʒə] *subst.* manager who deals with a certain part of the country *regionchef*

argue ['ɑːgjuː] *vb.* to discuss something about which you do not agree *diskutera, gräla;* **they argued over** *or* **about the design of the cover; we spent hours arguing with the managing director about the layout of the new factory** NOTE: you argue **with** someone **about** *or* **over** something

argument ['ɑːgjʊmənt] *subst.* **(a)** discussing something without agreeing *diskussion, gräl;* **they got into an argument with the customs officials over the documents; he was sacked after an argument with the managing director (b)** variable acted upon by an operator *or* function *argument; see also* OPERAND

arithmetic [ə'rɪθmətɪk] *subst.* concerned with mathematical functions such as addition, subtraction, division and multiplication *aritmetik;* **arithmetic capability =** ability of a device to perform mathematical functions *aritmetisk förmåga;* **arithmetic check =** further arithmetic operation carried out to ensure that a result is correct *aritmetisk kontroll;* **arithmetic functions =** calculations carried out on numbers, such as addition, subtraction, multiplication, division *aritmetiska funktioner;* **arithmetic instruction =** program instruction in which the operator defines the arithmetic operation to be carried out *aritmetisk instruktion; compare with* LOGICAL INSTRUCTION; **arithmetic logic unit (ALU)** *or* **arithmetic unit =** hardware section of a CPU that performs all the mathematical and logical functions *aritmetisk (logisk) enhet;* **arithmetic operation =** mathematical function carried out on data *aritmetisk operation;* **arithmetic operators =** symbol which indicates an arithmetic function (such as + for addition, x for multiplication) *aritmetiska operatorer, aritmetikoperatorer;* **arithmetic register =** memory location which stores operands *aritmetikregister;* **arithmetic shift =** word *or* data moved one bit to the left *or* right inside a register, losing the bit shifted off the end *aritmetiskt skift; compare with* LOGICAL SHIFT; **external arithmetic =** arithmetic

performed by a coprocessor *extern aritmetik;* **internal arithmetic =** arithmetic performed by the ALU *intern aritmetik*

aritmetik- och logikenhet ⇨ **unit**

aritmetisk instruktion ⇨ **instruction**

ark ⇨ **form, sheet**

arkivkopia ⇨ **file**

arkivskåp ⇨ **filing**

arkmatare ⇨ **cut, feed**

arkmatning ⇨ **feed**

arm [ɑːm] **1** *subst.* **access arm =** mechanical device in a disk drive used to position the read/write head over the correct track on a disk *sökarm* **2** *vb.* (i) to prepare a device *or* machine *or* routine for action *or* inputs *göra i ordning;* (ii) to define which interrupt lines are active *aktivera;* **armed interrupt =** interrupt line which has been made active (using an interrupt mask) *aktiverat avbrott, avmaskat avbrott*

array [ə'reɪ] *subst.* ordered structure containing individually accessible elements referenced by numbers, used to store tables *or* sets of related data *uppställning, vektor;* **alphanumeric array =** array whose elements are letters and numbers *alfanumerisk uppställning, alfanumerisk vektor;* **array bounds =** limits to the number of elements which can be stored in an array *vektorstorleksgräns;* **array dimension =** number of elements in an array, given as rows and columns *vektorstorlek;* **array element =** one individual piece of data within an array *vektorelement;* **array processor =** computer that can act upon several arrays of data simultaneously, for very fast mathematical applications *vektorprocessor;* **the array processor allows the array that contains the screen image to be rotated with one simple command; string array =** array whose elements can be strings (of alphanumeric characters) *strängvektor;* **three-dimensional array =** array made up of a number of two dimensional arrays, arranged in parallel, giving rows, columns and depth *tredimensionell vektor;* **two-dimensional array =** ordered structure whose elements are arranged as a table (of rows and columns) *tvådimensionell vektor*

arsenide ['ɑːsənaɪd] *see* GALLIUM ARSENIDE

article ['ɑːtɪkl] *subst.* **(a)** section of a newspaper *or* magazine *artikel;* **he wrote an article about the user group for the local newspaper (b)** section of an agreement *punkt, paragraf;* **see article 8 of the contract**

artificial intelligence (AI) [ˌɑːtɪ'fɪʃ(ə)l ɪn'telɪdʒ(ə)ns ('eɪ 'aɪ)] *subst.* the design and device of computer programs that attempt to imitate human intelligence and decision making functions, providing basic reasoning and other human characteristics *artificiell (konstgjord) intelligens (AI)*

artwork ['ɑːt,wɜːk] *subst.* graphical work *or* images which are to be printed *(monterade) bildoriginal;* **the artwork has been sent for filming**
NOTE: no plural

ASA ['eɪesˈeɪ] American Standards Association *den amerikanska standardiseringsorganisationen;* **ASA exposure index =** one standard method used to code the sensitivity of film *exponenttal, ljuskänslighet*

ascender [əˈsendə] *subst.* part of a character that rises above the main line of printed characters (as the 'tail' of a 'b', 'd', etc.) *stapel*

ASCII ['æskiː] = AMERICAN STANDARD CODE FOR INFORMATION INTERCHANGE code which represents alphanumeric characters in binary code *ASCII-kod;* **ASCII character =** character which is in the ASCII list of codes *ASCII-tecken;* **ASCII file =** stored file containing only ASCII coded character data *ASCII-fil;* **use a word processor *or* other program that generates a standard ASCII file; ASCII keyboard =** keyboard which gives all the ASCII characters *ASCII-tangentbord* NOTE: when speaking say "as-key"

ASIC ['eɪsɪk] = APPLICATION SPECIFIC INTEGRATED CIRCUITS specially designed ICs for one particular function *or* to special specifications *tillämpningsspecifika integrerade kretsar*

aspect ['æspekt] *subst.* way in which something appears *utseende;* **aspect card =** card containing information on documents in an information retrieval system *registerkort;* **aspect ratio =** ratio of the width to the height of pixel shapes *bildpunktsförhållande;* **aspect system =** method of storing and indexing documents in a retrieval system *arkivsystem*

ASR ['eɪesˈɑː] = AUTOMATIC SEND/RECEIVE device *or* terminal that can transmit *or* receive information *sändtagarterminal; compare* KSR

COMMENT: an ASR terminal can input information via a keyboard or via a tape cassette or paper tape. It can receive information and store it in internal memory or on tape

assemble [əˈsembl] *vb.* **(a)** to put a hardware *or* software product together from various smaller parts *sätta samman, montera;* **the parts for the disk drive are made in Japan and assembled in France (b)**

to translate assembly code into machine code *assemblera;* **there is a short wait during which time the program is assembled into object code; syntax errors spotted whilst the source program is being assembled (c)** to insert specific library routines *or* macros *or* parameters into a program *konfigurera program*

assemblerare ▷ **language, processor**

assemblerformat ▷ **format**

assembler (program) [əˈsemblə ˈprəʊɡræm] *subst.* assembly program *or* program which converts a program written in assembly language into machine code *assemblerare;* **absolute assembler =** type of assembly language program designed to produce code which uses only absolute addresses and values *absolutassemblerare;* **assembler error messages =** messages produced by an assembler program that indicate that errors have been found in the source code *felmeddelanden;* **cross-assembler =** assembler that produces machine-code code for one computer while running on another *korsassemblerare;* **single-pass assembler =** object code produced in one run through the assembler of the source program *enpassassemblerare;* **two-pass assembler =** assembler that converts an assembly language program into machine code in two passes, the first pass stores symbolic addresses, the second converts them to absolute addresses *tvåpassassemblerare*

assemblerspråk ▷ **low-level language (LLL)**

assembly [əˈsemblɪ] *subst.* **(a)** putting an item together from various parts *sammansättning, montering;* **there are no assembly instructions to show you how to put the computer together ; assembly plant =** factory where units are put together from parts made in other factories *monteringsfabrik* **(b)** converting a program into machine code *assemblera;* **assembly code =** mnemonics which are used to represent machine code instructions in an assembler program *assemblerkod;* **assembly language *or* assembler language =** programming language used to code information which will then be converted to machine code *assemblerspråk;* **assembly listing =** display of an assembly program ordered according to memory location *assemblerlistning;* **assembly (language) program =** number of assembly code instructions which perform a task *assemblerprogram;* **assembly routine *or* system =** *see* ASSEMBLER; **assembly time =** (i) time taken by an assembler program to translate a program *assembleringstid;* (ii) period during which an assembler is converting a program from assembly language into machine code *assembleringstid*

assertion [ə'sɜːʃ(ə)n] *subst.* (i) program statement of a fact *or* rule *påstående;* (ii) fact that is true *or* defined as being true *utsaga, försäkran*

assign [ə'saɪn] *vb.* (a) to give a computer *or* someone a job of work *tilldela;* **he was assigned the job of checking the sales figures; two PCs have been assigned to outputting the labels (b)** (i) to set a variable equal to a string of characters *or* numbers *tilldela;* (ii) to reserve part of a computer system for use while a program is running *tilldela;* **assigned frequency** = frequency reserved for one user *or* application *tilldelad frekvens*

assignment [ə'saɪnmənt] *subst.* **(a)** transfer of a property *or* of a right *överföring, överlåtelse;* **assignment of a copyright (b)** particular job of work *uppgift, tilldelning;* **he was appointed managing director with the assignment to improve the company's profits; the oil team is on an assignment in the North Sea (c)** setting a variable equal to a string of characters *or* a value *tilldelning;* **assignment statement** = basic programming command that sets a variable equal to a value *or* string *or* character *tilldelningssats*

assignor [ˌæsaɪ'nɔː] *subst.* person who assigns something to someone *överlåtare*

assist [ə'sɪst] *vb.* to help *hjälpa, assistera;* **can you assist the stock controller in counting the stock? he assists me with my income tax returns** NOTE: you assist someone **in** doing something or **with** something

assistance [ə'sɪstəns] *subst.* help *hjälp, assistans;* **financial assistance** = help in the form of money *finansiell hjälp* NOTE: no plural

assistant [ə'sɪstənt] *subst.* person who helps *or* an ordinary employee *medhjälpare;* **personal assistant** = secretary who also helps the boss in various ways *personlig medhjälpare (assistent);* **shop assistant** = person who serves the customers in a shop *(affärs)biträde;* **assistant manager** = person who helps a manager *biträdande chef*

associate [ə'səʊʃɪət] **1** *adj.* linked *förenad (med);* **associate company** = company which is partly owned by another *delägt företag* **2** *subst.* person who works in the same business as someone *kollega;* **she is a business associate of mine**

associational editing [əsəʊsɪ'eɪʃn(ə)l 'edɪtɪŋ] *subst.* way of editing a film *or* video so as to present together scenes which are similar to others *associativ redigering*

associative addressing [ə'səʊʃɪətɪv ə'dresɪŋ] *or* **content-addressable addressing** ['kɒntent ə'dresəbl ə'dresɪŋ] *subst.* location addressed by its contents rather than its address *associativ adressering;* **associative processor** = processor that uses associative storage *associativ processor;* **associative memory** *or* **storage** *or* **content-addressable storage** = method of data retrieval that uses part of the data rather than an address to locate the data *associativt minne;* **associative storage register** = register that is located by its contents rather than a name *or* address *associativt minnesregister*

astabil vippa ⇨ **multivibrator**

astable multivibrator [eɪ'steɪbl ˌmʌltɪvaɪ'breɪtə] *subst.* electronic circuit that repeatedly switches an output between two voltage levels *astabil vippa, astabil multivibrator*

asterisk ['æst(ə)rɪsk] *subst.* graphical symbol (*) used as a sign for multiplication *asterisk*

astigmatism [æs'tɪgmətɪz(ə)m] *subst.* optical lens disorder which prevents the light beams from converging properly *astigmatism*

async [æ'sɪŋk] *(informal)* = ASYNCHRONOUS

asynchronous [æ'sɪŋkrənəs] *adj.* serial data *or* equipment which does not depend on being synchronized with another piece of equipment *asynkron;* **asynchronous access** = communications using handshaking to synchronize data transmission *asynkron åtkomst;* **asynchronous communications** = data transmission between devices that is not synchronized to a clock, but is transmitted when ready *asynkron kommunikation;* **asynchronous communications interface adapter (ACIA)** = circuit that allows a computer to transmit and receive serial data using asynchronous access *anpassningsenhet för asynkron kommunikation;* **asynchronous computer** = (i) computer that changes from one operation to the next according to signals received when the process is finished *asynkron dator;* (ii) computer in which a process starts on the arrival of signals *or* data, rather than on a clock pulse *asynkron dator;* **asynchronous mode** = terminal linked to another piece of equipment in a way where the two need not be synchronized *asynkront läge, asynkront tillstånd;* **asynchronous port** = connection to a computer allowing asynchronous data access *asynkron (kommunikations)utgång;* **since asynchronous ports are used no special hardware is required; asynchronous transmission** = data transmission that uses handshaking signals rather than clock signals to synchronize data pulses *asynkron överföring*

> QUOTE each channel handles two forms of communication: asynchronous communication is mainly for transferring data between computers and peripheral devices, while character communication is for data transfer between computers
>
> **Electronics & Power**

asynkron bearbetning ⊳ **immediate, inline**

asynkron kommunikationsenhet ⊳ **ACIA**

ATC ['eɪtiː'siː] = AUTHORIZATION TO COPY software publisher granting the user the permission to make a certain number of copies of a program *tillåtelse att kopiera*

ATE ['eɪtiː'iː] = AUTOMATIC TEST EQUIPMENT computer controlled testing facilities, that can check a complex circuit *or* PCB for faults *or* problems *automatisk testutrustning*

ATM ['eɪtiː'em] = AUTOMATED TELLER MACHINE

atmosphere ['ætmə‚sfɪə] *subst.* gas which surrounds the earth *atmosfär*

atmospheric [‚ætməs'ferɪk] *adj.* referring to the atmosphere *atmosfärisk;* **atmospheric absorption** = energy loss of a radio signal due to atmospheric conditions causing dispersion of the signal *atmosfärisk absorbtion;* **atmospheric conditions** = state of the atmosphere (including clouds, pressures, etc.) *atmosfäriska förhållanden*

A to D ['eɪtə'diː] *or* **A/D** ['eɪ'diː] = ANALOG TO DIGITAL changing a signal from an analog form to a digitally coded form *analog till digital;* **A to D converter** = (analog to digital converter) device used to convert an analog input to a digital output form which can be understood by a computer *analog till digitalomvandlare;* **the speech signal was first passed through an A to D converter before being analysed;** *opposite is* DIGITAL TO ANALOG

atom ['ætəm] *subst.* **(a)** smallest particle of an element that has the same properties as the element *atom* **(b)** value *or* string that cannot be reduced to a simpler form *atom (jargong)*

atomic [ə'tɒmɪk] *adj.* referring to atoms *atomär;* **atomic clock** = very accurate clock which uses changes in energy of atoms as a reference *atomur*

attach [ə'tætʃ] *vb.* to fasten *or* to link *koppla in, ansluta;* **attached processor** = separate microprocessor in a system that performs certain functions under the control of a central processor *tillsatsprocessor*

attachment [ə'tætʃmənt] *subst.* device which is attached to a machine for a special purpose *tillbehör, tillsats;* **there is a special single sheet feed attachment**

attack [ə'tæk] *subst.* start of a sound *framkant, front;* **attack envelope** = shape of the initial section of a signal *framkantsutseende*

attend [ə'tend] *vb.* to be present at *närvara*

attended operation [ə'tendɪd ‚ɒpə'reɪʃ(ə)n] *subst.* process which has an operator standing by in case of problems *övervakad operation*

attend to [ə'tend tuː] *vb.* to give careful thought to (something) and deal with it *tillse, ägna uppmärksamhet åt;* **attend to this fault first - it's the worst**

attention [ə'tenʃ(ə)n] *subst.* giving careful thought, especially to processing a particular section of a program *uppmärksamhet;* **this routine requires the attention of the processor every minute; attention interruption** = interrupt signal that requests the attention of the processor *uppmärksamhetsavbrott;* **attention key** = key on a terminal that sends an interrupt signal to the processor *avbrottstangent*

attenuate [ə'tenjʊeɪt] *vb.* to reduce the strength *or* size of peaks (of a signal) *dämpa*

attenuation [ə‚tenjʊ'eɪʃ(ə)n] *subst.* reduction of a signal as it passes through a medium *dämpning*

attribute ['ætrɪbjuːt] *subst.* (i) field entry in a file *(fält)attribut;* (ii) information concerning the display *or* presentation of information *attribut;* **this attribute controls the colour of the screen; screen attributes** = variables defining the shape, size and colour of text *or* graphics displayed *skärmattribut*

auctioneering device [‚ɔːkʃə'nɪərɪŋ dɪ'vaɪs] *subst.* device that will select the maximum *or* minimum signal from a number of input signals *auktionsenhet*

audible ['ɔːdəbl] *adj.* which can be heard *hörbar;* **the printer makes an audible signal when it runs out of paper**

audience ['ɔːdjəns] *subst.* people who watch a TV programme *or* listen to a radio programme *publik;* **audience rating** = rating of a programme by calculating the number of people who have watched it *publiksiffra*

audio ['ɔːdɪəʊ] *adj. & subst.* referring to sound *or* to things which can be heard *hörbar, som har med ljud att göra;* **audio active** = system used in a learning laboratory, where the student can hear and respond to questions *inlärningsstudio;* **audio cassette** = reel of magnetic recording tape in a small protective casing inserted into a cassette recorder (for recording music *or* voice *or* data) *ljudkassett;* **audio compressor** = circuit that limits the maximum level of a signal by attenuating any peaks *ljudkompressor;* **audio conferencing** *see* TELECONFERENCING; **audio frequency** = frequency within the audio range that a human can hear *ljudfrekvens;* **audio range** = frequency range between 50-20000Hz *hörbarhetsområde;* **audio response unit** = speech synthesizer that allows a computer to speak responses to requests *syntetisk talmaskin;* **audio slide** = photographic slide that has magnetic tape along an edge allowing sound to be recorded *ljuddia*

audiovisual (AV) [ˌɔːdɪəʊ'vɪzjʊəl ('eɪ'viː)] *adj.* which uses sound and images *audiovisuell;* **audiovisual aids** = equipment used in teaching, which includes both sound and pictures *audiovisuella hjälpmedel*

audit ['ɔːdɪt] *subst.* noting tasks carried out by a computer *revision, loggning;* **audit trail** = recording details of use of a system by noting transactions carried out (used for checking on illegal use *or* to trace a malfunction) *revisionsloggning*

augend ['ɔːdʒend] *subst. (in an addition)* the number to which another number, the addend, is added to produce the sum *augend*

augment [ɔːg'ment] *vb.* to increase *utvidga, förstärka;* **augmented addressing** = producing a usable address word from two shorter words *utökad adressering*

augmenter [ɔːg'mentə] *subst.* value added to another *förstärkare*

aural ['ɔːr(ə)l] *adj.* by ear *hörsel-, öron-*

authentic [ɔː'θentɪk] *adj.* which is true *äkta*

authenticate [ɔː'θentɪkeɪt] *vb.* to say that something is true *or* genuine *intyga*

authentication [ɔːˌθentɪ'keɪʃ(ə)n] *subst.* making sure that something is authentic *certifiering, validering;* **authentication of messages** = using special codes to identify the sender of messages, so that the messages can be recognized as being genuine *meddelandevalidering*

author ['ɔːθə] *subst.* person who wrote a program *upphovsman, författare;* **author language** = programming language used to write CAL and training programs

verktygsspråk för pedagogiska ändamål; **authoring system** = computer system that is able to run an author language *system som kan köra "author language"*

authority [ɔː'θɒrətɪ] *subst.* power to do something *befogenhet, bemyndigande;* **he has no authority to delete your account;** **authority file** *or* **list** = list of special terms used by people compiling a database and also by the users of the database *befogenhetsfil*

authorization [ˌɔːθ(ə)raɪ'zeɪʃ(ə)n] *subst.* **(a)** permission *or* power to do something *tillåtelse, bemyndigande;* **authorization to copy (ATC)** = software publisher granting the user the permission to make a certain number of copies of a program *tillåtelse att kopiera*

COMMENT: some companies have introduced ATC schemes which allow users of certain software to make duplicates of the companies' programs for a fee

(b) giving a user permission to access a system *berättigad, bemyndigad, auktoriserad;* **authorization code** = code used to restrict access to a computer system to authorized users only *bemyndigandekod, form av lösenord* NOTE: no plural

authorize ['ɔːθəraɪz] *vb.* **(a)** to give permission for something to be done *tillåta;* **to authorize the purchase of a new computer system (b)** to give someone the authority to do something *bemyndiga*

authorized ['ɔːθəraɪzd] *adj.* permitted *tillåten;* **authorized user** = person who is allowed to access a system *bemyndigad användare*

auto ['ɔːtəʊ] *adj. & prefix* automatic *or* which works without the user needing to act *auto-;* **auto advance** = paper in a printer that is automatically moved forward to the next line at the end of a line *automatisk frammatning;* **auto-answer** = (modem) that will automatically answer a telephone when called *autosvar;* **auto-baud scanning** circuit that can automatically sense and select the correct baud rate for a line *automatisk hastighetsavsökning;* **auto boot** = computer system that will initiate a boot-up procedure when it is switched on *autostart;* **auto-dial** = to dial a number automatically using stored data *automatisk nummerslagning;* **auto-login** *or* **auto-logon** = phone number, password and user's number transmitted when requested by a remote system to automate logon *automatisk inloggning; see also* LOGIN, LOGON; **auto-redial** = (modem) that dials a telephone number again if engaged, until it replies *automatisk återuppringning;* **auto repeat** = facility where a character is automatically repeated if the key is kept pressed down *automatisk repetering;* **auto restart =** computer that can initialize and reload its operating system if there is a fault *or* power failure *or* at switch on *automatisk återstart;* **auto start =** facility to load a program automatically when the computer is switched on *autostart;* **auto stop =** feature of a tape player which stops when it has reached the end of a tape *autostopp;* **auto verify =** verification procedure carried out automatically, as soon as the data has been saved *automatisk kontroll*

QUOTE expansion accessories include auto-dial and auto-answer
Electronic & Wireless World

---

autografi ▷ **desktop**

automat ▷ **dispenser**

automate ['ɔːtəmeit] *vb.* to install machines to do work previously done by people *automatisera;* **the automated office =** office where many of the tasks are done by machines *"det automatiserade kontoret";* **automated teller machine (ATM) =** automatic telling machine *or* machine linked to a main computer that allows cash to be taken out of a bank account when a special card is inserted and special instructions given *uttagsautomat, ung. bankautomat*

automatic [ˌɔːtə'mætɪk] *subst.* which works by itself, without being worked by an operator *automatisk;* **automatic calling unit (ACU) =** device which allows a computer to call telephone numbers automatically *enhet för automatisk uppringning;* **automatic carriage return =** system where the cursor automatically returns to the beginning of a new line when it reaches the end of the previous one *automatisk radmatning;* **automatic checking =** error detection and validation check carried out automatically on received data *automatisk kontroll;* **automatic data capture =** system where data is automatically recorded in a computer system, as it is input *automatisk datainsamling;* **automatic data processing (ADP) =** data processing done by a computer *automatisk databehandling (ADB);* **automatic decimal adjustment =** process of lining up all the decimal points in a column of figures *automatisk decimaljustering;* **automatic error correction =** correction of received data, using error detection and correction codes *automatisk felkorrigering;* **automatic error detection =** use of an (alphanumeric) code, such as a gray code, that will allow any errors to be detected *automatisk feldetektering;* **automatic gain control (AGC) =** electronic device that provides a constant amplitude output signal from a varying input signal, by changing its gain *automatisk förstärkningskontroll;* **automatic letter**

writing = writing of form letters (using a wordprocessor) *kopplad brevutskrift, massbrevfunktion;* **automatic loader =** short program (usually in ROM) that will boot up a system and load a program *automatisk laddare;* **automatic message accounting =** system of logging telephone calls automatically so that details of them can be given to the user *automatisk samtalsredovisning;* **automatic programming =** process of producing an optimum (operating) system for a particular process *automatisk programmering;* **automatic repeat =** facility where a character is automatically repeated if the key is kept pressed down *automatisk repetering;* **automatic sequencing =** ability of a computer to execute a number of programs *or* tasks without extra commands *automatisk sekvensiering;* **automatic telephone exchange =** telephone exchange operated by a computer rather than a human operator *automatisk telefonväxel;* **automatic telling machine** *or* US **automatic teller machine =** machine which allows money to be taken out of a bank account when a special card is inserted and special instructions given *uttagsautomat, ung. bankautomat;* **automatic test equipment (ATE) =** computer controlled testing facilities, that can check a complex circuit *or* PCB for faults *or* problems *automatisk testutrustning;* **automatic vending machine =** machine which provides drinks, cigarettes, etc., when money is put in *varuautomat*

automatically [ˌɔːtə'mætɪk(ə)lɪ] *adv.* (machine) working without a person giving instructions *automatiskt;* **the statements are sent out automatically; addresses are typed in automatically; a demand note is sent automatically when payment is late; the compiler automatically corrected the syntax errors; a SBC automatically limits the movement of the machine; the program is run automatically when the computer is switched on**

automation [ˌɔːtə'meiʃ(ə)n] *subst.* use of machines to do work with very little supervision by people *automation*
NOTE: no plural
see AUTOMATE

automatiserat kontor ▷ **electronic**

automatisk avstavning ▷ **wraparound**

automatiskt system ▷ **hand**

automatuppringande ▷ **dial**

autopositive ['ɔːtə(ʊ)'pɒzitɪv] *subst.* photographic process that produces a positive image without a negative stage *omvändningsframkallning*

autosvarsmodem ▷ **modem**

auxiliary [ɔːgˈzɪljərɪ] *adj.* which helps *tillsats-, reserv-;* the computer room has an auxiliary power supply in case there is a mains failure; auxiliary equipment = backup *or* secondary equipment in case of a breakdown *tillsatsutrustning, reservutrustning;* auxiliary processor = extra, specialized processor, such as an array *or* numerical processor that can work with a main CPU to increase execution speed *tillsatsprocessor, hjälpprocessor;* auxiliary storage *or* memory *or* store = any data storage medium (such a magnetic tape *or* floppy disk) that is not the main high speed computer storage (RAM) *tillsatsminne, hjälpminne;* disk drives and magnetic tape are auxiliary storage on this machine

AV [ˈeɪˈviː] = AUDIOVISUAL

availability [əˌveɪləˈbɪlətɪ] *subst.* being easily obtained *tillgänglighet;* the availability of the latest software package is very good; offer subject to availability = the offer is valid only if the goods are available *erbjudandet gäller produkter i lager* NOTE: no plural

available [əˈveɪləbl] *adj.* which can be obtained *or* bought *tillgänglig;* available in all branches; item no longer available; items available to order only; available light = light which is present at a place where photographs are being taken, without needing additional artificial light *dagsljus;* available list = list of unallocated memory and resources in a system *lista över outnyttjade resurser;* available point = smallest single unit *or* point of a display whose colour and brightness can be controlled *pixel, minsta adresserbara bildpunkt;* available power = maximum electrical *or* processing power that a system can deliver *tillgänglig effekt;* available time = time during which a system may be used *tillgänglig tid*

avalanche [ˈævəlaːnʃ] *subst.* one action starting a number of other actions *lavin;* there was an avalanche of errors after I pressed the wrong key; avalanche photodiode (APD) = photodiode able to detect very low light levels (one photon received produces several electrons) *lavinfotodiod*

avbild ⇨ image

avbildningstabell ⇨ image

avbrott ⇨ break, interrupt

avbrottsbearbetning ⇨ interrupt

avbrottsfri kraft ⇨ uninterruptable **power supply (UPS)**

avbrottsförfrågan ⇨ interrupt

avbrottshanterare ⇨ interrupt

avbrottskoder ⇨ escape character

avbrottskommando ⇨ kill

avbrottslagring ⇨ interrupt

avbrottslinje ⇨ interrupt

avbrottsmask ⇨ mask

avbrottsnivå ⇨ interrupt

avbrottsprioritering ⇨ interrupt

avbrottspunkt ⇨ trace

avbrottstangent ⇨ escape character

avbrottstecken ⇨ escape character

avbrottstid ⇨ holdup

avbryta ⇨ abort, cancel, kill

average [ˈæv(ə)rɪdʒ] **1** *subst.* number calculated by adding together several figures and dividing by the number of figures added *medeltal, medelvärde;* the average for the last three months *or* the last three months' average; sales average *or* average of sales; weighted average = average which is calculated taking several factors into account, giving some more value than others *viktat medeltal;* on an average = in general *i genomsnitt;* we sell, on an average, five computers a day **2** *adj.* middle (figure) *genomsnittlig, medel-;* average cost per unit; average price; average sales per representative; average access time = the average time taken between a request being sent and data being returned from a memory device *medelåtkomsttid;* average delay = average time that a user must wait when trying to access a communication network *medelfördröjning; see also* MEAN the average delay increases at nine-thirty when everyone tries to log-in **3** *vb.* to produce as an average figure *beräkna medeltalet*

average out [ˈæv(ə)rɪdʒ aut] *vb.* to come to a figure as an average *jämna ut sig, fördela sig jämnt;* it averages out at 120 dpi

avfrågat avbrott ⇨ interrupt

avfrågning ⇨ polling

avfrågningstid ⇨ overhead

avgränsa ⇨ delimit

avgränsningstecken ⇨ delimiter

avkoda ⇨ decode

avkodare ⇨ decoder

avkodning ⇨ decoding

avkodningsenhet ⇨ de-scrambler

avkänningsmärken ⇨ mark

avlusa ⇨ debug

avmagnetisera ▷ degauss, demagnetize

avmagnetiserare ▷ head

avrundning ▷ rounding

avskärmning ▷ screen

avslutad ▷ complete, finished

avslutande systemadministrativa rutiner ▷ end

avslutning ▷ completion

avspelningshuvud ▷ head

avstavad ▷ hyphenated

avstava och justera ▷ justify

avstavning ▷ hyphenation

avstavning och radjustering ▷ justification

avstavningsprogram ▷ spacer

avstavningszon ▷ hot, soft

avsöka ▷ scan

avsökare ▷ scanner

avsökningsminne ▷ scanner

avtagande ▷ decay

avtal ▷ deal

axis ['æksɪs] *subst.* (i) line around which something turns *axel;* (ii) reference line which is the basis for coordinates on a graph *koordinat, axel;* **the CAD package allows an axis to be placed anywhere; horizontal axis** = reference line used for horizontal coordinates on a graph *horisontell axel;* **vertical axis** = reference line used for vertical coordinates on a graph *vertikal axel* NOTE: plural is **axes**

azerty keyboard [ə'zɜːtɪ 'kiːbɔːd] *subst.* method of arranging the keys on a keyboard where the first line begins AZERTY (used mainly in Europe) *azerty-tangentbord (användes främst i fransktalande länder); compare* QWERTY

azimuth ['æzɪməθ] *subst.* angle of a tape head to a reference (such as a tape plane) *azimut, vinkel;* **azimuth alignment** = correct horizontal angle of a tape head to the magnetic tape *azimutinställning, vinkelinställning;* **azimuth alignment is adjusted with this small screw; azimuth alignment might not be correct for tape recorded on a different machine**

Bb

B [biː] hexadecimal equivalent to decimal number 11 *talet elva skrivet med hexadecimal notation*

babble ['bæbl] *subst.* crosstalk *or* noise from other sources which interferes with a signal *interferens, överhöring*

BABT ['biːeɪbiː'tiː] = BRITISH APPROVAL BOARD FOR TELECOMMUNICATIONS; **BABT approval** = official approval for a device to be connected to the public telephone system *den engelska motsvarigheten till t. ex. televerkets "T"-märkning*

back [bæk] **1** *subst.* opposite side to the front *baksida;* **there is a wide range of connectors at the back of the main unit 2** *vb.* to help *stödja;* **battery-backed** = (volatile storage device) that has a battery backup *batterisäkrad;* **the RAM disk card has the option to be battery-backed; battery-backed CMOS memory replaces a disk drive in this portable**

backassemblera ▷ disassemble

back-end processor ['bæk end 'prəʊsesə] *subst.* special purpose auxiliary processor *stödprocessor*

background ['bækgraʊnd] *subst.* **(a)** past work *or* experience *bakgrund;* **his background is in the computer industry; the company is looking for someone with a background of success in the electronics industry; what is his background** *or* **do you know anything about his background? (b)** part of a picture which is behind the main object of interest *bakgrund;* **the new graphics processor chip can handle background, foreground and sprite movement independently; background colour** = colour of a computer screen display (characters and graphics are normally displayed in a different foreground colour) *bakgrundsfärg;* **white background colour with black characters is less stressful for the eyes; background noise** = noise which is present along with the required signal *bakgrundsbrus;* **the other machines around this device will produce a lot of background noise; the modem is sensitive to background noise; background projection** *or* **back projection** = film projected onto the back of a screen, in front of which further action is filmed *bakgrundsprojektion* **(c)** system in a computer where low-priority work can be done in the intervals when very important work is not being done *bakgrund;* **background job** = low priority task *bakgrundsjobb;* **background printing** =

printing from a computer while it is processing another task *utskrift i bakgrunden,* *bakgrundsutskrift;* **background printing can be carried out whilst you are editing another document; background program** = computer program with a very low priority *bakgrundsprogram;* **background task** = process executed at any time by the computer system, not normally noticed by the user *bakgrundsuppdrag*

background processing ['bækgraʊnd 'prəʊsesɪŋ] *subst.* **(a)** low priority job which is executed when there are no higher priority activities for the computer to attend to *bakgrundsbearbetning* **(b)** process which does not use the on-line capabilities of a system *bakgrundsbearbetning* NOTE: opposite is **foreground**

backing ['bækɪŋ] *subst.* **backing store** *or* **storage** *or* **memory** = permanent storage medium onto which data can be recorded before being processed by the computer *or* after processing for later retrieval *säkerhetsminne, stödminne;* **by adding another disk drive, I will increase the backing store capabilities; paper tape is one of the slowest access backing stores;** *compare with* MAIN MEMORY

backkompilator ⇨ **decompilation**

backlog ['bæklɒg] *subst.* work *or* tasks that have yet to be processed *arbete man inte hunnit med;* **the programmers can't deal with the backlog of programming work; the queue was too short for the backlog of tasks waiting to be processed** NOTE: no plural

back number ['bæk'nʌmbə] *subst.* old copy of a journal *or* periodical *gammal utgåva*

back pack ['bækpæk] *subst.* lightweight television recording equipment which the cameraman carries on his back when filming *ryggsäck*

backplane ['bæk,pleɪn] *subst.* part of the body of a computer which holds the circuit boards, buses and expansion connectors (the backplane does not provide any processing functions) *bakplan; see* MOTHERBOARD, RACK

back projection ['bæk prə(ʊ)'dʒekʃ(ə)n] *subst.* background projection *or* film projected onto the back of a screen, in front of which further action is filmed *bakåtprojektion*

backscatter ['bæk,skætə] *subst.* reflected *or* scattered radio wave travelling in the opposite direction to the original signal *bakåtstrålning*

backspace ['bækspeɪs] *subst.* movement of a cursor *or* printhead back by one character *backstegning, backning;* **backspace character** = code that causes a backspace action in a display device *back(stegnings)tecken;* **backspace key** = key which moves the cursor back one space *back(stegnings)tangent;* **if you make a mistake entering data, use the backspace key to correct it**

backstegning ⇨ **backspace**

backtrack ['bæktræk] *vb.* to carry out list processing in reverse, starting with the goal and working towards the proofs *baklänges härledning*

backup ['bæk'ʌp] *adj. & subst.* **(a)** helping *stöd;* **we offer a free backup service to customers; battery backup** = use of a battery to provide power to a volatile device (RAM chip) to retain data after a computer has been switched off *batterisäkring* **(b) backup** *or* **backup file** *or* **backup copy** = copy of a file *or* set of data kept for security against errors in the original *or* master copy *säkerhetskopia;* **backup copy** = copy of a computer disk to be kept in case the original disk is damaged *reservkopia;* **the most recent backup copy is kept in the safe; backup procedure** = method of making backup copies of files *säkerhetslagringsrutin;* **memory backup capacitor** = very high capacitance (small) device that can provide power for volatile RAM chips for up to two weeks (used instead of a battery) *minnessäkring med kondensator*

back up [bæk 'ʌp] *vb.* **(a)** to make a copy of a file *or* data *or* disk *säkerhetskopiera;* **the company accounts were backed up on disk as a protection against fire damage; the program enables users to back up hard disk files with a single command (b)** to help *stödja;* **he brought along a file of documents to back up his claim; the printout backed up his argument for a new system**

QUOTE the system backs up at the rate of 2.5Mb per minute
Microcomputer News
QUOTE the previous version is retained, but its extension is changed to .BAK indicating that it's a back-up
Personal Computer World

Backus-Naur-Form (BNF) ['bækəs'naʊə'fɔːm ('biːen'ef)] system of writing and expressing the syntax of a programming language *syntaxbeskrivande notation för programmeringsspråk*

backward ['bækwəd] *or* **backwards** ['bækwədz] *adj. & adv.* towards the back *or* in the opposite direction *baklänges, bakvänd;* **backward channel** = channel from the receiver to transmitter allowing the receiver to send control and handshaking signals *back-kanal;* **backward error correction =** correction of errors which are detected by the receiver and a signal is sent to the transmitter to request a re-transmission of the data *felkorrigering genom omsändning;* **backward mode =** negative displacement from an origin *bakvänt (omvänt) tillstånd;* **backward recovery =** data retrieval from a system that has crashed *baklänges (system)återställande;* **backwards supervision =** data transmission controlled by the receiver *mottagningsövervakning, mottagnings(styrd) övervakning*

COMMENT: backward recovery is carried out by passing the semi-processed data from the crashed computer through a routine that reverses the effects of the main program to return the original data

bad break ['bæd 'breik] *subst.* wrong hyphenation of a word at the end of a line of text *felavstavning*

bad copy ['bæd 'kɒpɪ] *subst.* illegible *or* badly edited manuscript which the typesetter will not accept *dålig kopia*

badge reader ['bædʒ 'riːdə] *subst.* machine that reads data from an identification badge *ID-kortläsare;* **a badge reader makes sure that only authorized personnel can gain access to a computer room**

bad sector ['bæd 'sektə] *subst.* sector which has been wrongly formatted *or* which contains an error *or* fault and is unable to be correctly written to or read from *dålig sektor;* **you will probably receive error messages when you copy files that are stored on bad sectors on a disk**

baffle ['bæfl] *subst.* sections of material placed in a loudspeaker, used to prevent unwanted internal resonating frequencies *baffel*

bag [bæg] *subst.* number of elements in no particular order *mängd*

bakgrundsbrus ⇨ ambient

bakgrundstillstånd ⇨ foreground

bakåtkompatibel ⇨ downward

bakåtstrålning ⇨ backscatter

balance ['bæləns] **1** *subst.* **(a)** placing of text and graphics on a page in an attractive way *lay-out, grafisk balans;* **the desktop publishing package allows the user to see if the overall page balance is correct (b)** positioning of musical instruments so that they may be recorded to their best advantage *balans, jämvikt* **(c)** amplitude control of left and right audio signals in a stereo system *balanskontroll;* **balance stripe =** thin magnetic stripe on a cine film on the

opposite side to the sound track, so that the whole film will lie flat when played back *balansspår* **2** *vb.* to plan something so that two parts are equal *utjämna, balansera;* **balanced circuit =** electronic circuit that presents a correct load to a communications line (the correct load is usually equal to the impedance of a line element) *balanserad krets;* **you must use a balanced circuit at the end of the line to prevent signal reflections; balanced error =** the probability of any error occurring (from a number of errors) is the same for all errors *utjämnat fel;* **balanced line =** communications line that is terminated at each end with a balanced circuit, preventing signal reflections *balanserad linje*

balanserad last ⇨ match

balanseringstransformator ⇨ match

band [bænd] *subst.* **(a)** range of frequencies between two limits *band;* **base band =** frequency range of a signal before it is processed *or* transmitted *basband;* **voice base band ranges from 20Hz to 15KHz; base band modem =** communications circuit that transmits an unmodulated (base band) signal over a short distance *basbandsmodem;* **do not use a base band modem with a normal phone line; base band local area network =** LAN using unmodulated signals transmitted over coaxial cable, often using a CSMA/CD protocol *basbandsnätverk* **(b)** group of tracks on a magnetic disk *spårgrupp*

band ⇨ ribbon, tape

bandformatsidentitet ⇨ identity

(band)huvud ⇨ head

bandinformation ⇨ header

banding ['bændɪŋ] *subst.* **elastic banding =** method of defining the limits of an image on the computer screen by stretching a boundary round it *ramsträckning, sträckvarning;* **elastic banding is much easier to control with a mouse**

bandkabel ⇨ tape

bandkassett ⇨ magnetic tape

bandlimited ['bænd,lɪmɪtɪd] *adj.* (signal) whose frequency range has been limited to one band *bandbegränsad*

bandpassfilter ⇨ filter

bandpass filter ['bændpɑːs 'fɪltə] *subst.* circuit that allows a certain band of frequencies to pass while stopping any that are higher *or* lower *bandpassfilter; compare with* LOW PASS, HIGH PASS

band printer ['bænd 'prɪntə] *subst.* printer in which the characters are located along a movable steel belt *(stål)bandskrivare*

bandslutssignal ⊳ end

bandstans ⊳ magnetic tape

bandstation ⊳ deck, magnetic tape

bandwidth ['bændwidθ] *subst.* the limits of frequencies used *bandbredd;* **telephone bandwidth is 3100 Hz**

bank [bæŋk] *subst.* collection of similar devices *bank;* **a bank of minicomputers process all the raw data; bank switching** = selection of a particular memory bank from a group *(minnes)bankväxling;* **memory bank** = collection of electronic memory devices connected together to form one large area of memory *minnesbank;* **an add-on card has a 128KB memory bank made up of 16 chips;** *see also* DATABANK

COMMENT: memory banks are used to expand the main memory of a CPU (often above the addressing range of the CPU) by having a number of memory chips arranged into banks. Each bank operates over the same address range but is selected independently by a special code

bank ⊳ bank

bankautomat ⊳ dispenser

banner ['bænə] *subst. (in printing)* heading *or* title extending to the width of a page *banderoll;* **banner headlines** = large headlines on a newspaper running across the width of the page *helsidesrubrik*

bar [bɑː] **1** *subst.* thick line *or* block of colour *band, streck* **2** *vb.* to stop someone from doing something *hindra;* **to bar entry to a file** = to stop someone accessing a file *att hindra tillträde till en fil*

bar chart ['bɑː tʃɑːt] *or* **bar graph** ['bɑː græf] *subst.* graph on which values are represented as vertical *or* horizontal bars *stapeldiagram*

bar code ['bɑː kəʊd] *or* US **bar graphics** ['bɑː ˌgræfiks] *subst.* data represented as a series of printed stripes of varying widths *stapelgrafik, linjegrafik;* **bar-code reader** *or* **optical scanner** = optical device that reads data from a bar code *streckkodsläsare*

COMMENT: bar codes are found on most goods and their packages; the width and position of the stripes is sensed by a light pen *or* optical wand and provides information about the goods, such as price, stock quantities, etc.

bar printer ['bɑː 'printə] *subst.* printer in which the characters are on arms which strike the paper to print characters *typstångsskrivare; see also* DAISY WHEEL

barrel ['bær(ə)l] *subst.* conducting post in a terminal *trumledning*

barrel distortion ['bær(ə)l disˈtɔːʃ(ə)n] *subst.* optical lens distortion causing sides of objects to appear curved *kudd-distorsion*

barrel printer ['bær(ə)l 'printə] *subst.* type of printer where characters are located around a rotating barrel *trumskrivare*

barrier box ['bæriə bɒks] *subst.* device that electrically isolates equipment from a telephone line to prevent damage *linjeisolering*

baryta paper [bəˈraitə 'peipə] *subst.* coated matt paper used to produce final high quality proofs before printing *barytpapper, originalpapper*

barytpapper ⊳ baryta paper

bas ⊳ baser, radix

base [beis] **1** *subst.* **(a)** lowest *or* first position *bas* **(b)** collection of files used as a reference *bas; see* DATABASE **(c)** place where a company has its main office or factory *or* place where a businessman has his office *bas;* **the company has its base in London and branches in all European countries (d)** initial *or* original position *bas;* **base address** = initial address in a program used as a reference for others *basadress;* **base addressing** = relative addressing *basadressering;* **base band** = frequency range of a signal before it is processed *or* transmitted *basband;* **base band modem** = communications circuit that transmits an unmodulated (base band) signal over a short range *basbandsmodem;* **base band local area network** = LAN for very short distances, in which devices use a base band modem *basbandsnätverk;* **base language** = assembly language *assemblerspråk;* **base line** = reference line used when printing to locate characters correctly *baslinje;* **base register** = register in a CPU (not usually in small computers) that contains the address of the start of a program *basregister* **(e)** (notation) referring to a number system *bas;* **base 2** = binary number system (using the two digits 0 and 1) *basen två (binärt);* **base 8** = octal number system (using the eight digits 0 - 7) *basen åtta (oktalt);* **base 10** = decimal number system (using the ten digits 0 - 9) *basen tio (decimalt);* **base 16** = hexadecimal number system (using the ten digits 0 - 9 and six letters A - F) *basen sexton (hexadecimalt)* **2** *vb.* **(a)** to start to calculate from a position *basera;* **we based our calculations on the basic keyboarding rate; based on** = calculating from *baserad på;* **based on last year's figures; the price is based on estimates of keyboarding costs (b)** to set up a company *or* a person in a place *basera, grunda;* **the European manager is**

based in our London office; a London-based system serves the whole country

basfilter ⇨ filter

bashögtalare ⇨ woofer

BASIC ['beɪsɪk] = BEGINNER'S ALL-PURPOSE SYMBOLIC INSTRUCTION CODE high-level programming language for developing programs in a conversational way, providing an easy introduction to computer programming *programmeringsspråket Basic*

basic ['beɪsɪk] *adj.* normal *or* from which everything starts *bas-, grund-, fundamental;* **the basic architechture is the same for all models in this range; basic code** = binary code which directly operates the CPU, using only absolute addresses and values (this is the final form of a program after a compiler *or* assembler pass) *maskinkod;* **basic control system satellite (BCS)** = system that runs dedicated programs *or* tasks for a central computer, controlled using interrupt signals *satellitstyrning;* **basic input/output operating system (BIOS)** = system routines that interface between high-level program instructions and the system peripherals to control the input and output to various standard devices, this often includes controlling the screen, keyboard and disk drives *Bios-program;* **basic instruction** = unmodified program instruction which is processed to obtain the instruction to be executed *basinstruktion, grundinstruktion;* **basic mode link control** = standardized control of transmission links using special codes *länkstyrning;* **basic operating system (BOS)** = software that controls the basic, low-level running of the hardware and file management *basoperativsystem;* **basic telecommunications access method (BTAM)** = method to provide access (read *or* write operations) to a remote device *fjärråtkomst över telenätet;* **basic weight** = weight of printing paper per 500 sheets *basvikt, engelsk pappersvikt*

basically ['beɪsɪk(ə)lɪ] *adv.* seen from the point from which everything starts *principiellt, i grund och botten;* **the acoustic coupler is basically the same as a modem**

basis ['beɪsɪs] *subst.* point *or* number from which calculations are made *grundval;* **we calculated keyboarding costs on the basis of 5,500 keystrokes per hour**

bas-minus-ett-komplement ⇨ diminished radix complement

bass [beɪs] *subst. & adj.* low sound *or* sound with a low frequency *bas;* **bass signal** = audio signals in the frequency range below 100Hz *bassignal;* **bass control** = knob used to vary the strength of the bass frequencies in an audio signal *baskontroll;* **bass driver** *or* **speaker** = large loudspeaker

able to produce low frequency sounds *bashögtalare;* **bass response** = characteristics of a circuit *or* device to bass signals *baskaraktäristik, basrespons*

batch [bætʃ] **1** *subst.* **(a)** group of items which are made at one time *sats;* **the last batch of disk drives are faulty (b)** (i) group of documents which are processed at the same time *sats;* (ii) group of tasks *or* amount of data to be processed as a single unit *sats;* **today's batch of orders; we deal with the orders in batches of fifty; batch file** = stored file containing a sequence of system commands, used instead of typing them in *kommandofil för satsvis bearbetning;* **this batch file is used to save time and effort when carrying out a routine task; (processing data in) batch mode** = (processing the data) in related groups in one machine run *satsvis bearbetning;* **batch region** = memory area where the operating system executes batch programs *område för satsvis bearbetning, minnesarea;* **batch system** = system that executes batch files *system för satsvis bearbetning;* **batch total** = sum of a number of batches of data, used for error checking, validation or to provide useful information *kontrollsumma för satsbearbetning* **2** *vb.* **(a)** to put data *or* tasks together in groups *gruppera;* **batched communication** = high-speed transmission of large blocks of data without requiring an acknowledgement from the receiver for each data item *satsvis kommunikation* **(b)** to put items together in groups *gruppera*

batch number ['bætʃ 'nʌmbə] *subst.* reference number attached to a batch *satsnummer*

batch processor ['bætʃ 'prəʊsesə] *subst.* system able to process groups of tasks *processor för satsvis bearbetning;* **batch processing** = system of data processing where information is collected into batches before being processed by the computer in one machine run *satsvis bearbetning*

COMMENT: batch processing is the opposite to interactive processing (where the user gives instructions and receives an immediate response)

batterisäkrad ⇨ back

batterisäkring ⇨ backup

battery ['bætərɪ] *subst.* chemical device that produces electrical current *batteri;* **battery backup** = use of a battery to provide power to volatile storage devices (RAM chips) to retain data after a computer has been switched off *batterisänkning;* **battery-backed** = (volatile storage device) that has a battery backup *batterisäkrad;* **battery voltage level** = size of voltage being provided by a battery *batterispänning(snivå)*

baud [bɔːd] *or* **baud rate** [ˈbɔːd ˈreɪt] *subst.* measure of the number of signal changes transmitted per second *baud;* the **baud rate of the binary signal was 300 bits per second; a modem with auto-baud scanner can automatically sense at which baud rate it should operate; baud rate generator** = device that produces various timing signals to synchronize data at different baud rates *klockgenerator, hastighetsgenerator;* **split baud rate** = modem which receives data at one baud rate but transmits data at another *delad överföringshastighet;* **the viewdata modem uses a 1200/75 split baud rate;** *see also* SCANNING

> COMMENT: baud rate is often considered the same as bits per second, but in fact it depends on the protocol used and the error checking (300 baud is roughly equivalent to 30 characters per second using standard error checking)

baudot code [ˈbəʊdɒtˈkəʊd] *subst.* five-bit character transmission code, used mainly in teletypewriters *baudotkod i 5-kanalig teletypkod*

B box [ˈbiː ˈbɒks] *subst.* register in a CPU (not usually in small computers) that contains the address of the start of a program *basregister*

BBS [ˈbiːbiːˈes] = BULLETIN BOARD SYSTEM information and message database accessible by modem and computer link *elektronisk anslagstavla i publikt meddelande (databassystem), elektroniskt klotterplank, elektronisk anslagstavla*

BCC [ˈbiːsiːˈsiː] = BLOCK CHARACTER CHECK error detection method for blocks of transmitted data *blockkontrolltecken*

BCD [ˈbiːsiːˈdiː] = BINARY CODED DECIMAL representation of single decimal digits as a pattern of four binary digits *binärkodad decimalrepresentation;* **the BCD representation of decimal 8 is 1000; BCD adder** = full adder able to add two four-bit BCD words *binärkodad decimaladderare*

BCH code [ˈbiːsiːˈeɪtʃˈkəʊd] = BOSE-CHANDHURI-HOCQUENGHEM CODE

BCPL [ˈbiːsiːpiːˈel] *subst.* high level programming language *programmerings-språket BCPL*

BCS [ˈbiːsiːˈes] **(a)** = BRITISH COMPUTER SOCIETY **(b)** = BASIC CONTROL SYSTEM (SATELLITE)

bead [biːd] *subst.* small section of a program that is used for a single task *sluten rutin, modul*

beam [biːm] *subst.* narrow radiated stream of waves *or* particles *stråle;* **the LASER produces a thin beam of light; beam deflection** = change in beam direction *strålavböjning;* **a magnetic field is used for beam deflection in a CRT; beam diversity** = using a single frequency communications band for two different sets of data *strålmångfald;* **beam splitter** = device to redirect a part of a beam *stråldelare;* **beam width** = maximum size of a transmission beam which should not be exceeded if a constant received power is to maintained *lobbredd*

beard [bɪəd] *subst.* blank section between bottom of a character and the type face limit *huvud, kött*

beep [biːp] **1** *subst.* audible warning noise *pip;* **the printer will make a beep when it runs out of paper 2** *vb.* to make a beep *pipa;* **the computer beeped when the wrong key was hit;** *see also* BLEEP

Beginner's All-Purpose Symbolic Instruction Code (BASIC) [bɪˈgɪnəz ˈɔːlˈpɜːpəs sɪmˈbɒlɪk ɪnˈstrʌkʃ(ə)n ˈkəʊd (ˈbeɪsɪk)] *subst.* high-level programming language for developing programs in a conversational way, providing an easy introduction to computer programming *programmeringsspråket Basic*

beginning [bɪˈgɪnɪŋ] *subst.* first part *början;* **beginning of file (bof)** = character *or* symbol that shows the start of a valid section of data *filstarttecken;* **beginning of information mark (bim)** = symbol indicating the start of a data stream stored on a disk drive *or* tape *informationstartmärke;* **beginning of tape (bot) marker** = section of material that marks the start of the recording area of a reel of magnetic tape *bandstartmärke*

begreppsordbok ▷ **thesaurus**

begränsa ▷ **restrict**

begynnelsevillkor ▷ **initial**

begära ▷ **request**

behovssignal ▷ **fetch**

behovsstyrd multiplexering ▷ **demand**

behörighetskontroll ▷ **access control**

bekräfta ▷ **validate**

bel [bel] *subst.* unit used when expressing ratio of signal power in logarithmic form (P bels = Log (A/B) where A and B are signal power) *Bel (B) (logaritmisk enhet för signalnivå), normalt dB decibel*

belastbarhet ▷ **fan**

bell character ['bel 'kærəktə] *subst.*
control code which causes a machine to
produce an audible signal *klocktecken*

belopp ⇨ rate

below-the-line [bɪ'ləʊ ðə 'laɪn] *adj.*
below-the-line expenditure = exceptional
payments which are separated from a
company's normal accounts *extraordinära
utgifter (bokförda separat från den normala
bokföringen);* **below-the-line costs** = costs
of crew and technicians used in making a
TV programme (as opposed to
scriptwriters, actors, etc., who are above-
the-line costs) *extraordinära kostnader*

beläggning ⇨ coating, deposit

benchmark ['ben(t)ʃmɑːk] *subst.* **(a)**
point in an index which is important, and
can be used to compare with other figures
riktmärke **(b)** program used to test the
performance of software *or* hardware *or* a
system *prestandatest;* **the magazine gave the
new program's benchmark test results**

benchmarking ['ben(t)ʃmɑːkɪŋ] *subst.*
testing a system *or* program with a
benchmark *prestandamätning*

COMMENT: the same task *or* program is given to different systems and their results and speeds of working are compared

benchmark problem ['ben(t)ʃmɑːk
'prɒbləm] *subst.* task *or* problem used to
test and evaluate the performance of
hardware *or* software *testproblem*

beredskapsström ⇨ hold

Bernoulli box [ber'nuːjɪ'bɒks] *subst.* high
capacity storage system using exchangeable
20MB cartridges *Bernoulli-minne*

QUOTE I use a pair of Bernoulli boxes for back up and simply do a disk-to-disk copy
PC Business World

beräkna ⇨ calculate, compute

beräkning ⇨ calculation, computation

beröringsfritt system ⇨ hand

beslutsstödssystem ⇨ decision

beslutabell ⇨ table

beslutsträd ⇨ decision

best fit ['best 'fɪt] *subst.* (i) (something)
which is the nearest match to a
requirement *bäst passande;* (ii) function
that selects the smallest free space in main
memory for a requested virtual page *bäst
passande*

bias ['baɪəs] *subst.* **(a)** electrical reference
level *förspänning, referensspänning* **(b)**
high frequency signal added to recorded
information to minimize noise and

distortion (the high frequency is removed
on playback) *förmagnetiseringssignal* **(c)**
deviation of statistical results from a
reference level *systematisk avvikelse från
referens*

biased ['baɪəst] *adj.* which has a bias
förutfattad mening; **biased data** = data *or*
records which point to one conclusion
partiska data; **biased exponent** = value of
the exponent in a floating point number
förskjuten exponent

bibliographic [ˌbɪblɪəʊ'græfɪk] *or*
bibliographical [ˌbɪblɪəʊ'græfɪk(ə)l] *adj.*
referring to books *or* to bibliographies
bibliografisk; **bibliographical information** =
information about a book (name of author,
number of pages, ISBN, etc.) which is used
for library cataloguing *bibliografisk
information*

bibliography [ˌbɪblɪ'ɒgrəfɪ] *subst.* **(a)** list
of documents and books which are relevant
to a certain subject *bibliografi;* **he printed a
bibliography at the end of each chapter (b)**
catalogue of books *bibliografi*

bid [bɪd] *vb. (of a computer)* to gain
control of a network in order to transmit
data *anropa, bjuda;* **the terminal had to bid
three times before there was a gap in
transmissions on the network**

bi-directional [ˌbaɪdɪ'rekʃənl] *adj.*
(operation *or* process) that can occur in
forward *or* reverse directions *dubbelriktad;*
**bi-directional file transfer; bi-directional
bus** = data *or* control lines that can carry
signals travelling in two directions
dubbelriktad buss; **bi-directional printer** =
printer which is able to print characters
from left to right and from right to left as
the head is moving forward *or* backward
across the paper (speeding up the printing
operation) *dubbelriktad skrivare; compare*
OMNIDIRECTIONAL

bifurcation [ˌbaɪfə'keɪʃ(ə)n] *subst.* system
where there are only two possible results
bifurkation, gaffelformig

Big Blue ['bɪg 'bluː] *informal name for* IBM

bild ⇨ image, picture

bildavkännare ⇨ image

bildbehandlare ⇨ image

bildbehandling ⇨ image

bildbehandlingsdator ⇨ processor

bildfångare ⇨ grabber

bildförsämring ⇨ degradation

bildförvrängning ⇨ distortion

bildinställning ⇨ framing

bildlagringsarea ⇨ image

bildlåsning ⇨ pix lock

bildläsare ⇨ scanner

bildplan ⇨ image

bildpunkt ⇨ pixel

bildruta ⇨ frame

bildskärm ⇨ display, monitor, screen, video

bildskärmsstyrkrets ⇨ display

bildskärmsstyrtecken ⇨ display

bildskärmsterminal ⇨ video, visual display terminal (VDT)

(bild)svepåtergivning ⇨ frame

(bild)svepåtergång ⇨ field

bildyta ⇨ field, image

billion ['bɪljən] number equal to one thousand million *or* one million million *i Europa miljard (1-10⁹), i USA biljon (1-10¹²)*

$$\text{billion} = \text{miljard } (1\text{-}10^9), \text{ biljon } (1\text{-}10^{12})$$

NOTE: in the US it means one thousand million, but in GB it usually means one million million. With figures it is usually written **bn: $5bn** (say 'five billion dollars')

BIM [bi:ai'em] = BEGINNING OF INFORMATION MARK symbol indicating the start of a data stream stored on a disk drive *or* tape *startmärke*

binary ['baɪnərɪ] *adj. & subst.* base 2 *or* number notation system which uses only the digits 0 and 1 *binär;* **binary adder =** device that provides the sum of two or more binary digits *binäradderare;* **binary arithmetic =** rules and functions governing arithmetic operations in base 2 *binäraritmetik;* **binary bit =** smallest single unit in (base 2) binary notation, either a 0 or a 1 *binär bit;* **binary cell =** storage element for one bit *binär cell;* **binary chop** *see* BINARY SEARCH; **binary code =** using different patterns of binary digits to represent various symbols, elements, etc. *binärkod;* **binary coded characters =** alphanumeric characters represented as patterns of binary digits *binärkodade tecken;* **binary coded decimal (BCD) =** representation of single decimal digits as a pattern of four binary digits *binärkodad decimal;* **binary counter =** circuit that will divide a binary input signal by two (producing one output pulse for two input pulses) *binärräknare;* **binary digit** *or* **bit =** smallest single unit in (base 2) binary notation, either a 0 or a 1 *binär siffra (tal med basen 2);* **binary dump =** display of a section of memory in binary form *binärdumpning;* **binary encoding =** representing a character *or* element with a unique combination *or* pattern of bits in a word *binärkodning;* **binary exponent =** one word that contains the sign and exponent of a binary number (expressed in exponent and mantissa form) *binär exponent;* **binary fraction =** representation of a decimal fraction in binary form *binär bråkdel;* **the binary fraction 0.011 is equal to one quarter plus one eighth (i.e. three eighths); binary half adder =** binary adder that can produce the sum of two inputs, producing a carry output if necessary, but cannot accept a carry input *binär halvadderare;* **binary loader =** short section of program code that allows programs in binary form (such as object code from a linker *or* assembler) to be loaded into memory *binär laddare;* **binary mantissa =** fractional part of a number (in binary form) *binär mantissa;* **binary notation** *or* **representation =** base 2 numerical system using only the digits 0 and 1 *binär notation;* **binary number =** quantity represented in base 2 *binärt tal;* **binary operation =** (i) operation on two operands *binär operation;* (ii) operation on an operand in binary form *binär operation;* **binary point =** dot which indicates the division between the whole unit bits and the fractional part of a binary number *binär punkt;* **binary scale =** power of two associated with each bit position in a word *binär skala;* **in a four bit word, the binary scale is 1,2,4,8; binary search** *or* **chop =** fast search method for use on ordered lists of data (the search key is compared with the data in the middle of the list and one half is discarded, this is repeated with the remaining half until only the required data item is left) *binär sökning;* **binary sequence =** series of binary digits *binär sekvens;* **binary signalling =** transmission using positive and zero voltage levels to represent binary data *binär signallering;* **binary synchronous communications (BSC) =** (old) standard for medium/high speed data communication links *BSC (binär synkronkommunikation);* **binary system =** use of binary numbers *or* operating with binary numbers *binärt system;* **binary-to-decimal conversion =** process to convert a binary number into its equivalent decimal value *binär till decimalomvandling;* **binary tree =** tree structure for data, where each item of data can have only two branches *binärt träd;* **binary variable =** variable that can contain either a one or zero *binär variabel*

QUOTE with this type of compression you can only retrieve words by scanning the list sequentially, rather than by faster means such as a binary search

Practical Computing

binaural ['baɪn'ɔ:r(ə)l] *adj.* method of recording two audio channels *binaural*

COMMENT: separate sound tracks for the left and right ears are recorded to provide enhanced depth of sound

bind [baind] *vb.* **(a)** to link and convert one or more object code programs into a form that can be executed *länka, fixera;* **binding time** = time taken to produce actual addresses from an object code program *länkningstid; see also* LINKER **(b)** to put a stiff cover on the printed pages of a book *binda in;* **the book is bound in laminated paper; a paperbound book; the sheets have been sent to the bindery for binding** NOTE: **binding - bound**

binder ['baində] *subst.* company which specializes in binding books *bokbindare*

bindery ['baindəri] *subst.* factory where books are bound *bokbinderi*

bindestreck ⇨ **dash, hyphen**

binding ['baindiŋ] *subst.* **(a)** action of putting a cover on a book *bokbindning* **(b)** cover of a book *bokband;* **the book has a soft plastic binding**

binär ⇨ **binary**

binärkodad decimal ⇨ **pack**

binär kodning ⇨ **encoding**

binär sökning ⇨ **binary look-up, dichotomizing search**

biologisk givare ⇨ **biosensor**

BIOS ['baios] = BASIC INPUT/OUTPUT SYSTEM system routines that interface between high-level program instructions and the system peripherals to control the input and output to various standard devices, this often includes controlling the screen, keyboard and disk drives *Bios, monitor*

biosensor [,baiə(ʊ)'sensə] *subst.* device that allows electrical impulses from an organism to be recorded *biogivare, biologisk givare;* **the nerve activity can be measured by attaching a biosensor to your arm**

bipolar [bai'pəʊlə] *adj.* with two levels *bipolär;* **bipolar coding** = transmission method which uses alternate positive and negative voltage levels to represent a binary one, with binary zero represented by zero level *bipolär kodning;* **bipolar signal** = use of positive and negative voltage levels to represent the binary digits *bipolär signal;* **bipolar transistor** = transistor constructed of three layers of alternating types of doped semiconductor (p-n-p or n-p-n) *bipolär transition*

> COMMENT: each layer has a terminal labelled emitter, base and collector, usually the base signal controls the current flow between the emitter and collector

bipolär transistor ⇨ **junction**

biquinary code [bai'kwinəri 'kəʊd] *subst.* decimal digits represented as two digits added together (for decimal digits less than 5, represented as 0 and the digit, for decimal digits greater than 4, represented as 5 and the digit minus 5) *bikvinär kod (talnotation med basen fem)*

bistable [bai'steibl] *adj.* (device *or* circuit) that has two possible states, on and off *bistabil;* **bistable circuit** *or* **multivibrator** = circuit which can be switched between two states *bistabil krets, bistabil vippa, multivibrator*

bit [bit] *subst.* **(a)** = BINARY DIGIT smallest unit in binary number notation, which can have the value 0 or 1 *bit* **(b)** smallest unit of data that a system can handle *bit;* **bit addressing** = selecting a register *or* word and examining one bit of it *bitadressering;* **bit density** = number of bits that can be recorded per unit of storage medium *bittäthet;* **bit handling** = CPU commands and processes that allow bit manipulation, changing, etc. *bithantering;* **bit manipulation** = various instructions that provide functions such as examine a bit, change *or* set *or* move a bit within a word *bitmanipulation;* **bit pattern** = certain arrangement of bits within a word, that represents a certain character *or* action *bitmönster;* **bit position** = place of a bit of data in a computer word *bitposition;* **bit rate** = measure of the number of bits transmitted per second *bithastighet;* **bit slice design** = construction of a large word size CPU by joining a number of smaller word size blocks *bituppdelad konstruktion;* **the bit slice design uses four four-bit word processors to construct a sixteen-bit processor; most significant bit (MSB)** = bit in a computer word that represents the greatest power of two (in an eight-bit word the MSB is in bit position eight and represents a decimal number of two to the power eight, or 128) *mest signifikant bit;* **bit stream** = binary data sequence that does not consist of separate, distinct character codes *or* groups *bitström;* **bit stuffing** = addition of extra bits to a group of data to make up a certain length required for transmission *bitfyllnad;* **bit track** = track on a magnetic disk along which bits can be recorded *or* read back *bitspår; compare* LOGICAL TRACK; **bits per inch (bpi)** = number of bits that can be recorded per inch of recording medium *bitar per tum;* **bits per second (bps)** = measure of the number of binary digits transmitted every second *bitar per sekund;* **check bit** = one bit of a binary word that is used to provide a parity check *kontrollbit;* **mask bit** = one bit (in a mask) used to select the required bit from a word *or* string *maskbit;* **sign bit** = single bit that indicates if a binary number is positive or negative (usually 0 = positive, 1 = negative) *teckenbit; see also* BYTE

QUOTE it became possible to store more than one bit per pixel

Practical Computing

bit ⊳ **bit, element**

bitbortfall ⊳ **drop out**

bit-map ['bɪt 'mæp] *vb.* to define events *or* data using an array of single bits *bitkarta;* (this can be an image *or* graphics *or* a table of devices in use, etc.) *punktavbildning;* **bit-mapped graphics** = image whose individual pixels can be controlled by changing the value of its stored bit (one is on, zero is off; in colour displays, more than one bit is used to provide control for the three colours - Red, Green, Blue) *punktavbildad grafik*

QUOTE the expansion cards fit into the PC's expansion slot and convert bit-mapped screen images to video signals

Publish

QUOTE it is easy to turn any page into a bit-mapped graphic

PC Business World

QUOTE microcomputers invariably use raster-scan cathode ray tube displays, and frequently use a bit-map to store graphic images

Soft

bittillskott ⊳ **drop in**

bituppdelad arkitektur ⊳ **slice**

bituppdelad processor ⊳ **microprocessor, processor**

black [blæk] *adj.* with no colour *svart;* **black and white** = use of shades of grey to represent colours on a monitor *or* display *svartvit;* **black box** = device that performs a function without the user knowing how *svart låda;* **black crush** = conversion of a television picture to one with no tones, only black or white *svarttryckning, kontrastökning;* **black level** = level of a TV signal that produces no luminescence on screen *svartnivå*

blackout ['blækaʊt] *or* **black out** ['blækaʊt] *subst.* complete loss of electrical power *strömavbrott; compare with* BROWN-OUT

black writer ['blæk 'raɪtə] *subst.* printer where toner sticks to the points hit by the laser beam when the image drum is scanned *laserskrivare; compare* WHITE WRITER

COMMENT: a black writer produces sharp edges and graphics, but large areas of black are muddy

blad ⊳ **form, sheet**

blanda ⊳ **mix**

blandat minne ⊳ **FEDS**

blandning ⊳ **mix**

blank [blæŋk] **1** *adj.* empty *or* with nothing written on it *tom, blank;* **blank character** = character code that prints a space *blanktecken;* **blank instruction** = program instruction which does nothing *blindinstruktion;* **blank tape** *or* **blank disk** = magnetic tape *or* disk that does not have data stored on it *tom tejp, tomt band, tom diskett;* **blank string** = (i) empty string *tom sträng;* (ii) string containing spaces *blanksträng* **2** *subst.* space on a form which has to be completed *tom plats att fylla i;* **fill in the blanks and insert the form into the OCR**

blanket agreement ['blæŋkɪt ə'griːmənt] *subst.* agreement which covers many items *generellt avtal;* **blanket cylinder** = rubber coated cylinder in a offset lithographic printing machine that transfers ink from the image plate to the paper *tryckcylinder*

blanketing ['blæŋkətɪŋ] *see* JAMMING

blankett ⊳ **form**

blankettfunktion ⊳ **form**

blankettset i löpande bana ⊳ **multipart stationery**

blanking ['blæŋkɪŋ] *subst.* preventing a television signal from reaching the scanning beam on its return trace *släckning;* **blanking interval** = time taken for the scanning beam in a TV to return from the end of a picture at the bottom right of the screen to top left *bildsläcktid;* **blanking pulse** = electrical signal used to start the blanking of a TV signal *släckpuls*

blast [blɑːst] *vb.* **(a)** to write data into a programmable ROM device *bränna* **(b)** to free sections of previously allocated memory *or* resources *blåsa ur*

blast-through alphanumerics ['blɑːstθruː ˌælfənjuːˈmrɪk] *subst.* characters that can be displayed on a videotext terminal when it is in graphics mode *videotexgrafiktecken*

bleed [bliːd] **1** *subst.* line of printing that runs off the edge of the paper *utfallande, utan marginalkant* **2** *vb.* **the photo is bled off** = the photograph is printed so that the image runs off the edge of the page *falla ut*

bleep [bliːp] **1** *subst.* audible warning noise *pip;* **the printer will make a bleep when it runs out of paper 2** *vb.* to make a bleep *pipa; see also* BEEP

bleeper [bliːpə] *subst.* device which bleeps (often used to mean radio pager) *personsökare;* **the doctor's bleeper began to ring, and he went to the telephone; he is in the factory somewhere - we'll try to find him on his bleeper**

blind [blaɪnd] *adj.* which will not respond to certain codes *blind*

blind dialling ['blaɪnd 'daɪəlɪŋ] *subst.* ability of a modem to dial out even if the line appears dead, used on certain private lines *blinduppringning;* **blind keyboard =** keyboard whose output is not displayed but is stored directly on magnetic tape *or* disk *blint tangentbord*

blindinstruktion ⊳ **do-nothing (instruction), instruction, non-operable instruction, operation**

blind variabel ⊳ **dummy**

B-line counter ['biː ˌlaɪn 'kaʊntə] *subst.* address register that is added to a reference address to provide the location to be accessed *baslinjeräknare*

blinkande tecken ⊳ **flash**

blinking ['blɪŋkɪŋ] *subst.* flashing effect caused by varying the intensity of a displayed character *blinkning*

blister pack ['blɪstə pæk] *subst.* type of packing where the item for sale is covered with a thin plastic sheet sealed to a card backing *krympförpackning, (krymp)plastförpackning*

blixtomvandlare ⊳ **flash**

block [blɒk] **1** *subst.* **(a)** (i) series of items grouped together *block;* (ii) number of stored records treated as a single unit *block;* **block character check (BCC) =** error detection method for blocks of transmitted data *blockteckenkontroll;* **block code =** error detection and correction code for block data transmission *blockkod;* **block compaction =** *see* COMPRESS, COMPACT; **block copy =** to duplicate a block of data to another section of memory *blockkopiering;* **block error rate =** number of blocks of data that contain errors compared with the total number transmitted *blockfelfrekvens;* **block header =** information at the start of a file describing content organization or characteristics *blockrubrik;* **block ignore character =** symbol at the start of a block indicating that it contains corrupt data *blockignoreringstecken;* **block input processing =** input system that requires a whole error-free block to be received before it is processed *blockbearbetning;* **block length =** number of bytes of data in a block *blocklängd;* **block list =** list of the blocks and records as they are organized in a file *blocklista;* **block mark =** code that indicates the end of a block *blockmarkering;* **block operation =** process carried out on a block of data *blockoperation;* **block parity =** parity error check on a block of data *blockparitet;* **block retrieval =** accessing blocks of data stored in memory *blockåtkomst;* **block**

synchronization = correct timing of start, stop and message bits according to a predefined protocol *blocksynkronisering;* **block transfer =** moving large numbers of records around in memory *blocköverföring;* **building block =** self-contained unit that can be joined to others to form a system *byggblock;* **data block =** all the data required for *or* from a process *datablock;* **end of block (EOB) =** code which indicates that the last byte of a block of a data has been sent *blockslutssignal;* **interblock gap (IBG) =** space between two blocks of stored data *blockmellanrum* **(b)** wide printed bar *klots (i tryck ett kort grovt streck);* **block diagram =** graphical representation of a system *or* program operation *blockdiagram* **(c)** block capitals *or* block letters = capital letters (such as A,B,C) *tryckbokstäver, versaler;* **write your name and address in block letters 2** *vb.* **(a)** to stop something taking place *hindra;* **the system manager blocked his request for more CPU time (b) to block in =** to sketch roughly the main items of a design *skissa*

blockeringssignal ⊳ **inhibit**

blocking factor ['blɒkɪŋ 'fæktə] *subst.* number of records in a block *blockfaktor*

blockmarkera ⊳ **mark**

blockmarkörer ⊳ **marker**

blockmellanrum ⊳ **interblock gap (IBG)**

blockslutssignal ⊳ **end**

blocköverföringskanal ⊳ **universal**

bloom [bluːm] *subst.* bright spot on the screen of a faulty television *ljusgårdseffekt*

bloop [bluːp] *vb.* to pass a magnet over a tape to erase signals which are not needed *radera*

blow [bləʊ] *vb.* to program a PROM device with data *bränna*

blueprint ['bluːprɪnt] *subst.* copy of an original set of specifications *or* design in graphical form *blåkopia*

blue-ribbon program [bluː 'rɪbən 'prəʊgræm] *subst.* perfect program that runs first time, with no errors *or* bugs *premiumprogram (existerar ej i verkligheten)*

blur [blɜː] **1** *subst.* image where the edges *or* colours are not clear *suddig* **2** *vb.* to make the edges *or* colours of an image fuzzy *göra suddig;* **the image becomes blurred when you turn the focus knob**

blytyp ⊳ **hot**

bläckstråleskrivare ⊳ **ink**

bn ['bɪljən] = BILLION

BNF ['biːen'ef] = BACKUS-NAUR-FORM system of writing and expressing the syntax of a programming language *syntaxbeskrivande notation för programmeringsspråk*

board [bɔːd] *subst.* **(a)** flat insulation material on which electronic components are mounted and connected *(krets)kort;* **bus board** = PCB containing conducting paths for all the computer signals (for the address, data and control buses) *busskort;* **daughter board** = add-on board that connects to a system motherboard *dotterkort;* **expansion board** *or* **add on board** = printed circuit board that is connected to a system to increase its functions *or* performance *tilläggskort, tillsatskort, expansionskort;* **motherboard** = main printed circuit board of a system, containing most of the components and connectors for expansion boards, etc. *moderkort;* **printed circuit board (PCB)** = flat insulating material that has conducting tracks of metal printed *or* etched onto its surface, which complete a circuit when components are mounted on it *kretskort* **(b)** people who run a group *or* society *or* company *styrelse;* **editorial board** = group of editors *redaktion*

> QUOTE both models can be expanded to the current maximum of the terminals by adding further serial interface boards
> **Micro Decision**

body ['bɒdɪ] *subst.* main section of text in a document *huvuddel, brödtext;* **body size** = length of a section of text from top to bottom in points *radfall;* **body type** = main style of type used in a text, as opposed to the style of type used for headings, notes, etc. *bröd(text)typsnitt, brödstil*

bof [beg'ınıŋɒv'faıl] = BEGINNING OF FILE character *or* symbol that shows the start of a valid section of data *filbörjan, filstart*

boilerplate ['bɔɪlə‚pleɪt] *subst.* final document that has been put together using standard sections of text held in a word processor *dokument sammansatt av standardmoduler*

boilerplating ['bɔɪlə‚pleɪtıŋ] *subst.* putting together a final document out of various standard sections of text *sammansättning av standarddokument*

bokstav ⇨ **character, letter**

bold [bəʊld] *adj. & subst.* **bold face** = thicker and darker form of a typeface *fet (stil)*

bomb [bɒm] **1** *vb. (of software), informal* to fail *"krascha" (programmet "hänger sig" och slutar fungera);* **the program bombed, and we lost all the data; the system can bomb if you set up several desk accessories or memory-resident programs at the same time 2** *subst.* **logic bomb** = section of code that performs various unpleasant functions such as system crash when a number of conditions are true (the logic bomb is installed by unpleasant hackers *or* very annoyed programmers) *logisk bomb, datavirus;* **the system programmer installed a logic bomb when they made him redundant**

bond paper ['bɒnd 'peɪpə] *subst.* heavy grade writing paper *brevpapper*

book [bʊk] **1** *subst.* **(a)** set of sheets of paper attached together *bok;* **they can print books up to 96 pages; the book is available in paperback and hard cover (b) cheque book** = book of new cheques *checkhäfte;* **phone book** *or* **telephone book** = book which lists names of people *or* companies with their addresses and telephone numbers *telefonkatalog, telefonbok* **2** *vb.* to order *or* to reserve something *boka, reservera;* **to book a room in a hotel** *or* **a table at a restaurant** *or* **a ticket on a plane; I booked a table for 7.45**

booklet ['bʊklət] *subst.* small book with a paper cover *broschyr, häfte*

bookseller ['bʊk‚selə] *subst.* person who sells books *bokhandlare*

bookshop ['bʊkʃɒp] *subst.* shop which sells books *boklåda, bokhandel*

bookstall ['bʊkstɔːl] *subst.* small open bookshop (as in a railway station) *bokstånd*

bookstore ['bʊkstɔː] *subst. US* bookshop *boklåda, bokhandel*

bookwork ['bʊkwɜːk] *subst.* **(a)** keeping of financial records *bokföring* **(b)** printing and binding of books *bokframställning* NOTE: no plural

Boolean algebra ['buːlıən 'ældʒıbrə] *or* **logic** ['lɒdʒık] rules set down to define, simplify and manipulate logical functions, based on statements which are true or false *boolesk algebra; see* AND, NOT, OR

Boolean connective ['buːlıən kə'nektıv] *subst.* symbol *or* character in a Boolean operation that describes the action to be performed on the operands *boolesk operationssymbol*

Boolean operation ['buːlıən ‚ɒpə'reɪʃ(ə)n] *subst.* logical operation on a number of operands, conforming to Boolean algebra rules *boolesk operation;* **Boolean operation table** = table showing two binary words (operands), the operation and the result *boolesk operationstabell;* **Boolean operator** = logical operator such as AND, OR etc.

booleoperator; **monadic Boolean operation** = logical operation on only one word, such as NOT *unär (enställig) booleoperation;* **dyadic Boolean operation** = logical operation producing a result from two words, such as AND *binär (tvåställig) booleoperation;* **Boolean value** = one of two values, either true or false *boolevärde;* **Boolean variable** = binary word in which each bit represents true or false, using the digits 1 or 0 *boolevariabel*

boom [buːm] **1** *subst.* **(a)** piece of metal which supports a microphone *or* antenna *bom* **(b)** time when sales *or* production *or* business activity are increasing *hausse, högkonjunktur;* **boom industry** = industry which is expanding rapidly *hausseindustri;* **the boom years** = years when there is a boom *högkonjunktur* **2** *vb.* to expand *or* to do well in business *öka, expandera;* **sales are booming; a booming industry** *or* **company; technology is a booming sector of the economy**

boost [buːst] **1** *subst.* help received *uppsving, puff;* **the prize was a real boost; the new model gave a boost to the sales figures 2** *vb.* to make something increase *öka, hjälpa fram;* **the extra hard disk will boost our storage capacity by 25Mb**

boot [buːt] *vb.* to execute a set of instructions automatically in order to reach a required state *ladda, starta*

booth [buːð] *subst.* small place for one person to stand *or* sit *hytt;* **telephone booth** = soundproof cabin with a public telephone in it *telefonhytt;* **ticket booth** = place outdoors where a person sells tickets *biljettstånd*

bootleg ['buːtleg] *subst.* illegal copy of recorded material *piratkopia*

bootstrap (loader) ['buːtstræp ('ləudə)] *subst.* set of instructions that are executed by the computer before a program is loaded, usually to load the operating system once the computer is switched on *självinmatande programladdare; compare* LOADER

QUOTE the digital signal processor includes special on-chip bootstrap hardware to allow easy loading of user programs into the program RAM
Electronics & Wireless World

boot up ['buːt ˌʌp] *or* **booting** ['buːtɪŋ] *subst.* automatic execution of a set of instructions usually held in ROM when a computer is switched on *autostart*

border ['bɔːdə] *subst.* area around printed *or* displayed text *ram*

"bordsdator" ⇨ **desktop**

borrow ['bɒrəu] *vb.* **(a)** to take something (such as money *or* a library book) from

someone for a time, returning it at the end of the period *låna;* **he borrowed £1,000 from the bank; she borrowed a book on computer construction (b)** operation in certain arithmetic processes, such as subtraction from a smaller number *låna*

borrower ['bɒrəuə] *subst.* person who borrows *låntagare;* **borrowers from the library are allowed to keep books for two weeks**

bortkopplad ⇨ **off-line**

BOS [bɒus] = BASIC OPERATING SYSTEM software that controls the basic, low-level running of the hardware and file management *basoperativsystem*

Bose-Chandhuri-Hocquenghem code (BCH) ['bɒus ˌtʃæn'djuː(ə)ri 'hɒkənəm 'kɒud ('biːsiː'eitʃ)] *subst.* error correcting code *felkorrigerande kod*

bot *or* **BOT** [biːɒuˈtiː] = BEGINNING OF TAPE; **BOT marker** = section of material that marks the start of the recording area of magnetic tape *bandstartmärke*

bottning ⇨ **underflow**

bottom space ['bɒtəm speis] *subst.* blank lines at the bottom of a page of printed text *botten(yta)*

bottom up method ['bɒtəm ʌp 'meθəd] *subst.* combining low-level instructions to form a high-level instruction (which can then be further combined) *'nedifrån och upp'*

bounce [bauns] *subst.* (error) multiple key contact caused by a faulty switch *studs;* **de-bounce** = preventing a single touch on a key producing multiple key contact *göra studsfri*

boundary ['baundə)ri] *subst.* limits of something *gräns;* **boundary protection** = preventing any program writing into a reserved area of memory *gränsskydd;* **boundary punctuation** = punctuation which marks the beginning *or* end of a file *gränsskiljetecken;* **boundary register** = register in a multi-user system that contains the addresses for the limits of one user's memory allocation *gränsregister*

bounds [baundz] *subst.* limits *or* area in which one can operate *tillåten yta;* **array bounds** = limits to the number of elements which can be given in an array *vektorgränser*

box [bɒks] *subst.* **(a)** cardboard *or* wood *or* plastic container *låda;* **the goods were sent in thin cardboard boxes; the keyboard is packed in plastic foam before being put into the box; black box** = device that performs a function without the user knowing how *svart låda* **(b) box number** = reference

box 36 **breakdown**

number used in a post office or an advertisement to avoid giving an address *boxnummer;* **please reply to Box No. 209; our address is: P.O. Box 74209, Edinburgh (c) cash box =** metal box for keeping cash *kassalåda;* **letter box** *or* **mail box =** place where incoming mail is put *brevlåda;* **call box =** outdoor telephone booth *telefonkiosk* **(d)** square of ruled lines round a text *or* illustration *ram;* **the comments and quotations are printed in boxes**

boxed [bɒkst] *adj.* put in a box *or* sold in a box *förpackad;* **boxed set =** set of items sold together in a box *förpackning med flera olika punkter*

box in [bɒks 'ɪn] *vb.* to surround a section of text with ruled lines *rama in*

BPI ['biːpiːˈaɪ] *or* **bpi** ['biːpiːˈaɪ] = BITS PER INCH number of bits that can be recorded per inch of recording medium *bitar per tum*

BPS ['biːpiːˈes] *or* **bps** ['biːpiːˈes] = BITS PER SECOND number of bits that can be transmitted per second *bitar per sekund;* **their transmission rate is 60,000 bits per second (bps) through a parallel connection**

bracket ['brækɪt] **1** *subst.* printing sign to show that an instruction *or* operations are to be separated *parentes, klammer;* **round brackets** *or* **square brackets =** different types of bracket (( ), [ ]) *parentes, klamrar* **2** *vb.* **to bracket together =** to print brackets round several items to show that they are treated in the same way and separated from the rest of the text *sätta inom parentes*

bracketed ['brækɪtɪd] *adj.* (characters) joined together with small lines between serif and main part *hårstreckstecken*

bracketing ['brækɪtɪŋ] *subst.* photographing the same scene with different exposures to make sure there is one good picture *säkerhetstagning, fotografering av samma motiv med olika exponering för att försäkra sig om att få en bra bild*

Braille [breɪl] *subst.* system of writing using raised dots on the paper to indicate letters, which allows a blind person to read by passing his fingers over the page *blindskrift enligt Braille;* **she was reading a Braille book; the book has been published in Braille; Braille marks =** raised patterns on equipment *or* in books to permit identification by touch *blindskriftstecken, Brailletecken*

branch [brɑːn(t)ʃ] **1** *subst.* **(a)** possible path *or* jump from one instruction to another *gren;* **branch instruction =** conditional program instruction that provides the location of the next instruction in the program (if a condition is met) *villkorlig hoppinstruktion,* *förgreningsinstruktion;* **program branch =** one or more paths that can be followed after a conditional statement *programgrening* **(b)** line linking one or more devices to the main network *gren;* **the faulty station is on this branch 2** *vb.* to jump from one section of a program to another *förgrena, hoppa*

branchpoint ['brɑːn(t)ʃ,pɔɪnt] *subst.* point in a program where a branch can take place *förgreningspunkt*

COMMENT: in BASIC, the instruction GOTO makes the system jump to the line indicated; this is an unconditional branch. The instruction IF...THEN is a conditional branch, because the jump will only take place if the condition is met

brand [brænd] *subst.* make of product, which can be recognized by a name *or* by a design *varunamn;* **the number one brand of magnetic tape; the company is developing a new brand of screen cleaner; brand name =** name of a brand *varumärkesnamn;* **brand image =** idea of a product which is associated with the brand name *märkesidentitet;* **own brand =** name of a store which is used on products which are specially packed for that store *eget märke*

branded ['brændɪd] *adj.* **branded goods =** goods sold under brand names *märkesvaror*

brand new ['bræn(d)'njuː] *adj.* quite new *or* very new *splitterny*

breach [briːtʃ] *subst.* failure to carry out the terms of an agreement *brott, avtalsbrott, löftesbrott;* **breach of contract =** failing to do something which is in a contract *kontraktsbrott;* **the company is in breach of contract =** it has failed to carry out the duties of the contract *företaget har brutit mot kontraktet;* **breach of warranty =** supplying goods which do not meet the standards of the warranty applied to them *sälja undermåliga varor*

breadboard ['bredbɔːd] *subst.* solderless connection board that allows prototypes of electronic circuits to be constructed quickly and easily *prototypkort*

break [breɪk] **1** *subst.* action *or* key pressed to stop a program execution *avbrott* **2** *vb.* **(a)** to fail to carry out the duties of an agreement *bryta;* **the company has broken the agreement (b)** to decipher a difficult code *knäcka;* **he finally broke the cipher system** NOTE: **breaking - broke - has broken**

breakdown ['breɪkdaʊn] *subst.* stopping work because of mechanical failure *haveri;* **we cannot communicate with our New York office because of the breakdown of the telex lines**

break down [breɪk 'daʊn] *vb.* to stop working because of mechanical failure *haverera;* **the modem has broken down; what do you do when your line printer breaks down?**

breaker ['breɪkə] *subst. brytare;* **circuit breaker** = device which protects equipment by cutting off the electrical supply *överspänningsskydd*

breakpoint ['breɪkpɔɪnt] *subst.* symbol inserted into a program which stops its execution at that point to allow registers, variables and memory locations to be examined (used when debugging a program) *brytpunkt;* **breakpoint instruction** *or* **halt** = halt command inserted in a program to stop execution temporarily, allowing the programmer to examine data and registers while debugging a program *brytpunktsinstruktion;* **breakpoint symbol** = special character used to provide a breakpoint in a program (the debugging program allows breakpoint symbols to be inserted, it then executes the program until it reaches one, then halts) *brytpunktssymbol*

breakup ['breɪkʌp] *subst.* loss *or* distortion of a signal *bortfall, degenering av signal*

bredbandsöverföring ⇨ **wideband**

breddsteg ⇨ **pitch**

breezeway ['briːzweɪ] *subst.* signal used to separate the colour information from the horizontal synchronizing pulse in a television signal

B register ['biː 'redʒɪstə] *subst.* (i) address register that is added to a reference address to provide the location to be accessed *basregister;* (ii) register used to extend the accumulator in multiplication and division operations *basregister*

bridge [brɪdʒ] *or* **bridging product** ['brɪdʒɪŋ 'prɒdʌkt] *subst.* **(a)** matching communications equipment that makes sure that power losses are kept to a minimum *brygga* **(b)** hardware *or* software that allows parts of an old system to be used on a new system *brygga;* **a bridging product is available for companies with both generations of machines**

bridgeware ['brɪdʒweə] *subst.* hardware *or* software used to make the transfer from one computer system to another easier (by changing file format, translation etc.) *brygga*

bridging ['brɪdʒɪŋ] *subst.* to use bridgeware to help transfer programs, data files etc., to another system *överbrygga*

brightness ['braɪtnəs] *subst.* luminance of an object which can be seen *ljusstyrka;* **a**

control knob allows you to adjust brightness and contrast; the brightness of the monitor can hurt the eyes; brightness range = variation of reflected light intensity *variationsområde för ljusstyrka*

QUOTE there is a brightness control on the front panel
Micro Decision

brilliance ['brɪljəns] *subst.* the luminance of an object as seen in a picture *briljans*

brilliant ['brɪljənt] *adj.* very bright and shining (light *or* colour) *glänsande, strålande, briljant;* **the background colour is a brilliant red; he used brilliant white for the highlights**

British Standards Institute (BSI) ['brɪtɪʃ 'stændədz 'ɪnstɪtjuːt ('biːesˈaɪ)] organization that monitors design and safety standards in the UK *engelska standardiseringsinstitutet*

broadband ['brɔːdbænd] *subst.* transmission channel whose bandwidth is greater than a voice channel (allowing faster data transmission) *bredband;* **broadband radio** = radio communications link using a broadband channel *bredbandsratio*

broadcast ['brɔːdkɑːst] **1** *subst.* data *or* voice transmission to many receivers *utsändning;* **broadcast homes** = homes with at least one TV *or* radio receiver *hushåll som har minst en TV eller radio;* **broadcast network** = network for sending data to a number of receivers *utsändningsnätverk;* **broadcast satellite technique** = method of providing greatest channel bandwidth for a geostationary satellite *rundsändningsteknik med satellit* **2** *vb.* to distribute information over a wide area *or* audience *sända ut;* **he broadcast the latest news over the radio** *or* **over the WAN; broadcasting station** = radio station that transmits received signals to other stations *publik radio- el. TV-station, rundradio-station*

broadsheet ['brɔːdʃiːt] *subst.* uncut sheet of paper *or* paper which has printing on one side only *plakat*

broadside ['brɔːdsaɪd] *subst. US* publicity leaflet *affisch, häfte, häftad broschyr*

brochure ['brəʊʃjʊə] *subst.* publicity booklet *broschyr;* **we sent off for a brochure about holidays in Greece** *or* **about maintenance services**

bromide ['brəʊmaɪd] *or* **bromide print** ['brəʊmaɪd 'prɪnt] *subst.* **(a)** positive photographic print from a negative *or* the finished product from a phototypesetting machine *bromsilvertryck;* **in 24 hours we**

had bromides ready to film (b) lithographic plate used for proofing *litografiskt avdrag*

brown-out ['braʊnaʊt] *subst.* power failure (low voltage level rather than no voltage level) *strömfall, spänningsfall; see also* BLACK-OUT

browse [braʊz] *vb.* to search through and access database material without permission *ögna igenom, bläddra*

brukstestad ▷ **field**

brum ▷ **hum**

brute force method ['bruːt ‚fɔːs 'meθəd] *subst.* problem-solving method which depends on computer power rather than elegant programming techniques *råstyrkelösning*

bruttovikt ▷ **weight**

brytpunkt ▷ **point**

brytpunktsinstruktion ▷ **instruction**

brytzon ▷ **hot**

bråkdel ▷ **fraction**

brädgård(stecken) ▷ **hashmark**

brädstapel(tecken) ▷ **hashmark**

bränna ▷ **blast**

brödstil ▷ **body**

brödtext ▷ **body**

BSC ['biːes'siː] = BINARY SYNCHRONOUS COMMUNICATIONS (old) standard for medium/high speed data communication links *binär synkronkommunikation*

BSI ['biːes'aɪ] = BRITISH STANDARDS INSTITUTE organization that monitors design and safety standards in the UK *engelska standardiseringsinstitutet*

BTAM ['biːtæm] = BASIC TELECOMMUNICATIONS ACCESS METHOD method to provide access (read *or* write operations) to a remote device *åtkomstmetod för telekommunikations-apparater*

bubbelminne ▷ **magnetic**

bubble memory ['bʌbl 'memərɪ] *subst.* method of storing binary data using the magnetic properties of certain materials, allowing very large amounts of data to be stored in primary memory *bubbelminne;* **bubble memory cassette =** bubble memory device on a removable cartridge that can be inserted into a controller card (like an audio cassette) to provide high capacity, high speed, removable memory *bubbelminneskassett*

bubble sort ['bʌbl 'sɔːt] *subst.* sorting method which repeatedly exchanges various pairs of data items until they are in order *utbytessortering, bubbelsortering*

bucket ['bʌkɪt] *subst.* storage area containing data for an application *ett (tillämpnings)programs dataarea*

buckling ['bʌklɪŋ] *subst.* distortion and bending of a film due to heat *or* dryness *filmdeformation*

buffer ['bʌfə] **1** *subst.* **(a)** (circuit) that isolates and protects a system from damaging inputs from circuits *or* peripherals *buffert; see also* DRIVER **(b)** temporary storage area for data waiting to be processed *buffert;* **buffer register =** temporary storage for data read from *or* being written to main memory *buffertregister;* **buffer size =** total number of characters that can be held in a buffer *buffertstorlek;* **data buffer =** temporary storage location for data received by a device that is not yet ready to process it *databuffert;* **dynamic** *or* **elastic buffer =** buffer whose size varies with demand *dynamisk buffert, elastisk buffert;* **I/O buffer =** temporary storage area for data waiting to be input *or* output *in- och utbuffert* **2** *vb.* using a temporary storage area to hold data until the processor *or* device is ready to deal with it *buffra;* **buffered input/output =** use of a temporary storage area on input *or* output ports to allow slow peripherals to operate with a fast CPU *buffrad in- och utmatning;* **buffered memory =** feature that allows instructions *or* data to be entered before the device has finished processing *buffrat minne;* **buffering =** using buffers to provide a link between slow and fast devices *buffring;* **double buffering =** two buffers working together so that one can be read while the other is accepting data *dubbel buffring, växelbuffring*

> COMMENT: buffers allow two parts of a computer system to work at different speeds (i.e. a high-speed central processing unit and a slower line printer)

> QUOTE the speed is enhanced by the 8K RAM printer buffer included
> QUOTE the software allocates a portion of cache as a print buffer to restore program control faster after sending data to the printer
> **Which PC?**

buffertminne ▷ **cache**

bug [bʌg] **1** *subst. informal* **(a)** error in a computer program which makes it run incorrectly *programfel, 'lus';* **bug patches =** (temporary) correction made to a program; small correction made to software by a user on the instructions of the software publisher *temporära åtgärder gjorda i ett program; see also* DEBUG **(b)** hidden microphone which records conversations secretly *hemlig avlyssning* **2** *vb.* to hide a microphone to allow conversations to be recorded secretly *avlyssna;* **the conference room was bugged**

buggy ['bʌgɪ] *subst.* small computer-controlled vehicle *buggy*

building block ['bɪldɪŋˌblɒk] *subst.* self-contained unit that can be joined to others to form a system *byggblock*

built-in ['bɪlt'ɪn] *adj.* (special feature) that is already included in a system *inbyggd;* **the built-in adapter card makes it fully IBM compatible; the computer has a built-in hard disk; built-in check =** error detection and validation check carried out automatically on received data *inbyggd kontroll;* **built-in function =** special function already implemented in a program *inbyggd funktion*

built into [bɪlt 'ɪntʊ] *adj.* feature that is already a physical part of a system *inbyggd;* **there are communications ports built into all modems**
NOTE: opposite is **add on**

bulk [bʌlk] *subst.* large quantity of something *parti, volym;* **in bulk =** in large quantities *partivis;* **bulk erase =** to erase a complete magnetic disk *or* tape in one action *volymradering;* **bulk storage medium =** medium that is able to store large amounts of data in a convenient way and form *volymminne;* **magnetic tape is a reliable bulk storage medium; bulk update terminal =** device used by an information provider to prepare videotext pages off-line, then transmit them rapidly to the main computer *terminal för satsvis volymuppdatering av videotexsidor*

bulletin board system (BBS) ['bʊlɪtɪn ˌbɔːd 'sɪstəm ('biːbiːˈes)] *subst.* information and message database accessible by modem and computer link *offentlig databas, elektroniskt klotterplank, elektronisk anslagstavla i publikt meddelande/databassystem*

bullets ['bʊlɪts] *subst.* **(a)** solid area of typeset tone indicating the required image intensity *bomber* **(b)** method of indicating an important section of text by the use of large dots on the page *bomber*

bundle ['bʌndl] *subst.* number of optic fibres gathered together *bunt, knippa*

bundled software ['bʌndld 'sɒftweə] *subst.* programs included in the price of a computer hardware package *medföljande program, i priset ingående program*

buntsteg ⇨ **gutter**

bureau ['bjʊərəʊ] *subst.* office which specializes in keyboarding data *or*

processing batches of data for other small companies *serivcebyrå;* **the company offers a number of bureau services, such as printing and data collection; our data manipulation is handled by a bureau; information bureau =** office which gives information *informationsbyrå;* **word-processing bureau =** office which specializes in word-processing *skrivbyrå;* **we farm out the office typing to a local bureau**
NOTE: the plural is **bureaux**

burner ['bɜːnə] *subst.* device which burns in programs onto PROM chips *(krets)brännare*

burn in ['bɜːn 'ɪn] *vb.* **(a)** to mark a (television *or* monitor) screen after displaying a high brightness image for too long *inbränning* **(b)** to write data into a PROM chip *inbränning*

burn-in ['bɜːnɪn] *subst.* heat test for electronic components *inkörning*

burn out ['bɜːnaʊt] *subst.* excess heat *or* incorrect use that causes an electronic circuit *or* device to fail *överhettning*

burst [bɜːst] *subst.* short isolated sequence of transmitted signals *skur, grupp;* **burst mode =** data transmission using intermittent bursts of data *intermittent gruppvis överföring;* **error burst =** group of several consecutive errors (in a transmission) *felskur*

burster ['bɜːstə] *subst.* machine used to separate the sheets of continuous fanfold paper *maskin för efterbehandling*

bus [bʌs] *subst.* **(a)** communication link consisting of a set of leads *or* wires which connects different parts of a computer hardware system, and over which data is transmitted and received by various circuits in the system *buss;* **address bus =** bus carrying address data between a CPU and a memory device *adressbuss;* **bi-directional bus =** data *or* control lines that can carry signals travelling in two directions *dubbelriktad buss;* **bus address lines =** wires, each of which carries one bit of an address word *bussadressledningar;* **bus arbitration =** protocol and control of transmission over a bus that ensures fair usage by several users *bussmedling;* **bus board =** PCB containing conducting paths for all the computer signals *buss(krets)kort;* **bus control lines =** wires, each of which carries one bit of a control word *busstyrledningar;* **bus data lines =** wires, each of which carries one bit of a data word *bussdataledningar;* **bus driver =** high power transistors *or* amplifier that can provide enough power to transmit signals to a number of devices *busstyrkrets;* **bus master =** data source that controls the bus whilst transmitting (bus master status moves between sending stations) *bussövervakare;* **bus network** = network of computers where the machines are connected to a central bus unit which transmits the messages it receives *bussnätverk;* **bus slave** = data sink which receives data from a bus master *busslav;* **bus structure** = way in which buses are organized, whether serial, parallel, bidirectional, etc. *busstruktur;* **control bus** = bus carrying control signals between a CPU and other circuits *styrbuss;* **daisy chain bus** = one communications bus that joins one device to the next, each device being able to receive *or* transmit *or* modify data as it passes through to the next device in line *kedjebuss;* **data bus** = bus carrying data between a CPU and memory and peripheral devices *databuss;* **dual bus system** = way of linking different parts of a system which keeps the memory bus separate from the input/output bus *dubbelt bussystem;* **input/output data bus (I/O bus)** = links allowing data and control transfer between a CPU and external peripherals *in- och utbuss;* **memory bus** = bus carrying address data between a CPU and memory devices *minnesbuss* **(b)** central source of information which supplies several devices *informationsbuss*

QUOTE mice can either be attached to the PC bus *or* a serial port
PC Business World
QUOTE both buses can be software controlled to operate as either a 16- or 32-bit interface
Electronics & Power

business ['bɪznəs] *subst.* **(a)** work in buying *or* selling *affärsverksamhet;* **business is expanding; business is slow; he does a good business in repairing computers; what's your line of business?; business computer** = powerful small computer which is programmed for special business tasks *affärsdator;* **business efficiency exhibition** = exhibition which shows products (computers, word-processors) which help a business to be efficient *engelsk benämning på kontors- el. datamässa;* **business system** *or* **business package** = set of programs adapted for business use (such as payroll, invoicing, customers file, etc.) *administrativt system* **(b)** commercial company *företag;* **he owns a small computer repair business; she runs a business from her home; he set up in business as an computer consultant; business address** = details of number, street and town where a company is located *företagsadress;* **business card** = card showing a businessman's name and the name and address of the company he works for *visitkort;* **business equipment** = machines used in an office *kontorsutrustning*
NOTE: no plural for (a); (b) has the plural **businesses**

buss(ledning) ⇨ **highway**

busy ['bɪzɪ] *adj.* **(a)** (i) occupied in doing something *or* in working *upptagen;* (ii) electrical signal indicating that a device is not ready to receive data *upptagetmarkerat;* **the line is busy** = the telephone line is being used *linjen är upptagen* **(b)** distracting *or* detailed (background to a film shot) *orolig, plottrig*

buzz [bʌz] **1** *subst.* sound like a loud hum *surr* **2** *vb.* to make a loud hum *surra*

buzzer ['bʌzə] *subst.* electrical device which makes a loud hum *summer*

buzzword ['bʌzwɜːd] *subst. informal* word which is popular among a certain group of people *modeord, slagord*

bypass ['baɪpɑːs] *subst.* alternative route around a component *or* device, so that it is not used *avledning, förbiledning;* **there is an automatic bypass around any faulty equipment**

byta ⇨ **change**

byte [baɪt] *subst.* group of bits *or* binary digits (usually eight) which a computer operates on as a single unit *byte;* **byte addresses** = location of data bytes in memory *byteadress;* **byte machine** = variable word length computer *bytemaskin;* **byte manipulation** = moving, editing and changing the contents of a byte *bytehantering;* **byte serial transmission** *or* **mode** = transmission of bytes of data sequentially, the individual bits of which can be sent in a serial *or* parallel way *bytevis överföringstillstånd*

QUOTE if you can find a way of packing two eight-bit values into a single byte, you save substantial amounts of RAM or disk space
Practical Computing

bytevis dataöverföring ⇨ **mode**

bärare ⇨ **carrier**

bärbar dator ⇨ **luggable, portable**

bärraket ⇨ **launch vehicle**

bärvåg ⇨ **carrier**

Cc

C [siː] high level programming language developed mainly for writing structured systems programs *programmeringsspråket C*

QUOTE these days a lot of commercial software is written in C
PC Business World

C [siː] hexadecimal number equivalent to decimal 12 *talet tolv skrivet med hexadecimal notation*

cable ['keɪbl] **1** *subst.* **(a)** flexible conducting electrical *or* optical link *kabel, sladd;* **cable television** *or* **cable TV** = television system where signals are broadcast to viewers' homes over cables *kabelteve;* **cable TV relay station** = receiving station which retransmits received television signals to a terminal point (where they are then distributed by cable to viewers' homes) *relästation för kabelteve; see also* CATV **(b)** telegram *or* message sent by telegraph *telegram;* **he sent a cable to his office asking for more money; cable address** = specially short address for sending cables *telegramadress* **2** *vb.* to send a message *or* money by telegraph *telegrafera;* **he cabled his office to ask them to send more money; the office cabled him £1,000 to cover his expenses**

cablegram ['keɪblgræm] *subst.* telegram *or* message sent by telegraph *telegram*

cabling ['keɪblɪŋ] *subst.* cable (as a material) *kablar, kablage;* **using high-quality cabling will allow the user to achieve very high data transfer rates; cabling costs up to £1 a foot**
NOTE: no plural

cache [kæʃ] **1** *subst.* **cache memory** = section of high-speed memory which stores data that the computer can access quickly *fickminne, buffertminne;* **file access time is much quicker if the most frequently used data is stored in cache memory; instruction cache** = section of high-speed memory which stores the next few instructions to be executed by a processor (to speed up operation) *instruktionsbuffert* **2** *vb.* to file *or* store in a cache *buffra;* **this program can cache any size font**

QUOTE the first range of 5.25 inch Winchester disk drives to feature inbuilt cache
Minicomputer News
QUOTE a serious user might also want a tape streamer and cache memory
PC Business World

CAD [kæd] = COMPUTER AIDED DESIGN *or* COMPUTER ASSISTED DESIGN the use of a computer and graphics terminal to help a designer in his work *datorstödd konstruktion;* **all our engineers design on CAD workstations; CAD/CAM** = CAD/COMPUTER AIDED MANUFACTURE interaction between computers used for designing and those for manufacturing a product *datorstödd konstruktion och tillverkning*

QUOTE CAD software is memory-intensive
PC Business World

CAI ['siːeɪ'aɪ] = COMPUTER AIDED INSTRUCTION *or* COMPUTER ASSISTED INSTRUCTION use of a computer to assist pupils in learning a subject *datorstödd undervisning*

CAL [kæl] = COMPUTER AIDED LEARNING *or* COMPUTER ASSISTED LEARNING use of a computer to assist pupils in learning a subject *datorstödd inlärning*

calculate ['kælkjʊleɪt] *vb.* **(a)** to find the answer to a problem using numbers *beräkna;* **the DP manager calculated the rate for keyboarding; you need to calculate the remaining disk space (b)** to estimate *uppskatta;* **I calculate that we have six months' stock left**

calculation [,kælkjʊ'leɪʃ(ə)n] *subst.* answer to a problem in mathematics *beräkning;* **rough calculation** = approximate answer *överslag(sberäkning);* **I made some rough calculations on the back of an envelope; according to my calculations, we have six months' stock left**

calculator ['kælkjʊleɪtə] *subst.* electronic machine which works out the answers to numerical problems *räknare, kalkylator;* **my pocket calculator needs a new battery; he worked out the discount on his calculator**

calibration [,kælɪ'breɪʃ(ə)n] *subst.* comparing the signal from an input with a known scale to provide a standardized reading *kalibrering*

call [kɔːl] **1** *subst.* conversation (between people *or* machines) on the telephone *samtal;* **local call** = call to a number on the same exchange *lokalsamtal;* **trunk call** *or* **long-distance call** = call to a number in a different zone *or* area *riks(samtal);* **person-to-person call** = call where you ask the operator to connect you with a named person *personsamtal;* **transferred charge call** *or* *US* **collect call** = call where the person receiving the call agrees to pay for it *samtal som mottagaren betalar, Ba-samtal;* **to make a call** = to dial and speak to someone on the telephone *ringa ett samtal;* **to take a call** = to answer the telephone *ta emot samtal, svara i telefon;* **to log calls** = to note all details of telephone calls made *bokföra samtal* **2** *vb.* **(a)** to transfer control to a separate program *or* routine from a main program *anropa;* **after an input is received, the first function is called up; the subroutine call instruction should be at this point; call instruction** = programming instruction that directs control to a routine (after saving the program counter contents to show the return instruction where to return to in the main program) *anropsinstruktion* **(b)** to try to contact another user by telephone *ringa upp;* **I'll call you at your office tomorrow; call**

accepted signal = signal sent by device meaning willing to accept caller's data *klarsignal;* **call control signal** = signal necessary to establish and end a call *anropssignal, slutsignal;* **call diverter** = device that on receiving a call, contacts another point and re-routes the call *vidarekopplare;* **call duration** = length of time spent between starting and ending a call *samtalskod, förbindelsetid;* **call duration depends on the complexity of the transaction; charges are related to call duration; call forwarding** = automatic redirection of calls to another user *or* station *vidarekoppling;* **we are having all calls forwarded from the office to home; called party** = person *or* station to which a call is made *mottagare*

call box ['kɔːlbɒks] *subst.* outdoor telephone booth *telefonkiosk*

caller ['kɔːlə] *subst.* person who telephones *or* requests a call *person som ringer upp*

callier effect ['kælɪəˈfekt] *subst.* scattering of light as it passes through one *or* more lenses *calliereffekt*

calligraphy [kəˈlɪgrəfɪ] *subst.* art of handwriting *kalligrafi*

call in [kɔːl ˈɪn] *vb.* to telephone to make contact *rapportera, kontakta, ringa (upp);* **we ask the representatives to call in every Friday to report the weeks' sales**

calling ['kɔːlɪŋ] *subst.* signal to request attention, sent from a terminal *or* device to the main computer *anrop;* **calling sequence** = series of program commands required to direct execution to or back from a subroutine *anropssekvens*

call up [kɔːl ˈʌp] *vb.* to ask for information from a backing store to be displayed *anropa, hämta (fram), visa;* **all the customers addresses were called up; call up the previous file**

CAM [kæm] **(a)** = COMPUTER AIDED MANUFACTURE *or* COMPUTER ASSISTED MANUFACTURING use of a computer to control machinery *or* assist in a manufacturing process *datorstödd tillverkning* **(b)** = CONTENT ADDRESSABLE MEMORY memory that is addressed and accessed by its contents rather than a location *associativt minne*

Cambridge ring ['keɪmbrɪdʒ rɪŋ] *subst.* local area networking standard used for connecting several devices and computers together in a ring with simple cable links *brittisk standard för lokalt nätverk*

cameo ['kæmɪəʊ] *subst.* **(a)** reverse characters, that is, white on a black background *inverterad bild, inverterad*

presentation **(b)** front-lit subject filmed in front of a dark background *förgrundsbelysning*

camera ['kæm(ə)rə] *subst.* (i) photographic device that transfers a scene onto a piece of film, usually via a lens *kamera;* (ii) device that transforms a scene into electronic signals that can be displayed on a television *tevekamera;* **camera chain** = pieces of equipment necessary to operate a television camera *kamerakedja;* **camera-ready copy (crc)** = final text *or* graphics ready to be photographed before printing *kamerafärdigt original*

cancel ['kæns(ə)l] *vb.* to stop a process *or* instruction before it has been fully executed *avbryta, stoppa, upphöra;* **cancel character** = control code used to indicate that the last data transmitted was incorrect *upphävningstecken;* **the software automatically sends a cancel character after any error; cancel page** = extra printed page inserted into a book to take the place of a page with errors on it *rättelseblad*

cancellation [ˌkænsəˈleɪʃ(ə)n] *subst.* action of stopping a process which has been started *upphävande*

candela [kænˈdiːlə] *subst.* SI unit of measurement of light intensity *candela (cd)*

canonical schema [kəˈnɒnɪk(ə)l ˈskiːmə] *subst.* model of a database that is independent of hardware *or* software available *kanoniskt schema*

capability [ˌkeɪpəˈbɪlɪtɪ] *subst.* being able to do something *förmåga, möjlighet;* **resolution capabilities; electronic mail capabilities; capability list** = list of operations that can be carried out *funktionslista*

capable ['keɪpəbl] *adj.* able to do something *duglig, som kan göra;* **that is the highest speed that this printer is capable of; the software is capable of far more complex functions** NOTE: a device is capable **of** something

capacitance [kəˈpæsɪt(ə)ns] *subst.* ability of a component to store electrical charge *kapacitans*

capacitative [kəˈpæsɪtətɪv] *or* **capacititive** [kəˈpæsɪtɪtɪv] *adj.* something which has capacitance *kapacitiv*

capacitor [kəˈpæsɪtə] *subst.* electronic component that can store charge *kondensator;* **capacitor microphone** = microphone that uses variations in capacitance due to sound pressure to generate an electrical signal *kondensatormikrofon;* **ceramic capacitors** = general purpose, non-polar small capacitors made from ceramic materials *keramisk kondensator;* **electrolytic capacitors** = polar, high-capacitance devices made in a variety of materials *elektrolyt(isk kondensator);* **non-electrolytic capacitors** = non-polar, low-capacitance devices made from a variety of materials *(icke-elektrolytisk) kondensator;* **variable capacitor** = device whose capacitance can be varied over a small range, used for tuning purposes *variabel kondensator;* **capacitor storage** = device using capacititive properties of a material to store data *kondensatorminne, kapacitivt minne;* **memory backup capacitor** = very high-capacitance, small device that can provide power for volatile RAM chips for up to two weeks (used instead of a battery) *batterisäkrad kondensator, säkring av minne; see also* BATTERY BACKUP

capacity [kəˈpæsətɪ] *subst.* **(a)** amount which can be produced *or* amount of work which can be done *kapacitet;* **industrial** *or* **manufacturing** *or* **production capacity; channel capacity** = maximum rate for data transmission over a channel *kanalkapacitet;* **to work at full capacity** = to do as much work as possible *utnyttja sin kapacitet maximalt;* **to use up spare** *or* **excess capacity** = to make use of time *or* space which is not fully used *utnyttja reservkapacitet (överskottskapacitet)* **(b)** amount of storage space available in a system *or* on a disk *kapacitet;* **storage capacity** = space available for storage *minneskapacitet;* **total storage capacity is now 3Mbyte**

capitals [ˈkæpɪtlz] *or informal* **caps** [kæps] *subst.* large form of letters (A,B,C,D, etc.) as opposed to lower case (a,b,c,d, etc.) *versaler;* **the word BASIC is always written in caps; caps lock** = key on a keyboard *or* typewriter that allows all characters to be entered as capitals *skiftlås;* **the LED lights up when caps lock is pressed** *kapstan*

capstan [ˈkæpstən] *subst.* device in a tape player which ensures that the tape moves at a constant speed *drivrulle*

caption [ˈkæpʃ(ə)n] *subst.* note *or* explanation under or next to a picture *or* diagram *bildtext, figurtext;* **the captions are printed in italics**

capture [ˈkæptʃə] **1** *subst.* **data capture** = action of obtaining data (either by keyboarding *or* by scanning *or* often automatically from a recording device *or* peripheral) *datafångst;* **data capture starts when an interrupt is received 2** *vb.* to take data into a computer system *fånga, mata in (data);* **the software allows captured images to be edited; scanners usually capture images at a resolution of 300 dots per inch (dpi)**

carbon [ˈkɑːbən] *subst.* **(a)** carbon paper *karbonpapper;* **you forgot to put a carbon in the typewriter (b)** carbon copy *karbonkopia;* **make a top copy and two carbons;** *see also* NCR

carbon copy [ˈkɑːbən ˈkɒpɪ] *subst.* copy made with carbon paper *karbonkopia;* **give me the original, and file the carbon copy**

carbonless [ˈkɑːbənlɪs] *adj.* which makes a copy without using carbon paper *självkopierande;* **our representatives use carbonless order pads; carbonless paper** = paper that transfers writing without carbon paper *självkopierande papper*

carbon microphone [ˈkɑːbən ˈmaɪkrəfəʊn] *subst.* microphone that uses changes of resistance in carbon granules due to sound pressure to produce a signal *kol(korns)mikrofon*

carbon paper [ˈkɑːbən ˈpeɪpə] *subst.* thin paper with a coating of ink on one side, used to make copies in a typewriter *or* printer *karbonpapper*

carbon ribbon [ˈkɑːbən ˈrɪbən] *subst.* thin plastic ribbon, coated with black ink, used in printers *karbonband; compare* FIBRE RIBBON

carbon set [ˈkɑːbən set] *subst.* forms with carbon paper attached *blankettset*

carbon tissue [ˈkɑːbən ˈtɪʃuː] *subst.* light-sensitive material used to transfer an image to the printing plate of a photogravure process *(ets)pigmentpapper, grafitfilm*

card [kɑːd] *subst.* **(a)** stiff paper *kartong;* **we have printed the instructions on thick white card** NOTE: no plural **(b)** small piece of stiff paper *or* plastic *kort;* **cash card** = plastic card containing the owner's details on a magnetic stripe, used to obtain money from a cash dispenser *uttagskort, bankautomatkort;* **charge card** = plastic card which allows you to buy goods and pay for them later *kontokort;* **credit card** = plastic card which allows you to borrow money *or* to buy goods without paying for them immediately *kreditkort;* **filing card** = card with information written on it, used to classify information in correct order *registerkort;* **index card** = card used to make a card index *katalogkort, registerkort;* **punched card** = card with holes punched in it that represent data *hålkort;* **smart card** = plastic card with a memory and microprocessor device embedded in it, so that it can be used for electronic funds transfer *or* for identification of the user *aktivt kort;* **smart cards reduce fraud; future smart cards could contain an image of the**

users fingerprint for identification (c) a punched card *hålkort;* **card code** = combination of punched holes that represent characters on a punched card *hålkortskod;* **card column** = line of punched information about one character, parallel to the shorter side of the card *kortkolumn;* **card feed** = device which draws punched cards into a reader automatically *kortmatning;* **card field** = part of a card column reserved for one type of data *kortfält;* **card format** = way in which columns and rows are arranged to represent data fields *or* characters in a punched card *kortformat;* **card image** = section of memory that contains an exact representation of the information on a card *minnesavbildning av hålkortsinformationen;* **card loader** = short program that transfers data from a punched card into main memory *kortladdare;* **card punch (CP)** = machine that punches the holes in punched cards *hålkortsstans;* **card reader** *or* **punched card reader** = device that transforms data on a punched card to a form that can be recognized by the computer *kortläsare;* **card row** = punch positions parallel to the longer edge of a card *kortrad* **(d)** sheet of insulating material on which electronic components can be mounted *kort, ledningskort;* **card cage** = metal supporting frame for circuit boards *kortlåda;* **card edge connector** = series of metal tracks ending at the edge and on the surface of a card, allowing it to be plugged into an edge connector to provide electrical contact (for data transmission, etc.) *kortkontakt;* **card extender** = card containing only conducting tracks, inserted between a motherboard connector and an expansion card, allowing the expansion card to be worked on and examined easily, outside the card cage *förlängningskort;* **expansion card** *or* **expansion board** = printed circuit board that is connected to a system (expansion connector) to increase its functions *or* performance *tillsatskort, expansionskort, instickskort;* **hard card** = board containing a hard disk drive and the required interfacing electronics, which can be slotted into a system (expansion connector) *fast skivminne på instickskort;* **card frame** *or* **card chassis** = frame containing a motherboard into which printed circuit boards can be plugged to provide a flexible system *kortchassi, kortlåda*

QUOTE this card does not occupy system memory space and provides fifty functions including programmable character sets

Computing Today

cardboard ['kɑːdbɔːd] *subst.* thick stiff brown paper *papp;* **cardboard box** = box made of cardboard *papplåda* NOTE: no plural

card index ['kɑːd'ɪndeks] *subst.* series of cards with information written on them, kept in special order so that the information can be found easily *kortregister, kortkatalog;* **card-index file** = information kept on filing cards *kortkatalog, kortlåda*

card-index ['kɑːd'ɪndeks] *vb.* to put information onto a card index *katalogisera, indexera*

card-indexing ['kɑːd'ɪndeksɪŋ] *subst.* putting information onto a card index *katalogisering, indexering;* **no one can understand her card-indexing system**

cardioid response ['kɑːdɪˌɔɪd rɪs'pɒns] *subst.* heart shaped response curve of an antenna *or* microphone when a signal source is moved around it *kardioidkaraktäristik*

caret mark ['kærət mɑːk] *or* **sign** [saɪn] *subst.* proofreading symbol to indicate that something has to be inserted in the text *inskjutningstecken*

carriage ['kærɪdʒ] *subst.* mechanical section of a typewriter *or* printer that correctly feeds *or* moves the paper that is being printed *vagn;* **carriage control** = codes that control the movements of a printer carriage *vagnstyrning;* **carriage control codes can be used to move the paper forward two lines between each line of text; carriage return (CR)** = signal *or* key to move to the beginning of the next line of print *or* display *vagnretur;* **the carriage return key is badly placed for touch-typists**

carrier ['kærɪə] *subst.* **(a)** substance that holds the ink for photocopying *or* printing processes *bärare, medium* **(b)** device that holds a section of microfilm *hållare* **(c)** continuous high frequency waveform that can be modulated by a signal *bärvåg;* **he's not using a modem - there's no carrier signal on the line; carrier sense multiple access - collision detection (CSMA/CD)** = network communications protocol that prevents two sources transmitting at the same time by waiting for a quiet moment, then attempting to transmit *standard för kommunikationsprotokoll (främst för lokala nätverk);* **carrier signalling** = simple data transmission (by switching on and off a carrier signal according to binary data) *bärvågssignalering;* **carrier system** = method of transmitting several different signals on one channel by using several different carrier frequencies *bärvågssystem;* **carrier telegraphy** = method of transmitting telegraph signals via a carrier signal *bärvågstelegrafi;* **carrier wave** = waveform used as a carrier *bärvåg;* **data carrier** = (i) any device *or* medium capable of storing data *datamedium;* (ii) a waveform used as a carrier for data signals *bärvåg;* **data carrier**

detect (DCD) = RS232C signal from a modem to a computer, indicating a carrier wave is being received *DCD-signal, bärvågsindikation;* **the call is stopped if the software does not receive a DCD signal from the modem**

carry ['kærɪ] **1** *subst.* (extra) digit due to an addition result being greater than the number base used *överföringssiffra;* **when 5 and 7 are added, there is an answer of 2 and a carry which is put in the next column, giving 12; carry bit** *or* **flag** = indicator that a carry has occurred *överföringssiffra;* **carry complete signal** = signal from an adder circuit indicating that all carry operations have been completed *överföringssiffra, färdigsignal;* **carry look ahead** = high speed adder that can predict if a carry will be generated by a sum and add it in, removing the delay found in an adder with ripple-through carry *framförhållande överföringssiffra;* **carry time** = period of time taken to transfer a carry digit to the next higher digit position *tid för överföringssiffra;* **cascade carry** = carry generated in an adder from an input carry signal *kaskad(kopplad) överföringssiffra;* **end-around carry** = most significant digit (the carry) is added into the least significant place (used in BCD arithmetic) *addering med överföringssssiffra (adderingsteknik i aritmetik med binärkodat decimaltal, överföringssiffran från en talposition adderas till den minst signifikanta biten i nästa talposition);* **high speed carry** = when a carry into an adder results in a carry out, all produced in one operation *höghastighetsöverföringssiffra;* **partial carry** = temporary storage of all carries generated in parallel adders, rather than a direct transfer *parallellmellan-lagring (för överföringssiffra);* **ripple-through carry** = carry generated by a carry in to an adder *serieöverförings-siffra* **2** *vb.* to move (something) from one place to another *bära;* **the fibre optic link carried all the data; the information-carrying abilities of this link are very good**

cartesian coordinates [kɑ:'ti:zjən kəʊ'ɔːdnəts] *subst.* positional system that uses two axes at right angles to represent a point which is located with two numbers, giving a position on each *kartesiska koordinater, rätvinkliga koordinater*

cartesian structure [kɑ:'ti:zjən 'strʌktʃə] *subst.* data structure whose size is fixed and the elements are in (a linear) order *kartesisk struktur; compare with* AXIS, POLAR COORDINATES

cartridge ['kɑ:trɪdʒ] *subst.* removable cassette, containing a disk *or* tape *or* program *or* data (usually stored in ROM) *kassett, patron;* **data cartridge** = cartridge that contains stored data *datakassett;* **disk cartridge** = removable hard disk *skrivminneskassett;* **ROM cartridge** = sealed module (with electrical connections) which can be plugged into a computer and contains data *or* extra programs stored in a ROM chip *läsminnespatron, "ROM-plugg";* **the portable computer has no disk drives, but has a slot for ROM cartridges;** **tape cartridge** = cassette box containing magnetic tape *bandkassett;* **cartridge drive** = drive which uses a disk *or* tape in a cartridge *kassettbandstation;* **cartridge fonts** = ROM cartridge which can be plugged into a printer, providing a choice of new typefaces, but still limited to the typefaces and styles included in the cartridge *typsnittspatron, typsnittskassett; compare* RESIDENT FONTS; **cartridge ribbon** = printer ribbon in a closed cartridge *färgbandspatron*

cartridge paper ['kɑ:trɪdʒ 'peɪpə] *subst.* good quality white paper for drawing *or* printing *korderspapper*

cascade carry [kæs'keɪd 'kærɪ] *subst.* carry generated in an adder from an input carry signal *kaskad(kopplad) överföringssiffra*

cascade connection [kæs'keɪd kə'nekʃ(ə)n] *subst.* number of devices *or* circuits arranged in series, the output of one driving the input of the next *kaskadkoppling*

cascade control [kæs'keɪd kən'trəʊl] *subst.* multiple control units, each controlling the next *kaskadstyrning*

case [keɪs] **1** *subst.* **(a)** protective container for a device *or* circuit *låda, hölje* **(b)** box containing metal characters used in composing *kast;* **upper case** *or* **lower case** = capital letters *or* ordinary letters *versaler, gemena;* **he corrected the word "coMputer", replacing the upper case M with a lower case letter; case change** = key used to change from upper to lower case on a keyboard *skift(tangent)* **(c)** cardboard cover for a book *box;* **the library edition has a case and jacket; have you remembered to order the blocking for the spine of the case?; case binding** = stiff cardboard cover *kartongband* **(d)** cardboard *or* wooden box for packing and carrying goods *låda;* **a packing case** = large wooden box for carrying items which can be easily broken *en packlår* **2** *vb.* **(a)** to bind a book in a stiff cardboard cover *kartongbinda;* **cased book** = book with a hard cover *kartongbunden bok* **(b)** to pack in a case *packa (i låda)*

case-making machine ['keɪs ˌmeɪkɪŋ mə'ʃi:n] *subst.* machine for cutting the cardboard which forms the cover of a book *bokbindningsmaskin*

casing ['keısıŋ] *subst.* solid protective box in which a computer *or* delicate equipment is housed *låda*

cassette [kə'set] *subst.* hard container used to store and protect magnetic tape *kassett;* **you must back up the information from the computer onto a cassette; audio cassette** = small cassette containing a reel of narrow magnetic tape on which audio signal can be recorded (used to store data in small home computers) *ljudkassett;* **data cassette** = special high-quality tape for storing data *datakassett;* **video cassette** = large cassette containing a reel of wide magnetic tape on which video data can be recorded *videokassett;* **cassette recorder** = machine to transfer audio signals onto magnetic tape *kassettbandspelare;* **cassette tape** = narrow reel of magnetic tape housed in a solid case for protection *kassettband*

COMMENT: using cassette tape allows data to be stored for future retrieval; it is used instead of a disk system on small computers or as a slow, serial access, high-capacity back-up medium for large systems

caster machine ['ka:stə mə'ʃi:n] *subst.* machine that produces metal type *blysättsmaskin*

casting off ['ka:stıŋ ɒf] *subst.* calculating the amount of space required to print text in a certain font *omfångsberäkning*

cast off ['ka:st 'ɒf] **1** *subst.* amount of space required to print a text in a certain font *omfång* **2** [ka:st 'ɒf] *vb.* to calculate the amount of space needed to print a text in a certain font *omfångsberäkna*

CAT [si:eı'ti:] **(a)** = COMPUTER AIDED *or* ASSISTED TRAINING use of a computer to demonstrate to and assist pupils in learning a skill *datorstödd utbildning* **(b)** = COMPUTER AIDED *or* ASSISTED TESTING use of a computer to test equipment *or* programs to find any faults *datorstödd provning*

catalogue ['kætəlɒg] **1** *subst.* list of contents *or* items in order *katalog;* **disk catalogue** *or* **directory** = list of files stored on a magnetic disk *skivminneskatalog;* **the entry in the disk catalogue is removed when the file is deleted 2** *vb.* to make a catalogue of items stored *katalogisera;* **all the terminals were catalogued, with their location, call sign and attribute table**

cataloguer ['kætə,lɒgə] *subst.* person who makes a catalogue *katalogredaktör*

catastrophe [kə'tæstrəfi] *subst.* serious fault, error *or* breakdown of equipment, usually leading to serious damage and shutdown of a system *katastrof*

catastrophic error [,kætə'strɒfık 'erə] *subst.* error that causes a program to crash *or* files to be accidentally erased *katastrofalt fel;* **catastrophic failure** = complete system failure *or* crash *katastrofalt fel*

catena [kə'ti:nə] *subst.* (i) number of items in a chained list *kedjelista;* (ii) series of characters in a word *sträng*

catenate ['kætəneıt] *vb.* to join together two *or* more sets of data *länka, förena, konkatenera, slå ihop*

cathode ['kæθəʊd] *subst.* negative electrical terminal of a device *or* battery *katod* NOTE: opposite is **anode**

cathode ray tube (CRT) ['kæθəʊd reı tju:b ('si: ɑ: 'ti:)] *subst.* device used for displaying characters *or* figures *or* graphical information, similar to a TV set *katodstrålerör;* **cathode ray tube storage** = a cathode ray tube with a long persistence phosphor screen coating that retains an image for a long time *bildrörsminne* NOTE: CRT is now often used to mean 'monitor'

COMMENT: cathode ray tubes are used in television sets, computer monitors and VDUs; a CRT consists of a vacuum tube, one end of which is flat and coated with phosphor, the other end containing an electron beam source. Characters *or* graphics are visible when the controllable electron beam strikes the phosphor causing it to glow

CATV ['si:eıtı'vi:] = COMMUNITY ANTENNA TELEVISION cable television system using a single aerial to pick up television signals and then distribute them over a wide area via cable *lokal kabeltev, centralantennsystem*

CB ['si:'bi:] = CITIZENS BAND RADIO cheap popular system of radio communications, usually between vehicles *privatradio, "medborgarradio"*

C band ['si:'bænd] *subst.* microwave communications frequency range of 3.9 - 6.2GHz *C-bandet (frekvensband i mikrovågsområdet)*

CBL ['si:'bi:'el] = COMPUTER BASED LEARNING learning mainly using a computer *datorbaserad inlärning*

CBMS ['si:bi:em'es] = COMPUTER BASED MESSAGE SYSTEM use of a computer system to allow users to send and receive messages from other users (usually in-house) *elektronisk post, meddelandehanteringssystem; see also BBS*

CBT ['si:bi:'ti:] = COMPUTER BASED TRAINING use of a computer system to train students *datorbaserad utbildning*

CBX ['si:bi:'eks] = COMPUTERIZED BRANCH EXCHANGE *datoriserad företagsväxel*

CCD ['si:si:'di:] = CHARGE COUPLED DEVICE; **CCD memory** = capacitors used (with MOS transistors) to store data, allowing either serial or random access *laddningskopplat minne*

CCD-element ⇨ **image**

CCITT ['si:si:'aɪti:'ti:] = COMITÉ CONSULTATIF INTERNATIONAL TÉLÉGRAPHIQUE ET TÉLÉPHONIQUE *internationell samarbetsorganisation mellan teleförvaltningar*

CCP ['si:si:'pi:] = COMMAND CONSOLE PROCESSOR software which interfaces between a user's terminal and system BIOS *kommandotolk*

CCTV ['si:si:ti:'vi:] = CLOSED CIRCUIT TELEVISION

CCU ['si:si:'ju:] = COMMUNICATIONS CONTROL UNIT *kommunikationsstyrenhet*

CD ['si:'di:] = COMPACT DISK; **CD-ROM** COMPACT DISK-READ ONLY MEMORY small plastic disk that is used as a high capacity ROM device, data is stored in binary form as holes etched on the surface which are then read by a laser *optisk skiva, optodiskett, CD*

CD ⇨ **compact, laser**

cedilla [sɪ'dɪlə] *subst.* accent under a letter c, used in certain languages to change the pronunciation *cedilj*

cell [sel] *subst.* **(a)** single function *or* number in a spreadsheet program *cell;* **cell reference variable** = register that contains the reference locating a certain cell that is being operated on *cellreferens* **(b)** single memory location, capable of storing a data word, accessed by an individual address *minnescell;* **cell phone** mobile telephone system that uses a network of stations to cover a large area *mobiltelefon*

cellar ['selə] *subst.* temporary storage for data *or* registers *or* tasks, in which items are added and retrieved from the same end of the list in a LIFO order *stack*

cellular ['seljʊlə] *adj.* **cellular radio** = radio telephone linked to a main telephone system, which uses a network of stations, each covering a certain area, to provide a service over a large area (the radio is switched from one station to another as it moves from area to area) *cellradiosystem (mobiltelefonsystem);* **cellular service** = changing from one transceiver station to another as a cellular radio *or* cell phone user moves from area to area *cellvalstjänst*

centering ['sentərɪŋ] *subst.* action of putting text in the centre of the screen *centrering;* **centering of headings is easily done, using this function key**

centi- ['sentɪ] *prefix* meaning one hundred *or* one hundredth *centi-;* **centimetre** = one hundredth of a metre *centimeter*

central ['sentr(ə)l] *adj.* in the middle *central;* **central computer** = HOST COMPUTER; **central memory (CM)** = area of memory whose locations can be directly and immediately addressed by the CPU *internminne, primärminne;* **central processing element (CPE)** = short (2, 4 or 8 bit) word length module that can be used to produce large word length CPUs using bit slice techniques *bituppdelad processor;* **central processing unit (CPU)** *or* **central processor** = group of circuits which perform the basic functions of a computer, made up of three parts: the control unit, the arithmetic and logic unit and the input/output unit *centralenhet;* **central terminal** = terminal which controls the communications between a central *or* host computer and remote terminals *centralterminal*

central ⇨ **central**

centralantennsystem ⇨ **master**

centralenhet ⇨ **central**

centraliserad ⇨ **centralized**

centraliserad databehandling ⇨ **centralized**

centraliserat datanät ⇨ **centralized**

centralized ['sentrəlaɪzd] *adj.* which is located in a central position *centraliserad;* **centralized data processing** = data processing facilities located in a centralized place that can be accessed by other users *centraliserad databehandling;* **centralized computer network** = network with processing power provided by a central computer *centraliserat datanätverk*

(central)processor ⇨ **CPU**

centre ['sentə] *or US* **center** ['sentə] **1** *subst.* point in the middle of something *centrum;* **centre holes** = location holes punched along the centre of paper tape *centrumhål;* **centre operator** = person who looks after central computer operations *chefsoperatör;* **centre sprocket feed** = centre (sprocket) holes that line up with coding hole positions on punched tape *frammatningshål, indexhål* **2** *vb.* **(a)** to align the read/write head correctly on a magnetic disk *or* tape *centrera* **(b)** to place a piece of text in the centre of the paper *or* display screen *centrera;* **which key do you press to centre the heading?**

centrering ⇨ centering

Centronics interface [sen'trɒnɪks 'ɪntəfeɪs] *subst.* parallel printer interface devised by Centronics Inc *Centronics-gränssnitt, parallellgränssnitt*

centrum ⇨ centre

CEPT standard ['siːiːpiːˈtiː 'stændəd] *subst.* videotex character standard defined by the Conference of European Post Telephone and Telegraph *en CEPT videotexstandard*

ceramic [sɪˈræmɪk] *adj.* made from baked clay *keramisk; see* CAPACITOR

CGA ['siːdʒiːˈeɪ] = COLOUR GRAPHICS ADAPTER popular microcomputer medium-resolution colour display system *CGA-grafik; see also* EGA

chad [tʃæd] *subst.* waste material produced from holes punched in tape *or* card *konfetti;* **chadded** *or* **chadless tape** = punched tape that retains chad by not punching holes through fully *genomslagsfri hålremsa*

chain [tʃeɪn] **1** *subst.* (i) series of files *or* data items linked sequentially *kedja;* (ii) series of instructions to be executed sequentially *kedja;* **chain code** = series of words, each word being derived (usually shifted by one bit) from the previous word *kedjekod;* **chain delivery mechanism** = mechanical system to move paper from machine to machine *kedjematning;* **chain list** = list of data with each piece of information providing an address for the next consecutive item in the list *kedjelista;* **chain printer** = printer whose characters are located on a continuous belt *kedjeskrivare;* **command chain** = list of commands (in a file) executed sequentially by a batch mode system *kommandokedja;* **daisy chain** = method of connecting equipment with a single cable passing from one machine *or* device to the next (rather than separate cables to each device) *kedjelänk;* **daisy chain bus** = one communications bus that joins one device to the next, each device being able to receive *or* transmit *or* modify data as it passes through to the next device in line *kedjebuss* **2** *vb.* to link files *or* data items in series by storing a pointer to the next file *or* item at each entry *länka;* **more than 1,000 articles or chapters can be chained together when printing;** *see also* CATENA; **chained** *or* **threaded file** = file in which an entry will contain data and an address to the next entry that has the same data content (allowing rapid retrieval of all identical data records) *länkad lista;* **chained list** = list in which each element contains data and an address to the next element in the list *länkad lista;* **chained record** = data

record in a chained file *länkad post;* **daisy-chain** = to connect equipment using the daisy chain method *kedjekoppling;* **daisy-chaining saves a lot of cable**

chaining ['tʃeɪnɪŋ] *subst.* execution of a very large program by executing small segments of it at a time, this allows programs larger than memory capacity to be run *länkning;* **chaining search** = search of a file of elements arranged in a chained list *kedjesökning;* **data chaining** = storing one record that holds the address of the next in the list *kedjelagring*

change [tʃeɪn(d)ʒ] *vb.* to make something different *ändra;* to use one thing instead of another *byta;* **change dump** = printout of locations where data has been changed *ändringsdump;* **change file** = file containing records that are to be used to update a master file *ändringsfil;* **change record** = record containing new data which is to be used to update a master record *ändringspost, ändringsfil;* **change tape** = (magnetic) tape containing recent changes *or* transactions to records which is used to update a master file *ändringsband*

change-over [tʃeɪn(d)ʒ 'əʊvə] *vb.* to switch from one computer system to another *växla system*

changer ['tʃeɪn(d)ʒə] *subst.* device which changes one thing for another *växlare;* **gender changer** = two connectors, used to change a female connector to a male one (or vice-versa) *omvandlingskontakt;* **you can interconnect all these peripherals with just two cables and a gender changer; record changer** = device on a turntable which allows records to be changed automatically *skivväxlare*

channel ['tʃænl] **1** *subst.* **(a)** physical connection between two points that allows data to be transmitted (such as a link between a CPU and a peripheral) *kanal;* **channel adapter** = interfacing device allowing different channels to be inter-connected *kanalanpassare;* **channel bank** = collection of a number of channels, and circuits to switch between them *kanalbank;* **channel capacity** = maximum rate of data transmission over a channel *kanalkapacitet;* **channel command** = instruction to a channel *or* control unit, providing control information such as data selection *or* routes *kanalkommando;* **channel group** = collection of twelve channels, treated as one group in a multiplexing system *kanalgrupp;* **channel isolation** = separation of channels measured as the amount of crosstalk between two channels (low crosstalk is due to good channel isolation) *kanalisolering;* **channel overload** = transmission of data at a rate greater than the channel capacity *kanalöverlastning;* **channel synchronizer** =

interface between a central computer and peripherals, providing a channel, **channel command** interpretation and status signals from the peripherals *kanalsynkroniserare;* **channel queue** = (i) queue of requests to use a channel *kanalkö;* (ii) queue of data that has yet to be sent over a channel *kanalkö;* **channel-to-channel connection** = direct link between the main I/O channels of two computers, allowing high speed data transfer *kanal(mellan)koppling;* **data channel** = communications link able to carry data signals *datakanal;* **dedicated channel** = communications channel reserved for a special purpose *specialiserad kanal;* **I/O channel** = link between a processor and peripheral allowing data transfer *in- och utkanal* **(b)** way in which information *or* goods are passed from one place to another *kanal;* **to go through the official channels** = to deal with government officials (especially when making a request) *gå genom de officiella kanalerna;* **to open up new channels of communication** = to find new ways of communicating with someone *öppna nya kommunikationskanaler;* **distribution channels** *or* **channels of distribution** = ways of sending goods from the manufacturer for sale in shops *distributionskanal* **2** *vb.* to send signals *or* data via a particular path *sända, kanalisera*

channelling ['tʃænlɪŋ] *subst.* protective pipe containing cables *or* wires *kabeltrumma, kabelränna*

chapter ['tʃæptə] *subst.* **(a)** section of a main program that can be executed in its own right, without the rest of the main program being required *delprogram* **(b)** sequence of frames on a video disk *avsnitt;* **chapter stop** = code at the end of a video disk chapter that enables rapid location of a particular chapter *avsnittskod* **(c)** section of a book *or* document *kapitel;* **chapter heading** = special heading at the beginning of each printed chapter *kapitelrubrik;* **chapter headings are in 12 point bold**

character ['kærəktə] *subst.* graphical symbol which appears as a printed *or* displayed mark, such as one of the letters of the alphabet, a number or a punctuation mark *tecken, bokstav;* **alphanumeric characters** = roman letters and arabic numerals (and other signs such as punctuation marks) *alfanumeriska tecken;* **cancel character** = control code used to indicate that the last data transmitted was incorrect *upphävningstecken;* **character assembly** = method of designing characters with pixels on a computer screen *teckenuppbyggnad;* **character blink** = character whose intensity is switched on and off (as an indicator) *blinkning;* **character block** = the pattern of dots that will make up a character on a screen *or* printer *teckenyta;* **character byte** = byte of

data containing the character code and any error check bits *teckenbyte;* **character check** = check to ensure that a character code protocol and format are correct *kodkontroll;* **character code** = system where each character is represented by a unique number *teckenkod;* **the ASCII code is the most frequently used character coding system; character density** = number of characters that can be stored *or* displayed per unit area *teckentäthet;* **character display** = device that displays data in alphanumeric form *teckenskärm;* **character fill** = writing one character to every location within an area of memory (for clearing and resetting the memory) *minnesfyllning;* **character generator** = ROM that provides the display circuits with a pattern of dots which represent the character (block) *teckengenerator;* **the ROM used as a character generator can be changed to provide different fonts; character key** = word processor control used to process text one character at a time *teckentangent;* **character machine** = computer in which the number of bits which make up a word is variable, and varies according to the type of data *teckenbaserad dator;* **character orientated** = computer that addresses character locations rather than words *teckenorienterad;* **character printer** = device that prints characters one at a time *teckenskrivare;* **a daisy wheel printer is a character printer; character recognition** = system that optically reads written *or* printed characters into a computer, using various algorithms to ensure that characters are correctly recognized *teckenigenkänning; see also* OCR; **character repertoire** = list of all the characters that can be displayed *or* printed *teckenuppsättning;* **character representation** = combination of bits used for each character code *teckenrepresentation;* **character rounding** = making a displayed character more pleasant to look at (within the limits of pixel size) by making sharp corners and edges smooth *konturutjämning;* **character set** = list of all the characters that can be displayed *or* printed *teckenuppsättning;* **character skew** = angle of a character in comparison to its correct position *teckenpositionsavvikelse;* **character string** = storage allocated for a series of alphanumeric characters *teckensträng; compare with* NUMERIC STRING; **characters per inch (cpi)** = number of printed characters which fit within the space of one inch *tecken per tum;* **you can select 10 or 12 cpi with the green button; characters per second (cps)** = number of characters which are transmitted *or* printed per second *tecken per sekund;* **character stuffing** = addition of blank characters to a file to increase its length to a preset size *teckenutfyllnad;* **check character** = additional character inserted into transmitted data to serve as an error detection check, its value is dependent on the text *kontrolltecken;* **device control character** = special code sent in a transmission to a device to instruct it to perform a special function *periferstyrtecken*

> QUOTE the screen displays very sharp and stable characters, each cell occupying an 8 by 11 dot matrix
> **Computing Today**

characteristic [ˌkærəktəˈrɪstɪk] **1** *subst.* **(a)** value of exponent in a floating point number *exponentvärde;* **the floating point number 1.345 x 10³, has a characteristic of 3; characteristic overflow** = exponent value of a floating point number that is greater than the maximum allowable *exponentspill* **(b)** measurements *or* properties of a component *mätbara egenskaper* **2** *adj.* which is typical *or* special *karaktäristisk;* **this fault is characteristic of this make and model of personal computer; characteristic curve** = response curve of an electronic component *or* circuit *karaktäristik, t. ex. förstärkningskurva*

charge [tʃɑːdʒ] *subst.* (i) a quantity of electricity *laddning;* (ii) the number of *or* excess of *or* lack of electrons in a material *or* component *laddning;* **charge-coupled device (CCD)** = electronic device operated by charge *laddningskopplad enhet;* **charge-coupled device memory** = capacitors used (with MOS transistors) to store data, allowing serial and random access *laddningskopplat minne;* **electric charge** = a number of atoms that are charged (due to an excess *or* deficiency of electrons) *elektrisk laddning* *vb.* to supply a device with an electric charge *ladda;* **battery charging** = to replenish the charge stored in a re-chargeable battery *omladdning av ett batteri*

chargeable [ˈtʃɑːdʒəbl] *adj.* which can be charged *laddningsbar;* **re-chargeable battery** = battery that can be used to supply power, and then have its charge replenished *(om)laddningsbart batteri, ackumulator;* **a re-chargeable battery is used for RAM back-up when the system is switched off**

chart [tʃɑːt] *subst.* diagram showing information as a series of lines *or* blocks, etc. *karta, diagram, schema;* **bar chart** = graph on which values are represented as vertical *or* horizontal bars of different heights *or* lengths *stapeldiagram;* **flowchart** = diagram showing the arrangement of various work processes as a series of stages *flödesdiagram;* **a flowchart is the first step to a well designed program; logical chart** = graphical representation of logic elements,

steps, decisions and interconnections in a system *logikschema;* **pie chart** = diagram where ratios are shown as slices of a circle *tårtdiagram;* **the memory allocation is shown on this pie chart; chart recorder** = mechanical device that records input values by drawing lines on a moving reel of paper *kurvritare*

chassis [ˈʃæsɪ] *subst.* metal frame that houses the circuit boards together with the wiring and sockets required in a computer system *or* other equipment *chassi; see also* RACK

check [tʃek] **1** *subst.* **(a)** act of making sure that something is correct *kontroll;* **character check** = check to ensure that a character code protocol and format are correct *teckenkontroll;* **check bit** = one bit of a binary word that is used to provide a parity check *kontrollbit;* **check character** = additional character inserted into transmitted text to serve as an (error detection) check for the text, its value is dependent on the text *kontrolltecken;* **check digit** *or* **number** = additional digit inserted into transmitted text to monitor and correct errors *kontrollsiffra;* **check indicator** = hardware *or* software device that shows that received text is not correct and a check has failed *kontrollindikator;* **check key** = series of characters derived from a text used to check for and correct errors *kontrollnyckel;* **check point** = point in a program where data and program status can be recorded *or* displayed *kontrollpunkt;* **check point dump** = printout of data and program status at a check point *kontrollpunktsdump;* **check register** = temporary storage for received data before it is checked against the same data received via another path *or* method *kontrollregister;* **check total** = CHECKSUM; **desk check** = dry run of a program *skrivbordstestning, torrkörning* **(b)** short fault *or* pause in a process (that does not stop the process) *kontroll;* **data check** = error in reading data due to a fault with the magnetic medium *datakontroll* **2** *vb.* to examine *or* to make sure than something is in good working order *kontrollera;* **the separate parts of the system were all checked for faults before being packaged; he checked the computer printout against the invoices** = he examined the printout and the invoices to see if the figures were the same *han kontrollerade datorutskriften mot fakturorna*

checkerboarding [ˈtʃekəˌbɔːdɪŋ] *subst.* (virtual page) memory organization that has resulted in odd pages *or* spread-out pages *or* segments of memory being filled, wasting memory by leaving unusable gaps inbetween *schackbrädeslagring*

checking [ˈtʃekɪŋ] *subst.* examination *kontroll, test;* **the maintenance engineer**

found some defects whilst checking the equipment; checking program = software that finds errors in program *or* data syntax, format and coding *testprogram;* **self-checking code** = error detection code *självtestande kod* NOTE: no plural

checksum ['tʃek,sʌm] *or* **check total** ['tʃek 'təʊtl] *subst.* program which checks that data is correct, by summing it and comparing the sum with a stored value *kontrollsumma;* **the data must be corrupted if the checksum is different**

chemical ['kemɪk(ə)l] **1** *adj.* referring to the interaction of substances *kemisk;* **chemical reaction** = interaction between two substances *or* elements *kemisk reaktion* **2** *subst.* product resulting from the interaction of other substances *or*elements *kemikalier*

chiffer ⇨ **cipher**

chiffrera ⇨ **encipher**

chip [tʃɪp] *subst.* device consisting of a small piece of a crystal of a semiconductor onto which are etched *or* manufactured (by doping) a number of components such as transistors, resistors and capacitors, which together perform a function *mikrokrets, chip;* **chip architecture** = design and layout of components on a chip *chiparkitektur, kretsarkitektur;* **chip card** = plastic card with a memory and microprocessor device embedded in it, so that it can be used for electronic funds transfer *or* identification of a user *aktivt kort;* **chip count** = number of chips on a PCB *or* in a device *kretsantal;* **it's no good, the chip count is still too high; chip select line** = connection to a chip that will enable it to function when a signal is present *aktiveringsledning;* **the data strobe line is connected to the latch chip select line; chip set** = chips which together will carry out a function *kretssats;* **diagnostic chip** = chip that contains circuits to carry out tests on circuits *or* other chips *diagnostikkrets;* **they are carrying out research on diagnostic chips to test computers that contain processors; single chip computer** = complete simple computer including CPU, memory and input/output ports on one chip *enkretsdator;* **sound chip** = device that will generate a sound *or* tune *ljudkrets*

chop [tʃɒp] *see* BINARY

chord keying ['kɔːd,kiːɪŋ] *subst.* action of pressing two *or* more keys at the same time to perform a function *samtidig tangenttryckning, ackord (särskilt vid snabbskriftstangentbord);* **to access the second window, press control and F2; shift and character delete keys will delete a line of text**

chroma ['krəʊmə] *subst.* colour hue and saturation measure *krominans, färgvärde;*

chroma control = circuit in a TV that alters the colour saturation *färgkontroll;* **chroma detector** = television circuit that checks whether a signal is monochrome*or* colour *färgdetektor*

chromatic [krə(ʊ)'mætɪk] *adj.* referring to colours *kromatisk;* **chromatic aberration** = optical lens that affects and focuses different colours in different ways *kromatiskt avbildningsfel;* **chromatic dispersion** = uneven refraction index across an optic fibre causing signal distortion *färgspridningsfel*

chromaticity [,krəmə'tɪsɪtɪ] *subst.* quality of light according to its most prominent colour and purity *kromacitet, färgvärde*

chrominance signal ['krəʊmɪnəns 'sɪgn(ə)l] *subst.* section of a colour monitor signal containing colour hue and saturation information *färgsignal, krominanssignal*

chronological order [,krɒnə'lɒdʒɪk(ə)l 'ɔːdə] *subst.* arrangement of records *or* files according to their dates *datumordning, kronologisk ordning*

CIM [sɪm] **(a)** = COMPUTER INPUT FROM MICROFILM coordinated use of microfilm for computer data storage and the method of reading the data *datoriserad mikrofilmläsning* **(b)** = COMPUTER INTEGRATED MANUFACTURE use of computers in every aspect of design and manufacturing *datorstödd tillverkning*

cine- [sɪnɪ] *prefix* meaning moving pictures *or* film *film-;* **cine camera** = camera that records motion pictures onto a roll of film *filmkamera;* **cine orientated image** = data *or* graphics on a microfilm where the image is at right angles to the long edge of the roll of film *sidfilmad mikrofilm*

cinema ['sɪnəmə] *subst.* **(a) the cinema** = making of films for showing to the public *filmen, filmindustrin* **(b)** building where films are shown to the public *biograf*

cinematography [,sɪnəmə'tɒgrəfɪ] *subst.* (i) motion picture photography *cinematografi, filmfoto;* (ii) effects giving impression of motion *filmkonst*

cipher ['saɪfə] *subst.* system of transforming a message into an unreadable form with a secret key (the message can be read normally after it has passed through the cipher a second time) *chiffer;* **always use a secure cipher when sending data over a telephone line; cipher key** = secret sequence of characters used with a cipher system to provide a unique ciphertext *chiffernyckel;* **cipher system** = formula used to transform text into a secret form *chiffersystem;* **public key cipher** = cipher that uses a public key to encrypt messages and a secret key to decrypt them (conventional ciphers use one secret key to encrypt and decrypt messages) *chiffer med öppna nycklar;* **ciphertext** = data output from a cipher *chiffertext* NOTE: opposite is **plaintext**

CIR ['si:aɪ'ɑ:] = CURRENT INSTRUCTION REGISTER CPU register that stores the instruction that is currently being executed *instruktionsregister*

circuit ['sɜ:kɪt] *subst.* connection between electronic components that perform a function *krets;* **circuit board** *or* **card** = insulating board used to hold components which are then connected together (electrically) to form a circuit *kretskort;* **circuit breaker** = device which protects equipment by cutting off the electrical supply when conditions are abnormal *överspänningsskydd;* **circuit capacity** = information carrying capacity of a particular circuit *kretskapacitet;* **circuit diagram** = graphical description of a circuit *kretsdiagram;* **the CAD program will plot the circuit diagram rapidly; circuit grade** = ability of a communication channel to carry information (the grades are: wideband, voice, subvoice and telegraph) *kanal(kvalitets)klassificering;* **circuit noise level** = amplitude of noise in a circuit compared to a reference level *kretsbrusnivå;* **circuit switched network** = communications network in which each link can be linked to another at a switching centre *kretskopplat nätverk;* **circuit switching** = communications circuit established on demand and held until no longer required *kretskoppling, uppringd förbindelse;* **data circuit** = circuit which allows bi-directional data communications *dubbelriktad kommunikationskrets, full-duplex dataförbindelse;* **decision circuit** = logical circuit that operates on binary inputs, producing an output according to the function set in hardware *beslutskrets;* **digital circuit** = electronic circuit that operates on digital information providing logical functions *or* switching *digital krets;* **logic circuit** = electronic circuit made up of various logical gates, such as AND, OR and EXOR *logisk krets;* **printed circuit board (PCB)** = flat insulating material that has conducting tracks of metal printed *or* etched onto its surface, which complete a circuit when components are mounted on it *tryckt kretskort, ledningskort*

circuitry ['sɜ:kɪtrɪ] *subst.* collection of circuits *elektroniska kretsar, kretskonstruktion;* **the circuitry is still too complex**
NOTE: no plural

circular ['sɜ:kjʊlə] *adj.* which goes round in a circle *rund, cirkelformad, cirkulär, rotations-;* **circular buffer** = computer-based queue that uses two markers, for top and bottom of the line of stored items (the markers move as items are read from *or* written to the stack) *cirkulär buffert;* **circular file** = a data file that has no visible beginning *or* end, each item points to the location of the next item with the last pointing back to the first *cirkulär fil;* **circular list** = list in which each element contains data and an address to the next element in the list with the last item pointing back to the first *cirkulär lista;* **circular orbit** = orbit of a satellite that is always at a constant distance from the centre of the earth *cirkulär bana;* **circular shift** = rotation of bits in a word with the previous last bit inserted in the first bit position *rundskift, cirkulärt skift;* **circular waveguide** = microwave beam carrying a channel, of circular cross-section, allowing high frequencies to be carried *cirkulär vågledare*

circulate ['sɜ:kjʊleɪt] *vb.* **(a)** to go round in a circle, and return to the first point *cirkulera* **(b)** to send information to *cirkulera, sända, skicka;* **they circulated the new list of prices to all their customers**

circulating ['sɜ:kjʊleɪtɪŋ] *adj.* which is moving about freely *cirkulerande, roterande;* **circulating register** = shift register whose output is fed back to its input to form a closed loop *cirkuleringsregister;* **circulating storage** = storage device that maintains stored data as a series of pulses, that move along the length of the medium, being regenerated and re-input when they reach the end *cirkulerande minne*

COMMENT: circulating storage devices are not often used now, being slow (serial access) and bulky: typical devices are acoustic or mercury delay lines

circulation [ˌsɜ:kjʊ'leɪʃ(ə)n] *subst.* **(a)** movement *cirkulation;* **the company is trying to improve the circulation of information between departments (b)** *(of a newspaper)* number of copies sold *upplaga;* **what is the circulation of this computer magazine? a specialized paper with a circulation of over 10,000**

circumflex ['sɜ:k(ə)mfleks] *subst.* printed accent (like a small 'v' printed upside down) placed above a letter, which may change the pronunciation *or* distinguish the letter from others *cirkumflex*

CISC ['si:aɪes'si:] = COMPLEX INSTRUCTION SET COMPUTER CPU design whose instruction set contains a number of long, complex instructions, that makes program writing easier, but reduces execution speed *komplexkodsdator; compare with* RISC

citationstecken ⇨ **invert, quotationmarks**

citizens band radio (CB) ['sɪtɪznz bænd 'reɪdɪəʊ (siː biː)] *subst.* cheap popular system of radio communications, usually between vehicles *privatradioband, "medborgarradio"*

cladding ['klædɪŋ] *subst.* protective material surrounding a conducting core *hölje;* **if the cladding is chipped, the fibre-optic cable will not function well**

clamp [klæmp] *vb.* to find the voltage of a signal *nivålåsning*

clapper ['klæpə] *subst.* mechanical part of a dot matrix printer that drives the printing needles onto the ribbon to print a character on the paper *hammare*

clarity ['klærətɪ] *subst.* being clear *klarhet;* **the atmospheric conditions affect the clarity of the signal**

classification [ˌklæsɪfɪ'keɪʃ(ə)n] *subst.* way of putting into classes *klassificering*

classify ['klæsɪfaɪ] *vb.* to put into classes *or* under various headings *klassificera;* **the diagnostic printouts have been classified under T for test results; classified directory** = book which lists businesses grouped under various headings (such as computer shops *or* newsagents) *yrkesregister (i telefonkatalog)*

clean [kliːn] **1** *adj.* not dirty *or* with no errors *or* with no programs *ren, felfri;* **I'll have to start again - I just erased the only clean file; clean copy** = copy which is ready for keyboarding, and does not have many changes on it *renskrift, renskrivet exemplar;* **clean machine** = computer that contains only the minimum of ROM based code to boot its system from disk, any languages required must be loaded in *tom maskin (dator);* **clean page** = page (of memory) that has not been changed since it was read *ren sida;* **clean proof** = proof without any corrections *korrekturfri, rentryck* **2** *vb.* to make something clean *tvätta, rengöra;* **data cleaning** = to remove errors from data *datarensning;* **head cleaning disk** = special disk which will clean dirt from the read/write head *rengöringsskiva;* **use a head cleaning disk every week; write errors occur if you do not use a head cleaning kit regularly; screen cleaning kit** = liquids and cloth which remove any static and dirt from a VDU screen *rengöringssats för bildskärmar*

clear [klɪə] **1** *adj.* easily understood *klart, enkelt;* **the program manual is not clear on copying files; the booklet gives clear instructions how to connect the different parts of the system; he made it clear that the system will only work on IBM-compatible**

hardware 2 *vb.* **(a)** to wipe out *or* erase *or* set to zero a computer file *or* variable *or* section of memory *radera;* **type CLS to clear the screen; all arrays are cleared each time the program is run; to clear an area of memory; to clear the data register (b)** to release a communications link when transmissions have finished *släppa, koppla ner;* **clear to send (CTS)** = RS232C signal that a line *or* device is ready for data transmission *CTS-signal, klarsignal, "datakanal klar"*

clearance ['klɪər(ə)ns] *subst.* authority to access a file *klartecken, tillstånd;* **you do not have the required clearance for this processor**

click [klɪk] **1** *subst.* **(a)** short duration sound, often used to indicate that a key has been pressed *klick* **(b)** pressing a key *or* button on a keyboard *tryck;* **you move through text and graphics with a click of the button 2** *vb.* to press a key *or* a button on a keyboard *or* the mouse *klicka;* **use the mouse to enlarge a frame by clicking inside its border**

clip [klɪp] **1** *subst.* short piece of (live) film *blänkare, "snutt";* **there was a clip of the disaster on the news 2** *vb.* **(a)** to attach papers together with a wire *binda;* **the corrections are clipped to the computer printout (b)** to cut out with scissors *klippa;* **clipping service** = service which cuts out references to someone in newspapers *or* magazines and sends them to him *presklippsservice*

clock [klɒk] *subst.* **(a)** machine which shows the time *klocka;* **the micro has a built-in clock; the time is shown by the clock in the corner of the screen; digital clock** = clock which shows the time using numbers (as 12:05) *digitalklocka* **(b)** circuit that generates pulses used to synchronize equipment *(synkroniserings)klocka;* **clock cycle** = time period between two consecutive clock pulses *klockcykel;* **clock pulse** = regular pulse used for timing *or* synchronizing purposes *klockpuls;* **clock rate** = number of pulses that a clock generates every second *klockfrekvens;* **clock track** = line of marks on a disk *or* tape which provides data about the read head location *synkroniseringsspår;* **main clock** = clock signal that synchronizes all the components in a system *systemklocka;* **programmable clock** = circuit whose frequency can be set by the user *programmerbar klocka vb.* to synchronize signals *or* circuits with a clock pulse *synkronisera;* **clocked signals** = signals that are synchronized with a clock pulse *synkroniserade signaler*

clone [kləʊn] *subst.* computer *or* circuit that behaves in the same way as the original it was copied from *kopia;* **they have copied our new personal computer and brought out**

a cheaper clone; higher performance clones are available for all the models in our range

close [kləʊz] *vb.* to shut down access to a file *or* disk drive *stänga;* **close file =** to execute a computer instruction to shut down access to a stored file *stänga en fil;* **closed loop =** number of computer instructions that are repeated *sluten slinga;* **closed subroutine =** number of computer instructions in a program that can be called at any time, with control being returned on completion to the next instruction in the main program *sluten subrutin;* **closed user group (CUG) =** to restrict the entry to a database *or* bulletin board *or* system (about or on a certain topic *or* subject) to certain known and registered users, usually by means of a password *sluten användargrupp; see also* USER GROUP

close up [kləʊz 'ʌp] *vb.* to move pieces of type *or* typeset words closer together *knipa, minska mellanrum;* **if we close up the lines, we should save a page**

close-up ['kləʊzʌp] *subst.* photograph taken very close to the subject *närbild*

cluster ['klʌstə] *subst.* number of terminals *or* stations *or* devices *or* memory locations grouped together in one place, controlled by a cluster controller *kluster;* **cluster controller =** central computer that controls communications to a cluster of devices *or* memory locations *klusterstyrenhet*

QUOTE cluster controllers are available with 8 or 16 channels
Microcomputer News

clustering ['klʌst(ə)rɪŋ] *subst.* series of elements, occurring in a sequential line within a hash table *kluster*

QUOTE these include IBM networking and clustering hardware and software
Personal Computer World

CM ['si:em] = CENTRAL MEMORY area of memory whose locations can be directly and immediately addressed by the CPU *primärminne*

C-MAC ['si:mæk] new direct-broadcast TV standard using time division multiplexing for signals *MAC-standarden för teve-signaler*

CMI ['si:em'aɪ] = COMPUTER MANAGED INSTRUCTION *datoriserad undervisning*

CML ['si:em'el] = COMPUTER MANAGED LEARNING *datoriserad inlärning*

CMOS ['si:mɒs] = COMPLEMENTARY METAL OXIDE SEMICONDUCTOR integrated circuit design and construction method (using a pair of complementary p- and n-type transistors) *Cmos-teknik*

COMMENT: the final package uses very low power but is relatively slow and sensitive to static electricity as compared to TTL integrated circuits; their main use is in portable computers where battery power is being used

CNC ['si:en'si:] = COMPUTER NUMERIC CONTROL machine operated automatically by computer *numerisk styrning; see also* NUMERICAL CONTROL

coalesce [ˌkəʊə'les] *vb.* to merge two or more files *slå samman*

coat [kəʊt] *vb.* to cover with a layer of liquid *täcka;* **coated papers =** papers which have been covered with a layer of clay to make them shiny *belagt (bestruket) papper*

coating ['kəʊtɪŋ] *subst.* material covering something *beläggning, hölje;* **paper which has a coating of clay** *belagt (bestruket) papper*

co-axial cable [ˌkəʊ'æksɪəl 'keɪbl] *subst.* cable made up of a central core, surrounded by an insulating layer then a second shielding conductor *koaxialkabel*

COMMENT: co-axial cable is used for high frequency, low loss applications such as TV aerials

COBOL ['kəʊˌbɒl] = COMMON ORDINARY BUSINESS ORIENTED LANGUAGE programming language mainly used in business applications *programmeringsspråket Cobol*

code [kəʊd] **1** *subst.* **(a)** rules used to convert instructions *or* data from one form to another *kod;* **code conversion =** rules used to change characters coded in one form, to another *kodomvandling* **(b)** sequence of computer instructions *kod;* **chain code =** series of words, each word being derived (usually shifted by one bit) from the previous word *kedjekod;* **code area =** section of main memory in which program instructions are stored *kodarea;* **code line =** one written *or* displayed computer program instruction *kodrad;* **computer *or* machine code =** programming language that consists of commands in binary code that can be directly understood by the central processing unit, without the need for translation *maskinkod;* **direct *or* one-level *or* specific code =** binary code which directly operates the central processing unit, using only absolute addresses and values (this is the final form of a program after a compiler *or* assembler pass) *absolutkod;* **macro code =** one word that is used to represent a number of instructions, simplifying program writing *makrokod;* **object code =** (i) binary code which directly operates a CPU *objektkod;* (ii) program code after it has been translated, compiled or assembled (into machine code) *objektkod;* **optimum code** = coding system that provides the fastest access and retrieval time for stored data items *optimal kod;* **source code** = set of codes (as a program) written by the programmer which cannot be directly executed by the computer, but have to be translated into an object code program by a compiler *or* assembler *or* interpreter *källkod;* **symbolic code** = instruction that is in mnemonic form rather than machine code *symbolisk kod* **(c)** system of signs *or* numbers *or* letters which mean something *kod;* **area code** = numbers which indicate an area for telephoning *riktnummer;* **what is the code for Edinburgh?; bar code** = data represented as a series of printed stripes of varying widths *streckkod;* **bar-code reader** = optical device that reads data from a bar code *streckkodsläsare;* **code element** = voltage *or* signal used to represent binary digits *kodelement;* **cyclic code** = coding system in which the binary representation of decimal numbers changes by only one bit at a time from one number to the next *cyklisk kod;* **device code** = unique identification and selection code for a peripheral *identifikationskod, enhetskod;* **error code** = code that indicates that a particular type of error has occurred *felkod;* **error correcting code** = coding system that allows bit errors occurring during transmission to be rapidly corrected by logical deduction methods *felkorrigerande kod;* **error detecting code** = coding system that allows bit errors occurring during transmission to be detected, but is not complex enough to correct them *feldetekterande kod;* **escape codes** = transmitted code sequence which informs the receiver that all following characters represent control actions *avbrottskoder;* **international dialling code** = numbers used for dialling to another country *landsnummer;* **machine-readable codes** = sets of signs *or* letters (such as bar codes *or* post codes) which can be read by computers *maskinläsbar kod;* **post code** *or* **US zip code** = letters and numbers used to indicate a town *or* street in an address on an envelope *postnummer;* **punched code** = combination of holes that represent characters in a punched card *hålkod;* **self-checking code** = error detecting code *självtestande kod;* **stock code** = numbers and letters which refer to an item of stock *varunummer, lagerkod* **2** *vb.* **(a)** to convert instructions *or* data into another form *koda* **(b)** to write a program in a programming language *koda, programmera*

CODEC ['kəʊdek] = CODER/DECODER device which encodes a signal being sent *or* decodes a signal received (used in many advanced PABX systems) *kodnings-avkodningsenhet*

coder ['kəʊdə] *subst.* device which encodes a signal *kodare, kodningsenhet*

coding ['kəʊdɪŋ] *subst.* act of putting a code on something *kodning;* **coding sheet** *or* **coding form** = special printed sheet used by programmers to write instructions for coding a certain type of program *kodningsformulär*

coercivity [ˌkəʊəˈsɪvɪtɪ] *subst.* magnetic field required to remove any flux saturation effects from a material *koercitivitet*

coherent [kə(ʊ)ˈhɪər(ə)nt] *adj.* referring to waveforms which are all in phase *koherent, sammanhällen, likfasig;* **the laser produces coherent light; coherent bundle** = number of optical fibres, grouped together so that they are all the same length and produce coherent signals from either end *koherent knippe*

coil [kɔɪl] *subst.* number of turns of wire *spole;* **an inductor is made from a coil of wire**

coincidence circuit [kəʊˈɪnsɪd(ə)ns ˈsɜːkɪt] *or* **element** ['elɪmənt] *subst.* electronic circuit that produces an output signal when two inputs occur simultaneously *or* two binary words are equal *och-krets; see also* AND

cold [kəʊld] *adj.* **(a)** not hot *kall;* **the machines work badly in cold weather (b)** without being prepared *"kall", ej ansluten;* **cold fault** = computer fault *or* error that occurs as soon as it is switched on *maskinfel;* **cold standby** = backup system that will allow the equipment to continue running, but with the loss of any volatile data *ej ansluten reservutrustning, passiv, reserv; compare with* HOT, WARM STANDBY; **cold start** = switching on a computer *or* to run a program from its original start point *kallstart; compare* WARM START

collate [kəˈleɪt] *vb.* (i) to compare and put items in order *kolla(tionera);* (ii) to put signatures in order for sewing and binding *blada samman ark för bindning;* **collating marks** = marks printed on the spine of a signature so that the binder can see if they have been collated in correct order *arkmarkeringar, ryggsignalsmarkeringar;* **collating sequence** = (i) characters ordered according to their codes *bindningsordning;* (ii) order in which signatures are stacked for binding *sekvenseringsordning*

collator [kəˈleɪtə] *subst.* (i) software that collates data *kollator;* (ii) device that collates punched cards *kollator*

collect [kəˈlekt] *vb.* to receive *or* capture data *samla in;* **data collection** = act of receiving data from various sources (either directly from a data capture device *or* from a cartridge) and inserting correctly in order into a database *datainsamling;* **data collection platform =** station that transmits collected data to a central point (usually via satellite) *datainsamlingsstation*

collect transfer [kə'lekt træns'fɜː] *subst.* to load a register with bits from a number of different locations *selektiv bitladdning*

collision detection [kə'lɪʒ(ə)n dɪ'tekʃ(ə)n] *subst.* the detecting and reporting of the coincidence of two actions *or* events *kollisionsupptäckt;* **carrier sense multiple access-collision detection (CSMA/CD) =** network communications protocol that prevents two sources transmitting at the same time by waiting for a quiet moment on the channel, then attempting to transmit *kommunikationsprotokoll CSMA/CD för lokala nätverk*

colon ['kəʊlən] *subst.* printing sign (:), which shows a break in a string of words *kolon;* **semi-colon =** printed sign (;) which marks the end of a program line *or* statement in some languages (such as C and Pascal) *satsslut, semikolon*

colophon ['kɒləfən] *subst.* design *or* symbol *or* company name, used on a printed item to show who are the publisher and the printer *kolofon, signet*

colour ['kʌlə] *subst.* sensation sensed by the eye, due to its response to various frequencies of light *färg;* **colour balance =** TV control adjustment to provide a pleasant image *or* various frequencies of light in a signal *färgbalans;* **colour burst =** part of a TV signal used to provide information about the hue of the colour *färgsynksignal;* **colour cell =** smallest area on a CRT screen that can display colour information *färgpunkt;* **colour decoder =** device which converts colour burst and picture signals so that they can be displayed on a screen *demodulator för färgsignal;* **colour display =** display device able to represent characters *or* graphics in colour *färgskärm;* **colour encoder =** device that produces a standard TV signal from separate Red, Green and Blue signals *modulator för färgsignal;* **colour graphics adapter (CGA) =** popular microcomputer colour display system *CGA-grafik; see also* EGA; **colour monitor =** screen that has a demodulator which shows information in colour *färgskärm;* **the colour monitor is great for games ; colour saturation =** purity of a colour signal *färgmättnad;* **colour separation =** process by which colours are separated into their primary colours *färgseparation;* **colour shift =** (unwanted) change in colour *färgskiftning;* **colour temperature =** method of standardizing the colour of a body (at a certain temperature) *färgtemperatur;* **colour transparency =** transparent positive film in colour, which

can be used to project on a screen *or* to make film for printing *färgdiapositiv (vanligen i storformat)*

> QUOTE as a minimum, a colour graphics adapter (CGA) is necessary, but for best quality of graphic presentation an enhanced graphics adapter (EGA) should be considered
>
> **Micro Decision**

column ['kɒləm] *subst.* **(a)** series of characters, printed one under the other *kolumn, spalt;* **to add up a column of figures; put the total at the bottom of the column; card column =** line of punched information about one character, parallel to the shorter side of the card *kortkolumn;* **column parity =** parity check on every punched card *or* tape column *kolumnparitet;* **80-column printer =** printer which has a maximum line width of 80 characters *80-teckens skrivare;* **an 80-column printer is included in the price (b)** section of printed words in a newspaper *or* magazine *spalt;* **column-centimetre =** space in centimetres in a newspaper column, used for calculating charges for advertising *spaltcentimeter*

columnar [kə'lʌmnə] *adj.* in columns *spaltvis;* **columnar graph =** graph on which values are shown as vertical *or* horizontal bars *spaltdiagram;* **columnar working =** showing information in columns *spaltsats, kolumnsats*

COM [kɒm] = COMPUTER OUTPUT ON MICROFILM recording the output from a computer directly onto microfilm *mikrofilmsutmatning*

coma ['kəʊmə] *subst.* lens aberration *koma, punktavbildningsfel (i lins)*

COMAL ['kəʊmæl] = COMMON ALGORITHMIC LANGUAGE structured programming language similar to BASIC *programmeringsspråket Comal*

combination [ˌkɒmbɪ'neɪʃ(ə)n] *subst.* several things which are joined together *kombination;* series of numbers which open a lock *kombination*

combinational [ˌkɒmbɪ'neɪʃənl] *adj.* which combines a number of separate elements *kombinerande;* **combinational circuit =** electronic circuit consisting of a number of connected components *logikkrets;* **combinational logic =** logic function made up from a number of separate logic gates *kombinationslogik*

combine [kəm'baɪn] *vb.* to join together *kombinera;* **combined head =** transducer that can read and write data from the surface of a magnetic storage medium, such as a floppy disk *kombinerat huvud, kombinationshuvud;* **combined station =** high-level data link control station that processes commands and responses *kombinerad station;* **combined symbol matching (CSM)** = efficient optical character recognition system *kombinerad symbolpassning*

comma ['kɒmə] *subst.* printed *or* written sign (,) which indicates a small break in the sense of a sentence *komma(tecken);* **inverted commas** = printing sign (") which marks the beginning and end of a quotation *citationstecken*

command [kə'mɑːnd] *subst.* **(a)** electrical pulse *or* signal that will start *or* stop a process *kommando* **(b)** word *or* phrase which is recognized by a computer system and starts *or* terminates an action *kommando;* **interrupt command; the command to execute the program is RUN; channel command** = instruction to a channel *or* control unit, providing control actions such as data filtering *or* routes *kanalkommando;* **command code** = binary code that starts *or* stops an instruction *or* action in a CPU *kommandokod;* **command console processor (CCP)** = software interface between a user's terminal and the BIOS *kommandotolk;* **command control language** = programming language that allows equipment to be easily controlled *kommandospråk;* **command-driven program** = program which requires the user to enter instructions at every stage *kommandostyrt program;* **command file** = sequence of frequently used commands stored in a file *kommandofil;* **command file processor** = execution of a user's command file, allowing the user to create a customized simple operating environment *or* to carry out a series of frequently used commands *kommandofil;* **command interface** = cue and prompts used by a program to inform and accept from a user required inputs (this can be user-friendly such as a WIMP environment, or not so friendly, such as a question mark) *kommandogränssnitt;* **command language** = programming language made up of procedures for various tasks, that can be called up by a series of commands *kommandospråk;* **command line** = program line that contains a command instruction *kommandorad;* **command prompt** = symbol displayed to indicate a command is expected *kommandomarkör;* **command register** = register that stores the instruction to be carried out *or* that is being processed *kommandoregister;* **command window** = area of a screen where commands are entered *kommandofönster;* **the user can define the size of the command window; dot command** = method of writing instructions, with a full stop followed by the command, used mainly for embedded commands in a word-processing system *punktkommando;* **embedded command** = printer control command, such as

indicating that text should be in italics, inserted into test and used by a word-processor when formatting text *integrerad styrkod*

comment ['kɒment] *subst.* helpful notes in a program to guide the user *kommentar;* **the lack of comments is annoying; BASIC allows comments to be written after a REM instruction; comment field** = section of a command line in an assembly language program that is not executed but provides notes and comments *kommentarfält*

commentary ['kɒmənt(ə)rɪ] *subst.* spoken information which describes a film *kommentar*

commercial [kə'mɜːʃ(ə)l] *subst.* advertising film on TV *tevereklam*

common ['kɒmən] *adj.* **(a)** which happens very often *vanlig, allmän;* **this is a common fault with this printer model (b)** belonging to several different people *or* programs *or* to everyone *vanlig, allmän;* **common carrier** = (i) firm which carries goods *or* passengers, and which anyone can use *allmänt färdmedel;* (ii) company which can provide information services to the public *informationsservice;* **common channel signalling** = one channel used as a communications link to a number of devices *or* circuits *allmän kanaldelning, gemensam kanalöverföring;* **common business orientated language (COBOL)** = programming language mainly used in business applications *programmeringsspråket Cobol;* **common hardware** = hardware items that can be used for a variety of tasks *generell maskinvara;* **common language** = data *or* program instructions in a standardized form that can be understood by other processors *or* compilers/interpreters *vanligt språk;* **common mode noise** = external noise on all power and ground lines *allmänt brus;* **common pricing** = illegal fixing of prices by several businesses so that they all charge the same price *kartellprissättning;* **common software** = useful (routines) that can be used by any program *allmänt programbibliotek;* **common storage area** = memory *or* storage area used by more than one program *allmän minnesarea;* **the file server memory is mainly common storage area, with a section reserved for the operating system**

communicate [kə'mjuːnɪkeɪt] *vb.* to pass information to someone *kommunicera;* **he finds it impossible to communicate with his staff; communicating with head office has been quicker since we installed the telex; communicating word processor** = word processor workstation which is able to transmit and receive data *kommunicerande skrivautomat*

communication [kə͵mjuːnɪˈkeɪʃ(ə)n]
subst. **(a)** passing of information
kommunikation; **communication with the
head office has been made easier by the
telex (b) communications** = process by
which data is transmitted and received, by
means of telephones, satellites, radio or
any medium capable of carrying signals
kommunikation; **communications buffer** =
terminal *or* modem that is able to store
transmitted data *kommunikationsbuffert;*
communications channel = physical link
over which data can be transmitted
kommunikationskanal; **communications
computer** = computer used to control data
transmission in a network
kommunikationsdator; **communications
control unit** = electronic device that
controls data transmission and routes in a
network *kommunikationsstyrenhet;*
communications executive = main set of
programs that ensure that protocol, format
and device and line handlers are correct for
the type of device *or* line in use
kommunikationsövervakningsprogram;
communications interface adapter =
electronic circuit that allows a computer to
communicate with a modem
kommunikationsgränssnittsanpassare;
communications link = physical path that
joins a transmitter to a receiver
(kommunikations)länk; **communications
link control** = processor that provides
various handshaking and error detection
functions for a number of links between
devices *(kommunikations)länkstyrning,
(kommunikations)länkstyrenhet;*
communications network = group of
devices such as terminals and printers that
are interconnected with a central
computer, allowing the rapid and simple
transfer of data *kommunikationsnät;*
communications network processor =
processor that provides various interfacing
and management (buffering *or* code
conversion) between a computer and
communications link control
nätverksprocessor; **communications port** =
connection allowing a device to
communicate *kommunikationsutgång;*
communications satellite = satellite used
for channelling radio *or* television *or* data
signals from one point on the earth to
another *kommunikationssatellit;*
communications scanner = line monitoring
equipment to check for data request signals
linjelyssnare; **data communications** =
transmission and reception of data rather
than speech *or* images *datakommunikation;*
data communications buffer = buffer on a
receiver that allows a slow peripheral to
accept data from a fast peripheral, without
slowing either down
datakommunikationsbuffert; **data
communications equipment (DCE)** =
equipment (such as a modem) which

receives *or* transmits data
kommunikationsutrustning

QUOTE it requires no additional hardware, other
than a communications board in the PC
Electronics & Power

community [kəˈmjuːnətɪ] *subst.* group of
people living *or* working in the same place
samhälle, församling, allmänhet, kommun;
the local business community = the business
people living and working in the area *de
lokala affärsmännen*

**community antenna television
(CATV)** [kəˈmjuːnətɪ ænˈtenə ˈtelɪˌvɪʒ(ə)n
(ˈsiːeɪtɪˈviː)] *subst.* cable television system
using a single aerial to pick up television
signals and then distribute them over a
wide area via cable *lokalt kabelnät,
centralantennssystem*

compact [kəmˈpækt] **1** *adj.* (thing) which
does not take up much space *kompakt;*
compact cassette = magnetic recording
tape contained inside a standard plastic
box, used in home personal computers for
data storage *(kompakt)kassett;* **compact
code** = minimum number of program
instructions required for a task
kompaktkod, optimal kod; **compact disk
(CD)** = small plastic disk that contains
audio signals in digital form etched onto
the surface *optisk skiva, optodiskett, CD;*
compact disk player = machine that reads
the digital data from a CD and converts it
back to its original form *CD-spelare;*
compact disk ROM = small plastic disk
that is used as a high capacity ROM device,
data is stored in binary form as holes
etched on the surface which are then read
by a laser *CD-skivminne, optiskt
lässkviminne;* **the compact disk ROM can
store as much data as a dozen hard disks;**
compacting algorithm = formula for
reducing the amount of space required by
text *kompakteringsalgoritm* **2** *vb.* to reduce
the space taken by something *kompaktera;*
data compacting = reducing the storage
space taken by data by coding it in a more
efficient way *datakompression*

companding [kəmˈpændɪŋ] =
COMPRESSING AND EXPANDING two
processes which reduce *or* compact data
before transmission *or* storage then restore
packed data to its original form
kompandera

compandor [kəmˈpændə] *subst.* =
COMPRESSOR/EXPANDER device used for
companding signals *kompander*

comparable [ˈkɒmp(ə)rəbl] *adj.* which
can be compared *jämförbar;* **the two sets of
figures are not comparable**

comparator [kəmˈpærətə] *subst.* logical
device whose output is true if there is a

difference between two inputs *jämförare, komparator*

compare [kəm'peə] *vb.* to check the differences between two pieces of information *jämföra*

compare with [kəm'peə wıð] *vb.* to put two things together to see how they differ *jämföra med*

comparison [kəm'pærısn] *subst.* way of comparing *jämförelse;* **there is no comparison between speeds of the two processors =** one of the two is much faster than the other *det går inte att jämföra hastigheten hos de två processorerna*

compatibility [kəm,pætə'bılətı] *subst. (of two hardware or software devices)* ability to function together *kompatibilitet, utbytbarhet*

> COMMENT: by conforming to the standards of another manufacturer *or* organization, compatibility of hardware *or* software allows programs *or* hardware to be interchanged with no modifications

> QUOTE check for software compatibility before choosing a display or graphics adapter
> **PC Business World**

compatible [kəm'pætəbl] **1** *adj.* (two hardware *or* software devices) that function correctly together *kompatibel;* **is the hardware IBM-compatible? 2** *subst.* hardware *or* software device that functions correctly with other equipment *or* is a clone *kompatibel;* **this computer is much cheaper than the other compatibles**

> QUOTE the compatibles bring computing to the masses
> **PC Business World**
> QUOTE low-cost compatibles have begun to find homes as terminals on LANS
> **Minicomputer News**
> QUOTE it is a fairly standard feature on most low-cost PC compatibles
> **Which PC?**
> QUOTE this was the only piece of software I found that wouldn't work, but it does show that there is no such thing as a totally compatible PC clone
> **Personal Computer World**

compilation [,kɒmpɪ'leɪʃ(ə)n] *subst.* translation of an encoded source program into machine readable code *kompilering;* **compilation error =** syntax error found during compilation *kompileringsfel;* **compilation errors result in the job being aborted; compilation time =** length of time it takes for a computer to compile a program *kompileringstid; compare with* DECOMPILATION

compile [kəm'paıl] *vb.* to convert a high level language program into a machine code program that can be executed by itself *kompilera;* **compiling takes a long time with this old version; debug your program, then**

compile it; compiled BASIC programs run much faster than the interpretor version; **compile and go =** computer program not requiring operator interaction that will load, compile and execute a high level language program *"kompilera och kör", körklart efter kompilering;* **compile phase =** the time during a program run, when the instructions are compiled *kompileringsfas*

compiler (program) [kəm'paılə ('prəʊɡræm)] *subst.* piece of software that converts an encoded program into a machine code program *kompilator;* **the new compiler has an in-built editor; this compiler produces a more efficient program; compiler diagnostics =** features in a compiler that help the programmer to find any faults *kompilatordiagnostik;* **compiler language =** high level language (such as C, Pascal) that will convert a source program that follows the language syntax into a machine code version, then run it *kompilatorspråk (motsatsen till interpreterande språk);* **cross-compiler =** assembler *or* compiler that compiles programs for one computer whilst running on another *korskompilator; compare with* INTERPRETER; **we can use the cross-compiler to develop the software before the new system arrives; language compiler =** software that converts an encoded source program into another (machine code) form *kompilator*

complement ['kɒmplɪmənt] **1** *subst.* (i) inversion of a binary digit *komplement;* (ii) result after subtracting a number from one less than the radix *komplement;* **the complement is found by changing the 1's to 0's and 0's to 1's; one's complement =** inversion of a binary digit *ett-komplement;* **nine's complement =** decimal complement (equivalent to binary one's complement) formed by subtracting each digit in the number from nine *nio-komplement;* **ten's complement =** formed by adding one to the nine's complement of the number *tio-komplement;* **two's complement =** formed by adding one to the one's complement of a number *två-komplement* **2** *vb.* to invert a binary digit *(binär)invertera;* **complemented =** (binary digit) that has had a complement performed *inverterad*

complementary [,kɒmplɪ'ment(ə)rɪ] *adj.* (two things) that complete each other *or* that go well together *komplementär;* **complementary colours =** two colours that when optically combined produce white *komplementärfärger;* **complementary operation =** logical operation that results in the logical NOT of a function *komplementär operation*

complementary metal oxide semiconductor (CMOS) [,kɒmplɪ'ment(ə)rɪ 'metl 'ɒksaıd 'semɪkən'dʌktə ('siːmɒs)] *subst.* integrated circuit design and construction method (using a pair of complementary p- and n-type transistors) *CMOS-teknik*

complementation [ˌkɒmplɪmən'teɪʃn] *subst.* number system used to represent positive and negative numbers *komplementärt system*

complete [kəm'pliːt] **1** *adj.* **(a)** finished *or* all ready *avslutad, klar;* **the spelling check is complete; when this job is complete, the next in the queue is processed (b)** requiring nothing else (in order to function) *fullständig, komplett;* **complete operation =** operation that retrieves the necessary operands from memory, performs the operation, returns the results and operands to memory and reads the next instruction to be processed *fullständig operation* **2** *vb.* to finish a task *avsluta;* **when you have completed the keyboarding, pass the text through the spelling checker**

completion [kəm'pliːʃ(ə)n] *subst.* time when something is complete *avslutning;* **completion date for the new software package is November 15th**

complex ['kɒmpleks] *adj.* very complicated *or* difficult to understand *komplex;* **the complex mathematical formula was difficult to solve; the controller must work hard to operate this complex network; complex instruction set computer (CISC) =** CPU design whose instruction set contains a number of long, complex instructions, that makes programming easier, but reduces execution speed *dator med komplex instruktionsuppsättning; compare* REDUCED INSTRUCTION SET COMPUTER

complexity [kəm'pleksətɪ] *subst.* being complicated *komplexitet;* **complexity measure =** measure of the system resources used in an operation *or* job *komplexitetsmått*

complicated ['kɒmplɪkeɪtɪd] *adj.* with many different parts *or* difficult to understand *komplicerad;* **this program is very complicated; the computer design is more complicated than necessary**

component [kəm'pəʊnənt] *subst.* (i) piece of machinery *or* section which will be put into a final product *komponent;* (ii) electronic device that affects an electrical signal *komponent;* **component density =** number of electronic components per unit area on a PCB *komponenttäthet;* **component density increases with production expertise; component density is so high on this motherboard, that no expansion connectors could be fitted; component error =** error introduced by a

malfunctioning device *or* component rather than incorrect programming *komponentfel*

compose [kəm'pəʊz] *vb.* to arrange the required type, in the correct order, prior to printing *sätta;* **composing room =** room in a typesetters *or* in a newspaper, where the text is composed by compositors *sätteri*

composite circuit ['kɒmpəzɪt 'sɜːkɪt] *subst.* electronic circuit made up of a number of smaller circuits and components *sammansatt krets, integrerad krets*

composite video signal ['kɒmpəzɪt 'vɪdɪəʊ 'sɪgn(ə)l] *subst.* single television signal containing synchronizing pulse and video signal in a modulated form *sammansatt videosignal*

composition [ˌkɒmpə'zɪʃ(ə)n] *subst.* creating typeset text, either using metal type *or* by keyboarding on a computer typesetter *typsats, sättning;* **composition size =** printing type size *satsstorlek*

compositor [kəm'pɒzɪtə] *subst.* person who sets up the required type prior to printing *sättare;* **electronic compositor =** computer that allows a user to easily arrange text on screen before it is electronically typeset *elektronisk sättmaskin*

compound ['kɒmpaʊnd] *adj.* **compound logical element =** logical circuit *or* function that produces an output from a number of inputs *sammansatt logikprodukt;* **compound statement =** a number of program instructions in one line of program *sammansatt instruktion;* **the debugger cannot handle compound statements**

compress [kəm'pres] *vb.* to squeeze something to fit into a smaller space *komprimera;* **use the archiving program to compress the file**

compression [kəm'preʃ(ə)n] *subst.* varying the gain of a device depending on input level to maintain an output signal within certain limits *signalkomprimering;* **data compression =** means of reducing the size of blocks of data by removing spaces, empty sections and unused material *data(volym)reduktion*

compressor [kəm'presə] *subst.* (i) electronic circuit which compresses a signal *kompressor;* (ii) (program *or* device) that provides data compression *komprimeringsenhet;* **audio compressor =** circuit which limits the maximum signal level *ljudkompressor*

comptometer [kɒmp'tɒmɪtə] *subst.* machine which counts automatically *kalkyleringsmaskin*

computable [kəm'pjuːtəbl] *adj.* which can be calculated *beräkningsbar*

computation [ˌkɒmpjʊ'teɪʃ(ə)n] *subst.* calculation *beräkning*

computational [ˌkɒmpjʊ'teɪʃ(ə)nl] *adj.* referring to computation *beräknings-;* **computational error** = mistake made in calculating *beräkningsfel*

compute [kəm'pjuːt] *vb.* to calculate *or* to do calculations *beräkna;* **connect charges were computed on an hourly rate**

computer [kəm'pjuːtə] *subst.* **(a)** machine that receives *or* stores *or* processes data very quickly according to a stored program *dator;* **analog computer** = computer which processes data in analog form (that is data which is represented by a continuously variable signal - as opposed to digital data) *analog dator;* **business computer** = powerful small computer which is programmed for special business uses *affärsdator;* **digital computer** = computer which processes data in digital form (that is data represented in discrete form) *digital dator;* **mainframe computer** = large scale powerful computer system that can handle high capacity memory and backing storage devices as well as a number of operators simultaneously *stordator, värddator;* **microcomputer** *or* **micro** = complete small-scale, cheap, low-power computer system based around a microprocessor chip and having limited memory capacity *mikrodator, smådator;* **minicomputer** *or* **mini** = small computer with a greater range of instructions and processing power than a microcomputer, but not able to compete with the speed or data handling capacity of a mainframe computer *minidator;* **personal computer (PC)** *or* **home computer** = small computer which can be used in the home, in which the various sections (screen, keyboard, disk drives, processing unit, memory etc.) are in one or two small compact cases *hemdator, persondator;* **single board computer (sbc)** = micro *or* mini computer whose components are all located on a single printed circuit board *enkortsdator;* **single chip computer** = complete simple computer, including CPU, memory and I/O ports on one chip *enkretsdator;* **supercomputer** = very powerful mainframe computer used for high speed mathematical tasks *superdator* **(b) computer animation** = making a series of computer-generated images displayed in sequence to emulate motion *datoranimering;* **computer applications** = the tasks and uses that a computer can carry out in a particular field *or* job *(dator)tillämpningar;* **computer architecture** = (i) layout and interconnection of a computer's internal hardware and the logical relationships between CPU,

memory and I/O devices *datorarkitektur;* (ii) way in which the CPU, terminals, printers and network connections are arranged *datorarkitektur;* **computer bureau** = office which offers to do work on its computers for companies which do not have their own computers *databehandlingsenhet;* **computer code** = programming language that consists of commands in binary code that can be directly understood by the central processing unit, without the need for translation *(maskinkods)program;* **computer conferencing** = connecting a number of computers *or* terminals together to allow a group of users to communicate *datorkonferens;* **computer crime** = theft, fraud or other crimes involving computers *datorbrott;* **computer dating** = use of a computer to match single people who may want to get married *dataträff;* **computer department** = department in a company which manages the company's computers *datoravdelning;* **computer engineer** = person who maintains *or* programs *or* designs computer equipment *datatekniker;* **computer error** = mistake made by a computer *datorfel;* **computer file** = section of information on a computer (such as the payroll, list of addresses, customer accounts) *fil;* **computer graphics** = information represented graphically on a computer display *datorgrafik;* **computer image processing** = analysis of information in an image, usually by electronic means *or* using a computer, also used for recognition of objects in an image *bildbehandling;* **computer independent language** = programming language that will operate on any computer that has a correct compiler *or* interpreter *datoroberoende språk;* **computer input from microfilm (CIM)** = use of microfilm for computer data storage, and the method of reading the data *mikrofilminläsning;* **computer language** = language (formed of figures *or* characters) used to communicate with a computer *programmeringsspråk;* **computer listing** = printout of a list of items taken from data stored in a computer *datorlistning;* **computer literacy** = understanding the basic principles of computers, related expressions and concepts, and being able to use computers for programming *or* applications *datormognad;* **computer-literate** = (person) able to understand how to use a computer, the expressions and concepts used *datormogen;* **the managing director is simply not computer-literate;** **computer logic** = way in which the various sections of the CPU, memory and I/O are arranged (in hardware) *datorlogik;* **computer mail** *or* **electronic mail** = messages sent between users of a bulletin board *or* network *elektronisk post;* **computer manager** = person in charge of a computer department *datachef;* **computer network** =

number of computers, terminals and peripherals connected together to allow communications between each *(data)nätverk;* **computer numeric control (CNC)** = control of a machine by computer *numerisk styrning;* **computer office system** = computer and related peripherals used for office tasks (filing, word processing, etc.) *kontorsdatorsystem;* **computer operator** = person who operates a computer *datoroperatör;* **computer organization** *see* COMPUTER ARCHITECTURE; **computer output** = data *or* information produced after processing by a computer *datorutskrift;* **computer output on microfilm (COM)** = information output from a computer, stored directly onto microfilm *datorutskrift på mikrofilm;* **computer power** = measure of speed and capacity of a computer (several tests exist, such as FLOPS *or* benchmark timings) *datorkapacitet;* **computer program** = series of instructions to a computer, telling it to do a particular piece of work *datorprogram;* **the user cannot write a computer program with this system; computer programmer** = person who writes computer programs *datorprogrammerare;* **computer run** = action of processing instructions in a program by a computer *datorkörning;* **computer science** = scientific study of computers, the organization of hardware and development of software *datorvetenskap;* **computer services** = work using a computer, done by a computer bureau *datatjänster;* **computer system** = a central processor with storage and associated peripherals that make up a working computer *datorsystem;* **computer time** = time when a computer is being used (paid for at an hourly rate) *datortid;* **running all those sales reports costs a lot in computer time; computer word** = number of bits that make up a standard word within a CPU (usually 8,16 *or* 32 bits long) *datorord*

computer- [kəmˈpjuːtə] *prefix* referring to a computer *dator-;* **computer-based learning (CBL)** = learning mainly using a computer *datorbaserad inlärning;* **computer-based message system (CBMS)** = use of a computer system to allow users to send and receive messages from other users (usually in-house) *datorbaserat meddelandehanteringssystem;* **computer-based training (CBT)** = use of a computer system to train students *datorbaserad utbildning;* **computer-generated** = which has been generated by a computer *datorgenererad;* **computer-generated graphics** *datorgenererad grafik;* **computer-integrated manufacturing (CIM)** = coordinated use of computers in every aspect of design and manufacturing *datorstödd tillverkning;* **computer-integrated systems** = coordinated use of computers and other related equipment in

a process *datorintegrerade system;* **this firm is a very well-known supplier of computer-integrated systems which allow both batch pagination of very long documents with alteration of individual pages; computer-managed instruction (CMI)** = using a computer to assist students in learning a subject *datoriserad undervisning;* **computer-managed learning (CML)** = using a computer to teach students and assess their progress *datoriserad inlärning*

computer-aided [kəmˈpjuːtərˌeɪdɪd] *or* **computer-assisted** [kəmˈpjuːtərəˈsɪstɪd] *adj.* which uses a computer to make the work easier *datorstödd;* **computer-aided** *or* **assisted design (CAD)** = the use of computer and graphics terminal to help a designer in his work *datorstödd konstruktion;* **computer-aided** *or* **assisted engineering (CAE)** = use of a computer to help an engineer solve problems *or* calculate design *or* product specifications *datorstödd konstruktion;* **computer-aided** *or* **assisted instruction (CAI)** = use of a computer to assist pupils in learning a subject *datorstödd undervisning;* **computer-aided** *or* **assisted learning (CAL)** = use of a computer to assist pupils to learn a subject *datorstödd undervisning;* **computer-aided** *or* **assisted manufacture (CAM)** = use of a computer to control machinery *or* to assist in a manufacturing process *datorstödd tillverkning;* **computer-aided** *or* **assisted testing (CAT)** = use of a computer to test equipment *or* programs to find any faults *datorstödd provning;* **computer-aided** *or* **assisted training (CAT)** = use of a computer to demonstrate to and assist pupils in learning a skill *datorstödd utbildning*

computer generations [kəmˈpjuːtə ˌdʒenəˈreɪʃnz] *subst.* way of defining the advances in the field of computing *datorgenerationer*

COMMENT: the development of computers has been divided into a series of "generations": *first generation:* computers constructed using valves having limited storage; *second generation:* computers where transistors were used in construction; *third generation:* use of integrated circuits in construction; *fourth generation:* most often used at present, using low cost memory and IC packages; *fifth generation:* future computers using very fast processors, large memory and allowing human input/output

computerization [kəmˌpjuːtəraɪˈzeɪʃn] *subst.* action of introducing a computer system *or* of changing from a manual to a computer system *datorisering;*

computerization of the financial sector is proceeding very fast

computerize [kəm'pjuːtəraɪz] *vb.* to change from a manual system to one using computers *datorisera;* **our stock control has been completely computerized; they operate a computerized invoicing system**

computer-readable [kəm'pjuːtə 'riːdəbl] *adj.* which can be read and understood by a computer *datorläsbar;* **computer-readable codes**

computing [kəm'pjuːtɪŋ] *adj. & subst.* referring to computers *or* work done on computers *som kan beräknas;* **computing power =** measure of speed and ability of a computer to perform calculations *beräkningskapacitet;* **computing speed =** speed at which a computer calculates *beräkningshastighet*

concatenate [kɒn'kætəneɪt] *vb.* to join together two *or* more sets of data *konkatenera, länka;* **concatenated data set =** more than one file *or* set of data joined together to produce one set *konkatenerad datamängd, länkad datamängd*

conceal [kən'siːl] *vb.* to hide *or* not display information *or* graphics from a user *gömma;* **the hidden lines are concealed from view with this algorithm**

concentrate ['kɒns(ə)ntreɪt] *vb.* (i) to focus a beam onto a narrow point *fokusera;* (ii) to combine a number of lines *or* circuits *or* data to take up less space *koncentrera;* **to concentrate a beam of light on a lens; the concentrated data was transmitted cheaply**

concentrator ['kɒns(ə)ntreɪtə] *subst.* device which combines intermittent data from various telephone lines and sends it along a single line in one go *koncentrator*

concertina fold [ˌkɒnsə'tiːnə ˌfəʊld] *subst.* accordion fold *or* method of folding continuous paper, one sheet in one direction, the next sheet in the opposite direction, allowing the paper to be fed into a printer continuously with no action on the part of the user *dragspelsvikning, löpande bana för papper*

concurrent [kən'kʌr(ə)nt] *adj.* almost simultaneous (actions *or* sets) *parallell;* **each concurrent process has its own window; three transputers provide concurrent processing capabilities for the entire department; concurrent operating system =** operating system software that allows several programs *or* activities to be processed at the same time *parallelloperativsystem;* **concurrent programming =** running several programs apparently simultaneously, achieved by executing small sections from each program in turn *parallellprogrammering*

concurrently [kən'kʌr(ə)ntlɪ] *adv.* running at almost the same time *parallellt; see also the four categories for processors* SISD, SIMD, MISD, MIMD

condenser lens [kən'densə ˌlenz] *subst.* optical device, usually made of glass, that concentrates a beam of light onto a certain area *lins, kondensor*

condition [kən'dɪʃ(ə)n] **1** *subst.* (i) state of a circuit *or* device *or* register *tillstånd;* (ii) series of requirements that have to be met before an action can occur *villkor, tillstånd;* **condition code register =** register that contains the state of the CPU after the execution of the last instruction *tillståndsregister; see also* FLAG; **error condition =** state that is entered if an attempt is made to operate on data containing errors *feltillstånd* **2** *vb.* to modify data that is to be transmitted so as to meet set parameters *trimma data, anpassa data;* **condition the raw data to a standard format**

conditional [kən'dɪʃ(ə)nl] *adj.* **(a)** provided that certain things take place *villkorlig* **(b)** (process) which is dependent on the result of another *villkorlig;* **conditional breakpoint =** breakpoint inserted, after which the programmer can jump to one of a number of sections, depending on data *or* program status *villkorlig brytpunkt;* **conditional jump** *or* **branch** *or* **transfer =** programming instruction that provides a jump to a section of a program if a certain condition is met *villkorligt hopp;* **the conditional branch will select routine one if the response is yes and routine two if no; conditional statement =** program instruction that will redirect program control according to the outcome of an event *villkorssats*

conduct [kən'dʌkt] *vb.* to allow an electrical current to flow through a material *leda;* **to conduct electricity; copper conducts well**

conduction [kən'dʌkʃ(ə)n] *subst.* ability of a material to conduct *ledning, överföring;* **the conduction of electricity by gold contacts**

conductive [kən'dʌktɪv] *adj.* referring to the ability of a material to conduct *ledande*

conductor [kən'dʌktə] *subst.* substance (such as a metal) which conducts electricity *ledare;* **copper is a good conductor of electricity ;** *see also* SEMICONDUCTOR

conduit ['kɒndɪt] *subst.* protective pipe *or* channel for wires *or* cables *kabelränna, kabeltrumma;* **the cables from each terminal are channelled to the computer centre by metal conduit**

cone [kəʊn] *subst.* moving section in most loudspeakers *kon*

conference [ˈkɒnf(ə)r(ə)ns] *subst.* meeting of people to discuss problems *konferens, möte;* **to be in conference =** to be in a meeting *sitta i möte;* **conference phone =** telephone so arranged that several people can speak into it from around a table *konferenstelefon;* **conference room =** room where small meetings can take place *konferensrum;* **conference call =** telephone call which connects together three or more telephone lines allowing each person or device to communicate with all the others *konferenssamtal;* **press conference =** meeting where newspaper and TV reporters are invited to hear news of a new product or a change of management, etc. *presskonferens*

conferencing [ˈkɒnf(ə)r(ə)nsiŋ] *subst.* teleconferencing or holding a meeting of people in different places, using the telephones to allow each person to communicate with the others *telefonkonferens;* **computer conferencing =** connecting a number of computers or terminals together to allow a group of users to communicate *datorkonferens, KOM-system;* **the multi-user BBS has a computer conferencing facility**

confidence level [ˈkɒnfɪd(ə)ns ˈlevl] *subst.* likelihood that a number will lie to within a range of values *sannolikhet, konfidensnivå*

configuration [kən.fɪgjʊˈreɪʃ(ə)n] *subst.* way in which the hardware and software of a computer system are planned and set up *konfigurering, konfiguration;* **configuration state =** state of a computer that allows it or the system or a program to be configured *konfigureringstillstånd, konfigureringsläge*

QUOTE the machine uses RAM to store system configuration information
                 PC Business World
QUOTE several configuration files are provided to assign memory to the program, depending on the available RAM on your system
                 PC Business World
QUOTE if you modify a program with the editor, or with a word-processor specified in the configuration file, it will know that the program has changed and will execute the new one accordingly
                 PC Business World

---

configure [kənˈfɪgə] *vb.* to select hardware, software and interconnections to make up a special system *konfigurera;* **this terminal has been configured to display graphics; you only have to configure the PC once - when you first buy it**

QUOTE users can configure four of the eight ports to handle links at speeds of 64K bit/sec
                 Computer News

---

configured-in [kənˈfɪgəd.ɪn] device whose configuration state indicates it is ready and available for use *körklar;* **configured-off** or **configured out =** device whose configuration state indicates it is not available for use *ej körklar*

conform [kənˈfɔːm] *vb.* to work according to set rules *följa (regler), anpassa;* **the software will not run if it does not conform to the operating system standards**

congestion [kənˈdʒestʃ(ə)n] *subst.* state that occurs when communication or processing demands are greater than the capacity of a system *stockning*

conjunct [ˈkɒndʒʌŋ(k)t] *subst.* one of the variables in an logical AND function *konjunkt*

conjunction [kənˈdʒʌŋ(k)ʃ(ə)n] *subst.* logical function whose output is true if all inputs are true *konjunktion*

connect [kəˈnekt] *vb.* to link together two points in a circuit or communications network *koppla;* **connect time =** length of time a user is logged onto an interactive system *(in)kopplingstid*

connection [kəˈnekʃ(ə)n] *subst.* link or something which joins *koppling;* **parallel connection =** connector on a computer allowing parallel data to be transferred *parallellkoppling;* **their transmission rate is 60,000 bps through parallel connection**

connective [kəˈnektɪv] *subst.* symbol between two operands that describes the operation to be performed *konnektiv*

connector [kəˈnektə] *subst.* physical device with a number of metal contacts that allow devices to be easily linked together *kontakt;* **the connector at the end of the cable will fit any standard serial port; card edge connector =** series of metal tracks ending at the edge and on the surface of a circuit board, allowing it to be plugged into an edge connector to provide electrical path (for data transmission, etc.) *kortkontakt; see also* FEMALE, MALE

conscious error [ˈkɒnʃəs ˈerə] *subst.* operator error that is immediately spotted, but cannot be prevented in time *uppenbart fel*

consecutive [kənˈsekjʊtɪv] *adj.* following one after another *efter varandra följande;* **the computer ran three consecutive files**

consecutively [kənˈsekjʊtɪvlɪ] *adv.* one after the other *efter varandra;* **the sections of the program run consecutively**

console [ˈkɒnsəʊl] *subst.* unit (keyboard and VDU, and usually a printer) which allows an operator to communicate with a computer system *manöverenhet, manöverbord, konsol;* **the console consists of input device such as a keyboard, and an output device such as a printer** *or* **CRT**

constant ['kɒnst(ə)nt] **1** *subst.* item of data, whose value does not change (as opposed to a variable) *konstant* **2** *adj.* which does not change *konstant;* **the disk drive motor spins at a constant velocity; constant length field** = data field that always contains the same number of characters *fält med konstant längd;* **constant ratio code** = character representation code that has a constant number of binary ones per word length *konstant förhållandekod*

construct [kən'strʌkt] *vb.* to build *or* to make (a device *or* a system) *konstruera*

construction [kən'strʌkʃ(ə)n] *subst.* building *or* making of a system *konstruktion;* **construction of the prototype is advancing rapidly; construction techniques have changed over the past few years**

consult [kən'sʌlt] *vb.* to ask an expert for advice *konsultera;* **he consulted the maintenance manager about the disk fault**

consultancy [kən'sʌltənsɪ] *subst.* act of giving specialist advice *konsultering;* **a consultancy firm; he offers a consultancy service**

consultant [kən'sʌltənt] *subst.* specialist who gives advice *konsult;* **they called in a computer consultant to advise them on the system design**

consulting [kən'sʌltɪŋ] *adj.* person who gives specialist advice *rådgivande;* **a consulting engineer**

consumables [kən'sjuːməblz] *subst pl.* small cheap extra items required in the day-to-day running of a computer system (such as paper and printer ribbons) *förbrukningsmaterial;* **put all the printer leads and paper with the other consumables**

contact ['kɒntækt] **1** *subst.* section of a switch *or* connector that provides an electrical path when it touches another conductor *kontakt;* **the circuit is not working because the contact is dirty; contact bounce** = *see* BOUNCE, DE-BOUNCE **2** *vb.* to try to call a user *or* device in a network *kontakta*

contact printing ['kɒntækt ˌprɪntɪŋ] *subst.* photographic printing process in which the negative touches the light-sensitive paper *kontaktkopiering*

contain [kən'teɪn] *vb.* to hold something inside *innehålla;* **each carton contains two computers and their peripherals; we have lost a file containing important documents**

content ['kɒntent] *subst.* the ideas inside a letter *or* other document *innehåll*

content-addressable ['kɒntent ə'dresəbl] *adj.* **content-addressable file** *or* **location** = method of storing data in which each item may be individually accessed *innehållsadresserbar fil;* **content-addressable memory (CAM)** *or* **associative storage** = method of data retrieval which uses part of the data rather than an address to locate the data *associativt minne*

contention [kən'tenʃ(ə)n] *subst.* situation that occurs when two or more devices are trying to communicate with the same piece of equipment *stockning, köbildning;* **contention bus** = communication control system in which a device must wait for a free moment before transmitting data *stockningsbuss;* **contention delay** = length of time spent waiting for equipment to become free for use *stockningsfördröjning*

contents ['kɒntents] *subst pl.* **(a)** things contained *or* what is inside something *innehåll;* **the contents of the bottle poured out onto the computer keyboard; the customs officials inspected the contents of the box; the contents of the letter** = the words written in the letter *brevets innehåll* **(b)** list of items in a file *innehåll*

context ['kɒntekst] *subst.* words and phrases among which a word is used *sammanhang;* **the example shows how the word is used in context**

contiguous [kən'tɪgjʊəs] *adj.* which touches the thing next to it *bredvidliggande, angränsande;* **contiguous file** = file stored in a series of adjacent disk sectors *sammanhängande fil;* **contiguous graphics** = graphic cells *or* characters that touch each other *sammanhängande grafik;* **most display units do not provide contiguous graphics: their characters have a small space on each side to improve legibility**

contingency plan [kən'tɪn(d)ʒ(ə)nsɪ ˌplæn] *subst.* secondary plan *or* equipment that will be used if the first fails to work *säkerhetsplan, nödfallsutrustning*

continual [kən'tɪnjʊəl] *adj.* which happens again and again *återkommande, ständig;* **the continual system breakdowns have slowed down the processing**

continually [kən'tɪnjʊəlɪ] *adv.* again and again *återkommande*

continuation [kənˌtɪnjʊ'eɪʃ(ə)n] *subst.* act of continuing *fortsättning;* **continuation page** = page *or* screen of text that follows on from a main page *fortsättningssida*

continue [kən'tınjʊ] *vb.* to go on doing something *or* to do something which you were doing earlier *fortsätta*

continuity [,kɒntı'njuːətı] *subst.* **(a)** clear conduction path between two points *sammanbindning, oavbruten övergång* **(b)** checking that the details of one scene in a film continue into the next scene to be shown, even if the two have been shot at different times *sammanhållning, oavbruten scenföljd*

continuous [kən'tınjuəs] *adj.* with no end *or* with no breaks *kontinuerlig, sammanhängande;* which goes on without stopping *i en följd;* **continuous data stream** = high speed serial data transmission, in which data words are not synchronized, but follow on immediately from each other *sammanhängande dataström;* **continuous feed** = device which feeds continuous stationery into a printer *löpande bana;* **continuous loop** = endless piece of recording *or* projection tape *oändlig slinga;* **continuous signal** = analog (continuously variable) signal *kontinuerlig signal;* **continuous stationery** = paper made as one long sheet, used in computer printers *papper i löpande bana;* **continuous wave** = high frequency waveform that can be modulated to carry data *kontinuerlig våg, bärvåg; see also* CARRIER

continuously [kən'tınjuəslı] *adv.* without stopping *oavbrutet, ständigt;* **the printer overheated after working continuously for five hours**

contrast ['kɒntrɑːst] **1** *subst.* **(a)** difference between black and white *kontrast;* **the control allows you to adjust brightness and contrast; contrast enhancement filter** = special filter put over a monitor to increase contrast and prevent eye-strain *kontrasthöjande filter* **(b)** control knob on a display that alters the difference between black and white tones *kontrast* **2** *vb.* to examine the differences between two sets of information *kontrastera;* **the old data was contrasted with the latest information**

contrasting ['kɒntrɑːstıŋ] *adj.* which show a sharp difference *kontrasterande;* **a cover design in contrasting colours**

control [kən'trəʊl] **1** *vb.* to be in charge of something *or* to make sure that something is kept in check *styra, kontrollera;* **controlled vocabulary** = set of terms *or* words used in an indexing language *styrt ordförråd* NOTE: **controlling - controlled 2** *subst.* **(a)** restricting *or* checking something *or* making sure that something is kept in check *kontrollstyrning;* **control computer** = dedicated computer used to control a process *or* piece of equipment *styrdator;* **control total** = result of summing certain fields in a computer file to provide error detection *kontrollsummering, kontrollsumma;* **out of control** = not kept in check *utan styrning* **(b)** (i) section of a computer *or* device that carries out instructions and processes signals, etc. *styrenhet;* (ii) conditional program statements *villkorliga instruktioner;* **control statement** = program instruction that redirects a program (to another branch etc.) *styrsats;* **control unit (CU)** = section of central processor that selects and executes instructions *styrenhet;* **control word** = word that defines the actions (in a particular process) that are to be followed *styrord;* **device control character** = special code sent in a transmission to a device to instruct it to perform a special function *styrtecken för kringutrustning;* **line control** = special code used to control a communications link *linjestyrning* **(c)** (i) key on a computer keyboard which sends a control character *kontroll(tangenten);* (ii) data *or* a key which controls something *styr-;* **control block** = reserved area of computer memory that contains control data *styrblock;* **control bus** = set of connections to a microcomputer that carry the control signals between CPU, memory and input/output devices *styrbuss;* **control cards** = in a punched card system, the first cards which contain the processor control instructions *styrkort;* **control character** = special character that provides a control sequence rather than a alphanumeric character *styrtecken;* **control cycle** = events required to retrieve, decode and execute an instruction stored in memory *instruktionscykel;* **control data** = data that controls the actions of a device *styrdata;* **control driven** = computer architecture where instructions are executed once a control sequence has been received *styrsekvensstyrd, kommandosekvensstyrd;* **control field** = storage area for control instructions *styrfält;* **control instruction** = program instruction that controls the actions of a device *styrinstruktion;* **the next control instruction will switch to italics; control language** = commands that describe the identification of and resources required by a job that a computer has to process *styrspråk;* **control memory** *or* **ROM** = memory which decodes control instructions into microinstructions which operate the computer *or* microcontroller *styrminne, styrkodsminne, läsminne;* **control mode** = state of a device in which control signals can be received to select options *or* functions *styrtillstånd;* **control panel** = main computer system control switches and status indicators *kontrollpanel, manöverpanel;* **control program/monitor** *or* **control program for microcomputers (CP/M)** = old-fashioned but still popular operating system for microcomputers *operativsystem för* *mikrodatorer;* **control register =** storage location only used for control data *styrregister, flaggregister;* **control signals =** electrical signals transmitted to control the actions of a circuit *styrsignaler;* **control sequence =** (series of) codes containing a control character and various arguments, used to carry out a process *or* change mode in a device *styrsekvens;* **control statement =** program instruction that directs a CPU to provide controlling actions *or* controls the operation of the CPU *styrsats;* **control token =** special sequence of bits transmitted over a LAN to provide control actions *styrstafettord;* **control transfer =** redirection of the CPU when a jump *or* call instruction is encountered *styröverföring, styrsekvensskifte* **(d) control group =** small group which is used to check a sample group *kontrollgrupp;* **control systems =** systems used to check that a computer system is working correctly *övervakningssystem*

> QUOTE there are seven print control characters which can be placed in a document
> **Personal Computer World**

controllable [kən'trəʊləbl] *adj.* which can be controlled *styrbar*

controller [kən'trəʊlə] *subst.* hardware *or* software device that controls a peripheral (such as a printer) *or* monitors and directs the data transmission over a local area network *styrenhet;* **display controller =** device that accepts character *or* graphical codes and instructions, and converts them into dot-matrix patterns that are displayed on a screen *bildskärmsstyrkrets, grafikstyrkrets;* **printer's controller =** main device in a printer that translates output from the computer into printing instructions *styrenhet för skrivare; see also* DEVICE DRIVER

> QUOTE a printer's controller is the brains of the machine. It translates the signals coming from your computer into printing instructions that result in a hard copy of your electronic document
> **Publish**

convention [kən'venʃ(ə)n] *subst.* well-known standards *or* rules which are followed, allowing hardware *or* software compatibility *konvention, överenskommelse, industristandard*

conversational (mode) [ˌkɒnvə'seɪʃ(ə)nl (məʊd)] *subst.* computer system that provides immediate responses to a user's input *dialog(tillstånd), interaktiv(t tillstånd); see also* INTERACTIVE MODE *compare with* BATCH MODE

conversion [kən'vɜːʃ(ə)n] *subst.* change from one system to another *övergång (överföring) (till nytt system);* **conversion equipment =** device that will convert data from one format to another (suitable for

another system) without changing the content *formatomvandlare;* **conversion tables** *or* **translation tables =** list of source codes *or* statements and their equivalent in another language *or* form *översättningstabeller;* **conversion tables may be created and used in conjunction with the customer's data to convert it to our systems codes; conversion program =** (i) program that converts programs written for one computer into a suitable form for another *konverteringsprogram;* (ii) program that converts data format, coding, etc. for use in another program *konverteringsprogram*

convert [kən'vɜːt] *vb.* to change one thing into another *omvandla*

converter [kən'vɜːtə] *or* **convertor** [kən'vɜːtə] *subst.* device *or* program that translates data from one form to another *omvandlare;* **the convertor allowed the old data to be used on the new system; analog to digital converter (ADC) =** device used to convert an analog signal to a digital output form, that can be understood by a computer *analog-digitalomvandlare;* **digital to analog converter (DAC) =** circuit that outputs an analog signal that is proportional to the input digital number *digital-analogomvandlare*

convertibility [kən,vɜːtə'bɪlətɪ] *subst.* ability to be changed *förändringsbarhet*

convertible [kən'vɜːtəbl] *adj.* which can be converted *som kan omvandlas*

convey [kən'veɪ] *vb.* to carry *or* import information *överföra (information);* **the chart conveyed the sales problem graphically**

conveyor [kən'veɪə] *subst.* method of carrying paper using a moving belt *bältmatning (i t. ex. kurvritare)*

coordinate [kəʊ'ɔːdnət] **1** *subst.* **coordinates =** values used to locate a point on a graph *or* map *koordinater;* **coordinate graph =** means of displaying one point on a graph, using two values referring to axes which are usually at right angles to each other *koordinat graf;* **polar coordinates =** use of a distance and a direction to locate a point *polära koordinater;* **rectangular coordinates =** two numbers referring to distances along axes at right angles from an origin *kartesiska koordinater, rektangulära koordinater* **2** *vb.* to organize complex tasks, so that they fit together efficiently *koordinera;* **she has to coordinate the keyboarding of several parts of a file in six different locations**

coordination [kəʊˌɔːdɪ'neɪʃ(ə)n] *subst.* organizing complex tasks; synchronizing two *or* more processes *koordinering*

copier [ˈkɒpɪə] or **copying machine** [ˈkɒpɪɪŋməˈʃiːn] subst. machine which makes copies of documents kopiator, kopieringsmaskin

copper [ˈkɒpə] subst. red-coloured soft metal, a good conductor of electricity, used in wires and as connecting tracks on PCBs koppar

copperplate printing [ˈkɒpəpleɪt ˈprɪntɪŋ] subst. printing method that uses a copper plate on which the image is etched djuptryck, kopparstick

coprocessor [ˌkəʊˈprəʊsesə] subst. extra, specialized processor, such as an array or numerical processor that can work with a main CPU to increase execution speed hjälpprocessor; **graphics coprocessor** = high speed display adapter that is dedicated to graphics operations such as line drawing, plotting, etc. grafikprocessor; **maths coprocessor** = dedicated processor that provides results to mathematical operations much faster than the ALU section of a CPU matematikprocessor

copy [ˈkɒpɪ] 1 subst. (a) document which looks the same as another kopia; duplicate of an original kopia; **file copy** = copy of a document which is filed in an office for reference filkopia (b) document kopia; **clean copy** = copy which is ready for keyboarding and does not have many changes to it renskrift, renskrivet exemplar; **fair copy** or **final copy** = document which is written or typed with no changes or mistakes slutlig renskriven version; **hard copy** = printout of text or data which is stored in a computer papperskopia; **rough copy** = draft of a program which, it is expected, will have changes made to it before it is complete koncept, utkast, kladd; **top copy** = first or top sheet of a document which is typed with carbon copies första sidan i ett blankettset, (maskinskrivet) original (c) text of material ready to be keyboarded text; **Tuesday is the last date for copy for the advertisement; copy reader** = person who checks copy before printing korrekturläsare (d) a book or a newspaper kopia, exemplar; **I kept yesterday's copy of "The Times"; I read it in the office copy of "Fortune"; where is my copy of the telephone directory?** 2 vb. to make a second document which is like the first kopiera (dokument); to duplicate original data kopiera (data); **he copied all the personnel files at night and took them home; there is a memory resident utility which copies the latest files onto backing store every 40 minutes**

copy protect [ˈkɒpɪ prəˈtekt] subst. & vb. switch to prevent copies of a disk being made kopieringsskydd, kopieringsskyddad; **the program is not copy protected**

copy protection [ˈkɒpɪ prəˈtekʃ(ə)n] subst. preventing copies being made kopieringsskydd; **a hard disk may crash because of copy protection; the new program will come without copy protection**

copyright [ˈkɒpɪraɪt] 1 subst. legal right (lasting for fifty years after the death of an artist whose work has been published) which a writer or programmer has in his own work, allowing him not to have it copied without the payment of royalties upphovsrätt; **Copyright Act** = Act of Parliament making copyright legal, and controlling the copying of copyright material "lagen om upphovsrätt"; **work which is out of copyright** = work by a writer, etc., who has been dead for fifty years, and which anyone can publish verk som ej är skyddat av upphovsrätt; **work still in copyright** = work by a living writer, or by a writer who has not been dead for fifty years verk som fortfarande är upphovsrättsskyddat; **infringement of copyright** or **copyright infringement** = act of illegally copying a work which is in copyright intrång i upphovsrätt; **copyright notice** = note in a book showing who owns the copyright and the date of ownership upphovsrättsangivelse; **copyright owner** = person who owns the copyright in a work upphovsrättsinnehavare 2 vb. to state the copyright of a written work by printing a copyright notice and publishing the work markera upphovsrätt 3 adj. covered by the laws of copyright upphovsrättsskyddad; **it is illegal to take copies of a copyright work**

copyrighted [ˈkɒpɪraɪtɪd] adj. in copyright upphovsrättsskyddad

CORAL [ˈkɒr(ə)l] = COMMON REAL-TIME APPLICATIONS LANGUAGE computer programming language used in a real-time system programmeringsspråket Coral

cord [kɔːd] subst. wire used to connect a device to a socket sladd, kabel t.ex. nätkabel

cordless telephone [ˈkɔːdlɪs ˈtelɪfəʊn] subst. telephone which is not connected to a line by a cord, but which uses a radio link sladdlös telefon

core [kɔː] subst. (a) central conducting section of a cable kärna (b) **core memory** or **store** = (i) central memory of a computer kärnminne; (ii) non-volatile magnetic storage method used in old computers kärnminne; **core program** = computer program stored in core memory kärnminnesprogram

coresident [ˌkəʊˈrezɪd(ə)nt] adj. (two or more programs) stored in main memory at the same time samexisterande, samtidigt laddade

coroutine [ˌkəʊruːˈtiːn] *subst.* section of a program *or* procedure that can pass data and control to another coroutine then halt itself *process, delprogram, underrutin*

correct [kəˈrekt] **1** *adj.* accurate *or* right *riktig, rätt* **2** *vb.* to remove mistakes from something *korrigera, rätta;* **error correcting code =** coding system that allows bit errors occurring during transmission to be rapidly corrected by logical deduction methods rather than retransmission *felkorrigerande kod*

correction [kəˈrekʃ(ə)n] *subst.* making something correct *korrigering;* change which makes something correct *rättning*

corrective maintenance [kəˈrektɪv ˈmeɪntənəns] *subst.* actions to trace, find and repair a fault after it has occurred *felåtgärdande underhåll*

correspond [ˌkɒrɪsˈpɒnd] *vb.* **(a) to correspond with someone =** to write letters to someone *korrespondera med någon* **(b) to correspond with something =** to fit *or* to match something *överensstämma med något*

correspondence [ˌkɒrɪsˈpɒndəns] *subst.* **(a)** letters and messages sent from one person to another *korrespondens, brevväxling;* **business correspondence =** letters concerned with a business *affärskorrespondens;* **to be in correspondence with someone =** to write letters to someone and receive letters back *bevväxla med någon;* **correspondence print quality =** quality of print from a computer printer that is acceptable for business letters (that is daisy-wheel rather than dot-matrixprinting) *skönskrift* NOTE: no plural **(b)** way in which something fits in with something *överensstämmelse*

correspondent [ˌkɒrɪsˈpɒndənt] *subst.* **(a)** person who writes letters *brevskrivare* **(b)** journalist who writes articles for a newspaper on specialist subjects *korrespondent;* **the computer correspondent; the "Times" business correspondent; he is the Paris correspondent of the "Telegraph"**

corrupt [kəˈrʌpt] **1** *adj.* data *or* program that contains errors *förvrängd, förvanskad* **2** *vb.* to introduce errors into data *or* a program *förvränga, förvanska;* **power loss during disk access can corrupt the data**

corruption [kəˈrʌpʃ(ə)n] *subst.* **data corruption =** errors introduced into data, due to noise *or* faulty equipment *datadistortion;* **acoustic couplers suffer from data corruption more than the direct connect form of modem; data corruption on the disk has made one file unreadable**

coulomb [ˈkuːlɒm] *subst.* SI unit of electrical charge *enheten coulomb* (C)

COMMENT: a coulomb is measured as the amount of charge flowing in a conductor when one amp of current is present for one second

count [kaʊnt] *vb.* to make a total of a number of items *räkna*

counter [ˈkaʊntə] *subst.* (i) device which counts *räknare;* (ii) register *or* variable whose contents are increased *or* decreased by a set amount every time an action occurs *räknare;* **the loop will repeat itself until the counter reaches 100; the number of items changed are recorded with the counter; instruction *or* program counter =** register in a CPU that contains the location of the next instruction to be processed *programräknare, instruktionsräknare*

counter- [ˈkaʊntə] *prefix* against *mot-*

counterprogramming [ˈkaʊntə ˈprəʊɡræmɪŋ] *subst.* running a popular TV programme at the same time as another station is running a popular series, to try to steal viewers *planerad (avsiktlig) kanalkrock*

counting perforator [ˈkaʊntɪŋ ˈpɜːfəreɪtə] *subst.* paper tape punch, used in typesetting, that keeps a record of the characters, their widths, etc., to allow justification operations *hålremsstans*

couple [ˈkʌpl] *vb.* to join together *förbinda, koppla;* **the two systems are coupled together**

coupler [ˈkʌplə] *subst.* mechanical device used to connect three or more conductors *kopplingsenhet;* **acoustic coupler =** device that connects to a telephone handset, converting binary computer data into sound signals to allow it to be transmitted down a telephone line *akustiskt modem*

coverage [ˈkʌvərɪdʒ] *subst.* size of the potential audience capable of receiving a broadcast *täckning, bevakning;* **press coverage *or* media coverage =** reports about something in the newspapers *or* on TV, etc. *press/mediabevakning;* **the company had good media coverage for the launch of its new model**

CP [ˈsiːpiː] = CARD PUNCH

cpi [ˈsiːpiːaɪ] = CHARACTERS PER INCH

CPM [ˈsiːpiːem] = CRITICAL PATH METHOD

CP/M [ˈsiːpiːem] = CONTROL PROGRAM/MONITOR popular operating system for microcomputers *operativsystemet CP/M*

cps [ˈsiːpiːes] = CHARACTERS PER SECOND number of characters printed *or* processed every second *tecken per sekund*

CPU ['siːpiː'juː] = CENTRAL PROCESSING UNIT group of circuits which perform the basic functions of a computer made up of three parts, the control unit, the arithmetic and logic unit and the input/output unit *(central)processor;* **CPU cycle =** period of time taken to fetch and execute an instruction (usually a simple ADD instruction) used as a measure of computer speed *processorcykel;* **CPU elements =** main sections that make up a CPU, including ALU, control unit, I/O bus, memory and various registers *processorelement;* **CPU handshaking =** interfacing signals between a CPU and a peripheral *or* I/O device *styrsignaler mellan processor och kringutrustning;* **CPU time =** total period of time that a CPU is used to actually process instructions *processortid*

> COMMENT: in a file handling program CPU time might be minimal, since data retrieval (from disk) would account for a large part of the program run; in a mathematical program, the CPU time could be much higher in proportion to the total run time

CR ['siːˈɑː] = CARRIAGE RETURN, CARD READER

crash [kræʃ] **1** *subst.* failure of a component *or* a bug in a program during a run, which halts and prevents further use of the system *stopp, krasch;* **disk crash =** fault caused by the read/write head touching the surface of the disk *skivkrasch* **2** *vb. (of a computer or program)* to come to a sudden stop *stoppa, krascha;* **the disk head has crashed and the data may have been lost**

> COMMENT: it is sometimes possible to recover data from a crashed hard disk before reformatting, if the crash was caused by a bad sector on the disk rather than contact between the r/w head and disk surface

crash-protected ['kræʃprəˈtektɪd] *adj.* (disk) which uses a head protection *or* data corruption protection system *kraschskyddad;* **if the disk is crash-protected, you will never lose your data**

crawl [krɔːl] *subst.* mechanical device that moves television *or* film titles down in front of a camera, to give the impression that they are moving up the screen *textrullningsmaskin*

CRC ['siːɑːˈsiː] = CAMERA-READY COPY, CYCLIC REDUNDANCY CHECK

create [krɪˈeɪt] *vb.* to make *skapa;* **a new file was created on disk to store the document; move to the CREATE NEW FILE instruction on the menu**

credit ['kredɪt] *subst.* **(a)** time given to a customer before he has to pay *kredit,* *kredittid;* **they have asked for six months' credit; credit card =** plastic card which allows the owner to borrow money and buy goods without paying for them immediately *kreditkort* **(b)** money received and placed in an account *or* in the balance sheet *kredit* **(c) credits =** text at the end of a film, giving the names of the actors *or* technical staff *eftertext*

crew [kruː] *subst.* group of technical staff who work together (as on filming a TV programme, recording an outside broadcast, etc.) *bemanning, lag, team;* **camera crew =** group of people who man a TV camera *kameralag;* **the camera crew had to film all day in the snow**

crippled leapfrog test ['krɪpld 'liːpfrɒg 'test] *subst.* standard leapfrog test that uses a single memory location rather than a changing location *minnescelltest*

criterion [kraɪˈtɪərɪən] *subst.* specification that has to be met *kriterium, villkor, kännemärke*
NOTE: plural is **criteria**

critical ['krɪtɪk(ə)l] *subst.* **critical fusion frequency** the rate of display of frames of graphics *or* text that makes them appear continuous *kritisk lägsta frekvens för rörliga bilder;* **critical path analysis =** the definition of tasks *or* jobs and the time each requires arranged in order to achieve certain goals *kritisk linjeanalys* NOTE: also called PERT (Program Evaluation and Review Techniques) **critical path method (CPM) =** use of analysis and projection of each critical step in a large project to help a management team *kritisk linjemetod (CPM);* **critical resource =** resource that can only be used by one process at a time *kritisk resurs*

CR/LF ['siːɑːreɪˈef] = CARRIAGE RETURN/LINE FEED

cropping ['krɒpɪŋ] *subst.* removal of areas of artwork *or* of a photograph which are not needed *beskärning;* **the photographs can be edited by cropping, sizing, touching up, etc.**

cross- [krɒs] *prefix* running from one side to another *kors-;* **cross fade =** to fade out one signal while bringing in another *balansering av mottagna radiosignaler ur fas;* **cross modulation =** two *or* more modulated signals on one channel interfering with each other *korsmodulation*

cross-assembler ['krɒs əˈsemblə] *subst.* assembler that produces machine-code code for one computer whilst running on another *korsassemblerare*

cross-check ['krɒsˈtʃek] *subst.* validation of an answer by using a different method of calculation *korsvis kontroll, dubbel kontroll*

cross-compiler [ˈkrɒskəmˈpaɪlə] assembler *or* compiler that compiles programs for one computer whilst running on another *korskompilator*

COMMENT: cross-compilers and assemblers are used to compile programs for micros, but are run on larger computers to make the operation faster

crossfire [ˈkrɒsfaɪə] *subst. see* CROSSTALK

crossover [ˈkrɒsˌəʊvə] *subst.* change from one system to another *övergång;* **the crossover to computerized file indexing was difficult**

cross-reference [ˈkrɒsˈref(ə)r(ə)ns] **1** *subst.* reference in a document to another part of the document *korsreferens, korshänvisning* **2** *vb.* to make a reference to another part of the document *korsreferera, korshänvisa;* **the SI units are cross-referenced to the appendix**

cross-reference generator [ˈkrɒsˈref(ə)r(ə)ns ˈdʒenəreɪtə] *subst.* section of an assembler *or* compiler *or* interpreter that provides a list of program labels, variables *or* constants with their location within the program *korsreferensgenerator*

cross-section [ˈkrɒsˈsekʃ(ə)n] *subst.* view of a material *or* object cut across its centre *genomskärning;* **the cross-section of the optical fibre showed the problem**

crosstalk [ˈkrɒstɔːk] *subst.* interference in one channel due to another nearby channel *or* signal (caused by badly isolated signals) *överhörning;* **the crosstalk was so bad, the signal was unreadable**

CRT [ˈsiːɑːˈtiː] = CATHODE RAY TUBE device used for displaying characters *or* figures *or* graphical information, similar to a TV set *katodstrålerör*

COMMENT: cathode ray tubes are used in television sets, computer monitors and VDUs; a CRT consists of a vacuum tube, one end of which is flat and coated with phosphor, the other end containing an electron beam source. Characters *or* graphics are visible when the controllable electron beam strikes the phosphor causing it to glow

cruncher [ˈkrʌn(t)ʃə] *or* **crunching** [ˈkrʌn(t)ʃɪŋ] *see* NUMBER

crushing [ˈkrʌʃɪŋ] *subst.* reduced contrast range on a TV image due to a fault *kontrastförlust*

cryogenic memory [ˈkraɪəʊˈdʒenɪk ˈmemərɪ] *subst.* storage medium operating at very low temperatures (4°K) to use the superconductive properties of a material *kryogent minne, supraledande minne*

cryptanalysis [ˌkrɪptəˈnæləsɪs] *subst.* study and methods of breaking ciphers *kryptoanalys, krypteringsanalys, chifferanalys*

cryptographic [ˌkrɪptəˈgræfɪk] *adj.* referring to cryptography *kryptografisk;* **cryptographic algorithm** = rules used to encipher and decipher data *chifferalgoritm, chiffreringsalgoritm;* **cryptographic key** = number *or* code that is used with a cipher algorithm to personalize the encryption and decryption of data *chiffernyckel*

cryptography [krɪpˈtɒgrəfɪ] *subst.* study of encryption and decryption methods and techniques *kryptografi, chifferteknik*

crystal [ˈkrɪstl] *subst.* small slice of quartz crystal which vibrates at a certain frequency, used as a very accurate clock signal for computer *or* other high precision timing applications *kristall;* **liquid crystal display (LCD)** = liquid crystals, that turn black when a voltage is applied, used in many watch, calculator and digital displays *bildskärm (teckenfönster) med flytande kristaller;* **crystal microphone** = microphone that uses a piece of piezo electric crystal which produces a signal when sound waves distort it *kristallmikrofon;* **crystal oscillator** = small piece of crystal that resonates at a certain frequency when a voltage is applied across it; this can be used as a high precision clock *kristalloscillator*

CSDC [ˈsiːesdiːˈsiː] = CIRCUIT SWITCHED DIGITAL CIRCUITRY

CSM [ˈsiːesˈem] = COMBINED SYMBOL MATCHING efficient optical character recognition system *matrismatchningsmetoden för optisk teckenläsning*

CSMA-CD [ˈsiːesemˈeɪˈsiːˈdiː] = CARRIER SENSE MULTIPLE ACCESS-COLLISION DETECTION

CTR *or* **CTRL** [kənˈtrəʊl] = CONTROL control key *or* key on a computer terminal that sends a control character to the computer when pressed *styr(tangent), kontroll(tangent)*

CTS [ˈsiːtiːˈes] = CLEAR TO SEND RS232C signal that a line *or* device is ready for data transmission *CTS-signal, klar att sända, "datakanal klar"*

CU [ˈsiːˈjuː] = CONTROL UNIT

cue [kjuː] *subst.* prompt *or* message displayed on a screen to remind the user that an input is expected *inmatningssignal*

CUG ['si:ju:'dʒi:] = CLOSED USER GROUP to restrict the entry to a database *or* bulletin board system (on a certain topic *or* subject) to certain known and registered users usually by means of a password *sluten användargrupp*

cumulative index ['kju:mjʊlətɪv 'ɪndeks] *subst.* index made up from several different indexes *samlingsregister*

current ['kʌr(ə)nt] **1** *adj.* referring to the present time *löpande, nuvarande, innevarande;* **current address** = address being used (accessed) at this time *löpande adress, nuvarande adress;* **current address register (CAR)** = CPU register that stores the address that is currently being accessed *aktivt (aktuellt) adressregister;* **current instruction register (CIR)** = CPU register that stores the instruction that is currently being executed *aktivt (aktuellt) instruktionsregister* **2** *subst.* movement of charge-carrying particles in a conductor *ström;* **direct current (DC)** = constant value electrical current supply that flows in one direction *likström;* **alternating current (AC)** = electrical current whose value varies with time in a regular sinusoidal way (changing direction of flow each half cycle) *växelström*

> COMMENT: mains electricity provides a 240v AC supply at 50Hz in the U.K. and 110v at 60Hz in the USA

cursor ['kɜ:sə] *subst.* marker on a display device which shows where the next character will appear *markör;* **cursor control keys** = keys on a keyboard that allow the cursor to be moved in different directions *markörflyttningstangenter;* **cursor home** = movement of the cursor to the top left hand corner of the screen *viloläge för markör;* **cursor pad** = group of cursor control keys *"pil-tangenter";* **addressable cursor** = cursor whose position on the screen can be defined by a program *adresserbar markör*

> COMMENT: cursors can take several forms, such as a square of bright light, a bright underline or a flashing light

> QUOTE above the cursor pad are the insert and delete keys, which when shifted produce clear and home respectively
> **Computing Today**
> QUOTE further quick cursor movements are available for editing by combining one of the arrow keys with the control function
> **Personal Computer World**

custom-built ['kʌstəmbɪlt] *adj.* made specially for one customer *specialbyggd, specialtillverkad*

customer ['kʌstəmə] *subst.* person who buys *or* uses a computer system *or* any peripherals *kund;* **customer engineering** =

maintenance and repair of a customer's equipment *kundunderhåll;* **customer service department** = department which deals with customers and their complaints and orders *kundserviceavdelning*

customize ['kʌstəmaɪz] *vb.* to modify a system to the customer's requirements *kundanpassa, specialanpassa;* **we used customized computer terminals**

custom ROM (PROM) ['kʌstəm 'rɒm ('prɒm)] *subst.* ROM produced (usually in small numbers) by a manufacturer to suit a customer's requirements *kundanpassat läsminne*

cut [kʌt] **1** *subst.* removing a piece from a file *or* text *klipp;* piece removed from a file *or* text *urklipp;* **the editors have asked for cuts in the first chapter 2** *vb.* **(a)** to divide something into parts, using scissors *or* knife *or*guillotine *klippa;* **cut in notes** = printed notes in the outer edge of a paragraph of a page *infällningsnotering;* **cut sheet feeder** mechanism that automatically feeds single sheets of paper into a printer *arkmatare* **(b)** to remove pieces of text *or* file to make it shorter *klippa, redigera;* **the author was asked to cut his manuscript to 250 pages** NOTE: NOTE: **cuts - cutting - has cut**

cut and paste ['kʌtənd'peɪst] *subst.* action of taking pieces of text from one point and inserting them at another (often used in dtp packages for easy page editing) *klippa-klistra*

cutoff ['kʌtɒf] *subst.* point at which (something) stops *stopp, stoppunkt;* **cutoff frequency** = frequency at which the response of a device drops off *gränsfrekvens*

cut off [kʌt 'ɒf] *vb.* **(a)** to remove part of something *skära av;* **six metres of paper were cut off the reel (b)** to stop something flowing *stänga av;* **the electricity supply was cut off**

cutting ['kʌtɪŋ] *subst.* action of cutting *klippning;* **cutting room** = room in a film studio where the unedited film is cut and joined together *klipprum;* **press cuttings** = pieces cut from newspapers *or* magazines which refer to someone*or* to a company *pressklipp*

CWP ['si:dʌblju:'pi:] = COMMUNICATING WORD PROCESSOR

cybernetics [,saɪbə'netɪks] *subst.* study of the mechanics of human *or* electronic machine movements, and the way in which electronic devices can be made to work and imitate human actions *cybernetik*

cycle ['saɪkl] **1** *subst.* (i) period of time when something leaves its original position and then returns to it *cykelperiod;* (ii) one completed operation in a repeated process *cykel;* **action cycle** = all the steps required to carry out a process *or* operation on data, (such as reading, processing, output and storage) *operationscykel, processcykel;* **clock cycle** = period of time between two consecutive clock pulses *klockcykel;* **cycle availability** = period of time in a cycle, during which data can be accessed *or* transmitted *tillgänglighetstid;* **cycle count** = number of times a cycle has been repeated *varvräkning;* **cycle index** = number of times a series of instructions have been *or* have to be repeated *indexregister, varvräknare;* **cycle shift** = to shift a pattern of bits within a word, with the bit(s) that are shifted off the end being inserted at the beginning of the word *(logisk) rundskrift;* **cycle stealing** = memory access operation by a peripheral that halts a CPU for one *or* more clock cycles whilst data is being transferred from memory to the device *"stöld av klockcykler", (klock)cykelstöld;* **cycle time** = time between start and stop of an operation, especially between addressing a memory location and receiving the data, and then ending the operation *cykeltid; compare* ADDRESS TIME **2** *vb.* to repeat an operation *or* series of instructions until instructed to stop *repetera, iterera*

cyclic ['saɪklɪk] *adj.* (operation) that is repeated regularly *regelbundet återkommande, cyklisk;* **cyclic access** = access to stored information that can only occur at a certain point in a cycle *regelbunden åtkomst;* **cyclic check** = error detection method that uses *or* examines a bit of data every n bits (one bit examined then n bits transmitted, then another bit examined, etc.) *cyklisk kontroll;* **cyclic code** *see* GRAY CODE; **cyclic decimal code** = cyclic code that refers to decimal digits *cyklisk decimalkod;* **cyclic redundancy check (CRC)** = error detection code for transmitted data *cyklisk överflödskontroll, cyklisk felövervakning;* **cyclic shift** = rotation of bits in a word with the previous last bit inserted in the first bit position *(logiskt) rundskift*

"cykelstöld" ⇨ DMA, cycle

cykeltid ⇨ execution

cylinder ['sɪlɪndə] *subst.* the tracks in a multi-disk device that can be accessed without moving the read/write head *cylinder*

cypher ['saɪfə] = CIPHER

Dd

D [diː] hexadecimal figure equivalent to decimal number 13 *talet tretton skrivet med hexadecimal notation*

3D [ˌθriːˈdiː] = THREE-DIMENSIONAL

QUOTE the software can create 3D images using data from a scanner or photographs from an electronic microscope
PC Business World

DAC ['diːeɪsiː] *or* **d/a converter** = DIGITAL TO ANALOG CONVERTER circuit that outputs an analog number that is proportional to the input digital signal, and so converts a digital input to an analog form *digitalanalogomvandlare;* **speech is output from the computer via a D/A converter; the D/A converter on the output port controls the analog machine**

COMMENT: a d/a converter allows the computer to work outside the computer environment, by driving a machine, imitating speech, etc.

DAD [dæd] = DIGITAL AUDIO DISK method of recording sound by converting and storing signals in a digital form on magnetic disk *magnetisk skiva för digital ljudlagring*

dagger ['dægə] *subst.* printing sign (†) used to mark a special word *kors, specialtecken i tryck;* **double dagger** = printing sign (‡) used to give a second reference level *dubbelt kors (som anger andra nivån av noter, hänvisningar)*

dagordning ⇨ agenda

daisy chain ['deɪzɪtʃeɪn] *subst.* method of connecting equipment with a single cable passing from one machine *or* device to the next (rather than separate cables to each device) *kedjekoppling;* **daisy chain bus** = communications bus that joins one device to the next, each device being able to receive *or* transmit *or* modify data as it passes through to the next device in line *kedjebuss;* **daisy chain interrupt** = line joining all the interrupt outputs of a number of devices to a CPU *kedjekopplad avbrottssignal;* **daisy chain recursion** = subroutines in a program that call another in the series, (the first routine calls the second routine which calls the third routine, etc.) *kedjekopplade subrutiner*

daisy-chain ['deɪzɪtʃeɪn] *vb.* to connect equipment using the daisy chain method *kedjekoppla*

QUOTE you can often daisy-chain cards or plug them into expansion boxes
Byte

daisy-wheel ['deɪzɪwiːl] *subst.* wheel-shaped printing head, with characters on the end of spokes, used in a serial printer *typhjul;* **daisy-wheel printer** *or* **daisy-wheel**

typewriter = serial character printer *or* typewriter with characters arranged on interchangeable wheels *typhjulsskrivare;* **a daisy-wheel printer produces much better quality text than a dot-matrix, but is slower**

DAMA ['diːeɪemˈeɪ] = DEMAND ASSIGNED MULTIPLE ACCESS

damage ['dæmɪdʒ] **1** *subst.* harm done to things *orsaka skada;* **to suffer damage** = to be harmed *lida skada;* **to cause damage** = to harm something *orsaka skada;* **the breakdown of the electricity supply caused damage estimated at £100,000** NOTE: no plural **2** *vb.* to harm *skada;* **the faulty read/write head appears to have damaged the disks; the hard disk was damaged when it was dropped**

damaged ['dæmɪdʒd] *adj.* which has suffered damage *or* which has been harmed *skadad;* **is it possible to repair the damaged files?**

dark current ['daːk 'kʌr(ə)nt] *subst.* amount of electrical current that flows in an optoelectrical device when there is no light falling on it *mörkerström, viloström*

darkroom ['daːkrʊm] *subst.* special room with no light, where photographic film can be developed *mörkrum*

dark trace tube ['daːktreɪs'tjuːb] *subst.* CRT with a dark image on a bright background *svart-på-vit-(bild)skärm*

DASD ['diːeɪesˈdiː] = DIRECT ACCESS STORAGE DEVICE storage medium whose memory locations can be directly read *or* written to *direktminne*

dash [dæʃ] *subst.* short line in printing *kort streck;* **em dash** *or* **em rule** = line as long as an em, used to separate one section of text from another *tankstreck, "pratminus";* **en dash** *or* **en rule** = line as long as an en, used to link two words or parts of words *bindestreck*

DAT [dæt] = DIGITAL AUDIO TAPE method of recording sound by converting and storing signals in a digital form on magnetic tape *digitalt ljudband, digital ljudlagring på band;* **DAT produces a very high quality sound**

data ['deɪtə] *subst.* collection of facts made up of numbers, characters and symbols, stored on a computer in such a way that it can be processed by the computer *data;* **programs act upon data files; data is input at one of several workstations; the company stores data on customers in its main computer file; a user needs a password to access data; raw data** = (i) pieces of information which have not been input into a computer system *rådata;* (ii) data (in a databank) which has to be processed to provide information to the

user *rådata;* (iii) unprocessed data *rådata;* **data above voice (DAV)** = data transmission in a frequency range above that of the human voice *frekvensdelad linje (med överlagrad datatrafik);* **data access management** = regulating the users who can access stored data *åtkomstadministration;* **data acquisition** = gathering data about a subject *datainsamling, datainmatning, datafångst;* **data adapter unit** = device that interfaces a CPU to one or more communications channels *anpassningsenhet;* **data administrator** = control section of a database management system *(data)administrationsprogram-(modul);* **data aggregate** = collection of items of data that are related *datamängd;* **data analysis** = extracting information and results from data *dataanalys;* **data area** = amount of storage space that contains data (rather than instructions) *dataarea;* **databank** = collection of data (usually on one theme) *databas;* **data block** = all the data required for *or* from a process *datablock;* **data break** = memory access operation by a peripheral that halts a CPU for one or more cycles whilst data is being transferred from memory to the device *dataavbrott;* **data buffer** = temporary storage location for data received by a device that is not yet ready to accept it *databuffert;* **data bus** = bus carrying the data between a CPU and memory and peripheral devices *databuss;* **data capture** = act of obtaining data (either by keyboarding or by scanning, or often automatically from a recording device *or* peripheral) *datafångst;* **data carrier** = (i) any device *or* medium capable of storing data *datalagringsmedium;* (ii) a waveform used as a carrier for data signals *databärvåg;* **data carrier detect (DCD)** = RS232C signal from a modem to a computer indicating a carrier wave is being received *DCD-signal, bärvågssignal;* **the call is stopped if the software does not receive a DCD signal from the modem; data cartridge** = cartridge that contains stored data *datapatron;* **data chaining** = one stored record that holds the address of the next in the list *(data)kedja, (data)länk;* **data channel** = communication link able to carry data signals *datakanal;* **data check** = error in reading data due to a fault with the magnetic medium *datafel, skivminnesfel;* **data circuit** = circuit which allows bi-directional data communications *dubbelriktad dataöverföring;* **data cleaning** = removing errors from data *datakontroll, dataadministration;* **data collection** = act of receiving data from various sources (either directly from a data capture device *or* from a cartridge) and inserting correctly in order into a database *datainsamling, datafångst;* **data collection platform** = station that transmits collected data to a central point (usually via satellite) *koncentratorcentral;*

data communications = transmission and reception of data rather than speech *or* images *datakommunikation;* **data communications buffer** = buffer on a receiver that allows a slow peripheral to accept data from a fast computer, without slowing either down *kommunikationsbuffert;* **data communications equipment (DCE)** = equipment (such as a modem) which receives *or* transmits data *datakommunikationsutrustning;* **data communications network** = number of computers, terminals, operators and storage units connected together to allow data transmission between devices *or* files *or* users *datanät;* **data compacting** = reducing the space taken by data by coding it in a more efficient way *datakompression;* **all the files were stored on one disk with this new data compacting routine;** **data compression** = means of reducing size of data by removing spaces, empty sections and unused material from the blocks of data *data(volym)reduktion;* **scanners use a technique called data compression which manages to reduce, even by a third, the storage required; data concentrator** = data which combines intermittent data from various lines and sends it along a single line in one go *koncentrator;* **data connection** = link which joins two devices and allows data transmission *datakommunikationslänk;* **data control** = data management to and from a database *or* processing system *datastyrning;* **data corruption** = errors introduced into data due to noise *or* faulty equipment *dataförvanskning;* **data corruption occurs each time the motor is switched on; data delimiter** = special symbol *or* character that marks the end of a file *or* data item *begränsningstecken;* **data description language (DDL)** = part of database system software which describes the structure of the system and data *strukturbeskrivningsspråk;* **data dictionary/directory (DD/D)** = software which gives a list of types and forms of data contained in a database *datakatalog;* **data division** = part of a (COBOL) program giving full definitions of the data types and structures *databeskrivningsdel i programmeringsspråket Cobol;* **data-driven** = (computer architecture) in which instructions are executed, once the relevant data has been received *datastyrd körning;* **data element** *see* DATA ITEM; **data element chain** = more than one data element treated as a single element *datakedja, kopplade data;* **data encryption** = encrypting data using a cipher system *datakryptering;* **data encryption standard (DES)** = standard for a block data cipher system *en kryptostandard som används av amerikanska statsförvaltningen;* **data entry** = method of entering data into a system

(usually using a keyboard but also direct from disks after data preparation) *datainmatning;* **data error** = error due to incorrect *or* illegal data *datafel;* **data field** = part of a computer instruction that contains the location of the data *datafält;* **data file** = file with data in it (as opposed to a program file) *datafil;* **the data file has to be analysed; data flow** = movement of data through a system *dataflöde;* **data flowchart** = diagram used to describe a computer *or* data processing system *flödesdiagram;* **the data flowchart allowed us to improve throughput, by using a better structure; data flow diagram (DFD)** = diagram used to describe the movement of data through a system *flödesdiagram;* **data format** = rules defining the way in which data is stored *or* transmitted *dataformat;* **data hierarchy** = data structure organized hierarchically *hierarkisk datastruktur;* **data highway** = bus carrying data signals between a CPU and peripherals *(data)buss; see also* BUS; **data independence** = structure of a database which can be changed without affecting what the user sees *dataoberoende;* **data input** = data transferred into a computer (from an I/O port or peripheral) *indata;* **data input bus (DIB)** = bus used when transferring data from one section of a computer to another, such as between memory and CPU *indatabuss;* **data integrity** = protection of data against damage *or* errors *dataintegritet;* **data in voice (DIV)** = digital data transmission in place of a voice channel *datatrafik på vanlig telefonförbindelse;* **data item** = one unit of data such as the quantity of items in stock, a person's name, age or occupation *dataelement;* **data level** = position of a data item within a database structure *(data)nivå;* **data link** = connection between two devices to allow the transmission of data *(data)länk, dataförbindelse;* **data link control** = protocol and rules used to define the way in which data is transmitted *or* received *datakommunikationsprotokoll;* **data link layer** = one layer in the ISO/OSI defined network that sends packets of data to the next link and deals with error correction *länkskiktet i kommunikationsstandarden OSI;* **data logging** = automatic data collection *(data)loggning, automatisk datainsamling;* **data management** = maintenance and upkeep of a database *databasadministration;* **data manipulation language (DML)** = database software that allows the user to access, store and change data *datahanteringsspråk;* **data medium** = medium which allows data to be stored *or* displayed (such as a VDU *or* magnetic disk *or* screen) *lagringsmedium, "visningsmedium";* **data migration** = data transfer (by a user's instruction) from an on-line device to an off-line device *dataflyttning;* **data name** = group of characters used to identify one item of data *fältnamn, postnamn;* **problems occur if an ambiguous data name is chosen; data network =** networking system which transmits data *datanät;* **data origination =** conversion of data from its original form to one which can be read by a computer *datakonvertering;* **data path =** bus *or* connections over which data is transmitted *dataväg;* **data pointer =** register containing the location of the next item of data *pekare;* **data preparation =** conversion of data into a machine-readable form (usually by keyboarding) before data entry *datakonvertering (stansning);* **data processing (DP** *or* **dp) =** selecting and operating on data to produce useful information *databehandling;* sorting *or* organizing data files *databehandling, datahantering;* **data processing manager =** person who runs a computer department *datachef;* **data protection =** means of making sure that data is private and secure *(logisk) datasäkerhet;* **data rate =** maximum rate at which data is processed *or* transmitted in a synchronous system, usually equal to the system clock rate *datahastighet;* **data record =** one record containing data for use with a program *datafält, datapost;* **data reduction =** production of compact, useful data from raw data *datareduktion;* **data register =** area within a CPU used to store data temporarily before it is processed *(data)register;* **data reliability =** measure of the number of data words with errors compared to the total number of words *datatillförlitlighet;* **data retrieval =** process of searching, selecting and reading data from a stored file *dataåtkomst, datahämtning;* **data routing =** defining the path to be taken by a message in a network *vägval;* **data security =** protection of data against corruption *or* unauthorized users *datasäkerhet;* **data services =** public services (such as the telephone system) which allow data to be transmitted *allmänna datakommunikationsnät och - tjänster;* **data set ready (DSR) =** signal from a device that is ready to accept data, this signal occurs after a DTR signal is received *redosignal, DSR-signal, modem klart;* **data signals =** electrical *or* optical pulses *or* waveforms that represent binary data *datasignaler;* **data signalling rate =** total amount of data that is transmitted through a system per second *dataöverföringshastighet;* **data sink =** device in a data terminal which receives data *mottagningsbuffert;* **data source =** device in a data terminal which sends data *datakälla;* **data station =** point that contains a data terminal and a data circuit *terminal;* **data storage =** medium able to store large quantities of data *datalagringsmedium; see also* BACKING STORE; **data stream =** data transmitted

serially one bit *or* character at a time *dataström, seriellt dataflöde;* **data strobe =** signal (in the control bus) that indicates that valid data is on the data bus *datapuls;* **data structure =** number of related items that are treated as one by the computer (in an address book record, the name, address and telephone number form separate entries which would be processed as one by the computer) *datastruktur;* **data switching exchange =** device used to direct and switch data between lines *dataväxel;* **data tablet** *see* GRAPHICS TABLET; **data terminal =** device that is able to display and transmit *or* receive data *(data)terminal;* **a printer is a data terminal for computer output; data terminal equipment (DTE) =** device at which a communications path starts *or* finishes *terminal(utrustning);* **data terminal ready (DTR) =** signal from a device that indicates that it is ready to send data *klarsignal, DTR-signal, "dataterminal klar";* **data transaction =** one complete operation on data *transaktion;* **data transfer rate =** rate at which data is moved from one point to another *överföringshastighet;* **data translation =** conversion of data from one system format to another *datakonvertering;* **data transmission =** process of sending data from one location to another over a data link *dataöverföring;* **data type =** sort of data which can be stored in a register (such as string, number, etc.) *datatyp;* **data validation =** process of checking data for errors and relevance in a situation *datavalidering;* **data vetting =** process of checking data as it is input for errors and validity *indatakontroll;* **data word =** piece of data stored as a single word *ord;* **data word length =** number of bits that make up a word in a computer *ordlängd;* **master data =** reference data which is stored in a master file *originaldata, referensdata;* **optical data link =** connection between two devices to allow the transmission of data using light (either line-of-sight or using fibre optics) *optisk länk;* **variable data =** data which can be modified, and is not write protected *variabel, variabla data*

COMMENT: Data is different from information in that it is facts stored in machine-readable form. When the facts are processed by the computer into a form which can be understood by people, the data becomes information

QUOTE data compression is the art of squeezing more and more information into fewer and fewer bytes
Practical Computing

databank ['deɪtəbæŋk] *subst.* (i) large amount of data stored in a structured form *databas;* (ii) personal records stored in a computer *databank*

databas ⇨ **data, database, databank**

> dataförbindelse ⇨ data link

databasdator ⇨ database

database ['deɪtəbeɪs] *subst.* integrated collection of files of data stored in a structured form in a large memory, which can be accessed by one or more users at different terminals *databas;* **database administrator (DBA)** = person in charge of running and maintaining a database system *databasadministratör;* **database language** = series of languages, such as data description language, that make up a database management system *databashanteringsspråk;* **database machine** = hardware and software combination designed for the rapid processing of database information *databasdator;* **database management system (DBMS)** *or* **database manager** = series of programs that allow the user to create and modify databases easily *databashanteringssystem, databashanterare;* **database mapping** = description of the way in which the records and fields in a database are related *strukturbeskrivning;* **database schema** = way in which a database is organized and structured *databasstruktur;* **database system** = series of programs that allows the user to create, modify, manage and use a database (often includes features such as a report writer *or* graphical output of data) *databashanteringssystem;* **on-line database** = interactive search, retrieve and update of database records using an on-line terminal *direktansluten databas*

QUOTE a database is a file of individual records of information which are stored in some kind of sequential order
Which PC?

databashanterare ⇨ database, DBMS

databashanteringssystem ⇨ database, DBMS

databasstruktur ⇨ database

databehandling ⇨ data

(data)buss ⇨ data

datadistortion ⇨ corruption

dataelement ⇨ data

datafel ⇨ data

datafil ⇨ file

dataflyttning ⇨ data

dataflöde ⇨ flow, throughput

dataflödesarkitektur ⇨ multiple

dataflödesdiagram ⇨ flowchart

dataformat ⇨ format

datafångst ⇨ capture, data

datafält ⇨ field

datagram ['deɪtəgræm] *subst.* packet of information in a packet switching system that contains its destination address and route *datapaket*

datagrupp ⇨ group

datahämtning ⇨ data

datainmatning ⇨ data, input (i/p *or* I/P)

datainsamling ⇨ acquisition, data

datakanal ⇨ highway

datakatalog ⇨ DD/D

datakompression ⇨ data

datakonvertering ⇨ data

datakälla ⇨ data

datalagring ⇨ information

datalagringsmedium ⇨ data

dataline ['deɪtəlaɪn] *subst.* one line of broadcast TV signal that contains the teletext signals and data (usually transmitted at the start of the image and identified with a special code) *videotexsignal, texttevesignal*

datamedium ⇨ carrier

dataminnesregister ⇨ memory

datamängd ⇨ aggregate, data

(data)nivå ⇨ data

datanät ⇨ data, network

dataomvandlare ⇨ encoder

datapaket ⇨ datagram, packet

(data)paketförmedlande nät ⇨ packet

datapapper ⇨ listing

datapatron ⇨ data

dataplex ['deɪtəpleks] *subst.* multiplexing of data signals *multiplexering*

datapuls ⇨ data

dataset ['deɪtəset] *subst.* US modem *modem;* **dataset ready (DSR)** = RS232C signal from a modem to a computer indicating it is ready for use *klarsignal, DSR-signal, "modem klart"*

dataslutssignal ⇨ end

dataspill ⇨ overrun

datastyrning ⇨ data

datasäkerhet ⇨ data

datatillförlitlighet ⇨ data

datatyp ⇨ data

datavirus ⇨ logic

data(volym)reduktion ⇨ data

dataväg ⇨ data

dataväxel ⇨ data

dataåtkomst ⇨ data

dataöverföring ⇨ data, electronic

dataöverföring på tallinje ⇨ in-band signalling

dataöverföringshastighet ⇨ data

date [deɪt] **1** *subst.* **(a)** number of day, month and year *datum;* **I have received your message of yesterday's date; the date of creation for the file was the 10th of June (b) up to date** = current *or* recent *or* modern *modern;* **an up-to-date computer system; to bring something up to date** = to add the latest information to something *uppdatera något;* **to keep something up to date** = to keep adding information to something so that it is always up to date *aktualisera något, hålla något aktualiserat;* **we spend a lot of time keeping our files up to date (c) out of date** = old-fashioned *föråldrad;* **their computer system is years out of date; they are still using out-of-date equipment 2** *vb.* to put a date on a document *datera*

dator ⇨ computer

datorgrafik ⇨ computer

datorisera ⇨ computerize

datorisering ⇨ computerization

datormognad ⇨ literacy

datorstödd ⇨ computer-aided

datorstödd konstruktion ⇨ CAD

datorstödd tillverkning ⇨ CAM

datorsäkerhet ⇨ hardware

daughter board ['dɔːtə,bɔːd] *subst.* add-on board that connects to a system mother board *instickskort*

DAV ['diːeɪviː] = DATA ABOVE VOICE

db ['diːbiː] *see* DECIBEL

DBA ['diːbiːeɪ] = DATABASE ADMINISTRATOR person in charge of running and maintaining a database system *data(bas)chef*

DBMS ['diːbiːemes] = DATABASE MANAGEMENT SYSTEM series of programs that allow the user to create and modify databases *databashanteringssystem, databashanterare*

DC ['diːsiː] = DIRECT CURRENT; **DC signalling** = method of communications

using pulses of current over a wire circuit, like a telegraph system *likströmssignalering*

DCD ['diːsiːdiː] = DATA CARRIER DETECT RS232C signal from a modem to a computer indicating a carrier is being received *bärvägsindikering, DCD-signal*

DCE ['diːsiːiː] = DATA COMMUNICATIONS EQUIPMENT

DD ['diːdiː] = DOUBLE DENSITY

DDC ['diːdiːsiː] = DIRECT DIGITAL CONTROL machine operated automatically by machine *direkt datorstyrning*

DD/M ['diːdiːem] = DATA DICTIONARY/DIRECTORY software which gives a list of types and forms of data contained in a database *datakatalog*

DDE ['diːdiːiː] = DIRECT DATA ENTRY keying in data directly onto magnetic tape *or* disk *direkt datainmatning*

DDL ['diːdiːel] = DATA DESCRIPTION LANGUAGE *strukturbeskrivningsspråk;* **many of DDL's advantages come from the fact that it is a second generation language**

DDP ['diːdiːpiː] = DISTRIBUTED DATA PROCESSING operations to derive information from data which is kept in different places *distribuerad databehandling*

dead [ded] *adj.* **(a)** not working *ur funktion;* (computer *or* piece of equipment) that does not function *ur funktion;* **dead halt** *or* **drop dead halt** = program instruction from the user *or* an error, that causes the program to stop without allowing recovery *systemavbrott;* **the manual does not say what to do if a dead halt occurs; dead keys** = keys on a keyboard that cause a function rather than a character to occur, such as the shift key *funktionstangenter, specialtangenter;* **dead matter** = type that has been used for printing and is no longer required *avläggningssats, dödmetall;* **dead time** = period of time between two events, in which nothing happens, to ensure that they do not interfere with each other *dödtid;* **efficient job management minimises dead time (b)** (room *or* space) that has no acoustical reverberation *tyst (ekofritt) rum*

deaden ['dedn] *vb.* to make a sound *or* colour less sharp *dämpa;* **acoustic hoods are used to deaden the noise of printers**

deadline ['dedlaɪn] *subst.* date by which something has to be done *gräns, sista tidpunkt;* **to meet a deadline** = to finish something in time *hålla en utlovad tid, hålla tidsplanen;* **we've missed our October 1st deadline**

deadlock ['dedlɒk] *subst.* situation when two users want to access two resources at the same time, one resource is assigned to each user but neither can use the other *systemlåsning*

deadly embrace ['dedlı ım'breıs] *subst.* = DEADLOCK

deaktivera avbrott ⇨ interrupt

deal [diːl] **1** *subst.* business agreement *or* contract *avtal;* **package deal** = agreement where several different items are agreed at the same time *avtalspaket;* **they agreed a package deal, which involves the development of software, customizing hardware and training of staff 2** *vb.* to deal with = to organize *behandla, ta itu med;* **leave it to the DP manager - he'll deal with it**

dealer ['diːlə] *subst.* person who buys and sells *återförsäljare;* **always buy hardware from a recognized dealer**

deallocate ['diːˈælə(ʊ)keɪt] *vb.* to free resources previously allocated to a job *or* process *or* peripheral *frigöra, friställa;* **when a reset button is pressed all resources are deallocated**

debit ['debɪt] *subst.* bit transmission rate that is twice the baud rate *dubbel överföringshastighet*

deblock ['diːblɒk] *vb.* to return a stored block of data to its original form (of individual records) *lösa upp datablock*

de-bounce ['diːˈbaʊns] *vb.* prevent a single touch on a key giving multiple key contact *göra studsfri;* **de-bounce circuit** = electronic circuit that prevents a key contact producing more than one signal when pressed *studsfri krets*

debug ['diːˈbʌg] *vb.* to test a program and locate and correct any faults *or* errors *felsöka, avlusa;* **they spent weeks debugging the system; debugging takes up more time than construction; debugged program =** software that works correctly and in which all the mistakes have been removed *or* corrected *felsökt (rättat, avlusat) program*

QUOTE the debug monitor makes development and testing very easy
Electronics & Wireless World

debugger ['diːˈbʌgə] *subst.* software that helps a programmer find faults *or* errors in a program *felsökningsprogram*

decade ['dekeɪd] *subst.* ten items *or* events *tiotal, dekad;* **decade counter =** electronic device able to count actions *or* events from 0-9 before resetting to zero and starting again *dekadräknare, decimalräknare, tiotalsräknare*

decay [dɪˈkeɪ] **1** *subst.* rate at which the electronic impulse *or* the amplitude of a signal fades away *avtagande, avklingande;* **decay time =** time taken for an impulse to fade *avklingningstid* **2** *vb.* to decrease gradually in amplitude *or* size *avta, avklinga;* **the signal decayed rapidly**

decentraliserad databehandling ⇨ decentralized data processing

decentraliserat datanät ⇨ decentralized computer network

decentraliserat system ⇨ distribute

decentralized computer network [diːˈsentrəlaɪzd kəmˈpjuːtə ˌnetwɜːk] *subst.* network where the control is shared between several computers *decentraliserat datanät*

decentralized data processing [diːˈsentrəlaɪzd ˈdeɪtə ˈprəʊsesɪŋ] *subst.* data processing and storage carried out at each location rather than in one central location *decentraliserad databehandling*

dechiffrera ⇨ decipher

deci- ['desı] *prefix* meaning one tenth of a number *deci-*

decibel ['desıbel] *subst.* unit of measurement of noise *decibel (dB);* **decibel meter =** signal power measuring device *decibelmätare*

decile ['desıl] *subst.* one of a series of nine figures below which one tenth *or* several tenths of the total fall *decil (del vid indelning av en fördelningsfunktion i tiondelar)*

decimal ['desım(ə)l] *subst.* **decimal (notation)** = arithmetic and number representation using the decimal system *decimalsystem, decimalrepresentation;* **correct to three places of decimals** = correct to three figures after the decimal point (e.g. 3.485) *tre decimalers noggrannhet;* **decimal point** = dot which indicates the division between the whole unit digits and the smaller (fractional) parts of a decimal number (such as 4.75) *decimalkomma (punkt i anglo-saxiska länder);* **decimal system** = number system using the digits 0 - 9 *decimala talsystemet;* **decimal tabbing** = adjusting a column of numbers so that the decimal points are vertically aligned *decimaltabulering;* **decimal tab key** = key for entering decimal numbers (using a word processor) so that the decimal points are automatically vertically aligned *decimaltabulator;* **decimal-to-binary conversion** = converting a decimal (base ten) number into a binary (base two) number *decimal-binär-omvandling*

decimalization [ˌdesɪmǝlaɪˈzeɪʃn] *subst.* changing to a decimal system *decimalomvandling*

decimalize [ˈdesɪmǝlaɪz] *vb.* to change to a decimal system *decimalomvandla*

decimalkomma ⇨ **decimal**

decimal notation ⇨ **denary notation**

decimalomvandling ⇨ **decimalization**

decimalt ⇨ **base**

decimonic ringing [desɪˈmɒnɪk ˈrɪŋɪŋ] *subst.* selecting one telephone by sending a certain ringing frequency *tonvalssystem*

decipher [dɪˈsaɪfǝ] *vb.* to convert an encrypted *or* encoded message (ciphertext) into the original message (plaintext) *dechiffrera*

decision [dɪˈsɪʒ(ǝ)n] *subst.* making up one's mind to do something *beslut;* **to come to a decision** *or* **to reach a decision; decision box** = graphical symbol used in a flowchart to indicate that a decision is to be made and a branch *or* path *or* action carried out according to the result *beslutsruta;* **decision circuit** *or* **element** = logical circuit that operates on binary inputs, providing an output according to the operation *(logisk) beslutskrets;* **decision** *or* **descrimination instruction** = conditional program instruction that directs control by providing the location of the next instruction to be executed if a condition is met *beslutsinstruktion, villkorsinstruktion;* **decision support system** = suite of programs that help a manager reach decisions using previous decisions, information and other databases *beslutsstödssystem;* **decision table** = chart which shows the relationships between certain variables and actions available when various conditions are met *beslutstabell;* **decision tree** = graphical representation of a decision table showing possible paths and actions if different conditions are met *beslutsträd*

deck [dek] *subst.* **(a) tape deck** = drive for magnetic tape *bandstation* **(b)** pile of punched cards *kortpacke*

deckle edge [ˈdeklˈedʒ] *subst.* rough edge of paper made by hand *rå kant*

declaration [ˌdeklǝˈreɪʃ(ǝ)n] *or* **declarative statement** [dɪˈklærǝtɪv ˈsteɪtmǝnt] *subst.* statement within a program that informs the compiler *or* interpreter of the form, type and size of a particular element, constant *or* variable *deklaration;* **procedure declaration** = to write and declare the variable types used and (if any) the routine name and location *procedurdeklaration*

declare [dɪˈkleǝ] *vb.* to define a computer program variable *or* to set a variable equal to a number *deklararera (variabel);* **he declared at the start of the program that X was equal to nine**

decode [ˈdiːˈkǝʊd] *vb.* to translate encoded data back to its original form *avkoda*

decoder [ˈdiːˈkǝʊdǝ] *subst.* program *or* device used to convert data into another form *avkodare;* **instruction decoder** = hardware that converts a machine-code instruction (in binary form) into actions *instruktionsavkodare*

decoding [ˈdiːˈkǝʊdɪŋ] *subst.* converting encoded data back into its original form *avkodning*

decollate [ˈdiːkɒˈleɪt] *vb.* to separate continuous stationery into single sheets *riva isär papper i löpande bana till enstaka blad;* to split two-part *or* three-part stationery into its separate parts (and remove the carbon paper) *riva isär blankettset*

decollator [ˈdiːkɒˈleɪtǝ] *subst.* machine used to separate continuous stationery into single sheets *or* to split 2-part or 3-part stationery into separate parts *efterbehandlare, dekollator*

decompilation [ˈdiːˌkɒmpɪˈleɪʃn] *subst.* conversion of a compiled program in object code into a source language *backkompilator, baklängeskompilator;* **fast incremental compilation and decompilation**

decrease 1 [dɪˈkriːs] **1** *subst.* fall *or* reduction *minskning;* **decrease in price; decrease in value; decrease in sales; sales show a 10% decrease on last year 2** *vb.* to fall *or* to become less *minska;* **sales are decreasing; the value of the pound has decreased by 5%**

decrement [ˈdekrɪmǝnt] *vb.* to subtract a set number from a variable *minska;* **the register contents were decremented until they reached zero**

decrypt [ˈdiːˈkrɪpt] *vb.* to convert encrypted data back into its original form *dekryptera;* **decryption is done using hardware to increase speed**

> QUOTE typically a file is encrypted using a password key and decrypted using the same key. A design fault of many systems means the use of the wrong password for decryption results in double and often irretrievable encryption
> **PC Business World**

decryption [ˈdiːˈkrɪpʃn] *subst.* converting of encrypted data back into its original form *dekryptering*

dedicated [ˈdedɪkeɪtɪd] *adj.* (program *or* procedure *or* system) reserved for a particular use *dedicerad, reserverad;* **there's only one dedicated graphics workstation in this network; dedicated channel =** communications line reserved for a special purpose *reserverad linje (kanal);* **dedicated computer =** computer which is only used for a single special purpose *dedicerad dator;* **dedicated line =** telephone line used only for data communications *reserverad linje;* **dedicated logic =** logical function implemented in hardware designed (usually for only one task *or* circuit) *dedicerad krets;* **the person appointed should have a knowledge of micro-based hardware and dedicated logic; the dedicated logic cuts down the chip count; dedicated word processor =** computer which has been configured specially for word processing and which cannot run any other programs *skrivautomat*

QUOTE the server should reduce networking costs by using standard networking cable instead of dedicated links
PC Business World

dedicerad dator ⇨ fix

deduct [dɪ'dʌkt] *vb.* to remove something from a total *dra av (ifrån)*

default [dɪ'fɔːlt] *subst.* predefined course of action *or* value that is assumed unless the operator alters it *grundvärde;* **default drive =** disk drive that is accessed first in a multi-disk system (to try and load the operating system *or* a program) *grundenhet, basenhet, startenhet;* **the operating system allows the user to select the default drive; default option =** preset value *or* option that is to be used if no other value has been specified *grundvärde;* **default rate =** baud rate (in a modem) that is used if no other is selected *grundhastighet;* **default response =** value which is used if the user does not enter new data *grundvärde;* **default value =** value which is automatically used by the computer if no other value has been specified *grundvärde;* **screen width has a default value of 80**

defect ['diːfekt] *subst.* something which is wrong *or* which stops a machine from working properly *fel;* **a computer defect** *or* **a defect in the computer**

defective [dɪ'fektɪv] *adj.* faulty *or* not working properly *felaktig, trasig;* **the machine broke down because of a defective cooling system**

defect skipping ['diːfekt 'skɪpɪŋ] *subst.* means of identifying and labelling defective magnetic tracks during manufacture so that they will not be used, instead pointing to the next good track to be used *leveransblockering (av felaktiga spår på skivminnen)*

defensive computing [dɪ'fensɪv kəm'pjuːtɪŋ] *subst.* method of programming that takes into account any problems *or* errors that might occur *konservativ programmering (för att klara "värsta fall")*

deferred addressing [dɪ'fɜːd ə'dresɪŋ] *subst.* indirect addressing, where the location accessed contains the address of the operand to be processed *indirekt adressering*

define [dɪ'faɪn] *vb.* (i) to assign a value to a variable *definiera variabelvärde;* (ii) to assign the characteristics of processes *or* data to something *definiera variabel;* **all the variables were defined at initialization**

definition [ˌdefɪ'nɪʃ(ə)n] *subst.* (i) ability of a screen to display fine detail *upplösning;* (ii) value *or* formula assigned to a variable *or* label *variabeldefinition, variabelvärde;* **macro definition =** description (in a program *or* to a system) of the structure, function and instructions that make up a macro operation *makrodefinition*

deflect [dɪ'flekt] *vb.* to change the direction of an object *or* beam *böja av*

deflection [dɪ'flekʃ(ə)n] *subst.* **deflection yokes =** magnetic coils around a cathode ray tube used to control the position of the picture beam on the screen *avböjningsspolar*

defocus ['diːˈfəʊkəs] *vb.* to move the point of focus of an optical system from an object, so that it appears out of focus *defokusera*

degauss ['diːˈgaʊs] *vb.* to remove unwanted magnetic fields and effects from magnetic tape, disks *or* read/write heads *avmagnetisera;* **the r/w heads have to be degaussed each week to ensure optimum performance**

degausser ['diːˈgaʊsə] *subst.* device used to remove unwanted magnetic fields from a disk *or* tape *or* recording head *avmagnetiseringsutrustning*

degradation [ˌdegrə'deɪʃ(ə)n] *subst.* **(a)** loss of picture *or* signal quality *degradering, försämring;* **image degradation =** loss of picture contrast and quality due to signal distortion *or* bad copying of a video signal *bildförsämring* **(b)** loss of processing capacity because of a malfunction *degradering, kapacitetsnedgång;* **graceful degradation =** allowing some parts of a system to continue to function after a part has broken down *mjuk kapacitetsnedgång*

dekompilera ⇨ unpack

dekryptera ⇨ decrypt

delad skärm ⇨ split screen

delad åtkomst ➭ share

delay [dɪ'leɪ] **1** *subst.* time when
something is later than planned
fördröjning; **there was a delay of thirty
seconds before the printer started printing;
we are sorry for the delay in supplying your
order, but the computer was not working;
delay distortion** = signal corruption due to
echoes *fördröjningsstörning, ekostörning;*
delay equalizer = electronic circuit
used to compensate for delays
caused by a communications line
fördröjningskompensering; **delay line** =
device that causes a signal to take a certain
time in crossing it *fördröjningsledning;*
delay line store = (old) method of storing
serial data as sound *or* pulses in a delay line,
the data being constantly read, regenerated
and fed back into the input
fördröjningslinjelagring; **delay vector** =
time that a message will take to pass from
one packet switching network node to
another *fördröjningsvektor* **2** *vb.* to cause
something to have a delay *fördröja*

delbild ➭ field

delbildfrekvens ➭ field

delbildssynkpuls ➭ field

(del)bildsvep ➭ field

delete [dɪ'liːt] *vb.* **(a)** to cut out words in a
document *radera* **(b)** to remove text *or* data
from a storage device *radera;* **the word-
processor allows us to delete the whole file
by pressing this key; delete character** =
special code used to indicate data *or* text to
be removed *raderingskod*

> COMMENT: when you delete a file, you are
> not actually erasing it but you are making
> its space on disk available for another file
> by instructing the operating system to
> ignore the file by inserting a special code in
> the file header and deleting the entry from
> the directory

deletion [dɪ'liːʃ(ə)n] *subst.* (i) making a
cut in a document *radering;* (ii) text
removed from a document *raderad text;*
**the editors asked the author to make several
deletions in the last chapter; deletion record**
= record containing new data which is to
be used to update *or* delete data in a master
record *uppdateringslista*

delimit [dɪ'lɪmɪt] *vb.* to set up the size of
data using delimiters *avgränsa*

delimiter [dɪ'lɪmɪtə] *subst.* (i) character *or*
symbol used to indicate to a language *or*
program the start *or* end of data *or* a record
or information *avgränsningstecken;* (ii) the
boundary between an instruction and its
argument *avgränsningstecken*

delprogram ➭ chapter, coroutine

delta ['deltə] *subst.* type of connection
used to connect the three wires in a 3-phase
electrical supply *deltakoppling,
trefaskoppling;* **delta clock** = clock that
provides timing pulses to synchronize a
system, and will restart (with an interrupt
signal) a computer *or* circuit that has had an
error *or* entered an endless loop *or* faulty
state *tidsutlöst återstart;* **delta-delta** =
connection between a delta source and load
trefaskoppling; **delta modulation** =
differential pulse coded modulation that
uses only one bit per sample
*deltamodulering (variant av
pulsmodulering);* **delta routing** = means of
directing data around a packet switching
network *deltavägval*

demagnetize ['diːmægnɪtaɪz] *vb.* to
remove stray *or* unwanted magnetic fields
from a disk *or* tape *or* recording head
avmagnetisera

demagnetizer ['diːmægnɪtaɪzə] *subst.*
device which demagnetizes something
avmagnetiseringsutrustning; **he used the
demagnetizer to degauss the tape heads**

demand [dɪ'mɑːnd] **1** *subst.* asking for
something to be done *förfrågan,
efterfrågan;* **demand assigned multiple
access (DAMA)** = means of switching in
circuits as and when they are required
behovsstyrd åtkomst; **demand multiplexing**
= time division multiplexing method
which allocates time segments to signals
according to demand *behovsstyrd
multiplexering;* **demand paging** = system
software that retrieves pages in a virtual
memory system from backing store when it
is required *styrd sidväxling;* **demand
processing** = processing data when it
appears, rather than waiting
realtidsbehandling; **demand reading/writing**
= direct data transfer between a processor
and storage *direktminneshantering;*
demand staging = moving files *or* data from
a secondary storage device to a fast access
device when required by a database
program *hämtning på förfrågan* **2** *vb.* to ask
for something and expect to get it
efterfråga; **she demanded her money back;
the suppliers are demanding immediate
payment**

demarcation [ˌdiːmɑː'keɪʃ(ə)n] *subst.*
showing the difference between two areas
begränsning; **demarcation strip** = device
that electrically isolates equipment from a
telephone line (to prevent damage)
nätisolering

democratic network [ˌdeməˈkrætɪk
'netwɜːk] *subst.* synchronized network
where each station has equal priority
demokratiskt nät, icke hierarkiskt nät

demodulation [ˌdiːmɒdjʊ'leɪʃn] *subst.*
recovery of the original signal from a

received modulated carrier wave *demodulering*

demodulator [diː'mɒdjuˌleɪtə] *subst.* circuit that recovers a signal from a modulated carrier wave *demodulerare*

demonstrate ['demənstreɪt] *vb.* to show how something works *demonstrera;* **he demonstrated the file management program**

demonstration [ˌdeməns'treɪʃ(ə)n] *subst.* act of showing how something works *demonstration;* **demonstration model =** piece of equipment in a shop, used to show customers how the equipment works *förevisningsmodell, demonstrationsexemplar*

demultiplex ['diː'mʌltɪpleks] *vb.* to split one channel into the original signals that were combined at source *demultiplexera*

demultiplexor ['diː'mʌltɪpleksə] *subst.* device that separates out the original multiplexed signals from one channel *demultiplexor*

denary notation ['diːnərɪ nə(ʊ)'teɪʃ(ə)n] *subst.* number system in base ten, using the digits 0 to 9 *decimal notation*

denial [dɪ'naɪ(ə)l] *subst.* **alternative denial =** logical function whose output is false if all inputs are true, and true if any input is false *negerad konjunktion;* **joint denial =** logical function whose output is false if any input is true *negerad disjunktion*

dense index ['dens 'ɪndeks] *subst.* database index containing an address *or* entry for every item *or* entry in the database *databasindex;* **dense list =** list that has no free space for new records *fylld lista*

densitometer [ˌdnsɪ'tɒmɪtə] *subst.* photographic device used to measure the density of a photograph *densitometer*

density ['densətɪ] *subst.* **(a)** amount of light that a photographic negative blocks *täthet, densitet* **(b)** darkness of a printed image *or* text *svärta (i utskrift);* **density dial =** knob that controls the density of a printed image *svärtningskontrollknapp;* **when fading occurs, turn the density dial on the printer to full black (c)** amount of data that can be packed into a space on a disk *or* tape *datatäthet;* **double density =** system to double the storage capacity of a disk drive by doubling the number of bits which can be put on the disk surface *dubbel täthet;* **double density disk (DD) =** disk that can store two bits of data per unit area compared to a standard disk, using a modified write process *diskett med dubbel lagringstäthet;* **packing** *or* **recording density =** number of bits that can be stored in a unit area on a magnetic disk *or* tape *lagringsdensitet;* **single density disk (SD) =**

standard magnetic disk able to store data *diskett med enkel lagringstäthet*

COMMENT: scanner software produces various shades of grey by using different densities; arrangements of black and white dots and/or different sized dots

QUOTE diode lasers with shorter wavelengths will make doubling of the bit and track densities possible
Byte

deny access [dɪ'naɪ 'ækses] *vb.* to refuse access to a circuit *or* system for reasons of workload *or* security *neka åtkomst*

dependent [dɪ'pendənt] *adj.* which is variable because of something *beroende;* **a process which is dependent on the result of another process; the output is dependent on the physical state of the link ; machine dependent =** not standardized *or* which cannot be used on hardware *or* software from a different manufacturer without modification *maskinberoende*

deposit [dɪ'pɒzɪt] **1** *subst.* thin layer of a substance which is put on a surface *beläggning* **2** *vb.* **(a)** to print out the contents of all *or* a selected area of memory *(utskrifts)dumpa* **(b)** to coat a surface with a thin layer of a substance *belägga* **(c)** to write data into a register *or* storage location *mellanlagra*

deposition [ˌdepə'zɪʃ(ə)n] *subst.* process by which a surface (of a semiconductor) is coated with a thin layer of a substance *beläggningsprocess*

depth [depθ] *subst.* **depth of field =** amount of a scene that will be in focus when photographed with a certain aperture setting *skärpedjup (i motivet);* **depth of focus =** position of film behind a camera lens that will result in a sharp image *skärpedjup (vid kamerainställningen)*

deque [dek] *subst.* = DOUBLE-ENDED QUEUE queue in which new items can be added to either end *dubbelsidig kö*

derivation graph [ˌderɪ'veɪʃ(ə)n ˌɡræf] *subst.* structure within a global database that provides information on the rules and paths used to reach any element *or* item of data *strukturdiagram*

derive [dɪ'raɪv] *vb.* to come from *härröra från, härleda;* **derived indexing =** library index entries produced only from material in the book *or* document *härledd indexering;* **derived sound =** sound signal produced by mixing the left and right hand channels of a stereo signal *sammanlagrat ljud (t.ex. för basåtergivning)*

DES ['diːiː'es] = DATA ENCRYPTION STANDARD standardized popular cipher system for data encryption *DES, krypteringsstandard (USA)*

descender [dɪ'sendə] *subst.* part of a character that goes below the line (such as the "tail" of a "g" or "p") *nedlöpande stapel; compare* ASCENDER

de-scramble ['diː'skræmbl] *vb.* to reassemble an original message *or* signal from its scrambled form *avkoda, återbilda*

de-scrambler ['diː'skræmblə] *subst.* device which changes a scrambled message back to its original, clear form *avkodningsenhet*

describe [dɪs'kraɪb] *vb.* to say what someone *or* something is like *beskriva;* **the leaflet describes the services the company can offer; the specifications are described in greater detail at the back of the manual**

description [dɪs'krɪpʃ(ə)n] *subst.* words which show what something is like *beskrivning;* **description list** = list of data items and their attributes *beskrivande katalog;* **data description language (DDL)** = part of a database system which describes the structure of the system and data *databeskrivningsspråk;* **page description programming language** = programming language that accepts commands to define the size, position and typestyle for text *or* graphics on a page *sidbeskrivningsspråk*

descriptor [dɪ'skrɪptə] *subst.* code used to identify a filename *or* program name *or* pass code to a file *identifierare, etikett, filbeteckning*

design [dɪ'zaɪn] **1** *subst.* planning *or* drawing of a product before it is built *or* manufactured *konstruktion;* **circuit design** = layout of components and interconnections in a circuit *krets(korts)konstruktion;* **industrial design** = design of products made by machines (such as cars and refrigerators) *(industriell) formgivning;* **product design** = design of products *produktutformning, konstruktion;* **design department** = department in a large company which designs the company's products *or* its advertising *(mekanisk) konstruktionsavdelning;* **design parameters** = specifications for the design of a product *konstruktionsspecifikation;* **design studio** = independent firm which specializes in creating designs *formgivare, formgivningsateljé* **2** *vb.* to plan *or* to draw something before it is built *or* manufactured *konstruera;* **he designed a new chip factory; she designs typefaces**

designer [dɪ'zaɪnə] *subst.* person who designs *konstruktör, formgivare;* **she is the designer of the new computer**

desk [desk] *subst.* writing table in an office, usually with drawers for stationery

skrivbord; **desk diary; desk drawer; desk light; desk check** = dry run of a program *skrivbordstest*

desktop ['desktɒp] *adj.* which sits on top of a desk *som kan ställas på skrivbordet;* which can be done on a desk *som kan utföras på skrivbordet;* **desktop computer (system)** = small microcomputer system that can be placed on a desk *"bordsdator";* **desktop publishing (DTP)** = design, layout and printing of documents using special software, a small computer and a printer *desktop publishing, autografi, datoriserat sidredigeringssystem*

QUOTE desktop publishing or the ability to produce high-quality publications using a minicomputer, essentially boils down to combining words and images on pages
                                                          Byte

despool ['diː'spuːl] *vb.* to print out spooled files *skriva ut sekundärbuffrade filer*

despotic network [des'pɒtɪk 'netwɜːk] *subst.* network synchronized and controlled by one single clock *hierarkiskt nätverk*

de-spun antenna ['diː'spʌn æn'tenə] *subst.* satellite aerial that always points to the same place on the earth *geosynkron antenn*

destination [ˌdestɪ'neɪʃ(ə)n] *subst.* place to which something is sent *or* to which something is going *destination;* location to which a data is sent *destination*

destructive addition [dɪs'trʌktɪv ə'dɪʃ(ə)n] *subst.* addition operation in which the result is stored in the location of one of the operands used in the sum, so overwriting it *överskrivande addition*

destructive cursor [dɪs'trʌktɪv 'kɜːsə] *subst.* cursor that erases the text as it moves over it *överskrivningsmarkör;* **reading the screen becomes difficult without a destructive cursor; destructive read** = read operation in which the stored data is erased as it is retrieved *inläsning utan återskrivning;* **destructive readout** = form of storage medium that loses its data after it has been read *utskrift utan återskrivning*

detail ['diːteɪl] **1** *subst.* small part of a description *detalj;* **detail file** = file containing records that are to be used to update a master file *uppdateringsfil;* **in detail** = giving many particulars *detaljerat;* **the catalogue lists all the products in detail; detail paper** = thin transparent paper used for layouts and tracing *ritpapper, transparent papper* **2** *vb.* to list in detail *precisera;* **the catalogue details the shipping arrangements for customers; the terms of the licence are detailed in the contract**

detailed ['diːteɪld] *adj.* in detail *detaljerad;* **detailed account** = account which lists every item *detaljerad katalogisering*

detect [dɪ'tekt] *vb.* to sense something (usually something very slight) *detektera, upptäcka;* **the equipment can detect faint signals from the transducer; detected error** = error noticed during a program run, but not corrected *upptäckt fel, registrerat fel;* **error detecting code** = coding system that allows errors occurring during transmission to be detected, but is not complex enough to correct the errors *felupptäckande kod*

detection [dɪ'tekʃ(ə)n] *subst.* process of detecting something *upptäckt;* **the detection of the cause of the fault is proving difficult**

detector [dɪ'tektə] *subst.* device which can detect *registrerande känselkropp, detektor;* **metal detector** = device which can sense hidden metal objects *metalldetektor*

deterministic [dɪˌtɜːmɪ'nɪstɪk] *adj.* (result of a process) that depends on the initial state and inputs *deterministisk*

develop [dɪ'veləp] *vb.* **(a)** to plan and produce *utveckla;* **to develop a new product (b)** to apply a chemical process to photographic film and paper to produce an image *framkalla*

developer [dɪ'veləpə] *subst.* **(a)** a **property developer** = person who plans and builds a group of new houses *or* new factories *byggherre, entreprenör;* **software developer** = person *or* company which writes software *programvaruutvecklare* **(b)** chemical solution used to develop exposed film *framkallare, framkallningsvätska*

development [dɪ'veləpmənt] *subst.* planning the production of a new product *utveckling;* **research and development** = investigating new products and techniques *forskning och utveckling;* **development software** = suite of programs that help a programmer write, edit, compile and debug new software *utvecklingsprogram för programmering;* **development time** = amount of time required to develop a new product *utvecklingstid*

device [dɪ'vaɪs] *subst.* small useful machine *or* piece of equipment *enhet, apparat, utrustning;* **device character control** = device control using various characters *or* special combinations to instruct the device *styrtecken;* **device code** = unique identification and selection code for each peripheral *identifikationskod, enhetskod;* **device control (character)** = special code sent in a transmission to a device to instruct it to perform a special function *styrkod;* **device driver** = program *or* routine used to interface and manage an I/O device *or* peripheral *styrprogram;* **device**

flag = one bit in a device status word, used to show the state of one device *statusbit, statusflagga;* **device independent** = programming technique that results in a program that is able to run with any peripheral hardware *enhetsoberoende, apparatoberoende, utrustningsoberoende;* **device priority** = the importance of a peripheral device assigned by the user *or* central computer which dictates the order in which the CPU will serve an interrupt signal from it *enhetsprioritet;* **the master console has a higher device priority than the printers and other terminals; device queue** = list of requests from users *or* programs to use a device *enhetskö, kö för att använda en enhet;* **device status word (DSW)** = data word transmitted from the device that contains information about its current status *enhetsstatus, DSW-signal;* **this routine checks the device status word and will not transmit data if the busy bit is set; I/O device** = peripheral (such as a terminal) which can be used for inputting or outputting data to a processor *in- och utenhet;* **output device** = device (such as a monitor *or* printer) which allows information to be displayed *utenhet*

devise [dɪ'vaɪz] *vb.* to plan *or* build a system *utforma (ett system);* **they devised a cheap method of avoid the problem**

Dewey decimal classification ['djuːɪ 'desɪm(ə)l ˌklæsɪfɪ'keɪʃən] *subst.* library cataloguing system using classes and subclasses that are arranged in groups of ten *katalogsystem för bibliotek*

DFD ['diːef'diː] = DATA FLOW DIAGRAM diagram used to describe the movement of data through a system *flödesplan, flödesdiagram*

diacritic [ˌdaɪə'krɪtɪk] *subst.* accent above *or* below a letter *diakritisk, diakritisk accent*

diagnose ['daɪəgnəʊz] *vb.* to find the cause and effect of a fault in hardware or error in software *felsöka*

diagnosis [ˌdaɪəg'nəsɪs] *subst.* finding of a fault *or* discovering the cause of a fault (results of diagnosing faulty hardware or software) *felsökning, identifiering av fel, identifiering av felorsak*

diagnostic [ˌdaɪəg'nɒstɪk] *adj.* diagnostic **aid** = hardware *or* software device that helps to find faults *felsökningshjälpmedel;* **diagnostic chip** = chip that contains circuits to carry out tests on other circuits *or* chips *felsökningskrets;* **diagnostic message** = message that appears to explain the type, location and probable cause of a software error *or* hardware failure *diagnosmeddelande, felmeddelande;* **diagnostic program** = software that helps find faults in a computer system *diagnostikprogram, felsökningsprogram;* **diagnostic routine** = routine in a program which helps to find faults in a computer system *felsökningsprogram, felsökningsrutin;* **diagnostic test** = means of locating faults in hardware and software by test circuits *or* programs *diagnostiskt prov;* **self-diagnostic** = computer that runs a series of diagnostic programs (usually when the computer is switched on) to ensure that all circuits, memory and peripherals are working correctly *självdiagnostisk*

QUOTE the implementation of on-line diagnostic devices that measure key observable parameters
Byte
QUOTE to check for any hardware problems, a diagnostic disk is provided
Personal Computer World

diagnostics [ˌdaɪəgˈnɒstiks] *subst.* functions *or* tests that help a user find faults in hardware *or* software *diagnostik(program), felsökningsprogram;* **compiler diagnostics** = function in a compiler that helps a programmer find faults in the program code *kompilatordiagnostik;* **thorough compiler diagnostics make debugging easy; error diagnostics** = information and system messages displayed when an error is detected to help a user debug and correct it *feldiagnostik*

diagonal cut [daɪˈægən ˈkʌt] *subst.* method of joining two pieces of film *or* magnetic tape together by cutting the ends at an angle so making the join less obvious *diagonalskarv*

diagram [ˈdaɪəgræm] *subst.* drawing which shows something as a plan *or* a map *diagram;* **flow diagram** = diagram showing the arrangement of work processes in a series *flödesdiagram*

diagram ⇨ **chart, figure**

diagramatically [ˌdaɪəgrəˈmætɪk(ə)lɪ] *adv.* using a diagram *grafiskt;* **the chart shows the sales pattern diagramatically**

diagrammall ⇨ **flowchart**

diagrammatic [ˌdaɪəgrəˈmætɪk] *adj.* in **diagrammatic form** = in the form of a diagram *i grafisk form;* **the chart showed the sales pattern in diagrammatic form**

diagramsymboler ⇨ **flowchart**

dial [ˈdaɪ(ə)l] **1** *vb.* to call a telephone number on a telephone *slå (ett telefonnummer), ringa (ett telefonsamtal);* **to dial a number; to dial the operator; he dialled the code for the USA; you can dial New York direct from London; to dial direct** = to contact a phone number without asking the operator to do it for you *slå direkt;* **auto-dial** = modem that can automatically dial a number (under the control of a computer) *automatuppringande;* **to dial into** = to call a telephone number, which has a modem and computer at the other end *ringa till;* **with the right access code it is possible to dial into a customer's computer to extract the files needed for the report** NOTE: GB English is **dialling - dialled,** but US spelling is **dialing - dialed 2** *subst.* (i) circular mechanical device which is turned to select something *nummerskiva;* (ii) round face on an instrument, with numbers which indicate something (such as the time on a clock) *instrumentskala, urtavla;* **to tune into the radio station, turn the dial; dial conference** = facility on a private exchange that allows one user to call a number of other extensions for a teleconference *konferenskoppling;* **dial pulse** = pulse-coded signals transmitted to represent numbers dialled *(ton)pulssignal(er) vid nummerslagning;* **dial tone** = sound made by a telephone that indicates that the telephone system is ready for a number to be dialled *kopplingston;* **dial-in modem** = auto-answer modem that can be called at any time *modem med autosvar;* **density dial** = knob that controls the density of a printed image *svärtningskontroll(knapp);* **if the text fades, turn the density dial on the printer to full black**

dialect [ˈdaɪəlekt] *subst.* slight variation of a standard language *dialekt;* **this manufacturer's dialect of BASIC is a little different to the one I'm used to**

dialling [ˈdaɪəlɪŋ] *subst.* act of calling a telephone number *uppringning;* **dialling code** = special series of numbers which you use to make a call to another town *or* country *riktnummer;* **dialling tone** = sound made by a telephone that indicates that the telephone system is ready for a number to be dialled *kopplingston;* **international direct dialling (IDD)** = calling telephone numbers in other countries direct *direktval till utlandet* NOTE: no plural

dialogue [ˈdaɪəlɒg] *subst.* speech *or* speaking to another person *dialog;* communication between devices such as computers *dialog;* **dialogue box** = on-screen message from a program to the user *meddelandefönster, meddelanderuta*

diameter [daɪˈæmɪtə] *subst.* distance across a round object *diameter*

DIANE [daɪˈæn] = DIRECT INFORMATION ACCESS NETWORK FOR EUROPE services offered over the Euronet network *databasnätet DIANE*

diaphragm [ˈdaɪəfræm] *subst.* **(a)** mechanical device in a camera that varies the aperture size *bländare* **(b)** moving part in a loudspeaker *or* microphone *membran;*

the diaphragm in the microphone picks up sound waves

diapositive [ˌdaɪəˈpɒzɪtɪv] *subst.* positive transparency *diapositiv bild (även av större format)*

diary [ˈdaɪərɪ] *subst.* book in which you can write notes *or* appointments for each day of the week *dagbok, almanacka;* **diary management =** part of an office computer program, which records schedules and appointments *kalenderprogram*

diascope [ˈdaɪəˌskəʊp] *subst.* slide projector *or* device that projects slide images onto a screen *diaprojektor*

diazo (process) [daɪˈeɪzəʊ (ˈprəʊses)] *subst.* method for copying documents (using sensitized paper exposed to the original) *diazoprocess för kopiering av pappersdokument*

DIB [ˈdiːaiˈbiː] = DATA INPUT BUS bus used when transferring data from one section of a computer to another, such as between memory and CPU *indatabuss*

dibit [ˈdɪbɪt] *subst.* digit made up of two binary bits *siffra lagrad som två bitar*

dichotomizing search [daɪˈkɒtəˌmaɪzɪŋ ˈsɜːtʃ] *subst.* fast search method for use on ordered lists of data (the search key is compared with the data in the middle of the list and one half is discarded, this is repeated with the half remaining until only one data item remains) *binär sökning, gaffling*

dichroic [daɪˈkrəʊɪk] *subst.* chemical coating on the surface of a lens *färgkorrigerande linsbeläggning*

dictate [dɪkˈteɪt] *vb.* to say something to someone who then writes down your words *diktera;* **to dictate a letter to a secretary; he was dictating orders into his pocket dictating machine; dictating machine =** small tape recorder that is used to record notes *or* letters dictated by someone, which a secretary can play back and type out the text *dikteringsapparat, diktafon*

dictation [dɪkˈteɪʃ(ə)n] *subst.* act of dictating *diktamen;* **to take dictation =** to write down what someone is saying *ta diktamen;* **dictation speed =** number of words per minute which a secretary can write down in shorthand *dikteringshastighet*

dictionary [ˈdɪkʃ(ə)nrɪ] *subst.* (i) book which lists words and meanings *ordbok;* (ii) data management structure which allows files to be referenced and sorted *filkatalog;* (iii) part of a spelling checker program: the list of correctly spelled words against which the program checks a text *ordlista*

dielectric [ˌdaɪɪˈlektrɪk] *subst.* insulating material that allows an electric field to pass, but not an electric current *dielektrisk isolator*

differ [ˈdɪfə] *vb.* not to be the same as something else *skilja sig från, vara olika;* **the two products differ considerably - one has an external hard disk, the other has internal hard disk and external magnetic tape drive**

difference [ˈdɪfr(ə)ns] *subst.* way in which two things are not the same *skillnad;* **what is the difference between these two products? differences in price** *or* **price differences; symmetric difference =** logical function whose output is true if either of the inputs is true, and false if both inputs are the same *symmetrisk differens*

different [ˈdɪfr(ə)nt] *adj.* not the same *olika;* **our product range is quite different in design from the Japanese models; we offer ten models each in six different colours**

differential [ˌdɪfəˈrenʃ(ə)l] *adj.* which shows a difference *olika, differentiell;* **differential PCM** DIFFERENTIAL PULSE CODED MODULATION pulse coded modulation that uses the difference in size of a sample value and the previous one, requiring fewer bits when transmitting *differentiell pulskodad modulation*

diffuse [dɪˈfjuːs] *vb.* to move *or* insert something over an area *or* through a substance *sprida, diffundera;* **the smoke from the faulty machine rapidly diffused through the building; the chemical was diffused into the substrate**

diffusion [dɪˈfjuːʒ(ə)n] *subst.* means of transferring doping materials into an integrated circuit substrate *spridning, diffusion*

digipulse telephone [ˈdɪdʒɪpʌls ˈtelɪfəʊn] *subst.* push button telephone dialling method using coded pulses *telefonapparat för tonval*

digit [ˈdɪdʒɪt] *subst.* symbol *or* character which represents an integer that is smaller than the radix of the number base used *siffra;* **a phone number with eight digits** *or* **an eight-digit phone number; the decimal digit 8; the decimal number system uses the digits 0123456789; check digit =** additional digit inserted into transmitted text to monitor and correct errors *kontrollsiffra, kontrolltecken;* **digit place** *or* **position =** position of a digit within a number *sifferposition; see also* RADIX

digital [ˈdɪdʒɪtl] *adj.* which represents data *or* physical quantities in numerical form (especially using a binary system in computer related devices) *digital;* **digital audio disk (DAD) =** method of recording sound by converting and storing signals in a digital form on magnetic disk, providing very high quality reproduction *magnetisk skiva för digital ljudlagring; see also* COMPACT DISK; **digital audio tape (DAT)** = method of recording sound by converting and storing signals in a digital form on magnetic tape, providing very high quality reproduction *digitalt ljudband, digital ljudlagring på band;* **digital cassette** = high quality magnetic tape housed in a standard size cassette with write protect tabs, and a standard format leader *digital ljudkassett;* **digital circuit** = electronic circuit that operates on digital information providing logical functions *or* switching *digital krets;* **digital clock** = clock which shows the time as a series of digits (such as 12:22:04) *digitalur;* **digital computer** = computer which processes data in digital form (that is data represented in discrete digital form) *digital dator; compare* ANALOG; **digital data** = data represented in (usually binary) numerical form *digitala data;* **digital logic** = applying Boolean algebra to hardware circuits *digital logik, digitala kretsar;* **digital multimeter (DMM)** = multimeter that uses a digital readout (giving better clarity than an AMM) *digital multimeter, digitalt universalinstrument;* **digital optical recording (DOR)** = recording signals in binary form as small holes in the surface of an optical *or* compact disk which can then be read by laser *digitaloptisk lagring;* **digital output** = computer output in digital form *digitala utdata; compare with* ANALOG OUTPUT; **digital plotter** = plotter whose pen position is controllable in discrete steps, so that drawings can be output graphically *digital kurvritare;* **digital read-out** = data displayed in numerical form, such as numbers on an LCD in a calculator *digitalt teckenfönster;* **digital recording** = conversion of sound signals into a digital form and storing them on magnetic disk *or* tape usually in binary form *digital inspelning, digital lagring;* **digital representation** = data *or* quantities represented using discrete quantities (digits) *digital datarepresentation;* **digital resolution** = smallest number that can be represented with one digit, the value assigned to the least significant bit of a word *or* number *digital upplösning;* **digital signal** = electric signal that has only a number of possible states, as opposed to analog signals which are continuously variable *digital signal;* **digital signalling** = control and dialling codes sent down a (telephone line) in digital form *digital signalering, digital överföring;* **digital signature** = unique identification code sent by a terminal *or* device in digital form *digital signatur;* **digital speech** *see* SPEECH SYNTHESIS; **digital system** = system that deals with digital signals *digitalt system;*

digital switching = operating communications connections and switches only by use of digital signals *digital koppling, digital växelfunktion;* **digital to analog converter** *or* **D to A converter (DAC)** = circuit that converts a digital signal to an analog one (the analog signal is proportional to an input binary number) *digitalanalogomvandlare;* **digital transmission system** = communications achieved by converting analog signals to a digital form then modulating and transmitting this (the signal is then converted back to analog form at the receiver) *system för digitalöverföring*

digitalanalogomvandlare ▷ DAC, D to A converter, digital

digital dator ▷ electronic

digitalisera ▷ digitize, quantize

digitaliserare ▷ digitizer, quantizer

digitaliseringsbräda ▷ tablet

digital kurvritare ▷ digital

digitally ['dɪdʒɪt(ə)lɪ] *adv.* (quantity represented) in digital form *digitalt;* **the machine takes digitally recorded data and generates an image**

digitalt data(kommunikationsnät) ▷ integrated

(digitalt) flertjänstnät ▷ integrated

digitalt kretskort ▷ logic

digitalt ljudband ▷ DAT

digitalt teckenfönster ▷ digital

digitize ['dɪdʒɪtaɪz] *vb.* to change analog movement *or* signals into a digital form which can be processed by computers, etc. *digitalisera;* **we can digitize your signature to allow it to be printed with any laser printer; digitized photograph** = image *or* photograph that has been scanned to produce an analog signal which is then converted to digital form and stored *or* displayed on a computer *digitaliserad bild;* **digitizing pad** = sensitive surface that translates the position of a pen into numerical form, so that drawings can be entered into a computer *digitaliseringstablett*

digitizer ['dɪdʒɪtaɪzə] *subst.* analog to digital converter *or* device which converts an analog movement *or* signal to a digital one which can be understood by a computer *digitaliserare*

diktafon ▷ machine

DIL [dɪl] = DUAL-IN-LINE PACKAGE standard layout for integrated circuit packages using two parallel rows of connecting pins along each side *tväraderskapsel (för integrerade kretsar)*

dimension [dɪ'menʃ(ə)n] *subst.* measurement of size *storlek;* **the dimensions of the computer are small enough for it to fit into a case**

dimensioning [dɪ'menʃ(ə)nɪŋ] *subst.* definition of the size of something (usually an array *or* matrix) *dimensionera;* **array dimensioning occurs at this line**

diminished radix complement [dɪ'mɪnɪʃt 'reɪdɪks 'kɒmplɪmənt] *subst.* number representation in which each digit of the number is subtracted from one less than the radix *bas-minus-ett-komplement; see also* ONE'S, NINE'S COMPLEMENT

DIN [dɪn] = DEUTSCHE INDUSTRIENORM German industry standards organization *DIN-norm (tysk industristandard)*

diode ['daɪəʊd] *subst.* electronic component that allows an electrical current to pass in one direction and not the other *diod;* **light-emitting diode (LED)** = semiconductor diode that emits light when a current is applied (used in clock and calculator displays, and as an indicator) *lysdiod*

diopter [daɪ'ɒptə] *or* **dioptre** [daɪ'ɒptə] *subst.* unit of measurement for the power of an optical lens *dioptrier;* **diopter lens** = optical device that is placed in front of a standard camera lens when close up shots are required *försättslins*

DIP [dɪp] = DUAL-IN-LINE PACKAGE standard layout for integrated circuit packages using two parallel rows of connecting pins along each side *tväraderskapsel (för integrerade kretsar)*

diplex ['daɪpleks] *subst.* simultaneous transmission of two signals over the same line *diplex*

dipole ['daɪpəʊl] *subst.* (i) material *or* molecule *or* object that has two potentials, one end positive and the other negative, due to electron displacement from an applied electric field *dipol;* (ii) short straight radio aerial that receives a signal from a central connector *dipolantenn*

direct [dɪ'rekt] **1** *vb.* to manage *or* to organize *leda, organisera;* **directed scan** = file *or* array search method in which a starting point and a direction of scan is provided, either up *or* down from the starting point (an address *or* record number) *direktsökning* **2** *adj.* straight or with no processing *or* going in a straight way *direkt;* **direct access** = storage and retrieval of data without the need to read other data first *direktåtkomst;* **direct (access) address** = ABSOLUTE ADDRESS;

direct access storage device (DASD) = storage medium whose memory locations can be directly read *or* written to *direktminne;* **direct addressing** = method of addressing where the storage location address given in the instruction is the location to be used *direktadressering;* **direct broadcast satellite (DBS)** = TV and radio signal broadcast over a wide area from an earth station via a satellite, received with a dish aerial *direktsändande satellit;* **direct change-over** = switching from one computer to another in one go *direktväxling;* **direct code** = binary code which directly operates the CPU, using only absolute addresses and values *absolutkod;* **direct coding** = program instructions written in absolute code *maskinkodning;* **direct connect** = (modem) which plugs straight into the standard square telephone socket *modem med jackkontakt;* **direct current (DC)** = constant value electric current that flows in one direction *likström;* **direct data entry (DDE)** = keying in data directly onto a magnetic disk *or* tape *direkt datainmatning;* **direct dialling** = calling a telephone number without passing through an internal exchange *ringa upp (via direktnummer);* **direct digital control (DDC)** = machine operated automatically by computer *datorstyrning;* **direct image film** = photographic film that produces a positive image *direktbildsfilm, omvändningsfilm;* **direct impression** = use of a typewriter to compose a piece of text that is to be printed *direktutskrift;* **direct information access network for Europe (DIANE)** = services offered over the Euronet network *DIANE-nätet;* **direct-insert routine** *or* **subroutine** = routine which can be directly copied (inserted) into a larger routine *or* program without the need for a call instruction *subrutin;* **direct instruction** = program command that contains an operand and the code for the operation to be carried out *direktadressinstruktion;* **direct inward dialling** = automatic routing of telephone calls in a private exchange *användning av direktnummer vid samtal till en abonnentväxel;* **direct mail** = selling a product by sending publicity material to possible customers through the post *direktreklam;* **these calculators are only sold by direct mail; the company runs a successful direct-mail operation; direct-mail advertising** = advertising by sending leaflets to people through the post *direktreklam;* **direct memory access (DMA)** = direct, rapid link between a peripheral and a computer's main memory which avoids the use of accessing routines for each item of data required *direkt minnesåtkomst;* **direct memory access transfer** between the main memory and the second processor; **direct memory access channel** = high speed data transfer link *kanal för direktminnesåtkomst;* **direct mode** = typing in a command which is executed once return is pressed *direktverkställelse;* **direct outward dialling** = automatic access to a telephone network from a private exchange *direktval av utgående linje;* **direct page register** = register that provides memory page access data when a CPU is carrying out a direct memory access, to allow access to any part of memory *sidregister för direktminnesåtkomst;* **direct reference address** = virtual address that can only be altered by indexing *direktreferensadress;* **direct transfer** = bit for bit copy of the contents of one register into another register (including any status bits, etc.) *direktöverföring* **3** *adv.* straight *or* with no third party involved *direkt;* **to dial direct** = to contact a phone number yourself without asking the operator to do it for you *ringa upp direkt;* **you can dial New York direct from London if you want**

direction [dɪ'rekʃ(ə)n] *subst.* **(a)** organizing *or* managing *ledning;* **he took over the direction of a software distribution group (b) directions for use** = instructions showing how to use something *bruksanvisning* NOTE: no plural for (a)

directional [dɪ'rekʃənl] *adj.* which points in a certain direction *riktad;* **directional antenna** = aerial that transmits *or* receives signals from a single direction *riktantenn;* **directional pattern** = chart of the response of an aerial *or* microphone to signals from various directions *täckningsdiagram, lobdiagram*

directive [dɪ'rektɪv] *subst.* programming instruction used to control the language translator, compiler, etc. *(kompilator)-direktiv*

> QUOTE directives are very useful for selecting parts of the code for particular purposes
> **Personal Computer World**

directly [dɪ'rektlɪ] *adv.* **(a)** immediately *direkt, omedelbart* **(b)** straight *or* with no third party involved *direkt;* **we deal directly with the manufacturer, without using a wholesaler**

director [dɪ'rektə] *subst.* **(a)** person appointed by the shareholders to help run a company *direktör;* **managing director** = director who is in charge of the whole company *verkställande direktör;* **board of directors** = all the directors of a company *styrelse (i företag)* **(b)** person who is in charge of a project, an official institute, etc. *styresman, direktör, chef;* **the director of the government computer research institute; she was appointed director of the organization** **(c)** person who controls the filming of a film *or* TV programme *regissör;* **casting director** = person in charge of choosing the actors for a film *or* TV programme *ung.*

producent; **lighting director** = person in charge of lighting in a film *or* TV studio *belysningschef;* **technical director** = person in charge of the technical equipment (especially the cameras) in a TV studio *teknisk chef*

directory [dɪ'rekt(ə)rɪ] *subst.* **(a)** list of people *or* businesses with information about their addresses and telephone numbers *katalog;* **classified directory** = list of businesses grouped under various headings, such as computer shops *or* newsagents *yrkesregister (i telefonkatalog);* **commercial directory** *or* **trade directory** = book which lists all the businesses and business people in a town *(geografiskt) företagsregister;* **street directory** = list of people living in a street *adressregister (för en gata);* map of a town which lists all the streets in alphabetical order in an index *gaturegister;* **telephone directory** = book which lists all people and businesses in alphabetical order with their phone numbers *telefonkatalog;* **to look up a number in the telephone directory; his number is in the London directory (b) disk directory** = list of names and information about files in a backing storage device *filkatalog;* **the disk directory shows file name, date and time of creation; directory routing** = means of directing messages in a packet switching network by a list of preferred routes at each node *vägvalskatalog*

direktadressering ▷ direct, immediate

direktadressinstruktion ▷ direct

direktansluten ▷ on-line

direktansluten databas ▷ on-line

direktansluten databehandling ▷ on-line

direktbearbetning ▷ immediate

direkt datainmatning ▷ DDE

direktinmatningsläge ▷ mode

direktinskrivning ▷ keyboard, key-to-disk

direktminne ▷ DASD, RAM

direktminnesåtkomst ▷ access

direktomvandlare ▷ flash

direktoperand ▷ immediate, zero

direktoperandinstruktion ▷ immediate

direktopereringstillstånd ▷ immediate

direktreklam ▷ mailing

direktsändning ▷ real time

direktval till utlandet ⊏⟩ **dialling**

direktåtkomst ⊏⟩ **random access**

direktåtkomstminne ⊏⟩ **DMA, random access**

dirty bit ['dɜːtɪ 'bɪt] *subst.* flag bit set by memory-resident programs (a utility *or* the operating system) to indicate that they have already been loaded into main memory *förändringsmarkering*

disable [dɪs'eɪbl] *vb.* to prevent a device *or* function from operating *koppla ur, blockera;* **he disabled the keyboard to prevent anyone changing the data; disable interrupt** = command to the CPU to ignore any interrupt signals *avbrottsblockering*

disarm [dɪs'ɑːm] *vb.* to prevent an interrupt having any effect *koppla från;* **disarmed state** = state of an interrupt that has been disabled, and cannot accept a signal *frånkopplat läge*

disassemble ['dɪsə'sembl] *vb.* to translate machine code instructions back into assembly language mnemonics *backassemblera, baklängesassemblera*

disassembler ['dɪsə'semblə] *subst.* software that translates a machine code program back into an assembly language form *backassemblerare*

disaster dump [dɪ'zɑːstə ˌdʌmp] *subst.* program and data dump just before *or* caused by a fatal error *or* system crash *systemdump, feldump*

disc [dɪsk] = DISK
NOTE: disc is the more usual spelling in the USA

discard [dɪs'kɑːd] *vb.* to throw out something which is not needed *förkasta, avlägsna*

disclose [dɪs'kləʊz] *vb.* to reveal details of something which were supposed to be secret *avslöja, offentliggöra*

disclosure [dɪs'kləʊʒə] *subst.* act of telling details about something *avslöjande, offentliggörande*

disconnect ['dɪskə'nekt] *vb.* to unplug *or* break a connection between two devices *koppla från (ur);* **do not forget to disconnect the cable before moving the printer**

discrete [dɪs'kriːt] *adj.* (values *or* events *or* energy *or* data) which occurs in small individual units *diskret;* **the data word is made up of discrete bits**

discretionary [dɪs'kreʃən(ə)rɪ] *adj.* which can be used if wanted *or* not used if not wanted *valbar;* **discretionary hyphen** *or* **soft hyphen** = hyphen which is inserted to show that a word is broken (as at the end of

a line), but which is not present when the word is written normally *mjukt bindestreck*

discrimination   instruction [dɪsˌkrɪmɪ'neɪʃ(ə)n   ɪn'strʌkʃn]   *subst.* conditional program instruction that directs control by providing the location of the next instruction to be executed (if a condition is met) *villkorlig instruktion, konditional instruktion; see also* BRANCH, JUMP, CALL

dish aerial ['dɪʃˌeərɪəl] *subst.* circular concave directional aerial used to pick up long distance transmissions *parabolantenn;* **we use a dish aerial to receive signals from the satellite**

disjointed [dɪs'dʒɔɪntɪd] *adj.* (set of information *or* data) that has no common subject *sönderdelad, osammanhängande*

disjunction [dɪs'dʒʌn(k)ʃ(ə)n] *subst.* logical function that produces a true output if any input is true *disjunktion, logiskt eller, logisk addition*

disjunctive search [dɪs'dʒʌn(k)tɪv 'sɜːtʃ] *subst.* search for data items that match at least one of a number of keys *disjunktiv sökning*

disk [dɪsk] *subst.* flat circular plate coated with a substance that is capable of being magnetized (data is stored on this by magnetizing selective sections to represent binary digits) *(minnes)skiva;* **backup disk** = disk which contains a copy of the information from other disks, as a security precaution *skivminne för säkerhetslagring, reserv;* **disk access** = operations required to read from or write to a magnetic disk, including device selection, sector and track address, movement of read/write head to the correct location, access location on disk *skivminnesåtkomst;* **disk-based (operating system)** = (operating system) held on floppy *or* hard disk *skivminnesorienterat operativsystem;* **disk cartridge** = protective case containing a removable hard disk *skivminnespacke, skivpacke;* **disk controller** = IC *or* circuits used to translate a request for data by the CPU into control signals for the disk drive (including motor control and access arm movement) *styrenhet för skivminne;* **disk-controller card** = add-on card that contains all the electronics and connectors to interface a disk drive to a CPU *styrkort för skivminne;* **disk crash** = fault caused by the read/write head touching the surface of the disk *skivminnesfel;* **disk drive** = device that spins a magnetic disk and controls the position of the read/write head *skivminnesenhet,   diskettenhet, diskettstation;* **disk file** = number of related records *or* data items stored under one name on disk *fil;* **disk formatting** = initial setting up of a blank disk with track and sector markers and other control information *preparering, formering, formatering (av skivminne);* **disk index holes =** holes around the hub of a disk that provide rotational information to a disk controller *or* number of holes providing sector location indicators on a hard-sectored disk *styrhål;* **disk map =** display of the organization of data on a disk *bild av skivminnesorganisation;* **disk operating system (DOS) =** section of the operating system software that controls disk and file management *skivminnessystem (för fil- och skivminnesorienterat operativsystem);* **MS disk operating system** *or* **Microsoft DOS (MS-DOS) =** popular DOS for microcomputers *operativsystemet MS-DOS från företaget Microsoft;* **disk pack =** number of disks on a single hub, each with its own read/write head *skivpacke;* **disk sector =** smallest area on a magnetic disk that can be addressed by a computer *sektor;* **disk storage =** using disks as a backing store *skivminne, skivminneslagring;* **disk track =** one of a series of (thin) concentric rings on a magnetic disk, which the read/write head accesses and along which data is stored in separate sectors *spår;* **disk unit =** disk drive *skivenhet;* **fixed disk =** magnetic disk which cannot be removed from the disk drive *fast skivminne, hårddisk;* **floppy disk =** small disk for storing information which can be removed from a computer *flexskiva, diskett;* **hard disk =** solid disk which will store a large amount of computer information in a sealed case, and cannot usually be removed from the computer *fast skivminne, hårddisk;* **optical disk =** disk which contains binary data in the form of small holes which are read by a laser beam (also called WORM (write one, read many) when used on computers) *optisk skiva;* **Winchester disk =** hard disk with a large storage capacity sealed in a computer *Winchesterminne, kapslat skivminne*

COMMENT: the disk surface is divided into tracks and sectors which can be accessed individually; magnetic tapes cannot be accessed in this way

diskantfilter ⇨ **filter**

diskanthögtalare ⇨ **tweeter**

diskett ⇨ **diskette, floppy disk**

diskette ['dıs'ket] *subst.* light, flexible disk that can store data in a magnetic form, used in most personal computers *flexskiva, diskett*

diskettenhet ⇨ **floppy disk**

diskettformat ⇨ **format**

diskettformatering ⇨ **format**

diskettsektor ⇨ **floppy disk**

diskettstation ⇨ **floppy disk**

diskless ['dıskl\ıs] *adj.* which does not use disks for data storage *utan skivminne;* **diskless system; they want to create a diskless workstation**

disorderly close-down [dıs'ɔːdəlı 'kləʊzdaʊn] *subst.* system crash that did not provide enough warning to carry out an orderly close-down *oförutsedd systemkrasch*

dispatch [dıs'pætʃ] *or* **despatch** [dıs'pætʃ] *subst.* action of sending material *or* information *or* messages to a location *sändning, expediering*

dispenser [dıs'pensə] *subst.* device which gives out something *automat;* **cash dispenser =** device which gives money when a card is inserted and special instructions keyed in *bankautomat*

dispersion [dıs'pɜːʃ(ə)n] *subst.* **(a)** separation of a beam of light into its different wavelengths *färgspridning* **(b)** logical function whose output is false if all inputs are true, and true if any input is false *negerad konjunktion*

displacement [dıs'pleısmənt] *subst.* offset used in an indexed address *adressförskjutning*

display [dıs'pleı] **1** *subst.* device on which information *or* images can be presented visually *bildskärm;* **display adapter =** device which allows information in a computer to be displayed on a CRT (the adapter interfaces with both the computer and CRT) *bildskärmsstyrkrets;* **display attribute =** variable which defines the shape *or* size *or* colour of text *or* graphics displayed *bildskärmsstyrtecken;* **display character =** graphical symbol which appears as a printed *or* displayed item, such as one of the letters of the alphabet *or* a number *(skärm)tecken;* **display character generator =** ROM that provides the display circuits with a pattern of dots which form the character *teckengenerator;* **display colour =** colour of characters in a (videotext) display system *teckenfärg;* **display controller =** device that accepts character *or* graphics codes and instructions, and converts them into dot-matrix patterns that are displayed on a screen *grafikstyrkrets, bildskärmsstyrkrets;* **display format =** number of characters that can be displayed on a screen, given as row and column lengths *skärmformat;* **display highlights =** emphasis of certain words *or* paragraphs by changing character display colour *framhävd presentation;* **display line =** horizontal printing positions for characters in a line of text *skärmlinje;* **display mode =** way of referring to the character set to be used, usually graphics *or* alphanumerics *skärmtillstånd;* **display processor** = processor that changes data to a format suitable for a display controller *grafikprocessor;* **display register** = register that contains character *or* control *or* graphical data that is to be displayed *videoregister;* **display resolution** = number of pixels per unit area that a display can clearly show *upplösning;* **display screen** = the physical part of a Visual Display Unit *or* terminal *or* monitor, which allows the user to see characters *or* graphics (usually a Cathode Ray Tube, but sometimes LCD *or* LED displays are used) *bildskärm;* **display scrolling** = movement of a screenful of information up or down one line or pixel at a time *skärmrullning;* **display size** = character size greater than 14 points, used in composition and headlines rather than normal text *rubrikstilstorlek;* **display space** = memory *or* amount of screen available to show graphics *or* text *skärmutrymme;* **display unit** = computer terminal *or* piece of equipment that is capable of showing data *or* information, usually by means of CRT *presentationsenhet;* **gas discharge** *or* **plasma** *or* **electroluminescent display** = flat lightweight display screen that is made up of two flat pieces of glass covered with a grid of conductors, separated by a thin layer of gas which luminesces when a point of the grid is selected by two electrical signals *plasmaskärm, EL-skärm; see also* VISUAL DISPLAY UNIT **2** *vb.* to show information *visa;* **the customer's details were displayed on the screen; by keying HELP, the screen will display the options available to the user**

QUOTE the review machine also came with a monochrome display card plugged into one of the expansion slots
Personal Computer World

distant ['dɪst(ə)nt] *adj.* which is located some way away *avlägsen;* **the distant printers are connected with cables**

distinguish [dɪs'tɪŋgwɪʃ] *vb.* to tell the difference between two things *särskilja;* **the OCR has difficulty in distinguishing certain characters**

distort [dɪs'tɔːt] *vb.* to introduce unwanted differences between a signal input and output from a device *störa, förvränga*

distortion [dɪs'tɔːʃ(ə)n] *subst.* unwanted differences in a signal before and after it has passed through a piece of equipment *störning;* **distortion optics** = special photographic lens used to produce a distorted image for special effects *förvrängningsoptik;* **image distortion** = fault in an optical lens causing the image to be distorted *bildförvrängning*

distribuerad databehandling ⇨ DDP

distribuerad processor ⇨ processor

distribuerat databassystem ⇨ distribute

distribuerat filsystem ⇨ file

distribute [dɪs'trɪbjuːt] *vb.* to send out data *or* information to users in a network *or* system *sända, distribuera;* **distributed adaptive routing** = directing messages in a packet network switching system by an exchange of information between nodes *adaptivt vägval;* **distributed database system** = data system where the data is kept on different disks in different places *distribuerat databassystem;* **distributed data processing (DDP)** = operations to derive information from data which is kept in different places *distribuerad databehandling;* **distributed file system** = system that uses files stored in more than one location *or* backing store but are processed at a central point *distribuerat filsystem;* **distributed intelligence** = decentralized system in which a number of small micros *or* mini-computers carry out a set of fixed (tasks rather than one large computer) *decentraliserat system;* **distributed (data) processing** = system of processing in a large organization with many small computers at different workstations instead of one central computer *distribuerad databehandling;* **distributed system** = computer system which uses more than one processor in different locations, all connected to a central computer *distribuerat system*

distribution [,dɪstrɪ'bjuːʃ(ə)n] *subst.* act of sending information out, especially via a network *utsändning;* **distribution network** *see* LAN, WAN; **distribution point** = point from which cable television *or* telephone signals are split up from a main line and sent to individual users' homes *förgreningspunkt*

dittogram ['dɪtəʊgræm] *subst.* printing error caused by repeating the same letter twice *oavsiktlig dubbelskrivning*

DIV ['diːaɪˈviː] = DATA IN VOICE digital satellite data transmission in place of a voice channel *digital dataöverföring i talkanal*

divergence [daɪ'vɜːdʒ(ə)ns] *subst.* failure of light *or* particle beams to meet at a certain point *divergens, avvikelse*

diversity [daɪ'vɜːsətɪ] *subst.* coming from more than one source *mångfald;* being aimed at more than one use *olikhet;* **beam diversity** = using a single frequency communications band for two different sets of data *strålmångfald*

diverter [daɪ'vɜːtə] *subst.* circuit *or* device that redirects a message *or* signal from one

path or route to another *stationsväxlare;*
call diverter = device which, on receiving a
telephone call, contacts another point and
re-routes the call *vidarekopplare*

divide [dɪ'vaɪd] *vb.* **(a) to divide a number
by four** = to find out how many fours can
be contained in the other number *dividera;*
twenty-one divided by three gives seven (b)
to cut *or* to split into parts *dela;* **in the
hyphenation program, long words are
automatically divided at the end of lines**

dividend ['dɪvɪdend] *subst.* operand that
is divided by a divisor in a division
operation *täljare, dividend*

> COMMENT: the dividend is divided by the
> divisor to form the quotient and a
> remainder

divider [dɪ'vaɪdə] *subst.* **frequency divider**
= circuit which divides the frequency of a
signal by a certain amount to change the
pitch *(frekvens)delare*

division [dɪ'vɪʒ(ə)n] *subst.* act of dividing
division

divisor [dɪ'vaɪzə] *subst.* operand used to
divide a dividend in a division operation
nämnare, divisor

DMA ['diːem'eɪ] = DIRECT MEMORY
ACCESS direct rapid link between a
peripheral and a computer's main
memory, which avoids the use of accessing
routines for each item of data read
direktåtkomstminne; **DMA controller** =
interface IC that controls high-speed data
transfer between a high-speed peripheral
and main memory, usually the controller
will also halt *or* cycle steal from the CPU
styrkrets för direktminne; **DMA cycle
stealing** = CPU allowing the DMA
controller to send data over the bus during
clock cycles when it performs internal *or*
NOP instructions *cykelstöld*

DML ['diːem'el] = DATA MANIPULATION
LANGUAGE

DMM ['diːem'em] = DIGITAL MULTIMETER

docket ['dɒkɪt] *subst.* US record of an
official proceeding *innehållsöversikt,
föredragningslista*

document ['dɒkjumənt] **1** *subst.* piece of
paper with writing on it *or* file containing
text *dokument;* **document assembly** *or*
document merge = creating a new file by
combining two *or* more sections *or*
complete documents
dokumentsammanslagning; **document
processing** = processing of documents
(such as invoices) by a computer
dokumentbehandling; **document reader** =
device which converts written *or* typed
information to a form that a computer can

understand and process *dokumentläsare,
sidläsare, textläsare;* **document recovery** =
program which allows a document which
has been accidentally deleted to be
recovered *dokumentåterställning,
räddningsprogram;* **document retrieval
system** = information storage and retrieval
system that contains complete documents
rather than just quotes *or* references
*dokumenthanteringssystem, (dokument)-
arkivsystem* **2** *vb.* to write a description of a
process *dokumentera*

documentation [ˌdɒkjumen'teɪʃ(ə)n]
subst. **(a)** all documents referring to
something *dokumentation;* **please send all
documentation concerning the product (b)**
information, notes and diagrams that
describe the function, use and operation of
a piece of hardware *or* software
dokumentation
NOTE: no plural

dokumentbehandling ▷ **document**

dokumenthanteringssystem ▷
document

dokumentläsare ▷ **scanner**

dolda linjer ▷ **hidden**

dold fil ▷ **file**

dollar sign ['dɒlə saɪn] *subst.* printed *or*
written character ($) used in some
languages to identify a variable as a string
type *dollartecken*

dolt fel ▷ **error**

domain [də(ʊ)'meɪn] *subst. domän;* **public
domain** = information *or* program which
belongs to and is available to the public *fri
programvara;* **program which is in the
public domain** = program which is not
copyrighted *fritt program*

domestic [də(ʊ)'mestɪk] *adj.* referring to
the home market *or* the market of the
country where the business is based
hemma; **domestic consumption** =
consumption on the home market
hemmakonsumtion; **domestic market** =
market in the country where a company is
based *hemmamarknad, lokalmarknad;*
**they produce goods for the domestic market;
domestic production** = production of goods
for domestic consumption *inhemsk
produktion, hemmamarknadsproduktion;*
domestic satellite = satellite used for
television *or* radio transmission, rather
than research *or* military applications *civil
kommmunikationssatellit*

dongle ['dɒŋgl] *subst.* coded circuit *or*
chip that has to be present in a system
before a piece of copyright software will
run *kodkrets*

do-nothing (instruction) [duː 'nʌθɪŋ (ɪn'strʌkʃn)] *subst.* programming instruction that does not carry out any action (except increasing the program counter to the next instruction address *blindinstruktion*

dopa ⇨ **dope, implant**

dopant ['dəʊpənt] *subst.* chemical substance that is diffused *or* implanted onto the substrate of a chip during manufacture, to provide it with n- *or* p-type properties *dopämne*

dope [dəʊp] *vb.* to introduce a dopant into a substance *dopa*

doped ['dəʊpt] *adj.* (chip) which has had a dopant added *dopad*

doping ['dəʊpɪŋ] *subst.* adding of dopant to a chip *dopning*

dopämne ⇨ **dopant**

DOR [diːəʊ'ɑː] = DIGITAL OPTICAL READING recording signals in binary form as small holes in the surface of an optical *or* compact disk which can then be read by laser *DOR-inspelning, CD-lagring, optisk lagring*

DOS [dɒs] = DISK OPERATING SYSTEM section of the operating system software, that controls the disk and file access *skivminnesorienterat operativsystem;* **boot up the DOS after you switch on the PC**

dossier ⇨ **file**

dot [dɒt] *subst.* small round spot *punkt;* **dot command** = method of writing instructions with a full stop followed by the command, used mainly for embedded commands in word-processor systems *punktkommando;* **dot matrix** = forming characters by use of dots inside a rectangular matrix *punktmatris;* **dots per inch** *or* **d.p.i.** *or* **dpi** = standard method used to describe the resolution capabilities of a page printer *or* scanner *punkter per tum;* **some laser printers offer high resolution printing: 400 dpi**

dot-matrix printer ['dɒt ˌmeɪtrɪks 'prɪntə] *subst.* printer in which the characters are made up by a series of closely spaced dots (it produces a page line by line; a dot-matrix printer can be used either for printing using a ribbon *or* for thermal *or* electrostatic printing) *matrisskrivare*

QUOTE the characters are formed from an array of dots like in a dot-matrix printer, except that much higher resolution is used
Practical Computing

double ['dʌbl] *adj.* twice *dubbel;* twice as large; twice the size *dubbelt så stor som;* **double buffering** = use of two buffers, allowing one to be read while the other is being written to *växelbuffert, dubbel buffert;* **double dagger** = typeset character used as a second reference mark *dubbelt kors (som anger andra nivån av noter, hänvisningar);* **double density** = system to double the storage capacity of a disk drive by doubling the number of bits which can be put on the disk surface *dubbel täthet;* **double-density disk** = disk that can store two bits of data per unit area, compared to a standard disk *diskett med dubbel lagringstäthet;* **double document** = error in photographing documents for microfilm, where the same image appears consecutively *dubbelbild;* **double ended queue (deque)** = queue in which new items can be added to either end *dubbelsidig kö;* **double exposure** = two images exposed on the same piece of photographic film, usually used for special effects *dubbelexponering;* **double-length** *or* **double precision arithmetic** = use of two data words to store a number, providing greater precision *aritmetik för dubbel precision (vid flyttalsberäkning);* **double precision arithmetic** = use of two data words to store a number, providing greater precision *aritmetik för dubbel precision;* **double sideband** = modulation technique whose frequency spectrum contains two modulated signals above and below the unmodulated carrier frequency *dubbelt sidband;* **double-sided disk** = disk which can store information on both sides *dubbelsidigt skivminne, dubbelsidig diskett;* **double-sided disk drive** = disk drive which can access data on double-sided disks *diskettstation för dubbelsidig läsning;* **double-sided printed circuit board** = circuit board with conducting tracks on both sides *dubbelsidigt kretskort;* **double-sided suppressed carrier (DSBSC)** = modulation technique that uses two modulated signal sidebands, but no carrier signal *dubbelt sidband med undertryckt bärvåg;* **double word** = two bytes of data handled as one word, often used for address data *dubbelord*

doublet ['dʌblət] *or* **diad** ['daɪəd] *subst.* word made up of two bits *dubblett*

down [daʊn] *adv. (of computers or programs)* not working *ur funktion, otillgänglig;* **the computer system went down twice during the afternoon; down stroke** = wide heavy section of a character written with an ink pen *(nedåtgående) stapel;* **down time** = period of time during which a computer system is not working *or* usable *otillgänglig tid*

download ['daʊnləʊd] *vb.* (i) to load a program *or* section of data from a remote computer via a telephone line *hämta (ner), ladda (ner);* (ii) to load data from a mainframe to a small computer *sända* *(ner), ladda (ner);* (iii) to send printer font data stored on a disk to a printer (where it will be stored in temporary memory *or* RAM) *ladda t.ex. typsnitt;* **there is no charge for downloading public domain software from the BBS**

downloadable ['daʊnˌlɔʊdəbl] *adj.* which can be downloaded *(ner)laddningsbar;* **downloadable fonts** = fonts *or* typefaces stored on a disk, which can be downloaded *or* sent to a printer and stored in temporary memory *or* RAM *laddningsbara typsnitt*

downtime ['daʊntaɪm] *subst.* period during which the computer *or* system is not usable *hindertid*

downward ['daʊnwəd] *adj.* towards a lower position *nedåt;* **downward compatibility** = ability of a complex computer system to work with a simple computer *bakåtkompatibel;* **the mainframe is downward compatible with the micro**

dp ['diːˈpiː] *or* **DP** ['diːˈpiː] = DATA PROCESSING operating on data to produce useful information *or* to sort and organize data files *ADB, TDB (administrativ teknisk databehandling)*

d.p.i. ['diːpiːˈaɪ] *or* **dpi** ['diːpiːˈaɪ] = DOTS PER INCH standard method used to describe the resolution capabilities of a dot-matrix *or* laser printer *or* scanner *punkter per tum;* **a 300 d.p.i. black and white A4 monitor; a 300 dpi image scanner**

COMMENT: 300 d.p.i. is the normal industry standard for a laser printer

DPM ['diːpiːˈem] = DATA PROCESSING MANAGER

draft [drɑːft] **1** *subst.* rough copy of a document before errors have been corrected *utkast, kladd;* **draft printing** = low quality, high speed printing *snabbutskrift* **2** *vb.* to make a rough copy *or* drawing *göra ett utkast till;* **he drafted out the details of the program on a piece of paper**

drag [dræg] *vb.* to move (a mouse) with a control key pressed, so moving an image on screen *dra ut, förflytta;* **you can enlarge a frame by clicking inside its border and dragging to the position wanted**

QUOTE press the mouse button and drag the mouse: this produces a dotted rectangle on the screen
QUOTE you can easily enlarge the frame by dragging from any of the eight black rectangles round the border, showing that it is selected
Desktop Publishing

drain [dreɪn] **1** *subst.* electrical current provided by a battery *or* power supply *ström;* connection to a FET **2** *vb.* to remove

or decrease power *or* energy from a device such as a battery *dra ström (ur t.ex. ett batteri)*

DRAM [dræm] = DYNAMIC RANDOM ACCESS MEMORY

QUOTE cheap bulk memory systems are always built from DRAMs
Electronics & Power

D-region ['diːriːdʒ(ə)n] *subst.* section of the ionosphere 50-90km above the earth's surface *D-skiktet;* **the D-region is the main cause of attenuation in transmitted radio signals**

drift [drɪft] *subst.* changes in the characteristics of a circuit with time *or* changing temperature *drift*

drift ⇨ **operation**

driftström ⇨ **hold**

drifttid ⇨ **up**

drive [draɪv] **1** *subst.* part of a computer which operates a tape *or* disk *band- eller diskettstation, skivminnesenhet, diskettenhet, diskettstation;* **disk drive** = device which spins a magnetic disk and controls the position of the read/write head *skivminnesenhet, diskettenhet, diskettstation;* **tape drive** = mechanism that carries magnetic tape over the drive heads *bandstation* **2** *vb.* to make a tape *or* disk work *driva;* **the disk is driven by a motor**

driven ['drɪvn] *adj.* operated by something *styrd;* **control driven** = computer architecture where instructions are executed once a control sequence has been received *kommandosekvensstyrd, styrsekvensstyrd;* **event-driven** = computer program *or* process where each step of the execution relies on external actions *händelsestyrd*

driver ['draɪvə] *or* **handler** ['hændlə] *subst.* program *or* routine used to interface and manage an input/output device *or* other peripheral *styrprogram, styrrutin;* **printer driver** = dedicated software that controls and formats users' commands ready for a printer *styrprogram för skrivare*

drivverk för utbytbart skivminne ⇨ **exchangeable**

DRO ['diːɑːˈrəʊ] = DESTRUCTIVE READOUT form of storage medium that loses its data after it has been read *förstörande läsning*

drop [drɒp] *subst.* fall to a lower position *falla;* **drop cap** = first letter in a sentence, printed in a larger typeface than the rest of the sentence *anfang;* **drop dead halt** *or* **dead halt** = program instruction from the user *or* an error that causes the program to stop without allowing recovery *tvärstopp;* **drop**

line = cable television line, running from a feeder cable to a user's home *anslutningskabel för kabelteve*

drop in ['drɒpɪn] *subst.* small piece of dirt that is on a disk *or* tape surface, which does not allow data to be recorded on that section *bittillskott, "skräp"*

drop out ['drɒpaʊt] *subst.* **(a)** failure of a small piece of tape *or* disk to be correctly magnetized for the accurate storage of data *bitbortfall* **(b)** loss of transmitted signals due to attenuation *or* noise *bitbortfall*

drossel ⇨ **inductor**

drum [drʌm] *subst.* early type of magnetic computer storage *trumminne;* **magnetic drum** = cylindrical magnetic storage device *minnestrumma;* **drum plotter** = computer output device that consists of a movable pen and a piece of paper around a drum that can be rotated, creating patterns and text when both are moved in various ways *trumkurvskrivare*

dry cell ['draɪˌsel] *subst.* battery that cannot be recharged *torrbatteri; compare with* RECHARGEABLE BATTERY

dry circuit ['draɪˌsɜːkɪt] *subst.* voice signal transmitting circuit that contains no DC signals *or* levels *torrsändningskrets*

dry contact ['draɪˌkɒntækt] *subst.* faulty electrical connection, often causing an intermittent fault *glappkontakt*

dry joint ['draɪˌdʒɔɪnt] *subst.* faulty *or* badly made electrical connection *kallödning*

dry run ['draɪˌrʌn] *subst.* running a program with test data to check everything works *provkörning, skrivbordstest*

DSBSC ['diːesˈbiːesˈsiː] = DOUBLE SIDEBAND SUPPRESSED CARRIER

DSE ['diːesˈiː] = DATA SWITCHING EXCHANGE

D-skiktet ⇨ **D-region**

DSR ['diːesˈɑː] = DATA SET READY signal from a device that it is ready to accept data, this signal occurs after a DTR signal is received *klarsignal, DSR-signal, "modem klart"*

DSW ['diːesˈdʌbljuː] = DEVICE STATUS WORD data word transmitted from a device that contains information about its current status *enhetsstatus, DSW-signal*

DTE ['diːtiːˈiː] = DATA TERMINAL EQUIPMENT device at which a communications path starts *or* finishes *(data)terminal*

DTMF ['diːtiːemˈef] = DUAL TONE, MULTIFREQUENCY communication signalling system, using two different frequencies to transmit binary data *tvåtonssignalering*

D to A converter ['diː tuː ˌeɪ kənˈvɜːtə] = DIGITAL TO ANALOG CONVERTER circuit that outputs an analog signal that is proportional to an input digital number *digitalanalogomvandlare*

DTP ['diːtiːˈpiː] = DESKTOP PUBLISHING the design, layout and printing of documents using special software, a desktop computer and a printer *desktop publishing, autografi, datorstödd typografi, datoriserat sidredigeringssystem*

DTR ['diːtiːˈɑː] = DATA TERMINAL READY signal from a device that indicates that it is ready to send data *redo-signal, DTR-signal, dataterminal klar*

D-type flip-flop ['diːtaɪp 'flɪp 'flɒp] *subst.* flip-flop device with one input and two outputs *d-vippa*

dual ['djuːəl] *adj.* using two *or* a pair *tvåfaldig, parvis;* **dual channel** = two separate audio recording paths, as found in stereo equipment *stereo;* **dual clocking** = multiplexed data, each set of data is available and valid on a different clock pulse *or* edge *parsändning;* **dual column** = two separate parallel lists of information *två spalter;* **dual-in-line package (DIL** *or* **DIP) =** standard layout for integrated circuit packages using two parallel rows of connecting pins along each edge *tvåraderskapsel (för integrerade kretsar);* **dual port memory** = memory with two sets of data and memory lines to allow communications between CPUs *tvåportsminne;* **dual processor** = computer system with two processors for faster program execution *dubbelprocessorsystem;* **dual systems** = two computer systems, working in parallel on the same data, with the same instructions, to ensure high reliability *parallelldatorsystem;* **dual tone, multifrequency (DTMF)** = communication signalling system using two different frequencies to transmit binary data *tvåtonssignalering*

dub [dʌb] *vb.* to add sound to a film after the film has been shot (usually to add a sound version in another language) *dubba;* **dubbed sound** = sound effects added after the film has been shot *dubbat ljud*

dubbelriktad ⇨ **bi-directional**

dubbelriktad radiokommunikation ⇨ **two way radio**

dubbelsidig kö ⇨ **double**

dubbel täthet ⇨ **double**

dubbing ['dʌbɪŋ] *subst.* action of adding sound to a film after the film has been shot *dubbning*

duct [dʌkt] *subst.* pipe containing cables, providing a tidy and protective surrounding for a group of cables *kabeltrumma, kabelränna*

dumb terminal ['dʌm 'tɜ:mɪnl] *subst.* peripheral that can only transmit and receive data from a computer, but is not capable of processing data *dum terminal; compare* INTELLIGENT TERMINAL

dummy ['dʌmɪ] *subst.* imitation product to test the reaction of potential customers to its design *testmodell;* **dummy instruction** = instruction in a program that is only there to satisfy language syntax *or* to make up a block length *blindinstruktion;* **dummy variable** = variable set up to satisfy the syntax of a language, but which is replaced when the program is executed *blind variabel*

dump [dʌmp] **1** *subst.* (i) data which has been copied from one device to another for storage *dump;* (ii) transferring of data to a disk for storage *dumpning;* (iii) *US* printout of the contents of all *or* selected data in memory *skrivardump;* **binary dump** = sections of memory dumped onto another medium *or* printed out in binary form *binärdump;* **change dump** = printout of all the locations whose contents have been changed during a program run *ändringsdump;* **dump and restart** = software that will stop a program execution, dump any relevant data or program status then restart the program *omstart efter dump;* **dump point** = point in a program where the program and its data are saved onto backing store to minimize the effects of any future faults *startmarkering (i ett program) för säkerhetslagring;* **screen dump** = outputting the text *or* graphics displayed on a screen to a printer *skärmutskrift* **2** *vb.* to move data from one device *or* storage area to another *dumpa (till/från);* **the account results were dumped to the backup disk**

duodecimal number system [ˌdjuː(ʊ)'desɪm(ə)l 'nʌmbə ˌsɪstəm] *subst.* number system with a radix of twelve *duodecimalt talsystem, talsystem med basen tolv*

duplex ['djuːpleks] *subst.* **(a)** photographic paper that is light sensitive on both sides *dubbelsidigt fotopapper* **(b)** simultaneous transmission of two signals on one line *duplex;* **duplex circuit** = electronic circuit used to transmit data in two directions simultaneously *duplexkrets;* **duplex computer** = two identical computer systems used in an on-line application, with one used as a backup in case of failure of the other *speglade system, dubbeldatorsystem, parallelldatorsystem;* **duplex operation** = transmission of data in two directions simultaneously *dubbelriktad sändning; see also* HALF-DUPLEX, FULL DUPLEX, SIMPLEX

duplicate ['djuːplɪkət] **1** *subst.* copy *kopia;* **he sent me the duplicate of the contract; duplicate receipt** *or* **duplicate of a receipt** = copy of a receipt *en (separat) kopia av ett kvitto;* **in duplicate** = with a copy *i två exemplar;* **receipt in duplicate** = two copies of a receipt *kvitto i två exemplar;* **to print an invoice in duplicate 2** ['djuːplɪkeɪt] *vb.* to copy *kopiera, duplicera;* **to duplicate a letter** = to make a copy of a letter *kopiera ett brev*

duplicating ['djuːplɪkeɪtɪŋ] *subst.* copying *kopiering;* **duplicating machine** = machine which makes copies of documents *kopieringsmaskin, dupliceringsmaskin;* **duplicating paper** = special paper to be used in a duplicating machine *kopieringspapper, dupliceringspapper*

duplication [ˌdjuːplɪ'keɪʃ(ə)n] *subst.* copying of documents *duplicering, mångfaldigande;* **duplication of work** = work which is done twice without being necessary *dubbelt arbete*

duplicator ['djuːplɪkeɪtə] *subst.* machine which produces multiple copies from a master *dupliceringsmaskin;* **duplicator paper** = absorbent paper used in a duplicator *dupliceringspapper, kopieringspapper*

duplicera ⇨ **duplicate, replicate**

durable ['djʊərəbl] *adj.* which will not be destroyed easily *hållbar, varaktig;* **durable cartridge**

duration [djʊ(ə)'reɪʃ(ə)n] *subst.* length of time for which something lasts *varaktighet;* **pulse duration modulation (PDM)** = pulse modulation where the pulse width depends on the input signal *pulsbreddsmodulering*

dustcover ['dʌstkʌvə] *subst.* protective cover for a machine *skyddsöverdrag*

duty-rated ['djuːtɪ'reɪtɪd] *adj.* referring to the maximum number of operations which a device can perform in a set time to a certain specification *nominell maximal kapacitet*

QUOTE the laser printer can provide letter-quality print on ordinary cut-sheet paper and is duty-rated at up to 3,000 pages per month
Minicomputer News

DUV ['diːjuː'viː] = DATA UNDER VOICE data transmission in a frequency range *or* channel lower than that of a human voice *frekvensdelad linje*

dyadic operation [dar'ædɪk ˌɒpə'reɪʃ(ə)n] *subst.* binary operation using two binary operands *dyadisk operation*

dyadisk operation ⇨ dyadic operation

dynamic [dar'næmɪk] *adj.* referring to data which can change with time *dynamisk, dynamisk data-;* **dynamic allocation** = system where resources are allocated during a program run, rather than being determined in advance *dynamisk tilldelning;* **dynamic buffer** = buffer whose size varies with demand *dynamisk buffert;* **dynamic data structure** = structure of a data management system which can be changed *or* adapted *dynamisk datastruktur;* **dynamic dump** = dump that is carried out periodically during a program run *dynamisk dump;* **dynamic memory** *or* **dynamic RAM** = random access memory that requires its contents to be updated regularly *dynamiskt direktminne;* **dynamic microphone** = microphone using a coil that moves and induces a voltage according to sound pressure *dynamisk mikrofon;* **dynamic multiplexing** = time division multiplexing method which allocates time segments to signals according to demand *dynamisk multiplexering;* **dynamic range** = range of softest to loudest sounds that a device *or* instrument can produce *dynamiskt omfång, dynamik;* **dynamic relocation (program)** = program that is moved from one section of memory to another during its run-time without affecting it *or* its data *dynamisk minnestilldelning;* **dynamic stop** = stop in a process where the system tells the user that some action must be taken before the processing will continue *dynamiskt avbrott;* **dynamic storage allocation** = to allocate memory to a program when it needs it rather than reserving a block before it has run *dynamisk minnestilldelning;* **dynamically redefinable character set** = computer *or* videotext character set that can be changed when required *teckenuppsättning med valbar betydelse;* **dynamic subroutine** = subroutine whose function must be defined each time it is called *dynamisk subrutin; compare* STATIC

dynamisk buffert ⇨ dynamic

dynamisk dump ⇨ dynamic

dynamisk fil ⇨ extend

dynamisk minnestilldelning ⇨ dynamic

dynamiskt direktminne ⇨ dynamic

dynamiskt minne ⇨ memory

dämpning ⇨ attenuation

Ee

E [iː] hexadecimal number equivalent to decimal number 14 *talet fjorton skrivet med hexadecimal notation*

EAN ['iːer'en] = EUROPEAN ARTICLE NUMBER numbering system for bar codes (European version of UPC)

EAPROM ['ıəprɒm] = ELECTRICALLY ALTERABLE PROGRAMMABLE READ-ONLY MEMORY version of EAROM which can be programmed *programmerbart läsminne*

EAROM ['ıərɒm] = ELECTRICALLY ALTERABLE READ-ONLY MEMORY

earth [ɜːθ] **1** *subst.* **(a)** the planet on which we live *jorden;* **earth coverage** = area of the earth's surface able to pick up a satellite's transmissions *jordtäckning;* **earth station** = dish antenna and circuitry used to communicate with a satellite *jordstation* **(b)** connection in a circuit representing zero potential *jord;* **all loose wires should be tied to earth; earth wire** = connecting wire between an electrical device and the earth, representing zero potential *jordledning* **2** *vb.* to connect an electrical device to the earth *jorda;* **all appliances must be earthed** NOTE: US English is **ground**

easy-to-use ['iːzɪtə'juːs] *adj.* that is simple to understand and operate *lättanvänd*

> QUOTE it is a really easy-to-use, menu-driven program that allows you to produce presentation quality graphics with little or no training
> *Soft*

EAX ['iːer'eks] = ELECTRONIC AUTOMATIC EXCHANGE

EBCDIC [eb'siːdɪk] = EXTENDED BINARY CODED DECIMAL INTERCHANGE CODE eight bit binary character coding system *standard för teckenrepresentation främst för stordatorer*

EBNF ['iːbiːen'ef] = EXTENDED BACKUS-NAUR FORM more flexible way of defining the syntax of a language *utökad syntaxbeskrivande notation för programmeringsspråk; see also* BNF

EBR ['iːbɪ'aː] = ELECTRON BEAM RECORDING recording the output from a computer directly onto microfilm using an electron beam *teknik för direktskrivning till mikrofilm*

echo ['ekəʊ] **1** *subst.* return of a signal back to the source from which it was transmitted *eko;* **echo chamber** = acoustic *or* electronic device used to increase the echo of a sound *ekorum, ekokammare;* **echo check** = each character received at a terminal is returned to the transmitter and checked to ensure accurate data transmission *ekokontroll;* **echo suppressor** = device used on long-distance speech lines to prevent echoing effects *ekodämpare* **2** *vb.* to return a received signal along the same transmission path *eka*

ECL ['i:si'el] = EMITTER COUPLED LOGIC high-speed logic circuit design using the emitters of the transistors as output connections to other stages *emitterkopplad logik*

ECMA ['i:si:em'eɪ] = EUROPEAN COMPUTER MANUFACTURERS ASSOCIATION *europeisk sammanslutning av datortillverkare verksam inom standardiseringsområdet;* **ECMA symbols** = standard set of symbols used to draw flowcharts *av ECMA föreslagen standard för flödesdiagram*

EDAC ['i:dæk] = ERROR DETECTION AND CORRECTION forward error correction system for data communications *system för felkorrigering i datakommunikation*

edge [edʒ] *subst.* side of a flat object *or* signal *or* clock pulse *kant, flank;* **edge board** *or* **card** = printed circuit board that has a series of contact strips along one edge allowing it to be inserted into an edge connector *instickskort;* **edge connector** = long connector with a slot containing metal contacts to allow it to make electrical contact with an edge card *kantkontakt;* **edge detection** = algorithm and routines used in image recognition to define the edges of an object *konturigenkänning;* **edge notched card** = paper card which has punched holes along an edge to represent data *kanthålkort;* **edge-triggered** = process *or* circuit which is clocked *or* synchronized by the changing level (edge) of a clock signal rather than the level itself *flanktriggad, flankutlöst*

edit ['edɪt] *vb.* to change, correct and modify text *or* programs *redigera;* **edit commands** = sequence of characters or keys that must be pressed to accomplish a function in an editor *redigeringskommandon;* **edit key** = key that starts a function that makes an editor easier to use *redigeringstangent;* **there are several special edit keys - this one will reformat the text; edit window** = area of the screen in which the user can display and edit text *or* graphics *redigeringsfönster;* **editing plan** = detailed plan of how a film *or* TV programme is to be edited before being shown *klippningsplan, redigeringsplan;* **editing run** = processing to check that new data meets certain requirements before actually analysing the data and its

implications *torrkörning (av dator), formatkontroll(körning) (av dator);* **editing symbol** = character on microfilm to aid positioning, cutting and editing of the frames *redigeringstecken;* **editing terms** = command words and instruction sequences used when editing *redigeringskommandon;* **linkage editing** = combining separate programs together, and standardizing the calls and references within them *länkning*

edition [ɪ'dɪʃ(ə)n] *subst.* all the copies of a book *or* newspaper printed at one time *utgåva;* **the second edition has had some changes to the text; did you see the late edition of the evening paper?**

editor ['edɪtə] *subst.* **(a)** person who edits a film *or* book *redaktör* **(b) editor program** = software that allows the user to select sections of a file and alter, delete or add to them *(fil- el. text)redigeringsprogram, textbehandlare, ordbehandlingsprogram;* **line editor** = software in which only one line of a source program can be edited at a time *radredigeringsprogram;* **text editor** = piece of software used to enter and correct text *or* modify programs under development *textredigeringsprogram, ordbehandlingsprogram* **(c)** person in charge of a newspaper *or* a section of a newspaper *redaktör;* **the editor of "The Times"; the paper's computer editor**

editorial [,edɪ'tɔ:rɪəl] **1** *adj.* referring to an editor *or* to editing *redaktionell;* **editorial processing centre** = number of small publishers that share a single computer to provide cheaper computing power *flera små förläggare som delar en dator* **2** *subst.* main article in a newspaper, written by the editor *ledare*

EDP ['i:di:'pi:] = ELECTRONIC DATA PROCESSING data processing using computers and electronic devices *ADB (automatisk databehandling);* **EDP capability** = word processor that is able to carry out certain data processing functions *textbehandlare med programmeringsfunktion* NOTE: **EDP** is more common in US English

EDS ['i:di:es] = EXCHANGEABLE DISK STORAGE disk drive using removable disk pack (as opposed to a fixed disk) *utbytbart skivminne*

educational [,edjʊ'keɪʃənl] *adj.* referring to education *utbildnings-;* which is used to teach *utbildnings-;* **educational TV** =

television programme that is in some way educational *utbildnings-TV*

EEPROM ['i:prɒm] = ELECTRICALLY ERASABLE PROGRAMMABLE READ-ONLY MEMORY *programmerbart läsminne, elektriskt raderminne*

QUOTE conventional EEPROM requires two transistors to store each bit of data
Electronics & Power

EEROM ['i:rɒm] = ELECTRICALLY ERASABLE READ-ONLY MEMORY

effective [ɪ'fektɪv] *adj.* which can be used to produce a certain result *ändamålsenlig, verksam, effektiv;* **effective address =** address resulting from the modification of an address *effektiv adress;* **effective bandwidth =** usable frequency range of a system *effektiv bandbredd;* **effective instruction =** the resulting instruction executed after the modification of an original instruction *effektivinstruktion;* **effective search speed =** rate of finding a particular section of information from a storage device *verklig sökhastighet;* **effective throughput =** average throughput of a processor *verklig (behandlings)kapacitet*

effective aperture [ɪ'fektɪv 'æpətjʊə] *subst.* **(a)** received signal power at the output of an aerial *effektiv antennförstärkning* **(b)** lens aperture after taking into account camera faults and lens defects *effektiv bländare*

COMMENT: the effective aperture is measured as the ratio of focal length of the lens to the diameter of the diaphragm

effektiv adress ⇨ **effective**

effektiv bandbredd ⇨ **effective**

efficiency [ɪ'fɪʃ(ə)nsɪ] *subst.* working well *effektivitet;* **he is doubtful about the efficiency of the new networking system**

efficient [ɪ'fɪʃ(ə)nt] *adj.* which works well *effektiv;* **the program is highly efficient at sorting files**

efficiently [ɪ'fɪʃ(ə)ntlɪ] *adv.* in an efficient way *effektivt;* **the word-processing package has produced a series of labelled letters very efficiently**

EFT ['i:ef'ti:] = ELECTRONIC FUNDS TRANSFER (SYSTEM) system where computers are used to transmit money to and from banks *elektronisk girering (mellan banker)*

efterbehandlingsprogram ⇨ **postprocessor**

efterlysning ⇨ **persistence, lag**

eftersända ⇨ **forward**

EFTPOS ['eftpɒs] = ELECTRONIC FUNDS TRANSFER POINT-OF-SALE terminal at a POS that is linked to a central computer which automatically transfers money from the customer's account to the shop's *butiksbetalterminal*

EGA ['i:dʒi:'eɪ] = ENHANCED GRAPHICS ADAPTER popular microcomputer high-resolution colour display standardized system *persondatorstandard för utökad (färg)grafikpresentation*

QUOTE although the video BIOS services are enhanced by adding an EGA card, the DOS functions are not
.EXE

EHF ['i:eɪtʃ'ef] = EXTREMELY HIGH FREQUENCY radio frequencies from 30 - 300GHz *extremt hög frekvens*

EIA ['i:aɪ'eɪ] = ELECTRONIC INDUSTRY ASSOCIATION; **EIA interface =** standard defining interface signals, transmission rate and power, usually used to connect terminals to modems *av EIA föreslaget standardgränssnitt för datakommunikation, EIA-gränssnitt*

eight-bit (system) ['eɪt,bɪt ('sɪstəm)] *subst.* referring to an (old) small, low cost, low power home computer in which the CPU can process eight-bit words *8-bitars(system);* **eight-bit byte** *or* **octet =** byte made up of eight binary digits *byte, ibland, särskilt i Frankrike, oktett; compare with* SIXTEEN, THIRTY-TWO BIT

eight-inch disk ['eɪt,ɪntʃdɪsk] *subst.* high-capacity floppy disk which is eight inches in diameter *åttatumsdiskett;* **eight-inch drive =** disk drive for a eight-inch disk *åttatumsdiskettenhet*

eighty-track disk ['eɪtɪ,træk 'dɪsk] *subst.* disk formatted to contain eighty tracks *åttiospårsskivminne;* **eighty-column screen =** screen that can display eighty characters horizontally *åttioteckensskärm*

either-or operation ['aɪðə,ɔ: ,ɒpə'reɪʃ(ə)n] *subst.* logical function that produces a true output if any input is true *antingen-ellerfunktion*

either-way operation ['aɪðə,weɪ ,ɒpə'reɪʃ(ə)n] *subst.* data transmission in one direction at a time over a bidirectional channel *halvduplex*

ekodämpare ⇨ **echo**

ekostörning ⇨ **delay**

ekvatororbital (omloppsbana) ⇨ **equatorial orbit**

ekvivalensoperation ⇨ **equivalence**

ekvivalent ⇨ **equal**

elapsed time [ɪ'læpst 'taɪm] *subst.* time taken by the user to carry out a task on a computer *använd tid*

elastic banding [ɪ'læstɪk 'bændɪŋ] *subst.* method of defining the limits of an image on a computer screen by stretching a boundary around it *ramsträckning*

elastic buffer [ɪ'læstɪk 'bʌfə] *subst.* buffer size that changes according to demand *elastisk buffert*

electret [ɪ'lektrət] *subst.* piece of dielectric that keeps an electronic charge after a voltage has been applied at manufacture *elektret-;* **electret microphone** = microphone using a section of dielectric as a transducer that provides an electric signal with varying sound pressure *elektretmikrofon*

electric [ɪ'lektrɪk] *adj.* worked by electricity *elektrisk;* **electric current** = mass movement of electric charge in a conductor *elektrisk ström;* **electric charge** = a number of atoms that are charged (due to excess *or* deficiency of electrons) *elektrisk laddning;* **electric typewriter** = typewriter whose keys are switches which control motors and solenoids to perform all the functions *elektrisk skrivmaskin*

electrical [ɪ'lektrɪk(ə)l] *adj.* referring to electricity *elektrisk;* **the engineers are trying to repair an electrical fault**

electrically [ɪ'lektrɪk(ə)lɪ] *adv.* referring to electricity *elektriskt;* **an electrically-powered motor; electrically alterable, programmable read-only memory (EAPROM)** = version of EAROM that can be programmed *programmerbart läsminne;* **electrically alterable read-only memory (EAROM)** = read-only memory chip whose contents can be programmed by applying a certain voltage to a write pin, and can be erased by light *or* a reverse voltage *raderbart läsminne, raderminne;* **electrically erasable programmable read-only memory (EEPROM)** = ROM storage chip which can be programmed and erased using an electrical signal *programmerbart läsminne, elektriskt raderminne;* **electrically erasable read-only memory (EEROM)** = EAROM memory chip whose contents can be programmed by applying a certain voltage to a write pin, and can be erased by light *or* a reverse voltage *raderbart läsminne, raderminne*

electricity [ɪlek'trɪsətɪ] *subst.* electric current used to provide light *or* heat *or* power *elektricitet;* **the electricity was cut off, and the computers crashed; electricity prices are an important factor in the production costs**

electrode [ɪ'lektrəʊd] *subst.* part of an electric circuit *or* device that collects, controls or emits electrons *elektrod*

electrographic printer [ɪ,lektrə(ʊ)'græfɪk 'prɪntə] *subst. see* ELECTROSTATIC PRINTER

electroluminescence [ɪ,lektrə(ʊ),luːmɪ'nesns] *subst.* light emitted from a phosphor dot when it is struck by an electron *or* charged particle *elektroluminescens*

electroluminescent [ɪ,lektrəʊ,luːmɪ'nesnt] *adj.* capable of emitting light due to electroluminescence *elektroluminescens;* **the screen coating is electroluminescent; electroluminescent display** = flat, lightweight display screen that is made up of two pieces of glass covered with a grid of conductors, separated by a thin layer of gas which luminesces when a point of the grid is selected by two electric signals *elektroluminescent bildskärm (EL-skärm)*

electroluminescing [ɪ,lektrə(ʊ),luːmɪ'nesɪŋ] *adj.* (object) which is emitting light due to electroluminescence *elektroluminescerande*

electromagnet [ɪ,lektrə(ʊ)'mægnət] *subst.* device that consists of a core and a coil of wire that produces a magnetic field when current is passed through the coil *elektromagnet*

electromagnetic [ɪ,lektrə(ʊ)mæg'netɪk] *adj.* generating a magnetic field *or* magnetic effect when supplied with electrical power *elektromagnetisk;* **electromagnetic interference** = corruption of data due to nearby electrically generated magnetic fields *elektromagnetisk interferens;* **electromagnetic spectrum** = frequency range of electromagnetic radiation (from light to radio wave) *elektromagnetiskt spektrum*

electromagnetically [ɪ,lektrə(ʊ)mæg'netɪklɪ] *adv.* working due to electromagnetic effects *elektromagnetiskt*

electromagnetic radiation [ɪ,lektrə(ʊ)mæg'netɪk ,reɪdɪ'eɪʃ(ə)n] *subst.* energy wave consisting of electric and/or magnetic fields *elektromagnetisk strålning*

COMMENT: electromagnetic radiation requires no medium to support it, travels approximately at the speed of light and can support frequency ranges from light to radio waves

electromechanical switching [ɪ,lektrə(ʊ)mə'kænɪk(ə)l 'swɪtʃɪŋ] *subst.* connection of two paths by an electrically operated switch *or* relay *elektromekanisk koppling, elektromekanisk växelfunktion*

electromotive force (EMF) [ˌɪlektrə(ʊ)'məʊtɪv fɔːs ('iːemˈef)] *subst.* difference in electrical potential across a source of electric current *elektromotorisk kraft (emk)*

electron [ɪ'lektrɒn] *subst.* elementary particle with an elementary negative charge *elektron;* **electron beam =** stream of electrons *elektronstråle;* **electron beam recording (EBR) =** (i) production of microfilm images by means of an electron beam *teknik för skrivning till mikrofilm med elektronstråle;* (ii) recording the output from a computer directly onto microfilm using an electron beam *teknik för direktskrivning till mikrofilm;* **electron gun =** electronic component that emits a large number of electrons (usually by heating a filament of metal) *elektronkanon*

COMMENT: mass of 9.109 x 10^{31} kg, and charge of 1.602 x10^{19} C

electronic [ɪlek'trɒnɪk] *adj.* referring to something which is controlled by *or* controls electron flow *elektronisk;* **electronic automatic exchange =** telephone routing system that uses electronic circuits to switch signals *elektronisk växel;* **electronic blackboard =** means of transmitting handwritten text and diagrams over a telephone line *elektronisk fax;* **electronic composition =** text manipulation by computer before typesetting *elektronisk sättning, elektronisk montering;* **electronic data processing (EDP) =** data processing using computers and electronic devices *ADB (automatisk databehandling;* **electronic data processing compatibility =** ability of a word processor to carry out certain data processing functions *förmåga hos en ordbehandlare att utföra vissa databehandlingsfunktioner;* **electronic digital computer =** digital computer constructed with electronic components (the basic form uses a CPU, main memory, backing storage and input/output devices; these are all implemented with electronic components and integrated circuits) *digital dator;* **electronic editing =** video film editing using computers, image storage, etc., rather than physically cutting the tape *elektronisk redigering;* **electronic engineer =** person who specializes in work on electronic devices *elektroniker, elektronikingenjör;* **electronic industry association interface (EIA) =** standard defining interface signals, transmission rate and power usually used to connect terminals to modems *EIA-standardgränssnitt;* **electronic filing =** system of storage of documents which can be easily retrieved *elektronisk lagring;* **electronic funds transfer (EFT) =**

using a computer to transfer money to and from banks *elektronisk girering (mellan banker);* **electronic funds transfer point of sale (EFTPOS) =** terminal at a POS that is linked to a central computer which automatically transfers money from the customer's account to the shop's *butiksbetalterminal;* **electronic keyboard =** keyboard that generates characters electronically in response to a switch making contact when pressed, rather than by mechanical means *(elektroniskt) tangentbord;* **electronic lock =** security device, usually in the form of a password (used to protect a file *or* piece of equipment from unauthorized use) *elektroniskt lås(sigill);* **electronic mail =** sending and receiving messages over a telephone network, usually using a bulletin board *elektronisk post;* **electronic mailbox =** system for holding messages sent by electronic mail until the person to whom they were sent is ready to accept them *elektronisk brevlåda;* **electronic money =** smart cards *or* phonecards, etc., which take the place of money *elektroniska betalningsmedel, aktivt plastkort;* **electronic news gathering (ENG) =** method of reporting news items for TV news programmes, where the reporter has a cameraman with a portable video camera which can transmit live pictures direct to the studio *elektronisk nyhetsbevakning (till teve);* **electronic office =** office where all the work is done using computers, which store information, communicate with different workstations, etc. *automatiserat kontor;* **electronic pen** *or* **stylus** *or* **wand =** light pen *or* wand; stylus used to draw on a graphics tablet *ljuspenna;* **electronic point-of-sale (EPOS) =** system that uses a computer terminal at a point-of-sale site for electronic funds transfer *or* stock control as well as product identification, etc. *kassaterminal, butiksterminal;* **electronic publishing =** (i) use of desktop publishing packages and laser printers to produce printed matter *datoriserad originalproduktion;* (ii) using computers to write and display information, such as viewdata *datorbaserad informationsverksamhet (t.ex. Videotex);* **electronic pulse =** short voltage pulse *elektrisk puls;* **electronic shopping =** system of shopping from the home, using computerized catalogues and paying by credit card, all by means of a home computer terminal *datoriserade inköp;* **electronic signature =** special code which identifies the sender of a coded message *elektronisk signatur;* **electronic smog =** excessive stray electromagnetic fields and static electricity generated by large numbers of electronic equipment (this can damage equipment *or* a person's health) *elektrisk strålning (ospecificerat);* **electronic stylus** *or* **wand** *see* LIGHT PEN; **electronic**

switching system = telephone routing using a computer system to control the lineswitching circuits *elektronisk telefonväxel;* **electronic traffic** = data transmitted in the form of electronic pulses *dataöverföring;* **electronic typewriter** = typewriter using an electronic keyboard linked, via a buffer, to an electrically driven printing mechanism, also with the facility to send *or* receive character data from a computer *elektrisk skrivmaskin;* **electronic viewfinder** = miniature cathode ray tube in a television *or* video camera that allows the camera operator to see the images being recorded *kameramonitor*

QUOTE electronic mail is a system which allows computer users to send information to each other via a central computer
Which PC?
QUOTE electronic publishing will be used for printing on paper, but it can be applied equally to data storage on a database, transmission via telecommunications or for use with visual presentation media such as AV slides or television
Electronic Publishing & Print Show
QUOTE electronic mail is a system which allows computer users to send information to each other via a central computer
Which PC?
QUOTE electronic publishing will be used for printing on paper, but it can be applied equally to data storage on a database, transmission via telecommunications or for use with visual presentation media such as AV slides or television
Electronic Publishing & Print Show

---

electronically [ɪlek'trɒnɪklɪ] *adv.* referring to operations using electronic methods *elektroniskt;* **the text is electronically transmitted to an outside typesetter**

electronics [ɪlek'trɒnɪks] *subst.* science of applying the study of electrons and their properties to manufactured products, such as components, computers, calculators or telephones *elektronik;* **the electronics industry; an electronics specialist** NOTE: takes a singular verb

electro-optic effect [ɪ'lektrəʊ 'ɒptɪk ɪ'fekt] *subst.* changes in the refractive index of a material due to a nearby electric field *elektro-optisk effekt, kerreffekt*

electrophotography [ɪˌlektrə(ʊ)fə'tɒgrəfɪ] *subst.* forming an image using electrical and optical effects *elektrofotografi, elektrostatiskt framställd bild*

electrosensitive [ɪˌlektrə(ʊ)'sensɪtɪv] *adj.* **electrosensitive paper** = metal-coated printing paper, which can display characters using localized heating with a special dot-matrix print head *aluminiumpapper;* **electrosensitive printing** = printing using electrosensitive paper *elektroutskrift*

electrostatic [ɪˌlektrə(ʊ)'stætɪk] *adj.* referring to devices using the properties of

static electrical charge *elektrostatisk;* **electrostatic printer** = type of printer which forms an image on the paper by charging certain regions to provide character shapes, etc., and using ink with an opposite charge which sticks to the paper where required *elektrostatisk skrivare;* **electrostatic screen** = metal cage surrounding sensitive equipment (and connected to ground) to protect it from interference *skärmbur, Faradays bur;* **electrostatic speaker** = loudspeaker containing two large charged plates, one flexible which moves when a signal is applied, creating sound signals *elektrostatisk högtalare;* **electrostatic storage** = data stored in the form of small electric charged regions on a dielectric material *elektrostatiskt minne*

electrostatically [ɪˌlektrə(ʊ)'stætɪklɪ] *adv.* using properties of static charge *elektrostatiskt*

electrothermal printer [ɪˌlektrə(ʊ)'θɜːml 'prɪntə] *subst.* printer that uses a printing head with a dot-matrix of heating elements to form characters on electrosensitive paper *termisk skrivare, termotransferskrivare, värmeöverföringsskrivare*

elegant ['elɪgənt] *adj.* **elegant programming** = writing a well-structured program using the minimum number of instructions *välgjord (elegant) programmering*

elektrisk skrivmaskin ⇨ **electric, electronic**

elektromagnet ⇨ **solenoid**

elektromagnetisk störning ⇨ **interference**

elektronisk anslagstavla ⇨ **BBS**

(elektronisk) brevlåda ⇨ **mailbox**

elektronisk etikett ⇨ **interior label**

elektronisk girering (mellan banker) ⇨ **electronic**

elektronisk post ⇨ **CBMS, electronic**

elektronisk redigering ⇨ **electronic**

elektronisk telefonväxel ⇨ **electronic**

elektroniskt klotterplank ⇨ **BBS**

elektroutskrift ⇨ **electrosensitive**

element ['elɪmənt] *subst.* **(a)** small part of an object which is made up of many similar parts *element, komponent;* **logic element** = gate *or* combination of gates *logisk krets;* **picture element** *or* **pixel** = smallest single unit *or* point on a display whose colour *or* brightness can be controlled *bildpunkt;* **signal element** = smallest basic unit used when transmitting digital data *bit* **(b)** one number *or* cell of a matrix *or* array *vektorelement;* **array element =** one individual piece of data within an array *element* **(c)** coil of resistive wire to which an electric current is applied to generate heat *värmeelement* **(d)** substance in which all the atoms have the same number of electrons and charge *grundämne*

elementary [,elɪ'ment(ə)rɪ] *adj.* made of many similar small sections *or* objects *elementbyggt;* **elementary cable section =** model of the characteristics of a short length of transmission cable that can be applied to the whole length of cable *kabelelement*

ELF ['iːel'ef] = EXTREMELY LOW FREQUENCY communications frequencies of less than 100Hz *extremt låg frekvens*

eliminate [ɪ'lɪmɪneɪt] *vb.* to remove something completely *eliminiera;* **using a computer should eliminate all possibility of error in the address system; the spelling checker does not eliminate all spelling mistakes**

QUOTE pointing with the cursor and pressing the joystick button eliminates use of the keyboard almost entirely
Soft

elimination [ɪ,lɪmɪ'neɪʃ(ə)n] *subst.* removing of something completely *eliminering;* **elimination factor =** during a search, the section of data that is not used *överflödsfaktor*

elite [eɪ'liːt] *subst.* typewriter typeface *typsnitt för skrivare och skrivmaskin (elite och prestige elite)*

eller-grind ⇨ **gate, OR function**

ellipse [ɪ'lɪps] *subst.* oval shaped; like an elongated circle *ellips*

elliptical orbit [ɪ'lɪptɪk(ə)l 'ɔːbɪt] *subst.* path of a satellite around the earth that is in the shape of an ellipse *elliptisk bana*

else rule ['els 'ruːl] *subst.* program logical rule used with an IF-THEN instruction to provide an alternative if the IF-THEN condition is not met *logiskt "annars" i programmeringsspråk (se följande programexempel);* **IF X=20 THEN PRINT 'X is 20' ELSE PRINT 'X not 20'**

EL-skärm ⇨ **electroluminescent**

ELT ['iːel'tiː] = ELECTRONIC TYPEWRITER

EM ['iː'em] = END OF MEDIUM

em [em] *subst.* space taken by an 'm' in a given typeface (equal to 12 point*or* pica) *typografiskt utrymmesmått motsvarande bokstaven "m" i graden 12 punkter, "trepinnars-block";* **em quad =** space printed of a size equal to an em *typografiskt*

utrymmesmått motsvarande bokstaven "m" i graden 12 punkter, "trepinnars-block";* **em dash** *or* **em rule =** dash as long as an 'm', showing that words are separated *tankstreck;* **ems per hour =** rate of production of characters from a machine *or* operator *typografiskt kapacitetsmått; see also* EN

E-mail ['iː 'meɪl] *or* **email** ['iː 'meɪl] = ELECTRONIC MAIL

QUOTE to collect telex messages from an e-mail system, you have to remember to dial the system and check whether there are any telex messages in your mailbox
Which PC?

embedded [ɪm'bedɪd] *adj.* **embedded code =** sections *or* routines written in machine code, inserted into a high-level program to speed up *or* perform a special function *inbäddad (maskin)kod, maskinkod i högnivåspråk;* **embedded command =** printer command (such as indicating that text should be in italic) inserted into the text and used by a word-processing system when producing formatted printed text *integrerad styrkod;* **embedded computer** *or* **system =** dedicated computer controlling a machine *inbyggd dator, integrerad dator;* dedicated computer within a larger system that performs one fixed function *integrerad specialdator*

emboldening [ɪm'bəʊld(ə)nɪŋ] *subst.* making a word print in bold type *utskrivning i halvfet stil*

embrace [ɪm'breɪs] *see* DEADLY

emf ['iːem'ef] = ELECTROMOTIVE FORCE

EMI ['iːem'aɪ] = ELECTROMAGNETIC INTERFERENCE corruption of data due to nearby electrically generated magnetic fields *magnetisk störning*

emission [ɪ'mɪʃ(ə)n] *subst.* sending out (of a signal *or* radiation, etc.) *utstrålning, avgivning, sändning;* **the emission of the electron beam; the receiver picked up the radio emission**

emit [ɪ'mɪt] *vb.* to send out *stråla ut, avge, sända*

emitter [ɪ'mɪtə] *subst.* connection to a bipolar transistor *emitter (en av anslutningarna till en bipolär transistor)*

emitter-coupled logic (ECL) [ɪ'mɪtə'kʌpld 'lɒdʒɪk ('iːsiː'el)] *subst.* high-speed logic circuit design using the emitters of the transistors as output connections to other stages *emitterkopplad logik*

emitterkopplad logik ⇨ **ECL**

empty ['em(p)tɪ] *adj.* with nothing inside *tom;* **empty** *or* **null list =** list with no elements *tom lista;* **empty medium** = blank but formatted storage medium that is ready to receive data *tomt medium;* **empty** *or* **null** *or* **void set** = reserved area for related data items, containing no data *tom dataarea;* **empty slot** = (i) packet of data in a packet-switching LAN that is carrying no information *tomt paket;* (ii) unused expansion edge connector on a motherboard *tom (ledig) kontakt;* **empty** *or* **null string** = variable containing no characters *nollvariabel*

emulate ['emjʊleɪt] *vb.* to copy *or* behave like something else *emulera, efterlikna;* **laser printer which emulates a wide range of office printers**

QUOTE some application programs do not have the right drivers for a laser printer, so look out for laser printers which are able to emulate the more popular office printers
Publish

emulation [ˌemjʊ'leɪʃ(ə)n] *subst.* behaviour by one computer *or* printer which is exactly the same as another, which allows the same programs to be run and the same data to be processed *emulering;* **emulation facility** = feature of hardware *or* software which emulates another system *emuleringsfunktion, emuleringsmöjlighet*

QUOTE full communications error checking built into the software ensures reliable file transfers and a terminal emulation facility enables a user's terminal to be used as if it were a terminal to the remote computer
Byte

emulator ['emjʊleɪtə] *subst.* software *or* hardware that allows a machine to behave like another *emulator, emulering*

emulera ⇨ **emulate**

emuleringsrutin ⇨ **extracode**

emulsion [ɪ'mʌlʃ(ə)n] *subst.* light-sensitive coating on photographic film *or* paper *emulsion;* **emulsion laser storage** = digital storage technique using a laser to expose light-sensitive material *filmlaserminne*

en [en] *subst.* half the width of an em *typografiskt mått omfattande ett halvt "m" i graden 12 punkter, en "pinne";* **en dash** *or* **en rule** = line as long as an en, showing that two words *or* parts of words are joined together *bindestreck;* **en quad** = space that is half the width of an em quad space *typografiskt mått omfattande ett halvt "m" i graden 12 punkter, en "pinne"; see also* EM

enable [ɪ'neɪbl] *vb.* **(a)** to allow something to happen *tillåta, möjliggöra;* **a spooling program enables editing work to be carried out which printing is going on (b)** to use an electronic signal to start a process *or* access a function (on a chip *or* circuit) *starta,*

öppna; **enabling signal** = signal that starts a process *or* allows one to take place *klarsignal, öppningssignal*

encipher [ɪn'saɪfə] *vb.* to convert plaintext into a secure coded form by means of a cipher system *chiffrera;* **our competitors cannot understand our files - they have all been enciphered**

enclose [ɪn'kləʊz] *vb.* to surround with something *omsluta;* to put something inside something else *innesluta*

enclosure [ɪn'kləʊʒə] *subst.* protective casing for equipment *förpackning, låda*

encode [ɪn'kəʊd] *vb.* to apply the rules of a code to a program *or* data *koda (in)*

encoder [ɪn'kəʊdə] *subst.* device that can translate data from one format to another *dataomvandlare;* **colour encoder** = device that produces a standard TV signal from separate Red, Green and Blue signals *färgkodare, färgmodulator*

encoding [ɪn'kəʊdɪŋ] *subst.* translation of a message *or* text according to a coding system *kodning;* **binary encoding** = representing a character *or* element with a unique combination *or* pattern of bits in a word *binär kodning;* **encoding format** = method of coding data stored on a magnetic disk (to avoid a series of similar bits) *kodningsformat;* **magnetic encoding** = storage of binary data signals on a magnetic medium *magnetisk lagring*

encrypt [ɪn'krɪpt] *vb.* to convert plaintext to a secure coded form, using a cipher system *kryptera;* **the encrypted text can be sent along ordinary telephone lines, and no one will be able to understand it**

encryption [ɪn'krɪpʃn] *subst.* conversion of plaintext to a secure coded form by means of a cipher system *kryptering;* **data encryption standard (DES)** = standard for a block data cipher system *DES, krypteringsstandard (USA)*

end [end] **1** *subst.* **(a)** final point *or* last part *slut(et);* **at the end of the data transmission;** **end product** = manufactured product, made at the end of a production process *slutprodukt;* **after six months' trial production, the end product is still not acceptable; in the end** = at last *or* after a lot of problems *till slut;* **in the end the company had to pull out of the US market; in the end the company had to call in a consultant engineer (b)** statement *or* character to indicate the last word of a source file *sluttecken;* **end about carry** = most significant digit is added into the least significant place (used in BCD arithmetic) *addering med överföringssiffra (adderingsteknik i aritmetik med binärkodat decimaltal, överföringssiffran* *från en talposition adderas till den minst signifikanta biten i nästa talposition);* **end about shift** = data movement to the left *or* right in a word, the bits falling outside the word boundary are discarded and replaced with zeros *vänsterskift (utan överföringssiffra);* **end of address (EOA)** = transmitted code which indicates that address data has been sent *adresslutsignal;* **end of block (EOB)** = code which shows that the last byte of a block of data has been sent through a communications link *blockslutssignal;* **end of data (EOD)** = code which shows that the end of a stored data file has been reached *dataslutssignal;* **end of document** *or* **end of file (EOF)** = marker after the last record in a file *filslutssignal;* **end of job (EOJ)** = code used in batch processing to show that a job has been finished *jobbslutssignal;* **end of medium (EM)** = code that indicates the end of usable physical medium *medieslutsignal;* **end of message (EOM)** = code used to separate the last character of one message from the first of another message *meddelandeslutsignal;* **end of page indicator** = indicator on a typewriter to show that a page is nearly finished *sidslutsignal;* **end of record (EOR)** = code used to show the end of a record *postslutssignal;* **end of run routines** = routines carried out before a program run finishes to perform certain system housekeeping functions *avslutande systemadministrativa rutiner;* **end of tape** = code used to indicate the end of a magnetic tape *bandslutssignal;* **end of text (EOT** *or* **ETX)** = code sent after last character of text *textslutssignal;* **end of transmission (EOT)** = sequence of characters that indicate that all the data from a terminal *or* peripheral has been transmitted *sändningslutssignal* **2** *vb.* to finish *or* to stop something *sluta*

ending ['endɪŋ] *subst.* **(a)** action of coming to an end *or* of stopping something *stopp* **(b)** end part of something *slut;* **line endings** = last words on each line of text, which may be hyphenated *radslut*

endless ['endləs] *adj.* with no end *oändlig;* **endless loop** = continuous piece of recording tape *or* number of computer instructions that are continuously repeated *oändlig slinga*

end user ['end,juːzə] *subst.* person who will use the device *or* program *or* product *(slut)användare;* **the company is creating a computer with a specific end user in mind**

energy ['enədʒɪ] *subst.* **(a)** force *or* strength; ability of a body *or* object to do work *energi, kraft, arbete* **(b)** power from electricity *or* metal, etc. *energi;* **we try to save energy by switching off the lights when the rooms are empty; if you reduce the room**

temperature to eighteen degrees, you will save energy NOTE: no plural for (b)

energy-saving ['enədʒɪ 'seɪvɪŋ] *adj.* which saves energy *energibesparande;* **the company is introducing energy-saving measures**

enfärgsskärm ⇨ **monochrome**

ENG ['iːen'dʒiː] = ELECTRONIC NEWS GATHERING

enhance [ɪn'hɑːns] *vb.* to make better *or* clearer *förbättra, utöka;* **enhanced dot matrix** = clearer character *or* graphics printout (using smaller dots and more dots per inch) *utökad utskriftsmatris;* **enhanced graphics adapter (EGA)** = popular standardized system of high-resolution colour display for microcomputers *persondatorstandard för grafikpresentation;* **enhanced graphics adapter screen** = high-resolution colour monitor that can display EGA system signals and graphics *EGA-skärm;* **enhanced small device interface (ESDI)** = interface standard between a CPU and peripherals such as disk drives *ESDI-gränssnitt*

> QUOTE the typefaces are fairly rudimentary, especially if you are not using an enhanced graphics adapter screen
> **Desktop Publishing**

enhancement [ɪn'hɑːnsmənt] *subst.* add-on facility which improves the output *or* performance of equipment *förbättring, utökning*

enhancer [ɪn'hɑːnsə] *subst.* device *or* software which enhances a process *or* product *(produkt)utökning*

enhet ⇨ **device, item, unit**

enhetsoberoende ⇨ **device**

enkelriktad sändning ⇨ **free**

enkelt ⇨ **clear**

enkortsdator ⇨ **microcomputer, single**

enkät ⇨ **questionnaire**

enlarge [ɪn'lɑːdʒ] *vb.* to make (a photograph) larger *förstora*

enlargement [ɪn'lɑːdʒmənt] *subst.* making larger; a larger version of a photograph *förstoring;* **an enlargement of the photograph was used to provide better detail**

ENQ ['iːen'kjuː] = ENQUIRY

enquiry [ɪn'kwaɪərɪ] *subst.* request for data *or* information from a device *or* database; accessing data in a computer memory without changing the data *förfrågan, fråga;* **enquiry character** = special control code that is a request for identification *or* status *or* data from a device *frägesymbol, frågetecken*

enställig operation ⇨ **monadic**
(Boolean) operator

enställig operator ⇨ **monadic**
(Boolean) operator

ensure [ɪnˈʃuə] *vb.* to make sure *garantera, se till;* **pushing the write-protect tab will ensure that the data on the disk cannot be erased**

enter [ˈentə] *vb.* to type in information on a terminal *or* keyboard *stansa, skriva in;* **to enter a name on a list; the data has been entered on data capture forms; enter key** = key pressed to indicate the end of an input *or* line of text *vagnreturtangent, returtangent*

entering [ˈent(ə)rɪŋ] *subst.* act of typing in data *or* writing items in a record *inskrivning, instansning*
NOTE: no plural

entity [ˈentətɪ] *subst.* subject to which the data stored in a file *or* database refers *entitet, objekt*

entry [ˈentrɪ] *subst.* **(a)** single record *or* data about one action *or* object in a database *or* library *objekt, objekt* **(b)** place where you can enter *ingång;* **entry condition** = condition that must be satisfied before a routine can be entered *startvillkor, ingångsvillkor;* **entry instruction** = first instruction executed in a called subroutine *startinstruktion, ingångsinstruktion;* **entry point** = address from which a program *or* subroutine is to be executed *startpunkt, ingångspunkt;* **entry time** = point in time when a program *or* job *or* batch will be executed by the operating system scheduler *starttid*

enumerated type [ɪˈnjuːməreɪtɪd ˈtaɪp] *subst.* data storage *or* classification using numbers to represent chosen convenient labels *uppräkningsbar datatyp*

> COMMENT: if 'man', 'horse', 'dog', 'cat' are the items of data, stored by the machine simply as 0, 1, 2, 3, they can still be referred to in the program as man, horse, etc., to make it easier for the user to recognize them

envelope [ˈenvələup] *subst.* **(a)** flat paper cover for sending letters *kuvert;* **air mail envelope** = very light envelope for air mail letters *flygpostkuvert;* **window envelope** = envelope with a hole covered with film so that the address on the letter inside can be seen *fönsterkuvert;* **sealed** *or* **unsealed envelope** = envelope where the flap has been stuck down to close it *or* envelope where the flap has been pushed into the back of the envelope *förseglat eller*

oförseglat kuvert **(b)** variation of amplitude of a signal *or* sound with time *envelopp, signalutseende;* **attack envelope** = shape of the initial section of a signal *framkantsutseende;* **envelope delay** *see* DELAY DISTORTION; **envelope detection** = technique of signal recovery from a modulated waveform *enveloppdetektering, detektion av signalutseende* **(c)** transmitted byte of data containing error and control bits *paketadministrationsbyte, "kuvert"*

environment [ɪnˈvaɪər(ə)nmənt] *subst.* **(a)** condition in a computer system of all the registers and memory locations *miljö* **(b)** surroundings *or* physical conditions *omgivning*

> QUOTE one of the advantages of working in a PC-based environment is the enormous range of software which can run on the same computer
> **ESL Newsletter**

envärd operation ⇨ **unary operation**

EOA [ˈiːəuˈeɪ] = END OF ADDRESS

EOB [ˈiːəuˈbiː] = END OF BLOCK

EOD [ˈiːəuˈdiː] = END OF DATA

EOF [ˈiːəuˈef] = END OF FILE

EOJ [ˈiːəuˈdʒeɪ] = END OF JOB

EOM [ˈiːəuˈem] = END OF MESSAGE

EOR [ˈiːəuˈɑː] = END OF RECORD

EOT [ˈiːəuˈtiː] = END OF TEXT *or* TRANSMISSION

episcope [ˈepɪskəup] *subst.* projector that can display opaque material and documents onto a screen *episkop*

epitaxial layer [ˌepɪˈtæksɪəl ˈleɪə] *subst.* very thin layer of material *or* doped semiconductor deposited onto a substrate base *epitaxiallager*

epitaxy [ˌepɪˈtæksɪ] *subst.* method of depositing very thin layers of materials onto a base, for use in chip manufacture *epitaxi*

EPOS [ˈiːpɒs] = ELECTRONIC POINT-OF-SALE system that uses a computer terminal at a point-of-sale site for electronic funds transfer *or* stock control as well as product identification *kassaterminal, butiksterminal*

EPROM [ˈiːprɒm] *subst.* **(a)** = ELECTRICALLY PROGRAMMABLE READ-ONLY MEMORY **(b)** = ERASABLE PROGRAMMABLE READ-ONLY MEMORY

> QUOTE the densest EPROMs commercially available today are at the 1Mbit level
> **Electronics & Power**

equal [ˈiːkw(ə)l] **1** *adj.* exactly the same *lika, samma som, ekvivalent* **2** *vb.* to be the same as *vara (bli) lik;* **production this month has equalled our best month ever** NOTE: NOTE: **equalling - equalled** but US: **equaling - equaled**

equality [ɪˈkwɒlətɪ] *subst.* logical function whose output is true if either of two inputs is true, and false if both inputs are the same *symmetrisk differens*

equalization [ˌiːkwəlaɪˈzeɪʃ(ə)n] *subst.* process of making a signal equal (to preset values) *anpassning, utjämning*

equalize [ˈiːkwəlaɪz] *vb.* to make equal (to preset values) *anpassa, utjämna;* **the received signal was equalized to an optimum shape**

equalizer [ˈiːkwəlaɪzə] *subst.* device which changes the amplitude of various parts of a signal according to preset values *equalizer, tonkontroll;* **frequency equalizer =** device that changes the amplitude of various frequency components of a signal according to preset values *equalizer, tonkontroll*

equally [ˈiːkwəlɪ] *adv.* in the same way *lika;* **they were both equally responsible for the successful launch of the new system**

equate [ɪˈkweɪt] *vb.* to make the same as *likställa, jämställa;* **the variable was equated to the input data**

equation [ɪˈkweɪʒ(ə)n] *subst.* formula *ekvation, formel;* **machine equation =** formula which an analog computer has been programmed to solve *(analog)maskinekvation*

equator [ɪˈkweɪtə] *subst.* imaginary line running round the middle of the earth *ekvator*

equatorial orbit [ˌekwəˈtɔːrɪəl ˈɔːbɪt] *subst.* satellite flight path that follows the earth's equator *ekvatororbital (omloppsbana)*

equip [ɪˈkwɪp] *vb.* to provide with machinery or equipment *utrusta, förse*

equipment [ɪˈkwɪpmənt] *subst.* machinery and furniture required to make a factory or office work *(kontors-)fabriksutrustning;* **office equipment** or **business equipment; computer equipment supplier; office equipment catalogue; equipment failure =** hardware fault, rather than a software fault *maskin(varu)fel* NOTE: no plural

equivalence [ɪˈkwɪvələns] *subst.* **(a)** being equivalent *likhet* **(b)** logical operation that is true if all the inputs are the same *likhet;* **equivalence function** or **operation =** (i) AND function *ekvivalensoperation;* (ii) logical function

whose output is true if both inputs are the same *ekvivalens;* **equivalence gate =** gate which performs an equivalence function *likhetsgrind;* **non-equivalence function (NEQ) =** logical function where the output is true if the inputs are not the same, otherwise the output is false *symmetrisk differens, icke-ekvivalens*

COMMENT: output is 1 if both inputs are 1 or if both are 0; if the two inputs are different, the output is 0

equivalent [ɪˈkwɪvələnt] *adj.* **to be equivalent to =** to have the same value as or to be the same as *motsvara, vara detsamma som;* **the total characters keyboarded so far is equivalent to one day's printing time**

erasable [ɪˈreɪzəbl] *adj.* which can be erased *raderbar;* **erasable storage** or **erasable memory =** (i) storage medium that can be re-used *raderbart minne;* (ii) temporary storage *mellanlagringsminne;* **erasable programmable read-only memory (EPROM) =** read-only memory chip that can be programmed by a voltage applied to a write pin and data applied to its output pins, usually erasable with ultraviolet light *raderbart läsminne, raderminne*

erase [ɪˈreɪz] *vb.* **(a)** to set all the digits in a storage area to zero *radera* **(b)** to remove any signal from a magnetic medium *radera;* **erase head =** small magnet that clears a magnetic tape or disk of recorded signals *raderhuvud*

erase character [ɪˈreɪzˌkærəktə] *subst.* character which means do nothing *radertecken, nolltecken*

eraser [ɪˈreɪzə] *subst.* device that erases the contents of an EPROM (usually using UV light) *läsminnesraderare*

ERCC [ˈiːɑːsiːˈsiː] = ERROR CHECKING AND CORRECTING memory which checks and corrects errors *felkorrigerande minne*

E-region [ˈiː ˈriːdʒ(ə)n] or **Heaviside-Kennelly layer** [ˈhevɪsaɪd ˈknɒlɪ ˈleɪə] *subst.* section of the ionosphere that is 90-150 km above the earth's surface *E-lagret*

ergonomics [ˌɜːgə(ʊ)ˈnɒmɪks] *subst.* study of people at work, and their working conditions, concerned with improving safety and making machines easy to use *ergonomi*

ergonomist [ɜːˈgɒnəmɪst] *subst.* scientist who studies people at work and tries to improve their working conditions *ergonom*

EROM [ˈiːrɒm] = ERASABLE READ-ONLY MEMORY *(same as* EAROM)

erratum [eˈrɑːtəm] *subst.* correction on a separate slip of paper to an error or

omission from a document *rättelseblad, tryckfelsförteckning*
NOTE: plural is **errata**

error ['erə] *subst.* mistake due to an operator *användarfel;* mistake caused by a hardware *or* software fault *maskin(varu)fel, program(varu)fel;* mistake in a program that prevents a program *or* system running correctly *programmeringsfel;* **he made an error in calculating the total; the secretary must have made a typing error; in error** *or* **by error** = by mistake *av misstag;* **margin of error** = number of mistakes which are acceptable in a document *or* in a calculation *felmarginal;* **error ambiguity** = error due to an incorrect selection from ambiguous data *tvetydighetsfel;* **error burst** = group of several consecutive errors (in a transmission) *felskur;* **error checking code** = general term used to describe all error correcting and error detecting codes *felkorrigeringskod;* **error code** = code that indicates that a particular type of error has occurred *felkod;* **error condition** = state that is entered if an attempt is made to operate on data containing errors *feltillstånd;* **error control** = routines that ensure that errors are minimised and any errors that occur are detected and dealt with rapidly *felhantering;* **error correcting code** = coding system that allows bit errors occurring during transmission to be rapidly corrected by logical deduction methods rather than re-transmission *felkorrigerande kod; see also* GRAY CODE; **error correction** = hardware *or* software that can detect and correct an error in a transmission *felkorrigering(sfunktion);* **error detecting codes** = coding system that allows errors occurring during transmission to be detected but is not complex enough to correct the errors *felupptäckskoder;* **error detection** = using special hardware *or* software to detect errors in a data entry *or* transmission, then usually ask for re-transmission *felupptäckt;* **error detection and correction (EDAC)** = forward error correction system for data communications *felupptäckt och felkorrigering;* **error diagnosis** = finding the cause of an error *felidentifiering;* **error diagnostics** = information and system messages displayed when an error is detected to help a user diagnose and correct an error *felmeddelanden;* **error handling** *or* **management** = routines and procedures that diagnose and correct errors *or* minimise the effects of errors, so that a system will run when an error is detected *felhantering;* **error interrupts** = interrupt signals sent due to an error in hardware *or* software *felavbrott;* **error logging** = recording errors that have occurred *felbokföring;* **features of the program include error logging; error message** = report that an error has occurred

felmeddelande; **error propagation** = one error causing another *felutbredning;* **error rate** = (i) number of mistakes per thousand entries *or* per page *felfrekvens;* (ii) number of corrupt bits of data in relation to the total transmission length *felfrekvens;* **the error rate is less than 1%; error recovery** = software *or* hardware that can continue after an error has occurred *återhämtning efter fel;* **error routine** = short routine within a main program that handles any errors when they occur *felhanteringsrutin;* **error trapping** = detecting and correcting errors before they cause any problems *felfälla, felfångst;* **compilation error** = error occurring during program compilation time *kompileringsfel;* **diagnostic error message** = explanatory line of text displayed when an error has been found *feldiagnosmeddelande, förklarande felmeddelande;* **execution error** = error occurring during program execution, due to bad inputs *or* a faulty program *driftsfel, körfel;* **logical error** = fault in a program design causing incorrect branching *or* operation *logikfel, logiskt fel;* **permanent error** = error in a system which cannot be repaired *permanent fel;* **quantization error** = error in converting an analog signal into a numerical form due to limited accuracy *or* a rapidly changing signal *kvantiseringsfel, digitaliseringsfel;* **recoverable error** = error that does not cause complete system shutdown, and allows the user to restart the program *fel efter vilket körningen kan återupptas;* **rejection error** = error by the scanner which is unable to read a character and leaves a blank *läsfel, avsökningsfel;* **scanning error** = error introduced while scanning an image *läsfel;* **a wrinkled or torn page may be the cause of scanning errors; substitution error** = error made by a scanner which mistakes one character *or* letter for another *läsfel;* **syntax error** = error resulting from incorrect use of programming language syntax *syntaxfel;* **transient read error** = error which can be recovered from (caused by bad data recording) *övergående (läs)fel;* **undetected error** = error which is not detected by a coding system *dolt fel, icke deklarerat fel*

QUOTE syntax errors, like omitting a bracket, will produce an error message from the compiler
Personal Computer World

ersättningstecken ⇨ **wild card**

ESC ['iːes'siː] escape character code *or* key on a computer *avbrottskod, avbrottstangent, escape-tangent*

escape character [ɪsˈkeɪp ˌkærəktə] *subst.* character used to represent an escape code *avbrottstecken;* **escape codes** = transmitted code sequence which informs the receiver that all following characters represent control actions *avbrottskoder;*

escape key = key on a keyboard which allows the user to enter escape codes to control the computer's basic modes *or* actions *avbrottstangent, escape-tangent*

escapement [ɪs'keɪpmənt] *subst.* preset vertical movement of a sheet of paper in a printer *or* in a typewriter *höjdstegsinställning, radavståndsinställning*

etikett ⇨ **external, key, label, tag**

escape-tangent ⇨ **escape character**

ESDI ['iːesdiˑ'aɪ] = ENHANCED SMALL DEVICE INTERFACE interface standard between a CPU and peripherals such as disk drives *ESDI-gränssnitt*

ESS ['iːes'es] = ELECTRONIC SWITCHING SYSTEM

establish [ɪs'tæblɪʃ] *vb.* (i) to discover and prove something *konstatera;* (ii) to define the use *or* value of something *fastställa;* **they established which component was faulty**

etch [etʃ] *vb.* to use an acid to remove selected layers of metal from a metal printing plate *or* printed circuit board *etsa;* **etch type** = type for printing produced from an etched plate *etsat typsnitt*

etikett ⇨ **external, key, label, tag**

ETV ['iːtiˑviː] = EDUCATIONAL TELEVISION

ETX ['iːtiˑ'eks] = END OF TEXT

Euronet ['jʊərə(ʊ)net] *subst.* telephone connected network, covering the EEC countries, that provides access to each country's scientific and economic information *EG:s telenät för intern företagsinformation*

evaluate [ɪ'væljʊeɪt] *vb.* to calculate a value *or* a quantity *utvärdera*

evaluation [ɪ,væljʊ'eɪʃ(ə)n] *subst.* action of calculating a value *or* a quantity *utvärdering*

evaluative abstract [ɪ'væljʊətɪv 'æbstrækt] *subst.* library abstract that contains details of the value and usefulness of the document *värderingsreferat*

even ['iːv(ə)n] *subst.* quantity *or* number that is a multiple of two *jämn(t tal);* **the first three even numbers are 2, 4, 6; even parity (check)** = error checking method that only transmits an even number of binary ones in each word *jämn paritet; compare* ODD PARITY; **even working** = section of printed material in 16, 32 or 64 page format *jämna ark*

event [ɪ'vent] *subst.* an action *or* activity *händelse*

event-driven [ɪ'vent 'drɪvn] *subst.* computer program *or* process where each step of the execution relies on external actions *händelsestyrd*

except [ɪk'sept] *prep. & conjunction* not including *utom;* **all the text has been keyboarded, except the last ten pages; except gate** = logical function whose output is true if either (of two) inputs is true, and false if both inputs are the same *antingen-grind*

exception [ɪk'sepʃ(ə)n] *subst.* thing which is different from all others *undantag;* **exception dictionary** = store of words and their special word-break requirements, for word-processing and photocomposition *undantagskatalog;* **exception report** = report which only gives items which do not fit in the general rule *or* pattern *undantagsrapport*

exceptional [ɪk'sepʃənl] *adj.* not usual *or* different *ovanlig, undantags-;* **exceptional items** = items in a balance sheet which do not appear there each year *extraordinära bokföringsposter*

excess [ɪk'ses] *subst.* too much of something *överflöd, överskjutande;* **excess-3 code** = code in which decimal digits are represented by the binary equivalent of three greater than the number *excess-tre-kod, plus-tre-kod;* **the excess-3 code representation of 6 is 1001**

excessive [ɪk'sesɪv] *adj.* too much *or* too large *överdriven;* **the program used an excessive amount of memory to accomplish the job**

excess-tre-kod ⇨ **excess**

exchange [ɪks'tʃeɪn(d)ʒ] **1** *subst.* **(a)** giving of one thing for another *utbyte;* **part exchange** = giving an old product as part of the payment for a new one *inbyte* **(b)** telephone equipment required to connect incoming and outgoing calls *telefonväxel;* **exchange line** = LOCAL LOOP **2** *vb.* **(a) to exchange one article for another** = to give one thing in place of something else *byta en artikel mot en annnan;* **exchange selection** = sorting method which repeatedly exchanges various pairs of data items until they are in order *utbytessortering* **(b)** to swap data between two locations *sidminnesbyte*

exchangeable [ɪks'tʃeɪn(d)ʒəbl] *adj.* which can be exchanged *utbytbar;* **exchangeable disk storage (EDS)** = disk drive using a removable disk pack (as opposed to a fixed disk) *drivverk för utbytbart skivminne*

exclamation mark [,eksklə'meɪʃ(ə)n mɑːk] *subst.* printed *or* written sign (!), which shows surprise *utropstecken*

exclude [ɪksˈkluːd] *vb.* to keep out *or* not to include *utesluta;* **the interest charges have been excluded from the document; the password is supposed to exclude hackers from the database**

excluding [ɪksˈkluːdɪŋ] *prep.* not including *uteslutande, utom, ej innefattande;* **all salesmen, excluding those living in London, can stay at hotels during the sales conference**

exclusion [ɪksˈkluːʒ(ə)n] *subst.* **(a)** act of not including *uteslutning;* **exclusion clause** = section of an insurance policy *or* warranty which says which items are not covered *undantagsklausul* **(b)** restriction of access to a telephone line *or* system *åtkomstbegränsning*

exclusive [ɪksˈkluːsɪv] *adj.* which excludes *uteslutande;* **exclusive agreement** = agreement where a person is made sole agent for a product in a market *exklusivt avtal;* **exclusive NOR (EXNOR)** = logical function whose output is true if all inputs are the same level, and false if any are different *symmetrisk negerad disjunktion;* **exclusive NOR gate** = electronic implementation of the EXNOR function *(logisk) negerad antingen-eller-grind (XNOR);* **exclusive OR (EXOR)** = logical function whose output is true if any input is true, and false if all the inputs are the same *symmetrisk differens;* **exclusive OR gate** = electronic implementation of the EXOR function *logisk antingen-eller-grind (XOR)*

executable form [ˈeksɪˌkjuːtəbl ˈfɔːm] *subst.* program translated *or* compiled into a machine code form that a processor can execute *exekverbar kod, körbar form, maskinkod*

execute [ˈeksɪkjuːt] *vb.* to run *or* carry out a computer program *or* process *(låta) köra (program), exekvera;* **execute cycle** = events required to fetch, decode and carry out an instruction stored in memory *exekveringscykel;* **execute mode** = state of a computer that is executing a program *körläge, exekveringstillstånd; compare with* DIRECT MODE; **execute phase** = section of the execute cycle when the instruction is carried out *körfas, exekveringsfas;* **execute signal** = signal that steps the CPU through the execute cycle *körsignal, exekveringsklocksignal;* **execute statement** = basic operating system command to start a program run *startkommando, exekveringsstart;* **execute time** = EXECUTION TIME; **fetch-execute cycle** = EXECUTE CYCLE

execution [ˌeksɪˈkjuːʃ(ə)n] *subst.* carrying out of a computer program *or* process *körning, exekvering;* **execution address** = location in memory at which the first instruction in a program is stored

startadress; **execution cycle** = period of time during which the instruction is executed *exekveringscykel;* **execution error** = error detected while a program is being run *exekveringsfel, driftsfel;* **execution phase** = EXECUTE PHASE; **execution time** = (i) time taken to run *or* carry out a program *or* series of instructions *körtid;* (ii) time taken for one execution cycle *cykeltid*

QUOTE fast execution speed is the single most important feature of a C compiler
.EXE

executive [ɪgˈzekjʊtɪv] **1** *adj.* **executive producer** = person who organizes and arranges for the finance for a film*or* TV programme but does not play an active part in making the film *ansvarig producent;* **executive program** *or* **supervisor program** = master program in a computer system that controls the execution of other programs *styrprogram, övervakningsprogram, operativsystem;* **executive control program** = OPERATING SYSTEM; **executive instruction** = instruction used to control and execute programs under the control of an operating system *operativsystemkommando; see also* SUPERVISOR INSTRUCTION **2** *subst.* person in a business who takes decisions (such a manager *or* director) *chef;* **executive terminal** = terminal which is specially adapted for use by company executives *chefsterminal*

exekvera ⇨ execute, run

exekvering ⇨ execution, run

exekveringscykel ⇨ execute, execution

exekveringstid ⇨ execution, run-time

exerciser [ˈeksəsaɪzə] *subst.* tester for a device *testenhet*

exhaustive search [ɪgˈzɔːstɪv ˈsɜːtʃ] *subst.* search through every record in a database *fullständig sökning, uttömmande sökning*

exit [ˈeksɪt] *vb.* to stop program execution *or* to leave a program and return control to the operating system *or* interpreter *gå ur, lämna;* **exit point** = point in a subroutine where control is returned to the main program *utgångspunkt;* **you have to exit to another editing system to add headlines**

exjunction [eksˈdʒʌŋ(k)ʃn] *subst.* logical function whose output is true if either (of two) inputs is true, and false if both inputs are the same *exjunktion*

EXNOR [ˈeksnɔː] = EXCLUSIVE NOR logical function whose output is true if all inputs are the same level, false if any are different *symmetrisk negerad disjunktion;* **EXNOR gate** = electronic implementation of the EXNOR function *(logisk) negerad antingen-eller-grind (XNOR); see also* NOR

EXOR ['ek'sɔː] = EXCLUSIVE OR logical function whose output is true if any input is true, and false if the all inputs are the same *symmetrisk differens;* **EXOR gate** = electronic implementation of the EXOR function *(logisk) antingen-eller-grind (XOR); see also* OR

expand [ɪks'pænd] *vb.* to make larger *utöka;* **if you want to hold so much data, you will have to expand the disk capacity**

expandable [ɪks'pændəbl] *adj.* which can be expanded *utbyggbar;* **expandable system** = computer system that is designed to be able to grow (in power *or* memory) by hardware *or* software additions *utbyggbart system*

expander [ɪks'pændə] *subst.* **video expander** = device that stores one frame of a video image as it is slowly received over a voice grade communications link, with a video compressor used at the transmitting end *videoexpander*

expansion [ɪks'pænʃ(ə)n] *subst.* increase in computing power *or* storage size *utökning, utbyggnad;* **expansion card** *or* **expansion board** = printed circuit board that is connected to a system to increase its functions *or* performance *instickskort, tillsatskort, expansionskort;* **expansion slot** = connector inside a computer into which an expansion card can be plugged *kortplats;* **insert the board in the expansion slot; macro expansion** = process in which a macro call is replaced with the instructions in the macro *makroexpansion*

> QUOTE it can be attached to most kinds of printer, and, if that is not enough, an expansion box can be fitted to the bus connector
> **Personal Computer World**

expansionskort ⇨ **card**

expert ['ekspɜːt] *subst.* person who knows a lot about something *expert;* **he is a computer expert; she is an expert in programming languages; expert system** = software that applies the knowledge, advice and rules defined by experts in a particular field to a user's data to help solve a problem *expertsystem*

expertsystem ⇨ **expert, knowledge**

expiration [ˌekspɪ'reɪʃ(ə)n] *subst.* coming to an end *upphörande;* **expiration date** = (i) last date at which photographic film *or* paper can be used with good results *sista användningsdag;* (ii) date when a computer file is no longer protected from deletion by the operating system *slutdatum*

expire [ɪks'paɪə] *vb.* to come to an end *or* to be no longer valid *upphöra att gälla, ta slut*

explicit address [ɪks'plɪsɪt ə'dres] *subst.* address provided in two parts, one is the reference point, the other a displacement *or* index value *explicit adress*

exponent [eks'pəʊnənt] *subst.* number indicating the power to which a base number is to be raised *exponent;* **binary exponent** = one word that contains the sign and exponent of a binary number (expressed in exponent and mantissa form) *binär exponent; see also* MANTISSA

exponent ⇨ **exponent, superscript**

exponentiation [ˌekspəʊnenʃɪ'eɪʃ(ə)n] *subst.* raising a base number to a certain power *upphöja*

express [ɪks'pres] *vb.* to state *or* to describe *uttrycka, beskriva;* **express the formula in its simplest form; the computer structure was expressed graphically**

expression [ɪks'preʃ(ə)n] *subst.* **(a)** mathematical formula *or* relationship *uttryck* **(b)** definition of a value *or* variable in a program *uttryck*

extend [ɪks'tend] *vb.* to make longer *förlänga, utöka;* **extended arithmetic element** = section of a CPU that provides hardware implementations of various mathematical functions *utökad aritmetisk modul;* **extended binary coded decimal interchange code (EBCDIC)** = 8-bit character coding system *teckenrepresentation, standard för EBCDIC-systemet främst för stordatorer;* **extended BNF (EBNF)** = more flexible way of defining the syntax of a language *utökad syntaxbeskrivande notation för programmeringsspråk;* **extending serial file** = file that can be added to *or* that has no maximum size *dynamisk fil*

extensible [ɪks'tensəbl] *adj.* which can be extended *utbyggbar;* **extensible language** = computer programming language that allows the user to add his own data types and commands *utbyggbart programmeringsspråk*

extension [ɪks'tenʃ(ə)n] *subst.* making longer *utökning;* thing which makes something longer *förlängning;* **extension cable** = cable that allows a device located at some distance to be connected *förlängningskabel;* **extension memory** = storage which is located outside the main computer system but which can be accessed by the CPU *tillsatsminne, utökningsminne;* **extension tube** = device that moves photographic lens away from the camera to allow close-up shots *mellanringar;* **filename extension** =

additional information after a filename, indicating the type *or* use of the file *filnamnsförlängning, filnamnstillägg*

extent [ɪks'tent] *subst.* number of pages in a printed document, such as a book *omfattning, omfång;* **by adding the appendix, we will increase the page extent to 256**

external [eks'tɜːnl] *adj.* outside a program *or* device *utanför, yttre;* **external clock =** clock *or* synchronizing signal supplied from outside a device *yttre klocka;* **external data file =** file containing data for a program that is stored separately from it *separat datafil;* **external device =** (i) item of hardware (such as terminals, printers, etc.) which is attached to a main computer *periferienhet;* (ii) any device that allows communications between the computer and itself, but which is not directly operated by the main computer *periferienhet;* **external disk drive =** device not built into the computer, but which is added to increase its storage capabilities *yttre skivminnesenhet, yttre diskettenhet;* **external interrupts =** interrupt signal from a peripheral device indicating that attention is required *periferiavbrottssignal;* **external label =** identifying piece of paper stuck to the outside of a device *or* disk *etikett;* **external memory =** memory which is located outside the main computer system confines but which can be accessed by the CPU *yttre minne, externminne, sekundärminne;* **external registers =** user's registers that are located in main memory rather than within the CPU *yttre register;* **external schema =** user's view of the structure of data *or* a program *användardiagram;* **external sort =** method of sorting which uses a file stored in secondary memory, such as a disk, as its data source and uses the disk as temporary memory during sorting *yttre sortering;* **external storage** *or* **external store =** storage device which is located outside the main computer system but which can be accessed by the CPU *yttre sekundärminne*

externminne ⇨ **memory**

externt minne ⇨ **storage**

extra ['ekstrə] **1** *adj.* added *or* which is more than usual *tilläggs-* **2** *subst.* **(a)** item which is additional to the package *lockvara, separat artikel, separat vara;* **the mouse and cabling are sold as extras (b)** mark at the end of a telegraphic transmission, induced by noise *störning;* **extra-terrestrial noise =** random noise coming from the air, space and planets *rymdbrus*

extracode ['ekstrə,kəʊd] *subst.* short routines within the operating system that emulate a hardware function *emuleringsrutin*

extract [ɪks'trækt] *vb.* to remove required data *or* information from a database *hämta (ut, fram);* **we can extract the files required for typesetting; extract instruction =** instruction to select and read required data from a database *or* file *urvalsinstruktion, sökinstruktion*

extractor [ɪks'træktə] *subst. see* MASK

extrapolation [eks,træpə(ʊ)'leɪʃn] *subst.* process of predicting future quantities *or* trends by the analysis of current and past data *extrapolering*

extremely [ɪks'triːmlɪ] *adv.* to a very high degree *extremt, i högsta grad;* **extremely high frequency (EHF) =** radio frequencies from 30-300GHz *EHF-bandet, extremt hög frekvens;* **extremely low frequency (ELF) =** communication frequencies of less than 100Hz *ELF-bandet, extremt låg frekvens*

eyepiece ['aɪpiːs] *subst.* camera viewfinder *okular, kamerasökare*

eye-strain ['aɪstreɪn] *subst.* pain in the eyes, caused by looking at bright lights *or* at a VDU for too long *överansträngning av ögonen*

QUOTE to minimize eye-strain, it is vital to have good lighting conditions with this LCD system
Personal Computer World

Ff

F [ef] = FARAD

F [ef] hexadecimal number equivalent to decimal number 15 *talet femton skrivet med hexadecimal notation*

f [ef] = FEMTO- *prefix* equal to one thousandth of a million millionth (10⁻¹⁵) *femto-*

fabriksutrustning ⇨ **equipment**

face [feɪs] *see* TYPEFACE

facet ['fæsɪt] *subst.* one surface *or* plane *facett*

faceted code ['fæsɪtɪd 'kəʊd] *subst.* code which indicates various details of an item, by assigning each one a value *facettkod*

facettkod ⇨ **faceted code**

facility [fə'sɪlətɪ] *subst.* **(a)** being able to do something easily *möjlighet;* **we offer facilities for processing a customer's own disks (b) facilities =** equipment *or* buildings which make it easy to do something *möjligheter, resurser, hjälpmedel;* **storage facilities (c)** communications path between two or more locations, with no ancillary line equipment *kommunikationsmöjlighet* **(d)** *US* single large building *anläggning, installation;* **we have opened our new data processing facility**

facsimile [fæk'sɪmɒlɪ] *subst.* exact copy of an original *faksimil;* **facsimile character generator =** means of displaying characters on a computer screen by copying preprogrammed images from memory *teckengenerator, symbolgenerator;* **facsimile copy =** exact copy of a document *faksimil;* **facsimile transmission (FAX) =** method of sending and receiving images in digital form over a telephone *or* radio link *(tele)fax, faksimilöverföring*

factor ['fæktə] *subst.* **(a)** thing which is important *or* which has an influence on something else *faktor;* **deciding factor =** most important factor which influences someone's decision *beslutsgrund;* **the deciding factor was the superb graphics; elimination factor =** during a search, the section of data that is not used *överflödsfaktor* **(b)** any number in a multiplication that is the operand *faktor;* **by a factor of ten =** ten times *en faktor tio*

factorial [fæk'tɔːrɪəl] *subst.* the product of all the numbers below a number *faktor;* **example: 4 factorial (written 4!) = 1x2x3x4 = 24**

factorize ['fæktəraɪz] *vb.* to break down a number into two whole numbers which when multiplied will give the original number *faktorisera;* **when factorized, 15 gives the factors 1, 15 or 3, 5**

factory ['fækt(ə)rɪ] *subst.* building where products are manufactured *fabrik;* **computer factory; they have opened a new components factory; factory price** *or* **price ex factory =** price not including transport from the maker's factory *pris fritt fabrik*

fade [feɪd] *vb. (of radio or electrical signal)* to become less strong *tona bort; (of colour or photograph)* to become less dark *blekna;* **to fade out =** to reduce the strength of an audio signal to create an effect *tona ner*

fading ['feɪdɪŋ] *subst.* (i) variation in strength of radio and television broadcast signals *signalstyrkevariation;* (ii) *(of photograph or colour)* becoming less dark *fading, fädning;* **when fading occurs turn the density dial on the printer to full black**

fail [feɪl] *vb.* not to do something which should be done *underlåta;* not to work properly *brista (i funktion), fela, fallera;* **the company failed to carry out routine maintenance of its equipment; the prototype disk drive failed its first test; a computer has failed if you turn on the power supply and nothing happens; fail safe system =** system that has a predetermined state it will go to

if a main program *or* device fails, so avoiding a total catastrophe that a complete system shutdown would produce *felsäkert system;* **fail soft system =** system that will still be partly operational even after a part of the system has failed *felsäkert system; see also* GRACEFUL DEGRADATION

QUOTE if one processor system fails, the other takes recovery action on the database, before taking on the workload of the failed system
Computer News

failure ['feɪljə] *subst.* breaking down *or* stopping *fel;* not doing something which should be done *underlåtelse;* **failure logging =** section of the operating system that automatically saves the present system states and relevant data when an error *or* fault is detected *felbokföring;* **failure rate =** number of a certain type of failure within a specified period of time *felfrekvens;* **failure recovery =** resuming a process *or* program after a failure has occurred and has been corrected *återhämtning efter fel;* **induced failure =** failure of a device due to external effects *fel av yttre orsak;* **mean time between failures (MTBF) =** average period of time that a piece of equipment will operate for between breakdowns *medeltid mellan fel, genomsnittlig drifttid;* **power failure =** loss of the electric power supply *strömavbrott; see also* BLACKOUT, BROWN OUT

faktor ⇨ **factor, factorial**

faktorisera ⇨ **factorize**

fall back ['fɔːlbæk] *subst.* special *or* temporary instructions *or* procedures *or* data used in the event of a fault *or* failure *säkerhetsprocedurer, säkerhetsdata, reservdataprocedurer;* **fall back recovery =** resuming a program after a fault has been fixed, from the point at which fall back routines were called *omstart, från avbrottspunkten;* **fall back routines =** routines that are called *or* procedures which are executed by a user when a machine *or* system has failed *säkerhetsrutiner, säkerhetsprocedurer, reservrutiner*

false [fɔːls] *adj.* (i) wrong *felaktig;* not true *or* not correct *falsk;* (ii) a logical term, equal to binary 0, opposite of true *falsk;* **false code =** code that contains values not within specified limits *felaktig kod;* **false drop** *or* **retrieval =** unwanted files retrieved from a database through the use of incorrect search codes *felhämtning;* **false error =** error warning given when no error has occurred *felaktigt felmeddelande*

falsk ⇨ **false**

FAM [fæm] = FAST ACCESS MEMORY

family ['fæm(ə)lɪ] *subst.* **(a)** range of different designs of a particular typeface *typsnittsfamilj* **(b)** range of machines from one manufacturer that are compatible with other products in the same line from the same manufacturer *maskinfamilj*

fan [fæn] **1** *subst.* (i) mechanism that circulates air for cooling *fläkt;* (ii) a spread of data items *or* devices *uppsättning;* **if the fan fails, the system will rapidly overheat 2** *vb.* (i) to cool a device by blowing air over it *fläkta;* (ii) to spread out a series of items *or* devices *sätta upp;* **fan antenna** = antenna whose elements are arranged in a semicircle *solfjädersantenn;* **fan-in** = maximum number of inputs that a circuit *or* chip can deal with *belastbarhet (antal logikkretsar som kan anslutas till en ingång);* **fan-out** = maximum number of outputs that a circuit *or* chip can drive without exceeding its power dissipation limit *belastbarhet (antal logikkretsar som kan anslutas till en utgång);* **fanning strip** = cable supporting insulated strip *stödkabel*

> QUOTE a filtered fan maintains positive air pressure within the cabinet, to keep dust and dirt from entering
> **Personal Computer World**

fanfold ['fænfəʊld] *or* **accordion paper** [ə'kɔːdjən peɪpə] *subst.* method of folding continuous paper, one sheet in one direction, the next sheet in the opposite direction, allowing the paper to be stored conveniently and fed into a printer continuously *dragspelsvikning (för papper i löpande bana)*

farad (F) ['færəd (ef)] *subst.* SI unit of capacitance, defined as coulombs over volts *(enheten) Farad (f)*

Faraday cage ['færədɪ 'keɪdʒ] *subst.* wire *or* metal screen, connected to ground, that completely encloses sensitive equipment to prevent any interference from stray electromagnetic radiation *Faradays bur*

Faradays bur ▷ **electrostatic, Faraday cage**

far end [fɑː'end] *see* RECEIVING END

fascia plate ['feɪʃə,pleɪt] *subst.* front panel on a device *frontpanel;* **the fascia plate on the disk drive of this model is smaller than those on other models**

fast [fɑːst] *adj.* **(a)** which moves quickly; which works quickly; (storage *or* peripheral device) that performs its functions very rapidly *snabb;* **fast program execution; this hard disk is fast, it has an access time of 28mS; fast access memory (FAM)** = storage locations that can be read from *or* written to very rapidly *snabb(åtkomst)minne;* **fast core** = high speed, low access time working memory for a CPU *kärnminne;* **the fast core is used as a scratchpad for all calculations in this system; fast line** =

special telecommunications line which allows data to be transmitted at 48K *or* 96K baud rates *höghastighetsförbindelse, snabb linje;* **fast peripheral** = peripheral that communicates with the computer at very high speeds, limited only by the speed of the electronic circuits, as opposed to a slow peripheral such as a card reader, where mechanical movement determines speed *snabb kringutrustning;* **fast time-scale** = operation in which the time-scale factor is less than one *kort tidsskala* **(b)** (photographic lens) with a very wide aperture *ljuskänslig;* highly light-sensitive photographic film *snabb*

fast fält ▷ **fix**

fast ordlängd ▷ **fix**

fast postlängd ▷ **fix**

fast skivminne ▷ **fix, hard, Winchester disk**

fast telefonanslutning ▷ **hardwired connection**

fast vägval ▷ **fix**

fatal error ['feɪtl 'erə] *subst.* fault in a program *or* device that causes the system to crash *systemfel*

father file ['fɑːðə,faɪl] *subst.* backup of the previous version of a file *faderfil, förra versionen; see also* GRANDFATHER, SON

fault [fɔːlt] *subst.* situation where something has gone wrong with software *or* hardware, causing it to malfunction *fel;* **the technical staff are trying to correct a programming fault; we think there is a basic fault in the product design;** *see also* BUG, ERROR; **fault detection** = (automatic) process which logically *or* mathematically determines that a fault exists in a circuit *(automatisk) felupptäckt;* **fault diagnosis** = process by which the cause of a fault is located *feldiagnos;* **fault location program** = routine that is part of a diagnostic program that identifies the cause of faulty data *or* equipment *felsökningsprogram;* **fault time** = period of time during which a computer system is not working *or* usable *feltid;* **fault trace** = program that checks and records the occurrences of faults in a system *felspåringsprogram*

fault tolerance ['fɔːlt 'tɒlər(ə)ns] *subst.* ability of a system to continue functioning even when a fault has occurred *feltolerans*

> QUOTE fault tolerance is usually associated with a system's reliability
> **Computer News**

fault-tolerant ['fɔːlt 'tɒlər(ə)nt] *adj.* (system *or* device) that is able to continue functioning even when a fault occurs *feltolerant;* **they market a highly successful range of fault-tolerant minis**

> QUOTE before fault-tolerant systems, users had to rely on cold standby
>
> **Computer News**

faulty ['fɔːltɪ] *adj.* which does not work properly *felaktig, trasig;* **there must be a faulty piece of equipment in the system; they traced the fault to a faulty cable; faulty sector** = sector of a magnetic disk that cannot be written to *or* read from correctly *felaktig sektor*

fax [fæks] *or* **FAX** [fæks] *subst. & vb. informal* = FACSIMILE COPY, FACSIMILE TRANSMISSION **we will send a fax of the design plan; I've faxed the documents to our New York office; the fax machine is next to the telephone switchboard**

> QUOTE investment in a good modem and communications system could reduce your costs considerably on both courier and fax services
>
> **Which PC?**

fax ⇨ **facsimile**

fd ['efdiː] *or* **FD** ['efdiː] **(a)** = FULL DUPLEX data transmission down a channel in two directions simultaneously *full duplex* **(b)** = FLOPPY DISK

fdc ['efdiːˈsiː] = FLOPPY DISK CONTROLLER

FDM ['efdiːˈem] = FREQUENCY DIVISION MULTIPLEXING transmission of several independent signals along a single channel achieved by shifting each signal up in frequency by a different amount *frekvensmultiplexering*

fdx ['efdiːˈeks] *or* **FDX** ['efdiːˈeks] = FULL DUPLEX

feasibility [ˌfiːzəˈbɪlətɪ] *subst.* ability to be done *möjlighet, genomförbarhet;* **he has been asked to report on the feasibility of a project; feasibility report** = report saying if something can be done *förstudierapport;* **feasibility study** = examination and report into the usefulness and cost of a new product that is being considered for purchase *möjlighetsanalys, förstudie;* **to carry out a feasibility study on a project** = to carry out an examination of costs and profits to see if the project should be started *göra en förstudie inför ett projekt* NOTE: no plural

feature ['fiːtʃə] *subst.* special function *or* ability *or* design of hardware *or* software *funktion, specialitet, egenskap;* **key feature** = most important feature *nyckelfunktion;* **the key features of this system are: 20Mb of formatted storage with an access time of 60ms**

FEDS [efiːdiːˈes] = FIXED AND EXCHANGEABLE DISK STORAGE magnetic disk storage system that contains some removable disks, such as floppy disks and some fixed *or* hard disk drives *blandat minne*

feed [fiːd] **1** *subst.* device which puts paper *or* tape into and through a machine, such as a printer *or* photocopier *matning;* **continuous feed** = device which feeds in continuous computer stationery into a printer *löpande bana;* **front feed** *or* **sheet feed attachment** = device which can be attached to a line printer to allow individual sheets of paper to be fed in automatically *arkmatare;* **feed holes** = punched sprocket holes along the edge of continuous paper *styrhål;* **feed horn** = microwave channelling device used to direct transmitted signals *matarhorn;* **feed reel** = reel of tape which is being fed into a machine *matningsrulle;* **paper feed** = mechanism which pulls paper through a printer *pappersmatning;* **sheet feed** = device which puts in one sheet at a time into a printer *arkmatning;* **tractor feed** = method of feeding paper into a printer, sprocket wheels on the printer connect with sprocket holes on each edge of the paper *traktormatning* **2** *vb.* to put paper into a machine *or* information into a computer *mata (in);* **this paper should be manually fed into the printer; data is fed into the computer** NOTE: **feeding - fed**

feedback ['fiːdbæk] *subst.* **(a)** adding part of the output of a circuit to the input *återkoppling;* **feedback loop** = path from output to input by which feedback occurs *återkopplingsslinga;* **negative feedback** = subtraction of part of the output from a device from its input signal *negativ återkoppling;* **positive feedback** = addition of part of the output from a device to its input *positiv återkoppling; see also* ACOUSTICAL **(b)** information from one source which can be used to modify something *or* provide a constructive criticism of something *synpunkter, återkoppling;* **we are getting customer feedback on the new system; they asked the sales teams for feedback on the reception of the new model; have you any feedback from the sales force about the customers' reaction to the new model?; feedback control** = information about the effects of a controlling signal on a machine *or* device, returned to the controlling computer *återkopplingsstyrning* NOTE: no plural

> COMMENT: negative or positive feedback can be accidental (when it may cause severe overloading of the circuit) or designed into the circuit to make it more stable

feeder ['fiːdə] *subst.* **(a)** channel that carries signals from one point to another *matare;* **feeder cable** = (i) main transmission line that carries signals from a central point for distribution *matarkabel;* (ii) cable from an antenna to a circuit *matarkabel* **(b)** mechanism that automatically inserts the paper into a printer *(pappers)matare*

feevee ['fiːviː] *subst.* US informal pay cable *or* form of cable TV where the viewer pays an extrafee for extra channels *betalteve*

feint [feint] *subst.* very light lines on writing paper *hårlinjer (på förlinjerat skrivpapper)*

felaktig ⇨ false, inaccurate

felaktig kod ⇨ false

felaktigt felmeddelande ⇨ false

felavbrott ⇨ error

felbokföring ⇨ failure, logging

feldiagnos ⇨ fault

feldiagnosmeddelande ⇨ error

felfrekvens ⇨ error, failure

felfri ⇨ clean

felfritt utförande ⇨ hazard

felfångst ⇨ error

felhantering ⇨ error

felhanteringsrutin ⇨ error

felhämtning ⇨ false

felkod ⇨ error

felkorrigerande minne ⇨ ERCC

felkorrigeringskod ⇨ error

felmarginal ⇨ error

felmeddelande ⇨ diagnostic, error

felpassning ⇨ mismatch

felskur ⇨ error

felspårningsprogram ⇨ fault, trace

felsäkert system ⇨ fail

felsäkert utförande ⇨ hazard

felsöka ⇨ debug, diagnose

felsökningsprogram ⇨ debugger, fault, program

felsökningsrutin ⇨ malfunction

feltid ⇨ fault

feltolerans ⇨ fault tolerance

feltolerant ⇨ fault-tolerant

felupptäckande kod ⇨ detect

felupptäckt och felkorrigering ⇨ error

felupptäcktskoder ⇨ error

female ['fiːmeɪl] *adj.* **female connector** = connector with connecting sockets into which the pins *or* plugs of a male connector can be inserted *honkontakt;* **female socket** = hole into which a pin *or* plug can be inserted to make a connection *honkontakt*

femte generationens datorer ⇨ fifth generation computers

femto- (f) [fem'tə (ef)] *prefix* equal to ten exponent minus fifteen (10^{-15}) *femto-;* **femto second** = thousandth of a picosecond *femtosekund*

FEP ['efiː'piː] = FRONT END PROCESSOR processor placed between an input source and the central computer, whose function is to preprocess received data to relieve the workload of the main computer *frontdator, kommunikationsdator*

ferric oxide ['ferɪk 'ɒksaɪd] *or* **ferrite** ['feraɪt] *subst.* substance (iron oxide) used as tape *or* disk coating that can be magnetized to store data *or* signals *järnoxid*

ferrite core ['feraɪt kɔː] *subst.* small bead of magnetic material that can hold an electromagnetic charge, used in (old) core memory *magnetkärna*

ferromagnetic material [,ferəʊmæg'netɪk mə'tɪərɪəl] *subst.* any ferrite material that can be magnetized *magnetiskt material*

FET ['efiː'tiː] = FIELD EFFECT TRANSISTOR electronic device that can act as a variable current flow control, an external signal varies the resistance of the device and current flow by changing the width of a conducting channel *fälteffekttransistor*

fetch [fetʃ] *subst.* command that retrieves the next instruction from memory *hämtkommando;* **demand fetching** = virtual page management system in which the pages are selected as required *hämtning vid behov, behovssignal;* **fetch cycle** = events that retrieve the next instruction to be executed from memory (by placing the program counter contents on the address bus) *hämtningscykel, hämtcykel;* **fetch-execute cycle** = events required to retrieve, decode and carry out an instruction stored in memory *hämt- och körcykel;* **fetch instruction** = computer instruction to select and read the next instruction *or* data to be processed *hämtningsinstruktion;* **fetch phase** = section of the fetch-execute cycle that retrieves and decodes the instructions from memory *hämtningsfas;* **fetch protect =** to restrict access to a section of memory *åtkomstbegränsning;* **fetch signal =** signal that steps the CPU through the fetch cycle *hämtsignal, klocksignal*

FF ['ef'ef] **(a)** = FORM FEED **(b)** = FLIP-FLOP

fiberoptik ⇨ optic fibres

fibre optics ['faɪbə 'ɒptɪks] *subst.* light transmission through thin strands of glass *or* plastic, which allows data to be transmitted *fiberoptik;* **fibre optic cable** *or* **connection =** fine strands of glass *or* plastic protected by a surrounding material, used for transmission of light signals *fiberoptisk kabel(överföring);* **fibre optic connections enabling nodes up to one kilometre apart to be used**

fibre ribbon ['faɪbə 'rɪbən] *subst.* fabric-based ribbon used in printers *färgband, textilband*

fiche [fiʃ] *see* MICROFICHE

fickminne ⇨ cache, memory

fidelity [fɪ'delətɪ] *subst.* ability of an audio system to reproduce sound correctly *trohet, originaltrohet;* **high fidelity system (hi fi) =** high-quality equipment for playing records *or* compact disks *or* tapes *or* for listening to the radio (tape recorder, turntable, amplifier and speakers) *högklassig ljudåtergivning, hi-fi-system; see also* HI FI

field [fiːld] *subst.* **(a)** area of force and energy distribution, caused by magnetic *or* electric energy sources *fält;* **field effect transistor (FET) =** electronic device that can act as a variable current flow control, an external signal varies the resistance of the device and current flow by changing the width of a conducting channel *fälteffekttransistor;* **field programmable device** *see* PLA; **field programming =** writing data into a PROM *läsminnesprogrammering; see also* BLOW; **field strength =** amplitude of the magnetic *or* electric field at one point in that field *fältstyrka* **(b)** section containing individual data items in a record *fält;* **the employee record has a field for age; address** *or* **operand field =** part of a computer instruction that contains the location of the operand *adressfält, operandfält;* **card field =** part of a card column reserved for one type of data *or* record *stansfält;* **data field =** part of a computer instruction that contains the location of the data *datafält;* **field label =** series of characters used to identify a field or its location *fältetikett;* **field length =** number of characters that a field can contain *fältlängd;* **field marker** *or* **separator =** code used to indicate the end of one field and the start of the next *fältgränstecken;*

protected field = storage *or* display area that cannot be altered by the user *skyddat fält, skyddad area* **(c)** method of building up a picture on a television screen *delbild;* **field blanking =** interval when television signal field synchronizing pulses are transmitted *(del)bildstäckning;* **field frequency =** number of field scans per second *delbildfrekvens;* **field flyback =** return of electron beam to top left hand corner of a screen *(bild)svepåtergång;* **field sweep =** vertical electron beam movement over a television screen *(del)bildsvep;* **field sync pulse =** pulse in a TV signal that makes sure that the receiver's field sweep is in sync *delbildssynkpuls* **(d)** section of an image that is available after the light has passed through the camera and lens *bildyta* **(e) in the field =** outside an office *or* factory *på fältet;* **field engineer =** engineer who does not work at one single company, but travels between customers carrying out maintenance on their computers *fälttekniker, fältingenjör;* **field sales manager =** manager in charge of a group of salesmen working in a particular area of the country *försäljningschef för ett visst område;* **field tested =** product tested outside a company *or* research laboratory, in a real situation *brukstestad;* **field work =** examining the situation among several potential customers *fältarbete*

fielding ['fiːldɪŋ] *subst.* arrangement of field allocations inside a record and file *fältuppställning, fältutseende*

FIFO ['faɪfəʊ] = FIRST IN FIRST OUT storage read/write method in which the first item stored is the first read *först in-först ut;* **FIFO memory =** memory using a FIFO access scheme *FIFU-minne, köminne;* **the two computers operate at different rates, but can transmit data using a FIFO memory; FIFO queue =** temporary (queue) storage, in which the first item written to the queue is the first to be read *FIFU-kö; compare* LIFO

fifth generation computers ['fɪfθ ˌdʒenə'reɪʃ(ə)n kəm'pjuːtəz] *subst.* next stage of computer system design using fast VLSI circuits and powerful programming languages to allow human interaction *femte generationens datorer*

FIFU-kö ⇨ FIFO

FIFU-minne ⇨ FIFO

figure ['fɪgə] *subst.* **(a)** printed line illustration in a book *figur, diagram; see* **figure 10 for a chart of ASCII codes (b)** printed number *siffra;* **figures case =** characters in a telegraphic transmission that are mainly numbers *or* signs *siffror;* **figures shift =** (i) transmitted code that indicates to the receiver that all following characters should be read as upper case

figure 120 **file**

sifferskift; (ii) mechanical switch which allows a typewriter to print *or* keyboard to produce special characters and symbols located on the same keys as the numbers *skifttangent;* **in round figures =** not totally accurate, but correct to the nearest 10 or 100 *avrundat, i runda tal;* **they have a workforce of 2,500 in round figures**

fil ⊳ computer, disk, file

filaddition ⊳ file

filbeskrivning ⊳ file

filcentral ⊳ local area network (LAN, lan)

filcentrum ⊳ file

fildisposition ⊳ file

file [faɪl] **1** *subst.* **(a)** cardboard holder for documents, which can fit in the drawer of a filing cabinet *mapp;* **put these letters in the customer file; look in the file marked "Scottish sales"; box file =** cardboard box for holding documents *mapp, (kort)låda* **(b)** documents kept for reference *akt, dossier;* **to place something on file =** to keep a record of something *lägga upp register över något;* **to keep someone's name on file =** to keep someone's name on a list for reference *ha någons namn i ett register;* **file copy =** copy of a document which is kept for reference in an office *arkivkopia;* **card-index file =** information kept on filing cards *kortregister* **(c)** section of data on a computer (such as payroll, address list, customer accounts), in the form of individual records which may contain data, characters, digits *or* graphics *fil;* **data file =** file containing data (as opposed to a program file) *datafil;* **disk file =** number of related records *or* data items stored under one name on disk *fil på skivminne;* **distributed file system =** system that uses files stored in more than one location *or* backing store, but which are processed at a central point *distribuerat filsystem;* **file activity ratio =** ratio of the number of different records accessed within a file compared to the total number in store *anropskvot;* **file cleanup =** tidying and removing out of date *or* unnecessary data from a file *filstädning, filverifiering, filunderhåll;* **file collating =** putting the contents of a file into order *filunderhåll;* **file control block =** list (in main memory) of files in use within the system *filkatalog (för fysisk placering), filkontrollblock;* **file conversion =** change of format *or* structure of a file system, usually when using a new program *or* file handling routine *filkonvertering;* **file creation =** writing file header information onto a disk and writing an entry into the directory *filgenerering, skapa en fil;* **file deletion =** erasing a file from storage *filradering, radera en fil; see*

also DELETE; **file descriptor =** code *or* series of characters used to identify a file *filbeskrivning, filidentifierare;* **file directory =** list of names and information about files in a backing storage device *filkatalog;* **file extent =** actual area *or* number of tracks required to store a file *filutrymme;* **file gap =** section of blank tape *or* disk that indicates the end of a file *filslut;* **file handling routine =** short computer program that manages the reading/writing and organization of stored files *filhanteringsprogram;* **file identification =** unique label *or* name used to identify and locate a file stored on baking store *filidentifierare;* **file index =** sorted table of the main entries in a file, with their address, allowing the rapid location of entries *filindex;* **file label =** character(s) used to identify a file *filidentifierare;* **file layout =** set of rules defining internal file structure *filstruktur, fildisposition;* **file maintenance =** process of updating a file by changing, adding *or* deleting entries *filunderhåll;* **file management (system) =** section of a DOS that allocates disk space to files, keeping track of the sections and their sector addresses *(fysiskt) filhanteringsunderhåll;* **file manager =** routines used to create, locate and maintain files on backing store *filhanterare;* **file merger =** (i) to combine two data files, but still retaining an overall structure *filkonkatenering, filsammanslagning;* (ii) one file created from more than one file written one after the other (no order preserved) *filaddition;* **file name =** word used to identify a particular stored file *filnamn;* **file organization** *see* FILE LAYOUT; **file processing =** applying a set of rules *or* search limits to a file, in order to update *or* find information *filhantering;* **file protection =** (i) software *or* physical device used to prevent any accidental deletion *or* modification of a file *or* its records *filskydd;* (ii) *see* FILE SECURITY; **file protect tab =** plastic tab on a disk which prevents accidental erasure of a file *(fil)skrivskydd;* **file purge =** erasing the contents of a file *filradering (endast av innehållet);* **file-recovery utility =** software that allows files that have been accidentally deleted *or* damaged to be read again *filräddningsprogram;* **a lost file cannot be found without a file-recovery utility; file security =** hardware *or* software organization of a computer system to protect users' files from unauthorized access *filskydd;* **file server =** small microcomputer and large backing store device that is used for the management and storage of a user's files in a network *nätcentral, nätminne, filcentrum;* **file set =** number of related files treated as one unit *filgrupp;* **file sort =** to put the contents of a file into order *sortering av fil;* **file storage =**

physical means of preserving data in a file, such as a disk drive *or* tape machine *lagringsmedium;* **file store =** files that are available in main memory at any time *filminne;* **file structure =** way in which a (data) file is organized *filstruktur;* **file transfer =** moving a file from one area of memory to another *or* to another storage device *filöverföring;* **file update =** (i) recent changes *or* transactions to a file *filuppdatering (lista el. tabell);* (ii) new version of software which is sent to users of an existing version *uppdaterad fil, aktualiserad fil;* **file validation =** *filvalidering;* **hidden file =** important system file which is not displayed in a directory and cannot normally be read by a user *dold fil;* **indexed file =** sequential file with an index of all the entries and their addresses *indexerad fil;* **inverted file =** file with an index entry for every data item *inverterad fil;* **output file =** set of records that have been completely processed according to various parameters *utdatafil;* **program file =** file containing a program rather than data *programfil;* **text file =** file that contains text rather than digits *or* data *textfil;* **threaded file =** file in which an entry will contain data and an address to the next entry that contains the same data (allowing rapid retrieval of all identical entries) *länkad fil;* **transaction** *or* **change** *or* **detail** *or* **movement file =** file containing recent changes to records *or* transactions used to update a master file *uppdateringsfil* **2** *vb.* **to file documents =** to put documents in order so that they can be found easily *lagra eller arkivera handlingar;* **the correspondence is filed under "complaints"; he filed the new papers in chronological order**

QUOTE it allows users to back up or restore read-only security files and hidden system files independently
Minicomputer News
QUOTE the lost file, while inaccessible without a file-recovery utility, remains on disk until new information writes over it
Publish

filename ['faɪl,neɪm] *subst.* unique identification code allocated to a program *filnamn;* **filename extension =** additional information after a filename, indicating the type *or* use of the file *filnamnstillägg, filnamnsförlängning;* **the filename extension SYS indicates that this is a system file**

QUOTE when the filename is entered at the prompt, the operating system looks in the file and executes any instructions stored there
PC User

filgrupp ⇨ **file**

filhanterare ⇨ **file**

filhantering ⇨ **file**

filhanteringsprogram ⇨ **file, manager**

filidentifierare ⇨ **file**

filindex ⇨ **file**

(fil)informationsblock ⇨ **header**

(fil)informationsetikett ⇨ **header**

filing ['faɪlɪŋ] *subst.* documents which have to be put in order *osorterat material;* **there is a lot of filing to do at the end of the week; the manager looked through the week's filing to see what letters had been sent; filing basket** *or* **filing tray =** container kept on a desk for documents which have to be filed *arkivkorg;* **filing cabinet =** metal box with several drawers for keeping files *arkivskåp;* **filing card =** card with information written on it, used to classify information into the correct order *registerkort* NOTE: no plural

filing system ['faɪlɪŋˌsɪstəm] *subst.* **(a)** way of putting documents in order for reference *arkiveringssystem* **(b)** software which organizes files *filsystem*

filkatalog ⇨ **directory, file**

filkatalog (för fysisk placering) ⇨ **file**

filkonkatenering ⇨ **file**

filkontrollblock ⇨ **file**

filkonvertering ⇨ **file**

filkö ⇨ **queue**

fill [fɪl] *vb.* **(a)** to make something full *fylla;* **the screen was filled with flickering images (b)** to put characters into gaps in a field so that there are no spaces left *fylla upp (ut);* **fill character =** character added to a string of characters to make up a required length *utfyllnadstecken;* **filled cable =** cable which uses a substance to fill any gaps between outer and conductors, so preventing water getting in *fylld kabel* **(c)** to draw an enclosed area in one colour *or* shading *fylla*

fill up [fɪl 'ʌp] *vb.* to make something completely full *fylla upp (ut);* **the disk was quickly filled up**

film [fɪlm] **1** *subst.* **(a)** transparent strip of plastic, coated with a light-sensitive compound and used to produce photographs with the aid of a camera *film;* **film advance =** (i) lever on a camera used to wind on a roll of film to the next frame *framdragningsvred, filmframmatningsarm;* (ii) the distance a phototypesetting machine has to move prior to the next line to be set *filmframdragare, filmframmatning;* **film assembly =** correct arrangement of photographs *or* negatives prior to the production of a printing plate *filmmonering;* **film base =** thin transparent roll of plastic used as a supporting material for photographic film *filmbas;* **film chain =**

all the necessary equipment needed when showing film *or* slides on television, such as a projector, TV camera and synchronizer *filmkanal;* **film optical scanning device for input into computers (FOSDIC)** = storage device for computer data using microfilm *mikrofilmläsare;* **film pickup** = transmission of a motion picture film by television by electronically scanning each frame *filmavsökning, filmöverföring (till video);* **film strip** = set of related images on a reel of film, usually for educational purposes *AV-diafilm;* **photographic film** = light-sensitive film used in a camera to record images *fotografisk film* **(b)** projection at high speed of a series of still images that creates the impression of movement *film* **2** *vb.* to expose a photographic film to light by means of a camera, and so to produce images *filma*

filming ['fɪlmɪŋ] *subst.* shooting of a cinema film *or* TV film *filmning;* **filming will start next week if the weather is fine**

filminne ⇨ **file**

filmsetting ['fɪlm,setɪŋ] *subst.* photocomposition *fotosättning*

filnamn ⇨ **file**

filnamnsförlängning ⇨ **filename**

filnamnstillägg ⇨ **filename**

filradering ⇨ **file**

filräddningsprogram ⇨ **file**

filsammanslagning ⇨ **file**

filskydd ⇨ **file**

filslut ⇨ **file**

filslutssignal ⇨ **end**

filstruktur ⇨ **file**

filstädning ⇨ **file**

filsystem ⇨ **filing system**

filter ['fɪltə] **1** *subst.* **(a)** electronic circuit that allows certain frequencies to pass while stopping others *filter;* **bandpass filter** = circuit that allows a certain band of frequencies to pass while stopping any that are higher or lower *bandpassfilter;* **high pass filter** = circuit that allows frequencies above a certain limit to pass, but blocks those below that limit *högpassfilter, basfilter;* **low pass filter** = circuit that blocks signals above a certain frequency *lågpassfilter, diskantfilter* **(b)** optical coloured glass, which stops certain frequencies of light *filter;* **absorption filter** = filter that blocks certain colours *absorptionsfilter, färgfilter;* **character enhancement filter** = filter placed over a monitor to increase contrast, and also to

prevent eye-strain *polariseringsfilter;* **filter factor** = indicator of the amount of light that an optical filter absorbs when light passes through it *filterfaktor* **(c)** pattern of binary digits used to select various bits from a binary word (a one in the filter retains that bit in the source word) *filter* **2** *vb.* **(a)** to remove unwanted elements from a signal *or* file *filtrera (bort)* **(b)** to select various bits *or* records from a word *or* file *filtrera (fram)*

filunderhåll ⇨ **file**

filutrymme ⇨ **file**

filvalidering ⇨ **file**

filverifiering ⇨ **file**

filöverföring ⇨ **file**

final ['faɪnl] *adj.* last *or* coming at the end of a period *slutlig;* **to keyboard the final data files; to make the final changes to a document**

find [faɪnd] **1** *vb.* to get something back which has been lost *finna, hitta;* **it took a lot of time to find the faulty chip; the debugger found the error very quickly** NOTE: **finding - found 2** *subst.* command to locate a piece of information *sökkommando;* **find and replace** = feature on a word-processor that allows certain words *or* sections of text to be located and replaced with others *sök- och ersättkommando*

fine [faɪn] *adj.* **(a)** very thin *or* very small *fin;* **the engraving has some very fine lines (b)** excellent *or* of very high quality *utsökt*

fine tune ['faɪn'tjuːn] *vb.* to adjust by small amounts the features *or* parameters of hardware *or* software to improve performance *finjustera;* **fine-tuning improved the speed by ten per cent**

finish ['fɪnɪʃ] **1** *subst.* **(a)** final appearance *utseende, polityr;* **the product has an attractive finish (b)** end of a process *or* function *slut* **2** *vb.* **(a)** to do something *or* to make something completely *avsluta;* **the order was finished in time; she finished all the keyboarding before lunch (b)** to come to an end *upphöra;* **the contract is due to finish next month**

finished ['fɪnɪʃt] *adj.* which has been completed *avslutad;* **finished document** = document which is typed, and is ready to be printed *färdigt dokument;* **finished goods** = manufactured goods which are ready to be sold *färdiga varor*

finite-precision numbers ['faɪnaɪt prɪ'sɪʒ(ə)n 'nʌmbəz] *subst.* use of a fixed number of bits to represent numbers *tal med ändligt antal siffror*

finjustera ⇨ **tune**

firmware ['fɜːmweə] *subst.* computer program *or* data that is permanently stored in a hardware memory chip, such as a ROM *or* EPROM *inbyggt program; compare with* HARDWARE, SOFTWARE

first fit ['fɜːst 'fɪt] *subst.* routine *or* algorithm that selects the first, largest section of free memory in which to store a (virtual) page *snabbpassning*

first generation computer ['fɜːst ˌdʒenə'reɪʃ(ə)n kəm'pjuːtə] *subst.* original computer made with valve based electronic technology, started around 1951 *första generationens dator;* **first generation image** = master copy of an original image, text *or* document *originalkopia;* **first in first out (FIFO)** = temporary queue where the first item stored is the first read *först in-först ut;* **first party release** = ending of a telephone connection as soon as either party puts his phone down *or* disconnects his modem *enkel slutsignalering*

first-level address ['fɜːst 'levl ə'dres] *subst.* computer storage address that directly, without any modification, accesses a location *or* device *förstanivåadress*

fisheye lens ['fɪʃaɪˌlenz] *subst.* extremely wide angle photographic lens that has a field of view of 180 degrees and produces a distorted circular image *fisköga*

fix [fɪks] **1** *subst.* chemical stage in processing a film that sets permanently the developed image on a film *or* paper *fixering* **2** *vb.* **(a)** to make something permanent *or* to attach something permanently *fixera;* **the computer is fixed to the workstation; fixed and exchangeable disk storage (FEDS)** = magnetic disk storage system that contains some removable disks, such as floppy disks and some fixed *or* hard disk drives *blandat minne;* **fixed cycle operation** = (i) process in which each operation is allocated a certain, fixed time limit *klockfixerad process;* (ii) actions within a process that are synchronized to a clock *klockfixerad process;* **fixed data** = data written to a file *or* screen for information *or* identification purposes and which cannot be altered by the user *fasta data;* **fixed disk storage** = hard disk *or* magnetic disk which cannot be removed from the disk drive *fast skivminne;* **fixed field** = area in a stored record that can only contain a certain amount of data *fast fält, fält med fast storlek;* **fixed head disk (drive)** = use of a separate immovable read/write head over each disk track making access time very short *skivmekanism med fasta huvuden;* **fixed-length record** = record whose size cannot be changed *fast postlängd;* **fixed-length word** = preset number of bits that make up a computer word *fast ordlängd;* **fixed program computer** = (hardwired)

computer program that cannot be altered and is run automatically *dedicerad dator, specialiserad dator;* **fixed routing** = communications direction routing that does not consider traffic *or* efficient paths *fast vägval;* **fixed word length** = computer whose word size (in bits) cannot be changed *fast ordlängd* **(b)** to mend *laga, fixa;* **the technicians are trying to fix the switchboard; can you fix the photocopier?**

fixed-point notation = ['fɪkstˌpɔɪnt nə(ʊ)'teɪʃ(ə)n] *subst.* number representation that retains the position of the digits and decimal points in the computer, so limiting the maximum manageable numbers *fixtalsnotation;* **storage of fixed point numbers has two bytes allocated for the whole number and one byte for the fraction part; fixed-point arithmetic** = arithmetic rules and methods using fixed-point numbers *fixtalsaritmetik; compare with* FLOATING POINT

fixtalsaritmetik ⇨ **fixed-point notation**

fixtalsnotation ⇨ **fixed-point notation**

fjärransluten terminal ⇨ **terminal**

fjärrbearbetning ⇨ **teleprocessing (TP)**

fjärrkommunikationsnät ⇨ **long haul network**

fjärrskriftsmaskin ⇨ **teleprinter**

fjärrskriftsterminal ⇨ **teletype (TTY)**

fjärrskrivargränssnitt ⇨ **teleprinter**

fjärrskrivarpapper ⇨ **teleprinter**

fladder ⇨ **flutter**

flag [flæg] **1** *subst.* (i) way of showing the end of field *or* of indicating something special in a database *flagga, flaggtecken;* (ii) method of reporting the status of a register after a mathematical *or* logical operation *flagga, flaggtecken;* **if the result is zero, the zero flag is set; carry flag** = indicator that a carry has occurred after a subtraction *or* addition *överföringsflagga;* **device flag** = one bit in a device status word, used to show the state of a device *statusflagga;* **overflow bit** *or* **flag** = single bit in a word that is set to one (1) if a mathematical overflow has occurred *spillindikering;* **zero flag** = indicator that the contents of a register *or* result is zero *nollflagga;* **flag bit** = single bit of a word used as a flag for certain operations *flaggbit;* **flag code** = code sequence which informs the receiver that following characters represent control actions *flaggtecken;* **flag event** = process *or* state *or* condition that sets a flag *flagghändelse;* **flag register** = register that contains the status and flag bits of a CPU *flaggregister;* **flag**

sequence = sequence of codes sent on a packet switching network as identification of the start and finish of a frame of data *flaggsekvens* **2** *vb.* to attract the attention of a program while it is running to provide a result *or* to report an action *or* to indicate something special *flagga för*

flagging ['flægɪŋ] *subst.* **(a)** putting an indicator against an item so that it can be found later *utsättande av flagga* **(b)** picture distortion from a video recorder due to incorrect synchronization of tape playback head *synkroniseringsfel*

flanktriggad ⇨ **edge**

flare [fleə] *subst.* unwanted light due to internal lens *or* camera reflections causing bright spots on a photographic film *ljusinfall, flare*

flared [fleəd] *adj.* image with unwanted bright spots *or* lines due to internal lens *or* camera reflections *infallsstörd*

flash [flæʃ] *vb.* to switch a light on and off *blinka;* to increase and lower the brightness of a cursor to provide an indicator *blinka;* **flash A/D** = parallel high speed A/D converter *direktomvandlare, blixtomvandlare;* **flash card** = card containing indexing information photographed with a document *referenskort;* **flashing character** = character intensity that is switched on and off (as an indicator) *blinkande tecken*

flat [flæt] *adj.* **(a)** lacking contrast (in an image *or* photograph) *kontrastlöst, flackt* **(b)** smooth (surface) *flat, plan;* **flat file** = two-dimensional file of data items *tvådimensionell datastruktur;* **flat pack** = integrated circuit package whose leads extend horizontally, allowing the device to be mounted directly onto a PCB without the need for holes *komponent för ytmontering* **(c)** fixed *or* not changing *fast, fix;* **flat rate** = set pricing rate that covers all the uses of a facility *enhetspris*

flatbed ['flætbed] *subst.* printing *or* scanning machine that holds the paper *or* image on a flat surface while processing *flatbädd;* **scanners are either flatbed models or platen type, paper-fed models; paper cannot be rolled through flatbed scanners; flatbed plotter** = movable pen that draws diagrams under the control of a computer onto a flat piece of paper *flatbäddsritare;* **flatbed press** = mechanical printing machine where the inked printing plate lies flat on the bed of the machine *flatbäddspress, plantryckpress;* **flatbed transmitter** = device that keeps a document flat while it is being scanned before being transmitted by facsimile means *flatbäddsfax*

flatbäddsritare ⇨ **flatbed**

fleradressinstruktion ⇨ **multi-**

fleranvändarsystem ⇨ **multi-**

flerbussystem ⇨ **multi-bus system**

flerdimensionell vektor ⇨ **multidimensional**

flerfunktionskort ⇨ **multifunction**

flerkortsdator ⇨ **multi-board computer**

flerlagerskort ⇨ **multilayer**

flernivåsignal ⇨ **multilevel**

flerprocessorssystem ⇨ **multiprocessing system**

flerpunkts- ⇨ **multipoint**

flerpunktsnät ⇨ **multidrop circuit**

flersystemsskivenhet ⇨ **multi-disk**

flerterminalsystem ⇨ **multi-terminal system**

fleruppdragskörning ⇨ **multitasking, task**

fleruppdragssystem ⇨ **multiprogramming**

fleråtkomsttillstånd ⇨ **free**

flex [fleks] *subst.* wire *or* cable used to connect an appliance to the mains electricity supply *kabel (nätsladd)*
NOTE: no plural: **a piece of flex**

flexibility [,fleksə'bɪlətɪ] *subst.* ability of hardware *or* software to adapt to various conditions *or* tasks *flexibilitet*

flexible ['fleksəbl] *adj.* which can be altered *or* changed *flexibel;* **flexible array** = array whose size and limits can be altered *variabel vektor;* **flexible disk** = FLOPPY DISK; **flexible disk cartridge** = FLOPPY DISK; **flexible machining system (FMS)** = computer numeric control (CNC) *or* control of a machine by a computer *numerisk styrning;* **flexible manufacturing system (FMS)** = use of CNC machines, robots and other automated devices in manufacturing *FMS-system, flexibelt tillverkningssystem;* **flexible working hours** = system where workers can start *or* stop working at different hours of the morning *or* evening, provided that they work a certain number of hours per week *flextid*

flexskiva ⇨ **diskette, floppy disk**

flicker ['flɪkə] **1** *subst.* **(a)** random variation of brightness in a television picture *flimmer* **(b)** effect that occurs when a frame from a video disk is frozen and two different pictures are displayed alternately at high speed due to the incorrect field matching *flimmer* **(c)** computer graphic image whose brightness alternates due to a low image refresh rate *or* signal corruption *flimmer* 2 *vb.* to move very slightly *flimra;* **the image flickers when the printer is switched on**

flicker-free ['flıkə,friː] *adj.* (display) that does not flicker *flimmerfri*

QUOTE the new 640 by 480 pixel standard, coupled with the flicker-free displays on the four new monitors and a maximum of 256 colours from a palette of more than quarter of a million
PC User

flier ['flaɪə] *subst.* small advertising leaflet designed to encourage customers to ask for more information about a product *or* service *flygblad, reklamblad*

flimmer ⇨ **flicker**

flimmerfri ⇨ **flicker-free**

flimmerfrihet ⇨ **image**

flip-flop (FF) ['flıpflɒp ('efef)] *subst.* electronic circuit *or* chip whose output can be one of two states, which is determined by one or two inputs, can be used to store one bit of digital data *vippa, flipp-flopp;* **JK-flip-flop** = flip-flop device with two inputs (J and K) and two outputs whose states are always complementary and dependent on the inputs *JK-vippa;* **D-flip-flop** = flip-flop device with one input and two outputs *D-vippa*

flippy ['flıpı] *subst.* disk that is double-sided but used in a single-sided drive, so it has to be turned over to read the other side *vändbar diskett*

float [fləʊt] *subst.* addition of the origin address to all indexed *or* relative addresses to check the amount of memory a program will require *minnesutrymmesberäkning;* **float factor** = location in memory at which the first instruction of a program is stored *startläge, grundläge;* **float relocate** = to convert floating addresses to absolute addresses *adresskonvertering*

floating ['fləʊtıŋ] *adj.* not fixed *flytande;* character which is separate from the character it should be attached to *lös;* **floating accent** = method of printing an accent in text where the accent is separate from the letter above which it is printed (on a typewriter, an accented letter may need three keystrokes, one for the accent, then backspace, then key the letter) *lös accent;* **floating address** = location specified in relation to a reference address *relativadress;* **floating head** = FLYING HEAD; **floating point arithmetic** = arithmetic operations on floating point numbers *flyttalsaritmetik;* **floating point (notation)** = numerical notation in which a fractional number is represented with a point after the first digit and a power of ten, so that any number can be stored in a

standard form *flyttalsnotation;* **the fixed number 56.47 in floating-point arithmetic would be 0.5647 and a power of 2; floating point number** = number represented using floating point notation *flyttal;* **floating point operation (FLOP)** = mathematical operation carried out on a floating point number *flyttalsberäkning;* **floating point processor** = specialized CPU that can process floating point numbers very rapidly *flyttalsprocessor;* **the floating point processor speeds up the processing of the graphics software; this model includes a built-in floating point processor; floating symbolic address** = symbol *or* label that identifies a particular instruction *or* word, regardless of its location *relativ symboladress;* **floating voltage** = voltage in a network *or* device that has no related ground *or* reference plane *flytande spänning, utan referenspunkt*

flooding ['flʌdıŋ] *subst.* rapid, reliable but not very efficient means of routing packet-switched data, in which each node sends the data received to each of its neighbours *flödessändning*

FLOP [flɒp] = FLOATING POINT OPERATION; **FLOPs per second** = measure of computing power as the number of floating point operations that a computer can execute every second *flyttalsoperationer per sekund*

floppy disk ['flɒpı 'dısk] *or* **floppy** ['flɒpı] *or* **FD** ['efdiː] *subst.* secondary storage device, in the form of a flat, circular flexible disk onto which data can be stored in a magnetic form (a floppy disk cannot store as much data as a hard disk, but is easily removed, and is protected by a flexible paper *or* plastic sleeve) *diskett, flexskiva;* **floppy disk controller (FDC)** = combination of hardware and software devices that control and manage the read/write operations of a disk drive from a computer *styrenhet för diskettenhet;* **floppy disk sector** = smallest area on a magnetic (floppy) disk that can be individually addressed by a computer *diskettsektor;* **floppy disk drive** *or* **unit** = disk drive for floppy disks and ancillary electronics as a separate assembly *diskettenhet, diskettstation;* **floppy tape** *or* **tape streamer** = continuous loop of tape, used for backing storage *strömbandsminne, bandminne för kontinuerlig kopiering; see also* MICROFLOPPY

COMMENT: floppies are available in various sizes: the commonest are 3.5 inch, 5.25 inch and 8 inch. The size refers to the diameter of the disk inside the sleeve

flow [fləʊ] **1** *subst.* regular movement *flöde;* **automatic text flow across pages; the device controls the copy flow; current flow is**

regulated by a resistor; **flow control** = management of the flow of data into queues and buffers, to prevent spillage *or* lost data *flödesstyrning* **2** *vb.* to move smoothly *flyta;* **work is flowing normally again after the breakdown of the printer; data flow** = movement of data through a system *dataflöde*

flowchart ['fləʊtʃɑːt] *or* **flow diagram** ['fleʊˌdaɪəgræm] **1** *subst.* chart which shows the arrangement of the steps in a process *or* program *flödesschema, flödesdiagram;* **data flowchart** = diagram used to describe a computer *or* data processing system structure *dataflödesdiagram;* **flowchart symbols** = special symbols used to represent devices, decisions and operations in a flowchart *diagramsymboler;* **flowchart template** = plastic sheet with template symbols cut out, to allow symbols to be drawn quickly and clearly *diagrammall;* **logical flowchart** = diagram showing where the logical decisions occur in a structure and their effects on program execution *logiskt flödesschema* **2** *vb.* to describe a process, its control and routes graphically *beskriva med flödesdiagram;* **flow diagram** = FLOWCHART; **flow direction** = order in which events occurring a flowchart *flödesriktning;* **flowline** = lines connecting flowchart symbols, showing the direction of flow within a flowchart *flödeslinje*

fluctuate ['flʌktjʊeɪt] *vb.* to move up and down *variera, fluktuera;* **the electric current fluctuates between 1 Amp and 1.3 Amp**

fluctuating ['flʌktjʊeɪtɪŋ] *adj.* moving up and down *varierande, fluktuerande;* **fluctuating signal strength**

fluctuation [ˌflʌktjʊˈeɪʃ(ə)n] *subst.* up and down movement *variation, fluktuation;* **voltage fluctuations can affect the functioning of the computer system**

flush [flʌʃ] **1** *vb.* to clear *or* erase all the contents of a queue, buffer, file or section of memory *radera;* **flush buffers** = to erase any data remaining in a buffer, ready for a new job *or* after a job has been aborted *radera buffert, tömma buffert* **2** *adj.* level *or* in line with *jäms med;* **the covers are trimmed flush with the pages; flush left** *or* **flush right** *see* JUSTIFY LEFT, JUSTIFY RIGHT

flutter ['flʌtə] *subst.* fluctuations of tape speed due to mechanical *or* circuit problems, causing signal distortion *fladder;* **wow and flutter are common faults on cheap tape recorders**

fly [flaɪ] *vb.* to move through the air *flyga;* **flying spot scan** = method of transferring a frame of film to television by scanning it with a light beam *ljusfläcksavsökning*

flyback ['flaɪbæk] *subst.* electron picture beam return from the end of a scan to the beginning of the next *svepåtergång*

flying head ['flaɪŋˌhed] *subst.* hard disk read/write head that is wing-shaped to fly just above the surface of the spinning disk *svävande läs- och skrivhuvud*

flyktigt minne ▷ volatile memory

flytta ▷ move, remove, recode

flyttal ▷ floating

flyttalsaritmetik ▷ floating

flyttalsberäkning ▷ floating

flyttalsnotation ▷ floating

flyttalsprocessor ▷ floating

flyttbar ▷ movable, removable

flyttbarhet ▷ portability

flödesdiagram ▷ data, DFD, flowchart

flödeslinje ▷ flowchart

flödesriktning ▷ flowchart

flödesschema ▷ flowchart

flödesstyrning ▷ flow

flödessändning ▷ flooding

FM ['efem] = FREQUENCY MODULATION

FMS ['efem'es] = FLEXIBLE MACHINING SYSTEM, FLEXIBLE MANUFACTURING SYSTEM computer numeric control (CNC) *or* control of a machine by a computer *FMS-system*

FNP ['efen'piː] = FRONT END NETWORK PROCESSOR

f-number ['ef'nʌmbə] *subst.* measurement of the amount of light that an optical lens can collect, measured as the ratio of focal length to maximum aperture *bländartal*

focal length ['fəʊk(ə)l 'leŋθ] *subst.* distance between the centre of an optical lens and the focusing plane, when the lens is focused at infinity *brännvid*

focus ['fəʊkəs] **1** *subst.* image *or* beam that is clear and well defined *fokus;* **the picture is out of focus** *or* **is not in focus** = the picture is not clear *bilden är ofokuserad* **2** *vb.* to adjust the focal length of a lens *or* beam deflection system so that the image *or* beam is clear and well defined *fokusera;* **the camera is focused on the foreground; they adjusted the lens position so that the beam focused correctly**

fog [fɒg] *subst.* effect on photographic material which has been accidentally exposed to unwanted light, causing a loss of picture contrast *slöja*

fokusera ⇨ concentrate

fold [fəʊld] *vb.* to bend a flat thing, so that part of it is on top of the rest *vika;* **she folded the letter so that the address was clearly visible; accordion** *or* **fanfold =** method of folding continuous stationery, one sheet in one direction, the next sheet in the opposite direction *dragspelsvikning (för papper i löpande bana)*

-fold [fəʊld] *suffix* times *gånger;* **four-fold =** four times *fyra gånger*

folder [ˈfəʊldə] *subst.* cardboard envelope for carrying papers *mapp;* **put all the documents in a folder for the chairman**

folding [ˈfəʊldɪŋ] *subst.* hashing method (that generates an address by splitting the key into parts and adding them together) *(samman)vikning, hopslagning*

folding machine [ˈfəʊldɪŋ məˈʃiːn] *subst.* machine which automatically folds sheets of paper *vikmaskin*

folio [ˈfəʊliəʊ] **1** *subst.* page with a number, especially two facing pages in an account book which have the same number *folioark bundet till kvartsformat* **2** *vb.* to put a number on a page *numrera, paginera*

font [fɒnt] *or* **fount** [faʊnt] *subst.* set of characters all of the same style, size and typeface *typsnitt;* **font change =** function on a computer to change the style of characters used on a display screen *typsnittsbyte;* **font disk =** (i) transparent disk that contains the master images of a particular font, used in a phototypesetting machine *typsnittsskiva;* (ii) magnetic disk that contains the data to drive a character generator to make up the various fonts on a computer display *typsnittsdiskett;* **downloadable fonts** *or* **resident fonts =** fonts *or* typefaces which are stored on a disk and can be downloaded to a printer and stored in temporary memory *minnesresidenta typsnitt*

> QUOTE laser printers store fonts in several ways: as resident, cartridge and downloadable fonts
> **Desktop Publishing Today**

foolscap [ˈfuːlzkæp] *subst.* large size of writing paper, longer than A4 *folioark;* **the letter was on six sheets of foolscap; a foolscap envelope =** large envelope which takes foolscap paper *foliokuvert*
NOTE: no plural

foot [fʊt] *subst.* bottom part *nedre del;* **he signed his name at the foot of the letter** *han skrev sitt namn nedtill på brevet*

foot candle [ˈfʊtˌkændl] *subst.* amount of light illumination in one square foot when the incident flux is one lumen *anglosaxiskt mått på belysningsyta*

footer [ˈfʊtə] *or* **footing** [ˈfʊtɪŋ] *subst.* message at the bottom of all the pages in a printed document (such as the page number) *fottext*

footnote [ˈfʊtnəʊt] *subst.* note at the bottom of a page, which refers to the text above it, usually using a superior number as a reference *fotnot*

footprint [ˈfʊtprɪnt] *subst.* **(a)** area covered by a transmitting device such as a satellite *or* antenna *täckning* **(b)** area that a computer takes up on a desk *(bords)utrymme*

forbid [fəˈbɪd] *vb.* to say that something must not be done *förbjuda;* **the contract forbids sale of the goods to the USA; forbidden character** *or* **combination =** bit combination in a computer word that is not allowed according to the rules defined by the programmer *or* system designer *otillåten kombination*
NOTE: **forbidding - forbade - forbidden**

force [fɔːs] **1** *subst.* strength *kraft;* **to come into force =** to start to operate *or* work *träda i kraft;* **the new regulations will come into force on January 1st 2** *vb.* to make someone do something *tvinga;* **competition has forced the company to lower its prices; forced page break =** embedded code which indicates a new page start *tvångsbrytning*

foreground [ˈfɔːɡraʊnd] *subst.* **(a)** front part of an illustration (as opposed to the background) *förgrund;* **foreground colour =** colour of characters and text displayed on a screen *förgrundsfärg* **(b)** high priority task done by a computer *förgrundsuppdrag, högprioritetsuppdrag;* **foreground/background modes =** computer system in which two modes for program execution are possible: foreground mode for interactive user programs, background mode for housekeeping and other necessary system programs *förgrundstillstånd, bakgrundstillstånd;* **foreground processing** *or* **foregrounding =** region of a multitasking operating system in which high priority jobs *or* programs are executed *förgrundsbearbetning;* **foreground program =** high priority program in a multitasking system, whose results are usually visible to the user *förgrundsprogram; compare* BACKGROUND; **foregrounding =** execution of high priority jobs *or* programs in a multitasking operating system *förgrundsdrift*

forest [ˈfɒrɪst] *subst.* number of interconnected data structure trees *strukturskog*

form [fɔːm] **1** *subst.* **(a)** preprinted document with blank spaces where information can be entered *formulär, blankett* **(b)** complete plate *or* block of type, ready for printing *sats* **(c)** page of computer stationery *blad, ark;* **form feed** = command to a printer to move to the next sheet of paper *sidmatning;* **form flash** = text heading held in store and printed out at the same time as the text *sidhuvudutskrift;* **form handling equipment** = peripherals (such as decollator) which deal with output from a printer *utrustning för efterbearbetning;* **form letter** = standard letter into which personal details of each addressee are inserted, such as name, address and job *standardbrev;* **form mode** = display method on a data entry terminal, the form is displayed on the screen and the operator enters relevant details *formulärfunktion, blankettfunktion;* **form overlay** = heading *or* other matter held in store and printed out at the same time as the text *formulärpåtryck, utskriftsrubrik;* **form stop** = sensor on a printer which indicates when the paper has run out *pappersslutssensor* **2** *vb.* to create a shape *forma;* to construct *konstruera;* **the system is formed of five separate modules**

form ⇨ **format**

format [ˈfɔːmæt] **1** *subst.* **(a)** size and shape of a book *pappersformat;* **the printer can deal with all formats up to quarto (b)** specific method of arranging text *or* data *dataformat;* way of arranging data on disk *skivminnesformat, diskettformat;* **address format** = way in which address data is stored including which bits select pages, memory protect, etc. *adressformat;* **card format** = way in which columns and rows are arranged to represent data *or* characters in a punched card *kortformat;* **data format** = rules defining the way in which data is stored *or* transmitted *dataformat;* **display format** = number of characters that can be displayed on a screen, given as row and column lengths *skärmformat;* **format mode** = use of protected display fields on a screen to show a blank form *or* page which cannot be altered, but into which a user can enter information *formulärfunktion;* **instruction format** = rules defining the way the operands, data and address are arranged in an instruction *instruktionsformat;* **local format storage** = format of a empty form *or* repeated page stored in a terminal rather than being repeatedly transmitted *lokalt formulärminne;* **variable format** = changing method of arranging data *or* text within an area *variabelt format* **(c)** precise syntax of instructions and arguments *syntax, format;* **symbolic-coding format** = assembly language instruction syntax, using a label, operation and operand fields

assemblerformat **(d)** way of arranging a TV programme *form;* **magazine format** = type of information programme which contains several different items linked together *magasinsform* **2** *vb.* **(a)** to arrange text as it will appear in printed form on paper *sidbrytning;* **style sheets are used to format documents; formatted dump** = text *or* data printed in a certain format *formaterad dump* **(b)** to **format a disk** = (i) to set up a blank disk so that it is ready for data, by writing control and track location information on it *formatera en skiva (en diskett);* (ii) to define the areas of a disk reserved for data and control *formatera en skiva;* **disk formatting** = setting up a blank disk by writing control and track location information on it *skivformatering, diskettformatering;* **disk formatting has to be done before you can use a new floppy disk**

> QUOTE there are three models, offering 53, 80 and 160 Mb of formatted capacity
> **Minicomputer News**

formatera ⇨ **format**

formatering ⇨ **disk**

formatter [ˈfɔːmætə] *subst.* hardware *or* software that arranges text *or* data according to certain rules *formaterare;* **print formatter** = software that converts embedded codes and print commands to printer control signals *utskriftsformaterare, formatstyrprogram;* **text formatter** = program that converts text to a new form *or* layout according to parameters *or* embedded codes (such as line width, page size, justification, etc.) *textbrytningsprogram, textformaterare*

formel ⇨ **equation, formula**

formering ⇨ **disk**

formula [ˈfɔːmjʊlə] *subst.* set of mathematical rules applied to solve a problem *formel;* **formula portability** = feature in a spreadsheet program to find a value in a single cell from data in others, with the possibility of using the same formula in other cells *formelflyttbarhet;* **formula translator** = FORTRAN
NOTE: plural is **formulae**

formulär ⇨ **form**

formulärfunktion ⇨ **form**

formulärmall ⇨ **overlay**

for-next loop [ˈfə ˈnekst ˈluːp] *subst.* loop or routine that is repeated until a condition no longer occurs *slinga i programmeringsspråket Basic;* **for X=1 to 5: print X: next X - this will print out 1 2 3 4 5**

forskning ⇨ **research**

FORTH [fɔːθ] computer programming language mainly used in control applications *programmeringsspråket Forth*

> QUOTE the main attraction of FORTH over other computer languages is that it is not simply a language, rather it is a programming tool in which it is possible to write other application specific languages
>
> **Electronics & Power**

FORTRAN ['fɔːtræn] = FORMULA TRANSLATOR programming language developed in the first place for scientific use *programmeringsspråket Fortran*

fortsätta ⇨ **continue**

fortsättning ⇨ **continuation**

forty-track disk ['fɔːtɪ,træk 'dɪsk] *subst.* floppy disk formatted to contain forty tracks of data *40-spårsskiva*

forward ['fɔːwəd] **1** *adj.* moving in advance *or* in front *framåt;* **forward channel** = communications line containing data transmitted from the user to another party *utdatalinje;* **forward clearing** = switching telephone systems back to their clear state, starting from the point where the call was made and travelling forward towards the destination *framåtriktad slutsignalering;* **forward error correction** = method of detecting and correcting certain error conditions with the use of redundant codes *felkorrigering vid mottagning;* **forward reference** = reference to something which has not yet been established *framåtreferens;* **forward scatter** = scattered sections of wave travelling in the same direction as the incident *fortplantning av radiovågor genom spridningsfenomen i jonosfären* **2** *vb.* to pass a call on to another point *vidarekoppla, eftersända*

forward mode ['fɔːwəd,məud] *subst.* to add a number *or* index *or* displacement to an origin *framåtläge*

FOSDIC ['fɒzdɪk] = FILM OPTICAL SCANNING DEVICE FOR INPUT INTO COMPUTERS storage device for computer data using microfilm *mikrofilmläsare*

fotosättning ⇨ **photocomposition, phototypesetting**

fottext ⇨ **footer**

fount [faunt] = FONT set of characters all of the same style, size and typeface *typsnitt*

four-address instruction ['fɔːrə,dres ɪn'strʌkʃ(ə)n] *subst.* program instruction which contains four addresses within its address field, usually the location of the two operands, the result and the location of the next instruction *fyradressinstruktion;* **four-plus-one address** = instruction that contains the locations of four registers and

the location of the next instruction *fyra-plus-en-adress*

Fourier series ['fuərɪ,ei 'sɪəriːz] *subst.* mathematical representation of waveforms by a combination of fundamental and harmonic components of a frequency *Fourierserie*

fourth generation computers ['fɔːθ,dʒenə'reiʃ(ə)n kəm'pjuːtəz] *subst.* computer technology using LSI circuits, developed around 1970 and still in current use *fjärde generationens datorer;* **fourth generation languages** = languages that are user-friendly and have been designed with the non-expert in mind *fjärde generationens programmeringsspråk, 4 G-språk*

four-track recorder ['fɔː 'træk rɪ'kɔːdə] *subst.* tape recorder that is able to record and play back four independent audio tracks at once *fyrkanalsbandspelare*

fps ['efpiː'es] = FRAMES PER SECOND

fraction ['frækʃ(ə)n] *subst.* (i) part of a whole unit, expressed as one figure above another (such as ½, ¾, etc.) *bråkdel;* (ii) mantissa of a floating point number *mantissa*

fractional ['frækʃənl] *adj.* made of fractions; referring to fractions *bråkdels-;* **the root is the fractional power of a number;** **fractional part** = mantissa of a floating point number *mantissa*

fragmentation [,frægmen'teiʃ(ə)n] *subst.* main memory allocation to a number of files, which has resulted in many small, free sections *or* fragments that are too small to be of any use, but waste a lot of space *fragmentering, splittring*

frame [freim] *subst.* **(a)** (i) space on magnetic tape for one character code *teckenlängd;* (ii) packet of transmitted data including control and route information *paket;* **frame error** = error due to a faulty bit within a frame on magnetic tape *teckenfel* **(b)** one complete television *or* photographic image *ruta, bildruta;* **video frame** = one image on a video film *videobildruta;* **with the image processor you can freeze a video frame;** **frame flyback** = electron beam return from the bottom right to the top left corner of the screen to start building up a new field *(bild)svepåtergivning;* **frame frequency** = number of television frames transmitted per second *bildfrekvens;* **in the UK the frame frequency is 25 fps; frame grabber** = high speed digital sampling circuit that stores a television picture frame in memory so that it can then be processed by a computer *bildfångare, lagring i bildminne;* **frame store** = digital storage of analog TV signals on disk *videoskivlagring;* **the image**

processor allows you to store a video frame in a built-in 8-bit frame store; the frame store can be used to display weather satellite pictures

frames per second (fps) ['freɪmz pɜː 'sek(ə)nd (ˌefpiː'es)] *subst.* **(a)** speed of single frames of a motion picture through a projector *or* camera every second *bilder per sekund* **(b)** number of television picture frames transmitted per second *bilder per sekund*

framework ['freɪmwɜːk] *subst.* basic structure of a database *or* process *or* program *ramverk, specifikation, struktur;* **the program framework was designed first**

framing ['freɪmɪŋ] *subst.* **(a)** positioning of a camera's field of view for a required image *bildinställning* **(b)** synchronization of time division multiplexed frames of data *synkronisering;* **framing bit =** sync bit *or* transmitted bit used to synchronize devices *synkroniseringsbit;* **framing code =** method of synchronizing a receiver with a broadcast teletext stream of data *synkroniseringskod*

framsida ⇨ **front, front-end**

framtidsdatorer ⇨ **generation**

framåtläge ⇨ **forward mode**

fraud [frɔːd] *subst.* making money by tricking people *or* by making them believe something which is not true *bedrägeri;* **computer fraud =** theft of data *or* dishonest use *or* other crimes involving computers *databrott*

> QUOTE the offences led to the arrest of nine teenagers who were all charged with computer fraud
> **Computer News**

free [friː] **1** *adj.* available for use *or* not currently being used *tom, fri, ledig;* (spare bytes) available on disk *or* in memory *ledigt utrymme;* **free indexing =** library entries having references to documents which the indexer considers useful, even if they do not appear in the text *fri indexering;* **free line =** telephone line that is not connected and so is available for use *ledig linje;* **free running mode =** interactive computer mode that allows more than one user to have simultaneous use of a program *fleråtkomsttillstånd;* **free space loss =** measure of the loss of transmitted signals from a satellite antenna to an earth station *förluster i fri rymd;* **free space media =** empty space between a transmitter and a receiving aerial which is used for transmission *antennavstånd;* **free wheeling =** transmission protocol where the computer transmitting receives no status signals from the receiver *enkelriktad sändning* **2** *vb.* to erase *or* remove *or* backup

programs *or* files to provide space in memory *radera, frigöra*

freedom ['friːdəm] *subst.* being free to do something without restriction *frihet;* **freedom of information =** being able to examine computer records (referring both to government activities and to records kept about individuals) *informationsfrihet;* **freedom of the press =** being able to write and publish in a newspaper what you wish without being afraid of prosecution, provided that you do not break the law *pressfrihet;* **freedom of speech =** being able to say what you want without being afraid of prosecution, provided that you do not break the law *yttrandefrihet*

freely ['friːlɪ] *adv.* with no restrictions *fritt*

freeze [friːz] *vb.* **to freeze (frame) =** to stop and display a single frame from a film *or* TV *or* videodisk *or* video tape machine *frysa (en bild);* **the image processor will freeze a single TV frame**

F-region ['ef 'riːdʒ(ə)n] section of the ionosphere that is 150 - 400Km from the earth's surface *F-skiktet*

frekvensmultiplexering ⇨ **FDM**

frequency ['friːkwənsɪ] *subst.* number of cycles *or* periods of a regular waveform that are repeated per second *frekvens;* **frequency changer =** electronic circuit that shifts the frequency of a signal up *or* down *frekvensbytare;* **frequency divider =** electronic circuit that reduces the frequency of a signal by a multiple of two *frekvensdelare;* **frequency division multiplexing (FDM) =** transmission of several independent signals along a single channel, achieved by shifting each signal up in frequency by a different amount *frekvensmultiplexering;* **frequency domain =** effects of a certain circuit on the frequency range of a signal *(i) frekvensplanet, frekvenskaraktäristik;* **frequency modulation (FM) =** varying the frequency of a carrier waveform according to a signal amplitude *frekvensmodulering;* **frequency range =** range of allowable frequencies, between two limits *frekvensområde;* **frequency response =** electronic circuit parameter given as the ratio of output to input signal amplitudes at various frequencies *frekvenskaraktäristik;* **frequency shift keying (FSK) =** transmission system using the translation of two state binary data into two different frequencies, one for on, one for off *tvåtonsmodulering;* **frequency variation =** change of frequency of a signal from normal *frekvensvariation;* **clock frequency =** frequency of the main clock that synchronizes a computer system *klockfrekvens;* **the main clock frequency is 10MHz**

frequent ['fri:kwənt] *adj.* which comes *or* goes *or* takes place often *ofta förekommande, vanlig;* **we send frequent telexes to New York; how frequent are the planes to Birmingham?**

frequently ['fri:kwəntlı] *adv.* often *ofta;* **the photocopier is frequently out of use; we telex our New York office very frequently - at least four times a day**

friction feed ['frıkʃ(ə)n,fi:d] *subst.* printer mechanism where the paper is advanced by holding it between two rollers (as opposed to tractor feed) *friktionsmatning*

fristående ⊳ off-line

fristående databehandling ⊳ processing

FROM [from] = FUSIBLE READ ONLY MEMORY

front [frʌnt] *subst.* part of something which faces away from the back *framsida;* **the disks are inserted in slots in the front of the terminal; front panel** = main computer system control switches and status indicators *frontpanel;* **front porch** = section of television signal between the line blanking pulse and the line sync pulse *linjesläcktid (tidigare delen);* **front projection** = projection of background images onto a screen located behind a person *backprojicering*

frontdator ⊳ FEP

front-end ['frʌntend] *adj.* located at the start *or* most important point of a circuit *or* network *ingång, framsida, startpunkt;* **front-end processor (FEP)** = processor placed between an input source and the central computer whose function is to preprocess received data to relieve the workload of the main computer *frontdator;* **front-end system** = typesetting system, where text is keyboarded on a terminal directly connected to the typesetting computer *frontsystem*

frontprocessor ⊳ processor

fråga ⊳ inquiry, query, question

frågebearbetning ⊳ query

frågebehandling ⊳ processing

frågeformulär ⊳ questionnaire

frågeprogram ⊳ query

frågespråk ⊳ language, query

frågeterminal ⊳ inquiry

FSK ['efes'keı] = FREQUENCY SHIFT KEYING

full [fʊl] *adj.* **(a)** with as much inside as possible *full;* **the disk is full, so the material will have to be stored on another disk (b)** complete *or* including everything *full, fullständig;* **full adder** = binary addition circuit that can produce the sum of two inputs and can also accept a carry input, producing a carry output if necessary *heladderare;* **full duplex** = data transmission down a channel in two directions simultaneously *full duplex; see also* DUPLEX, HALF-DUPLEX, SIMPLEX; **full-frame time code** = standard method of counting video frames rather than using a time check signal for synchronization with music and effects *(fullbilds)tidskod(ning);* **full-size display** = large screen VDU which can display a whole page of text *fullskaleskärm, helsidesskärm;* **full subtractor** = binary subtractor circuit that can produce the difference of two inputs and can also accept a carry input, producing a carry output if necessary *helsubtraherare*

QUOTE transmitter and receiver can be operated independently, making full duplex communication possible
Electronics & Power

fullständig handskakning ⊳ handshake

fullständig operation ⊳ operation

fullständig sökning ⊳ exhaustive search

fully ['fʊlı] *adv.* completely *fullständig;* **fully connected network** = situation where each node in a network is connected with every other *fullt uppkopplat datanät;* **fully formed characters** = characters produced by a printer in a single action *enanslagstecken;* **a daisy wheel printer produces fully formed characters**

function ['fʌŋ(k)ʃ(ə)n] **1** *subst.* **(a)** mathematical formula, where a result is dependent upon several other numbers *funktion* **(b)** sequence of computer program instructions in a main program that perform a certain task *rutin, funktion;* **function digit** = code used to instruct a computer as to which function *or* branch in a program to follow *funktionssiffra, operationssiffra;* **function table** = list that gives the relationship between two sets of instructions *or* data *funktionstabell* **(c)** special feature available on a computer *or* word-processor *funktion;* **the word-processor had a spelling-checker function but no built-in text-editing function; function code** = printing codes that control an action rather than representing a character *funktionskod* **2** *vb.* to operate *or* perform correctly *fungera;* **the new system has not functioned properly since it was installed**

QUOTE they made it clear that the PC was to take its place as part of a much larger computing function that comprised of local area networks, wide area networks, small systems, distributed systems and mainframes
Minicomputer News
QUOTE if your computer has a MOD function, you will not need the function defined in line 3010
Computing Today

functional ['fʌŋ(k)ʃənl] *adj.* which refers to the way something works *funktionell;* **functional diagram** = drawing of the internal workings and processes of a machine *or* piece of software *funktionsdiagram;* **functional specification** = specification which defines the results which a program is expected to produce *funktionsspecifikation;* **functional unit** = hardware *or* software that works as it should *fungerande enhet*

function key ['fʌŋ(k)ʃ(ə)n,kiː] *or* **programmable function key** [prəʊ'græməbl 'fʌŋ(k)ʃ(ə)n,kiː] *subst.* key *or* switch that has been assigned a particular task *or* sequence of instructions *funktionstangent;* **tags can be allocated to function keys; hitting F5 will put you into insert mode**

COMMENT: function keys often form a separate group of keys on the keyboard, and have specific functions attached to them. They may be labelled F1, F2, etc.

QUOTE the final set of keys are to be found above the main keyboard and comprise 5 function keys, which together with shift, give 10 user-defined keys
Computing Today

fundamental frequency [,fʌndə'mentl 'friːkwənsɪ] *subst.* most prominent frequency in a complex signal *grundfrekvens, grundton*

COMMENT: almost all signals contain parts of other frequencies (harmonics) at lower amplitudes to the fundamental, which often causes distortion

funktion ⇨ feature, function

funktionstangent ⇨ function key

funktionstid ⇨ operation

fuse [fjuːz] **1** *subst.* electrical protection device consisting of a small piece of metal, which will melt when too much power passes through it *säkring;* **to blow a fuse** = to melt a fuse by passing too much current through it *utlösa en säkring* **2** *vb.* to draw too much current, causing a fuse to melt *utlösa en säkring;* **when the air-conditioning was switched on, it fused the whole system**

fusible link ['fjuːzəbl 'lɪŋk] *subst.* small link in a PLA that can be blown to program the device permanently *programmerbar bit (en programmerbar logikkrets eller grindmatris)*

fusible read only memory (FROM) ['fjuːzəbl 'riːd əʊnlɪ 'memərɪ (from)] *subst.* PROM that is made up of a matrix of fusible links which are selectively blown to program it *programmerbart läsminne*

fusion ['fjuːʒ(ə)n] *subst.* combining two hardware devices *or* programs *or* chemical substances to create a single form *sammanslagning, förening*

fuzzy ['fʌzɪ] *subst.* not clear *suddig;* **top quality paper will eliminate fuzzy characters; fuzzy logic** *or* **fuzzy theory** = type of logic applied to computer programming, which tries to replicate the reasoning methods of the human brain *statistisk logik*

fyllnadsbit ⇨ **pad**

fyradressinstruktion ⇨ **instruction**

fyra G-språk ⇨ **generation**

fyrdubbel täthet ⇨ **quad**

fälla ⇨ **trap**

fälteffekttransistor ⇨ **FET**

fältgränstecken ⇨ **field**

fältlängd ⇨ **field**

fältmarkör ⇨ **marker**

fälttekniker ⇨ **field**

färdig ⇨ **ready**

färgband ⇨ **ribbon**

fönsterhantering ⇨ **windowing**

fönstermeny ⇨ **pop**

fönsterorienterat användargränssnitt ⇨ **WIMP**

förbehandla ⇨ **preprocess**

förberedande handbok ⇨ **primer**

förbinda ⇨ **couple**

förbrukningsmaterial ⇨ **consumables**

fördela ⇨ **allocate**

fördröjning ⇨ **delay, lag, latency**

fördröjningskompensering ⇨ **delay**

fördröjningsledning ⇨ **delay**

förebyggande underhåll ⇨ **preventive**

föredragningslista ⇨ **agenda**

förfrågningstecken ⇨ **inquiry**

förgrundsbearbetning ⇨ **foreground**

förgrundsdrift ⇨ **foreground**

förgrundsprogram ⇨ **foreground**

förgrundstillstånd ⇨ foreground

förhämtning ⇨ look ahead, pre-

förkasta ⇨ reject

förlängningskabel ⇨ extension

förmagnetiseringssignal ⇨ bias

förminska ⇨ reduce

förmåga ⇨ capability

förskjuten exponent ⇨ biased

förskjutning ⇨ offset

förspänning ⇨ bias

först in-först ut ⇨ FIFO

förstudie ⇨ feasibility

förstudierapport ⇨ feasibility

förstärkning ⇨ amplification

förteckna ⇨ index

förvanskad ⇨ corrupt

förvrängd ⇨ corrupt

föräldrafil ⇨ ancestral file

förändringsmarkering ⇨ dirty bit

förändringssteg ⇨ increment

Gg

G [dʒiː] = GIGA *prefix* **GHz =** gigahertz *giga;* meaning one thousand million *G*

COMMENT: in computing G refers to 2^{30}, equal to 1,073,741,824

GaAs ['dʒiːeɪ'eɪes] = GALLIUM ARSENIDE

gain [geɪn] **1** *subst.* increase *or* becoming larger *vinst, tillsats, förstärkning;* amount by which a signal amplitude is changed as it passes through a circuit, usually given as a ratio of output to input amplitude *förstärkning;* **gain control =** variable control that sets the amount of gain a circuit *or* amplifier will provide *förstärkningskontroll* **2** *vb.* to obtain *or* to get *vinna, få;* **to gain access to a file =** to be able to access a file *få åtkomst till en fil;* **the user cannot gain access to the confidential information in the file without a password**

galactic noise [gə'læktɪk 'nɔɪz] *subst.* random electrical noise which originates from planets and stars in space *bakgrundsbrus, rymdbrus*

galley proof *or* **slip** ['gælɪ 'pruːf 'gælɪ 'slɪp] *subst.* rough initial proof of a column *or* section of text, printed on a long piece of paper *spaltkorrektur*

gallium arsenide (GaAs) ['gælɪəm 'ɑːsənaɪd ('dʒiːeɪ'eɪes)] *subst.* semiconductor compound, a new material for chip construction, that allows faster operation than silicon chips *galliumarsenid*

game [geɪm] *subst.* something which is played for enjoyment *or* relaxation *spel;* **computer game =** game played on a computer, using special software *datorspel;* **game paddle =** device held in the hand to move a cursor *or* graphics in a computer game *styrspak (för spel)*

gamma ['gæmə] *subst.* (i) measure of the development of a photographic image, and so its contrast range *gamma-värde, kontrastvärde;* (ii) logarithm of the luminescence of the image on a TV screen, in relation to that of the original scene when filmed *gradationskaraktäristik*

ganged [gæŋd] *adj.* mechanically linked devices that are operated by a single action *kedjekopplade enheter;* **ganged switch =** series of switches that operate on different parts of a circuit, but which are all switched by a single action *kedjekopplad brytare;* **a ganged switch is used to select which data bus a printer will respond to**

gap [gæp] *subst.* **(a)** space between recorded data *mellanrum;* **block** *or* **interblock gap (IBG) =** blank magnetic tape between the end of one block of data and the start of the next in backing store *blockmellanrum;* **gap character =** an extra character added to a group of characters (for parity or another purpose, but not data *or* instructions) *mellantecken;* **gap digit =** an extra digit added to a group of data (for parity or another purpose, but not data *or* instructions) *mellansiffra;* **record gap =** blank section of magnetic tape between two consecutive records *blockmellanrum, postmellanrum* **(b)** space between a read head and the magnetic medium *gap mellan läs/skrivhuvud och magnetskiva;* **gap loss =** signal attenuation due to incorrect alignment of the read/write head with the storage medium *signalförlust i skriv/läshuvudet;* **air** *or* **head gap =** narrow gap between a recording *or* playback head and the magnetic medium *luftspalt* **(c)** method of radio communications using a carrier signal that is switched on and off, as in a telegraphic system *paus, mellanrum*

garanti ⇨ warranty

garbage ['gɑːbɪdʒ] *subst.* **(a)** radio interference from adjacent channels *störsignaler* **(b)** data *or* information that is no longer required because it is out of date *or* contains errors *skräpdata;* **garbage collection** = reorganization and removal of unwanted *or* out of date files and records; clearing a section of memory of a program *or* its data that is not in use *minneskompaktering, skräpminnesinsamling;* **garbage in garbage out (GIGO)** = expression meaning that the accuracy and quality of information that is output depends on the quality of the input *"skräp in skräp ut"*

> COMMENT: GIGO is sometimes taken to mean "garbage in gospel out": i.e. that whatever wrong information is put into a computer, people will always believe that the output results are true

gas discharge display ['gæs dɪs'tʃɑːdʒ dɪs'pleɪ] *or* **gas plasma display** ['gæs ˌplæzmə dɪs'pleɪ] *subst.* flat, lightweight display screen that is made of two flat pieces of glass covered with a grid of conductors, separated by a thin layer of a gas which luminesces when one point of the grid is selected by two electric signals *plasmaskärm*

> COMMENT: mainly used in modern portable computer displays, but the definition is not as good as in cathode ray tube displays

gate [geɪt] *subst.* **(a)** logical electronic switch whose output depends on the states of the inputs and the type of logical function implemented *grind;* **AND gate** = gate that performs a logical AND function *(logisk) och-grind;* **EXNOR gate** = electronic implementation of the EXNOR function *(logisk) negerad antingen-eller-grind;* **EXOR gate** = electronic implementation of the EXOR function *(logisk) antingen-eller-grind;* **NAND gate** = electronic circuit that provides a NAND function *(logisk) icke-och-grind;* **negation** *or* **NOT gate** = single input gate whose output is equal to the logical inverse of the input *(logisk) icke-grind, negerande grind, inverterare;* **NOR gate** = electronic circuit which performs a NOR function *(logisk) varken-eller-grind;* **OR gate** = electronic circuit that provides the OR function *(logisk) eller-grind;* **gate array** = number of interconnected logic gates built into an integrated circuit to perform a complex function *grindkrets;* **gate delay** *or* **propagation time** = time taken for a gate to produce an output after it has received inputs *grindfördröjning;* **gate circuit** = electronic components that implement a logical function *grindmatris* **(b)** connection pin of a FET device *kontaktstift* **(c)** mechanical film *or* slide frame a ligner in a camera *or* projector *filmförare*

gateway ['geɪtweɪ] *subst.* hard *or* software protocol translation device that allows users working in one network to access another *nätport*

gather ['gæðə] *vb.* to receive data from various sources (either directly from a data capture device or from a cartridge) and sort and insert in correct order into a database *samla (in);* **gather write** = to write a group of separate records as one block of data *samlingsinskrivning*

gauge [geɪdʒ] **1** *subst.* device which measures thickness *or* width *skjutmått* **2** *vb.* to measure the thickness *or* width of something *mäta*

gender changer ['dʒendəˌtʃeɪn(d)ʒə] *subst. informal* device for changing a female connection to a male or vice versa *könsbyteskontakt*

general ['dʒen(ə)r(ə)l] *adj.* **(a)** ordinary *or* not special *vanlig, normal, generell;* **general office** = main administrative office *huvudkontor* **(b)** dealing with everything *generell;* **general purpose computer** = computer whose processing power may be applied to many different sorts of applications, depending on its hardware *or* software instructions *generell dator;* **general purpose interface bus (GPIB)** = standard for an interface bus between a computer and laboratory equipment *GPIB-bussen, IEEE 488-buss, IEC 625-1-buss;* **general purpose program** = program *or* device able to perform many different jobs *or* applications *generellt program;* **general register** *or* **general purpose register (gpr)** = data register in a computer processing unit that can store items of data for many different mathematical *or* logical operations *generellt register*

generate ['dʒenəreɪt] *vb.* to use software *or* a device to produce codes *or* a program automatically *generera;* **to generate an image from digitally recorded data; the graphics tablet generates a pair of co-ordinates each time the pen is moved; computer-generated** = produced using a computer *datorgenererad;* **they analyzed the computer-generated image; generated address** = location used by a program that has been produced by instructions within the program *(själv)genererad adress;* **generated error** = error occurring due to inaccuracies in data used (such as a sum total error due to a series of numbers which are rounded up) *självgenererat fel*

generation [ˌdʒenə'reɪʃ(ə)n] *subst.* **(a)** producing data *or* software *or* programs using a computer *generering;* **the computer is used in the generation of graphic images; code generation is automatic; program generation** *see* GENERATOR **(b)** state *or* age of the technology used in the design of a system *generation;* **first generation** = earliest type of technology *första* *generationen;* **first generation computers** = original computers made with valve-based electronic technology, started around 1951 *första generationens datorer, tidiga datorer;* **first generation image** = master copy of an original image, text *or* document *originalkopia;* **second generation computers** = computers which used transistors instead of valves *andra generationens datorer, transistoriserade datorer;* **third generation computers** = computers which used integrated circuits instead of transistors *tredje generationens datorer, datorer med integrerade kretsar;* **fourth generation computers** = computer technology using LSI circuits, developed around 1970 and still in current use *fjärde generationens datorer, moderna datorer;* **fourth generation languages** = languages that are user-friendly and have been designed with the non-expert in mind *fjärde generationens programmeringsspråk, fyra G-språk;* **fifth generation computers** = next stage of computer system design using fast VLSI circuits and powerful programming languages to allow human interaction *femte generationens datorer, framtidsdatorer* **(c)** distance between a file and the original version, used when making backups *lagringsversion;* **the father file is a first generation backup**

QUOTE vector and character generation are executed in hardware by a graphics display processor
Computing Today

generator ['dʒenəreitə] *subst.* **(a)** (program) that generates new programs according to rules *or* specifications set out by the user *kodgenerator* **(b)** device which generates electricity *generator;* **the computer centre has its own independent generator, in case of mains power failure**

generell dator ⇨ **general**

generellt register ⇨ **gpr**

generic [dʒi'nerik] *adj.* (something) that is compatible with a whole family of hardware *or* software devices from one manufacturer *generisk, släkt-, familjetypisk*

genomföra ⇨ **implement**

genomgående utbyte ⇨ **global**

genomlysbarhet ⇨ **transmittance**

genomskriven nolla ⇨ **slashed zero**

genomskärning ⇨ **cross-section**

genomsnittlig drifttid ⇨ **MTBF**

genomströmning ⇨ **throughput**

genuine ['dʒenjuin] *adj.* real *or* correct *äkta, autentisk;* **authentication allows the**

system to recognize that a sender's message is genuine

geometric distortion [,dʒiə'metrik dis'tɔːʃ(ə)n] *subst.* linear distortion of a television picture, which can becaused by video tape speed fluctuations *geometrisk distorsion*

geostationary satellite [,dʒiːəʊ'steiʃnəri 'sætəlait] *subst.* satellite which moves at the same velocity as the earth, so remains above the same area of the earth's surface, and appears stationary when viewed from the earth *geostationär satellit*

germanium [dʒɜː'meiniəm] *subst.* semiconductor material, used as a substrate in some transistors instead of silicon *germanium*

get [get] *subst.* instruction to obtain a record from a file *or* database *hämta*

ghost [gəʊst] *subst.* effect on a television image where a weaker copy of the picture is displayed to one side of the main image, caused by signal reflections *spöksignal;* **ghost cursor** = second cursor which can be used in some programs *spökmarkör*

GHz ['gigəhɜːts] = GIGAHERTZ

gibberish ['dʒibəriʃ] *subst.* useless and meaningless information *rappakalja, babbel*

giga- ['giːgə] *or* **G** [dʒiː] *prefix* meaning one thousand million *en miljard;* **gigabyte** = 10^9 bytes *gigabyte;* **gigahertz** = frequency of 10^9 *gigahertz*

COMMENT: in computing giga refers to 2^{30}, which is equal to 1,073,741,824

GIGO ['gaigəʊ] = GARBAGE IN GARBAGE OUT expression meaning that the accuracy and quality of information that is output depends on the quality of the input *"skräp in skräp ut"*

COMMENT: GIGO is sometimes taken to mean "garbage in gospel out": i.e. that whatever wrong information is put into a computer, people will always believe that the output results are true

giltighetskontroll ⇨ **validation**

giltighetskontrollera ⇨ **validate**

GINO ['gainəʊ] = GRAPHICAL INPUT OUTPUT graphical control routine written in FORTRAN *grafiskt styrprogram*

GKS ['dʒiːkeies] = GRAPHICS KERNEL SYSTEM standard for software command and functions describing graphical input/output to provide the same functions etc. on any type of hardware *standard för grafikrepresentation*

glappkontakt ⇨ **dry contact**

glare [gleə] *subst.* very bright light reflections, especially on a VDU screen *blänk;* **the glare from the screen makes my eyes hurt**
NOTE: no plural

gles vektor ⇨ **sparse array**

glitch [glɪtʃ] *subst. informal* anything which causes the sudden unexpected failure of a computer *or* equipment *hake, något oväntat som förorsakar problem i systemet*

global ['gləub(ə)l] *adj.* covering everything *global, allmän, genomgående;* **global exchange =** replace function which replaces one piece of text (such as a word) with another throughout a whole text *genomgående utbyte;* **global knowledge =** all the knowledge about one problem *or* task *fullständig kunskap;* **global search and replace =** word-processor search and replace function covering a complete file *or* document *genomgående sök- och utbytesfunktion;* **global variable =** variable *or* number that can be accessed by any routine *or* structure in a program *allmän variabel; compare* LOCAL VARIABLE

globalt nät ⇨ **wide area network (WAN)**

glossy ['glɒsɪ] **1** *adj.* shiny (paper) *glättad;* **the illustrations are printed on glossy art paper 2** *subst. informal* **the glossies =** expensive magazines *den glättade veckopressen*

GND ['dʒiːen'diː] = GROUND electrical circuit connection to earth *or* to a point with a zero voltage level *jord*

go ahead ['gəuəhed] *subst.* signal to indicate that a receiver *or* device is ready to accept information *fortsätt-signal*

goal [gəul] *subst.* (i) aim *or* what you are trying to do *mål;* (ii) final state reached when a task has been finished *or* has produced satisfactory results *mål*

gofer ['gəufə] *subst. US informal* person who does all types of work in an office *or* studio, etc. *allt-i-allo*

gold contacts ['gəuld͵kɒntækts] *subst.* electrical contacts, (usually for low-level signals) that are coated with gold to reduce the electrical resistance *förgyllda kontakter*

golf-ball ['gɒlfbɔːl] *subst.* metal ball with characters on its surface, which produces printed characters by striking a ribbon onto paper *typkula;* **golf-ball printer =** computer printer using a golf-ball as a printing head *kulskrivare, kulskrivmaskin*

COMMENT: a golf-ball contains all the characters of a single typeface; to change the face, the ball is taken out and replaced by another. The main defect of a golf-ball typewriter when used as a printer, is that it is slower than a dot-matrix printer

gospel ['gɒsp(ə)l] *see note at* GARBAGE

GOTO ['gəutuː] programming command which instructs a jump *hoppinstruktion;* **GOTO 105 instructs a jump to line 105**

COMMENT: GOTO statements are frowned upon by software experts since their use discourages set, structured programming techniques

GPIB ['dʒiːpiːaɪ'biː] = GENERAL PURPOSE INTERFACE BUS standard for an interface bus between a computer and laboratory equipment *GPIB-buss, IEEE 488-buss, IEC 625-1-buss*

GPIB-buss ⇨ **GPIB**

gpr ['dʒiːpiːɑː] = GENERAL PURPOSE REGISTER data register in a computer processing unit that can store items of data for many different mathematical *or* logical operations *generellt register*

grab [græb] *vb.* to take something and hold it *gripa, hugga tag i*

QUOTE sometimes a program can grab all the available memory, even if it is not going to use it
Byte

grabber ['græbə] *subst.* **frame grabber =** high speed digital sampling circuit that stores a TV picture in memory so that it can then be processed by a computer *bildfångare, lagring i bildminne*

QUOTE the frame grabber is distinguished by its ability to acquire a TV image in a single frame interval
Electronics & Wireless World

graceful degradation ['greɪsf(u)l ͵degrə'deɪʃ(ə)n] *subst.* allowing some parts of a system to continue to function after a part has broken down *mjuk kapacitetsnedgång*

grade [greɪd] *subst.* level *or* rank *nivå;* **a top-grade computer expert; grade of service =** quality of telephone service at a given time, defined by the likelihood of a successful connection via a telephone network at its busiest time *servicenivå*

graduated ['grædʒueɪtɪd] *adj.* which has a scale *or* measurements marked on it *graderad*

grafikprocessor ⇨ **display**

grafisk formgivare ⇨ **typographer**

grain [greɪn] *subst.* spotted effect on fast photographic films due to the size of the light-sensitive silver halide crystals *korn, kornighet*

gram [græm] *or* **gramme** [græm] *subst.* unit of measurement of weight, one thousandth of a kilogram *gram;* **the book is printed on 70 gram paper**

grammage ['græmɪdʒ] *subst.* weight of paper, calculated as grams per square metre *gramvikt*
NOTE: usually shown as **gsm : 80 gsm paper**

grammar ['græmə] *subst.* rules for the correct use of language *grammatik*

grammatical error [grə'mætɪk(ə)l 'erə] *subst.* incorrect use of a computer programming language syntax *grammatiskt fel, grammatikaliskt fel*

grandfather file ['græn(d)fɑːðə,faɪl] *subst.* third most recent version of a backed up file, after father and son files *ursprungsversion;* **grandfather cycle** = period in which the grandfather file is retrieved and updated to produce a new father file, the old father file becoming the new grandfather file *versionscykel*

granska ⇨ **review**

granularity [,grænjʊ'lærɪtɪ] *subst.* size of memory segments in a virtual memory system *kornighet*

graph [græf] *subst.* diagram showing the relationship between two *or* more variables as a line *or* series of points *grafisk framställning, diagram, kurva;* **graph paper** = paper with many little squares, used for drawing graphs *(millimeter)rutat papper;* **graph plotter** = printing device with a pen which takes data from a computer and plots it in graphic form *kurvritare, kurvskrivare*

graphic ['græfɪk] *adj.* (representation of information) in the form of pictures *or* plots instead of by text *grafisk;* **graphic data** = stored data that represents graphical information (when displayed on a screen) *grafikdata;* **graphic display** = computer screen able to present graphical information *grafisk skärm;* **graphic display resolution** = number of pixels that a computer is able to display on the screen *grafikupplösning;* **graphic language** = computer programming language with inbuilt commands that are useful when displaying graphics *grafiskt programmeringsspråk;* **this graphic language can plot lines, circles and graphs with a single command**

graphical ['græfɪkl] *adj.* referring to something represented by graphics *grafisk*

graphically ['græfɪklɪ] *adv.* using pictures *grafiskt;* **the sales figures are graphically represented as a pie chart**

graphics ['græfɪks] *subst.* pictures *or* lines which can be drawn on paper *or* on a screen to represent information *grafik;* **graphics output such as bar charts, pie charts, line drawings, etc.;; graphics art terminal** = typesetting terminal that is used with a phototypesetter *grafikterminal;* **graphics character** = preprogrammed shape that can be displayed on a non-graphical screen instead of a character, used extensively in videotext systems to display simple pictures *grafiktecken;* **graphics kernel system (GKS)** = standard for software command and functions describing graphical input/output to provide the same functions etc. on any type of hardware *standard för grafikrepresentation, GKS-systemet;* **graphics library** = number of routines stored in a library file that can be added to any user program to simplify the task of writing graphics programs *grafikbibliotek;* **graphics light pen** = high-accuracy light pen used for drawing onto a graphics display screen *ljuspenna;* **graphics mode** = videotext terminal whose displayed characters are taken from a range of graphics characters instead of text *grafikläge;* **graphics pad** *or* **tablet** = flat device that allows a user to input graphical information into a computer by drawing on its surface *tablett;* **graphics processor** = dedicated processor and memory used only to produce and control images on a display, to provide high speed graphics handling capabilities *grafikprocessor;* **graphics software** = prewritten routines that perform standard graphics commands such as line drawing, plotting, etc., that can be called from within a program to simplify program writing *grafikprogram;* **graphics terminal** = special terminal with a high-resolution graphic display and graphics pad *or* other input device *grafikterminal;* **graphics VDU** = special VDU which can display high-resolution *or* colour graphics as well as text *grafikskärm*

QUOTE one interesting feature of this model is graphics amplification, which permits graphic or text enlargement of up to 800 per cent
QUOTE the custom graphics chips can display an image that has 640 columns by 400 rows of 4-bit pixel
QUOTE several tools exist for manipulating image and graphical data: some were designed for graphics manipulation
Byte

gravure [grə'vjʊə] *see* PHOTOGRAVURE

Gray code ['greɪkəʊd] *subst.* coding system in which the binary representation of decimal numbers changes by only one bit at a time from one number to the next *Gray-kod*

COMMENT: used in communications systems to provide error detection facilities

green phosphor ['gri:n 'fɒsfə] *subst.* most commonly used phosphor for monochrome screen coating, which displays green characters on a black background *grön fosfor*

COMMENT: a new popular screen type is paper-white, using a white phosphor to display black characters on a white background

gremlin ['gremlɪn] *subst. informal* unexplained fault in a system *"troll i systemet"*; **there is a line gremlin =** unexplained fault when data is lost during transmission *"linjen spökar"*

grey scale ['greɪˌskeɪl] *subst.* **(a)** shades of grey that are used to measure the correct exposure when filming *gråskala* **(b)** shades which are produced from displaying what should be colour information on a monochrome monitor *gråskala*

grid [grɪd] *subst.* system of numbered squares used to help when drawing *stödraster;* matrix of lines at right angles allowing points to be easily plotted *or* located *rutraster*

grind ▷ gate

grindfördröjning ▷ gate

grindkrets ▷ gate

grip [grɪp] **1** *subst.* person who works on the stage in a film *or* TV studio *studioarbetare, passare* **2** *vb.* to hold something tightly *gripa, klämma;* **in friction feed, the paper is gripped by the rollers**

groda ▷ howler

ground [graʊnd] *subst.* **(a)** electrical circuit connection to earth *or* to a point with a zero voltage level *jord* NOTE: **ground** is more common in US English; the U.K. English is **earth (b)** the earth's surface *jordytan;* **ground absorption =** loss of transmitted power in radio waves that are near the ground *jordabsorption;* **ground station =** equipment and antenna on the earth used to communicate with an orbiting satellite *markstation*

group [gru:p] **1** *subst.* **(a)** set of computer records that contain related information *datagrupp;* **group mark** *or* **marker =** code used to identify the start and end of a group of related records *or* items of data *gruppmarkör;* **group poll =** polling a number of devices at once *gruppavfrågning* **(b)** six-character word used in telegraphic communications *(fråge)grupp* **(c)** single communications channel made up from a number of others that have been multiplexed together *multiplexerad linje* **2** *vb.* to bring several things together *samla, gruppera*

grundadress ▷ address

grundfrekvens ▷ fundamental frequency

grundläge ▷ float

grundläggande enhet ▷ primitive

grundvärde ▷ default, value

gruppavfrågning ▷ group

gruppmarkör ▷ group

gränssnitt ▷ interface, interfacing

gränssnittskort ▷ interface

gsm ['dʒi:es'em] *or* **g/m²** = GRAMS PER SQUARE METRE (PER SHEET) way of showing the weight of paper used in printing *g/m²*, *pappersvikt;* **the book is printed on 70 gsm coated paper**

guarantee [ˌgær(ə)n'ti:] *subst.* legal document promising that a machine will work properly *or* that an item is of good quality *garanti;* **the system is still under guarantee and will be repaired free of charge**

guard band ['gɑ:dbænd] *subst.* **(a)** frequency gap between two communication bands to prevent data corruption due to interference between each other *skyddsgap* **(b)** section of magnetic tape between two channels recorded on the same tape *kanalmellanrum*

guard bit ['gɑ:dbɪt] *subst.* one bit within a stored word that indicates to the computer whether it can be altered or if it is protected *skyddsbit*

guarding ['gɑ:dɪŋ] *subst.* joining a single sheet to a book *or* magazine *bindning*

guide bars ['gaɪdbɑ:z] *subst.* special lines in a bar code that show the start and finish of the code *start och stopplinjer;* **the standard guide bars are two thin lines that are a little longer than the coding lines**

guillotine [ˌgɪlə'ti:n] *subst.* office machine for cutting paper *skärmaskin, skärapparat*

gulp [gʌlp] *subst.* a group of words, usually two bytes *grupp, ordgrupp; see also* BYTE, NIBBLE

gun [gʌn] *or* **electron gun** [ɪ'lektrɒn ˌgʌn] *subst.* source of an electron beam located inside a cathode ray tube *elektronkanon*

COMMENT: black and white monitors have a single beam gun, while colour monitors contain three, one for each primary colour (Red, Green and Blue) used

gutter ['gʌtə] *subst.* inside margin between two pages of type *buntsteg, innermarginal*

gå ur ⇨ exit

gömma ⇨ conceal

Hh

hack [hæk] *vb.* **(a)** to experiment and explore computer software and hardware *"hacka", knappa, leka, experimentera* **(b)** to break into a computer system for criminal purposes *"hacka sig in", bryta sig in (i datorsystem)*

hacker ['hækə] *subst.* person who hacks *hacker*

QUOTE software manufacturers try more and more sophisticated methods to protect their programs and the hackers use equally clever methods to break into them
Electronics & Wireless World
QUOTE The hackers used their own software to break into the credit card centre
Computer News
QUOTE any computer linked to the system will be alerted if a hacker uses its code number
Practical Computing

halation [hə'leɪʃn] *subst.* photographic effect seen as a dark region with a very bright surround, caused by pointing the camera into the light *haloeffekt*

half [hɑːf] *subst.* one of two equal parts *hälft;* **half the data was lost in transmission; the second half of the program contains some errors; half adder** = binary adder that can produce the sum of two inputs, producing a carry output if necessary, but cannot accept a carry input *halvadderare;* **half duplex** = data transmission in one direction at a time over a bidirectional channel *halv duplex;* **half-duplex modem** = modem which works in one mode at a time (either transmitting *or* receiving) *halvduplexmodem;* **some modems can operate in half-duplex mode if required;** *see also* DUPLEX; **half-height drive** = disk drive whose front is half the height of a standard drive (half height drives, usually 5.25 inches are now the norm on PCs) *halvhöjds(diskett)station;* **half-intensity** = character *or* graphics display at half the usual display brightness *halvljusstyrka;* **half space** = paper movement in a printer by a half the amount of a normal character *halvsteg;* **half title** = first page of a book,

with the title, but not the publisher's colophon *or* details of the author *(smuts)titelsida;* **half wave rectifier** = circuit that allows current to pass in one direction only *halvvågslikriktare;* **half word** = sequence of bits occupying half a standard computer word, but which can be accessed as a single unit *halvord*

halftone ['hɑːftəʊn] *or* **half-tone** *subst.* **(a)** (i) continuous shading of a printed area *halvtonsraster;* (ii) grey shade halfway between white and black *halvton;* **halftone process** *or* **half-toning** = making halftones from photographs *halvtonsprocess* **(b)** illustration made using the halftone process *halvtonsbild;* **the book is illustrated with twenty halftones**

halide ['hælaɪd] *subst.* silver compound that is used to provide a light-sensitive coating on photographic film and paper *halider, ljuskänslig silversalter*

hall effect ['hɔːlɪˌfekt] *subst.* description of the effect of a magnetic field on electron flow *hall-effekten;* **hall effect switch** = solid state electronic switch operated by a magnetic field *halleffektsbrytare*

halo ['heɪləʊ] *subst.* photographic effect seen as a dark region with a very bright line around it, caused by pointing the camera into the light *halo*

halt [hɔːlt] **1** *subst.* computer instruction to stop a CPU carrying out any further instructions until restarted, or until the program is restarted, usually by external means (such as a reset button) *stopp;* **dead** *or* **drop-dead halt** = program instruction from the user *or* an error that causes the program to stop without allowing recovery *tvärstopp, totalstopp;* **halt instruction** = program instruction that causes a CPU to halt, suspending operations, usually until it is reset *stoppinstruktion;* **programmed halt** = instruction within a program which when executed, halts the processor (to restart the program, a reset is usually required) *programmerat stopp;* **halt condition** = operating state reached when a CPU reaches a fault or faulty instruction *or* halt instruction *or* halt instruction in the program that is being run *stoppläge, stoppvillkor* **2** *vb.* to stop *stoppa;* **hitting CTRL S will halt the program**

halvadderare ⇨ half

halvduplex ⇨ either-way operation

halvfet stil ⇨ emboldening

halvhöjds(diskett)station ⇨ half

halvledare ⇨ semiconductor

halvledarkrets ⇨ semiconductor

halvledarlaser ⇨ semiconductor

halvledarminne ⇨ **semiconductor**

ham [hæm] *subst.* **radio ham** = private radio operator who works especially with a short-wave transceiver *sändaramatör*

Hamming code [ˈhæmɪŋˈkəʊd] *subst.* coding system that uses check bits and check sums to detect and correct errors in transmitted data, mainly used in teletext systems *Hamming-kod;* **Hamming distance** = the number of digits that are different in two equal length words *Hammingavstånd*

hand [hænd] *subst.* **hands off** = working system where: (i) the operator does not control the operation which is automatic *automatiskt system;* (ii) the operator does not need to touch the device in use *beröringsfritt system;* **hands on** = working system where the operator controls the operations by keying instructions on the keyboard *operatörsberoende system;* **the sales representatives have received hands-on experience of the new computer; the computer firm gives a two day hands-on training course; hand portable set** *or* **handy talkies** *or* **HT's** = small low-range portable transceiver *hand(kommunikations)radio, kommunikationsradio;* **hand receiver** = hand-held device containing all necessary electronics to allow reception of broadcast radio signals *fickradio(mottagare);* **hand viewer** = hand-held magnifying lens with a mount to allow photographic slides to be viewed *diabetraktare*

handbok ⇨ **manual**

hand-held [ˈhænd,held] *adj.* which can be held in the hand *hand-, bärbar;* **hand-held computer** *or* **programmable** = very small computer which can be held in the hand, useful for basic information input, when a terminal is not available *handdator*

> QUOTE all acquisition, data reduction, processing, and memory circuitry is contained in the single hand-held unit
> **Byte**

handledning ⇨ **manual**

handler [ˈhændlə] *or* **driver** [ˈdraɪvə] *subst.* section of the operating system *or* program which controls a peripheral *hanteringsmodul, styrprogram*

hand off [hænd ˈɒf] *vb.* to pass control of a communications channel from one transmitter to another *överlämna*

handset [ˈhæn(d)set] *subst.* telephone receiver, with both microphone and loudspeaker *telefonlur, mikrotelefon; see also* ACOUSTIC COUPLER

handshake [ˈhæn(d)ʃeɪk] *or* **handshaking** [ˈhæn(d)ʃeɪkɪŋ] *subst.* standardized signals between two devices to make sure that the system is working

correctly, equipment is compatible and data transfer is correct (signals would include ready to receive, ready to transmit, data OK) *handskakning;* **full handshaking** = signals transmitted between two communicating devices indicating ready-to-transmit, ready-to-receive, received, transmitted, etc. *fullständig handskakning;* **handshake I/O control** = use of handshake signals meaning ready-to-send and ready-to-receive, that allow a computer to communicate with a slower peripheral *handskakningsstyrning*

> QUOTE if a line is free, the device waits another 400ms before reserving the line with a quick handshake process
> **Practical Computing**

handskakning ⇨ **handshake**

handstans ⇨ **key**

handwriting [ˈhænd,raɪtɪŋ] *subst.* words written by hand *handskrift;* **the keyboarders are having difficulty in reading the author's handwriting**

handwritten [ˈhænd,rɪtn] *adj.* written by hand, using a pen or pencil, not typed *handskriven;* **the author sent in two hundred pages of handwritten manuscript**

hang [hæŋ] *vb.* to enter an endless loop and not respond to further instruction *hänga (sig)*

hangover [ˈhæŋ,əʊvə] *subst.* **(a)** effect on a TV screen where the previous image can still be seen when the next image appears *eftersläpning* **(b)** sudden tone change on a document that is transmitted over a fax machine as a gradual change, caused by equipment faults *logisk smetning*

hangup [ˈhæŋʌp] *subst.* sudden stop of a working program (often due to the CPU executing an illegal instruction *or* entering an endless loop) *hängning*

hang up [hæŋ ˈʌp] *vb.* to cut off a communications line *lägga på, bryta;* **after she had finished talking on the telephone, she hung up**

hankontakt ⇨ **male connector**

hanteringsmodul ⇨ **handler**

hard [hɑːd] *adj.* **(a)** solid, as opposed to soft *hård, fast;* (parts of a computer system) that cannot be programmed *or* altered *maskin(vara);* **hard card** = board containing a hard disk drive and the required interfacing electronics, which can be slotted into a system's expansion connector *styrkort för fast skivminne;* **hard copy** = printed document *or* copy of information contained in a computer *or* system, in a form that is readable (as opposed to soft copy) *papperskopia;* **hard**

copy interface = serial *or* parallel interface used to transmit data between a computer and a printer *skrivargränssnitt;* hard disk = rigid magnetic disk that is able to store many times more data than a floppy disk, and usually cannot be removed from the disk drive *fast skivminne, hårddisk;* hard disk drive = unit used to store and retrieve data from a spinning hard disk (on the commands of a computer) *drivenhet för fast skivminne;* hard disk model = model of computer with a hard disk *modell med fast skivminne;* hard error = error which is permanent in a system *permanent fel;* hard failure = fault (in hardware) that must be mended before a device will function correctly *maskinfel;* the hard failure was due to a burnt-out chip (b) high contrast (photographic paper *or* film) *med hög kontrast, hårt*

hardbound ['hɑːdˌbaʊnd] *adj.* (book) with a hard cased cover, as opposed to a paperback *inbunden*

hardcover ['hɑːdˌkʌvə] *subst. & adj.* version of a book with a cased binding (as opposed to paperback) *inbunden (bok);* we printed 4,000 copies of the hardcover edition, and 10,000 of the paperback

hard-sectoring ['hɑːdˌsekt(ə)rɪŋ] *subst.* method of permanently formatting a disk, where each track is split into sectors, sometimes preformatted by a series of punched holes around the central hub, where each hole marks the start of sector *permanent sektoriserad, permanent formaterad*

hardware ['hɑːdwə] *subst.* physical units, components, integrated circuits, disks and mechanisms that make up a computer *or* its peripherals *maskinvara;* **hardware compatibility** = architecture of two different computers that allows one to run the programs of the other without changing any device drivers *or* memory locations, or the ability of one to use the add-on boards of the other *maskinvarukompatibilitet;* **hardware configuration** = way in which the hardware of a computer system is connected together *(maskinvaru) konfiguration;* **hardware interrupt** = interrupt signal generated by a piece of hardware rather than by software *maskinavbrott;* **hardware reliability** = ability of a piece of hardware to function normally over a period of time *(maskinvaru)tillförlitlighet, pålitlighet;* **hardware security** = making a system secure by means of hardware (such as keys, cards, etc.) *datorsäkerhet* NOTE: no plural *compare* SOFTWARE

COMMENT: computer hardware can include the computer itself, the disks and disk drive, printer, VDU, etc.

hardwired connection ['hɑːdˈwaɪəd kəˈnekʃ(ə)n] *subst.* permanent phone line connection, instead of a plug and socket *fast telefonanslutning*

hardwired logic ['hɑːdˈwaɪəd 'lɒdʒɪk] *subst.* logical function *or* program, which is built into the hardware, using electronic devices, such as gates, rather than in software *inbyggt program*

hardwired program ['hɑːdˈwaɪəd 'prəʊɡræm] *subst.* computer program built into the hardware, and which cannot be changed *inbyggt program*

harmonic [hɑːˈmɒnɪk] *subst.* frequency of an order of magnitude greater *or* smaller than a fundamental *överton;* **harmonic distortion** = unwanted harmonics produced by a non-linear circuit from an input signal *övertonsdistorsion;* **harmonic telephone ringer** = telephone that will only detect a certain range of ringing frequencies, this allows many telephones on a single line to be rung individually *linjedelningstelefon*

hartley ['hɑːtlɪ] *subst.* unit of information, equal to 3.32 bits, or the probability of one state out of ten equally probable states *hartleyenhet, hartleys informationsenhet*

hash [hæʃ] **1** *vb.* to produce a unique number derived from the entry itself, for each entry in a database *hasha, identitetsnumrera;* **hashing function** = algorithm used to produce a hash code for an entry and ensure that it is different from every other entry *hashningsfunktion* **2** *subst.* **(a)** *see* # MARK **(b)** hash code = coding system derived from the ASCII codes, where the code numbers for the first three letters are added up, giving a new number used as hash code *hashkod;* **hash-code system** = coding system using hash codes *hashkodat system;* **hash index** = list of entries according to their hashed numbers *hashindex;* **hash table** = list of all entries in a file with their hashed key address *hashtabell;* **hash total** = total of a number of hashed entries used for error detection *nonsenssumma, kontrollsumma;* **hash value** = number arrived at after a key is hashed *hashningsvärde*

hashmark ['hæʃmɑːk] *or* **hash mark** ['hæʃmɑːk] *subst.* printed sign (#) used as a hard copy marker *or* as an indicator *brädgård(stecken), brädstapel(tecken)*
NOTE: in US usage (#) means number; #32 = number 32 (apartment number in an address, paragraph number in a text, etc.). In computer usage, the pound sign (£) is often used in the US instead of the hash to avoid confusion

hashningsfunktion ⇨ **hash**

hastighet ⇨ **speed, velocity**

hazard ['hæzəd] *subst.* fault in hardware due to incorrect signal timing *fel, signalfel, tidsfel;* **hazard-free implementation** = logical function design that has taken into account any hazards that could occur and solved them *felfritt utförande, felsäkert utförande*

HD ['eitʃ'di:] = HALF DUPLEX data transmission in one direction only, over a bidirectional channel *halvduplex*

HDLC ['eitʃdi:el'si:] = HIGH LEVEL DATA LINK CONTROL

HDVS ['eitʃdi:vi:es] = HIGH DEFINITION VIDEO SYSTEM proposed new television format made up of 1125 lines and requiring a wide screen and high bandwidth equipment to view it on, so limited at present to satellite and cable television installations *högupplösande teve*

HDX ['eitʃdi:eks] = HALF DUPLEX

head [hed] **1** *subst.* **(a) combined head** *or* **read/write head** = transducer that can read *or* write data from the surface of a magnetic storage medium, such as a floppy disk *läs- och skrivhuvud;* **head alignment** = (i) correct position of a tape *or* disk head in relation to the magnetic surface, to give the best performance and correct track location; (ii) location of the read head in the same position as the write head was (in relation to the magnetic medium) *huvudjustering, huvudinställning;* **head cleaning disk** = special disk which is used to clean the disk read/write heads *rengöringsskiva;* **head crash** = component failure in a disk drive, where the head is allowed to hit the surface of the spinning disk, causing disk surface damage and data corruption *skivminneskrasch;* **head demagnetizer** = device used to remove any stray magnetic effects that might have built up on the tape head *avmagnetiserare;* **head park** = to move the read/write head in a (hard) disk drive to a safe position, not over the disk, so that if the unit is knocked *or* jarred the head will not damage the disk surface *parkering av huvudet;* **head wheel** = wheel that keeps video tape in contact with the head *tryckrulle;* **disk head** = head which reads *or* writes on a floppy disk *läs- och skrivhuvud;* **flying head** = hard disk read/write head that uses a 'wing' to fly just over the surface of the spinning disk *svävande läs- och skrivhuvud;* **playback head** = transducer that reads signals recorded on a storage medium and usually converts them to an electrical signal *avspelningshuvud;* **read head** = transducer that can read data from a magnetic storage medium such as a floppy disk *läshuvud;* **tape head** = head which reads *or* writes signals on a magnetic tape *(band)huvud, avspelningshuvud, inspelningshuvud;* **write head** = transducer that can write data onto

a magnetic medium *skrivhuvud, inspelningshuvud* **(b)** data that indicates the start address of a list of items stored in memory *startindikering* **(c)** top edge of a book *or* of a page *sidhuvud;* **head of form** = first line on a form *or* sheet of paper that can be printed on *sidhuvud* **(d)** start of a reel of recording tape *or* photographic film *startsladd* **(e)** top part of a device, network *or* body *överdel;* **head end** = interconnection equipment between an antenna and a cable television network *huvudända* **2** *vb.* to be the first item of data in a list *leda;* **the queue was headed by my file**

header ['hedə] *subst.* **(a)** in a local area network, a packet of data that is sent before a transmission to provide information on destination and routing *startpaket* **(b)** information at the beginning of a list of data relating to the rest of the data *listetikett, listrubrik;* **header block** = block of data at the beginning of a file containing data about file characteristics *startblock, (fil)informationsblock;* **header card** = punched card containing information about the rest of the cards in the set *startkort, informationskort;* **header label** = section of data at the beginning of a magnetic tape, that contains identification, format and control information *startetikett, (fil)informationsetikett;* **tape header** = identification information at the beginning of a tape *bandinformation, magnetisk (band)etikett* **(c)** words at the top of a page of a document (such as title, author's name, page number, etc.) *sidhuvud; see also* FOOTER

heading ['hedɪŋ] *subst.* **(a)** title *or* name of a document or file *rubrik* **(b)** header *or* words at the top of each page of a document (such as the title, the page numbers, etc.) *sidhuvud*

headlife ['hedlaɪf] *subst.* length of time that a video *or* tape head can work before being serviced *or* replaced *livslängd (hos video- eller bandhuvud)*

headline ['hedlaɪn] *subst.* = HEADING

headset ['hedset] *or* **headphones** ['hedfəʊnz] *subst.* small speakers with padding, worn over a person's ears (used for private listening, instead of loudspeakers) *hörlur, hörtelefon*

headword ['hedwɜːd] *subst.* main entry word in a printed dictionary *huvudord*

heap [hi:p] *subst.* **(a)** temporary data storage area that allows random access *heap, extrautrymme; compare with* STACK **(b)** binary tree

heat sensitive paper ['hi:t,sensətɪv 'peɪpə] *subst. see* ELECTROSTATIC PRINTING

heat-sink ['hi:tsɪŋk] *subst.* metal device used to conduct heat away from an electronic component to prevent damage *kylfläns*

Heaviside-Kennelly layer ['hevɪsaɪd 'kenəlɪ 'leɪə] *see* E-REGION

heladderare ⇨ **full**

helical scan ['helɪk(ə)l 'skæn] *subst.* method of accessing data stored on video tape which is stored at an angle to the tape edge *spiralsökning, helixavsändning*

helios noise ['hi:lɪjəs'nɔɪz] *subst.* noise originating from the sun that is picked up by an earth-based antenna when it points in the direction of the sun *solbrus*

helixavsändning ⇨ **helical scan**

help [help] *subst.* **(a)** thing which makes it easy to do something *hjälp;* **he finds his word-processor a great help in the office; they need some help with their programming (b)** function in a program *or* system that provides useful information about the program in use *hjälpfunktion;* **hit the HELP key if you want information about what to do next**

helsidesskärm ⇨ **full**

helskiveintegration ⇨ **wafer scale integration**

heltal ⇨ **integer**

heltal i (dubbel)precision ⇨ **integer**

heltals-BASIC ⇨ **integer**

hemdator ⇨ **home**

Hertz [hɜːts] *subst.* SI unit of frequency, defined as the number of cycles per second of time *Herz (Hz)*

> COMMENT: Hertz rate is the frequency at which mains electricity is supplied to the consumer. The Hertz rate in the USA and Canada is 60; in Europe it is 50

heterodyne ['hetərə(ʊ)daɪn] *subst.* circuit producing two outputs equal to the sum and difference in frequency of two inputs *heterodyn frekvensblandare*

heterodyn frekvensblandare ⇨ **heterodyne**

heterogeneous network ['hetərə(ʊ)'dʒiːnjəs 'netwɜːk] *subst.* computer network joining computers of many different types and makes *heterogent nätverk;* **heterogeneous multiplexing** = communications multiplexing system that can deal with channels with different transmission rates and protocols *heterogen multiplexering*

heuristic [hjʊ(ə)'rɪstɪk] *adj.* which learns from past experiences *heuristisk, läraktig;* **a heuristic program learns from its previous actions and decisions**

hex [heks] *or* **hexadecimal notation** ['heksə'desɪm(ə)l nə(ʊ)'teɪʃ(ə)n] *subst.* number system using base 16 and digits 0-9 and A-F *hexadecimal notation;* **hex dump** = display of a section of memory in hexadecimal form *hexdump;* **hex pad** = keypad with keys for each hexadecimal digit *hexadecimalt tangentbord*

hexadecimal notation ⇨ **hex**

hexadecimalt ⇨ **base**

hexadecimalt tangentbord ⇨ **hex, keypad**

HF ['eɪtʃ'ef] = HIGH FREQUENCY radio communications range of frequencies from 3 - 30 MHz *högfrekvens, kortvåg*

hidden ['hɪdn] *adj.* which cannot be seen *gömd, dold;* **hidden defect in a program** = defect which was not seen when the program was tested *dolt fel i ett program;* **hidden files** = important system files which are not displayed in a directory listing and cannot normally be read by a user *dolda filer;* **it allows users to backup or restore hidden system files independently; hidden lines** = lines which make up a three-dimensional object, but are obscured when displayed as a two-dimensional image *dolda linjer;* **hidden line algorithm** = mathematical formula that removes hidden lines from a two-dimensional computer image of a 3-D object *algoritm för att undertrycka dolda linjer;* **hidden line removal** = erasure of lines which should not be visible when looking at a two-dimensional image of a three-dimensional object *undertryckning av dolda linjer*

hierarchical classification [ˌhaɪəˈrɑːkɪkl ˌklæsɪfɪkeɪʃ(ə)n] *subst.* library classification system where the list of subjects is divided down into more and more selective subsets *hierarkisk klassificering;* **hierarchical communications system** = network in which each branch has a number of separate minor branches dividing from it *hierarkiskt kommunikationssystem;* **hierarchical computer network** = method of allocating control and processing functions in a network to the computers which are most suited to the task *hierarkiskt datanät;* **hierarchical database** = database in which records can be related to each other in a defined structure *hierarkisk databas;* **hierarchical directory** = directory listing of files on a disk, showing the main directory and its files, branches and any sub-directories *hierarkisk filkatalog*

hierarchy ['haɪərɑːkɪ] *subst.* way in which objects *or* data *or* structures are organized, usually with the most important *or* highest priority *or* most general item at the top, then working down a tree structure *hierarki;* **data hierarchy** = data structure organized hierarchically *datahierarki*

hierarkisk datastruktur ⇨ **data**

hierarkiskt nätverk ⇨ **despotic network**

hi fi ['haɪ'faɪ] *or* **hifi** ['haɪ'faɪ] = HIGH FIDELITY accurate reproduction of audio signals by equipment such as a record player and amplifier *hifi (hög trovärdighet), hög ljudkvalitet;* **a hi fi system** *or* **a hi fi** = equipment for playing records *or* compact disks *or* tapes *or* listening to the radio (including tape recorder, turntable, amplifier and speakers) *stereoanläggning*

high [haɪ] *adj.* **(a)** large *or* very great *hög, stor;* **high density storage** = very large number of bits stored per area of storage medium *högtäthetsminne;* **a hard disk is a high density storage medium compared to paper tape; high fidelity** *or* **hifi** *or* **hi fi** = accurate reproduction of audio signals by equipment such as a record player and amplifier *hifi;* **high frequency** = radio communications range of frequencies between 3-30 Mhz *högfrekvens, kortvåg;* **high-level data link control (HDLC)** = ISO defined communications interface protocol which allows several computers to be linked *HDLC (kommunikationsprotokoll från ISO);* **high-level data link control station** = equipment and programs which correctly receive and transmit standard HDLC data frames *styrenhet för HDLC-protokoll;* **high-level (programming) language (HLL)** = computer programming language that is easy to learn and allows the user to write programs using words and commands that are easy to understand and look like English words, the program is then translated into machine code, with one HLL command often representing a number of machine code instructions *högnivåspråk;* **programmers should have a knowledge of high-level languages, particularly PASCAL;** *compare* LOW-LEVEL LANGUAGE; **high order** = digit with the greatest weighting within a number *mest signifikanta siffra;* **high-order language** = HIGH-LEVEL LANGUAGE; **high pass filter** = circuit that allows frequencies above a certain limit to pass, while blocking those below that frequency limit *högpassfilter;* **high performance equipment** = very good quality *or* high specification equipment *högpresterande utrustning;* **high priority program** = program that is important *or* urgent and is processed before

others *högprioriterat program;* **high reduction** = reduction of text *or* graphics for use in micrographics, usually reduced by 30 to 60 times *stark förminskning;* **high specification** *or* **high spec** = giving a high degree of accuracy *or* having a large number of features *noggrann specifikation;* **high spec cabling needs to be very carefully handled; high speed carry** = single operation in which a carry into an adder results in a carry out *höghastighetsöverföringssiffra;* **high usage trunk** = main communications line that carries a large number of calls *stamlinje* **(b) logical high** = equal to logic TRUE state or 1 *sann; compare* LOGICAL LOW; FALSE

QUOTE they have proposed a standardized high-level language for importing image data into desktop publishing and other applications programs
Byte

highlight ['haɪlaɪt] **1** *subst.* **highlights** = characters *or* symbols treated to make them stand out from the rest of the text, often by using bold type *markerade tecken* **2** *vb.* to make part of the text stand out from the rest *markera, lysa upp;* **the headings are highlighted in bold**

high-resolution ['haɪˌrezəˈluːʃ(ə)n] *or* **hi-res** *subst.* ability to display *or* detect a very large number of pixels per unit area *hög upplösning;* **high-resolution graphics; this high-resolution monitor can display 640 x 320 pixels; the new hi-res optical scanner can detect 300 dots per inch**

QUOTE the computer is uniquely suited to image processing because of its high-resolution graphics
Byte

high-speed ['haɪspiːd] *adj.* which operates faster than normal data transmission *or* processing *höghastighets-;* **high-speed duplicator** = machine that copies video *or* audio tapes by running them at a faster speed than normal *höghastighetsduplikator;* **high-speed skip** = rapid movement in a printer to miss the perforations in continuous stationery *snabbmatning*

highway ['haɪweɪ] *or* **bus** [bʌs] *subst.* communications link consisting of a set of leads *or* wires which connect different parts of a computer hardware system and over which data is transmitted and received by various circuits inside the system *buss(ledning);* **address highway** = physical connections that carry the address data in a parallel form between the central processing unit and memory *or* external devices *adresskanal;* **data highway** = bus carrying the data signals in parallel form between the central processing unit and memory *or* external devices *datakanal*

hill climbing ['hɪl,klaɪmɪŋ] *subst.* method of achieving a goal in an expert system *måluppfyllelse ('på toppen')*

hi-res ['haɪ'rez] = HIGH RESOLUTION **hi-res graphics** *hög upplösning;* **this hi-res monitor can display 640 x 320 pixels; the new hi-res optical scanner can detect 300 dots per inch**

hiss [hɪs] *subst.* high-frequency noise mixed with a signal *högfrekvent brus*

histogram ['hɪstəgræm] *subst.* graph on which values are represented as vertical *or* horizontal bars *stapeldiagram, histogram*

hit [hɪt] **1** *subst.* successful match *or* search of a database *träff, överensstämmels (med t.ex. sökprofil);* **there was a hit after just a few seconds; there are three hits for this search key; hit on the line =** short period of noise on a communications line, causing data corruption *intermittent brusstörning* **2** *vb.* to press a key *slå ned, trycka på;* **to save the text, hit ESCAPE S**

QUOTE the cause of the data disaster is usually due to your finger hitting the wrong key
PC Business World

H & J ['eɪtʃən'dʒeɪ] = HYPHENATION AND JUSTIFICATION

hjul ⇨ **reel**

hjälpfunktion ⇨ **help**

hjälpprocessor ⇨ **coprocessor**

hjälpprogram ⇨ **utility (program)**

HLDLC ['eɪtʃel'diːel'siː] = HIGH-LEVEL DATA LINK CONTROL

HLL ['eɪtʃel'el] = HIGH-LEVEL LANGUAGE

HMI ['eɪtʃem'aɪ] = HUMAN-MACHINE INTERACTION facilities provided to improve the interaction betweeen a user and a computer system *människa-maskin-gränssnitt, växelverkan mellan människa och maskin*

HOF ['eɪtʃəʊ'ef] = HEAD OF FORM

hold [həʊld] **1** *subst.* synchronization timing pulse for a television time base signal *synkroniseringssignal* **2** *vb.* to retain *or* keep a value *or* communications line *or* section of memory *hålla;* **hold current =** amount of electrical current that has to be supplied to keep a device in its operating state, but not operating *driftström, hållström, beredskapsström;* **holding line =** boundary line indicating the limits of an area of artwork *ortone råm;* **holding loop =** section of program that loops until it is broken by some action, most often used when waiting for a response from the keyboard *or* a device *ställprogram, väntprogram, väntslinga;* **holding time =**

time spent by a communications circuit on call *upptagettid*

COMMENT: the hold feature keeps the picture steady and central on the screen; some televisions have horizontal and vertical hold controls to allow the picture to be moved and set up according to various conditions

holdup ['həʊldʌp] *subst.* (i) time period over which power will be supplied by a UPS *avbrottstid, drifttid i ett reservkraftaggregat;* (ii) pause in a program *or* device due to a malfunction *stopp, avbrott*

hole [həʊl] *subst.* **(a)** punched gap in a punched paper tape *or* card, representing data *hål;* **index hole =** hole in the edge of a hard-sectored disk *indexhål* **(b)** method of describing the absence of an electron from an atomic structure *elektronhål*

COMMENT: a hole may move, but in the opposite direction to the flow of electrons in a material; it is also considered to have a positive charge as compared to a electron. This concept is mostly used in semiconductor physics, where the bulk movement of holes and electrons in an electronic device are studied

Hollerith code ['hɒlərɪθ,kəʊd] *subst.* coding system that uses punched holes in a card to represent characters and symbols, the system uses two sets of twelve rows to provide possible positions for each code *hollerithkod*

hologram ['hɒlə(ʊ)græm] *subst.* imagined three-dimensional image produced by the interference pattern when a part of a coherent light beam is reflected from an object and mixed with the main beam *hologram*

holograph ['hɒlə(ʊ)grɑːf] *subst.* handwritten manuscript, as written by the author using a pen *or* pencil, but not typed *handskrivet manuskript, egenhändigt skrivet original*

holographic image [,hɒlə'græfɪk 'ɪmɪdʒ] *subst.* hologram of a three-dimensional object *hologram;* **holographic storage =** storage of data as a holographic image which is then read by a bank of photocells and a laser (a new storage medium with massive storage potential) *holografiskt minne*

holography [hɒ'lɒgrəfɪ] *subst.* science and study of holograms and their manufacture *holografi*

home [həʊm] *subst.* **(a)** place where a person lives *hem;* **home banking =** method of examining and carrying out bank transactions via a terminal and modem in the user's home *bankservice i hemmet;* **home computer** = microcomputer designed for home use, whose applications might include teaching, games, personal finance and word-processing *hemdator* **(b)** starting point for printing on a screen, usually taken as the top left hand corner *startpunkt;* **home record** = first *or* initial data record in a file *startdata*

homing ['həʊmɪŋ] *subst.* location of the source of a transmitted signal *or* data item *pejling, spärning*

homogeneous computer network [,hɒmə(ʊ)'dʒiːnjəs kəm'pjuːtə 'netwɜːk] *subst.* network made up of similar machines, that are compatible *or* from the same manufacturer *homogent nätverk;* **homogeneous multiplexing** = switching multiplexer system where all the channels contain data using the same protocol and transmission rate *homogen multiplexering*

homogent nätverk ⇨ **homogeneous computer network**

honkontakt ⇨ **female**

hood [hʊd] *subst.* cover which protects something *huv;* **acoustic hood** = soundproof cover put over a line printer to cut down its noise *ljudhuv*

hooking ['hʊkɪŋ] *subst.* distortion of a video picture caused by tape head timing errors *avsökningsstörning, tidsfel*

hop [hɒp] *subst.* direct transmission path, using the reflections from only the ionosphere, not the earth, to propagate the signal from one point on the earth to another *kortvågsöverföring med endast atmosfärisk reflexion*

hopper ['hɒpə] *subst.* device which holds punched cards and feeds them into the reader *kortmatare*

hoppinstruktion ⇨ **GOTO, instruction**

hoppoperation ⇨ **jump (instruction)**

horizontal [,hɒrɪ'zɒntl] *adj.* lying flat *or* going from side to side, not up and down *horisontell, vågrät;* **horizontal blanking** = prevention of a picture signal reaching a television beam during the time it contains no picture information on its returntrace *släckpuls (efter avsökt linje);* **horizontal check** = error detection method for transmitted data *horisontell kontroll; see also* CYCLIC CHECK; **horizontal synchronization pulse** = pulse in a television broadcast signal that synchronizes the receiver sweep circuitry *horisontell synkronisering;* **horizontal wraparound** = movement of a cursor on a computer display from the end of one line to the beginning of the next *horisontell radbrytning*

horn [hɔːn] *subst.* directional radio device with a wider open end leading to a narrow section, used for the reception and transmission of radiowaves *horn;* **feed horn** = microwave channelling device used to direct transmitted signals *matarhorn*

horunge ⇨ **orphan**

host [həʊst] *subst. & adj.* **host adapter** = adapter which connects to a host computer *värddatoranpassningsenhet;* **the cable to connect the scanner to the host adapter is included**

host computer ['həʊst kəm'pjuːtə] *subst.* **(a)** main controlling computer in a multi-user *or* distributed system *värddator* **(b)** computer used to write and debug software for another computer, often using a cross compiler *värddator, utvecklingsdator* **(c)** computer in a network that provides special services *or* programming languages to all users *värddator*

> QUOTE you select fonts manually or through commands sent from the host computer along with the text
>
> *Byte*

hot ['hɒt] *adj.* **hot chassis** = metal framework *or* case around a computer that is connected to a voltage supply rather than being earthed *ledande chassi;* **hot frame** = very bright film frame caused by over exposure *överexponerad filmruta;* **hot metal composition** = old method of producing typeset pages from individual metalletters which were cast from hot liquid metal, now mainly replaced by phototypesetting *blysättning;* **hot spot** = region of high brightness on a film *or* display screen *glansfläck, ljusaste punkten;* **hot standby** = piece of hardware that is kept operational at all times and is used as backup in case of system failure *(direkt insatsberedd) aktiv säkerhetsenhet;* **hot type** = characters cast from hot liquid metal *blytyp;* **hot zone** = text area to the left of the right margin in a word-processed document (if a word does not fit in completely, a hyphen is automatically inserted) *brytzon, avstavningszon*

house [haʊs] **1** *subst.* company (especially a publishing company) *bolag, förlag;* **one of the biggest software houses in the US; house corrections** = printing *or* composition errors, caused by and corrected by the printers of a document *tryckerikorrektur;* **house style** = (i) style of spelling and layout, used by a publishing company in all its books *språkliga och grafiska regler;* (ii) method *or* design of a company's products, used to identify them from the products of competitors *företagets egen design (grafiska profil)* **2** *vb.* to put a device in a case *bygga in, kapsla (in);* **the**

magnetic tape is housed in a solid plastic case

housekeeping ['haʊsˌkiːpɪŋ] *subst.* tasks that have to be regularly carried out to maintain a computer system (checking backups, deleting unwanted files, etc.) *rutinuppgifter, (system)administration;* **housekeeping routine =** set of instructions executed once, at the start of a new program to carry out system actions such as clear memory, configure function keys or change screen display mode *startrutin, konfigureringsrutin; see also* IN-HOUSE

housing ['haʊzɪŋ] *subst.* solid case *låda, skåp;* **the computer housing was damaged when it fell on the floor**

howler ['haʊlə] *subst.* **(a)** buzzer that indicates to a telephone exchange operator that a user's telephone handset is not on the receiver *upptagetsignal* **(b)** very bad and obvious mistake *groda, grovt fel;* **what a howler, no wonder your program won't work**

HRG ['eɪtʃɑːˈdʒiː] = HIGH RESOLUTION GRAPHICS ability to display a large number of pixels per unit area *högupplösningsgrafik;* **the HRG board can control up to 300 pixels per inch**

HT ['eɪtʃˈtiː] = HANDY TALKIES small portable transceivers *hand(kommunikations)radio, (bärbar) kommunikationsradio*

hub [hʌb] *subst.* central part of a disk, usually with a hole and a ring which the disk drive grips to spin the disk *nav*

huffman code ['hʌfmənˌkəʊd] *subst.* data compression code, where frequent characters occupy less bit space than less frequent ones *huffmankod*

hum [hʌm] *subst.* low frequency electrical noise *or* interference on a signal *brum*

human-computer ['hjuːmən kəmˈpjuːtə] *or* **human-machine interface (HMI)** ['hjuːmən məˈʃiːn ˈɪntəfeɪs ('eɪtʃemˈaɪ)] *subst.* facilities provided to improve the interaction between a user and a computer system *människa-maskin-gränssnitt, växelverkan mellan människa och maskin*

hunting ['hʌntɪŋ] *subst.* process of searching out a data record in a file *sökning*

huv ⇨ **hood**

huvudbuss ⇨ **A-bus**

huvuddator ⇨ **master**

huvuddiskett ⇨ **master**

huvudinställning ⇨ **head**

huvudjustering ⇨ **head**

huvudledning ⇨ **trunk**

huvudlob ⇨ **main**

huvudminne ⇨ **main**

huvudrutin ⇨ **main**

huvudsökord ⇨ **main**

huvudterminal ⇨ **key**

hybrid circuit ['haɪbrɪd 'sɜːkɪt] *subst.* connection of a number of different electronic components such as integrated circuits, transistors, resistors and capacitors in a small package, which since the components are not contained in their own protective packages, requires far less space than the individual discrete components *hybridkrets;* **hybrid computer =** combination of analog and digital circuits in a computer system to achieve a particular goal *hybriddator;* **hybrid interface =** one-off interface between a computer and a piece of analog equipment *hybridgränssnitt;* **hybrid system =** combination of analog and digital computers and equipment to provide an optimal system for a particular task *hybridsystem*

hyphen ['haɪf(ə)n] *subst.* printing sign (-) to show that a word has been split *bindestreck;* **soft** *or* **discretionary hyphen =** hyphen which is inserted when a word is split at the end of a line in word-processed text, but is not present when the word is written normally *mjuk avstavning*

hyphenated ['haɪfəneɪtɪd] *adj.* written with a hyphen *avstavad;* **the word 'high-level' is usually hyphenated**

hyphenation [ˌhaɪfəˈneɪʃn] *subst.* splitting of a word (as at the end of a line, when the word is too long to fit) *avstavning;* **hyphenation and justification** *or* **J =** justifying lines to a set width, splitting the long words correctly at the end of each line *avstavning och radjustering;* **an American hyphenation and justification program will not work with British English spellings**

> QUOTE the hyphenation program is useful for giving a professional appearance to documents and for getting as many words onto the page as possible
> **Micro Decision**

hypo ['haɪpəʊ] *abbreviation* photographic fixing solution *fixerlösning*

Hz [hɜːts] = HERTZ

hålkort ⇨ **punch**

hållkrets ⇨ **sample**

hållström ⇨ **hold**

hålremsa ⇨ **perforated tape, tape**

hålremskod ⇨ **tape**

hårddisk ⇨ **hard**

hårt bindestreck ▷ required hyphen

hämtcykel ▷ fetch

hämtningscykel ▷ fetch

hämtningsfas ▷ fetch

hämtningsinstruktion ▷ fetch

hämtning vid behov ▷ fetch

hämt- och körcykel ▷ fetch

hämtsignal ▷ fetch

händelsestyrd ▷ event-driven

högerskift ▷ right

höggradig integration ▷ LSI

högnivåspråk ▷ high

högpassfilter ▷ filter

högpresterande utrustning ▷ high

högprioriterat avbrott ▷ non-maskable interrupt (NMI)

högprioriterat program ▷ high

högupplösande teve ▷ HDVS

hölje ▷ case

Ii

IAM ['aɪeɪ'em] = INTERMEDIATE ACCESS MEMORY memory storage that has an access time between that of main memory and a disk based system *mellanminne, medelåtkomstminne*

IAR ['aɪeɪ'ɑː] = INSTRUCTION ADDRESS REGISTER register in a CPU that contains the location of the next instruction to be processed *instruktionsadressregister, instruktionspekare*

IAS ['aɪeɪ'es] = IMMEDIATE ACCESS STORE high-speed main memory area in a computer system *snabbåtkomstminne*

IBG ['aɪbiː'dʒiː] = INTERBLOCK GAP

IC ['aɪ'siː] = INTEGRATED CIRCUIT
NOTE: plural is **ICs**

icand ['ɪ'kænd] *subst.* = MULTIPLICAND

icke-flyktigt minne ▷ non-volatile

icke-grind ▷ gate

icke-och-grind ▷ gate, NAND function

icke-permanent minne ▷ volatile memory

icon ['aɪkɒn] *or* **ikon** ['aɪkɒn] *subst.* graphic symbol *or* small picture displayed on screen, used in an interactive computer system to provide an easy way of identifying a function *ikon, symboltecken;* **the icon for the graphics program is a small picture of a palette; click twice over the wordprocessor icon - the picture of the typewriter**

> QUOTE the system has on-screen icons and pop-up menus and is easy to control using the mouse
> **Electronics & Power**
> QUOTE an icon-based system allows easy use of a computer without the need to memorize the complicated command structure of the native operating system
> **Micro Decision**

ID ['aɪ'diː] = IDENTIFICATION; **ID card =** card which identifies a person *ID-kort;* **ID code =** password *or* word that identifies a user so that he can access a system *ID-kod;* **after you wake up the system, you have to input your ID code then your password**

IDA ['aɪdiː'eɪ] = INTEGRATED DIGITAL ACCESS

IDD ['aɪdiː'diː] = INTERNATIONAL DIRECT DIALLING

ideal [aɪ'dɪəl] *adj.* perfect *or* very good for something *idealisk;* **she is the ideal designer for children's books; ideal format =** standard large format for photographic negatives, used mainly in professional equipment *idealformat*

identical [aɪ'dentɪk(ə)l] *adj.* exactly the same *identisk;* **the two systems use identical software; the performance of the two clones is identical**

identification [aɪˌdentɪfɪ'keɪʃ(ə)n] *subst.* procedure used by a host computer to establish the identity and nature of the calling computer *or* user (this could be for security and access restriction purposes *or* to provide transmission protocol information) *identifiering, identifikation;* **identification character =** single character sent to a host computer to establish the identity and location of a remote computer *or* terminal *identifieringstecken;* **identification division =** section of a COBOL program source code, in which the identifiers and formats for data and variables to be used within the program are declared *deklarationsdel i programmeringsspråket Cobol*

identifier [aɪ'dentɪfaɪə] *subst.* set of characters used to distinguish between different blocks of data *or* files *identifierare, identifieringstecken;* **identifier word =** word that is used as a block *or* file identifier *identifieringsord*

identifiering ▷ identification, recognition

identifikation ⇨ **identification**

identifikationskod ⇨ **device**

identify [aɪ'dentɪfaɪ] *vb.* to establish who someone is *or* what something is *identifiera;* **the user has to identify himself to the system by using a password before access is allowed; the maintenance engineers have identified the cause of the system failure**

identitetsnumrera ⇨ **hash**

identity [aɪ'dentətɪ] *subst.* who someone *or* what something is *identitet;* **identity burst** = pattern of bits before the first block of data on a magnetic tape that identifies the tape format used *bandformatsidentitet;* **identity gate** *or* **element** = logical gate that provides a single output that is true if the inputs are both the same *likhetsgrind, likhetselement;* **identity number** = unique number, used usually with a password to identify a user when logging into a system *identitetsnummer;* **don't forget to log in your identity number; identity operation** = logical function whose output is true only if all the operands are of the same value *identitetsoperation*

idiot tape ['ɪdɪət‚teɪp] *subst.* tape containing unformatted text, which cannot be typeset until formatting data, such as justification, line width, and page size, has been added by a computer *rådataband*

idle ['aɪdl] *adj.* (machine *or* telephone line *or* device) which is not being used, but is ready and waiting to be used *vilande, passiv, väntande;* **idle character** = symbol *or* code that means 'do nothing' *or* a code that is transmitted when there is no data available for transmission at that time *väntetecken;* **idle time** = period of time when a device is switched on but not doing anything *vilotid, passiv tid*

IDP ['aɪdiː'piː] = INTEGRATED DATA PROCESSING

IEC 625-1-buss ⇨ **GPIB**

IEE ['aɪiː'iː] *U.K.* = INSTITUTION OF ELECTRICAL ENGINEERS

IEEE ['aɪiː'iː'iː] *USA* = INSTITUTE OF ELECTRICAL AND ELECTRONIC ENGINEERS; **IEEE bus** = interface that conforms to IEEE standards *IEEE-buss;* **IEEE-488** = interfacing standard as laid down by the IEEE, where only data and handshaking signals are used, mainly used in laboratories to connect computers to measuring equipment *IEEE-488-standarden/GBIP-buss*

IEEE 488-buss ⇨ **GPIB**

ier ['aɪi'ɑː] *subst.* = MULTIPLIER

if [ɪf] = INTERMEDIATE FREQUENCY

IF statement ['ɪf 'steɪtmənt] *subst.* computer programming statement, meaning do an action IF a condition is true (usually followed by THEN) *logisk "om-och-endast-om"-sats;* **IF-THEN-ELSE** = high-level programming language statement, meaning IF something cannot be done, THEN do this, or ELSE do that *"om-så-annars"-sats*

ignore [ɪg'nɔː] *vb.* not to recognize *or* not to do what someone says *ignorera, bortse från;* **this command instructs the computer to ignore all punctuation; ignore character** = null *or* fill character *fyllnadstecken*

IH ['aɪ'eɪtʃ] = INTERRUPT HANDLER

IIL ['aɪaɪ'el] = INTEGRATED INJECTION LOGIC

IKBS ['aɪkeɪbiː'es] = INTELLIGENT KNOWLEDGE-BASED SYSTEM

ikon ['aɪkɒn] *or* **icon** ['aɪkɒn] *subst.* graphic symbol *or* picture displayed on screen, used in an interactive computer system to provide an easy way of identifying a function *ikon, symboltecken; see also* ICON

ikon ⇨ **icon**

ILF ['aɪel'ef] = INFRA LOW FREQUENCY

ILL ['aɪel'el] = INTER-LIBRARY LOAN

illegal [ɪ'liːg(ə)l] *adj.* which is not legal *or* which is against the law *or* against rules of syntax *olaglig, ogiltig;* **illegal character** = invalid combination of bits in a computer word, according to preset rules *ogiltigt tecken;* **illegal instruction** = instruction code not within the repertoire of a language *ogiltig instruktion;* **illegal operation** = instruction *or* process that does not follow the computer system's protocol *or* language syntax *ogiltig operation*

illegally [ɪ'liːgəlɪ] *adv.* against the law *or* against rules *olagligen;* **the company has been illegally copying copyright software**

illegible [ɪ'ledʒəbl] *adj.* which cannot be read *oläslig;* **if the manuscript is illegible, send it back to the author to have it typed**

illiterate [ɪ'lɪt(ə)rət] *adj.* (person) who cannot read *analfabet, som inte är läs- och skrivkunnig;* **computer illiterate** = (person) who does not understand computer-related expressions *or* operations *ej datamogen, dataanalfabet; see also* LITERATE

QUOTE three years ago the number of people who were computer illiterate was much higher than today
Minicomputer News

illuminance [ɪ'luːmɪnəns] *subst.* measurement of the amount of light that strikes a surface, measured in lux *belysningsstyrka*

illuminate [ɪˈljuːmɪneɪt] *vb.* to shine a light on something *belysa, upplysa;* **the screen is illuminated by a low-power light**

illumination [ɪˌljuːmɪˈneɪʃ(ə)n] *subst.* lighting *belysning;* **aperture illumination =** pattern generated from an aperture antenna *spaltspridning*

illustrate [ˈɪləstreɪt] *vb.* to add pictures to a text *illustrera;* **the book is illustrated in colour; the manual is illustrated with charts and pictures of the networking connections**

illustration [ˌɪləsˈtreɪʃ(ə)n] *subst.* picture (in a book) *illustration;* **the book has twenty-five pages of full-colour illustrations**

iläggsetikett ⇨ **inlay card**

image [ˈɪmɪdʒ] *subst.* **(a)** exact duplicate of an area of memory *avbild, kopia, bild* **(b)** copy of an original picture *or* design *avbild, kopia, bild;* **image area =** region of microfilm *or* display screen on which characters *or* designs can be displayed *bildyta;* **image carrier =** storage medium containing data that defines the typefaces used in a phototypesetter *skiva eller band med program för typsnitten till en fotosättare, typsnittsmaster, fotosättarmatrisdata, fotosättarpatrisdata;* **image degradation =** picture contrast and quality loss due to signal distortion *or*bad copying of a video signal *bildförsämring;* **image distortion =** optical lens fault causing an image to be distorted *bildförvrängning;* **image enhancer =** electronic device that improves the clarity of an image *bildförbättrare, "bildtvättare";* **image master =** data describing fonts and character shapes in a phototypesetter *typsnittsmatris (i elektronisk form), typsnittsmaster;* **image plane =** region where the photographic film is located in a camera, where a sharp image of a scene is formed when the lens is correctly focused *bildplan;* **image processing =** analysis of information contained in an image, usually by electronic means *or* using a computer which provide the analysis *or* recognition of objects in the image, etc. *bildbehandling;* **image processor =** electronic *or* computer system used for image processing, and to extract information from the image *bildbehandlare;* **image retention =** time taken for a TV image to disappear after it has been displayed, caused by long persistence phosphor *bildefterlysning;* **image scanner =** input device which converts documents *or* drawings *or* photographs into a digitized, machine-readable form *bildläsare, scanner;* **image sensor =** photoelectric device that produces a signal related to the amount of light falling on it (this scans horizontally over an image, reading in one line at a time) *bildavkännare, CCD-element;* **image stability =** ability of a display screen to provide a flicker-free picture *bildstabilitet, flimmerfrihet;* **image storage space =** region of memory in which a digitized image is stored *bildlagringsarea;* **image table =** two bit-mapped tables used to control input and output devices *or* processes *avbildningstabell*

imaging [ˈɪmɪdʒɪŋ] *subst.* technique for creating pictures on a screen (in medicine used to provide pictures of sections of the body, using scanners attached to computers) *(medicinsk) bildbehandling;* **magnetic resonance imaging =** scanning technique, using magnetic fields and radio waves *bildgenerering med magnetresonansteknik;* **X-ray imaging =** showing X-ray pictures of the inside of part of the body on a screen *röntgenbildbehandling*

immediate [ɪˈmiːdjət] *adj.* which happens at once *omedelbar;* **immediate access store (IAS) =** high-speed main memory area in a computer system *snabbåtkomstminne;* **immediate addressing =** accessing data immediately because it is held in the address field of an instruction *direktadressering;* **immediate instruction =** computer instruction in which the operand is included within the instruction, rather than an address of the operand location *direktoperandinstruktion;* **immediate mode =** mode in which a computer executes an instruction as soon as it is entered *direktopereringstillstånd;* **immediate operand =** operand which is fetched at the same time as the instruction (within an immediate addressing operation) *direktoperand;* **immediate processing =** processing data when it appears, rather than waiting for a synchronizing clock pulse *or* time *direktbearbetning, asynkron bearbetning, realtidsbearbetning; compare with* BATCH

immunity [ɪˈmjuːnətɪ] *see* INTERFERENCE

impact [ˈɪmpækt] *subst.* hitting *or* striking something *anslag;* **impact printer =** printer that prints text and symbols by striking an ink ribbon onto paper with a metal character, such as a daisy-wheel printer (as opposed to a non-impact printer like a laser printer) *anslagsskrivare; see also* DAISY-WHEEL PRINTER, DOT MATRIX PRINTER

impedance [ɪmˈpiːd(ə)ns] *subst.* measurement of the effect an electrical circuit has on signal current magnitude and phase when a steady voltage is applied *impedans;* **impedance matching =** means of making the best signal power transfer between two circuits by making sure that their output and input impedances are the same as the transmission line *impedansbalansering;* **impedance matching a transmitter and receiver minimizes power losses to transmitted signals; impedance mismatch** = situation where the impedance of the transmission *or* receiving end of a system does not match the other, resulting in loss of signal power (due to increased attenuation effects of the two different impedances) *impedansmissanpassning; see also* OHM

impedans ⇨ **impedance, load**

impedansbalansering ⇨ **impedance**

implant [ɪm'plɑːnt] *vb.* to fix deeply into something *inplantera, prägla in;* to bond one substance into another chemically *inplantera, dopa;* **the dopant is implanted into the substrate**

implement ['ɪmplɪmənt] *vb.* to carry out *or* to put something into action *genomföra, realisera*

implementation [ˌɪmplɪmen'teɪʃ(ə)n] *subst.* version of something that works *realisering, implementation;* **the latest implementation of the software runs much faster**

implementation ⇨ **implementation**

implication [ˌɪmplɪ'keɪʃ(ə)n] *subst.* logical operation that uses an IF-THEN structure, if A is true and if B is true this implies that the AND function of A and B will be true *implikation*

implied addressing [ɪm'plaɪd ə'dresɪŋ] *subst.* assembler instruction that operates on only one register (this is preset at manufacture and the user does not have to specify an address *underförstådd adressering;* **implied addressing for the accumulator is used in the instruction LDA,16**

import [ɪm'pɔːt] *vb.* (a) to bring goods into a country for sale *importera* (b) to bring something in from outside a system *importera;* **you can import images from the CAD package into the DTP program; imported signal** = broadcast television signal from outside a normal reception area, that is routed into and distributed over a cable network *importerad signal*

importation [ˌɪmpɔː'teɪʃ(ə)n] *subst.* the act of importing something into a system from outside *import*

QUOTE text and graphics importation from other systems is possible
                                              Publish

impression [ɪm'preʃ(ə)n] *subst.* number of books *or* documents printed all on the same printrun *upplaga;* **impression cylinder** = roller in a printing press that presses the

sheets of paper against the inked type *tryckcylinder*

imprint ['ɪmprɪnt] *subst.* publisher's *or* printer's name which appears on the title page*or* in the bibliographical details of a book *kolofon, boktryckarmärke, tryckort;* **imprint position** = on a sheet of paper, place where the next letter *or* symbol is to be printed *nästa teckenläge*

impulse ['ɪmpʌls] *subst.* (voltage) pulse which lasts a very short time *puls*

impulsive [ɪm'pʌlsɪv] *adj.* lasting a very short time *snabb, hastig, kortvarig;* **impulsive noise** = interference on a signal caused by short periods of noise *pulsbrus*

inaccuracy [ɪn'ækjʊrəsɪ] *subst.* mistake *or* error *felaktighet;* **the bibliography is full of inaccuracies**

inaccurate [ɪn'ækjʊrət] *adj.* not correct *or* wrong *felaktig, fel, inte (tillräckligt) noggrann;* **he entered an inaccurate password**

inactive [ɪn'æktɪv] *adj.* not working *or* running *väntande, vilande, inaktiv*

inaktiv ⇨ **inactive**

in-band signalling ['ɪn,bænd 'sɪgnəlɪŋ] *subst.* use of a normal voice grade channel for data transmission *dataöverföring på tallinje*

inbladad ⇨ **interleaved**

inbladning ⇨ **interleaving**

inbuilt ['ɪn'bɪlt] *adj.* (feature *or* device) included in a system *inbyggd;* **this software has inbuilt error correction**

inbyggd ⇨ **integral, integrated**

inbyggd adressering ⇨ **inherent addressing**

inbyggd databas ⇨ **integrated**

inbyggd dator ⇨ **embedded**

inbyggd periferienhet ⇨ **integrated**

inbyggd slinga ⇨ **inner loop**

inbyggt modem ⇨ **integrated**

inbyggt program ⇨ **firmware, internally stored program, program**

in camera process [ˌɪn 'kæm(ə)r(ə) 'prəʊses] *subst.* film processing which takes place inside the camera *direktframkallande process*

incandescence ['ɪnkæn'desns] *subst.* generation of light by heating a wire in an inert gas (as in a light bulb) *glödgning*

incandescent [ˈɪnkænˈdesnt] *adj.* shining because of heat produced in an inert gas *(vit)glödande;* **current passing through gas and heating a filament in a lightbulb causes it to produce incandescent light**

inches-per-second (ips) [ˈɪn(t)ʃɪz pɜːˈsek(ə)nd (ˈaɪpiːˈes)] way of showing the speed of tape past the read/write heads *tum per sekund*

in-circuit emulator [ˈɪnˌsɜːkɪt ˈemjʊleɪtə] *subst.* (circuit) that emulates a device *or* integrated circuit and is inserted into a new or faulty circuit to test it working correctly *kretsemulator;* **this in-circuit emulator is used to test the floppy disk controller by emulating a disk drive**

inclined orbit [ɪnˈklaɪnd ˈɔːbɪt] *subst.* orbit that is not polar *or* equatorial *lutande omloppsbana*

inclusion [ɪnˈkluːʒ(ə)n] *subst.* logical operation that uses an IF-THEN structure, if A is true and if B is true this implies that the AND function of A and B will be true *inklusion*

inclusive [ɪnˈkluːsɪv] *adj.* which counts something in with other things *inklusive;* **prices are inclusive of VAT; inclusive OR** *see* OR

incoming [ˈɪnˌkʌmɪŋ] *adj.* which is coming in from outside *inkommande;* **incoming message =** message received in a computer *inkommande meddelande;* **incoming traffic =** amount of data *or* messages received *inkommande trafik, inkommande signaler*

incompatible [ˌɪnkəmˈpætəbl] *adj.* not compatible *or* which cannot work together *inte kompatibel;* **they tried to link the two systems, but found they were incompatible**

incorrect [ˌɪnkəˈrekt] *adj.* not correct *or* with mistakes *felaktig;* **the input data was incorrect, so the output was also incorrect**

incorrectly [ˌɪnkəˈrektlɪ] *adv.* not correctly *or* with mistakes *felaktigt, fel;* **the data was incorrectly keyboarded**

increment [ˈɪnkrɪmənt] **1** *subst.* **(a)** addition of a set number, usually one, to a register, often for counting purposes *steg, inkrement, stegvis ökning;* **an increment is added to the counter each time a pulse is detected (b)** value of the number added to a register *förändringssteg;* **increase the increment to three 2** *vb.* **(a)** to add something *or* to increase a number *öka;* **the counter is incremented each time an instruction is executed (b)** to move forward to the next location *stega (fram)* **(c)** to move a document *or* card forward to its

next preset location for printing *or* reading *stega (fram)*

incremental computer [ˌɪnkrɪˈmentl kəmˈpjuːtə] *subst.* computer that stores variables as the difference between their actual value and an absolute initial value *stegdator, stegad dator, inkrementell dator;* **incremental data =** data which represents the difference of a value from an original value *stegade data, inkrementella data;* **incremental plotter =** graphical output device that can only move in small steps, with input data representing the difference between present position and the position required, so drawing lines and curves as a series of short straight lines *stegritare*

indata ⇨ **information, input (i/p** *or* **I/P)**

indataarea ⇨ **input (i/p** *or* **I/P)**

indatabegränsad ⇨ **input (i/p** *or* **I/P), input-bound**

indatablock ⇨ **input (i/p** *or* **I/P)**

indatabuffert ⇨ **input (i/p** *or* **I/P)**

indataenhet ⇨ **input (i/p** *or* **I/P)**

indataingång ⇨ **input (i/p** *or* **I/P)**

indatakontroll ⇨ **data**

indatakö ⇨ **input (i/p** *or* **I/P)**

indataledning ⇨ **input (i/p** *or* **I/P)**

indatamodul ⇨ **input (i/p** *or* **I/P)**

indataregister ⇨ **input (i/p** *or* **I/P)**

indatasignaler ⇨ **input (i/p** *or* **I/P)**

indent [ˈɪndent] **1** *subst.* space *or* series of spaces from the left margin, when starting a line of text *indrag* **2** *vb.* to start a line of text with a space in from the left margin *indragning;* **the first line of the paragraph is indented two spaces**

indentation [ˌɪndenˈteɪʃ(ə)n] *subst.* leaving a space at the beginning of a line of text *indrag*

independent [ˌɪndɪˈpendənt] *adj.* free *or* not controlled by anyone *oberoende*

independently [ˌɪndɪˈpendəntlɪ] *adv.* freely *or* without being controlled *or* without being connected *oberoende (av);* **in spooling, the printer is acting independently of the keyboard; the item is indexed independently**

indeterminate system [ˌɪndɪˈtɜːmɪnət ˈsɪstəm] *subst.* system whose logical (output) state cannot be predicted *oförutsägbart system*

index [ˈɪndeks] **1** *subst.* **(a)** list of items in a computer memory, usually arranged alphabetically *innehållslista, innehållsfil;*

index build = creation of an ordered list from the results of a database *or* file search *rapportbyggnad;* **index page** = videotext page that tells the user the locations of other pages *or* areas of interest *innehållssida;* **index register** = computer address register that is added to a reference address to provide the location to be accessed *indexregister* **(b)** list of subjects and contents of a book in alphabetical order (usually at the back of a book) *innehållsförteckning* **(c)** list of terms classified into groups *or* put in alphabetical order *index, katalog;* **index card** = small card used for storing information *katalogkort;* **index letter** *or* **index number** = letter *or* number which identifies an item in an index *indexbokstav, indexnummer* **(d)** address to be used that is the result of an offset value added to a start location *indexadress; see* INDEXED ADDRESSING; **index register (IR)** = computer address register that is added to a reference address to provide the location to be accessed *indexregister;* **index value word** = offset value added to an address to produce a usable address *indexvärde* **(e)** guide marks along the edge of a piece of film *or* strip of microfilm *styrmarkering;* **index hole** = hole in the edge of a hand-sectored disk *styrhål* **2** *vb.* **(a)** to write an index (for a book) *förteckna, innehållsförteckna, indexera;* **the book was sent out for indexing; the book has been badly indexed (b)** to put marks against items, so that they will be selected and sorted to form an index *indexera;* **indexed address** = address of the location to be accessed which is found in an index register *indexerad adress;* **indexed addressing** = method of addressing where the storage location is addressed with a start address and an offset word, which is added to give the destination address *indexerad adressering;* **indexed file** = sequential file with an index of all entries and their addresses *indexerad fil;* **indexed instruction** = instruction that contains an origin and offset that are added to provide the location to be accessed *indexerad instruktion;* **indexed sequential access method (ISAM)** = data retrieval method using a list containing the address of each stored record, where the list is searched, then the record is retrieved from the address in the list *ISAM-metoden för datasökning;* **indexed sequential storage** = method of storing records in a consecutive order, but in such a way that they can be accessed rapidly *indexerad sekvensiell lagring*

QUOTE in microcomputer implementations of COBOL, indexed files are usually based on some type of B-tree structure which allows rapid data retrieval based on the value of the key being used

PC-User

index ▷ index, inferior figures, subscript

indexadress ▷ index

indexbokstav ▷ index

indexer ['ɪndeksə] *subst.* person who writes an index *katalogredaktör*

indexera ▷ index

indexerad adress ▷ index

indexerad adressering ▷ index

indexerad fil ▷ index

indexerad instruktion ▷ instruction

indexerad sekvensiell lagring ▷ index

indexfält ▷ key

indexing ['ɪndeksɪŋ] *subst.* **(a)** use of indexed addressing methods in a computer *indexering* **(b)** process of building and sorting a list of records *indexering;* **indexing language** = language used in building library *or* book indexes *indexeringsspråk* **(c)** writing an index for a book *indexering;* **computer indexing** = using a computer to compile an index for a book by selecting relevant words *or* items from the text *datoriserad indexering*

indexnummer ▷ index

indexregister ▷ index

indextext ▷ master

indexvärde ▷ index

indicate ['ɪndɪkeɪt] *vb.* to show *visa, peka ut, indikera*

indication [ˌɪndɪ'keɪʃ(ə)n] *subst.* sign *or* thing which shows *indikation*

indicator ['ɪndɪkeɪtə] *subst.* something which shows the state of a process, usually a light *or* buzzer *indikator, signal, (larm)signal;* **indicator chart** = graphical representation of the location and use of indicator flags within a program *indikeringsdiagram;* **indicator flag** = register *or* single bit that indicates the state of the processor and its registers, such as a carry *or* overflow *indikatorflagga;* **indicator light** = light used to warn *or* to indicate the condition of equipment *indikatorlampa, larmsignal*

indirect [ˌɪndɪ'rekt] *adj.* not direct *indirekt;* **indirect addressing** = way of addressing data, where the first instruction refers to an address which contains a second address *indirekt adressering;* **indirect ray** = transmission path of a radio wave that does not take the shortest route, such as a reflection *indirekt överföringsväg, reflekterad stråle*

indirekt adressering ⇨ **addressing**

individual [ˌɪndɪ'vɪdjuəl] **1** *subst.* single person *individ;* **each individual has his own password to access the system 2** *adj.* single *or* belonging to a single person *enskild;* **the individual workstations are all linked to the mainframe**

indrag ⇨ **indent, indentation**

indragning ⇨ **indent**

induce [ɪn'djuːs] *vb.* (i) to generate an electrical current in a coil of wire by electromagnetic effects *inducera;* (ii) to prove (something) mathematically *härleda;* **induced failure** = failure of a device due to external effects *fel p.g.a. yttre påverkan, inducerat fel;* **induced interference** = electrical noise on a signal due to induced signals from nearby electromagnetic sources *inducerat brus*

inductance [ɪn'dʌktəns] *subst.* measurement of the amount of energy a device can store in its magnetic field *induktans*

induction [ɪn'dʌkʃ(ə)n] *subst.* (i) generation of an electrical current due to electromagnetic effects from a nearby source *induktion;* (ii) mathematically proving a formula *or* fact *härledning;* **induction coil** = transformer consisting of two nearby coils of insulated wire, one inducing a signal in the other; is often used either to isolate a signal supply from a some equipment *or* as a method of stepping up *or* down a voltage *induktionsspole; see also* TRANSFORMER

inductive coordination [ɪn'dʌktɪv kəʊˌɔːdɪ'neɪʃn] *subst.* agreement between electrical power suppliers and communication providers on methods of reducing induced interference *överenskommelse mellan elkraftindustrin och kommunikationsföretagen om att minska inducerade störningar*

inductor [ɪn'dʌktə] *subst.* electrical component consisting of a coil of wire used to introduce inductance effects into a circuit (by storing energy in its magnetic field) *spole, drossel*

induktion ⇨ **inference**

inequivalence [ˌɪnɪ'kwɪvələns] *subst.* logical function whose output is true if either of two inputs is true, and false if both inputs are the same *olikhet*

inert [ɪ'nɜːt] *adj.* (chemical substance *or* gas) that does not react with other chemicals *inert*

COMMENT: inert gas is used to protect a filament from oxidizing

inference ['ɪnf(ə)r(ə)ns] *subst.* **(a)** deduction of results from data according to certain rules *slutsats;* **inference engine** *or* **machine** = set of rules used in an expert system to deduce goals *or* results from data *(expertsystems) regelverk* **(b)** method of deducing a result about confidential information concerning an individual by using various data related to groups of people *slutledning, induktion;* **inference control** = determining which information may be released without disclosing personal information about a single individual *kontroll att data är avpersonifierade*

inferior figures [ɪn'fɪərɪə 'fɪgəz] *subst.* smaller numbers *or* characters that are printed slightly below normal characters, used in mathematical and chemical formulae *index, siffror i underkant; see also* SUBSCRIPT, SUPERSCRIPT, SUPERIOR
NOTE: used in formulae: CO_2

infinite ['ɪnfɪnət] *adj.* with no end *oändlig;* **infinite loop** = loop which has no exit (except by ending the running of the program by switching off the machine *or* resetting) *oändlig slinga*

infinity [ɪn'fɪnɪtɪ] *subst.* **(a)** very large incomprehensible quantity even bigger than the biggest you can think of *oändligheten* **(b)** distance of an object from a viewer where beams of light from the object would be seen to be parallel (i.e. very far away) *oändlighet*

infix notation ['ɪnfɪks nə(ʊ)'teɪʃ(ə)n] *subst.* method of computer programming syntax where operators are embedded inside operands (such as C - D or X + Y) *infixnotation; compare with* PREFIX, POSTFIX NOTATION

infogad subrutin ⇨ **insert**

informatics [ˌɪnfə'mætɪks] *subst.* science and study of ways and means of information processing and transmission *informatik*
NOTE: no plural

informatik ⇨ **informatics**

information [ˌɪnfə'meɪʃ(ə)n] *subst.* **(a)** knowledge presented to a person in a form which can be understood *information* **(b)** data that has been processed *or* arranged to provide facts which have a meaning *information;* **information bearer channel** = communications channel that is able to carry control and message data, usually at a higher rate than a data only channel *integrerad signalkanal;* **information content** = measurement of the amount of information conveyed by the transmission of a symbol *or* character, often measured in shannons *informationsinnehåll;* **information flow control** = regulation of access to certain information *informationsflödesstyrning;* **information input** = information received from an input device *indata;* **information line** = line running across the screen which gives the user information about the program running *or* the file being edited, etc. *informationsmeny, informationsrad, meddelanderad;* **information management system** = computer program that allows information to be easily stored, retrieved, searched and updated *informationshanteringssystem;* **information networks** = number of databases linked together, usually by telephone lines and modems, allowing a large amount of data to be accessed by a wider group of users *informationsnätverk;* **information output** = display of information on an output device *utdata;* **information processing** = organizing, processing and extracting information from data *informationsbehandling;* **information processor** = machine that processes a received signal, according to a program, using stored information to provide an output (this is an example of a computer that is not dealing with mathematical functions) *dator;* **information provider (IP)** = company *or* user that provides an information source for use in a videotext system (such as the company providing weather information *or* stock market reports) *informationslämnare;* **information rate** = amount of information content per character multiplied by the number of characters transmitted per second *informationsmängd per sekund;* **information retrieval (IR)** = locating quantities of data stored in a database and producing useful information from the data *informations(åter)sökning;* **information retrieval centre** = information search system, providing specific information from a database for a user *system för informationsåtervinning;* **information storage** = storing data in a form which allows it to be processed at a later date *datalagring;* **information storage and retrieval (ISR)** = techniques involved in storing information and retrieving data from a store *teknik för informationslagring och återsökning;* **information structure** *see* DATA STRUCTURE; **information system** = computer system which provides information according to a user's requests *informationssystem;* **information technology (IT)** = technology involved in acquiring, storing, processing and distributing information by electronic means (including radio, television, telephone, computers) *informationsteknik;*

information theory = formulae and mathematics concerned with data transmission equipment and signals *informationsteori;* **information transfer channel** = connection between a data transmitter and a receiver *kommunikationskanal; see also* DATA TERMINAL EQUIPMENT

QUOTE Information Technology is still too young to be an established discipline. However, the national and international IT research programmes are reasonably agreed that it comprises electronics, computing and telecommunications

Electronics and Power

informationsbehandling ⇨ information

informationsflödesstyrning ⇨ information

informationshanteringssystem ⇨ information

informationsinnehåll ⇨ information

informationskort ⇨ header

informationslämnare ⇨ information, ip

informationsmeny ⇨ information

informationsnätverk ⇨ network

informationsteknik ⇨ technology

informationsteori ⇨ information

infra- ['ınfrə] *prefix* meaning below *or* less than *infra-;* **infra-low frequency (ILF)** = range of audio frequencies between 300Hz-3KHz *talfrekvens*

infrared ['ınfrəred] *adj.* section of the electromagnetic radiation spectrum extending from visible red to microwaves *infraröd;* **infrared communications** = line of sight of communications path using a modulated infrared light beam rather than electrical signals down a cable *infraröd överföring;* **infrared detector** = photoelectric cell that is sensitive to the infrared region of the electromagnetic spectrum *infrarödavkännare;* **infrared photography** = type of photography that uses a special film which is sensitive to infrared radiation and so can be used in situations where the light level is very low; **infrared sights** = *infrarödfotografi;* camera and specialized optical equipment that can be used insituations where the light level is low, providing bright, enhanced images *infrarödoptik, bildförstärkare*

infrasonic frequency [ˌınfrəˈsɒnık ˈfriːkwənsı] *subst.* sound wave frequency that is in the range below that audible by the human ear *infraljud*

infrastructure ['ɪnfrəˌstrʌktʃə] *subst.* basic structure *or* basic services *infrastruktur*

infringement [ɪn'frɪn(d)ʒmənt] *subst.* breaking the law *or* a rule *intrång, inbrott;* **copyright infringement =** illegally making a copy of a book *or* program which is in copyright *intrång i upphovsrätt*

ingång ▷ entry, front-end, port

inherent addressing [ɪn'hɪər(ə)nt ə'dresɪŋ] *subst.* instruction that contains all the data required for the address to be accessed with no further operation *inbyggd adressering; compare with* EXTENDED, INDEXED

inherited error [ɪn'herɪtɪd 'erə] *subst.* error that is the result of a fault in a previous process *or* action *medfött fel*

inhibit [ɪn'hɪbɪt] *vb.* to stop a process taking place *or* to prevent an integrated circuit *or* gate from operating, (by means of a signal *or* command) *inhibera, hindra;* **inhibiting input =** one input of a gate which blocks the output signal *inhiberingssignal, blockeringssignal*

in-house ['ɪn'haʊs] *adv. & adj.* working inside a company *inom företaget, företagsegen;* **all the data processing is done in-house; the in-house maintenance staff deal with all our equipment**

initial [ɪ'nɪʃ(ə)l] **1** *adj.* first *or* at the beginning *begynnelse-;* **initial address =** address at which the first instruction of a program is stored *initialadress;* **initial condition =** condition that must be satisfied before a routine can be entered *begynnelsevillkor;* **initial error =** error in data that is the difference between the value of the data at the start of processing and its present actual value *initialfel;* **initial instructions =** routine that acts as an initial program loader *initialinstruktioner;* **initial program header =** small machine-code program usually stored in a read-only memory device that directs the CPU to load a larger program *or* operating system from store into main memory (such as a boot up routine that loads the operating system when a computer is switched on) *startprogram;* **initial program loader (IPL) =** short routine that loads a program (the operating system) from backing store into main memory *startprogram;* **initial value =** starting point (usually zero) set when initializing variables at the beginning of a program *startvärde* **2** *subst.* first letter of a word, especially of a name *initial;* **what do the initials IBM stand for?**

initial ▷ initial

initialadress ▷ initial

initialfel ▷ initial

initialinstruktioner ▷ initial

initialization [ɪnˌɪʃəlaɪ'zeɪʃn] *subst.* process of initializing *startprocess, initialisering;* **initialization is often carried out without the user knowing**

initialize [ɪ'nɪʃəˌlaɪz] *vb.* to set values *or* parameters *or* control lines to their initial values, to allow a program *or* process to be re-started *initialisera, återställa*

injection laser [ɪn'dʒekʃ(ə)n 'leɪzə] *subst.* solid state laser device used to transmit data as pulses of light down an optic fibre *signallaser*

injection logic [ɪn'dʒekʃ(ə)n 'lɒdʒɪk] *see* INTEGRATED

ink [ɪŋk] **1** *subst.* dark liquid used to mark *or* write with *bläck;* **ink-jet printer =** computer printer that produces characters by sending a stream of tiny drops of electrically charged ink onto the paper (the movement of the ink drops is controlled by an electric field; this is a non-impact printer with few moving parts) *bläckstråleskrivare;* **colour ink-jet technology and thermal transfer technology compete with each other 2** *vb.* to draw lines on paper with a pen *or* using a plotter device *rita, färga in*

> QUOTE ink-jet printers work by squirting a fine stream of ink onto the paper
> **Personal Computer World**

(in)kapslad slinga ▷ loop, nest

inkapslat makro ▷ nest

inkrement ▷ increment

inkrementella data ▷ incremental computer

inkrementell dator ▷ incremental computer

inlay card ['ɪnleɪ kɑːd] *subst.* identification card inside a tape *or* disk box *iläggsetikett*

inline ['ɪnlaɪn] **1** *subst.* connection pins on a chip arranged in one or two rows *in-ledning* **2** *adv.* way in which unsorted *or* unedited data is processed *linjärt;* **in-line program =** program that contains no loops *linjärt program;* **in-line processing =** processing data when it appears rather than waiting for a synchronizing *or* clock pulse *asynkron bearbetning, realtidsbearbetning*

inloggningsspärr ▷ interlock

inläsare ▷ scanner

inmatningskontroll ▷ keystroke

inmatningsläge ▷ input (i/p *or* I/P)

inmatningsrutin ⊳ input (i/p *or* I/P)

inmatningssats ⊳ input (i/p *or* I/P)

innehåll ⊳ content, contents

innehålla ⊳ contain

innehållsfil ⊳ index

innehållsförteckna ⊳ index

innehållsförteckning ⊳ index, table

innehållslista ⊳ index

innehållssida ⊳ index

inner loop ['ınə'lu:p] *subst.* loop contained inside another loop *inbyggd slinga; see also* NESTED LOOP

innermarginal ⊳ gutter

in- och utdata ⊳ output (o/p or O/P)

in- och utenhet ⊳ device

in phase ['ın'feız] *adv.* **(a)** (two electrical signals) that have no phase difference between them, i.e. there is no delay *or* a delay of one complete cycle between them *i fas* **(b)** synchronization of film frames and projector shutter timing *i fas*

inplantera ⊳ implant

input-bound ['ınput baʊnd] *or* **limited** ['lımıtıd] *adj.* (program) which is not running as fast as it could due to limiting input rate from a slower peripheral *indatabegränsad*

input (i/p *or* **I/P)** ['ınput] **1** *vb.* to transfer data *or* information from outside a computer to its main memory *sända (indata);* **the data was input via a modem** NOTE: **inputs - inputting - input 2** *subst.* **(a)** action of inputting information *datainmatning* **(b)** data *or* information that is transferred into a computer *indata;* **input area** = section of main memory that holds data transferred from backing store until it is processed *or* distributed to other sections *indataarea;* **input block** = block of data transferred to an input area *indatablock;* **input buffer register** = temporary store for data from an input device before it is transferred to main *or* backing store *indatabuffert;* **input device** = device such as a keyboard *or* bar code reader, which converts actions *or* information into a form which a computer can understand and transfers the data to the processor *indataenhet;* **input lead** = lead which connects an input device to a computer *indataledning;* **input limited** = (program) which is not running as fast as it could due to limiting input rate from a slower peripheral *indatabegränsad;* **input mode** = computer which is receiving data *inmatningsläge;* **input port** = circuit *or*

connector that allows a computer to receive data from other external devices *indataingång;* **input register** = temporary store for data received at slow speeds from an I/O device, the data is then transferred at high speed to main memory *indataregister;* **input routine** = set of instructions which control an I/O device and direct data received from it to the correct storage location *inmatningsrutin;* **input section** = (i) input routine *indatamodul;* (ii) input area *indataarea;* **input statement** = computer programming command that waits for data entry from a port *or* keyboard *inmatningssats;* **input storage** *see* INPUT AREA; **input unit** = an input device *indataenhet;* **input work queue** = list of commands to be carried out in the order they were entered (or in order by priority) *indatakö* **(c)** electrical signals which are applied to relevant circuits to perform the operation *indatasignaler*

input/output (I/O) ['ınput'aʊtput] *subst.* receiving *or* transmitting data between a computer and its peripherals, and other points outside the system *in-utdatasändning;* **input/output buffer** = temporary storage area for data waiting to be output *or* data input *in-utbuffertminne;* **input/output bus** = links allowing data and control signal transfer between a CPU and memory *or* peripheral devices *in-ut(data)buss;* **input/output channel** = link between a processor and peripheral allowing data transfer *in-utkanal;* **input/output control program** = monitoring and control of I/O operations and data flow by a section of the operating system *or* supervisory program *in-utdatastyrprogram;* **input/output controller** = intelligent device that monitors, directs and controls data flow between a CPU and I/O devices *in-utstyrenhet;* **input/output device** *or* **unit** = peripheral (such as a terminal in a workstation) which can be used both for inputting and outputting data to a processor *in-utenhet;* **input/output executive** = master program that controls all the I/O activities of a computer *in-utstyrprogram;* **input/output instruction** = computer programming instruction that allows data to be input *or* output from a processor *in-utinstruktion;* **input/output interface** = circuit allowing controlled data input and output from a CPU, consisting usually of: input/output channel, parallel input/output port and a DMA interface *in-utgränssnitt;* **input/output interrupt** = interrupt signal from a peripheral device *or* to indicate that an input or output operation is required *in-utavbrott;* **input/output library** = set of routines that can be used by the programmer to help simplify input/output tasks (such as printer drivers *or* port control routines) *in-utbibliotek;* **input/output port** = circuit *or* connector that provides an input/output channel to another device *in-utanslutning;* **the joystick can be connected to the input/output port; input/output processor (IOP) =** processor that carries out input/output transfers for a CPU, including DMA and error correction facilities *in-utprocessor;* **input/output referencing =** use of labels to refer to specific input/output devices, the actual address of the device being inserted at run-time *in-utdatareferens;* **input/output register =** temporary store for data received from main memory before being transferred to an I/O device (or data from an I/O device to be stored in main memory *or* processed) *in-utregister;* **input/output request (IORQ) =** request signal from the CPU for data input or output *in-utfrågessignal;* **input/output status word =** word whose bits describe the state of peripheral devices (busy, free, etc.) *in-utdatastatusord;* **parallel input/output (PIO) =** data input *or* output from a computer *parallelldataöverföring*

QUOTE inputs include raster scan files and ASCII files
Byte

inquiry [ɪnˈkwaɪərɪ] *subst.* (i) asking a question *fråga, förfrågan;* (ii) accessing data held in a computer system *söka;* **inquiry character (ENQ) =** code transmitted by a computer to a remote terminal, asking for a response *förfrågningstecken;* **inquiry station =** terminal that is used to access and interrogate files stored on a remote computer *frågeterminal;* **inquiry/response =** interactive computer mode in which a user's commands and enquiries are responded to very quickly *interaktivitetsläge*

insamla ⇨ **collect, gather**

insatt subrutin ⇨ **insert**

insert [ɪnˈsɜːt] *vb.* **(a)** to put something into something *sticka in, sätta in;* **first insert the system disk in the left slot (b)** to add new text inside a word *or* sentence *sätta in;* **inserted subroutine =** series of instructions that are copied directly into the main program where a call instruction appears *or* where a user requires *infogad subrutin, inskjuten subrutin, insatt subrutin*

insertion loss [ɪnˈsɜːʃ(ə)n lɒs] *subst.* attenuation to a signal caused by adding a device into an existing channel *or* circuit *inkopplingsförlust*

insert mode [ˈɪnsɜːt məʊd] *subst.* interactive computer mode used for editing and correcting documents *insättningsläge*

COMMENT: this is a standard feature on most word-processing packages where the cursor is placed at the required point in the document and any characters typed will be added, with the existing text moving on as necessary

inskjuten subrutin ⇨ **insert**

inskrivning ⇨ **entering, keyboarding**

inspelning ⇨ **recording**

inspelningshuvud ⇨ **head**

install [ɪnˈstɔːl] *vb.* to put a machine into an office *or* factory *installera;* to set up a new computer system to the user's requirements *or* to configure a new program to the existing system capabilities *installera;* **the system is easy to install and simple to use**

installation [ˌɪnstəˈleɪʃ(ə)n] *subst.* **(a)** computer and equipment used for one type of work and processing *installation;* **the engineers are still testing the new installation (b)** setting up a new computer system *installation;* **the installation of the equipment took only a few hours**

installationshandbok ⇨ **manual**

instansning ⇨ **entering, keyboarding**

instantaneous access [ˌɪnst(ə)nˈteɪnjəs ˈækses] *subst.* extremely short access time to a random access device *omedelbar åtkomst*

instant replay [ˈɪnstənt ˈriːpleɪ] *subst.* feature found in video recording systems that allows the action that has just been recorded to be viewed immediately *omedelbar uppspelning*

instickskort ⇨ **daughter board, expansion**

instruct [ɪnˈstrʌkt] *vb.* to tell someone *or* a computer what to do *instruera*

instruction [ɪnˈstrʌkʃ(ə)n] *subst.* word used in a programming language that is understood by the computer to represent an action *instruktion;* **the instruction PRINT is used in this BASIC dialect as an operand to display the following data; absolute instruction =** instruction which completely describes the operation to be performed (i.e. no other data is required) *absolutinstruktion;* **arithmetic instruction =** instruction to perform an arithmetic operation on data rather than a logical function *aritmetisk instruktion;* **blank** *or* **null** *or* **dummy instruction =** instruction in a program that is only there to satisfy language syntax *or* to make up a block length *blindinstruktion;* **breakpoint instruction =** halt command inserted in a program to temporarily stop execution, allowing the programmer to examine data and registers whilst debugging a program *brytpunktsinstruktion;* **decision** *or* **discrimination instruction** = conditional program instruction that directs control by providing the location of the next instruction to be executed (if a condition is met) *villkorsinstruktion, val;* **executive instruction** = instruction used to control and execute programs under the control of an operating system *styrinstruktion, verkställande instruktion;* **four-address instruction** = program instruction which contains four addresses within its address field, usually the location of the two operands, the result and the location of the next instruction *fyradressinstruktion;* **indexed instruction** = instruction that contains an origin and location of an offset that are added together to provide the address to be accessed *indexerad instruktion;* **input/output instruction** = computer programming instruction that allows data to be input *or* output from a processor *in-utinstruktion;* **jump instruction** = program command to end one set of instructions and direct the processor to another section of the program *hoppinstruktion;* **macro instruction** = one programming instruction that refers to a number of instructions within a routine *or* macro *makroinstruktion;* **no-op instruction** = instruction that does not carry out any functions, but increments the program counter *blindinstruktion;* **n-plus-one instruction** = instruction made up of a number (n) of addresses and one other address that is the location of the next instruction to be executed *N-plus-ett- (N+1)stegsinstruktion;* **supervisory instruction** = instruction used to control and execute programs under the control of an operating system *övervakningsinstruktion;* **three-address-instruction** = instruction format which contains the addresses of two operands and the location where the result is to be stored *treadressinstruktion;* **two-address-instruction** = instruction format containing the locations of two operands, the result being stored in one of the operand locations *tväadressinstruktion;* **two-plus-one-address instruction** = instruction containing locations of two operands and an address for the storage of the result *tvä-plus-ett-instruktion;* **instruction address** = location of an instruction *instruktionsadress;* **instruction address register (IAR)** register in a CPU that contains the location of the next instruction to be processed *instruktionsadressregister, instruktionspekare;* **instruction area** = section of memory that is used to store instructions *instruktionsarea;* **instruction cache** = area of high-speed memory which stores the next few instructions to be executed by a processor *instruktionsbuffertminne;* **instruction character** = special character that provides a control sequence rather than an alphanumeric character *instruktionstecken;* **instruction codes** = set of symbols *or* codes that a CPU can directly understand and execute *instruktionskoder;* **instruction counter** *or* **instruction address register (IAR)** *or* **program counter** = register in a CPU that contains the location of the next instruction to be processed *instruktionsräknare, programräknare;* **instruction cycle** = sequence of events and their timing that is involved when fetching and executing an instruction stored in memory *instruktionscykel;* **instruction cycle time** = amount of time taken for one instruction cycle *instruktionstid;* **instruction decoder** = program which decodes instructions in machine code *instruktionsavkodare;* **instruction execution time** = time taken to carry out an instruction *instruktionscykeltid;* **instruction format** = rules defining the way the operands, data and addresses are arranged in an instruction *instruktionsformat;* **instruction modification** = altering a part of an instruction (data *or* operator) so that it carries out a different function when next executed *modifiering av instruktion;* **instruction pipelining** = beginning processing a second instruction while still processing the present one (this increases program speed of execution) *parallellbearbetning med rörledning(steknik);* **instruction processor** = section of the central processing unit that decodes the instruction and performs the necessary arithmetic and logical functions *instruktionsprocessor;* **instruction register (IR)** = register in a central processing unit that stores an instruction during decoding and execution operations *instruktionsregister;* **instruction repertoire** *or* **set** = total number of instructions that a processor can recognize and execute *instruktionsuppsättning;* **instruction storage** *see* INSTRUCTION AREA; **instruction time** = amount of time taken for a central processing unit to carry out a complete instruction *instruktionstid;* **instruction word** = fixed set of characters used to initiate an instruction *instruktionsord;* **the manufacturers of this CPU have decided that JMP will be the instruction word to call the jump function**

COMMENT: in a high level language the instructions are translated by the compiler *or* interpreter to a form that is understood by the central processing unit

instruktionsadress ⇨ **instruction**

instruktionsadressregister ⇨ **IAR**

instruktionsarea ⇨ **instruction**

instruktionsavkodare ⇨ instruction

instruktionsbok ⇨ manual

instruktionsbuffertminne   ⇨ instruction

instruktionscykel   ⇨ instruction, operation

instruktionscykeltid ⇨ instruction

instruktionsformat ⇨ format

instruktionskoder ⇨ instruction

instruktionspekare ⇨ instruction

instruktionstecken ⇨ instruction

instruktionstid ⇨ instruction

instruktionsuppsättning ⇨ instruction

instrumentation [ˌɪnstrʊmenˈteɪʃ(ə)n] *subst.* equipment for testing, display or recording signals *instrumentering;* **we've improved the instrumentation on this model to keep you better informed of the machine's position**

insufficient [ˌɪnsəˈfɪʃ(ə)nt] *adj.* not enough *otillräcklig;* **there is insufficient time to train the keyboarders properly**

insulate [ˈɪnsjʊleɪt] *vb.* to prevent a voltage *or* energy from a conductor reaching another point by separating the two points with an insulation material *isolera*

insulation material [ˌɪnsjʊˈleɪʃ(ə)n məˈtɪərɪəl] *subst.* substance that is very bad conductor, used to prevent a voltage *or* energy reaching a point *isoleringsmaterial, isolerande material*

insulator [ˈɪnsjʊleɪtə] *subst.* material that can insulate *isolator (i fråga om elektrisk isolering), isoleringsmaterial el. isolerande material (i fråga om värmeisolering)*

insättningsläge ⇨ insert mode

integer [ˈɪntɪdʒə] *subst.* mathematical term to describe a whole number (it may be positive *or* negative *or* zero) *heltal;* **double-precision integer** = two computer words used to store an integer *heltal i (dubbel)precision;* **integer BASIC** = faster version of BASIC that uses only integer mathematics and cannot support fractions *heltals-BASIC*

integral [ˈɪntɪgr(ə)l] *subst.* add-on device *or* special feature that is already built into a system *inbyggd, integrerad;* **the integral disk drives and modem reduced desk space**

> QUOTE an integral 7 inch amber display screen, two half-height disk drives and terminal emulation for easy interfacing with mainframes
> **Computing Today**

integrated [ˈɪntɪgreɪtɪd] *adj.* (system) that contains many peripherals grouped together in order to provide a neat, complete system *inbyggd, integrerad;* **integrated database** = database that is able to provide information for varied requirements without any redundant data *inbyggd databas;* **integrated data processing (IDP)** = organizational method for the entry and retrieval of data to provide maximum efficiency *integrerad databehandling;* **integrated device** = device that is part of another machine *or* device *inbyggd periferienhet;* **our competitor's computer doesn't have an integrated diskdrive like this model; integrated digital access (IDA)** = system where subscribers can make two telephone calls and be linked (from their office *or* home) to a database, and send material by fax, all at the same time *samåtkomst;* **integrated digital network** = communications network that uses digital signals to transmit data *digitalt data(kommunikationsnät);* **integrated emulator** = emulator program run within a multitasking operating system *integrerat emuleringsprogram;* **integrated injection logic (IIL)** = method of designing and constructing logical circuits on an integrated circuit to provide low power consumption with medium speed gates *metod för kretskonstruktion;* **integrated modem** = modem that is a internal part of the system *inbyggt modem;* **integrated office** = office environment in which all operations are carried out using a central computer (to store information, print, etc.) *integrerad kontorsfunktion, "elektroniskt kontor";* **integrated optical circuit** = optoelectronic circuit that can generate, detect and transmit light for communications over optical fibres *integrerad optisk krets;* **integrated services digital network (ISDN)** = international digital communications network which can transmit sound, fax and data over the same channel *(digitalt) flertjänstnät;* **integrated software** = software such as an operating system *or* word-processor that is stored in the computer system and has been tailored to the requirements of the system *integrerat program(system)*

integrated circuit (IC) [ˈɪntɪgreɪtɪd ˈsɜːkɪt (ˈaɪsiː)] *subst.* circuit where all the active and passive components are formed on one small piece of semiconductor, by means of etching and chemical processes *integrerad krets*

COMMENT: integrated circuits can be classified as follows: Small Scale Integration (SSI): 1 to 10 components per IC; Medium Scale Integration (MSI): 10 to 500 components per IC; Large Scale Integration (LSI): 500 to 10,000 components per IC; Very Large Scale Integration (VLSI): 10,000 to 100,000 components per IC

integration [ˌɪntɪˈgreɪʃ(ə)n] *subst.* bringing several operations together *integration;* **small scale integration (SSI); medium scale integration (MSI); large scale integration (LSI); very large scale integration (VLSI)** *termer för integrationsnivån i kretsens konstruktion (hur många transistorer som syns på chippet)*

integration ⇨ integration

integrerad ⇨ integral, integrated

integrerad databehandling ⇨ integrated

integrerad kontorsfunktion ⇨ integrated

integrerad krets ⇨ composite circuit, integrated circuit (IC), micro-

integrerad signalkanal ⇨ information

integrerad styrkod ⇨ embedded code

integrerat emuleringsprogram ⇨ integrated

integrerat program(system) ⇨ integrated

integrity [ɪnˈtegrətɪ] *subst.* reliability of data (when being processed *or* stored on disk) *(data)integritet, tillförlitlighet;* **integrity of a file =** the fact that a file that has been stored on disk is not corrupted *or* distorted in any way *dataintegritet;* **the data in this file has integrity =** the data has not been corrupted *data i den här filen är tillförlitliga*

QUOTE it is intended for use in applications demanding high data integrity, such as archival storage or permanent databases
Minicomputer News

intelligence [ɪnˈtelɪdʒ(ə)ns] *subst.* (i) ability to reason *intelligens;* (ii) ability of a device to carry out processing *or* run a program *"lokal intelligens", egen beräkningskapacitet;* **artificial intelligence (AI) =** the design of computer programs and systems that attempt to imitate human intelligence and decision-making functions, providing basic reasoning and human characteristics *artificiell intelligens*

intelligent [ɪnˈtelɪdʒ(ə)nt] *adj. (of a machine)* (program *or* device) that is capable of limited reasoning facilities, giving it human-like responses *intelligent;*

intelligent device = peripheral device that contains a central processing unit allowing it to process data *"intelligent periferienhet";* **intelligent knowledge-based system (IKBS)** *or* **expert system =** software that applies the knowledge, advice and rules defined by an expert in a particular field to a user's data to help solve a problem *expertsystem, kunskapsbaserat system;* **intelligent spacer =** facility on a word-processing system used to prevent words from being hyphenated *or* separated at the wrong point *avstavningsprogram;* **intelligent tutoring system =** computer-aided learning system that provides responsive and interactive teaching facilities for users *datorstött utbildningssystem;* **intelligent terminal =** computer terminal which contains a CPU and memory, usually with a facility to allow the user to program it independently of the main CPU *intelligent terminal* NOTE: the opposite is **dumb terminal**

"intelligent periferienhet" ⇨ intelligent

INTELSAT [ɪnˈtelsæt] = INTERNATIONAL TELECOMMUNICATIONS SATELLITE ORGANIZATION international group that deals with the design, construction and allocation of space to various communications satellite projects *internationella organisationen för företag och organisationer som driver telekommunikationssatelliter*

intensity [ɪnˈtensɪtɪ] *subst.* measure of the strength of a signal *or* the brightness of a light source *or* the loudness of a noise *intensitet, styrka, signalstyrka*

COMMENT: sound intensity is usually measured in decibels

inter- [ˈɪntə] *prefix* meaning between *inter-;* **interblock =** between blocks *mellanblock*

interact [ˌɪntərˈækt] *vb. (of two things)* to act on each other *interagera, samverka*

interaction [ˌɪntərˈækʃ(ə)n] *subst.* action of two things on each other *interaktion, samverkan*

interactive [ˌɪntərˈæktɪv] *adj.* (system *or* piece of software) that allows communication between the user and the computer (in conversational mode) *interaktiv;* **interactive cable television =** cable television system that allows the viewer to transmit signals such as program choice, teleshopping *or* answers to game questions back to the television transmission centre *interaktiv kabelteve;* **interactive debugging system =** software development tool that allows the user to run a program under test, set breakpoints, examine source and object code, examine registers and memory contents and trace the instruction execution *interaktivt felsökningssystem;* **interactive graphics** = display system that is able to react to different inputs from the user *interaktiv grafik;* **the space invaders machine has great interactive graphics, the player controls the position of his spaceship on the screen with the joystick; interactive media** = communication between a group of people using different transmission means *samkommunikation, samverkande (kommunikations)media;* **interactive mode** *or* **processing** = computer mode that allows the user to enter commands *or* programs *or* data and receive immediate responses *interaktivt läge, interaktiv körning; see also* INQUIRY/RESPONSE; **interactive routine** = computer program that can accept data from an operator, process it and provide a real-time reaction to it *interaktivt program, interaktiv rutin;* **interactive system** = system which provides an immediate response to the user's commands *or* programs *or* data *interaktivt system;* **interactive terminal** = terminal in an interactive system which sends and receives information *interaktiv terminal;* **interactive videotext** = viewdata service that allows the operator to select pages, display them, ask questions use a service such as teleshopping *interaktiv teletext (videotex)*

QUOTE interactivity is a buzzword you've been hearing a lot lately. Resign yourself to it because you're going to be hearing a lot more of it
Music Technology

interactive video [ˌɪntərˈæktɪv ˈvɪdɪəʊ] *subst.* system that uses a computer linked to a video disk player to provide processing power and real images *or* moving pictures *interaktiv video*

COMMENT: this system is often used in teaching to ask a student questions, which if answered correctly will provide him with a filmed sequence from the videodisk

QUOTE soon pupils will be able to go shopping in a French town from the comfort of their classroom - carried to their destination by interactive video, a medium which combines the power of the computer with the audiovisual impact of video
Electronics & Power

interaktivitetsläge ⇨ inquiry

interaktivt felsökningssystem ⇨ interactive

interaktivt läge ⇨ interactive, mode

interblock gap (IBG) [ˈɪntəblɒk ˈgæp (ˈaɪbiːˈdʒiː)] *subst.* blank magnetic tape between the end of one block of data and the start of the next in backing store *blockmellanrum*

intercarrier noise [ˌɪntəˈkærɪə ˈnɔɪz] *subst.* interference caused by two different signal carriers getting mixed *interferensstörning;* **television intercarrier noise is noticed when the picture and the sound signal carriers clash**

interchange [ˌɪntəˈtʃeɪn(d)ʒ] **1** *subst.* exchange of one thing for another *utbyte;* **the machine allows document interchange between it and other machines without reformatting 2** *vb.* to exchange one thing for another *byta*

interchangeable [ˌɪntəˈtʃeɪn(d)ʒəbl] *adj.* which can be exchanged *utbytbar*

intercharacter spacing [ˌɪntəˈkærəktə ˈspeɪsɪŋ] *subst.* word-processor feature that provides variable spacing between words to create a justified line *knipning, tillriktning*

intercom [ˈɪntəkɒm] *subst.* short-range voice communications system *snabbtelefon*

COMMENT: used mainly in offices *or* in automatic door systems where room-to-room communication of voice signals is required

interconnect [ˈɪntəkəˈnekt] *vb. (of several things)* to connect together *koppla samman;* **a series of interconnected terminals**

interconnection [ˈɪntəkəˈnekʃ(ə)n] *subst.* **(a)** section of connecting material between two devices *sammankoppling* **(b)** connection between a telephone set and a telephone network *koppling, anslutning*

interface [ˈɪntəfeɪs] **1** *subst.* (i) point at which one computer system ends and another begins *gränssnitt;* (ii) circuit *or* device *or* port that allows two or more incompatible units to be linked together in a standard communication system, allowing data to be transferred between them *gränssnitt;* (iii) section of a program which allows transmission of data to another program *gränssnitt;* **EIA interface** = standard defining interface signals, transmission rate and power usually used to connect terminals to modems *EIA-gränssnitt;* **general purpose interface adapter (GPIA)** = usually used to interface a processing unit to a IEEE-488 bus *IEEE-488-anpassare;* **general purpose interface bus (GPIB)** = standard for an interface bus between a computer and laboratory equipment *GPIB-buss;* **input/output interface** = circuit allowing controlled data input and output from a CPU, consisting usually of: input/output channel, parallel input/output port and a DMA interface *in-utgränssnitt;* **interface card** = add-on board that allows a computer to interface to certain equipment *or* conform to a certain standard *gränssnittskort;* **interface message processor** = computer in a packet switching network that deals with the flow of data, acting as an interface processor *paketkanalomvandlare, paketstyrenhet;* **interface processor** = computer that controls data transfer between a processor and a terminal *or* network *terminalstyrenhet;* **interface routines** = software that allows programs *or* data for one system to run on another *omvandlingsprogram;* **parallel interface** = computer circuit *or* connector that allows parallel data to be transmitted *or* received *parallellgränssnitt* NOTE: parallel interfaces are usually used to drive printers **serial interface** = circuit that converts parallel data in a computer to and from a serial form, allowing serial data to be transmitted to *or* received from other equipment *seriellt gränssnitt* NOTE: the most common serial interface is RS232C **2** *vb.* (i) to modify a device by adding a circuit *or* connector to allow it to conform to a standard communications system *anpassa (till ett gränssnitt);* (ii) to connect two or more incompatible devices together with a circuit, to allow them to communicate *koppla (samman)*

interfacing ['ɪntəfeɪsɪŋ] *subst.* hardware *or* software used to interface two computers *or* programs *or* devices *gränssnitt*

interfere [ˌɪntə'fɪə] *vb.* **to interfere with something** = to stop something working properly *or* to get in the way *hindra, störa*

interference [ˌɪntə'fɪər(ə)ns] *subst.* **(a)** unwanted addition of signals *or* noise to a transmitted signal *störning* **(b)** effect seen when two signals are added, creating constructive interference when both signals are in phase *or* destructive interference when they are out of phase *interferens;* **interference fading** = effect in radio reception when destructive interference occurs *interferensstörning;* **interference immunity** = ability of a system (i) to ignore interference signals *störsäkerhet;* (ii)to function correctly even with interference *interferenssäkerhet;* **interference pattern** = effect seen when light *or* radio *or* x-ray waves interact and produce destructive and constructive interference, causing patterns *interferensmönster;* **constructive interference** = increase in peak and trough amplitude when two in phase signals are added *konstruktiv interferens;* **destructive interference** = cancellation of peaks and troughs when two out of phase signals are added (if the signals are exactly out of phase, they completely cancel out each other) *destruktiv interferens;* **electromagnetic interference** = corruption of data due to nearby electrically generated magnetic fields *elektromagnetisk störning;* **induced interference** = electrical noise on a

signal due to induced signals from nearby electromagnetic sources *inducerad störning*

COMMENT: interference can be due to electrical noise (such as from a relay), natural galactic noise or two signals mixing due to insufficient insulation

interferens ⇨ **babble**

interferensljusledare ⇨ **multimode fibre**

interferensstörning ⇨ **intercarrier noise**

interfolierad ⇨ **interleaved**

interfoliering ⇨ **interleaving**

interior label [ɪn'tɪərɪə 'leɪbl] *subst.* identification label stored on a storage medium (magnetic tape *or* disk) rather than an exterior *or* physical label stuck to the case *elektronisk etikett*

interlace [ˌɪntə'leɪs] *vb.* to build up an image on a television screen using two passes, each displaying alternate lines *sammanfläta*

COMMENT: this system uses two picture fields made up of alternate lines to reduce picture flicker effects

interleaved [ˌɪntə'liːvd] *adj.* **(a)** (thin sheets of paper) which are stuck between the pages of a book *inbladad, interfolierad;* **blank paper was interleaved with the newly printed text to prevent the ink running (b)** sections of two programs executed alternately to give the impression that they are running simultaneously *överlagrad, växelvis tidsdelad*

QUOTE there are two separate 40-bit arrays on each card to allow interleaved operation, achieving data access every 170ns machine cycle
Minicomputer News

interleaving [ˌIntə'liːvɪŋ] *subst.* **(a)** processor dealing with slices *or* sections of processes alternately, so that they appear to be executed simultaneously *tidsdelning* **(b)** addition of blank paper between printed sheets to prevent the ink from making other sheets dirty *inbladning, interfoliering* **(c)** dividing data storage into sections so that each can be accessed separately *överlagring, överlappning*

inter-library loan (ILL) ['ɪntə'laɪbr(ə)rɪ 'ləʊn ('aɪel'el)] *subst.* lending of books *or* documents between from one library to another *lån mellan bibliotek*

interlinear spacing [ˌɪntə'lɪnɪə 'speɪsɪŋ] *subst. (on a phototypesetter)* insertion of spaces between lines of text *justering av radmellanrum*

interlock 1 ['ɪntəlɒk] *subst.* **(a)** security device which is part of the logon prompt and requires a password *inloggningsspärr* **(b)** [,ɪntə'lɒk] method of synchronizing audio tape with a video *or* filmed sequence (this can be achieved by using a frame counter *or* a timer*or* by running both audio and visual tapes on the same motor) *synkronisering;* **interlock projector** = film display machine that can also provide synchronized sound *ljudfilmprojektor* **2** [,ɪntə'lɒk] *vb.* to prevent a device from performing another task until the present one has been completed *låsa, spärra*

interlude ['ɪntəlu:d] *subst.* small initial routine at the start of a program that carries out housekeeping tasks *konfigurering(srutin), start(rutin)*

intermediate [,ɪntə'mi:djət] *adj.* which is at a stage between two others *mellanliggande;* **intermediate access memory (IAM)** = memory storage that has an access time between that of main memory and disk based systems *mellanminne, medelåtkomstminne;* **intermediate code** = code used by a computer *or* assembler during the translation of a high-level code to machine code *mellankod, intermediär kod;* **intermediate file** = series of records that contain partially processed data, that will be used at a later date to complete that task *mellanfil;* **intermediate materials** = medium *or* format used for recording prior to the transfer to another format *mellanlagringsmedium, mellanformat;* **those slides, photographs, video and film are the intermediate materials to be mastered onto the video disk; intermediate storage** = temporary area of memory for items that are currently being processed *mellanlagringsminne*

intermediate frequency (if) [,ɪntə'mi:djət 'fri:kwənsɪ (ɪf)] *subst.* frequency in a radio receiver to which the incoming received signal is transformed *mellanfrekvens*

COMMENT: this is to allow high frequency signals to be converted to a lower intermediate frequency so that they can be processed with standard components, rather than more expensive high-frequency versions

intermediär kod ➪ **intermediate**

intermittent error [,ɪntə'mɪt(ə)nt 'erə] *subst.* error which apparently occurs randomly in a computer *or* communications system due to a program fault *or* noise *intermittent fel, återkommande fel*

COMMENT: these errors are very difficult to trace and correct due to their apparent random appearance

internal [ɪn'tɜ:nl] *adj.* which is inside *intern, inbyggd;* **internal arithmetic** = arithmetic operations performed by the ALU *intern aritmetik;* **internal character code** = representation of characters in a particular operating system *intern teckenkod;* **internal format** = way in which data and instructions are represented within a CPU *or* backing store *internt format;* **internal language** = language used in a computer system that is not under the direct control of the operator *internspråk*

COMMENT: many compiled languages are translated to an internal language

internally stored program [ɪn'tɜ:nəlɪ 'stɔ:əd 'prəʊgræm] *subst.* computer program code that is stored in a ROM device in a computer system (and does not have to be loaded from backing store) *inbyggt program, läsminneslagrat program*

internal memory [ɪn'tɜ:nl 'memərɪ] *or* **store** [stɔ:] *subst.* section of RAM and ROM to which the central processing unit is directly connected without the use of an interface (as in external memory devices such as disk drives) *internminne*

internal sort [ɪn'tɜ:nl sɔ:t] *subst.* sorting program using only the main memory of a system *internsortering*

intern aritmetik ➪ **internal**

international [,ɪntə'næʃ(ə)nl] *adj.* referring to different countries *internationell;* **international direct dialling (IDD)** = system using an international dialling code that allow a user to telephone any country without going through an operator *internationell direktuppringning;* **international dialling code** INTERNATIONAL PREFIX CODE; **international number** = digits to be dialled after the international prefix code to reach a subscriber in another country *landsnummer;* **international prefix code** = code number to be dialled at the start of a number to select another country's exchange system *utlandsprefix, utlandskod, (009);* **international standard book number (ISBN)** = ten-digit identifying number allocated to every new book published *ISBN-nummer;* **international standard serial number (ISSN)** = identifying number allocated to every journal *or* magazine published *ISSN-nummer*

International Standards Organization (ISO) [,ɪntə'næʃ(ə)nl 'stændədz ,ɔ:gənaɪ'zeɪʃ(ə)n ('aɪes'əʊ)] *subst.* organization which regulates standards for many types of product *internationella standardorganisationen;* **International Standards Organization Open System Interconnection (ISO/OSI)** = standardized ISO network design which is constructed in layered form, with each layer having a specific task, allowing different systems to communicate if they conform to the standard *OSI-standarden för nätverk*

internminne ⇨ **internal memory**

internsortering ⇨ **internal sort**

intern teckenkod ⇨ **internal**

interpolation [ɪn,tɜːpə(ʊ)'leɪʃ(ə)n] *subst.* calculation of intermediate values between two points *interpolering*

interpret [ɪn'tɜːprɪt] *vb.* to translate what is said in one language into another *översätta, tolka;* **interpreted language** = programming language that is executed by an interpreter *interpreterat språk*

interpretative [ɪn'tɜːprɪtətɪv] *adj.* **interpretative code** = code used with an interpretative program *interpretativ kod;* **interpretative program** = software that translates (at run-time) high level interpretative code into machine code instructions *interpretator, interpretativt program, översättningsprogram, tolk*

interpreter [ɪn'tɜːprɪtə] *subst.* software that is used to translate (at the time of execution) a user's high-level program into machine code *interpretator, översättare, tolk; compare with* COMPILER

> COMMENT: a compiler translates the high-level language into machine code and then executes it, rather than the real-time translation by an interpreter

interpreterare ⇨ **processor**

interrecord gap ['ɪntə,rekɔːd 'gæp] = INTERBLOCK GAP

interrogation [ɪn,terə(ʊ)'geɪʃ(ə)n] *subst.* asking questions *fråga;* **file interrogation** = questions asked to select various records *or* data items from a file *filförfrågan*

interrupt [,ɪntə'rʌpt] **1** *vb.* to stop something happening while it is happening *avbryta* **2** *subst.* **(a)** stopping of a transmission due to an action at the receiving end of a system *avbrott* **(b)** signal which diverts a central processing unit from one task to another which has higher priority, allowing the CPU to return to the first task later *avbrott;* **this printer port design uses an interrupt line to let the CPU know it is ready to receive data; armed interrupt** = interrupt line which has been made active (using an interrupt mask) *aktivt avbrottssignal (avbrottslinje);* **interrupt enable** = to arm an interrupt (by

setting a bit in the interrupt mask) *aktivera avbrott;* **interrupt disable** = to disable an interrupt (by resetting a bit in the interrupt mask to zero) *deaktivera avbrott;* **interrupt handler (IH)** = software that accepts interrupt signals and acts on them (such as running a special routine *or* sending data to a peripheral) *avbrottshanterare;* **interrupt level** = priority assigned to the interrupt from a peripheral *avbrottsnivå;* **interrupt line** = connection to a central processing unit from outside the system that allows external devices to use the CPU's interrupt facility *avbrottslinje;* **interrupt mask** = term in computer programming that selects which interrupt lines are to be activated *avbrottsmask;* **interrupt priorities** = deciding which interrupt is given highest priority *avbrottsprioritering; see also* NON-MASKABLE INTERRUPT; **interrupt request** = signal from a device that indicates to the CPU that it requires attention *avbrottsförfrågan;* **interrupt servicing** = carrying out some action when an interrupt is detected, such as running a routine *avbrottsbearbetning;* **interrupt signal** *see* INTERRUPT; **interrupt stacking** = storing interrupts in a queue and processing according to priority *avbrottslagring;* **maskable interrupt** = interrupt line that can be disabled and ignored using an interrupt mask *maskerbart avbrott;* **non-maskable interrupt (NMI)** = high priority interrupt signal that cannot be blocked and overrides all other commands *högprioriterat avbrott;* **polled interrupt** = interrupt signal determined by polling *avfrågat avbrott;* **transparent interrupt** = mode in which if an interrupt occurs, all machine and program states are saved, the interrupt is serviced then the system restores all previous states and continues normally *osynligt avbrott, omärkbart avbrott, avbrott med återställning;* **vectored interrupt** = interrupt which directs the CPU to transfer to a particular location *vektoriserat avbrott*

intersection [,ɪntə'sekʃ(ə)n] *subst.* logical function whose output is only true if both its inputs are true *konjunktion (i satslogik), snitt (i mängdlära)*

interstation muting ['ɪntə,steɪʃn 'mjuːtɪŋ] *subst.* ability of a radio receiver to prevent the noise found between radio stations from being amplified and heard by the user *brusdämpning*

interval ['ɪntəv(ə)l] *subst.* short pause between two actions *intervall, paus, mellanrum;* **there was an interval between pressing the key and the starting of the printout**

intervention [,ɪntə'venʃ(ə)n] *subst.* acting to make a change in a system *ingrepp*

interword spacing ['ıntə,wɜːd 'speısıŋ] *subst.* variable spacing between words in a text, used to justify lines *ordmellanrum*

intimate ['ıntımət] *subst.* software that operates and interacts closely with hardware in a system *systemnära program*

intrinsic [ın'trınsık] *adj.* pure (substance) which has had no other chemicals (such as dopants) added *naturlig, kemiskt ren;* **the base material for ICs is an intrinsic semiconductor which is then doped**

introduce [,ıntrə'djuːs] *vb.* to put something into something *införa, föra in;* **errors were introduced into the text at keyboarding**

intrusion [ın'truːʒ(ə)n] *subst.* action by a telephone operator to allow both parties on each end of the telephone line to hear his *or* her message *intrång, inkräktande*

intrång ⇨ **infringement**

in-ut ⇨ **I/O**

in-utanslutning ⇨ **input/output (I/O)**

in-utavbrott ⇨ **input/output (I/O)**

in-utbegränsad ⇨ **I/O**

in-utbibliotek ⇨ **input/output (I/O)**

in-utbuffert ⇨ **I/O**

in-utbuffertminne ⇨ **input/output (I/O)**

in-utbuss ⇨ **I/O**

in-utdata ⇨ **output (o/p**

in-ut(data)buss ⇨ **input/output (I/O)**

in-utdatareferens ⇨ **input/output (I/O)**

in-utdatastatusord ⇨ **input/output (I/O)**

in-utdatastyrprogram ⇨ **input/output (I/O)**

in-utdatasändning ⇨ **input/output (I/O)**

in-utenhet ⇨ **input/output (I/O), I/O, unit**

in-utfil ⇨ **I/O**

in-utfrågessignal ⇨ **input/output (I/O)**

in-utgränssnitt ⇨ **input/output (I/O), interface**

in-utgång ⇨ **I/O**

in-utinstruktion ⇨ **input/output (I/O), instruction, I/O**

in-utkanal ⇨ **input/output (I/O), I/O**

in-utkanalisering ⇨ **I/O**

in-utprocessor ⇨ **input/output (I/O), processor**

in-utregister ⇨ **input/output (I/O)**

in-utstyrenhet ⇨ **input/output (I/O)**

in-utstyrprogram ⇨ **input/output (I/O)**

invalid [ın'vælıd] *adj.* not valid *ogiltig;* **he tried to use an invalid password; the message was that the instruction was invalid**

inverse ['ın'vɜːs] *subst.* changing the logical state of a signal *or* device to its logical opposite *invertering;* **the inverse of true is false; the inverse of 1 is 0; inverse video =** television effect created by swapping the background and foreground text display colours *omvänd bild*

inversion [ın'vɜːʃ(ə)n] *subst.* changing over the numbers in a binary word (one to zero, zero to one) *inversion;* **the inversion of a binary digit takes place in one's complement**

invert [ın'vɜːt] *vb.* to change all binary ones to zeros and zeros to ones *invertera;* **inverted commas =** printing sign (") which is usually used to indicate a quotation *citationstecken;* **inverted file =** file with an index entry for all the data items *inverterad fil*

inverter [ın'vɜːtə] *subst.* **(a)** logical gate that provides inversion facilities *inverterare (fasvändare)* **(b)** circuit used to provide alternating current supply from a DC battery source *växelriktare, omformare;* **inverter (AC/DC) =** device which changes alternating current to direct current, or direct current to alternating current *likriktare, omformare*

inverterad fil ⇨ **file**

inverterare ⇨ **gate, NOT function**

invitation [,ınvı'teıʃ(ə)n] *subst.* action by a processor to contact another device to allow it to send a message *inbjudan, förfrågan, erbjudande;* **invitation to send (ITS) =** special character transmitted to indicate to a device that the host computer is willing to receive messages *sändningsbegäran*

invite [ın'vaıt] *vb.* to ask someone to do something *inbjuda, be*

invoke [ın'vəuk] *vb.* to start *or* run a program (often a memory resident utility) *väcka, kalla fram*

QUOTE when an error is detected, the editor may be invoked and positioned at the statement in error
Personal Computer World

involve [ın'vɒlv] *vb.* to have to do with; to include (something) in a process *inkludera, dra in, medföra;* **backing up involves**

copying current working files onto a separate storage disk

I/O ['input'autput] = INPUT/OUTPUT referring to the receiving *or* transmitting of data *in-ut;* **I/O bound** = processor that is doing very little processing since its time is taken up reading *or* writing data from a I/O port *in-utbegränsad;* **I/O buffer** = temporary storage area for data waiting to be input *or* output *in-utbuffert;* **I/O bus** = links allowing data and control signal transfer between a CPU and memory *or* peripheral devices *in-utbuss;* **I/O channel** = link between a processor and peripheral, allowing data transfer *in-utkanal;* **I/O device** = peripheral (such as a terminal in a workstation) which can be used for both inputting and outputting data to a processor *in-utenhet;* **I/O file** = file whose contents have been *or* will be transferred from storage to a peripheral *in-utfil;* **I/O instruction** = computer programming instruction that allows data to be input *or* output from a processor *in-utinstruktion;* **I/O mapping** = method of assigning a special address to each I/O port that does not use any memory locations *in-utkanalisering; compare with* MEMORY MAPPING; **I/O port** = circuit *or* connector that provides an input/output channel from a CPU to another device *in-utgång; see also* SERIAL PORT, PARALLEL PORT

ion ['aɪən] *subst.* charged particle *jon*

COMMENT: an ion is an atom that has gained *or* lost an extra electron, producing a negative *or* positive ion

ionosphere [aɪ'ɒnəsfɪə] *subst.* layer of charged particles surrounding the earth *jonosfär*

COMMENT: the ionosphere extends from 50km above the surface of the earth

IOP ['aɪəʊ'piː] = INPUT/OUTPUT PROCESSOR

IORQ ['aɪəʊɑː'kjuː] = INPUT/OUTPUT REQUEST

ip ['input] = INFORMATION PROVIDER company *or* user that provides an information source for use in a videotext system *informationslämnare;* **ip terminal** = special visual display unit that allows users to create and edit videotext pages before sending to the main videotext page database *redigeringsterminal*

i/p *or* **I/P** ['input] = INPUT

IPL ['aɪpiːel] = INITIAL PROGRAM LOADER

ips ['ɪn(t)ʃɪzpɜː'sek(ə)nd] = INCHES PER SECOND

IPSE [aɪpiːes'iː] = INTEGRATED PROJECT SUPPORT ENVIRONMENT

QUOTE one of the first aims of an IPSE is to provide a centralized information base into which all project data can be deposited in a form which enables all tools to exchange data
Electronics & Power

IR ['aɪɑː] **(a)** = INFORMATION RETRIEVAL **(b)** = INDEX REGISTER **(c)** = INSTRUCTION REGISTER

IRC ['aɪɑː'siː] = INFORMATION RETRIEVAL CENTRE

irretrievable [ɪrɪ'triːvəbl] *adj.* which cannot be retrieved *oåtkomlig, oåterhämtbar;* **the files are irretrievable since the computer crashed**

irreversible process [ɪrɪ'vɜːsəbl 'prəʊses] *subst.* process which, once carried out, cannot be reversed *oåterkallerlig process*

i runda tal ⇨ **figure**

IS ['aɪes] = INDEXED SEQUENTIAL

ISAM ['aɪeseɪem] = INDEXED SEQUENTIAL ACCESS METHOD

ISBN [aɪesbiː'en] = INTERNATIONAL STANDARD BOOK NUMBER

ISDN ['aɪesdiː'en] = INTEGRATED SERVICES DIGITAL NETWORK

ISO ['aɪes'əʊ] = INTERNATIONAL STANDARDS ORGANIZATION; **ISO/OSI** = INTERNATIONAL STANDARDS ORGANIZATION OPEN SYSTEM INTERCONNECTION

isolate ['aɪsəleɪt] *vb.* (i) to separate something from a system *isolera;* (ii) to insulate (something) electrically *isolera;* **isolated adaptive routing** = method of controlling message transmission path *isolerat anpassat vägval, isolerat adaptivt vägval;* **isolated location** = (hardware) storage location which cannot be directly accessed by a user's program, protecting it against accidental erasure *skyddad minnesposition (minnesarea)*

isolation [aɪsə(ʊ)'leɪʃ(ə)n] *subst.* being isolated *isolering;* **isolation transformer** = transformer used to isolate equipment from direct connection with the mains electricity supply, in case of voltage spikes etc. *isolationstransformator*

isolator ['aɪsəleɪtə] *subst.* device *or* material which isolates *isolator*

isotropic [aɪsə(ʊ)'trɒpɪk] *adj.* with the same properties in all dimensions and directions *isotrop;* **isotropic radiator** = antenna that transmits in all directions *isotropantenn*

ISR ['aɪesɑː] = INFORMATION STORAGE AND RETRIEVAL

ISSN ['aɪesesˈen] = INTERNATIONAL STANDARD SERIAL NUMBER

IT ['aɪˈtiː] = INFORMATION TECHNOLOGY

italic [ɪˈtælɪk] *adj. & subst.* type of character font in which the characters slope to the right *kursiv;* **the headline is printed in italic and underlined; italics =** italic characters *kursiv stil;* **all the footnotes are printed in italics; hit CTRL I to print the text in italics**

item ['aɪtəm] *subst.* single thing among many *enhet;* **a data item can be a word** *or* **a series of figures** *or* **a record in a file; item size =** number of characters *or* digits in an item of data *enhetsstorlek*

iterate ['ɪtəreɪt] *or* **iterative routine** ['ɪtərətɪv ruːˈtiːn] *subst.* loop *or* series of instructions in a program which repeat over and over again until the program is completed *slinga, iterering*

iteration [ˌɪtəˈreɪʃ(ə)n] *subst.* repeated application of a program to solve a problem *iteration*

iterative process ['ɪtərətɪv 'prəʊses] *subst.* process that is continuously repeated until a condition is met *iterativ process*

ITS ['aɪtiˈes] = INVITATION TO SEND

Jj

jack [dʒæk] *subst.* plug which consists of a single pin *(tele)plugg;* **data jack =** plug that allows a modem to be connected directly to the telephone system *modemkontakt*

jacket ['dʒækɪt] *subst.* cover for a book *or* disk *skyddsomslag;* **the book jacket has the author's name on it**

jam [dʒæm] **1** *subst.* process *or* mechanism which has stopped working due to a fault *krångel, stopp, låsning;* **a jam in the paper feed 2** *vb.* **(a)** *(of a device)* to stop working because something is blocking the functioning *krångla, fastna, låsa sig;* **the recorder's not working because the tape is jammed in the motor; lightweight copier paper will feed without jamming (b)** to prevent a transmission from being correctly received by transmitting a strong noise at the same frequency (often used to prevent unauthorized transmission) *störa, blockera;* **the TV signals are being jammed from that tower**

jar [dʒɑː] *vb.* to give a sharp shock to a device *skaka till;* **you can cause trouble by turning off or jarring the PC while the disk**

read heads are moving; hard disks are very sensitive to jarring

JCL ['dʒeɪsiˈel] = JOB CONTROL LANGUAGE commands that describe the identification of and resources required by a job that a computer has to process *jobbstyrspråket JCL från IBM (avsett för programmering av styrning av satsvisa körningar i stordatorer)*

jet [dʒet] *see* INK-JET

jingle ['dʒɪŋgl] *subst.* short easily-remembered tune used to advertise a product on television *jingel, musiksnutt*

jitter ['dʒɪtə] *subst.* fault where there is rapid small up-and-down movement of characters *or* pixels on a screen of image bits in a facsimile transmission *jitter;* **looking at this screen jitter is giving me a headache**

JK-flip-flop ['dʒeɪˈkeɪ 'flɪpflɒp] *subst.* flip-flop device with two inputs (J and K) and two complementary outputs that are dependent on the inputs *JK-vippa*

job [dʒɒb] *subst.* task *or* number of tasks *or* work to be processed as a single unit *uppgift, uppdrag, jobb;* **the next job to be processed is to sort all the records; job control file =** file which contains instructions in a JCL *jobbstyrfil;* **job control language (JCL) =** commands that describe the identification of and resources required by a job that a computer has to process *jobbstyrspråk;* **job control program =** short program of job control instructions loaded before a particular application is run, that sets up the system as required by the application *jobbstyrprogram;* **job file =** file containing jobs *or* job names waiting to be processed *jobbfil;* **job mix =** the jobs being executed at any one time in a system *uppdragsmix;* **job number =** number which is given to a job in a queue, waiting to be processed *jobbnummer;* **job orientated language =** computer programming language that provides specialized instructions relating to job control tasks and processing *uppdragsorienterat språk;* **job orientated terminal =** computer terminal designed for and used for a particular task *specialiserad terminal;* **job priority =** importance of a job compared to others *uppdragsprioritet;* **job processing =** to read in job control instructions from an input source and execute them *jobbearbetning;* **job queue** *or* **job stream =** number of tasks arranged in an order waiting to be processed in a multitasking *or* batch system *jobbkö, jobbström;* **job scheduling =** arranging the order in which jobs are processed *jobbplanering;* **job statement control =** use of instructions and statements to control the actions of the operating system of a computer *uppdragsstyrning;* **job step** *or* **stream** = one unit of processing involved in a task *arbetssteg;* **remote job entry (RJE)** = use of an interactive user terminal to enter job control instructions *fjärrinmatning av jobb enligt IBMs RJE-system;* **stacked job control** = queue of job control instructions that are processed in the order in which they were received *jobbkö*

jobbearbetning ⇨ **job**

jobbfil ⇨ **job**

jobbing printer ['dʒɒbɪŋ 'prɪntə] *subst.* person who does small printing jobs, such as printing business cards *accidenstryckare*

jobbkö ⇨ **job**

jobbnummer ⇨ **job**

jobbplanering ⇨ **job**

jobbslutssignal ⇨ **end**

jobbström ⇨ **job**

jobbstyrfil ⇨ **job**

jobbstyrprogram ⇨ **job**

jobbstyrspråk ⇨ **job**

jog [dʒɒg] *vb.* to advance a video tape by one frame at a time *enbildsmatning*

joggle ['dʒɒgl] *vb.* to align a stack of punched cards *or* sheets of paper *stöta, kupera*

join [dʒɔɪn] **1** *vb.* **(a)** to put several things together *lägga samman* **(b)** to combine two or more pieces of information to produce a single unit of information *lägga samman, kombinera;* **join files** = instruction to produce a new file consisting of one file added to the end of another *slå samman filer, kombinera filer* **2** *subst.* logical function that produces a true output if any input is true *konjunktion*

joint denial ['dʒɔɪntdɪ'naɪ(ə)l] *subst.* logical function whose output is false if any input is true *negerad konjunktion*

jord ⇨ **earth, ground, neutral**

jorda ⇨ **earth**

jordledning ⇨ **earth**

journal ['dʒɜːnl] *subst.* **(a)** record of all communications to and from a terminal *journal, loggfil, felkatalogfil;* **journal file** = stored record of every communication between a user and the central computer, used to help retrieve files after a system crash *or* fault *loggfil* **(b)** list of any changes *or* updates to a file *aktualiseringsfil;* **the modified records were added to the master file and noted in the journal (c)** learned

journal = specialized magazine *facktidskrift*

journalist ['dʒɜːnəlɪst] *subst.* person who writes for a newspaper *journalist*

joystick ['dʒɔɪstɪk] *subst.* device that allows a user to move a cursor around the screen by moving an upright rod connected to an I/O port on the computer *styrspak;* **joystick port** = circuit and connector used to interface a joystick with a computer *ingång för styrspak;* **a joystick port is provided with the home computer**

COMMENT: mostly used for computer games or CAD or desktop publishing packages

judder ['dʒʌdə] *subst.* unwanted movement in a printing *or* facsimile machine that results in a distorted picture *skakning, vibration*

jumbo chip ['dʒʌmbəʊ 'tʃɪp] *subst.* integrated circuit made using the whole of a semiconductor wafer *jättekrets; see also* WAFER SCALE INTEGRATION

COMMENT: these devices are very new and proving rather difficult to manufacture without faults to any of the thousands of gates on the surface; when working, these devices will be extremely powerful

jumper ['dʒʌmpə] *subst.* temporary wire connection on a circuit board *omkopplare;* **jumper-selectable** = circuit *or* device whose options can be selected by positioning various wire connections *omkopplingsbar (med strömställare);* **the printer's typeface was jumper-selectable**

jump (instruction) [dʒʌmp (ɪn'strʌkʃ(ə)n] **1** *subst.* programming command to end one set of instructions and direct the processor to another section of the program *hopp;* **conditional jump** = situation where the processor is directed to another section of the program only if a condition is met *villkorat hopp;* **jump operation** = situation where the CPU is sent from the instruction it is currently executing to another point in the program *hoppoperation;* **unconditional jump** = instruction which transfers control from one point in the program to another, without requiring any condition to be met *ovillkorligt hopp* **2** *vb.* **(a)** to direct a CPU to another section of a program *hoppa;* **jump on zero** = conditional jump executed if a flag *or* register is zero *hoppa om flaggan är noll* **(b)** to miss a page *or* a line *or* a space when printing *hoppa över;* **the typewriter jumped two lines; the paging system has jumped two folio numbers**

junction ['dʒʌŋ(k)ʃ(ə)n] *subst.* **(a)** connection between wires *or* cables *koppling;* **junction box** = small box where a number of wires can be interconnected *kopplingslåda* **(b)** region between two areas of semiconductor which have different doping levels (such as a p-type and n-type area), resulting in a potential difference between them *övergång, övergångsskikt;* **bipolar junction transistor (BJT)** = transistor constructed of 3 layers of alternating types of doped semiconductor (p-n-p *or* n-p-n), each layer having a terminal labelled as emitter, base and collector *bipolär transistor;* usually the base controls the current flow between emitter and collector *övergång*

junk [dʒʌŋk] **1** *subst.* information *or* hardware which is useless *or* out-of-date *or* non-functional *skräp;* **junk mail** = form letters containing special offers *or* advertisements *direktreklam;* **space junk** = satellites and hardware that are out of action and no longer used, but are still in orbit in space *rymdskrot* **2** *vb.* to get rid of a file *radera, skrota;* to make a file *or* piece of hardware redundant *radera, skrota;* **to junk a file** = to erase *or* delete from storage a file that is no longer used *radera en fil*

justera ⊳ adjust, justify

justification [ˌdʒʌstɪfɪˈkeɪʃ(ə)n] *subst.* moving data bits *or* characters to the left *or* right so that the lines have straight margins *utslutning, radjustering;* **hyphenation and justification** *or* **J** = justifying lines to a set width, splitting the long words correctly at the end of each line *avstavning och radjustering;* **an American hyphenation and justification program will not work with British English spellings**

justify [ˈdʒʌstɪfaɪ] *vb.* **(a)** to change the spacing between words *or* characters in a document so that the left and right margins will be straight *justera;* **justify inhibit** = to prevent a word processor justifying a document *förhindra radjustering;* **justify margin** *see* LEFT *or* RIGHT JUSTIFY; **hyphenate and justify** = to break long words correctly where they split at the ends of lines, so as to give a straight right margin *avstava och justera;* **left justify** = to print with a straight left-hand margin *rak vänstermarginal;* **right justify** = to print with a straight right-hand margin *rak högermarginal* **(b)** to shift the contents of a computer register by a set amount *skifta*

juxtaposition [ˌdʒʌkstəpəˈzɪʃ(ə)n] *subst.* arranging *or* placing items next to or adjacent to each other *sammanställning*

jämföra ⊳ compare

jämförbar ⊳ comparable

jämn paritet ⊳ parity

järnoxid ⊳ ferric oxide

jättekrets ⊳ jumbo chip

Kk

K [keɪ] *prefix* **(a)** = KILO symbol used to represent one thousand *k, kilo-***(b)** symbol used to represent 1,024, equal to 2^{10} *k, kilo*

kabel ⊳ cable

kabeltrumma ⊳ duct

kablage ⊳ cabling

kalenderprogram ⊳ diary

kalibrering ⊳ calibration

kalkylator ⊳ calculator

kalkyl(matris)program ⊳ spreadsheet

kalligrafi ⊳ calligraphy

kallödning ⊳ dry joint

kamera ⊳ camera

kanal ⊳ channel

kanalkö ⊳ queue

kanalmellanrum ⊳ guard band

kantkontakt ⊳ edge

kantperforering ⊳ sprocket holes

kapacitans ⊳ capacitance

kapacitet ⊳ capacity, throughput

kapitäler ⊳ small

Karnaugh map [ˈkɑːnɔːˌmæp] *subst.* graphical representation of states and conditions in a logic circuit *Karnaughdiagram;* **the prototype was checked for hazards with a Karnaugh map**

karta ⊳ chart, map

kassaterminal ⊳ EPOS, point-of-sale (POS)

kassera ⊳ reject

kassett ⊳ cartridge, cassette, magnetic

katalog ⊳ catalogue, index, main

katalogkort ⊳ index

katod ⊳ cathode

katodsstrålerör ⊳ CRT

katodstrålerör ⊳ cathode ray tube (CRT), television (TV)

KB ['kɪlə(ʊ)baɪt] *or* **K byte** ['kɪlə(ʊ)baɪt] = KILOBYTE unit of measure for high capacity storage devices meaning 1,024 bytes *kbyte;* **the new disk drive has a 100KB capacity; the original PC cannot access more than 640K bytes of RAM**

COMMENT: 1,024 is the strict definition in computer or electronics applications, being equal to a convenient power of two; these abbreviations can also be taken to equal approximately one thousand, even in computing applications. 1KB is roughly equal to 1,000 output characters in a PC

Kb ['kɪləbɪt] = KILOBIT ['kɪlə(ʊ)baɪt] measure of 1,024 bits *kbit*

kbit ⇨ **Kb**

kbyte ⇨ **KB**

kedja ⇨ **chain**

kedjebuss ⇨ **chain**

kedjekoppla ⇨ **daisy-chain**

kedjekopplade enheter ⇨ **ganged**

kedjekoppling ⇨ **daisy chain**

kedjelista ⇨ **list**

kedjelänk ⇨ **chain**

kedjeskrivare ⇨ **printer**

kedjesökning ⇨ **search**

kernel ['kɜːnl] *subst.* basic essential instruction routines required as a basis for any operations in a computer system *kärna;* **graphics kernel system (gks)** = number of basic commands required to illuminate in various shades and colours the pixels on a screen (these are then used to provide more complex functions such as line *or* shape plotting) *GKS-systemet*

COMMENT: kernel routines are usually hidden from the user; they are used by the operating system for tasks such as loading a program or displaying text on a screen

kerning ['kɜːnɪŋ] *subst.* slight overlapping of certain printed character areas to prevent large spaces between them, giving a neater appearance *kerning*

kerning ⇨ **kerning**

key [kiː] **1** *subst.* **(a)** button on a keyboard that operates a switch *tangent;* **there are 64 keys on the keyboard; key click** = sound produced by a computer to allow the operator to know that the key he pressed has been registered *tangentklick;* **key force** = pressure required to close the switch in a key *anslagskraft;* **key matrix** = design of interconnections between keys on a keyboard *tangentmatris;* **key number** = numeric code used to identify which key

has been pressed *tangentnummer;* **key overlay** = paper placed over the keys on a keyboard describing their functions for a particular application *tangentbordsmall;* **without the key overlay, I would never remember which function key does what; key punch** = machine used for punching data into punched cards by means of a keyboard *kortstans, handstans;* **key rollover** = use of a buffer between the keyboard and computer to provide rapid key stroke storage for fast typists who hit several keys in rapid succession *tangentbordsbuffert;* **key strip** = piece of paper above certain keys used to remind the operator of their special functions *tangentbordsmall;* **key travel** = distance a key has to be pressed before it registers *anslagsanhåll* **(b)** *(names of keys)* **alphanumeric key** *or* **character key** = key which produces a character (letter *or* symbol *or* figure) *teckentangent;* **carriage return key** = key which moves a cursor *or* printhead to the beginning of the next line on screen *or* on a typewriter *or* in printing *(vagn)returtangent;* **function key** = key which has a specific task *or* sequence of instructions *funktionstangent;* **tags can be allocated to function keys; shift key** = key which provides a second function for a key (usually by moving the output into upper case) *skifttangent* **(c)** important object *or* group of characters in a computer system, used to represent an instruction *or* set of data *nyckel-;* **key plate** = initial printing plate used when printing colour images *konturplåt;* **key terminal** = most important terminal in a computer system *or* one with the highest priority *huvudterminal, konsolsystem* **(d)** special combination of numbers *or* characters that are used with a cipher to encrypt *or* decrypt a message *nyckel;* **type this key into the machine, that will decode the last message; key management** = the selection, protection and safe transmission of cipherkeys *nyckelhantering* **(e)** identification code *or* word used for a stored record *or* data item *nyckel, etikett;* **we selected all the records with the word DISK in their keys; index key** = one field which is used to index a record *nyckelfält, indexfält;* **key field** = field which identifies entries in a record *nyckelfält, indexfält;* **keyed sequential access method (KSAM)** = file structure that allows data to be accessed using key fields or key field content *KSAM (metod för datasökning)* **2** *vb.* **to key in** = to enter text *or* commands via a keyboard *skriva in;* **they keyed in the latest data**

QUOTE where large orders are being placed over the telephone it is easy to key them into the micro
Micro Decision

keyboard ['kiːbɔːd] **1** *subst.* number of keys fixed together in some order, used to enter information into a computer *or* to produce characters on a typewriter *tangentbord;* **keyboard to disk entry** = system where information entered on a keyboard is stored directly on to disk with no processing *direktinskrivning;* **ANSI keyboard** = standard for a keyboard that provides either upper case or upper and lower case characters on a typewriter style keyboard *ANSI-tangentbord;* **ASCII keyboard** = keyboard that provides a key for every ASCII code *ASCII-tangentbord;* **ASR keyboard** = communications console keyboard that has all the characters and punctuation keys and special control, send and receive keys *ASR-tangentbord;* **AZERTY keyboard** = non-English language key layout (the first six letters on the top left row of the keyboard being AZERTY) *AZERTY-tangentbord;* **interactive keyboard** = keyboard that helps to direct the user *or* prompts for an input by lighting up certain keys on the keyboard (under program control) *interaktivt tangentbord;* **keyboard contact bounce** = multiple signals from a key pressed just once, due to a faulty switch and key bounce *kontaktstuds(signaler);* **keyboard encoder** = way in which each key generates a unique word when pressed *tangentbordskodare;* **keyboard layout** = way in which various function and character keys are arranged *tangentbordslayout;* **keyboard overlay** = paper placed over the keys on a keyboard describing their special functions for a particular application *tangentbordsmall;* **keyboard scan** = method for a computer to determine if a key has been pressed by applying a voltage across each key switch (if the key is pressed a signal will be read by the computer) *tangentbordsavsökning;* **keyboard send/receive (KSR)** = terminal which has a keyboard and monitor, and is linked to a CPU *tangentbordsterminal;* **keyboard to disk entry** = system where information entered on a keyboard is stored directly onto disk with no processing *direktinskrivning;* **QWERTY keyboard** = standard English language key layout (the first six letters on the top left row of keys are QWERTY) *QWERTY-tangentbord;* **touch sensitive keyboard** = thin, flat membrane type keyboard whose keys are activated by touching the particular key, with no movement involved (often used for heavy duty or dirty environments where normal keys would not function correctly) *membrantangentbord* **2** *vb.* to enter information by using a keyboard *skriva in;* **it was cheaper to have the manuscript keyboarded by another company**

QUOTE the new keyboard is almost unchanged, and features sixteen programmable function keys
Micro Decision
QUOTE the main QWERTY typing area is in the centre of the keyboard with the 10 function keys on the left
Personal Computer World

keyboarder ['ki:,bɔːdə] *subst.* person who enters data via a keyboard *stansare, stansoperatör/stansoperatris, inskrivare*

keyboarding ['ki:,bɔːdɪŋ] *subst.* action of entering data using a keyboard *instansning, inskrivning;* **the cost of keyboarding is calculated in keystrokes per hour**

keypad ['ki:pæd] *subst.* group of special keys used for certain applications *tangentbord, knappsats;* **you can use the numeric keypad to enter the figures; hex keypad** = keypad with 16 keys (0-9 and A-F) for all the hexadecimal digits *hexadecimalt tangentbord;* **numeric keypad** = set of ten keys with figures (0-9), included in most computer keyboards as a separate group, used for entering large amounts of data in numeric form *numeriskt tangentbord*

QUOTE it uses a six button keypad to select the devices and functions
Byte

keystroke ['ki:strəʊk] *subst.* action of pressing a key *anslag, nedslag;* **he keyboards at a rate of 3500 keystrokes per hour; keystroke count** = counting of each keystroke made, often used to calculate keyboarding costs *nedslagsräkning;* **keystroke verification** = check made on each key pressed to make sure it is valid for a particular application *teckenkontroll, inmatningskontroll*

key-to-disk ['ki:tuːˈdɪsk] *subst.* system where data is keyed in and stored directly on disk without any processing *direktinskrivning*

keyword ['ki:wɜːd] *subst.* (i) command word used in a programming language to provide a function *kommando(ord);* (ii) important *or* informative word in a title *or* document that describes its contents *nyckelord;* (iii) word which is relevant *or* important to a text *nyckelord;* **the BASIC keyword PRINT will display text on the screen; computer is a keyword in IT; keyword and context (KWAC)** = library index system using important words from the text and title as index entries *KWAC-register;* **keyword in context (KWIC)** = library index system that uses keywords from the title *or* text of a book *or* document as an indexed entry, followed by the title *or*text it relates to *KWIC-register;* **keyword out of context (KWOC)** = library index system that indexes book *or* document titles under any relevant keywords *KWOC-register*

kHz ['kɪlə(ʊ)hɜːts] = KILOHERTZ unit of frequency measurement equal to one thousand Hertz *kHz; see also* HERTZ

kill [kɪl] *vb.* to erase a file *or* stop a program during execution *radera, avbryta;*

kill file = command to erase a stored file completely *raderingskommando;* **kill job** = command to halt a computer job while it is running *avbrottskommando*

kilo ['ki:ləʊ] *prefix* **(a)** meaning one thousand *kilo, k;* **kilobaud** = 1,000 bits per second *kilobaud;* **kilohertz** *or* **KHz** = unit of frequency measurement equal to one thousand Hertz *kHz;* **kilo instructions per second (KIPS)** = one thousand computer instructions processed every second, used as a measure of computer power *tusen instruktioner per sekund;* **kilo-ohm** = resistance of one thousand ohms *kohm;* **kiloVolt-ampere output rating (KVA)** = method of measuring the power rating of a device *(effektmått) kVA;* **kilowatt** *or* **kW** = power measurement equal to one thousand watts *kW* **(b)** meaning 1,024 units, equal to 2^{10} (used only in computer and electronics applications) *kilo, k;* **kilobit** *or* **Kb** = 1,024 bits of data *kbit (Kb);* **kilobyte** *or* **KB** *or* **Kbyte** = unit of measurement for high capacity storage devices meaning 1,024 bytes of data *kbyte (KB);* **kiloword** *or* **KW** = unit of measurement of 1,024 computer words *kord (KW)*

kimball-etikett ⇨ **kimball tag**

kimball tag ['kɪmbəltæg] *subst.* coded card attached to a product in a shop, containing information about the product that is read by a scanner when the product is sold *streckkodsetikett, magnetetikett, kimball-etikett*

KIPS [kips] = KILO INSTRUCTIONS PER SECOND one thousand computer instructions processed every second, used as a measure of computer power *kips*

kisel ⇨ **silicon**

kiselchip ⇨ **silicon**

kiselkrets ⇨ **silicon**

kiselskiva ⇨ **silicon, wafer**

klar ⇨ **complete**

klarsignal ⇨ **enable**

klick ⇨ **click**

klippa-klistra ⇨ **cut and paste**

klocka ⇨ **clock**

klockfixerad process ⇨ **fix**

klockfrekvens ⇨ **frequency**

klockregister ⇨ **timer**

klocksignal ⇨ **fetch**

klocktecken ⇨ **bell character**

kludge [klu:dʒ] *or* **kluge** [klu:dʒ] *subst. informal* (i) temporary correction made to

a badly written *or* constructed piece of software *or* to a keyboarding error *hoplappning, fix;* (ii) hardware which should be used for demonstration purposes only *demonstrationsmaskin, prototyp*

kluged [klu:dʒd] *adj.* temporarily repaired *hoplappad*

knapp ⇨ **knob**

knappsats ⇨ **keypad**

knapptelefon ⇨ **pushbutton**

knipning ⇨ **intercharacter spacing**

knob [nɒb] *subst.* round button (such as on a monitor), which can be turned to control some process *ratt, knapp;* **turn the on/off knob; the brightness can be regulated by turning a knob at the back of the monitor**

knowledge ['nɒlɪdʒ] *subst.* what is known *kunskap;* **intelligent-knowledge based system (IKBS)** = software that applies the knowledge, advice and rules defined by experts in a particular subject, to a user's data to help solve a problem *expertsystem, kunskapsbaserat system;* **knowledge-based system** = computer system that applies the stored reactions, instructions and knowledge of experts in a particular field to a problem *kunskapsbaserat system; see also* EXPERT SYSTEM; **knowledge engineering** = designing and writing expert computer systems *kunskapsingenjörsarbete*

kod ⇨ **code, language**

koda (in) ⇨ **encode**

kodgenerator ⇨ **generator**

kodkrets ⇨ **dongle**

kodning ⇨ **encoding**

kodningsformat ⇨ **encoding**

kolpulver ⇨ **toner**

kombinera ⇨ **combine**

kombinerande ⇨ **combinational**

kommando ⇨ **command**

kommandofönster ⇨ **window**

kommando(ord) ⇨ **keyword**

kommandospråk ⇨ **language**

komma(tecken) ⇨ **comma**

kommentar ⇨ **annotation, comment**

kommunicera ⇨ **communicate**

kommunikation ⇨ **communication**

kommunikationsbuffert ⇨ **data**

kommunikationsdator ⇨ **FEP**

kommunikationskanal ⇨ information

kommunikationslänk ⇨ link

kommunikationsnät ⇨ network

kompakt ⇨ compact

kompandera ⇨ companding

kompatibilitet ⇨ compatibility

kompilator ⇨ compiler (program), language

kompilering ⇨ compilation

kompileringsfel ⇨ error

komplement ⇨ complement

komplementär ⇨ complementary

komplex ⇨ complex

komplexitet ⇨ complexity

komplicerad ⇨ complicated

komponent ⇨ component

komprimera ⇨ compress

koncentrator ⇨ data

koncentratorcentral ⇨ data

kondensator ⇨ capacitor

konferens ⇨ conference

konfiguration ⇨ configuration

konfigurering ⇨ configuration

konfigurering(s rutin) ⇨ interlude

konjunktion ⇨ conjunction, intersection, join

konkatenera ⇨ concatenate

konsol ⇨ console

konstant ⇨ constant

konstgjord ⇨ man-made

konstruera ⇨ construct

konstruerad ⇨ man-made

konstruktion ⇨ construction

konsult ⇨ consultant

konsultera ⇨ consult

kontakt ⇨ connector, contact, socket

kontakta ⇨ call in

kontaktstift ⇨ pin

kontaktstuds(signaler) ⇨ keyboard

kontorsautomation ⇨ office

kontorsutrustning ⇨ equipment

kontrast ⇨ contrast

kontroll ⇨ check

kontrollera ⇨ check, control

kontrollpunkt ⇨ trace, trap

kontrollsiffra ⇨ digit

kontrollstavning ⇨ spellcheck

kontrollstyrning ⇨ control

kontrollsumma ⇨ hash, total

kontroll(tangent) ⇨ CTR

kontrolltecken ⇨ digit

konturigenkänning ⇨ edge

koordinater ⇨ coordinate

kopia ⇨ clone, copy, duplicate, image

kopiator ⇨ copier, machine

kopiera ⇨ copy, duplicate, replicate

kopiering ⇨ replication, transcription

kopieringsmaskin ⇨ copier, duplicating, machine

kopieringspapper ⇨ duplicating

kopieringsskydd ⇨ copy protection

koppar ⇨ copper

koppla ⇨ connect, couple

koppla samman ⇨ interconnect

koppling ⇨ interconnection, junction

kopplingslåda ⇨ junction

kopplingston ⇨ dialling

kord ⇨ kilo

korrektur ⇨ machine, proof

korrektur(avdrag) ⇨ proof

korrekturtecken ⇨ mark

korrigera ⇨ correct, rectify

korsassemblerare ⇨ assembler (program)

korskompilator ⇨ cross-compiler

(kors)referenstabell ⇨ table

kort ⇨ card

kortkatalog ⇨ card index

kortläsare ⇨ card, magnetic

kortmatare ⇨ hopper

kortpacke ⇨ deck, pack

kortplats ⇨ expansion, slot

kortregister ⇨ card index, file

kortstans ⇨ key

kraftaggregat ⇨ PSU

kraftigt olinjär ⇨ transient

krasch ⇨ crash

kraschskyddad ⇨ crash-protected

krav ⇨ requirements

kredit ⇨ credit

kredittid ⇨ credit

krets ⇨ circuit

kretsemulator ⇨ in-circuit emulator

kretskort ⇨ laminate

krets(korts)konstruktion ⇨ design

kretsvalssignal ⇨ select

kringutrustning ⇨ peripheral

kristall ⇨ crystal

kryptera ⇨ encrypt

kryptografisk ⇨ cryptographic

KSR ['keɪes'ɑː] = KEYBOARD SEND/RECEIVE terminal which has a keyboard and monitor, and is linked to a CPU *tangentbordsterminal; compare with* ASR

kulskrivare ⇨ golf-ball

kulskrivmaskin ⇨ golf-ball

kund ⇨ customer

kundanpassa ⇨ customize

kunskapsbaserat system ⇨ knowledge

kunskapsingenjörsarbete ⇨ knowledge

kupera ⇨ joggle

kursiv ⇨ italic

kursiv stil ⇨ italic

kurvritare ⇨ graph, plotter

kurvskrivare ⇨ graph, plotter

KVA ['keɪviːˈeɪ] = KILOVOLT-AMPERE OUTPUT RATING

kvalitet ⇨ quality

kvantiseringsbrus ⇨ quantize

kvantiseringsfel ⇨ error

kvantitet ⇨ quantity

kvartil ⇨ quartile

kvartsur ⇨ quartz (crystal) clock

kvicksilverminne ⇨ mercury delay line

kvintett ⇨ quintet

kvittenssignal ⇨ ACK

kvitteringssignal ⇨ acknowledge

KW ['kiːlə(ʊ)wɜːd] = KILOWORD

KWAC [kwæk] = KEYWORD AND CONTEXT library indexing system using important words from the text and title as indexed entries *KWAC-register*

KWIC [kwɪk] = KEYWORD IN CONTEXT library indexing system that uses keywords from the title *or* text of a book *or* document as an indexed entry followed by the text it relates to *KWIC-register*

KWOC [kwɒk] = KEYWORD OUT OF CONTEXT library indexing system that indexes books *or* document titles under any relevant keywords *KWOC-register*

kylfläns ⇨ heat-sink

källkod ⇨ source

källspråk ⇨ language

känna igen ⇨ recognize

känselåterkoppling ⇨ tactile

kärna ⇨ core

kärnminne ⇨ magnetic

kö ⇨ queue

köhanterare ⇨ queue

kömellanlagring ⇨ spooling

köminne ⇨ FIFO

kömodell ⇨ queue

köra ⇨ execute, run

körfas ⇨ execute

körfel ⇨ error

körläge ⇨ execute

körning ⇨ execution, run

körsignal ⇨ execute

körtid ⇨ execution, run-time

kötid ⇨ time

Ll

label ['leɪbl] **1 (a)** *subst.* (i) word *or* other symbol used in a computer program to

identify a routine *or* statement *etikett;* (ii) character(s) used to identify a variable *or* piece of data *or* a file *etikett;* **BASIC uses many program labels such as line numbers; label field =** an item of data in a record that contains a label *etikettfält;* **label record =** record containing identification for a stored file *filetikett* **(b)** piece of paper *or* card attached to something to show instructions for use *or* an address *etikett;* **external label =** identifying piece of paper stuck to the outside of a device *or* disk *etikett* **2** *vb.* to print an address on a label *etikettera, märka*
NOTE: **labelling - labelled** but US **labeling - labeled**

labelling ['leɪblɪŋ] *subst.* printing labels *etikettering;* **the word-processor has a special utility allowing simple and rapid labelling**
NOTE: no plural

laboratory [ləˈbɒrət(ə)rɪ] *subst.* place where scientists work on research and development of new products *laboratorium;* **the new chip is being developed in the university laboratories**

ladda om ⇨ **reload**

laddläge ⇨ **load point**

laddning ⇨ **charge**

laddningsband ⇨ **trailer**

laddningsrutin ⇨ **loader**

lag [læg] *subst.* **(a)** time taken for a signal to pass through a circuit, such that the output is delayed compared to the input *eftersläpning, fördröjning;* **time lag is noticeable on international phone calls (b)** time taken for an image to be no longer visible after it has been displayed on a CRT screen (this is caused by long persistence phosphor) *efterlysning*

lagra ⇨ **save, store**

lagring efter frekvens ⇨ **activity**

lagringsmedium ⇨ **file**

lagringsversion ⇨ **generation**

laminate ['læmɪneɪt] **1** *vb.* to cover a paper with a thin film of plastic, to give it a glossy look *laminera, lamellera;* **the book has a laminated cover 2** *subst.* *kretskortslaminat, kretskort*

LAN [læn] *or* **lan** = LOCAL AREA NETWORK network where various terminals and equipment are all within a short distance of one another (at a maximum distance of about 500m, for example in the same building), and can be interconnected by cables *lokalt nät, lokalt datanät;* **LAN server =** dedicated computer and backing storage facility used by terminals and operators of a LAN *nätcentral, filcentral; compare* WAN

> QUOTE since most of the LAN hardware is already present, the installation costs are only $50 per connection
> **Practical Computing**

landledning ⇨ **landline**

landline ['lændlaɪn] *subst.* permanent direct link using cables laid in the ground between two points *landledning*

landsnummer ⇨ **international**

language ['læŋgwɪdʒ] *subst.* **(a)** spoken *or* written words which are used to communicate with other people *språk;* **he speaks several European languages; foreign language =** language which is spoken by people of another country *främmande språk* **(b)** system of words *or* symbols which allows communication with computers (such as one that allows computer instructions to be entered as words which are easy to understand, and then translates them into machine code) *programmeringsspråk, kod;* **assembly language** *or* **assembler language =** programming language using mnemonics to code instructions which will then be converted to machine code *assemblerspråk;* **command language =** programming language made up of procedures for various tasks, that can be called up by a series of commands *kommandospråk;* **control language =** commands that identify and describe the resources required by a job that a computer has to perform *styrspråk;* **graphic language =** computer programming language with inbuilt commands that are useful when displaying graphics *grafiskt programmeringsspråk;* **high-level language (HLL) =** computer programming language that is easy to learn and allows the user to write programs using words and commands that are easy to understand and look like English words, the program is then translated into machine code, with one HLL instruction often representing more than one machine code instruction *högnivåspråk;* **low-level language (LLL) =** language which is fast, but long and complex to program in, where each instruction represents a single machine code instruction *maskinkod, assemblerspråk;* **machine language =** programming language that consists of commands in binary code form that can be directly understood by the CPU *maskinkod;* **programming language =** software that allows a user to enter a program in a certain language and then to execute it *programmeringsspråk;* **query language =** language in a database management system that allows a database to be easily searched and queried *frågespråk;* **source language** = original language in which a program is written prior to processing by a computer *källspråk;* **language assembler** = program used to translate and assemble a source code program into a machine executable binary form *assemblerare;* **language compiler** = software that converts an encoded source program into another (machine code) form, and then executes it *kompilator;* **language interpreter** = any program that takes each consecutive line of source program and translates it into another (machine code) language at run-time *interpretator, översättare, tolk;* **language processor** = language translator from one language to machine code (there are three types of language processor:(i) assembler *assemblerare;* (ii) compiler *kompilator;* (iii) interpreter *interpreterare, tolk;* **language rules** = syntax and format for instructions and data items used in a particular language *språkstruktur, syntax;* **language support environment** = hardware and software tools supplied to help the programmer write programs in a particular language *programmeringsmiljö;* **language translation** = using a computer to translate text from one language to another *maskinöversättning;* **language translator** = program that converts code written in one language into equivalent instructions in another language *översättningsprogram*

COMMENT: There are three main types of computer languages: machine code, assembler and high-level language. The higher the level the language is, the easier it is to program and understand, but the slower it is to execute. The following are the commonest high-level languages: ADA, ALGOL, APL, BASIC, C, COBOL, COMAL, CORAL, FORTH, FORTRAN, LISP, LOGO, PASCAL, PL/1, POP-2, PROLOG. Assembly language uses mnemonics to represent machine code instructions; machine code is the basic binary patterns that instruct the processor to perform various tasks

lansera ⇨ **launch, release**

lansering ⇨ **launch**

lap [læp] *subst.* **(a)** a person's knees, when he is sitting down *knä;* **he placed the computer on his lap and keyboarded some orders while sitting in his car (b)** overlap of printed colours which prevents any gaps showing *överlappning*

lapel microphone [lə'pel 'maɪkrəfəʊn] *subst.* small microphone that is pinned to someone's jacket *rockslagsmikrofon, mygga*

lapheld computer ['læp,held kəm'pju:tə] *or* **laptop computer** ['læp,tɒp kəm'pju:tə] *subst.* computer that is light enough to carry but not so small as to fit in a pocket, usually containing a screen, keyboard and disk drive *portföljdator*

QUOTE in our summary of seven laphelds we found features to admire in every machine
QUOTE the idea of a hard disk in a lapheld machine which runs on batteries is not brand new
PC Business World

large-scale computer ['lɑːdʒskeɪl kəm'pju:tə] *subst.* high-powered (large word size) computer system that can access high capacity memory and backing storage devices as well as multiple users *stort system*

large-scale integration (LSI) ['lɑːdʒskeɪl ,ɪntɪ'greɪʃ(ə)n ('eles'aɪ)] *subst.* integrated circuit with 500 to 10,000 components *höggradig integration*

larmsignal ⇨ **indicator**

laser ['leɪzə] *subst.* = LIGHT AMPLIFICATION BY STIMULATED EMISSION OF RADIATION device that produces coherent light of a single wavelength in a narrow beam, by exciting a material so that it emits photons of light *laser;* **laser beam recording** = production of characters on a light-sensitive film by a laserbeam controlled directly from a computer *laserinspelning;* **laser beam communications** = use of a modulated laser beam as a line-of-sight communications medium *laseröverföring;* **laser disk** = plastic disk containing binary data in the form of small etched dots that can be read by a laser, used to record high quality TV images *or* sound in digital form *optisk skiva, CD;* **laser emulsion storage** = digital storage technique using a laser to expose light-sensitive material *(film)laserminne;* **laser printer** = high-resolution computer printer that uses a laser source to print high-quality dot matrix character patterns on paper (these have a much higher resolution than normal printers, usually 300 dpi) *laserskrivare, sidskrivare med laserteknik;* **injection laser** = solid-state laser device used to transmit data as pulses of light down an optic fibre *laserdiod*

laserdiod ⇨ **laser**

laserskrivare ⇨ **printer**

last ⇨ **match**

lastbarhet ⇨ **fan**

last in first out (LIFO) ['lɑːst'ɪn 'fɜːst'aʊt ('laɪfəʊ)] *subst.* queue system that reads the last item stored, first *sist in-först ut;* **this computer stack uses a last in first out data retrieval method;** *compare with* FIRST IN FIRST OUT

latch [lætʃ] **1** *subst.* electronic component that maintains an output condition until it receives an input signal to change *låskrets; see also* FLIP-FLOP **2** *vb.* to set an output state *låsa;* **the output latched high until we reset the computer**

> QUOTE other features of the device include a programmable latch bypass which allows any number of latches from 0 to 8 so that this device may be used as latched or combinatorial
> *Electronics & Power*

latency [ˈleɪt(ə)nsɪ] *subst.* time delay between the moment when an instruction is given to a computer and the execution of the instruction *or* return of a result (such as the delay between a request for data and the data being transferred from memory) *fördröjning*

latent image [ˈleɪt(ə)nt ˈɪmɪdʒ] *subst.* image formed before developing on light sensitive film after it has been exposed *latent bild*

lateral reversal [ˈlæt(ə)r(ə)l rɪˈvɜːs(ə)l] *subst.* creating the mirror image of a picture by swapping left and right *spegelvändning*

launch [lɔːn(t)ʃ] **1** *subst.* (i) putting a new product on the market *lansering;* (ii) putting a satellite into space *uppskjutning;* **the launch of the new PC has been put back six months; the launch date for the network will be September 2** *vb.* (i) to put a new product on the market *lansera;* (ii) to put a satellite into space *skjuta upp;* **the new PC was launched at the Personal Computer Show; launching costs for the computer range were calculated at $250,000**

launch amplifier [ˈlɔːn(t)ʃ ˈæmplɪfaɪə] *subst.* amplifier used to boost the television signals before they are transmitted over a cable network *signalförstärkare*

launch vehicle [ˈlɔːn(t)ʃ ˌviːɪkl] *subst.* spacecraft used to transport a satellite from earth into space *bärraket*

layer [ˈleɪə] *subst.* **(a)** division of sections of space at certain distances from the earth into separate regions for various radio communications (these are: D-Region from 50 - 90km above earth's surface, E-Region from 90 - 150km above earth's surface, F-Region from 150- 400km above earth's surface) *skikt* **(b)** ISO/OSI standards defining the stages a message has to pass through when being transmitted from one computer to another over a network *skikt enligt ISO/OSI-modellen;* **application layer** = the program that requests a transmission *tillämpningsskikt;* **data link layer** = layer that sends packets of data to the next link, and deals with error correction *länkskikt;* **network layer** = layer that decides on the routes to be used, the costs, etc. *nätskikt;* **physical layer** = layer that defines the rules for bit rate, power, medium for transmission, etc. *fysiskt skikt;*

presentation layer = section that agrees on format, codes and request for start/end of a connection *presentationsskikt;* **session layer** = layer that makes the connection/disconnection between a transmitter and receiver *sessionsskikt;* **transport layer** = layer that checks and controls the quality of the connection *transportskikt*

layered [ˈleɪəd] *adj.* consisting of layers *skiktad;* **the kernel has a layered structure according to user priority**

lay in [leɪ ˈɪn] *vb.* to synchronize a frame of film with the music *or* sound tracks *lägga på*

layout [ˈleɪaʊt] *subst.* **(a)** mock-up of a finished piece of printed work showing the positioning and sizes of text and graphics *skiss, uppställning;* **the design team is working on the layouts for the new magazine** **(b)** rules governing the data input and output from a computer *regler för in-utmatning*

lay out [leɪ ˈaʊt] *vb.* to plan and design the positions and sizes of a piece of work to be printed *layouta, sidplanera, sidbryta;* **the designers have laid out the pages in A4 format**

LBR [ˈelbiːˈɑː] = LASER BEAM RECORDING producing characters on a light sensitive film by laser beam directly controlled from a computer *laserinspelning*

LC circuit [ˈelˌsiː ˈsɜːkɪt] *subst.* simple inductor-capacitor circuit that acts as a filter *or* oscillator *LC-krets*

LCD [ˈelsiːˈdiː] = LIQUID CRYSTAL DISPLAY liquid crystal that turns black when a voltage is applied, used in many watches, calculators and other small digital displays *flytande kristallskärm*

> QUOTE LCD screens can run for long periods on ordinary or rechargeable batteries
> *Micro Decision*

LCP [ˈelsiːˈpiː] = LINK CONTROL PROCEDURE rules defining the transmission of data over a channel *länkstyrningsprotokoll*

LDS [ˈeldiːˈes] = LOCAL DISTRIBUTION SERVICE TV signal relay station that transmits signals to another point from which they are distributed over cable *lokal TV-station*

lead *subst.* **(a)** [liːd] electrical conducting wire *ledare* **(b)** [led] thin piece of metal used to give extra space between lines of type before printing *reglett, mellanslag*

leader [ˈliːdə] *subst.* **(a)** section of magnetic tape *or* photographic film that contains no signal *or* images, used at the beginning of the reel for identification and to aid the tape machine to pick up the tape *ledspår;* **leader record =** initial record containing information (such as titles, format, etc.) about following records in a file *etikettsfält* **(b)** row of printed dots *streckad linje, punktutföring*

leading ['ledɪŋ] *subst.* extra space between lines of print *(extra) radavstånd, kägel*

leading edge ['liːdɪŋ'edʒ] *subst.* first edge of a punched card that enters the card reader *framkant*

leading zero ['liːdɪŋ'zɪərəʊ] *subst.* zero digit used to pad out the beginning of a stored number *inledande nolla*

lead in page ['liːdɪn'peɪdʒ] *subst.* videotext page that directs the user to other pages of interest *innehållssida*

leaf [liːf] *subst.* **(a)** page of a book (printed on both sides) *blad* **(b)** final node in a data tree structure *blad*

leaflet ['liːflət] *subst.* small publicity sheet (usually one page folded in half) *flygblad, broschyr*

leak [liːk] **1** *subst.* **(a)** loss of secret documents *or* a breach of security *läcka;* **a leak informed the press of our new designs** **(b)** gradual loss of charge from a charged component due to imperfect insulation *läckage* **2** *vb.* **(a)** to provide secret information to unauthorized people *läcka;* **the details of our new software package have been leaked to the press (b)** to lose electric charge gradually; **in this circuit, the capacitor charge leaks out at 10% per second**

leakage ['liːkɪdʒ] *subst.* loss of signal strength *läckage*

> QUOTE signal leakages in both directions can be a major problem in co-axial cable systems
> **Electronics & Wireless World**

leap-frog test ['liːpfrɒg'test] *subst.* memory location test, in which a program skips from one location to another random location, writing data then reading and comparing for faults, until all locations have been tested *slumpvis minnestest;* **crippled leap-frog test =** standard leap-frog test that uses a single memory location rather than a changing location *minnescelltest*

learning curve ['lɜːnɪŋkɜːv] *subst.* the rate at which someone can acquire knowledge about a subject *inlärningskurva*

lease [liːs] **1** *subst.* written contract for letting *or* renting a piece of equipment for a period against payment of a fee *uthyrning* **2** *vb.* **(a)** to let *or* rent equipment for a period

hyra ut; **the company has a policy of only using leased equipment; leased circuit =** electronic circuit *or* communications channel rented for a period *hyrd förbindelse, fast förbindelse;* **leased line =** communications channel, such as a telephone line, which is rented for the exclusive use of the subscriber *hyrd ledning, fast ledning* **(b)** to use equipment for a time and pay a fee *hyra;* **the company leases all its computers**

least cost design ['liːst,kɒst dɪ'zaɪn] *subst.* best money-saving use of space *or* components *kostnadseffektiv konstruktion;* **the budget is only £1000, we need the least cost design for the new circuit**

least recently used algorithm ['liːst 'riːsntlɪ 'juːzd 'ælgərɪθm] *subst.* algorithm which finds the page of memory that was last accessed before any other, and erases it to make room for another page *minst-senast-använd-algoritm, lägsta-frekvens-algoritm*

least significant digit (LSD) ['liːst sɪg'nɪfɪkənt 'dɪdʒɪt ('eles'diː)] *subst.* digit which occupies the right hand position in a number and so carries the least power (equal to the number radix raised to zero = 1) *minst signifikanta siffra;* **least significant bit (LSB) =** binary digit occupying the right hand position of a word and carrying the least power of two in the word (usually equal to two raised to zero = 1) *misnt signifikanta bit*

leaving files open ['liːvɪŋ 'faɪlz 'əʊp(ə)n] *fras* meaning that a file has not been closed *or* does not contain an end of text marker (this will result in the loss of data since the text will not have been saved) *lämna filer öppna*

LED [eliː'diː] = LIGHT EMITTING DIODE semiconductor diode that emits light when a current is applied *lysdiod*

> COMMENT: LED displays are used to display small amounts of information, as in pocket calculators, watches, indicators, etc.

leda ⇨ **conduct**

ledande chassi ⇨ **hot**

ledning ⇨ **management**

ledningskort ⇨ **printed circuit**

left justification ['left ,dʒʌstɪfɪ'keɪʃ(ə)n] *subst.* **(a)** shifting a binary number to the left hand end of the word containing it *vänsterjustering* **(b)** making the left hand margin of the text even *vänsterställning, rak vänstermarginal*

left justify ['left 'dʒʌstɪfaɪ] *vb.* printing command that makes the left hand margin of the text even *vänsterställa, trycka med rak vänster*

left shift ['left'ʃɪft] *subst.* left arithmetic shift by one bit of data in a word, a binary number is doubled for each left shift *vänsterskift*

leg [leg] *subst.* one possible path through a routine *väg, gren*

legal ['liːg(ə)l] *adj.* statement or instruction that is acceptable within language syntax rules *giltig*

legibility [,ledʒɪ'bɪlətɪ] *subst.* being able to be read *läslighet, läsbarhet;* **the keyboarders find the manuscript lacks legibility**

legible ['ledʒəbl] *adj.* which can be read easily *läslig, läsbar;* **the manuscript is written in pencil and is hardly legible**

length [leŋθ] *subst.* how long something is *längd;* the number of data items in a variable *or* list *längd, storlek;* **block length** = number of records *or* fields *or* characters in a block of data *blocklängd;* **buffer length** = number of data items that can be stored in a buffer while waiting for the processor to attend to them *buffertstorlek;* **field length** = number of characters stored in a field *fältlängd;* **file length** = number of characters *or* bytes in a stored file *fillängd;* **length of filename** = number of characters allowed for identification of a file *filnamnslängd;* **line length** = number of characters which can be displayed horizontally on one line of a display (CRT displays often use an 80 character line length) *radlängd;* **record length** = total number of characters contained in the various fields within a stored record *postlängd, poststorlek;* **register length** = number of bits that make up a register *registerstorlek*

lens [lenz] *subst.* shaped glass that changes the path of a light beam *lins;* **concave lens** = lens that is thinner in the centre than at the edges, bending light out *konkav lins;* **convex lens** = lens that is thicker in the centre than the edges, bending light in *konvex lins;* **lens speed** = the maximum aperture of a lens, relating to the amount of light that can enter the lens *ljusstyrka (hos en lins);* **lens stop** = lens aperture size *maximal bländaröppning*

letter ['letə] *subst.* **(a)** piece of writing sent from one person to another *or* from a company to another, to give information, to send instructions, etc. *brev;* **form letter** *or* **standard letter** = letter sent to several addressees by name without any change to the text *standardbrev* **(b)** written *or* printed sign, which goes to make up a word (such as A,B, C, etc.) *bokstav;* **his name was written in capital letters**

letterhead ['letəhed] *subst.* name and address of a company printed at the top of the company's notepaper *brevhuvud;* **business forms and letterheads can now be designed on a PC**

letter-quality (LQ) printing ['letə'kwɒlətɪ 'prɪntɪŋ] *subst.* feature of some dot-matrix printers to provide characters of the same quality as a typewriter by using dots which are very close together *skönskrift;* **near-letter-quality (NLQ) printing** = printing by a dot-matrix printer that provides higher quality type, which is almost as good as a typewriter, by decreasing the space between the dots *skönskrift (med matrisskrivare)*

level ['levl] *subst.* **(a)** strength *or* power of an electrical signal *nivå, styrka;* **turn the sound level down, it's far too loud; sound pressure level (SPL)** = measurement of the magnitude of the pressure wave conveying sound *ljudtrycksnivå, signalstyrka* **(b)** quantity of bits that make up a digital transmitted signal *signallängd, signalnivå;* **quatenary level quantization** = use of four bits of data in an A/D conversion process *fyrbitskvantisering*

leveranskontroll ⇨ **acceptance**

leveransprov ⇨ **acceptance**

lexical analysis ['leksɪk(ə)l ə'næləsɪs] *subst.* stage in program translation when the compiling *or* translating software replaces program keywords with machine code instructions *lexikal analys, syntaxanalys*

lexicographical order [,leksɪkə(u)'græfik(ə)l 'ɔːdə] *subst.* order of items, where the words are listed in the order of the letters of the alphabet, as in a dictionary *bokstavsordning*

LF ['el'ef] **(a)** = LOW FREQUENCY range of audio frequencies between 5 - 300Hz *or* range of radio frequencies between 30 - 300KHz *lågfrekvens* **(b)** = LINE FEED

librarian [laɪ'breərɪən] *subst.* person who works in a library *bibliotekarie*

library ['laɪbr(ə)rɪ] *subst.* **(a)** collection of files *or* documents *or* books *or* records, etc., which can be consulted *or* borrowed by the public, usually kept in a public place *bibliotek;* **the editors have checked all the references in the local library; a copy of each new book has to be deposited in the British Library; look up the bibliographical details**

in the library catalogue **(b)** collection of programs *or* books belonging to a person *bibliotek;* **he has a large library of computer games; library function =** software routine that a user can insert into his program to provide the function with no effort *biblioteksfunktion;* **library program =** (i) number of specially written *or* relevant software routines, which a user can insert into his own program, saving time and effort *programbibliotek;* (ii) group of functions which a computer needs to refer to often, but which are not stored in main memory *programbibliotek;* **the square root function is already in the library program; macro library =** number of useful, independent routines that can be incorporated into any program to ease program writing *makrobibliotek;* **library routine =** prewritten routine that can be inserted into a main program and called up when required *biblioteksrutin;* **library subroutine =** tried and tested subroutine stored in a library, and which can be inserted into a user's program when required *biblioteks(sub)rutin;* **library track =** one track on a magnetic disk *or* tape used to store information about the contents (such as titles, format and index data) *biblioteksspår*

licence ['laɪs(ə)ns] *subst.* permission given by one manufacturer to another manufacturer to make copies of his products against payment of a fee *licens;* **the software is manufactured in this country under licence**

LIFO ['laɪfəʊ] = LAST IN FIRST OUT queue system that reads the last item stored, first *sist in-först ut;* **this computer stack uses a LIFO data retrieval method;** *see also* FIFO

lifter ['lɪftə] *subst.* mechanical device that lifts magnetic tape away from the heads when rewinding the tape *lyftare*

ligature ['lɪgətʃʊə] *subst.* two characters printed together to form a combined character *or* a short line connecting two characters *ligatur*

light [laɪt] **1** *subst.* perception of brightness due to electromagnetic effects in the frequency range 400 - 750 nm, which allows a person to see *ljus;* **the VDU should not be placed under a bright light; light conduit =** fibre optics used to transmit light from one place to another rather than for the transmission of data *optisk fiber, ljusledare;* **light emitting diode (LED) =** semiconductor diode that emits light when a current is applied (used in calculators and clock displays and as indicators) *lysdiod;* **light guide =** fine strands of glass *or* plastic protected by a surrounding material, used for the transmission of light *optisk fiber, ljusledare;* **light pen =** computer accessory in the shape of a pen that contains a light-sensitive device that can detect pixels on a video screen (often used with suitable software to draw graphics on a screen *or* position a cursor) *ljuspenna;* **light pipe** *see* LIGHT GUIDE; **coherent light =** light beam in which all the waveforms are in phase *koherent ljus;* **visible light =** range of light colours that can be seen with the human eye *synligt ljus;* **ultra-violet light (UV light) =** electromagnetic radiation with wavelengths just greater than the visible spectrum, from 200 to 4,000 angstroms (often used to erase data from EPROMs) *ultraviolett ljus;* **infrared light (IR light) =** electromagnetic radiation just below visible red (often used for communications purposes such as remote control) *infrarött ljus* **2** *adj.* not dark *ljus;* **light face =** typeface with thin lines, which appears light on the page *magert typsnitt*

light-sensitive ['laɪt,sensətɪv] *adj.* which is sensitive to light *ljuskänslig;* **the photograph is printed on light-sensitive paper; light-sensitive device =** device (such as a phototransistor) which is sensitive to light, and produces a change in signal strength *or* resistance *fotocell*

lightweight ['laɪtweɪt] *adj.* which is not heavy *lättvikts-;* **a lightweight computer which can easily fit into a suitcase**

likhet ⇨ equivalence

likhetselement ⇨ identity

likhetsgrind ⇨ identity

likriktare ⇨ inverter, rectifier

limited distance modem ['lɪmɪtɪd 'dɪst(ə)ns 'məʊdem] *subst.* data transmission device with a very short range that sends pure digital data rather than a modulated carrier *korthållsmodem*

limiter ['lɪmɪtə] *subst.* electronic circuit that prevents a signal from going above a certain level *nivåbegränsare*

limiting resolution ['lɪmɪtɪŋ ,rezə'luːʃ(ə)n] *subst.* maximum number of lines that make up a television picture *maximal upplösning*

limits ['lɪmɪts] *subst.* predefined maximum ranges for numbers in a computer *gränser*

line [laɪn] *subst.* **(a)** physical connection for data transmission (such as a cable between parts of a system *or* a telephone wire) *linje, ledning;* **access line =** permanently connected communications line between a terminal and a DSE *fast ledning, terminalledning;* **fast line =** special communications link that allows data to be transmitted at 48K *or* 96K baud *höghastighetslinje, snabb förbindelse;* **line busy tone =** signal indicating that a telephone link cannot be made since the intended receiver is busy *upptagetsignal;* **line communications** = signal transmission using a cable link *or* telegraph wire *linjeöverföring, ledningsbunden överföring;* **line control** = special codes used to control a communications channel *linjestyrsignaler;* **line driver** = high power circuit and amplifier used to send signals over a long distance line without too much loss of signal *(linje)drivsteg;* **line extender** = circuit used to boost a television signal *linjeförstärkare;* **line impedance** = impedance of a communications line *or* cable (equipment should have a matching load to minimize power loss) *ledningsimpedans;* **line level** = amplitude of a signal transmitted over a cable *signalnivå;* **line load** = number of messages transmitted over a line compared to the maximum capacity *trafik, belastning;* **line speed** = rate at which data is sent along a line *överföringshastighet;* **line switching** = communications line and circuit established on demand and held until no longer required *linjeuppkoppling, linjeväxling;* **line transient** = large voltage spike on a line *(linje)spänningsstopp* **(b)** single long thin mark drawn by a pen *or* printed on a surface *linje;* **the printer has difficulty in reproducing very fine lines; line art** = black and white graphics, with no shades of grey *streckteckning;* **line drawings** = drawings made of lines drawn by the artist *streckteckning;* **the book is illustrated with line drawings and halftones (c)** one trace by the electron picture beam on a screen *or* monitor *linje;* **line blanking interval** = period of time when the picture beam is not displayed, this is during line flyback *linjesläcktid;* **line drive signal** = signal to start the scanning procedure in a television camera *styrsignal;* **line flyback** = electron beam returning from the end of one line to the beginning of the next *linjeåtergång;* **line frequency** = number of picture lines that are scanned per second *linjefrekvens* **(d)** row of characters (printed on a page *or* displayed on a computer screen *or* printer) *rad;* **each page has 52 lines of text; several lines of manuscript seem to have been missed by the keyboarder; can we insert an extra line of spacing between the paragraphs?; command line** = program line that contains a command *kommandorad;* **information line** = line running across the screen which gives the user information about the program being executed *or* the file being edited *informationsrad, meddelanderad;* **line editor** = piece of software that allows the operator to modify one line of text from a file at a time *radredigeringsprogram;* **line ending** = character which shows that a line has ended (instructed by pressing the carriage return key) *radslut;* **line feed (LF)** = control on a printer *or* computer terminal that moves the cursor down by one line

radmatning; **line folding** = move a section of a long line of text onto the next row *radbrytning;* **line increment** = minimum distance between two lines of type, which can be as small as one eighteenth of a point *radmellanrum;* **line length** = number of characters contained in a displayed line (on a computer screen this is normally 80 characters, on a printer often 132 characters) *radlängd;* **line spacing** = distance between two rows of characters *radmellanrum, kägel;* **lines per minute (LPM)** = number of lines printed by a line printer per minute *rader per minut* **(e)** series of characters received as a single input by a computer *rad;* **line input** = command to receive all characters including punctuation entered up to a carriage return code *radinmatning* **(f)** one row of commands *or* arguments in a computer program *rad;* **line number** = number that refers to a line of program code in a computer program *radnummer*

COMMENT: the programming language will sort out the program into order according to line number

QUOTE straight lines are drawn by clicking the points on the screen where you would like the line to start and finish
Personal Computer World
QUOTE while pixel editing is handy for line art, most desktop scanners have trouble producing the shades of grey or half-tones found in black and white photography
Publish

linear ['lɪnɪə] *adj.* (circuit output) that varies directly with the input signal so that the output to input characteristics are a straight line (in practice this is never achieved since all components have maximum and minimum output limits at which points the signal becomes distorted) *linjär;* **linear array** = antenna whose elements lie in a straight line *antennuppsättning, antenngrupp (antennsystem där antennelementen är uppställda på rad);* **linear function** = mathematical expression where the input is not raised to a power above one and contains no multiplications other than by a constant *linjär funktion;* **the expression Y = 10 + 5X - 3W is a linear function; the expression $Y = (10 + 5X^2)$ is not a linear function; linear integrated circuit** = electronic device whose output varies linearly with its input over a restricted range (device usually used to provide gain to an analog signal) *linjär integrerad krets;* **linear list** = list that has no free space for new records within its structure *linjär lista;* **linear program** = computer program that contains no loops *or* branches *linjärt program;* **linear programming** = method of mathematically breaking down a problem so that it can be solved by computer *linjäroptimering, linjärprogrammering;*

linear search = search method which compares each item in a list with the search key until the correct entry is found (starting with the first item and working sequentially towards the end) *linjärsökning*

line of sight ['laɪnəv'saɪt] *subst.* clear transmission path for radio communications in a straight line *siktlinje*

COMMENT: line of sight paths are used with a very directional transmission medium such as a laser beam rather than uni-directional one such as radio

line printer ['laɪn,prɪntə] *subst.* device for printing draft quality information at high speeds, typical output is 200 to 3000 lines per minute *radskrivare*

COMMENT: line printers print a whole line at a time, running from right to left and left to right, and are usually dot matrix printers with not very high quality print. Compare page printers, which print a whole page at a time

linjedelningstelefon ⇨ **harmonic**

linjegrafik ⇨ **bar code**

linjeisolering ⇨ **barrier box**

linjär sökning ⇨ **search**

linjärt ⇨ **inline**

linjärt program ⇨ **inline**

link [lɪŋk] **1** *subst.* **(a)** communications path *or* channel between two components *or* devices *kommunikationslänk;* **to transmit faster, you can use the direct link with the mainframe; data link layer** = ISO/OSI layer that sends packets of data to the next link, and deals with error correction *länkskikt;* **link control procedure (LCP)** = rules defining the transmission of data over a channel *länkstyrningsprotokoll;* **link loss** = attenuation of signals transmitted over a link *länkdämpning;* **satellite link** = use of a satellite to allow the transmission of data from one point on earth to another *satellitlänk* **(b)** software routine that allows data transfer between incompatible programs *överföringsprogram;* **link trials** = testing computer programs so as to see if each module works in conjunction with the others *länkningsprov* **2** *vb.* to join *or* interface two pieces of software *or* hardware *länka;* **the two computers are linked; link files** = command to merge together a list of separate files *länka filer;* **linked list** = list of data where each entry carries the address of the next consecutive entry *länkad lista;* **linked subroutine** = number of computer instructions in a program that can be called at any time, with control being returned on completion to the next instruction in the main program *länkad subrutin*

linkage ['lɪŋkɪdʒ] *subst.* act of linking two things *länkning;* **linkage editing** = combining separate programs together, and standardizing the calls *or* references within them *länkningsredigering;* **linkage software** = special software which links sections of program code with any library routines *or* other code *länkningsprogram;* **graphics and text are joined without linkage software**

linking ['lɪŋkɪŋ] *subst.* merging of a number of small programs together to enable them to run as one unit *länkning;* **linking loader** = short software routine that merges sections of programs to allow them to be run as one *länkningsladdare*

LIPS [elaɪpiːˈes] = LOGICAL INFERENCES PER SECOND standard for the measurement of processing power of an inference engine *LIPS (logiska slutsatser per sekund)*

COMMENT: one inference often requires thousands of computer instructions

liquid crystal display (LCD) ['lɪkwɪd 'krɪstl dɪs'pleɪ ('elsiːˈdiː)] *subst.* liquid crystals that turn black when a voltage is applied, used in many watch, calculator and digital displays *flytande kristallskärm*

COMMENT: LCDs do not generate light and so cannot be seen in the dark without an external light source (as opposed to LEDs)

LISP [lɪsp] = LIST PROCESSING high-level language used mainly in processing lists of instructions *or* data and in artificial intelligence work *programmeringsspråket LISP*

list [lɪst] **1** *subst.* series of ordered items of data *lista;* **chained list** = list in which each element contains data and an address to the next element in the list *kedjelista;* **linear list** = list that has no free space for new records within its structure *linjär lista;* **linked list** = list of data where each entry carries the address of the next consecutive entry *länkad lista;* **pushdown list** = temporary storage, in a LIFO format, for a list of items of data *stack;* **reference list** = list of routines *or* instructions and their location within a program *referenslista;* **stop list** = list of words that are not to be used *or* are not significant for a file search *stopplista;* **list processing** = (i) computation of a series of items of data such as adding *or* deleting *or* sorting *or* updating entries *listbearbetning;* (ii) LISP *or* a high-level language used mainly in processing lists of instructions *or* data, and in artificial intelligence work *programmeringsspråket LISP* **2** *vb.* to print *or* display certain items of information *lista;* **to list a program** = to display a program line by line in correct order *lista ett program*

listetikett ⇨ **header**

listing ['lıstıŋ] *subst.* **(a)** program lines printed *or* displayed in an ordered way *listning, programlistning;* **computer listing** = printout of a list of items, taken from data stored in a computer *datalistning;* **a program listing** = a printed copy of the lines of a program *programlistning;* **listing paper** = continuous stationery *datapapper* **(b) listings** = series of information items (such as cinema times, etc.) listed in a newspaper *listningar, sammanställningar, tabeller*

listrubrik ⇨ **header**

literacy ['lıt(ə)rəsı] *subst.* being able to read *läskunnighet;* **computer literacy** = understanding the basic principles of computers, related expressions and being able to use computers for programming *or* applications *datormognad*

literal ['lıt(ə)r(ə)l] *subst.* **(a)** (operand) computer instruction that contains the actual number *or* address to be used, rather than a label *or* its location *litteral, strängkonstant* **(b)** printing error when one character is replaced by another *or* when two characters are transposed *tryckfel*

literate ['lıtərət] *adj.* (person) who can read *läskunnig;* **computer-literate** = able to understand expressions relating to computers and how to use a computer *datormogen person*

lith film ['lıθfılm] *subst.* high quality and contrast photographic film used in lithographic printing *lithfilm*

lithographic [ˌlıθə(ʊ)'græfık] *adj.* referring to lithography *litografisk;* **lithographic film** LITH FILM

lithography [lı'θɒgrəfı] *or informal* **litho** *subst.* **offset lithography** = printing process used for printing books, where the ink sticks to dry areas on the film and is transferred to rubber rollers from which it is printed on to the paper *lito-, litografi*

liveware ['laıvweə] *subst.* the operators and users of a computer system (as opposed to the hardware and software) *användare (av datorer)*

ljudhuv ⇨ **hood**

ljudisolerad ⇨ **soundproof**

ljudtät ⇨ **soundproof**

ljuspenna ⇨ **electronic, graphics**

ljustäthet ⇨ **luminance**

LLL ['elel'el] = LOW-LEVEL LANGUAGE

load [ləʊd] **1** *subst.* **(a)** job *or* piece of work to be done *last, belastning;* **load sharing** = use of more than one computer in a network to even out the work load on each processor *lastfördelning;* **line load** = number of messages transmitted over a line compared to the maximum capacity of the line *linjebelastning, last (på en överföringslinje);* **work load** = number of tasks that a machine has to complete *belastning, last* **(b)** impedance presented to a line *or* device *impedans, last;* **load life** = length of time an impedance can operate with a certain power before it is no longer usable *belastningslivslängd;* **matched load** = load that is the same as the impedance of the transmission line *or* device connected to it *balanserad last* **2** *vb.* **(a)** to transfer a file *or* program from disk *or* tape to main memory *ladda;* **scatter load** = loading sequential data into various non-continuous locations in memory *spridningslagring;* **load and run** *or* **load and go** = computer program that is loaded into main memory and then starts to execute itself automatically *ladda och starta, "tuta och kör"* **(b)** to put a disk *or* tape into a computer, so that it can be run *ladda, sätta in* **(c)** to place an impedance *or* device at the end of a line *belasta*

loader ['ləʊdə] *subst.* program which loads another file *or* program into computer memory *laddningsprogram, laddare;* **absolute loader** = program that loads a section of code into main memory *absolutladdare; compare* BOOTSTRAP; **binary loader** = short section of program code that allows programs in binary form (such as object code from a linker *or* assembler) to be loaded into memory *binärladdare;* **card loader** = short program that transfers data from a punched card into main memory *kortladdare;* **initial program loader (IPL)** = short routine that loads the first section of a program, after which it continues the loading process itself *laddningsrutin*

QUOTE this windowing system is particularly handy when you want to load or save a file or change directories
Byte

loading ['ləʊdıŋ] *subst.* action of transferring a file *or* program from disk to memory *(in)laddning;* **loading can be a long process**

load point ['ləʊdpɔınt] *subst.* start of a recording section in a reel of magnetic tape *laddläge, startpunkt*

lobe [ləʊb] *subst.* section of a response curve around an antenna *or* microphone *lob*

local ['ləʊk(ə)l] *adj. & subst.* **(a)** (variable *or* argument) that is only used in a certain section of a computer program *or* structure *lokal;* **local declaration** = assignment of a variable that is only valid in a section of a computer program *or* structure *lokaldeklaration;* **local memory** = high speed RAM that is used instead of a hardware device to store bit streams *or* patterns *lokalt minne;* **local variable** = variable which can only be accessed by certain routines in a certain section of a computer program *lokal variabel; compare* GLOBAL VARIABLE **(b)** referring to a system with limited access *lokalt; (of a terminal)* **on local** = not working with a CPU, but being used as a stand-alone terminal *urkopplad, ej ansluten;* **local mode** = operating state of a computer terminal that does not receive messages *urkopplat läge, lokalt läge*

local area network (LAN *or* **lan)** ['ləʊk(ə)l 'eərɪə 'netwɜːk (læn)] *subst.* network where various terminals and equipment are all a short distance from one another (at a maximum distance of about 500m, for example in the same building) and can be interconnected by cables *lokalt nät, lokalt datanät; compare with* WAN; **local area network server** = dedicated computer and backing storage facility used by terminals and operators of a LAN *nätcentral, filcentral*

COMMENT: LANs use cables *or* optical fibre links; WANs use modems, radio and other long distance transmission methods

locate [lə(ʊ)'keɪt] *vb.* (i) to place *or* to set *placera;* (ii) to find *finna, hitta;* **the computer is located in the main office building; have you managed to locate the programming fault?**

location [lə(ʊ)'keɪʃ(ə)n] *subst.* **(a)** number *or* absolute address which specifies the point in memory where a data word can be found and accessed *position, plats, läge* **(b) on location** = filming in real situations, and not in the studio *utomhus (i motsats till studio);* **location shots** = sections of a film which are shot on location *utomhusscener*

lock [lɒk] *vb.* to prevent access to a system *or* file *låsa;* **locking a file** = the action of preventing any further writing to a file *låsa en fil;* **to lock onto** = to synchronize an internal clock with a received signal *låsa på (en signal), synkronisera med*

lockout ['lɒkaʊt] *subst.* preventing a user sending messages over a network by continuously transmitting data *utlåsning*

lock up ['lɒkʌp] *subst.* faulty operating state of computer that cannot be recovered from without switching off the power *låsning*

COMMENT: this can be caused by an infinite program loop *or* a deadly embrace

log [lɒg] **1** *subst.* record of computer processing operations *logg* **2** *vb.* to record a series of actions *logga, föra logg(bok), föra bok över;* **to log in** *or* **log on** = to enter various identification data, such as a password, usually by means of a terminal, to the central computer before accessing a program *or* data (used as a means of making sure that only authorized users can access the computer system) *logga in;* **automatic log on** = telephone number, password and user number transmitted when requested by a remote system to automate logon *automatisk inloggning;* **to log off** *or* **log out** = to enter a symbol *or* instruction at the end of a computing session to close all files and break the channel between the user's terminal and the main computer *logga ut* NOTE: the verbs can be spelled **log on, log-on,** or **logon; log off, log-off** or **logoff**

logarithm ['lɒgərɪð(ə)m] *subst.* mathematical operation that gives the power a number must be raised to, to give the required number *logaritm;* **decimal logarithm of 1,000 is 3 (= 10 x 10 x 10)**

logarithmic [,lɒgə'rɪðmɪk] *adj.* referring to variations in the logarithm of a scale *logaritmisk;* **bel is a unit in the logarithmic scale; logarithmic graph** = graph whose axes have a scale that is the logarithm of the linear measurement *kurva med logaritmisk skala*

logg ⇨ **log, trail**

logger ['lɒgə] *subst.* **call logger** = device which logs telephone calls (and notes the number called, the time when the call was made, and the length of the call) *samtalsräknare*

loggfil ⇨ **journal**

logging ['lɒgɪŋ] *subst.* input of data into a system *logga;* **logging on** *or* **logging off** = process of opening *or* ending operations with a system *logga in (ur);* **call logging** = system of monitoring telephone calls *räkna (logga) samtal;* **error logging** = recording errors met *felbokföring;* **features of the program include error logging**

QUOTE logging on and off from terminals is simple, requiring only a user name and password
QUOTE once the server is up and running it is possible for users to log-on
Micro Decision
QUOTE facilities for protection against hardware failure and software malfunction include log files
Computer News

loggning ⇨ **audit**

logic ['lɒdʒɪk] *subst.* **(a)** science which deals with thought and reasoning *logik;* **formal logic** = treatment of form and structure, ignoring content *formell logik* **(b)** mathematical treatment of formal logic operations such as AND, OR, etc., and their transformation into various circuits *logik; see also* BOOLEAN ALGEBRA; **logic map** = graphical representation of states and conditions in a logic circuit *logikdiagram;* **logic state** = one out of two possible levels in a digital circuit, the levels being 1 and 0 or TRUE and FALSE *logiskt tillstånd, logiskt läge;* **logic state analyzer** = test equipment that displays the logic states of a number of components *or* circuits *logikanalysator;* **logic symbol** = graphical symbol used to represent a type of logic function *logisk symbol* **(c)** system for deducing results from binary data *logiksystem;* **logic bomb** = section of code that performs various unpleasant functions such as system crash when a number of conditions are true (the logic bomb is installed by unpleasant hackers *or* very annoyed programmers) *logisk bomb, datavirus;* **logic level** = voltage used to represent a particular logic state (this is often five volts for a one and zero volts for a zero) *logiknivå;* **logic operation** = computer operation *or* procedure in which a decision is made *logikoperation* **(d)** components of a computer *or* digital system *logikkretsar;* **sequential logic** = logic circuit whose output depends on the logic state of the previous inputs *sekventiell logik;* **logic card** *or* **logic board** = printed circuit board containing binary logic gates rather than analog components *digitalt kretskort;* **logic circuit** = electronic circuit made up of various logical gates such as AND, OR and EXOR *logisk krets;* **logic element** = gate *or* combination of logic gates *logikelement;* **logic flowchart** = graphical representation of logic elements, steps and decisions and the interconnections *logikdiagram;* **logic gate** = electronic circuit that applies a logical operator to an input signal and produces an output *logisk grind; see also* GATE

logical ['lɒdʒɪk(ə)l] *adj.* that uses logic in its operation *logisk;* **logical reasoning can be simulated by an artificial intelligence machine; logical channel** = electronic circuit between a terminal and a network node in a packet switching system *logisk kanal;* **logical chart** = graphical representation of logic elements, steps and decisions and their interconnections *logikdiagram;* **logical comparison** = function to see if two logic signals are the same *logisk jämförelse;* **logical decision** = one of two paths chosen as a result of one of two possible answers to a question *logiskt beslut;* **logical error** = fault in a program design causing incorrect branching *or* operations *logikfel, logiskt fel;* **logical expression** = function made up from a series of logical operators such as AND and

OR *logiskt uttryck;* **logical high** = equal to logic true state *or* 1 *logiskt sann;* **logical low** = equal to logic false state *or* 0 *logiskt falsk;* **logical operator** = character *or* word that describes the logical action it will perform (the most common logical operators are AND, NOT, and OR) *logisk operator;* **logical record** = unit of information ready for processing that is not necessarily the same as the original data item in storage, which might contain control data, etc. *logisk post;* **logical shift** = data movement to the left *or* right in a word, the bits falling outside the word boundary are discarded, the free positions are filled with zeros *logiskt skift; compare with* ARITHMETIC SHIFT

logic-seeking ['lɒdʒɪk,siːkɪŋ] *adj.* printer that can print the required information with the minimum head movement, detecting ends of lines, justification commands, etc. *logisk avsökning*

> QUOTE a reduction in the number of logic gates leads to faster operation and lower silicon costs
> QUOTE the removal of complex but infrequently used logic makes the core of the processor simpler and faster, so simple operations execute faster
> **Electronics & Power**

logikfel ▷ **error**

login ['lɒgɪn] = LOGGING IN

logisk antingen-eller-grind ▷ **exclusive, EXOR, gate**

(logisk) antingen-grind ▷ **except**

logisk avsökning ▷ **logic-seeking**

logisk bomb ▷ **Trojan Horse**

(logisk) eller-grind ▷ **gate, OR function**

(logisk) icke-grind ▷ **gate**

(logisk) icke-och-grind ▷ **gate, NAND function**

(logisk) negerad antingen-eller-grind (XNOR) ▷ **exclusive, EXNOR, gate**

(logisk) och-grind ▷ **AND, gate**

logiskt falsk ▷ **logical**

logiskt flödesschema ▷ **flowchart**

logiskt sann ▷ **logical**

(logisk) varken-eller-grind ▷ **gate, NOR function**

LOGO ['lɒgəʊ] *subst.* high-level programming language used mainly for educational purposes, with graphical commands that are easy to use *programmeringsspråket LOGO*

logo ['lɒgəʊ] *subst.* special printed set of characters *or* symbols used to identify a company *or* product *logotyp*

logoff ['lɒg'ɒf] = LOG OFF, LOGGING OFF

logon ['lɒg'ɒn] = LOG ON, LOGGING ON

logotyp ⇨ logo

logout ['lɒg'aʊt] = LOGGING OUT

lokal nätcentral ⇨ server

lokalt nät ⇨ network

long haul network ['lɒŋhɔːl 'netwɜːk] *subst.* communications network between distant computers that usually uses the public telephone system *fjärrkommunikationsnät*

long persistence phosphor ['lɒŋpɜːˌsɪst(ə)ns 'fɒsfə] *subst.* television screen coating that retains the displayed image for a period of time longer than the refresh rate, reducing flicker effects *fosfor med lång efterlysning*

look ahead ['lʊkə'hed] *subst.* action by some CPUs to fetch instructions and examine them before they are executed (to speed up operations) *förhämtning, framförhållning;* **carry look ahead** = high speed adder that can predict if a carry will be generated by a sum and add it in, removing the delay found in a ripple through carry adder *framförhållande överföringssiffra*

binary look-up ['baɪnərɪ 'lʊkʌp] *subst.* fast search method for use on ordered lists of data; the search key is compared with the data in the middle of the list and one half is discarded, this is repeated with remaining half until only one data item remains *binär sökning*

look-up table ['lʊkʌp 'teɪbl] *or* LUT ['elju:'ti:] *subst.* collection of stored results that can be accessed very rapidly by a program without the need to calculate each result whenever needed *(kors)referenstabell;* **lookup tables are preprogrammed then used in processing so saving calculations for each result required**

QUOTE a lookup table changes a pixel's value based on the values in a table
Byte

loop [lu:p] **1** *subst.* **(a)** procedure *or* series of instructions in a computer program that are performed again and again until a test shows that a specific condition has been met *or* until the program is completed *slinga;* **closed loop** = computer control operation in which data is fed back from the output of the controlled device to the controlling loop *sluten slinga;* **endless loop** *or* **infinite loop** = loop which has no end, except when the program is stopped *oändlig slinga;* **holding loop** = section of program that loops until it is broken by some action, most often used when waiting for a response from the keyboard *or* a device *vänteslinga;* **modification loop** = instructions within a loop that change other instructions *or* data within a program *modifierande slinga;* **nested loop** = loop contained inside another *(in)kapslad slinga;* **loop body** = main section of instructions within a loop that carry out the primary function rather than being used to enter or leave or setup the loop *slingans huvuddel;* **loop check** = check that data has been correctly transmitted down a line by returning the data to the transmitter *återkopplingskontroll;* **loop counter** = register that contains the number of times a loop has been repeated *(sling)räknare;* **loop program** = sequence of instructions that are repeated until a condition is met *slinga* **(b)** (i) long piece of tape with the two ends joined *ögla;* (ii) communications channel that is passed via all receivers and is terminated where it started from *slinga, slingledning;* **loop film** = endless piece of magnetic *or* photographic film that plays continuously *oändligt band, oändlig film* **(c)** length of wire coiled in the shape of a circle *cirkel;* **loop antenna** = aerial in the shape of a circle *ramantenn;* **loop network** = communications network that consists of a ring of cable joining all terminals *ringnät* **2** *vb.* to make a piece of wire *or* tape into a circle *göra en ögla;* **looping program** = computer program that runs continuously *kontinuerligt program*

lose [lu:z] *vb.* not to have something any more *förlora, tappa;* **we have lost the signal in the noise; all the current files were lost when the system crashed and we had no backup copies; lost call** = telephone call that cannot be established *tappat samtal;* **lost time** = period of a transmitted facsimile signal when the image is being scanned, that contains no image data *förlorad tid*

loss [lɒs] *subst.* the power of a signal that is lost when passing through a circuit *förlust*

loudness ['laʊdnəs] *subst.* volume of a signal which you can hear *(fysiologisk) ljudstyrka*

loudspeaker ['laʊd'spi:kə] *subst.* electromagnetic construction that moves a paper cone according to an input signal so producing sound waves from an electrical input *högtalare*

lower case ['ləʊə'keɪs] *subst.* small characters (such as a, b, c, as opposed to upper case A, B, C) *gemena bokstäver*

low frequency (LF) ['ləʊ 'friːkwənsɪ ('el'ef)] *subst.* range of audio frequencies between 5-300Hz *or* range of radio frequencies between 30-300kHz *lågfrekvens, långvåg;* **low pass filter =** electronic circuit that blocks signals above a certain frequency *lågpassfilter;* **low-priority work =** task which is not particularly important *lågprioriterat arbete;* **low-resolution graphics** *or* **low-res graphics =** ability to display character-sized graphic blocks *or* preset shapes on a screen rather than using individual pixels *lågupplösande grafik; compare* HIGH-RESOLUTION; **low speed communications =** data transmission at less than 2400 bits per second *långsam överföring*

low-level language (LLL) ['ləʊ,levl 'læŋgwɪdʒ ('elel'el)] *subst.* programming language similar to assembler and in which each instruction has a single equivalent machine code instruction (the language is particular to one system *or* computer) *lågnivåspråk, maskinkod, assemblerspråk; see also* HIGH-LEVEL LANGUAGE

low-order digit ['ləʊ,ɔːdə 'dɪdʒɪt] *subst.* digit in the position within a number that represents the lowest weighting of the number base *minst signifikanta siffra;* **the number 234156 has a low-order digit of 6**

low-res ['ləʊ'rez] *see* LOW-RESOLUTION

LPM ['elpiː'em] = LINES PER MINUTE

LQ ['el'kjuː] = LETTER QUALITY

LSB ['eles'biː] = LEAST SIGNIFICANT BIT binary digit occupying the right hand position of a word and carrying the least power of two in the word, usually equal to two raised to zero = 1 *minst signifikanta bit*

LSD ['eles'diː] = LEAST SIGNIFICANT DIGIT digit which occupies the right hand position in a number and so carries least power (equal to the number radix raised to zero = 1) *minst signifikanta siffra*

LSI ['eles'aɪ] = LARGE SCALE INTEGRATION system with between 500 and 10,000 circuits on a single IC *höggradig integration*

luftprodukt ⇨ vapourware

luggable ['lʌgəbl] *subst.* personal computer that is just about portable and usually will not run off batteries (it is much heavier and less compact than a lap-top or true transportable machine) *bärbar ("släpbar") persondator*

lumen ['luːmən] *subst.* SI unit of illumination, defined as the amount of flux emitted from a candela into an angle of one steradion *lumen (lm)*

luminance ['luːmɪnəns] *subst.* amount of light radiated from a source *ljustäthet, luminans;* **luminance signal =** part of television signal providing luminance data *luminanssignal*

'lus' ⇨ bug

LUT ['elju:'tiː] = LOOK-UP TABLE

> QUOTE an image processing system can have three LUTs that map the image memory to the display device
> *Byte*

lux [lʌks] *subst.* SI unit of measurement of one lumen per square metre *lux (lx)*

lågnivåspråk ⇨ low-level language (LLL)

lågpassfilter ⇨ filter

(långsam) svajning ⇨ wow

långvåg ⇨ low frequency (LF)

låsa ⇨ interlock, lock

låskrets ⇨ latch

läge ⇨ location, mode

länk ⇨ thread

länka ⇨ chain, concatenate, link

länkad fil ⇨ thread

länkdämpning ⇨ link

länkning ⇨ linkage, linking

läraktig ⇨ heuristic

läsa ⇨ read

läsare ⇨ reader, scanner

läsbar ⇨ readable

läsfel ⇨ error

läshuvud ⇨ head

läsminne ⇨ ROM

läsminneslagrat program ⇨ internally stored program

läsminnesprogrammering ⇨ field

läsminnesraderare ⇨ eraser

läs- och skivminne ⇨ memory

läs- och skrivhuvud ⇨ head, tape

löpande bana ⇨ feed

lösenord ⇨ access, password

löstagbart skivminne ⇨ Winchester disk

Mm

M [em] *prefix* = MEGA **(a)** one million *M, mega;* **Mbps** = MEGA BITS PER SECOND number of million bits transmitted every second *Mbit/s, Mbit per sekund;* **MFLOPS** = MEGA FLOATING POINT OPERATIONS PER SECOND measure of computing power and speed, equal to one million floating point operations per second *miljoner flyttalsoperationer per sekund* **(b)** symbol for 1,048,576, used only in computer and electronic related applications, equal to 2^{20} *M, mega;* **Mbyte (MB)** = measurement of mass storage equal to 1,048,576 bytes *Mbyte;* **the latest model has a 30Mbyte hard disk**

m [em] *prefix* = MILLI one thousandth *m, milli*

MAC [mæk] **(a)** = MULTIPLEXED ANALOG COMPONENTS standard television broadcast signal format *standardiserat tevesignalsformat* **(b)** = MESSAGE AUTHENTICATION CODE special code transmitted at the same time as a message as proof of its authenticity *valideringskod* = MEDIA ACCESS BAND *gränssnitt med det fysiska lagret i datakommunika- tionsprotokollet från OSI*

machine [məˈʃiːn] *subst.* **(a)** number of separate moving parts *or* components, acting together to carry out a process *maskin;* **copying machine** *or* **duplicating machine** = machine which makes copies of documents *kopiator, kopieringsmaskin;* **dictating machine** = recording machine which records what someone dictates, so that the text can be typed *diktafon, dikteringsbandspelare;* **machine proof** = proof of sheets of a book, taken from the printing machine *korrektur* **(b)** computer *or* system *or* processor made of various components connected together to provide a function *or* perform a task *system, maskin, maskinvara;* **clean machine** = computer that contains only the minimum of ROM based code to boot its system from disk, any languages required must be loaded separately *tom dator, ren maskin;* **source machine** = computer which can compile source code *källkodsdator;* **virtual machine** = simulated machine and its operations *virtuell (simulerad) maskin, virtuell dator;* **machine address** = number *or* absolute address which specifies the point in memory where a data word can be found and accessed *maskinadress, absolutadress;* **machine check** = fault caused by equipment failure *maskinfel, maskinvarutest;* **machine code** *or* **machine language** = programming language that consists of commands in binary code that

can be directly understood by the central processing unit without the need for translation *maskinkod;* **machine code format** = a machine code instruction is usually made up of 1, 2 or 3 bytes for operand, data and address *maskinkodsformat;* **machine code instruction** = instruction that directly controls the CPU and is recognized without the need for translation *maskinkodsinstruktion;* **machine cycle** = minimum period of time taken by the CPU for the execution of an instruction *maskincykel;* **machine dependent** = not standardized *or* which cannot be used on hardware *or* software from a different manufacturer without modifications *maskinberoende;* **machine equation** = formula which an analog computer has been programmed to solve *förprogrammerad formel;* **machine independent** = (computer software) that can be run on any computer system *maskinoberoende;* **machine independent language** = programming language that can be translated and executed on any computer that has a suitable compiler *maskinoberoende programmeringsspråk;* **machine instruction** = an instruction which can be recognized by a machine and is part of its limited set of commands *maskininstruktion;* **machine intelligence** = the design of computer programs and devices that attempt to imitate human intelligence and decision-making functions, providing basic reasoning and other human characteristics *artificiell intelligens;* **machine intimate** = software that operates and interacts closely with the hardware in a system *lågnivåprogram;* **machine language** = (i) the way in which machine code is written *maskinspråk;* (ii) MACHINE CODE *maskinkod;* **machine language compile** = to generate a machine code program from a HLL program by translating and assembling each HLL instruction *kompilera;* **machine language programming** = slowest and most complex method of programming a CPU, but the fastest in execution, achieved by entering directly into RAM or ROM the binary representation for the machine code instructions to be carried out (rather than using an assembler with assembly language programs *or* a compiler with HLL programs) *maskinkodsprogrammering;* **machine-readable** = (commands *or* data) stored on a medium that can be directly input to the computer *maskinläsbar;* **the disk stores data in machine-readable form;** **machine run** = action of processing instructions in a program by a computer *körning;* **machine translation** = computer system that is used to translate text and commands from one language and syntax to another *maskinöversättning, datoröversättning;* **machine word** = number of bits of data operated on simultaneously by a CPU in one machine cycle, often 8, 16 or 32 bits *dataord, maskinord*

machinery [mə'ʃiːnərɪ] *subst.* machines *maskiner, maskinutrustning*
NOTE: no plural

machining [mə'ʃiːnɪŋ] *subst.* making a product using a machine *(maskin)bearbetning;* printing the sheets of a book *tryckning*

machinist [mə'ʃiːnɪst] *subst.* person who works a machine *maskinist, operatör*

macro ['mækrəʊ] *subst.* program routine *or* block of instructions identified by a single word *or* label *makro;* **macro assembler** *or* **assembly program** = assembler program that is able to decode macro instructions *makroassembler;* **macro call** = use of a label in an assembly language program to indicate to an assembler that the macro routine is to be inserted at that point *makroanrop;* **macro code** *or* **macro command** *or* **macro instruction** = one word that is used to represent a number of instructions, simplifying program writing *makrokod, makroinstruktion;* **macro definition** = description (in a program *or* to the operating system) of the structure, function and instructions that make up a macro operation *makrodefinition;* **macro expansion** = process in which a macro call is replaced with the instructions in the macro *makroutvidgning;* **macro flowchart** = graphical representation of the logical steps, stages and actions within a routine *makrodiagram;* **macro language** = programming language that allows the programmer to define and use macro instructions *makrospråk;* **macro programming** = writing a program using macro instructions *or* defining macro instructions *makroprogrammering*

macro- ['mækrəʊ] *prefix* very large *or* applying to the whole system *makro-*

macroelement ['mækrəʊ'elɪmənt] *subst.* number of data items treated as one element *makroelement*

macroinstruction ['mækrəʊɪnˌstrʌkʃ(ə)n] *subst.* one programming instruction that refers to a number of instructions within a routine *or* macro *makroinstruktion*

magazine [ˌmægə'ziːn] *subst.* **(a)** paper, usually with illustrations which comes out regularly, every month or every week *tidskrift, veckotidning;* **a weekly magazine; he edits a computer magazine (b)** number of pages in a videotext system *magasin* **(c)** container for photographic film *magasin*

magnet ['mægnɪt] *subst.* something that produces a magnetic field *magnet*

magnetetikett ⇨ **kimball tag**

magnetic [mæg'netɪk] *adj.* which has a magnetic field associated with it *magnetisk;* **magnetic bubble memory** = method of storing large amounts of binary data as small magnetized areas in the medium (made of certain pure materials) *bubbelminne;* **magnetic card** = plastic card with a strip of magnetic recording material on its surface, allowing data to be stored (used in automatic cash dispensers) *magnetkort;* **magnetic card reader** *or* **magnetic strip reader** = machine that can read data stored on a magnetic card *kortläsare;* **magnetic cartridge** *or* **cassette** = small box containing a reel of magnetic tape and a pick up reel *kassett;* **magnetic cell** = small piece of material whose magnetic field can be altered to represent the two states of binary data *magnetisk cell;* **magnetic core** = early main memory system for storing data in the first types of computer, each bit of data was stored in a magnetic cell *kärnminne;* **magnetic disk** = flat circular piece of material coated with a substance, allowing signals and data to be stored magnetically *skiva i skivminne; see also* FLOPPY DISK, HARD DISK; **magnetic disk unit** = computer peripheral made up of a disk drive and necessary control electronics *skivminnesenhet;* **magnetic drum** = computer data storage peripheral that uses a coated cylinder to store data magnetically (not often used now) *trumminne;* **magnetic encoding** = storage of (binary) data signals on a magnetic medium *magnetisk datalagring;* **magnetic field** = description of the polarity and strength of magnetic effects at a point *magnetfält;* **magnetic flux** = measure of magnetic field strength per unit area *magnetiskt flöde;* **magnetic focusing** = use of magnetic field to focus a beam of electrons (in a television) *magnetisk fokusering;* **magnetic head** = electromagnetic component that converts electrical signals into a magnetic field, allowing them to be stored on a magnetic medium *magnethuvud;* **magnetic ink** = printing ink that contains a magnetic material, used in some character recognition systems *magnetiskt bläck;* **magnetic ink character recognition (MICR)** = system that identifies characters by sensing the magnetic ink patterns (as used on bank cheques) *magnetisk teckenläsning;* **magnetic master** = original version of a recorded tape *or* disk *originalband, originalskiva;* **magnetic material** *or* **medium** = substance that will retain a magnetic flux pattern after a magnetic field is removed *magnetiskt material, magnetmedium;* **magnetic media** = magnetic materials used to store signals, such as disk, tape, etc.

magnetmedier; **magnetic memory** *or* **store** = storage that uses a medium that can store data bits as magnetic field changes *magnetminne;* **magnetic recording** = transferring an electrical signal onto a moving magnetic tape *or* disk by means of an magnetic field generated by a magnetic head *magnetisk inspelning;* **magnetic screen** = metal screen used to prevent stray magnetic fields affecting electronic components *magnetisk skärm;* **magnetic storm** = disturbance in the earth's magnetic fields affecting radio and cable communications *magnetisk storm;* **magnetic strip** = layer of magnetic material on the surface of a plastic card, used for recording data *magnetremsa;* **magnetic thin film storage** = high-speed access RAM device using a matrix of magnetic cells and a matrix of read/write heads to access them *tunnfilmsminne;* **magnetic transfer** = copy signals stored on one type of magnetic medium to another *magnetisk överföring*

magnetic tape [mæg'netık 'teıp] *subst.* narrow length of thin plastic coated with a magnetic material used to store signals magnetically *magnetband;* **magnetic tape cartridge** *or* **cassette** = small box containing a reel of magnetic tape and a pick up reel, used in a cassette player *or* tape drive *bandkassett;* **magnetic tape encoder** = device that directly writes data entered at a keyboard onto magnetic tape *bandstans;* **magnetic tape reader** = machine that can read signals stored on magnetic tape and convert them to an electrical form that can be understood by a computer *bandstation (enbart för läsare), (magnet)bandläsare;* **magnetic tape recorder** = device with a magnetic head, motor and circuitry to allow electrical signals to be recorded onto *or* played back from a magnetic tape *bandstation;* **magnetic tape transport** = computer-controlled magnetic tape drive mechanism *band(matnings)mekanism, bandmatning*

(magnetiska) avkänningsmärken ▷ **mark**

magnetisk teckenläsare ▷ **mark**

magnetiskt material ▷ **ferromagnetic material**

magnetize ['mægnətaız] *vb.* to convert a material *or* object into a magnet *magnetisera*

COMMENT: magnetic tape is available on spools of between 200 and 800 metres. The tape is magnetized by the read/write head. Tape is a storage medium which only allows serial access, that is, all the tape has to be read until the required location is found (as opposed to disk storage, which can be accessed randomly)

magnetkort ▷ **magnetic**

magnetkärna ▷ **ferrite core**

magnification [,mægnıfı'keıʃ(ə)n] *subst.* amount by which something has been made to appear larger *förstoring;* **the lens gives a magnification of 10 times**

magnify ['mægnıfaı] *vb.* to make something appear larger *förstora;* **the photograph has been magnified 200 times**

magnitude ['mægnıtjuːd] *subst.* level *or* strength of a signal *or* variable *storlek, stryka, magnitud;* **signal magnitude** = strength of an electrical current and voltage *or* power signal *signalstyrka*

mag tape ['mæg,teıp] *subst. informal* = MAGNETIC TAPE

mail [meıl] **1** *subst.* **(a)** system of sending letters and parcels from one place to another *post* **(b)** letters sent *or* received *post* **(c)** electronic messages to and from users of a bulletin board *or* network *elektronisk post;* **electronic mail** *or* **email** *or* **e-mail** = messages sent between users of a bulletin board *or* interconnecting network *elektronisk post* **2** *vb.* to send something by post *posta;* **to mail a letter; we mailed our order last Wednesday**

mailbox ['meılbɒks] *or* **mail box** *subst.* electronic storage space with an address in which a user's incoming messages are stored *(elektronisk) brevlåda*

mailing ['meılıŋ] *subst.* sending something using the post *posta, skicka ut;* **the mailing of publicity material; direct mailing** = sending of publicity material by post to possible buyers *direktreklam;* **mailing list** = list of names and addresses of people who might be interested in a product *or* list of names and addresses of members of a society *adresslista;* **his name is on our mailing list; to build up a mailing list; to buy a mailing list** = to pay a society, etc. money to buy the list of members so that you can use it to mail publicity material *köpa en adresslista;* **mailing piece** = leaflet suitable for sending by direct mail *reklambroschyr;* **mailing shot** = leaflets sent by mail to possible customers *direktutskick*

mail-merge ['meıl'mɜːdʒ] *subst.* word-processing program which allows a standard form letter to be printed out to a series of different names and addresses *massbrevsfunktion, (register)kopplad (brev)utskrift*

main [meın] *adj.* most important *huvudsaklig, viktigast;* **main beam** = direction of the central most powerful region of an antenna's transmission pattern *huvudlob;* **main clock** = clock signal that synchronizes all the components in a system *systemklocka;* **main distributing frame** = racks of termination circuits for the cables in a telephone network *korskoppling(sstativ);* **main entry** = entry in a catalogue under which is contained the most important information about the document *huvudsökord;* **main index** = more general index that directs the user gradually to more specific index areas *huvudindex, katalog;* **main memory** *or* **main storage** = fast access RAM whose locations can be directly and immediately addressed by the CPU *primärminne, huvudminne;* **the 16-bit system includes up to 3Mb of main memory; main routine** = section of instructions that make up the main part of a program (a program often consists of a main routine and several subroutines, which are called from the main routine) *huvudrutin*

mainframe (computer) ['meɪn,freɪm (kəm'pjuːtə)] *subst.* large-scale high power computer system that can handle high capacity memory and backing storage devices as well as a number of operators simultaneously *stordator;* **mainframe access** = using microcomputers to access a mainframe computer *stordatoråtkomst*

mains electricity [meɪnz ɪlek'trɪsətɪ] *subst.* normal domestic electricity supply to consumers *nätspänning, hushållsström (i Sverige 230v vid 50Hz)*

> COMMENT: in UK this is 240 volts at 50Hz; in the USA, it is 120 volts at 60Hz

maintain [meɪn'teɪn] *vb.* to ensure a system is in good condition and functioning correctly *underhålla, upprätthålla;* **well maintained** = well looked after *välskött*

maintainability [meɪn,teɪnə'bɪlətɪ] *subst.* the ability to have repairs carried out quickly and efficiently if a failure occurs *underhållsbarhet*

maintenance ['meɪntənəns] *subst.* (i) keeping a machine in good working condition *underhåll, skötsel;* (ii) tasks carried out in order to keep a system running, such as repairing faults, replacing components, etc. *underhåll;* **file maintenance** = process of updating a file by changing *or* adding *or* deleting entries *filunderhåll;* **preventive maintenance** = regular inspection and cleaning of a system to prevent faults occurring *förebyggande underhåll;* **maintenance contract** = arrangement with a repair company that provides regular checks and special repair prices in the event of a fault *underhållskontrakt, serviceavtal;* **maintenance routine** = software diagnostic tool used by an engineer during

preventative maintenance operations *underhållsrutin*

major cycle ['meɪdʒə 'saɪkl] *subst.* minimum access time of a mechanical storage device *huvudcykel*

majuscule ['mædʒəskjuːl] *subst.* capital letter *versal, majuskel*

make-ready time ['meɪk'redɪ 'taɪm] *subst.* time taken by a printer to prepare the machines and film for printing *färdigställningstid*

make up [meɪk 'ʌp] *vb.* to arrange type into the correct page formats before printing *bryta, ombryta*

make up ['meɪkʌp] *or* **makeup** *subst.* arrangement and layout of type into correct page formats before printing *ombrytning;* **corrections after the page makeup are very expensive**

makroexpansion ⇨ **expansion**

makroinstruktion ⇨ **instruction**

male connector ['meɪl kə'nektə] *subst.* plug with conducting pins that can be inserted into a female connector to provide an electrical connection *hankontakt*

malfunction [mæl'fʌŋ(k)ʃ(ə)n] **1** *subst.* (of hardware *or* software) not working correctly *fel;* **the data was lost due to a software malfunction; malfunction routine** = software routine used to find and help diagnose the cause of an error or fault *felsökningsrutin* **2** *vb.* not to work properly *fungera dåligt;* **some of the keys on the keyboard have started to malfunction**

malfunctioning [mæl'fʌŋ(k)ʃ(ə)nɪŋ] *subst.* not working properly *felfunktion*

mall ⇨ **template**

manage ['mænɪdʒ] *vb.* to direct *or* to be in charge of *ha hand om, leda, sköta*

manageable ['mænɪdʒəbl] *adj.* which can be dealt with easily *hanterlig;* **processing problems which are still manageable; the problems are too large to be manageable; data should be split into manageable files**

management ['mænɪdʒmənt] *subst.* directing *or* organizing (work *or* a business) *ledning;* **network management** = organization, planning, running and upkeep of a network *nätverkshantering, nätadministration;* **product management** = directing the making and selling of a product as an independent item *produktledning;* **management information system (MIS)** = computer system that provides management staff with relevant, up-to-date information *administrativ databehandling, informationssystem för* *företagsledning;* **management training =** training managers by making them study problems and work out ways of solving them *chefsutbildning* NOTE: no plural

manager ['mænɪdʒə] *subst.* **(a)** user-friendly front end software that allows easy access to operating system commands *(användar)gränssnittshanterare;* **file manager =** section of a disk operating system that allocates disk space to files, keeping track of the file sections (if it has to be split) and their sector addresses *filhanteringsprogram;* **queue manager =** software which orders tasks waiting to be processed *köhanterare;* **records manager =** program which maintains records and can access and process them *posthanterare;* **text manager =** facilities that allow text to be written, stored, retrieved, edited and printed *textbehandlare* **(b)** head of a department in a company *chef;* **a department manager; data processing manager; production manager**

managerial [,mænə'dʒɪərɪəl] *adj.* referring to managers *direktörs-;* **managerial staff**

manipulate [mə'nɪpjʊleɪt] *vb.* to move, edit and change text *or* data *hantera, manipulera;* **an image processor that captures, displays and manipulates video images**

manipulation [mə,nɪpjʊ'leɪʃ(ə)n] *subst.* moving *or* editing *or* changing text *or* data *hantering, manipulering;* **the high-speed database management program allows the manipulation of very large amounts of data**

man machine interface (MMI) ['mæn mə'ʃiːn 'ɪntəfeɪs ('emem'aɪ)] *subst.* hardware and software designed to make it easier for users to communicate effectively with a machine *användargränssnitt*

man-made ['mænmeɪd] *adj.* not natural, produced by man *konstruerad, konstgjord;* **man-made noise =** electrical interference caused by machines *or* motors *radiostörningar; compare* GALACTIC NOISE

mantissa [mæn'tɪsə] *subst.* fractional part of a number *mantissa;* **the mantissa of the number 45.897 is 0.897**

mantissa ⇨ **fraction**

manual ['mænjʊəl] **1** *subst.* document containing instructions about the operation of a system *or* piece of software *handbok, handledning;* **the manual is included with the system; installation manual =** booklet showing how a system should be installed *installationshandbok;* **instruction manual =** document describing how to use a system *or* software *instruktionsbok;* **user's manual =** booklet

showing how a device *or* system should be used *användarhandbok* **2** *adj.* (work) done by hand; (process) carried out by the operator without the help of a machine *(utförd) med händerna, manuell;* **manual data processing =** sorting and processing information without the help of a computer *manuell behandling, handsortering;* **manual entry** *or* **manual input =** act of entering data into a computer, by an operator via a keyboard *manuell inmatning, instansning*

manually ['mænjʊəlɪ] *adv.* done by hand, not automatically *för hand, manuellt;* **the paper has to be fed into the printer manually**

manufacture [,mænjʊ'fæktʃə] *vb.* to make in a factory *tillverka;* **the company manufactures diskettes and magnetic tape**

manufacturer [,mænjʊ'fæktʃ(ə)rə] *subst.* company which manufactures a product *tillverkare;* **if the system develops a fault it should be returned to the manufacturer for checking; the manufacturer guarantees the system for 12 months**

manuscript ['mænjʊskrɪpt] *or* **MS** ['em'es] *subst.* original draft copy of a book written *or* typed by the author *manuskript, manus;* **this manuscript was all written on computer**

manöverbord ⇨ **console**

manöverenhet ⇨ **console**

map [mæp] **1** *subst.* diagram representing the internal layout of a computer's memory *or* communications regions *karta;* **memory map =** diagram indicating the allocation of address ranges to various memory devices, such as RAM, ROM and memory-mapped input/output devices *minnesavbildning* **2** *vb.* to retrieve data and display it as a map *avbilda data;* **database mapping =** description of the way in which the records and fields in a database are related *strukturbeskrivning;* **I/O mapping =** method of assigning a special address to each (I/O) port in a microcomputer rather than a memory location *in-utkanalisering;* **to map out =** to draw *or* set down the basic way in which something should be done *skissa, specifiera;* **memory-mapped (input/output) =** allocation of addresses to a computer's input/output devices to allow them to be accessed as if they are a memory location *minnesavbildad (in-uthantering);* **a memory-mapped screen has an address allocated to each pixel allowing direct access to the screen by the CPU;** *see also* BIT-MAP, BIT-MAPPED

mapp ⇨ **file**

MAR ['emeɪ'ɑː] = MEMORY ADDRESS REGISTER register within the CPU that

contains the next location to be accessed
minnesadressregister

marching display ['mɑːtʃɪŋ dɪs'pleɪ]
subst. display device that contains a buffer
to show the last few characters entered
teckenfönster

margin ['mɑːdʒɪn] *subst.* **(a)** blank space
around a section of printed text *marginal;*
**when typing the contract leave wide
margins; the left margin and right margin
are the two sections of blank paper on either
side of the page; to set the margin =** to
define the size of a margin *sätta marginaler*
(b) extra time *or* space *marginal;* **safety
margin =** time *or* space allowed for
something to be safe *säkerhetsmarginal;*
margin of error = number of mistakes
which are accepted in a document *or* in a
calculation *felmarginal*

marginal ▷ margin

margination [ˌmɑːdʒɪ'neɪʃ(ə)n] *subst.*
giving margins to a printed page *sättning av
marginaler*

mark [mɑːk] **1** *subst.* **(a)** sign put on a
page to show something *märke, markering;*
proof correction marks = special marks
used to show changes to a proof
korrekturtecken **(b)** transmitted signal that
represents a logical one *or* true condition
markering, märke; **mark hold =**
continuously transmitted mark signal that
indicates there are no messages on the
network *uppehållsmarkering;* **mark space =**
two-state transmission code using a mark
and a space (without a mark) as signals
(mellanrums)kod **2** *vb.* to put a mark on
something *markera, märka;* **mark block =**
to put a block marker at the beginning and
end of a block of text *blockmarkera;*
marking interval = time when a mark
signal is being carried out
markeringsintervall; **mark sense =** to write
characters with conductive *or* magnetic ink
so that they are then machine readable
(magnetiska) avkänningsmärken; **mark
sense device** *or* **reader =** device that reads
data from special cards containing
conductive *or* magnetic marks *(magnetisk)
avläsningsanordning, magnetisk
teckenläsare, magnetisk avläsare;* **mark
sensing card =** preprinted card with spaces
for mark sense characters *magnetkort, kort
för magnetisk avläsning*

marker ['mɑːkə] *subst.* **(a) marker pen =**
coloured pen used to indicate *or* highlight
sections of text *överstrykningspenna* **(b)**
code inserted in a file *or* text to indicate a
special section *markör, märke;* **block
markers =** two markers inserted at the start
and finish of a section of data *or* text to
indicate a special block which can then be
moved *or* deleted *or* copied as a single unit
blockmarkörer; **field marker =** code used to

indicate the end of one field and the start of
the next *fältmarkör;* **word marker =** symbol
indicating the start of a word in a variable
word length machine *ordmarkör*

markerade tecken ▷ highlight

markering ▷ mark

markeringsintervall ▷ mark

mark up [mɑːk 'ʌp] *vb.* to prepare copy
for the compositor to set, by showing on
the copy the typeface to be used, the line
width, and other typesetting instructions
sättkoda, förbereda för sättning

markör ▷ cursor, prompt

MASER ['meɪzə] = MICROWAVE
AMPLIFICATION BY STIMULATED
EMISSION OF RADIATION low noise
amplifier, formerly used for microwave
signals from satellites *MASER*

mask [mɑːsk] **1** *subst.* **(a)** integrated
circuit layout stencil that is used to define
the pattern to be etched *or* doped onto a
slice of semiconductor *mask, mall;* **a mask**
or **stencil is used to transfer the transistor
design onto silicon (b)** photographic device
used to prevent light reaching selected
areas of the film *mask* **(c)** pattern of binary
digits used to select various bits from a
binary word (a one in the mask retains that
bit in the word) *mask(ering);* **mask bit =**
one bit used to select the required bit from
a word *or* string *maskeringsbit;* **mask
register =** storage location in a computer
that contains the pattern of bits used as a
mask *maskeringsregister, maskregister;*
interrupt mask = data word in a computer
that selects which interrupt lines are to be
activated *avbrottsmask* **2** *vb.* to cover an
area of (something) with (something)
maskera, maska av; **masked ROM =** read-
only memory device that is programmed
during manufacture, by depositing metal
onto selected regions dictated by the shape
of a mask *maskerat läsminne*

maskable ['mɑːskəbl] *adj.* which can be
masked *maskerbar;* **maskable interrupt =**
interrupt which can be activated by using
an interrupt mask *maskerbart avbrott;* **non-
maskable interrupt (NMI) =** high priority
interrupt signal that cannot be deactivated
högprioriterat avbrott

> QUOTE the device features a maskable interrupt
> feature which reduces CPU overheads
> **Electronics & Power**

maskerbart avbrott ▷ interrupt

maskeringsbit ▷ mask

maskeringsregister ▷ mask

maskinavbrott ▷ hardware

maskinberoende ▷ dependent

maskinfamilj ⇨ family

maskinfel ⇨ hard

masking ['mɑːskɪŋ] *subst.* operation used to select various bits in a word *maskering*

maskinkod ⇨ **actual address, basic, code, executable form, low-level language (LLL)**

maskinskrivare ⇨ typist

maskinskriverska ⇨ typist

maskinskrivning ⇨ typing

maskinvara ⇨ hard, hardware

maskinvarufel ⇨ equipment

maskinvarukompatibilitet ⇨ hardware

(maskinvaru)konfiguration ⇨ hardware

(maskinvaru)tillförlitlighet ⇨ hardware

maskinöversättning ⇨ language

masknät ⇨ mesh

maskregister ⇨ mask

mass media ['mæs'miːdjə] *subst.* media which aim to reach a large public (such as television, radio, mass-market newspapers) *massmedier*

mass storage ['mæs'stɔːrɪdʒ] *subst.* storage and retrieval of large amounts of data *massminne;* **mass storage device** = computer backing store device that is able to store large amounts of data *massminnesenhet;* **the hard disk is definitely a mass storage device; mass storage system** = data storage system that can hold more than one million million bits of data *massminnessystem*

mast [mɑːst] *subst.* **radio mast** *or* **TV mast** = tall structure used to position an aerial above natural obstacles (such as houses, hills, etc.) *radiomast, TV-mast*

master ['mɑːstə] **1** *subst.* main *or* most important device *or* person in a system *övervakande-, huvud-, överordnad-;* most up-to-date and correct file *huvudfil, referensfil;* **the master computer controls everything else; master antenna television system (MATV)** = single main receiving antenna that provides television signals to a number of nearby receivers *centralantennsystem;* **master card** = first punched card in a pack that provides information about the rest of the pack *registerkort, indextext;* **master clock** = timing signal to which all components in a system are synchronized *systemklocka;* **master computer** = computer in a

multiprocessor system that controls the other processors and allocates jobs, etc. *övervakande dator, huvuddator;* **master control program (MCP)** = software that controls the operations in a system *primärt styrprogram;* **master data** = reference data which is stored in a master file *referensdata, originaldata;* **master disk** = (i) disk containing all the files for a task *huvuddiskett;* (ii) disk containing the code for a computer's operating system that must be loaded before the system will operate *systemskiva, systemskiva;* **master file** = set of all the reference data required for an application, which is updated periodically *referensfil;* **master/master computer system** = system in which each processor is a master, dedicated to one task *symmetriskt multiprocessorsystem, symmetrisk paralelldator;* **master program file** = magnetic medium which contains all the programs required for an application *huvudfil;* **master proof** = final proof of a section of text before it is printed *slutkorrektur;* **master/slave computer system** = system with a master controlling computer and a slave that takes commands from the master *system med överordnad dator och slavdator;* **master tape** = magnetic tape which contains all the vital operating system routines, loaded once when the computer is switched on (by the initial program loader) *systemband;* **master terminal** = one terminal in a network that has priority over any other, used by the system manager to set up the system *or* carry out privileged commands *systemkonsol;* **image master** = data describing fonts and character shapes in a phototypesetter *fil med typsnittsdata, matrisfil, patrisfil* **2** *vb.* bemästra, behärska; **we mastered the new word-processor quite quickly; the user-friendly package is easier to master**

matare ⇨ feeder

match [mætʃ] *vb.* **(a)** to search through a database for a similar piece of information *matcha* **(b)** to set a register *or* electrical impedance equal to another *balansera;* **matched load** = impedance of the same value as the cable across which it is connected, so minimizing signal reflections *balanserad last;* **matching transformer** = transformer used to connect and match two lines of differing impedance, while isolating them electrically *balanseringstransformator;* **impedance matching** = means of making the best signal power transfer between two circuits by making sure that their output and input impedances are the same *impedans-balansering*

material [mə'tɪərɪəl] *subst.* **(a)** substance which can be used to make a finished product *material;* **gold is the ideal material**

for electrical connections; **synthetic materials** = substances made as products of a chemical process *syntetmaterial;* **materials control** = system to check that a company has enough materials in stock to do its work *materialstyrning;* **materials handling** = moving materials from one part of a factory to another in an efficient way *materialhantering* **(b) display material** = posters, photographs, etc., which can be used to attract attention to goods which are for sale *reklammateriel*

mathematical [ˌmæθəˈmætɪk(ə)l] *adj.* referring to mathematics *matematisk;* **mathematical model** = representation of a system using mathematical ideas and formulae *matematisk modell;* **mathematical subroutines** = library routines that carry out standard mathematical functions, such as square root, logarithm, cosine, sine, etc. *matematiska subrutiner*

mathematics [ˌmæθəˈmætɪks] *subst.* study of the relationship between numbers, their manipulation and organization to (logically) prove facts and theories *matematik; see also* ALGEBRA

maths [mæθs] *or US* **math** [mæθ] *informal* = MATHEMATICS; **maths chip** *or* **coprocessor** = dedicated IC that can be added to a system to carry out mathematical functions far more rapidly than a standard CPU, speeding up the execution of a program *matematikprocessor*

matningsrulle ⇨ **feed**

matris ⇨ **matrix**

matrisrotation ⇨ **matrix**

matrisskrivare ⇨ **matrix**

matrix [ˈmeɪtrɪks] *subst.* **(a)** array of numbers *or* data items arranged in rows and columns *matris;* **matrix rotation** = swapping the rows with the columns in an array (equal to rotating by 90 degrees) *matrisrotation* **(b)** array of connections between logic gates providing a number of possible logical functions *matris;* **key matrix** = way in which the keys of a keyboard are arranged as an array of connections *tangentbordsmatris* **(c)** pattern of the dots that make up a character on a computer screen *or* dot-matrix *or* laser printer *punktmatris;* **matrix printer** *or* **dot-matrix printer** = printer in which the characters are made up by a series of dots printed close together, producing a page line by line *matrisskrivare;* a dot-matrix printer can be used either for printing using a ribbon or for thermal *or* electrostatic printing; **character matrix** = pattern of dots that makes up a displayed character *teckenmatris*

matt [mæt] *or* **matte** [mæt] **1** *subst.* **(a)** addition of an image onto a film of a background *överlägg* **(b)** mask used to prevent light reaching certain areas on a film *överlägg, mask* **2** *adj.* (print) which is not shiny *matt*

matter [ˈmætə] *subst.* **(a)** question *or* problem to be discussed *fråga, angelägenhet;* it is a matter of concern to the members of the committee = the members of the committee are worried about it *det är ett bekymmer för medlemmarna i kommittçen* **(b)** main section of text on a page as opposed to titles *or* headlines *sats;* **printed matter** = printed books, newspapers, publicity sheets, etc. *trycksak;* **publicity matter** = sheets *or* posters *or* leaflets used for publicity *reklamtrycksak* **(c)** question *or* problem to be discussed *ärende, fråga;* the most important matter on the agenda; we shall consider first the matter of last month's fall in prices NOTE: no plural for (b)

MATV [ˈemeɪtiːˈviː] = MASTER ANTENNA TELEVISION SYSTEM

maximum [ˈmæksɪməm] *adj. & subst.* highest value used *or* which is allowed *maximum;* **maximum capacity** = greatest amount of data that can be stored *maximal kapacitet;* **maximum reading** = greatest signal magnitude recorded *maximal signal;* **maximum transmission rate** = greatest number of data that can be transmitted every second *maximal överföringshastighet;* **maximum usable frequency** = highest signal frequency which can be used in a circuit without distortion *maximal användbar frekvens;* **maximum users** = greatest number of users that a system can support at any one time *maximalt antal användare*

MB [ˈmegəbaɪt] *or* **Mb** *or* **Mbyte** = MEGABYTE equal to 1,048,576 bytes of storage, equal to 2^{20} bytes *Mbyte*

> QUOTE the maximum storage capacity is restricted to 8 Mbytes
> **Micro Decision**

Mbps [ˈembiːpiːˈes] = MEGA BITS PER SECOND

MBR [ˈembiːˈɑː] = MEMORY BUFFER REGISTER register in a CPU that temporarily buffers all inputs and outputs *buffertregister*

Mbyte ⇨ **M**

mC [ˈmɪliˌkuːlɒm] = MILLICOULOMB

MCP [ˈemsiːˈpiː] = MASTER CONTROL PROGRAM

MDR [ˈemdiːˈɑː] = MEMORY DATA REGISTER register in a CPU that holds data before it is processed *or* moved to a memory location *dataregister*

mean [miːn] **1** *subst. & adj.* average value of a set of numbers *or* values *medelvärde;* **mean time between failures (MTBF) =** average period of time that a piece of equipment will operate between failures *medeltid mellan fel, genomsnittlig drifttid;* **mean time to failure (MTF) =** average period of time for which a device will operate (usually continuously) before failing *medeltid till fel, genomsnittlig (kontinuerlig) drifttid;* **mean time to repair =** average period of time required to repair a faulty piece of equipment *medelreparationstid, genomsnittlig drifttid innan reparation* **2** *vb.* to signify something *betyda;* **the message DISK FULL means that there is no more room on the disk for further data**

measure ['meʒə] **1** *subst.* **(a)** way of calculating size *or* quantity *mått;* **square measure =** area in square feet *or* metres, calculated by multiplying width and length *ytmått, area* **(b)** **tape measure =** long tape with centimetres *or* inches marked on it, used to measure how long something is *måttband* **(c)** total width of a printed line of text (shown in picas) *radbredd* **(d)** type of action *åtgärd;* **to take measures to prevent something happening =** to act to stop something happening *vidta åtgärder för att förhindra att något inträffar;* **safety measures =** actions to make sure that something is safe *säkerhetsåtgärder* **2** *vb.* to find out the size *or* quantity of something; to be of a certain size *or* quantity *mäta*

measurement ['meʒəmənt] *subst.* **(a)** **measurements =** size *mått;* **to write down the measurements of a package (b)** way of judging something *mätning;* **performance measurement** *or* **measurement of performance is carried out by running a benchmark program**

mechanical [mə'kænɪk(ə)l] *adj.* referring to machines *mekanisk;* **mechanical paper =** paper (such as newsprint) made from rough wood, which has not been processed *slippapper*

mechanism ['mekənɪz(ə)m] *subst.* piece of machinery *mekanism;* **the printer mechanism is very simple; the drive mechanism appears to be faulty**

meddelande ⇨ **message**

meddelandehanteringssystem ⇨ **CBMS**

meddelandeslutsignal ⇨ **end**

medeltal ⇨ **average**

medelvärde ⇨ **average**

medelåtkomstminne ⇨ **IAM**

medfött fel ⇨ **inherited error**

media ['miːdjə] **(a)** means of communicating information to the public (such as television, radio, newspapers) *medium;* **the product attracted a lot of interest in the media** *or* **a lot of media interest; media analysis** *or* **media research =** examining different types of media (such as the readers of newspapers, television viewers) to see which is best for advertising a certain type of product *medieanalys;* **media coverage =** number of reports about an event *or* product in newspapers, magazines and on TV *mediebevakning;* **we got good media coverage for the launch of the new model** NOTE: **media** is followed by a singular or plural verb **(b)** *see* MEDIUM; **magnetic media =** magnetic materials used to store signals, such as disk, tape, etc. *magnetmedier, magnetiska medier*

medieslutsignal ⇨ **end**

medium ['miːdjəm] **1** *adj.* middle *or* average *medelstor;* **a medium-sized computer system 2** *subst.* **(a)** way of doing something *or* means of doing something *medium;* **advertising medium =** type of advertisement (such as a TV commercial) *annonsmedium;* **the product was advertised through the medium of the trade press (b) storage medium =** any physical material that can be used to store data for a computer application *lagringsmedium, minnesmedium;* **data storage mediums such as paper tape, magnetic disk, magnetic tape, paper, card and microfiche are available; data medium =** medium which allows data to be stored *or* displayed such as magnetic disk *or* a VDU *datamedium;* **empty medium =** blank but formatted storage medium that is ready to accept data *tomt medium;* **magnetic medium** *or* **material =** substance that will retain a magnetic flux pattern after a magnetic field is removed *magnetiskt medium* NOTE: plural is **mediums** or **media**

medium ⇨ **carrier, media, medium**

medium frequency ['miːdjəm 'friːkwənsɪ] *subst.* radio frequency range between 300 to 3000KHz (often referred to as medium wave (MW), especially on radio receivers) *mellanvåg, medelfrekvens*

medium lens ['miːdjəm 'lenz] *subst.* optical photographic lens that has a focal length near the standard for the film size *normalobjektiv*

medium scale integration (MSI) ['miːdjəm 'skeɪl ˌɪntɪ'greɪʃ(ə)n ('emesˈaɪ)] *subst.* integrated circuit with 10 to 500 components *medelskaleintegration (se LSI och ULSI)*

medium speed ['miːdjəm spiːd] *subst.* data communication speed between 2400 and 9600 bits per second *medelhastighet*

COMMENT: medium speed transmission describes the maximum rate of transfer for a normal voice grade channel

medium wave (MW) ['miːdjəm‚weɪv ('em'dʌblju:)] *see* MEDIUM FREQUENCY

meet [miːt] *subst.* logical function whose output is true if both inputs are true *konjunktion*

mega- ['megə] *prefix* (a) meaning one million *M, mega-;* **megabits per second (Mbps)** = number of million bits transmitted every second *Mbit/s, Mbit per sekund;* **megaflops (MFLOPS)** measure of computing power and speed equal to one million floating point instructions per second *Mflops* **(b)** meaning 1,048,576 (equal to 2^{20}) and used only in computing and electronic related applications *M, mega;* **megabit (Mb)** = equal to 1,048,576 bits *Mbit;* **megabyte (MB)** equal to 1,048,576 bytes of storage *Mbyte*

QUOTE adding multiple megabytes of memory is a simple matter of plugging memory cards into the internal bus
Byte

mellanfil ⇨ **intermediate**

mellanformat ⇨ **intermediate**

mellankod ⇨ **intermediate**

mellanlagra ⇨ **deposit**

mellanlagringsarea ⇨ **save**

mellanlagringsmedium ⇨ **intermediate**

mellanlagringsminne ⇨ **intermediate**

mellanliggande ⇨ **intermediate**

mellanminne ⇨ **IAM**

mellanrum ⇨ **gap, space**

mellansiffra ⇨ **gap**

mellanslag ⇨ **space**

mellantecken ⇨ **gap**

member ['membə] *subst.* individual record *or* item in a field *individ*

membrantangentbord ⇨ **keyboard**

memomotion [‚memə(ʊ)'məʊʃn] *subst.* method of filming an action by taking one frame every few seconds *enbildstagning*

memorize ['meməraɪz] *vb.* to remember *or* to retain in the memory *memorera*

memory ['memərɪ] *subst.* storage space in a computer system *or* medium that is

capable of retaining data *or* instructions *minne;* **associative memory** = method of data retrieval that uses part of the data rather than an address to locate data *associativt minne;* **backing memory** = any data storage medium, such as a magnetic tape *or* floppy disk, that is not the main high speed memory *säkerhetsminne, reservminne;* **bootstrap memory** = permanent memory within a terminal *or* microcomputer, that allows a user to customize the attributes, booting the system and loading programs *startminne;* **bubble memory** = method of storing large amounts of binary data, as small magnetized areas in the medium (certain pure materials) *bubbelminne;* **cache memory** = section of high-speed memory which stores data that the CPU needs to access quickly *fickminne, snabbt buffertminne;* **charge coupled device (CCD) memory** = volatile, low-cost, high-storage capability memory device *CCD-minne;* **content-addressable memory** = memory that is addressed and accessed by its contents rather than a location *innehållsadresserat minne;* **control memory** = memory which decodes control instructions into microinstructions which operate the computer *or* microcontroller *styrkodsminne, mikrokodsminne;* **core memory** *or* **primary memory** = central fast-access memory which stores the programs and data currently in use *primärminne;* **disk memory** = data stored on magnetic disk, not on tape *skivminne;* **dynamic memory** = random access memory that requires its contents to be updated regularly *dynamiskt minne;* **external memory** = memory which is located outside the main computer system confines, but which can be accessed by the CPU *externminne, sekundärminne, yttre minne;* **fast access memory (FAM)** = storage locations that can be read from *or* written to very rapidly *snabbåtkomstminne;* **FIFO memory** *or* **first in first out memory** = memory using a FIFO access scheme *köminne, först in-först utminne;* **internal memory** = storage available within and under the direct control of the main computer, such as main memory *internminne;* **magnetic memory** = storage that uses a medium that can store data bits as magnetic field changes *magnetminne;* **main memory** = fast access RAM whose locations can be directly and immediately addressed by a CPU *primärminne;* **non-volatile memory** = storage medium that retains data even when power has been switched off *icke-flyktigt minne, permanent minne;* **random access memory (RAM)** = memory that allows access to any location in any order without having to access the rest of memory *direktminne, läs- och skivminne;* **read only memory (ROM)** = memory device that has had data written into it at manufacture, which can only be read *läsminne;* **scratchpad memory =** workspace *or* area of high-speed memory that is used for the temporary storage of data currently in use *slaskminne, anteckningsblock;* **serial memory =** storage whose locations can only be accessed in a serial way, locating one item requires a search through every location *seriellt minne;* **magnetic tape is a high capacity serial memory; static memory =** non-volatile memory that does not require refreshing *statiskt minne;* **virtual memory =** system where the workspace is held in both backing store and memory at the same time *virtuellt minne;* **volatile memory =** memory *or* storage medium which loses data stored in it when its power supply is switched off *flyktigt minne, icke-permanent minne;* **memory access time =** time delay between requesting access to a location and being able to do so *åtkomsttid;* **memory address register (MAR) =** register within the CPU that contains the address of the next location to be accessed *minnesadressregister;* **memory bank =** number of smaller storage devices connected together to form one large area of memory *minnesbank;* **memory board =** printed circuit board containing memory chips *minneskort;* **memory buffer register (MBR) =** register in a CPU that temporarily buffers all inputs and outputs *(minnes)buffertregister;* **memory capacity =** number of bits *or* bytes that can be stored within a memory device *minneskapacitet;* **memory cell =** smallest location that can be individually accessed *minnescell;* **memory chip =** electronic component that is able to store binary data *minneskrets;* **memory cycle =** period of time from when the CPU reads *or* writes to a location and the action being performed *minnescykel;* **memory data register (MDR) =** register in a CPU which holds data before it is processed *or* moved to a memory location *dataminnesregister;* **memory diagnostic =** software routine that checks each memory location in main memory for faults *minnesdiagnosprogram;* **memory dump =** printout of all the contents of an area of memory *minnesdump;* **memory edit =** to change (selectively) the contents of various memory locations *minnesredigering;* **memory hierarchy =** the different types (capacity and access time) of memory available in a system *minneshierarki;* **memory intensive =** software that uses large amounts of RAM or disk storage during run-time, such as programs whose entire code has to be in main memory during execution *minneskrävande;* **memory management =** software that controls and regulates the flow and position in memory of files and data *minneshantering;* **memory map =** diagram indicating the allocation of address ranges to various devices such as

RAM, ROM and memory-mapped input/output devices *minneskarta, minnesavbildning;* **memory-mapped =** with addresses allocated to a computer's input *or* output devices to allow them to be accessed as if they were a memory location *minnesavbildad;* **a memory-mapped screen has an address allocated to each pixel, allowing direct access to the screen by the CPU; memory-mapped I/O =** an I/O port which can be accessed as if it were a memory location within the CPU's normal address range *minnesavbildad in- och utgång;* **memory page =** one section of main store which is divided into pages, which contains data *or* programs *minnessida;* **memory protect =** feature on most storage systems to prevent the accidental overwriting of data *minnesskydd;* **memory-resident =** (program) that is held permanently in memory *minnesresident;* **the system can bomb if you set up too many memory-resident programs at the same time; memory switching system =** system which communicates information, stores it in memory and then transmits it according to instructions *mellanlagringssystem, förmedlingssystem;* **memory workspace =** amount of extra memory required by a program to store data used during execution *arbetsarea*

QUOTE when a program is loaded into memory, some is used for the code, some for the permanent data, and some is reserved for the stack which grows and shrinks for function calls and local data
Personal Computer World

menu ['menjuː] *subst.* list of options *or* programs available to the user *meny;* **menu-driven software =** program where commands *or* options are selected from a menu by the operator *menystyrt program, menystyrd programvara;* **menu selection =** choosing commands from a list of options presented to the operator *menyval;* **main menu =** list of primary options available *huvudmeny;* **pop-up menu** *or* **pull-down menu =** menu of options that can be displayed at any time, usually overwriting any other text *fönstermeny, rullgardinsmeny;* **the pull-down menu is viewed by clicking over the icon at the top of the screen**

QUOTE when the operator is required to make a choice a menu is displayed
Micro Decision

mercury delay line ['mɜːkjʊrɪ dɪ'leɪ 'laɪn] *subst.* (old) method of storing serial data as pulses in a length of mercury, the data was constantly read, regenerated and fed back into the input *kvicksilverminne*

merge [mɜːdʒ] *vb.* to combine two data files, but still retaining an overall order *slå samman;* **the system automatically merges text and illustrations into the document;**

merge sort = software application in which the sorted files are merged into a new file *sammanslagningssortering, samsortering; see also* MAIL-MERGE

mervärdesnät ⇨ value added network (VAN)

mesh [meʃ] *subst.* any system with two *or* more possible paths at each interconnection *galler, nät;* **mesh network** = method of connecting several machines together, where each pair of devices has two *or* more connections *masknät*

message ['mesɪdʒ] *subst.* **(a)** information sent from one person to another *meddelande* **(b)** certain defined amount of information *meddelande;* **message format** = predetermined rules defining the coding, size and speed of transmitted messages *meddelandeformat;* **message heading** = section of a message that contains routing and destination information *huvud(meddelande);* **message numbering** = identification of messages by allocating a number to each one *meddelandenumrering;* **message routing** = selection of a suitable path between the source and destination of a message in a network *vägval;* **message slot** = number of bits that can hold a message which circulates around a ring network *meddelandeplats;* **message switching** = storing, arranging and making up batches of convenient sizes of data to allow for their economical transmission over a network *meddelandeförmedling;* **message text** = information that concerns the user at the destination without routing *or* network control data *meddelandetext*

metabit ['metəbɪt] *subst.* extra identifying bit for each data word *metabit*

metacompilation ['metəkɒmpɪ'leɪʃ(ə)n] *subst.* compiling a program that will compile other programs when executed *metakompilering*

metalanguage ['metəˌlæŋgwɪdʒ] *subst.* language which describes a programming language *metaspråk*

metal oxide semiconductor (MOS) ['metl 'ɒksaɪd 'semɪkən'dʌktə (mɒs)] *subst.* production and design method for a certain family of integrated circuits using patterns of metal conductors and oxide deposited onto a semiconductor *MOS-metoden för kretstillverkning med halvledare;* **metal oxide semiconductor field effect transistor (MOSFET)** = high-powered and high-speed field effect transistor manufactured using MOS techniques *MOSFET-krets;* **complementary metal oxide semiconductor (CMOS)** = integrated circuit design and construction method, using a pair of complementary p- and n-type transistors *CMOS-krets*

meter ['miːtə] **1** *subst.* device which counts *or* records something *mätare, räknare;* **an electricity meter; a meter attached to the photocopier records the number of copies made;** *see also* MULTIMETER **2** *vb.* to record and count *mäta, räkna;* **the calls from each office are metered by the call logger**

metod ⇨ procedure

MF ['em'ef] = MEDIUM FREQUENCY

MFLOPS ['emflɒps] = MEGA FLOATING POINT INSTRUCTIONS PER SECOND

MHz ['megəhɜːts] = MEGAHERTZ one million cycles per second *MHz*

MICR ['emaɪsiːɑː] = MAGNETIC INK CHARACTER RECOGNITION system that identifies characters by sensing magnetic ink patterns (as used on bank cheques) *magnetisk teckenigenkänning*

micro ['maɪkrəʊ] *subst.* = MICROCOMPUTER

micro- ['maɪkrə(ʊ)] *prefix* **(a)** meaning one millionth of a unit *mikro-;* **micrometre** = one millionth of a metre *mikrometer;* **microsecond** = one millionth of a second *mikrosekund* **(b)** meaning very small *mikro-;* **microcassette** = small format audio cassette used mainly in pocket dictating equipment *minikassett, mikrokassett;* **microchip** = circuit in which all the active and passive components are formed on one small piece of semiconductor, by means of etching and chemical processes *integrerad krets;* **microcircuit** = complex integrated circuit *mikrokrets;* **microcode** = ALU control instructions implemented as hardwired software *mikrokod*

microcomputer ['maɪkrə(ʊ)kəm'pjuːtə] *or* **micro** ['maɪkrə(ʊ)] *subst.* complete small-scale, cheap, low-power computer system based around a microprocessor chip and having limited memory capacity *mikrodator, persondator;* **microcomputer architecture** = layout and interconnection of a microcomputer's internal hardware *datorarkitektur;* **microcomputer backplane** = main printed circuit board of a system, containing most of the components and connections for expansion boards, etc. *bakplan;* **microcomputer bus** = main data, address and control buses in a microcomputer *buss;* **microcomputer development kit** = basic computer based around a new CPU chip that allows hardware and software designers to experiment with the new device *utvecklingssats (för persondatorbyggare);* **single-board microcomputer** = microcomputer whose components are all

contained on a single printed circuit board
enkortsdator

> COMMENT: micros are particularly used as
> home computers *or* as small office
> computers

microcomputing ['maɪkrə(ʊ)kəm'pjuːtɪŋ]
subst. referring to microcomputers and
their use *personlig databehandling;* **the
microcomputing industry**

microcontroller ['maɪkrə(ʊ)kən'trəʊlə]
subst. small self-contained microcomputer
for use in dedicated control applications
styrprocessor; **single-chip microcontroller =**
one integrated circuit that contains a CPU,
I/O ports, RAM and often a basic
programming language *enkretsstyr-
processor*

microcycle ['maɪkrə(ʊ),saɪkl] *subst.* unit
of time (usually a multiple of the system
clock period) used to give the execution
time of instructions *mikrocykel*

microdevice ['maɪkrəʊdɪ'vaɪs] *subst.*
very small device, such as a microprocessor
mikroenhet

microelectronics
['maɪkrə(ʊ)ɪ,lek'trɒnɪks] *subst.* design and
manufacture of electronic circuits with
integrated circuits and chips
mikroelektronik

microfiche ['maɪkrə(ʊ)fiʃ] *subst.* sheet of
text and graphics in highly reduced form on
a photographic film *mikrofiche*

microfilm ['maɪkrə(ʊ)fɪlm] **1** *subst.* reel of
film containing a sequence of very small
images used for document storage
mikrofilm; **we hold all our records on
microfilm 2** *vb.* to take very small
photographs *mikrofilma;* **the 1985 records
have been sent away for microfilming**

microfloppy ['maɪkrə(ʊ),flɒpɪ] *subst.*
small size magnetic floppy disk (usually
refers to 3.5 inch disks) *liten diskett*

microform ['maɪkrə(ʊ)fɔːm] *subst.*
medium used for storing information in
microimage form *mikrofilmsmedium*

micrographics [,maɪkrə(ʊ)'græfiks]
subst. images and graphics stored as
microimages *mikrografi*

microimage ['maɪkrə(ʊ),ɪmɪdʒ] *subst.*
graphical image too small to be seen with
the naked eye *mikroskopisk bild*

microinstruction
[,maɪkrə(ʊ)ɪn'strʌkʃ(ə)n] *subst.* one
hardwired instruction (part of a
microcode) that controls the actions of the
ALU *mikroinstruktion*

micron ['maɪkrɒn] *subst.* one millionth of
a metre *mikrometer*

microphone ['maɪkrəfəʊn] *subst.* device
that converts sound waves into an
electrical signal *mikrofon;* **dynamic
microphone =** microphone using a coil that
moves and induces a voltage according to
sound pressure *dynamisk mikrofon;* **lapel
microphone =** small microphone that is
pinned to someone's jacket
rockslagsmikrofon, mygga; **moving coil
microphone =** microphone that uses a coil
of wire moved by sound waves to generate
an electrical signal *dynamisk mirkofon,
mikrofon med rörlig spole*

microphotography [,maɪkrə(ʊ)fə'tɒgrəfɪ]
subst. photographic production of
microimages (too small to be seen with the
naked eye) *mikrofotografi*

microprocessor [,maɪkrə(ʊ)'prəʊsesə]
subst. central processing unit elements,
often contained on a single integrated
circuit chip, which when combined with
other memory and I/O chips will make up a
microcomputer *mikroprocessor;* **bit-slice
microprocessor =** large word size CPU
constructed by joining a number of smaller
word size blocks *bituppdelad processor;* **the
bit-slice microprocessor uses four 4-bit
processors to make a 16-bit word processor;
microprocessor addressing capabilities =**
highest address that a CPU can directly
address, without special features (this
depends on the address word size - the
bigger the word the greater the addressing
capacity) *mikroprocessorns adressomfång;*
microprocessor architecture = layout of the
basic parts within a CPU (I/O, ALU, etc.)
datorarkitektur; **microprocessor chip =**
integrated circuit that contains all the
elements of a central processing unit,
connected with other memory and I/O
chips to make a microcomputer *mikrochip;*
microprocessor unit (MPU) = unit
containing the main elements of a
microprocessor *mikroprocessor*

microprogram ['maɪkrə(ʊ),prəʊgræm]
subst. series of microinstructions
mikroprogram, mikrokod; **microprogram
assembly language =** each assembly
language instruction of a computer is
carried out by a microprogram
assemblerspråk; **microprogram counter =**
register that stores the address of the next
microinstruction to be carried out (the
microprogram counter is the same as the
memory address register) *programräknare;*
microprogram instruction set = complete
set of basic microinstructions available in a
CPU *uppsättning mikrokodsinstruktioner;*
microprogram store = storage device used
to hold a microprogram *mikroprogram,
minne*

microprogramming
['maɪkrə(ʊ),prəʊgræmɪŋ] *subst.* writing microcode using microinstructions *mikroprogrammering*

microsecond ['maɪkrə(ʊ),sek(ə)nd] *subst.* one millionth of a second *mikrosekund*

microsequence ['maɪkrə(ʊ),siːkwəns] *subst.* series of microinstructions *mikrosekvens*

microwave ['maɪkrə(ʊ)weɪv] *subst.* radio frequency range from 1 to 3000GHz *mikrovågor;* **microwave communications link** = use of a microwave beam to transmit data between two points *mikrovågslänk;* **microwave relay** = radiocommunications equipment used to receive microwave signals, then boost and retransmit them *mikrovågsrelä;* **microwave transmission** = communication using modulated microwaves allowing high datarates, used for international telephone and satellite communications *mikrovågsöverföring*

microwriter ['maɪkrə(ʊ),raɪtə] *subst.* portable keyboard and display, used for keyboarding when travelling *miniterminal*

middleware ['mɪdlweə] *subst.* system software that has been customized by a dealer for a particular user *systemanpassad programvara*

mid-user ['mɪd,juːzə] *subst.* operator who retrieves relevant information from a database for a customer *or* end user *operatör*

migration [maɪ'greɪʃ(ə)n] *subst.* **data migration** = moving data between a high priority or on-line device to a low-priority or off-line device *dataförflyttning*

mikrokodsminne ⇨ **memory**

mikrotelefon ⇨ **handset**

milk disk ['mɪlkdɪsk] *subst.* disk used to transfer data from a small machine onto a larger computer, which provides greater processing power *mellanlagringsskiva*

milking machine ['mɪlkɪŋməˌʃiːn] *subst.* portable machine which can accept data from different machines, then transfer it to another larger computer *maskin för dataöverföring*

milli- ['mɪlɪ] *prefix* meaning one thousandth *m, milli-;* **milliampere** *or* **mA** = electrical current measure equal to one thousandth of an ampere *mA;* **millisecond** *or* **ms** = one thousandth of a second *ms*

MIMD ['emaɪem'diː] = MULTIPLE INSTRUCTION STREAM - MULTIPLE DATA STREAM architecture of a parallel processor that uses a number of ALUs and memory devices in parallel to provide high speed processing *parallelldator som arbetar enligt MIMD-principen*

mini- ['mɪnɪ] *prefix* meaning small *mini-;* **miniaturization** = making something very small *miniatyrisering;* **minidisk** = magnetic disk smaller than the 5.25 inch standard, usually 3.5 inch *liten diskett;* **minifloppy** = magnetic disk (usually refers to the 5.25 inch standard) *diskett; (slang)* **miniwinny** = small Winchester hard disk *litet skivminne*

minicomputer ['mɪnɪkəm'pjuːtə] *or* **mini** ['mɪnɪ] *subst.* small computer, with a greater range of instructions and processing power than a microcomputer, but not able to compete with the speed *or* data handling capacity of a mainframe computer *minidator*

minimal latency coding ['mɪnɪm(ə)l 'leɪt(ə)nsɪ 'kəʊdɪŋ] *see* MINIMUM ACCESS CODE

minimal tree ['mɪnɪm(ə)l 'triː] *subst.* tree whose nodes are organized in the optimum way, providing maximum efficiency *minimiträd*

minimize ['mɪnɪmaɪz] *vb.* to make as small as possible *förminska, minimera;* **we minimized costs by cutting down the number of components**

minimum ['mɪnɪməm] *subst.* the smallest amount of something *minimum;* **minimum access code** *or* **minimum delay code** = coding system that provides the fastest access and retrieval time for stored data items *minimikod;* **minimum weight routing** = method of optimizing the transmission path of a message through a network *minsta-trafikvägval*

minmax ['mɪnmæks] *subst.* method used in artificial intelligence to solve problems *minimaxmetoden*

minnesavbildning ⇨ **map**

(minnes)bankväxling ⇨ **bank**

minneskompaktering ⇨ **garbage**

minneskrets ⇨ **memory**

(minnes)skiva ⇨ **disk**

minnessökning ⇨ **search**

minnestrumma ⇨ **drum**

minnesutrymmesberäkning ⇨ **float**

minuend ['mɪnjʊənd] *subst.* number from which another is subtracted *subtrahend*

minus ['maɪnəs] *or* **minus sign** ['maɪnəs ˌsaɪn] *subst.* printed *or* written sign (like a small dash) to indicate subtraction *or* to show a negative value *minustecken*

minuscule ['mɪnəskjuːl] *subst.* lower case printed character *gemen, minuskel*

MIPS [mɪps] = MILLION INSTRUCTIONS PER SECOND measure of computing power of a computer *MIPS*

mirror ['mɪrə] **1** *subst.* glass with a metal backing, which reflects an image *spegel;* **mirror image** = image produced that is equivalent to that which would be seen in a mirror *spegelbild* **2** *vb.* to create an identical copy *spegla*

> QUOTE they also offer mirror-disk protection against disk failure, providing automatic backup of a database
> QUOTE disks are also mirrored so that the system can continue to run in the event of a disk crash
> QUOTE mirroring of the database is handled automatically by systems software
> **Computer News**

MIS [emæɪˈes] = MANAGEMENT INFORMATION SYSTEM

MISD [emæɪesˈdiː] = MULTIPLE INSTRUCTION STREAM - SINGLE DATA STREAM architecture of a parallel computer that has a single ALU and data bus with a number of control units *parallelldator som arbetar enligt MISD-principen, dataflödesartiklar*

mismatch [mɪsˈmætʃ] *subst.* situation occurring when two things are not correctly matched *felpassning;* **impedance mismatch** = situation where the impedance of the transmission *or* receiving end of a system does not match the other, resulting in loss of signal power *impedansanpassningsfel*

mix [mɪks] **1** *subst.* way in which different signals have been combined to form a single signal (usually audio) *blandning* **2** *vb.* to combine several separate signals into a single signal *blanda;* **to mix down** = to combine the signals from several sources such as a number of recorded audio tracks *or* instruments into a single signal *blanda, mixa*

mixed highs ['mɪkst haɪz] *subst.* fine colour detail that is in monochrome in a TV signal *färgkontraster*

mixer ['mɪksə] *subst.* electronic circuit used to combine two *or* more separate signals into a single output *blandare, mixer*

mixing ['mɪksɪŋ] *subst.* **(a)** combining several audio signals into a single signal *blandning, mixning;* **mixing studio** = room with audio mixers and sound processors used when recording music *mixningsstudio* **(b)** printing a line of text with several different typefaces *blandad sats*

mjuk avstavning ⇨ hyphen

mjukt bindestreck ⇨ discretionary

MKS ['emkeɪˈes] = METRE KILOGRAM SECOND widely used measurement system based on the metre, kilogram and second *MKSA-systemet; see also* SI UNITS

MMI ['ememˈaɪ] = MAN MACHINE INTERFACE hardware and software designed to make it easier for users to communicate effectively with a machine *användargränssnitt*

mnemonic [niːˈmɒnɪk] *subst.* shortened form of a word *or* function that is helpful as a reminder (such as INCA for increment register A) *mnemoteknisk, som stöder minnet;* **assembler mnemonics** *or* **mnemonic operation codes** = standard word abbreviations used when writing a program for a particular CPU in assembly language (such as LDA for load register A) *mnemoniska koder*

mobile ['məʊbaɪl] *adj.* (i) which can move about *rörlig;* (ii) *informal* meaning a travelling radio base such as a car transceiver *rörlig, mobil;* **mobile earth terminal** = satellite communications equipment that is mobile *rörlig markstation;* **mobile unit** = complete set of television filming and editing equipment carried in a vehicle (for outside broadcasts) *fältenhet;* **mobile radiophone** = radio telephone linked to a main telephone system, which uses a network of stations, each covering a certain area, to provide a service over a large area *mobiltelefon*

mock-up ['mɒkʌp] *subst.* model of a new product for testing *or* to show to possible customers *testmodell, attrapp*

modal ['məʊdl] *adj.* referring to modes *modal*

mode [məʊd] *subst.* **(a)** way of doing something *metod;* method of operating a computer *läge, tillstånd;* **when you want to type in text, press this function key which will put the terminal in its alphanumeric mode; burst mode** = data transmission using intermittent bursts of data *intermittent gruppvis överföring;* **byte mode** = data transmitted one byte at a time *bytevis dataöverföring;* **control mode** = state of a device in which control signals can be received to select options *or* functions *styrläge;* **deferred mode** = entering a command as a program line, then executing the program *interaktivt läge;* **direct mode** = typing in a command which is executed once carriage return has been pressed *direktinmatningsläge;* **execute mode** = command entered in direct mode to start a program run *körläge;* **form mode** = display method on a data entry terminal, the form is displayed on the screen and the operator enters relevant details *formulärfunktion;* **input mode** = computer which is receiving data *inmatningsläge;* **insert mode** = interactive computer mode in which new text is entered within the previous text, which adjusts to make room for it *insättningsläge;* **interactive mode** = computer that allows the user to enter commands *or* programs *or* data and receive an immediate response *interaktivt läge;* **noisy mode** = floating point arithmetic in which a digit other than a zero is deliberately added in the least significant position during the normalization of a floating point number *normaliseringstillstånd;* **replace mode** = interactive computer mode in which new text entered replaces any previous text *utbytesläge;* **sequential mode** = each instruction in a program is stored in consecutive locations *sekventiellt läge* **(b)** number of paths taken by light when travelling down an optical fibre *väg;* **mode dispersion** = loss of power in a light signal transmitted down an optic fibre due to dispersion from transmission paths that are not directly along the axis of the fibre *spridningsförlust;* *see* MONOMODE, MULTIMODE **(c)** number that occurs most frequently in a series of samples *median, tyngdpunkt*

> QUOTE the printer gives print quality in three modes: high speed, data processing and letter-quality
> **Minicomputer News**

model ['mɒdl] **1** *subst.* **(a)** small copy of something to show what it will look like when finished *modell;* **he showed us a model of the new computer centre building (b)** style *or* type of product *modell;* version of a product *modell;* **the new model B has taken the place of model A; this is the latest model; the model on display is last year's; they are selling off the old models at half price; demonstration model** = piece of equipment used in demonstrations (and then sold cheaply) *demonstrationsexemplar* **2** *adj.* which is a perfect example to be copied *modell-, mönster-;* **a model agreement 3** *vb.* to make a computerized model of a new product *or* of the economic system, etc. *modellera* NOTE: **modelling - modelled** but US **modeling - modeled**

modelling ['mɒd(ə)lɪŋ] *subst.* creating computer models *modellering*

modem ['məudem] *or* **MODEM** *subst.* = MODULATOR/DEMODULATOR device that allows data to be sent over telephone lines by converting binary signals from a computer into analog sound signals which can be transmitted over a telephone line *modem;* **dial-in modem** = auto-answer modem that can be called at any time to access a system *autosvarsmodem; see also*

STANDARD; *compare with* ACOUSTIC COUPLER

> COMMENT: the process of converting binary signals to analog is called "modulation". When the signal is received, another modem reverses the process (called "demodulation"). Both modems must be working according to the same standards

modem ▷ **dataset, modem**

modification [ˌmɒdɪfɪ'keɪʃ(ə)n] *subst.* change made to something *förändring, modifiering;* **the modifications to the system allow it to be run as part of a LAN; modification loop** = instructions within a loop that changes other instructions *or* data within a program *modifierande slinga*

modified frequency modulation ['mɒdɪfaɪd 'friːkwənsɪ ˌmɒdjʊ'leɪʃ(ə)n] *subst.* method of frequency modulation used to record data onto a magnetic medium *frekvensmoduleringslagring*

modifier ['mɒdɪfaɪə] *subst.* programming instruction that alters the normal action of a command *modifierande instruktion*

modifiering av instruktion ▷ **instruction**

modify ['mɒdɪfaɪ] *vb.* to change something *or* to make something fit a different use *modifiera, ändra;* **the keyboard was modified for European users; we are running a modified version of the mail-merge system; the software will have to be modified to run on a small PC**

modular ['mɒdjʊlə] *adj.* (method of constructing hardware *or* software products) by connecting several smaller blocks together to produce a customized product *modulär;* **modular programming** = programming small individually written sections of computer code that can be made to fit into a structured program and can be called up from a main program *modulär programmering*

modularity [ˌmɒdjʊ'lærɪtɪ] *subst.* being made up from modules *modularitet;* **the modularity of the software or hardware allows the system to be changed**

modularization [ˌmɒdjʊləraɪ'zeɪʃ(ə)n] *subst.* designing programs from a set of standard modules *modularisering*

modulate ['mɒdjʊleɪt] *vb.* to change a carrier wave so that it can carry data *modulera;* **modulated signal** = constant frequency and amplitude carrier signal that is used in a modulated form to transmit data *modulerad signal;* **modulating signal** = signal to be transmitted that is used to modulate a carrier *modulerande signal*

modulation [ˌmɒdjuˈleɪʃ(ə)n]   *subst.* process of varying a carrier's amplitude *or* frequency *or* phase according to an applied signal *modulering;* **amplitude modulation (AM) =** system that varies the amplitude of a constant carrier signal according to an external signal *amplitudmodulering;* **frequency modulation (FM) =** system that varies the frequency of a constant amplitude carrier signal according to an external signal *frekvensmodulering*

modulator [ˈmɒdjuleɪtə]   *subst.* electronic circuit that varies a carrier signal according to an applied signal *modulator;* **modulator/demodulator =** MODEM

module [ˈmɒdjuːl]   *subst.* **(a)** small section of a large program that can if required function independently as a program in its own right *modul* **(b)** self-contained piece of hardware that can be connected with other modules to form a new system *modul;* **a multifunction analog interface module includes analog to digital and digital to analog converters**

modulo arithmetic [ˈmɒdʒələʊ əˈrɪθmətɪk]   *subst.* branch of arithmetic that uses the remainder of one number when divided by another *modularitmetik;* **modulo-N =** modulo arithmetic using base N *modulo-N;* **modulo-N check =** error detection test using the remainder from a modulo arithmetic operation on data *modulo-N-kontroll*

modulus [ˈmɒdjʊləs] *or* **MOD** [mɒd]   *subst.* the remainder after the division of one number by another *rest (efter en modulo-N beräkning);* **7 mod 3 = 1**

momentary switch [ˈməʊmənt(ə)rɪ ˈswɪtʃ]   *subst.* switch that only conducts while it is being pressed *strömställare med momentan slutning*

monadic (Boolean) operator [mɒˈnædɪk (ˈbuːliən) ˈɒpəreɪtə]   *subst.* logical operator with only one operand *enställig operator;* **the monadic operator NOT can be used here; monadic operation =** operation that uses one operand to produce one result *enställig operation*

monitor [ˈmɒnɪtə]   **1** *subst.* **(a)** visual display unit used to display high quality text *or* graphics, generated by a computer *(bild)skärm;* **multi-scan** *or* **multi-sync monitor =** monitor which has circuitry to lock onto the required scanning frequency for any type of graphics card *(själv)synkroniserande bildskärm;* **monitor unit** *see* VDU **(b)** (i) loudspeaker used to listen to the sound signals produced during recording *or* mixing *avlyssningshögtalare, studiohögtalare;* (ii) TV screen in a TV studio control room, which shows the image being filmed by one of the cameras

monitor (c) **monitor program =** computer program that allows basic commands to be entered to operate a system (such as load a program, examine the state of devices, etc.) *övervakningsprogram; see also* OPERATING SYSTEM; **firmware monitor =** monitor program that is resident in a ROM device, used to load in the operating system when a machine is switched on *inbyggt övervakningsprogram* **(d)** system that watches for faults *or* failures in a circuit *övervakningsfunktion;* **power monitor =** circuit that shuts off the electricity supply if it is faulty *or* likely to damage equipment *nätspänningsövervakning(skrets)* **2** *vb.* (i) to check *or* to examine how something is working *kontrollera, bevaka;* (ii) to look after and supervise a process *or* experiment to make sure it is operating correctly *övervaka, överse;* **he is monitoring the progress of the trainee programmers; the machine monitors each signal as it is sent out**

mono- [ˈmɒnəʊ]   *prefix* meaning single *or* one *mono-*

monoaural [ˌmɒnə(ʊ)ˈɔːr(ə)l]   *adj.* single audio channel presented to only one ear *enkanals-, mono (i ett öra)*

monochrome [ˈmɒnəkrəʊm]   *adj. & subst.* (image) in one colour, usually shades of grey and black and white *monokrom;* **monochrome monitor =** computer monitor that displays text and graphics in black, white and shades of grey instead of colours *monokrom skärm, svart-vit skärm, enfärgsskärm*

monolithic [ˌmɒnə(ʊ)ˈlɪθɪk]   *adj.* (integrated circuit) manufactured on a single crystal of semiconductor *monolitisk krets*

monomode fibre [ˈmɒnə(ʊ)ˌməʊd ˈfaɪbə]   *subst.* optical fibre that only allows light to travel along its axis without any internal reflections, as the result of having a very fine core diameter *envägsfiber; see also* MODE

monophonic [ˌmɒnə(ʊ)ˈfɒnɪk]   *adj.* system where one audio signal is used to feed one *or* more loudspeakers *monofonisk; compare with* STEREOPHONIC

monoprogramming system [ˌmɒnə(ʊ)ˈprəʊgræmɪŋ ˈsɪstəm]   *subst.* computer batch processing system that executes one program at a time *satsvis programmering; compare with* MULTIPROGRAMMING SYSTEM

monospacing [ˈmɒnə(ʊ)ˌspeɪsɪŋ]   *subst.* system of printing where each character occupies the same amount of space, as on a typewriter (as opposed to proportional spacing) *fast teckenindelning*

monostable [ˌmɒnə(ʊ)'steɪbl] *subst.* electronic circuit that produces an output pulse for a predetermined period when it receives an input signal *monostabil krets*

Monte Carlo method [ˌmɒntɪ'kɑːləʊ 'meθəd] *subst.* statistical analysis technique *Monte Carlo-metoden*

montera ⇨ **mount**

Morse code ['mɔːs'kəʊd] *subst.* system of signalling using only two symbols: dots and dashes *Morsekod;* **morse key** = switch used to send morse messages by hand *telegrafinyckel*

MOS [mɒs] = METAL OXIDE SEMICONDUCTOR production and design method for a certain family of integrated circuits using patterns of metal conductors and oxide deposited onto a semiconductor *MOS-metoden för kretstillverkning med halvledare; see also* MOSFET; CMOS; **MOS memory** = solid-state memory using MOSFETs to store binary data *MOS-minne;* **CMOS** = COMPLEMENTARY METAL OXIDE SEMICONDUCTOR integrated circuit design and construction method (using a pair of complementary p- and n- type transistors) *CMOS*

> QUOTE integrated circuits fall into one of two distinct classes, based either on bipolar or metal oxide semiconductor (MOS) transistors
> **Electronics & Power**

mosaic [mə(ʊ)'zeɪɪk] *subst.* display character used in videotext systems that is made up of small dots *mosaiktecken*

MOSFET ['mɒsfet] = METAL OXIDE SEMICONDUCTOR FIELD EFFECT TRANSISTOR high power and high speed field effect transistor manufactured using MOS techniques *MOSFET-krets*

most significant bit ['məʊst sɪg'nɪfɪkənt 'bɪt] *or* **msb** *or* **MSB** ['emes'biː] *subst.* bit in a word that represents the greatest value *or* weighting (usually the bit which is furthest to the left) *mest signifikant bit;* **the most significant bit in an eight bit binary word represents 128 in decimal notation**

most significant character ['məʊst sɪg'nɪfɪkənt 'kærəktə] *or* **most significant digit (MSD)** *subst.* digit at the far left of a number, that represents the greatest power of the base *mest signifikanta tecken* NOTE: the opposite is **LSB, LSD**

motherboard ['mʌðəˌbɔːd] *subst.* main printed circuit board of a system, containing most of the components and connections for expansion boards, etc. *moderkort*

motion picture ['məʊʃ(ə)n 'pɪktʃə] *subst.* projection at high speed of a series of still images that creates the impression of movement *film*

motor ['məʊtə] *subst.* electromagnetic machine that converts an electrical supply into (rotary) motion (by means of a magnetic field) *elmotor*

motstå ⇨ **resist**

motta ⇨ **receive**

mottagare ⇨ **receiver**

mottagningsbuffert ⇨ **data**

mottagningsterminal ⇨ **receive**

mount [maʊnt] *vb.* to fix a device *or* a circuit onto a base *montera;* **the chips are mounted in sockets on the PCB**

mouse [maʊs] *subst.* small hand-held input device moved on a flat surface to control the position of a cursor on the screen *mus;* **mouse-driven** = (software) which uses a mouse rather than a keyboard for input *musstyrd;* **mouse driver** = program which converts data from a mouse to a standard form that can be used by any software *musstyrprogram* NOTE: the plural is **mice** or sometimes **mouses**

> QUOTE a powerful new mouse-based editor:- you can cut, paste and copy with the mouse
> **Personal Computer World**
> QUOTE you can use a mouse to access pop-up menus and a keyboard for a word-processor
> **Byte**

mouth [maʊθ] *subst.* open end of an antenna *horn, tratt*

M out of N code ['em aʊt əv 'en 'kəʊd] *subst.* coding system providing error detection, each valid character which is N bits long must contain M binary "one" bits *M-av-N-kod*

movable ['muːvəbl] *adj.* which can be moved *flyttbar;* **movable head disk** = magnetic disk head assembly that moves across the disk until the required track is reached *skivminne med rörligt huvud*

move [muːv] *vb.* to change the place of something *flytta;* **move block** = command which changes the place of a block of text identified by block markers *"flytta block"-kommando;* **moving coil microphone** = microphone which uses a coil of wire moved by sound waves to generate an electrical signal *dynamisk mikrofon, mikrofon med rörlig spole*

movement ['muːvmənt] *subst.* changing the place of something *flyttning;* **movement file** = file containing recent changes *or* transactions to records, which is then used to update a master file *loggfil*

MPS ['empiːes] = MICROPROCESSOR SYSTEM

MPU ['empi:'ju:] = MICROPROCESSOR UNIT

MS ['em'es] = MANUSCRIPT
NOTE: plural is **MSS**

ms ['mɪlɪˌsekənd] = MILLISECOND one thousandth of a second *ms*

msb ['emes'biː] *or* **MSB** = MOST SIGNIFICANT BIT bit in a word that represents the greatest value *or* weight (usually the bit furthest to the left) *mest signifikanta bit*

MSD ['emes'diː] = MOST SIGNIFICANT DIGIT

MSI ['emes'aɪ] = MEDIUM SCALE INTEGRATION

M signal ['em 'sɪgn(ə)l] *subst.* signal produced from the sum of left and right signals in a stereophonic system *summasignal*

MSX ['emes'eks] *subst.* hardware and software standard for home computers that can use interchangeable software *MSX-standarden*

MTBF ['emti:bi:'ef] = MEAN TIME BETWEEN FAILURES average period of time that a piece of equipment will operate between failures *genomsnittlig drifttid, medeltid mellan fel*

MTF ['emti:'ef] = MEAN TIME TO FAILURE average period of time for which a device will operate (usually continuously) before failing *genomsnittlig drifttid, medeltid till fel*

multi- ['mʌltɪ] *prefix* meaning many *or* more than one *multi-, fler-;* **multimegabyte memory card; a multistandard unit; multi-access system** = computer system that allows several users to access one file *or* program at the same time *fleranvändarsystem; see also* MULTI-USER; **multi-address** *or* **multi-address instruction** = instruction that contains more than one address (of data *or* locations *or* input/output) *fleradressinstruktion*

multi-board computer ['mʌltɪbɔːd kəm'pjuːtə] *subst.* computer which has several integrated circuit boards connected to a mother board *flerkortsdator*

multiburst signal ['mʌltɪbɜːst 'sɪgn(ə)l] *subst.* television test signal *testbild, testsignal*

multi-bus system ['mʌltɪbʌs 'sɪstəm] *subst.* computer architecture that uses a high speed bus between CPU and main memory and a slower bus between CPU and other peripherals *flerbussystem*

multicasting ['mʌltɪˌkɑːstɪŋ] *subst.* broadcasting to a number of receivers *or*

nodes, with an address in each message to indicate the node required *fleradressändning*

multichannel ['mʌltɪˌtʃænl] *adj.* with more than one channel *flerkanals-*

multicolour ['mʌltɪˌkʌlə] *adj.* with several colours *flerfärgs-*

multidimensional [ˌmʌltɪdɪ'menʃənl] *adj.* with features in more than one dimension *flerdimensionell;* **multidimensional array** = number of arrays arranged in parallel, providing depth *flerdimensionell vektor;* **multidimensional language** = programming language that can be represented in a number of ways *flerdimensionellt programmeringsspråk*

multi-disk ['mʌltɪdɪsk] *adj.* referring to several types of disk *flerskivminnes-;* **multi-disk option** = system that can have disk drives installed in a number of sizes *flerskivminnessystem;* **multi-disk reader** = device which can read from various sizes and formats of disk *flersystemsskivenhet*

multidrop circuit ['mʌltɪdrɒp 'sɜːkɪt] *subst.* network allowing communications between a number of terminals and a central computer, but not directly between terminals *flerpunktsnät*

multifrequency ['mʌltɪ'friːkwənsɪ] *subst.* **dual tone, multifrequency (DTMF)** = communication signalling system using two different frequencies to transmit binary data *tvåtonssignalering*

multifunction ['mʌltɪ'fʌŋkʃ(ə)n] *adj.* which has several functions *flerfunktions-;* **a multifunction analog interface module includes analog to digital and digital to analog converters; multifunction card** = add-on circuit board that provides many features to upgrade a computer *flerfunktionskort;* **multifunction workstation** = workstation where several tasks can be carried out *flerfunktionsarbetsplats*

multifunctional ['mʌltɪ'fʌŋkʃənl] *adj.* which has several functions *flerfunktions-;* **a multifunctional scanner**

multikörning ⇨ **task**

multilayer [ˌmʌltɪ'leɪə] *subst.* printed circuit board that has several layers *or* interconnecting conduction tracks *flerlagerskort*

multilevel [ˌmʌltɪ'levl] *subst.* signal with a number of possible values (quaternary signals have four levels) *flernivåsignal*

multilink system ['mʌltɪlɪŋk 'sɪstəm] *subst.* system where there is more than one connection between two points *flergrenssystem, förgrenat system*

multimedia [ˌmʌltɪ'miːdɪə] *adj.* referring to several forms of media *multimedia-;* **multimedia mail** = messages that can contain voice, sound, images or data *multimediala meddelanden*

multimeter ['mʌltɪˌmiːtə] *subst.* testing equipment that provides an indication of the voltage *or* current *or* impedance at a point or of a component *universalinstrument, multimeter;* **analog multimeter (AMM)** = testing equipment using a moving needle to indicate voltage, current *or* impedance levels *analogt universalinstrument, analog multimeter;* **digital multimeter (DMM)** = multimeter that uses a digital readout to indicate voltage, current *or* impedance levels *digitalt universalinstrument, digital multimeter*

multimode fibre ['mʌltɪˌməʊd 'faɪbə] *subst.* optical fibre that allows many different paths in addition to the direct straight path for light beams, causing pulse stretching and interference on reception of the signal *interferensljusledare*

multi-part stationery ['mʌltɪpɑːt 'steɪʃ(ə)nərɪ] *subst.* continuous stationery with two or more sheets together, either with carbons between *or* carbonless *blankettset i löpande bana*

multipass overlap ['mʌltɪpɑːs ˌəʊvə'læp] *subst.* system of producing higher quality print from a dot matrix printer by repeating the line of characters but shifted slightly, so making the dots less noticeable *repetitionsskrivning*

multiphase program ['mʌltɪfeɪz 'prəʊgræm] *subst.* program that requires more than one fetch operation before execution is complete *flerfasprogram*

multiple ['mʌltɪpl] *adj.* having many parts *or* acting in many ways *fler-, multipel;* **multiple access** *see* MULTI-ACCESS; **multiple address code** = instruction with more than one address for the operands, result and the location of the next instruction to be executed *fleradresskod; see also* THREE-PLUS-ONE; FOUR-PLUS-ONE ADDRESS; **multiple bus architecture** = computer architecture that uses a high speed bus between CPU and main memory and a slower bus between CPU and other peripherals *flerbussarkitektur;* **multiple instruction stream - multiple data stream (MIMD)** = architecture of a parallel processor that uses a number of ALUs and memories in parallel to provide high speed processing *parallellarkitektur, MIMD-arkitektur;* **multiple instruction stream - single data stream (MISD)** = architecture of a parallel computer that has a single ALU and data bus with a number of control units *dataflödesarkitektur, MISD-arkitektur (jämför även SIMD);* **multiple**

precision = use of more than one byte of data for number storage to increase possible precision *multipel precision*

multiplex ['mʌltɪpleks] *vb.* to combine several messages in the same transmission medium *multiplexera;* **multiplexed analog components (MAC)** = standard television broadcast signal format *MAC-systemet för tevesändning;* **multiplexed bus** = one bus used to carry address, data and control signals at different times *multiplexerad buss*

multiplexing ['mʌltɪpleksɪŋ] *subst.* combining several messages in the same transmission medium *multiplexering;* **dynamic multiplexing** = multiplexing method which allocates time segments to signals according to demand *dynamisk multiplexering;* **homogeneous multiplexing** = switching multiplexor system where all the channels contain data using the same protocol and transmission rate *homogen multiplexering;* **optical multiplexing** = sending several light beams down a single path *or* fibre *optisk multiplexering*

multiplexor (MUX) ['mʌltɪpleksə ('emjuːˈeks)] *subst.* circuit that combines a number of inputs into a smaller number of outputs *multiplexor, Mux; compare with* DEMULTIPLEXOR **a 4 to 1 multiplexor combines four inputs into a single output**

multiplicand [ˌmʌltɪplɪ'kænd] *subst.* number which is multiplied by another number *multiplikand*

multiplication [ˌmʌltɪplɪ'keɪʃ(ə)n] *subst.* mathematical operation that adds one number to itself a number of times *multiplikation;* **the multiplication of 5 and 3 = 15; multiplication sign** = printed *or* written sign (x) used to show that numbers are multiplied *multiplikationstecken*

multiplier ['mʌltɪplaɪə] *subst.* number which multiplies a multiplicand *multiplikator*

multiply ['mʌltɪplaɪ] *vb.* to perform a multiplication of a number (the multiplier) *multiplicera*

multipoint ['mʌltɪpɔɪnt] *adj.* (connection) with several lines, attaching several terminals to a single line to a single computer *flerpunkts-*

multiprecision ['mʌltɪprɪ'sɪʒn] *subst.* use of more than one data word to represent numbers (increasing the range *or* precision possible) *multipel precision*

multiprocessing system ['mʌltɪ'prəʊsesɪŋ 'sɪstəm] *subst.* system where several processing units work together sharing the same memory *flerprocessorssystem*

multiprocessor ['mʌltɪ'prəʊsesə] *subst.* number of processing units acting together *or* separately but sharing the same area of memory *flerprocessor;* **multiprocessor interleaving =** each processor in a multiprocessor system dealing with a section of one or more processes *flerprocessoröverlappning*

multi-programming [ˌmʌltɪ'prəʊgræmɪŋ] *subst.* operating system used to execute more than one program apparently simultaneously (each program being executed a little at a time) *fleruppdragssystem, multiprogramkörning*

multi-scan ['mʌltɪskæn] *or* **multi-sync monitor** ['mʌltɪsɪŋk 'mɒnɪtə] *subst.* monitor which contains circuitry to lock onto the required scanning frequency of any type of graphics card *självsynkroniserande bildskärm*

multi statement line ['mʌltɪ 'steɪtmənt 'laɪn] *subst.* line from a computer program that contains more than one instruction *or* statement *programrad med fler än en sats*

multi-strike printer ribbon ['mʌltɪstraɪk 'prɪntəˌrɪbən] *subst.* inked ribbon in a printer that can be used more than once *flergångsfärgband*

multitasking [ˌmʌltɪ'tɑːskɪŋ] *or* **multitasking** *subst.* ability of a computer system to run two or more programs at the same time *fleruppdragskörning;* **the system is multi-user and multi-tasking; real-time multitasking =** executing several (real-time) tasks simultaneously without slowing the execution of any of the processors *fleruppdragskörning i realtid, realtidskörning*

COMMENT: few small systems are capable of simultaneous multitasking, since each program would require its own processor; this is overcome by allocating to each program an amount of processing time, executing each a little at a time so that they will appear to run simultaneously due to the speed of the processor and the relatively short gaps between programs

QUOTE this is a true multi-tasking system, meaning that several computer applications can be running at the same time
Which PC?
QUOTE page management programs are so greedy for memory that it is not a good idea to ask them to share RAM space with anything else, so the question of multi-tasking does not arise here
Desktop Publishing

multi-terminal system ['mʌltɪˌtɜːmɪnl 'sɪstəm] *subst.* system where several terminals are linked to a single CPU *flerterminalsystem*

multithread ['mʌltɪθred] *subst.* program design using more than one logical path through it, each path being concurrently executed *flerprocessarkitektur*

multi-user system ['mʌltɪˌjuːzə 'sɪstəm] *subst.* computer system that can support more than one user at a time *fleranvändarsystem;* **the program runs on a standalone machine or a multi-user system**

multivibrator [ˌmʌltɪvaɪ'breɪtə] *subst.* electronic circuit that switches continuously between two output states, often used for clock generation *multivibrator, astabil vippa;* **astable multivibrator =** electronic circuit that repeatedly switches an output between two voltage levels *astabil vippa*

multi-window editor ['mʌltɪˌwɪndəʊ 'edɪtə] *subst.* program used for creating and editing a number of applications programs independently, each in a separate window on screen at the same time *redigeringsprogram med flera fönster*

mung up [mʌŋ ʌp] *vb. informal* to distort data *or* to ruin a file *klanta till det*

Murray code ['mʌrɪ'kəʊd] *subst.* code used for teleprinters that uses only 5 bits *Murray-kod*

mush [mʌʃ] *subst.* distortion and loss of signal *störning, smet;* **mush area =** distortion and loss of signal due to two transmissions interfering *smetfläck i överföringen*

music chip ['mjuːzɪktʃɪp] *subst.* integrated circuit capable of generating musical sounds and tunes *musikkrets;* **music synthesizer =** device able to generate musical notes which are similar to those made by musical instruments *synthesizer*

musstyrd ⇨ **mouse**

musstyrprogram ⇨ **mouse**

muting ['mjuːtɪŋ] *subst.* **interstation muting =** ability of a radio receiver to prevent the noise found between radio stations from being amplified and heard by the user *brusdämpning*

MUX ['mʌltɪpleks] = MULTIPLEXOR circuit that combines a number of inputs into a smaller number of outputs *multiplexerare;* compare DEMULTIPLEXOR

MW ['em'dʌbljuː] = MEDIUM WAVE

mått ⇨ **rate**

människa-maskin-gränssnitt ⇨ **HMI, human-computer**

märke ⇨ **mark, tag**

mättnadsprov ⇨ **test**

mättning ⇨ **saturation**

möjlighetsanalys ⇨ **feasibility**

mörkerström ⇨ **dark current**

möte ⇨ **conference**

Nn

n ['næɲə(ʊ)] *prefix* meaning nano-*nano-*

NAK ['eneɪ'keɪ] = NEGATIVE ACKNOWLEDGEMENT

name [neɪm] *subst.* **(a)** word used to call a thing *or* a person *namn;* **brand name** = name of a particular make of product *varumärke;* **corporate name** = name of a large corporation *företagsnamn, firma;* **the company buys computer parts from several suppliers, and packages them together to make their own name product (b)** ordinary word used to identify an address in machine language *adresskod;* **file name** = word used to identify a particular stored file *filnamn;* **program name** = identification name for a stored program file *filnamn på programfil;* **name table** *or* **symbol table** = list of reserved words *or* commands in a language and the addresses in the computer that refer to them *namntabell;* **variable name** = word used to identify a variable in a program *variabelnamn*

NAND function ['nænd 'fʌŋ(k)ʃ(ə)n] *subst.* logical function whose output is false if all inputs are true, and true if any input is false *negerad konjunktion;* **NAND gate** = electronic circuit that provides a NAND function *(logisk) icke-och-grind* NOTE: the NAND function is equivalent to an AND function with a NOT function at the output

COMMENT: the output is 0 only if both inputs are 1; if one input is 1 and the other 0, or if both inputs are 0, then the output is 1

nano- *or* **N** ['næɲə(ʊ)] *prefix* meaning one thousand millionth *or nano-;* *US* one billionth *nano-;* **nanocircuit** *or* **nanosecond circuit** = electronic and logic circuits that can respond to impulses within nanoseconds *nanosekundkrets;* **nanometre** *or* **nm** = one thousand millionth of a metre *nanometer;* **nanosecond** *or* **ns** = one thousand millionth of a second *nanosekund* NOTE: US billion is the same as UK one thousand million (10 to the power of nine); UK billion is one million million (10 to the power of 10)

QUOTE the cache's internal RAM is accessed in under 70ns from address strobe to ready signal
Electronics & Power

narrative ['nærətɪv] *subst.* explanatory notes or comments to help a user operate a program *hjälpkommentarer*

narrative statement ['nærətɪv 'steɪtmənt] *subst.* statement which sets variables and allocates storage at the start of a program *kommentarsats, initieringssats*

narrow band ['nærəʊ 'bænd] *subst.* communication method that uses a bandwidth less than that of a voice channel *smalband;* **narrow band FM (NBFM)** = frequency modulation system using very small bandwidth (with only one pair of sidebands) *smalbandig frekvens-modulering; compare* WIDE BAND

National Television Standards Committee (NTSC) ['næʃənl 'telɪˌvɪʒ(ə)n 'stændədz kə'mɪtɪ] *subst.* official body that defines television and video formats *or*standards used mainly in the USA and in Japan *TV-standard för videosignaler; see also* VIDEO STANDARDS

COMMENT: NTSC standards are based on 525 horizontal lines and 60 frames per second

native ['neɪtɪv] *adj.* **native format** = first *or* basic format *ursprungsformat*

natural ['nætʃr(ə)l] *adj.* occurring in nature *or* not created artificially *naturlig;* **natural binary coded decimal (NBCD)** = representation of single decimal digits as a pattern of 4 bits *naturlig binärkodad decimal;* **natural language** = language that is used *or* understood by humans *naturligt språk;* **the expert system can be programmed in a natural language**

QUOTE there are two main types of natural-language interface: those based on menus, and those where the user has to discover what questions the computer will respond to by trial and error
Electronics & Power

nav ⇨ **hub**

NBCD ['enbiːsiːˈdiː] = NATURAL BINARY CODED DECIMAL

NBFM ['enbiːefˈem] = NARROW BAND FREQUENCY MODULATION

NC ['en'siː] = NUMERICAL CONTROL machine operated automatically by computer *or* circuits controlled by a stored program *or* data *numeriskt styrd*

n-channel metal oxide semiconductor ['enˌtʃænl 'metl 'ɒksaɪd ˌsemɪkən'dʌktə] *subst.* transistor design, with MOS techniques, that uses an n-type region for conduction *N-dopad halvledare*

NCR paper ['ensiː'ɑː'peɪpə] = NO CARBON REQUIRED paper *see* CARBONLESS PAPER

NDR ['endiː'ɑː] = NON DESTRUCTIVE READOUT display system that continues to display previous characters when new ones are displayed *oförstörande läsning*

near letter-quality (NLQ) ['nɪə,letə'kwɒlətɪ ('enel'kjuː)] *subst.* printing by a dot-matrix printer that provides higher quality type, which is almost as good as a typewriter, by decreasing the spaces between the dots *skönskrift;* **switch the printer to NLQ for these form letters**

nedslag ⇨ **keystroke**

nedslagsräkning ⇨ **keystroke**

needle ['niːdl] *subst.* tiny metal pin on a dot matrix printer which prints one of the dots *nål, stift*

negate [nɪ'geɪt] *vb.* to reverse the sign of a number *negera;* **if you negate 23.4 the result is -23.4**

negation [nɪ'geɪʃ(ə)n] *subst.* reversing the sign of a number (such as from 5 to -5) *negation, byte av tecken*

negative ['negətɪv] **1** *adj.* meaning "no" *negativ, icke-, minus-;* **negative acknowledgement (NAK)** = signal sent by a receiver to indicate that data has been incorrectly *or* incompletely received *negativ bekräftelse, negativ kvittens;* **negative feedback** = loop around a circuit in which part of the output signal is subtracted from the input signal *negativ återkoppling;* **negative number** = number which represents the number subtracted from zero, indicated by a minus sign in front of the number *negativt tal;* **negative-true logic** = use of a lower voltage level to represent binary 1 than for binary 0 *negativ logik* **2** *subst.* normal photographic film where the colours are reversed (black is white and white is black) *negativ;* **contact negative** = film which can be used to produce a print without any reduction *or* enlargement *kontaktfilm, kontaktnegativ*

negativ återkoppling ⇨ **feedback**

negerad antingen-eller-grind ⇨ EXNOR, exclusive, gate

negerad disjunktion ⇨ **denial**

negerad konjunktion ⇨ **denial, joint denial**

neither-nor function ['naɪðə'nɔː 'fʌŋ(k)ʃ(ə)n] *subst.* logical function whose output is false if any input is true *negerad disjunktion*

neka åtkomst ⇨ **deny access**

NEQ ['eniː'kjuː] = NON-EQUIVALENCE; **NEQ function** = logical function where the output is true if the inputs are not the same, otherwise the output is false *icke-ekvivalens, symmetrisk differens;* **NEQ gate** = electronic implementation of an NEQ function *antingen-eller-grind*

(ner)laddningsbar ⇨ **downloadable**

nest [nest] *vb.* (i) to insert a subroutine within a program *or* another routine *bygga in, kapsla in;* (ii) to use a routine that calls itself recursively *använda inkapsling;* **nested loop** = loop inside another loop in the same program *(in)kapslad slinga;* **nested macrocall** = a macro called from within another macro *inkapslat makro;* **nesting level** = number of subroutines within a subroutine *kapslingsnivå;* **nesting store** = hardware stack (normally stacks are implemented with software) *stack i maskinvara, kapslad stack*

nettovikt ⇨ **weight**

network ['netwɜːk] **1** *subst.* any system made of a number of points *or* circuits that are interconnected *nät, nätverk;* **communications network** = group of devices such as terminals and printers that are interconnected with a central computer allowing the rapid and simple transfer of data *kommunikationsnät;* **computer network** = shared use of a series of interconnected computers, peripherals and terminals *datanät;* **information network** = number of databases linked together, usually using telephone lines and modems, allowing a large amount of data to be accessed by a wider number of users *informationsnätverk;* **local area network (LAN)** = network where the various terminals and equipment are all within a short distance of one another (at a maximum distance of 500m, for example in the same building) and can be interconnected by cables *lokalt nät, lokalt datanät;* **long haul network** = communications network between distant computers that usually uses the public telephone system *längdistansnät;* **radio** *or* **television network** = series of local radio *or* TV stations linked to a main central station *radio- eller tevenät;* **wide area network (WAN)** = network where the various terminals are far apart and linked by radio *or* satellite *globalt nät, längdistansnät;* **network analysis** = study of messages, destinations and routes in a network to provide a better operation *nätanalys;* **network architecture** = method in which a network is constructed, such as layers in an OSI system *nätarkitektur;* **network control program** = software that regulates the flow of and channels for data transmitted in a network *nätstyrningsprogram;* **network controller** = network user responsible for allocating disk space, answering queries and solving problems from other users of the same network *nätstyrenhet;* **network database** = database structure in which data items can be linked together *nätverksdatabas;* **network diagram** = graphical representation describing the interconnections between points *nätverksdiagram;* **network hardware** = physical links, computers and control equipment that make up a network *nätutrustning;* **network layer** = ISO/OSI standard layer that decides on the routes to be used, the costs, etc. *nätskikt; see also* LAYER; **network management** = organization, planning, running and upkeep of a network *nätadministration, näthantering;* **network processor** = signal multiplexer controlled by a microprocessor in a network *nätprocessor;* **network redundancy** = extra links between points allowing continued operation in the event of one failing *nätredundans;* **network software** = software which is used to establish the link between a user's program and the network *nätprogramvara;* **network structure** = data structure that allows each node to be connected to any of the others *nätstruktur;* **network timing** = signals that correctly synchronize the transmission of data *nätklocka; see also* BUS, MESH, PROTOCOL, RING, STAR, TOPOLOGY **2** *vb.* to link points together in a network *koppla samman (i nät);* **they run a system of networked micros; the workstations have been networked together rather than used as standalone systems; networked TV programme** = programme which is broadcast (usually simultaneously) by all the stations in a TV network *samtidig utsändning över alla stationer i ett tevenät*

QUOTE the traditional way of operating networks involves having a network manager and training network users to familiarize themselves with a special set of new commands
Which PC?
QUOTE workstations are cheaper the more you buy, because they are usually networked and share resources
PC Business World

networking ['netwɜːkɪŋ] *subst.* **(a)** broadcasting a prime-time TV programme over several local stations at the same time *samtidig utsändning* **(b)** (i) working *or* organization of a network *nätuppbyggnad, nätarkitektur;* (ii) interconnecting two *or* more computers either in the same room *or* different buildings, in the same town *or* different towns, allowing them to exchange information *sammankoppling, inkoppling på nät;* **networking hardware** *or* **network hardware** = physical links, computers and control equipment that make up a network *nätutrustning, nät(system)komponenter;* **networking software** *or* **network software** = software which is used to establish the link between a user's program and the network

nätprogramvara; **networking specialist** = company *or* person who specializes in designing and setting up networks *nätexpert, nätingenjör;* **this computer firm is a UK networking specialist**

COMMENT: networking allows a machine with a floppy disk drive to use another PC's hard disk when both machines are linked by a cable and are using networking software

neutral ['njuːtr(ə)l] *adj.* with no state *or* bias *or* voltage *neutral, jord;* **neutral transmission** = (transmission) system in which a voltage pulse and zero volts represent the binary digits 1 and 0 *neutral överföring*

new [njuː] *adj.* recent *or* not old *ny;* **they have installed a new computer system; the new programmer does not seem as efficient as the old one; new (command)** = program command that clears main memory of the present program ready to accept a new program to be entered *nystartskommando;* **new line character** = character that moves a cursor *or* printhead to the beginning of the next line *vagnreturtecken; see also* CARRIAGE RETURN (CR), LINEFEED (LF); **new technology** = electronic instruments which have recently been invented *ny teknik*

news [njuːz] *subst.* information about things which have happened *nyheter;* **business news; financial news; financial markets were shocked by the news of the collapse of the computer company; news agency** = office which distributes news to newspapers and television companies *nyhetsbyrå;* **news release** = sheet giving information about a new event which is sent to newspapers and TV and radio stations so that they can use it *pressrelease;* **the company sent out a news release about the new managing director**

newsletter ['njuːzˌletə] *subst.* **company newsletter** = printed sheet *or* small newspaper giving news about a company *nyhetsbrev*

newsprint ['njuːzprɪnt] *subst.* mechanical paper used for printing newspapers *slippapper, tidningspapper*
NOTE: no plural

next instruction register ['nekst ɪn'strʌkʃ(ə)n 'redʒɪstə] *subst.* register in a CPU that contains the location where the next instruction to be executed is stored *programpekare; see also* REGISTER

nexus ['neksəs] *subst.* connection point between units in a network *nod, knut*

nibble ['nɪbl] *or* **nybble** ['nɪbl] *subst.* half the length of a standard byte *halvbyte*

NOTE: a nibble is normally 4 bits, but can vary according to different micros or people

nil pointer ['nɪl 'pɔɪntə] *subst.* pointer used to indicate the end of a chained list of items *nollpekare*

nine's complement ['naɪnz 'kɒmplɪmənt] *subst.* decimal complement (equivalent to the binary one's complement) formed by subtracting each digit in the number from nine *niokomplement; see also* TEN'S COMPLEMENT

N-key rollover ['en'ki:'rəʊləʊvə] *subst.* facility on a keyboard where each keystroke (up to a maximum of N) is registered in sequence even if they are struck very fast *tangentbordsbuffert*

n-level logic ['en'levl 'lɒdʒɪk] *subst.* logic gate design in which no more than n gates occur in a series *maximal signalfördrivning i logikkonstruktion*

NLQ ['enel'kju:] = NEAR LETTER-QUALITY

NMI ['enem'aɪ] = NON-MASKABLE INTERRUPT

NMOS ['enmɒs] = N-CHANNEL METAL OXIDE SEMICONDUCTOR

no-address operation [ˌnəʊə'dres ˌɒpə'reɪʃ(ə)n] *subst.* instruction which does not require an address within it *adressfri operation*

node [nəʊd] *subst.* interconnection point in a structure *or* network *nod;* **a tree is made of branches that connect together at nodes; this network has fibre optic connection with nodes up to one kilometre apart**

noise [nɔɪz] *subst.* random signal present in addition to any wanted signal, caused by static, temperature, power supply, magnetic or electric fields and also from stars and the sun *brus;* **noise immunity** = ability of a circuit to ignore *or* filter out *or* be protected from noise *störsäkerhet;* **noise margin** = maximum amplitude of noise that will affect a device, such as switch a logic gate *störmarginal;* **noise temperature** = temperature of a component for it to produce the same thermal noise as a source *brustemperatur, brusvärde;* **galactic noise** = electrical noise which originates from planets and stars in space *rymdbrus;* **impulsive noise** = interference on a signal caused by short periods of noise *pulsbrus;* **thermal noise** = background noise signal caused by temperature variations incomponents *termiskt brus, värmebrus*

QUOTE the photographs were grainy, out of focus, and distorted by signal noise
Byte

noisy mode ['nɔɪzɪ 'məʊd] *subst.* floating point arithmetic system, in which a digit other than a zero is deliberately added in the least significant position during the normalization of a floating point number *slumpmässig avrundning;* **noisy digit** = digit, usually not zero, added during the normalization of a floating point number when in noisy mode *slumpmässig avrundningssiffra*

nollflagga ⇨ **flag**

nollpekare ⇨ **nil pointer**

nolltecken ⇨ **erase character**

nollvariabel ⇨ **empty, null**

nomenclature [nə(ʊ)'menklətʃə] *subst.* predefined system for assigning words and symbols to represent numbers or terms *nomenklatur*

nomogram ['nɒməgræm] *or* **nomograph** ['nɒməgrɑːf] *subst.* graphical system for solving one value given two others *nomogram*

non- [nɒn] *prefix* meaning not *icke-*

nonaligned ['nɒnə'laɪnd] *adj.* two devices that are not correctly positioned in relation to each other, for optimum performance *ur fas;* **nonaligned read head** = read head that is not in the same position on a magnetic medium as the write head was, producing a loss of signal quality *läshuvud ur fas*

non-arithmetic shift ['nɒnə'rɪθmətɪk 'ʃɪft] *see* LOGICAL SHIFT

noncompatibility ['nɒnkəmˌpætə'bɪlətɪ] *subst.* two or more pieces of hardware *or* software that cannot exchange data *or* use the same peripherals *icke-kompatibilitet*

noncounting keyboard ['nɒn'kaʊntɪŋ 'kiːbɔːd] *subst.* entry keyboard on a phototypesetter that does not allow page format instructions to be entered *oformaterande inmatning*

non-destructive cursor ['nɒndɪs'trʌktɪv 'kɜːsə] *subst.* cursor on a display that does not erase characters already displayed as it passes over them *(oförstörande) inskrivningsmarkör;* **the screen quickly became unreadable when using a non-destructive cursor; non-destructive readout (NDR)** = display device that retains previous characters when displaying new characters *icke-raderande skrivning (på skärmen);* **non-destructive test** = series of tests carried out on a piece of equipment without destroying it *oförstörande provning;* **I will carry out a number of non-destructive tests on your computer, if it passes, you can start using it again; non-scrollable** = part of the screen display which is always displayed (in a WP, the text can scroll whilst instructions, etc., are non-scrollable) *skärmresident; see also* STATUS LINE

non-equivalence function (NEQ) ['nɒnɪ'kwɪvələns 'fʌŋ(k)ʃ(ə)n (ˌenɪ'kjuː)] *subst.* logical function where the output is true if the inputs are not the same, otherwise the output is false *icke-ekvivalens, symmetrisk differens;* **non-equivalence gate** = electronic implementation of an NEQ function *antingen-eller-grind*

nonerasable storage ['nɒnɪ'reɪzəbl 'stɔːrɪdʒ] *subst.* storage medium that cannot be erased and re-used *permanentminne;* **paper tape is a nonerasable storage**

non-impact printer ['nɒn'ɪmpækt 'prɪntə] *subst.* printer (like an ink-jet printer) where the character form does not hit a ribbon onto the paper *anslagsfri skrivare*

nonlinear ['nɒn'lɪnɪə] *adj.* electronic circuit whose output does not change linearly in proportion to its input *olinjär (krets)*

non-maskable interrupt (NMI) ['nɒn'maːskəbl ˌɪntə'rʌpt (ˈenemˈaɪ)] *subst.* high priority interrupt signal that cannot be blocked by software and overrides other commands *högprioriterat avbrott*

non-operable instruction ['nɒn'ɒp(ə)rəbl ɪn'strʌkʃ(ə)n] *subst.* instruction that does not carry out any function, but increments the program counter *blindinstruktion*

non-printing codes ['nɒn'prɪntɪŋ kəʊdz] *subst.* codes that represent an action of the printer rather than a printed character *skrivarstyrkoder;* **the line width can be set using one of the non-printing codes, .LW, then a number**

non return to zero (NRZ) ['nɒnrɪ'tɜːn tə 'zɪərəʊ (ˈenɑː'zed)] *subst.* signalling system in which a positive voltage represents one binary digit and a negative voltage the other *NRZ(0)-representation;* representation of binary data in which the signal changes when the data changes state, and does not return to zero volts after each bit of data *sätt att representera data med hjälp av signalförändringar*

nonsenssumma ⇨ **hash, total**

non-volatile ['nɒn'vɒlətaɪl] *adj.* **non-volatile memory** *or* **non-volatile store** *or* **storage** = storage medium *or* memory that retains data even when the power has been switched off *permanent minne, icke-flyktigt minne;* **bubble memory is a non-volatile storage; using magnetic tape provides non-volatile memory**
NOTE: opposite is **volatile**

COMMENT: disks (both hard and floppy) and tapes are non-volatile memory stores; solid-state memory, such as RAM chips are volatile unless battery backed

no op ['nəʊ'ɒp] *or* **no operation instruction** ['nəʊ ˌɒpə'reɪʃ(ə)n ɪn'strʌkʃ(ə)n] = NO OPERATION programming instruction which does nothing *blindinstruktion*

NOR function [nɔː 'fʌŋ(k)ʃ(ə)n] *subst.* logical function whose output is false if either input is true *negerad disjunktion;* **NOR gate** = electric circuit *or* chip which performs a NOR function *(logisk) varken-eller-grind*

COMMENT: the output is 1 only if both inputs are 0; if the two inputs are different or if both are 1, the output is 0

normal ['nɔːm(ə)l] *adj.* usual *or* which happens regularly *normal, vanlig;* **the normal procedure is for backup copies to be made at the end of each day's work; normal format** = standardized format for data storage *normalformat;* **normal range** = expected range for a result *or* number, any outside this range are errors *normalomfång*

normaliseringstillstånd ⇨ **mode**

normalization [ˌnɔːməlaɪ'zeɪʃ(ə)n] *subst.* process of normalizing data *normalisering;* **normalization routine** = routine that normalizes a floating point number and adds extra (noisy) digits in the least significant position *normaliseringsrutin*

normalize ['nɔːməlaɪz] *vb.* **(a)** to convert data into a form which can be read by a particular computer system *formatera* **(b)** to convert characters into just capitals or into just a lower case form *versal/gemenformatera* **(c)** to store and represent numbers in a pre-agreed form, usually to provide maximum precision *normalisera;* **all the new data has been normalized to 10 decimal places; normalized form** = floating point number that has been normalized so that its mantissa is within a certain range *normaliserad form*

notation [nə(ʊ)'teɪʃ(ə)n] *subst.* method of writing *or* representing numbers *notation, (tal)representation;* **binary notation** = base two numerical system using only the digits 0 and 1 *binär notation;* **decimal notation** = number representation in base 10, using the digits 0-9 *decimalnotation;* **hexadecimal notation** = number system using base 16 and the digits 0-9 and A-F *hexadecimal notation;* **infix notation** = mathematical syntax where operators are embedded inside operands (such as C - D or X + Y) *infixnotation;* **octal notation** = number system using base 8 and the digits 0-7 *oktalnotation;* **postfix notation** =

mathematical operations written in a logical way, so that the operator appears after the operands, this removes the need for brackets *postfixnotation, omvänd polsk notation;* **normal notation: (x-y) + z, but using postfix notation: xy - z +; prefix notation** = mathematical operations written in a logical way, so that the operator appears before the operands, this removes the need for brackets *prefixnotation, polsk notation*

notched [nɒtʃt] *see* EDGE NOTCHED CARD

notepad ['nəʊtpæd] *subst.* **screen notepad** = part of the screen used to store information even when the terminal is switched off *permanent skärmminne*

NOT function [nɒt 'fʌŋ(k)ʃ(ə)n] *subst.* logical inverse function where the output is true if the input is false *negation;* **NOT-AND** = equivalent to the NAND function *negerad konjunktion;* **NOT gate** = electronic circuit *or* chip which performs a NOT function *(logisk) icke-grind, negerande grind, inverterare*

> COMMENT: if the input is 1, the output is 0; if the input is 0, the output is 1

notice board ['nəʊtɪs bɔːd] *subst.* (i) board fixed to a wall where notices can be pinned up *anslagstavla;* (ii) type of bulletin board on which messages to all users can be left *elektronisk anslagstavla*

N-plus-ett-(N+1)stegsinstruktion ⇨ instruction

n-plus-one address instruction ['en'plʌs 'wʌn ə'dres ɪn'strʌkʃ(ə)n] *subst.* instruction made up of a number (n) of addresses and one other address that is the location of the next instruction *N-plus-ett-instruktion*

npn transistor ['enpiː'en træn'zɪstə] *subst.* bipolar transistor design using p-type semiconductor for the base and n-type for the collector and emitter *NPN-transistor; see also* TRANSISTOR, BIPOLAR

NRZ ['enɑː'zed] = NON RETURN TO ZERO

ns ['nænə(ʊ)ˌsek(ə)nd] = NANOSECOND one thousand millionth of a second *nanosekund*

NTSC ['entiːesˈsiː] = NATIONAL TELEVISION STANDARDS COMMITTEE official body that defines television and video formats *or* standards used mainly in the USA and in Japan *TV-standard för videosignaler; see also* VIDEO STANDARDS

> COMMENT: the NTSC standard is based on 525 horizontal lines and 60 frames per seconds

> QUOTE the system has a composite video output port that conforms to the NTSC video specification
> **Byte**

n-type material ['en'taɪp mə'tɪərɪəl] *or* **N-type material** *or* **n-type semiconductor** ['en 'taɪp 'semɪkɒn'dʌktə] *subst.* semiconductor that has been doped with a substance that provides extra electrons in the material, giving it an overall negative charge compared to the intrinsic semiconductor *n-dopat material, N-material; see also* NPN TRANSISTOR

null [nʌl] *subst.* nothing *noll, blind, null, icke, tom;* **null character** = character which means nothing (usually code 0) *tomt tecken;* **null instruction** = program instruction that does nothing *blindinstruktion;* **null list** = list which contains nothing *tom lista;* **null modem** = emulator circuit that allows two pieces of equipment that normally require modems to communicate, to be connected together over a short distance *korthållsmodem, nollmodem;* **this cable is configured as a null modem, which will allow me to connect these 2 computers together easily; null set** = set that only contains zeros *nollmängd;* **null string** = string that contains no characters *nollvariabel*

> QUOTE you have to connect the two RS232 ports together using a crossed cable, or null modem
> **PC Business World**

number ['nʌmbə] **1** *subst.* **(a)** representation of a quantity *tal, antal;* **number cruncher** = dedicated processor used for high-speed calculations *beräkningsmaskin, "siffertuggare";* **number crunching** = performing high-speed calculations *beräkningsarbete, "taltuggning";* **a very powerful processor is needed for graphics applications which require extensive number crunching capabilities; number range** = set of allowable values *omfång, talbredd* **(b)** written figure *siffra, nummer;* **each piece of hardware has a production number; please note the reference number of your order; box number** = reference number used when asking for mail to be sent to a post office *or* to a newspaper, in reply to advertisements *boxnummer;* **check number** = number produced from data for parity *or* error detection *kontrollsiffra, kontrollsumma* **2** *vb.* **(a)** to put a figure on a document *numrera;* **the pages of the manual are numbered 1 to 395 (b)** to assign digits to a list of items in an ordered manner *numrera, indexera*

numeral ['njuːm(ə)r(ə)l] *subst.* character *or* symbol which represents a number *siffra, nummer;* **Arabic numerals** = figures written 1, 2, 3, 4, etc. *arabiska siffror;*

Roman numerals = figures written I, II, III, IV, etc. *romerska siffror*

numeric [njʊ'merɪk] *adj.* (i) referring to numbers *numerisk;* (ii) (field, etc.) which contains only numbers *numeriskt fält;* **numeric array** = array containing numbers *numerisk vektor;* **numeric character** = letter used in some notations to represent numbers (for example in hex the letters A-F are numeric characters) *numeriskt tecken;* **numeric keypad** = set of ten keys with figures, included in most computer keyboards as a separate group, used for entering large amounts of data in numeric form *numeriskt tangentbord;* **numeric operand** = operand that only uses numerals *numerisk operand;* **numeric pad** = numeric keypad *numeriskt tangentbord;* **numeric punch** = punched hole in rows 0-9 of a punched card *sifferstans, sifferstansning*

numerical [njʊ'merɪk(ə)l] *adj.* referring to numbers *numerisk;* **numerical analysis** = study of ways of solving mathematical problems *numerisk analys;* **numerical control (NC)** *or* **computer numerical control (CNC)** = machine operated automatically by computer *or* circuits controlled by stored data *numeriskt styrd*

numerisk styrning ⊳ **CNC, flexible**

numeriskt styrd ⊳ **NC**

numeriskt tangentbord ⊳ **keypad**

nybble ['nɪbl] *or* **nibble** ['nɪbl] *subst. informal* half the length of a standard byte *halvbyte*
NOTE: a nybble is normally 4 bits, but can vary according to different micros

nyckelfunktion ⊳ **feature**

nyckelfärdigt system ⊳ **turnkey system**

nyckelhantering ⊳ **key**

nyckelord ⊳ **keyword**

nämnare ⊳ **divisor**

nätadministration ⊳ **management**

nätaggregat ⊳ **PSU**

nätcentral ⊳ **file, local area network (LAN or lan), server**

nätisolering ⊳ **demarcation**

nätminne ⊳ **file, server**

nätport ⊳ **gateway**

nätprocessor ⊳ **processor**

nätskikt ⊳ **network**

nätspänningsövervakning(skrets) ⊳ **monitor**

nätstruktur ⊳ **structure**

nätverkshantering ⊳ **management**

nödfallsutrustning ⊳ **contingency plan**

Oo

OA ['ʒu'eɪ] = OFFICE AUTOMATION

object ['ɒbdʒɪkt] *subst.* **(a)** variable used in an expert system within a reasoning operation *objekt* **(b)** data in a statement which is to be operated on by the operator *objekt; see also* ARGUMENT, OPERAND; **object** *or* **object-orientated architecture** = structure where all files, outputs, etc., in a system are represented as objects *objektorienterad arkitektur;* **object code** = binary code which directly operates a central processing unit (a program code after it has been translated, compiled or assembled into machine code) *objektkod;* **object computer** = computer system for which a program has been written and compiled *måldator;* **object deck** = punched cards that contain a program *programpacke för måldator;* **object language** = the language of a program after it has been translated *målspråk; compare with* SOURCE LANGUAGE; **object program** = computer program in object code form, produced by a compiler *or* assembler *målprogram*

objective [əb'dʒektɪv] *subst.* **(a)** something which someone tries to do *mål* **(b)** optical lens nearest the object viewed *objektiv*

objekt ⊳ **entity, object**

obtain [əb'teɪn] *vb.* to get *or* to receive *nå, erhålla, få;* **to obtain data from a storage device; a clear signal is obtained after filtering**

OCCAM ['ɔkæm] computer programming language, used in large multiprocessor *or* multi-user systems *programmeringsspråket OCCAM*

COMMENT: this is the development language for transputer systems

occur [ə'kɜː] *vb.* to happen *or* to take place *hända, ske;* **data loss can occur because of power supply variations**

och-funktion ⊳ **AND**

och-grind ⊳ **AND, gate**

OCP ['ʒusi'piː] = ORDER CODE PROCESSOR *(in a multiprocessor system)* a processor which decides and performs the arithmetic and logical operations according to the program code *OC-processor, huvudprocessor*

OCR ['əusiː'ɑː] **(a)** = OPTICAL CHARACTER READER device which scans printed *or* written characters, recognizes them, and converts them into machine-readable form for processing in a computer *optisk teckenläsare* **(b)** = OPTICAL CHARACTER RECOGNITION process that allows printed *or* written characters to be recognized optically and converted into machine-readable code that can be input into a computer, using an optical character reader *optisk teckenläsning;* **OCR font** = character design that can be easily read using an OCR reader *OCR-typsnitt, optiskt läsbart typsnitt*

COMMENT: there are two OCR fonts in common use: OCR-A, which is easy for scanners to read, and OCR-B, which is easier for people to read than the OCR-A font

octal (notation) ['ɒktəl (nə(ʊ)'teɪʃ(ə)n)] *subst.* number notation using base 8, with digits 0 to 7 *oktal notation;* **octal digit** = digit (0 to 7) used in the octal system *oktal siffra;* **octal scale** = power of eight associated with each digit position in a number *oktalskala*

COMMENT: in octal, the digits used are 0 to 7; so decimal 9 is octal 11

octave ['ɒktɪv] *subst.* series of 8 musical notes, each a semitone higher than the previous one *oktav*

octet [ɒk'tet] *subst.* a group of eight bits treated as one unit; word made up of eight bits *byte, ibland, särskilt i Frankrike, oktett; see also* BYTE

odd [ɒd] *adj.* (number, such as 5 or 7) which cannot be divided by two *udda;* **odd-even check** = method of checking that transmitted binary data has not been corrupted *udda-jämn-kontroll;* **odd parity (check)** = error checking system in which any series of bits transmitted must have an odd number of binary ones *udda paritetskontroll* (NOTE: opposite is **even**)

OEM ['əuiː'em] = ORIGINAL EQUIPMENT MANUFACTURER company which produces equipment using basic parts made by other manufacturers, and customizes the product for a particular application *ursprungstillverkare, underleverantör av färdig utrustning*

off-cut ['ɒfkʌt] *subst.* scrap paper that is left when a sheet is trimmed to size *kantmakulatur*

off hook ['ɒf'hʊk] *adv.* state of a telephone unit indicating to incoming calls that it is being used *upptagen*
NOTE: opposite is **on hook**

office ['ɒfɪs] *subst.* room *or* building where a company works *or* where business is done *kontor;* **office automation (OA)** = use of machines and computers to carry out normal office tasks *kontorsautomation;* **office computer** = small computer (sometimes with a hard disk and several terminals) suitable for office use *kontorsdator;* **office copier** = copying machine in an office *kontorskopiator;* **office equipment** = desks, typewriters, and other furniture and machines needed in an office *kontorsutrustning;* **office of the future** = design of an office that is completely coordinated by a computer *framtidskontoret; see also* PAPERLESS OFFICE

off-line ['ɒflaɪn] *adv. & adj.* (i) (processor *or* printer *or* terminal) that is not connected to a network *or* central computer (usually temporarily) *fristående, urkopplad;* (ii) (peripheral) connected to a network, but not available for use *fristående, bortkopplad;* **before changing the paper in the printer, switch it off-line; off-line printing** = printout operation that is not supervised by a computer *fristående utskrift;* **off-line processing** = processing by devices not under the control of a central computer *fristående databehandling*
NOTE: opposite is **on-line**

offprint ['ɒfprɪnt] *subst.* section of a journal reprinted separately *särtryck*

off screen ['ɒf'skriːn] *adv.* TV action that is taking place off the screen, outside the viewer's field of vision *utanför bild*

offset ['ɒfset] *subst.* **(a) offset lithography** = printing process used for printing books, where the ink sticks to dry areas on the film and is transferred to rubber rollers from which it is printed on to the paper *offsettryck;* **offset printing** = printing method that transfers the ink image to the paper via a second roller *offsettryck* **(b)** quantity added to a number *or* address to give a final number *förskjutning;* **offset value** *or* **offset word** = value to be added to a base address to provide a final indexed address *förskjutningsvärde*

oförutsägbart system ⇨ **indeterminate system**

ogiltig instruktion ⇨ **illegal**

ogiltig operation ⇨ **illegal**

ogiltigt tecken ⇨ **illegal**

ohm [əʊm] *subst.* unit of measurement of electrical resistance *ohm;* **this resistance**

has a value of 100 ohms; kilo-ohm = one thousand ohms *kohm*

Ohm's Law [ˈəʊmzˈlɔː] *subst.* definition of one ohm as: one volt drop across a resistance of one ohm when one amp of current is flowing *Ohms lag*

O.K. [ˈəʊˈkeɪ] used as a prompt in place of 'ready' in some systems *redomarkör, redomarkering*

oktalt ⇨ **base**

okular ⇨ **viewfinder**

olikhet ⇨ **inequivalence**

oläslig ⇨ **illegible**

omdirigera ⇨ **redirect, re-route**

omedelbar åtkomst ⇨ **instantaneous access**

omega wrap [ˈəʊmɪgə ˈræp] *subst.* system of threading video tape around a video head *omegamatning*

COMMENT: the tape passes over most of the circular head and is held in place by two small rollers

omformare ⇨ **alternator, inverter**

omformattera ⇨ **reformat**

omgivningstemperatur ⇨ **ambient**

omission factor [ə(ʊ)ˈmɪʃ(ə)n ˈfæktə] *subst.* number of relevant documents that were missed in a search *bortfallsfaktor*

omkastning ⇨ **transposition**

omkopplare ⇨ **jumper**

omnidirectional [ˈɒmnɪdɪˈrekʃənl] *adj.* device that can pick up signals from all directions *rundstrålande;* **omnidirectional aerial; omnidirectional microphone**

omodifierad instruktion ⇨ **unmodified instruction**

OMR [ˈəʊemˈɑː] **(a)** = OPTICAL MARK READER device that can recognize marks *or* lines on a special form (such as on an order form *or* a reply to a questionnaire) and that inputs them into a computer *optisk markeringsläsare* **(b)** = OPTICAL MARK RECOGNITION process that allows certain marks *or* lines on special forms (such as on an order form *or* a reply to a questionnaire) to be recognized by an optical mark reader, and input into a computer *optisk markeringsigenkänning*

omsluta ⇨ **enclose**

omstart ⇨ **dump, fall back**

omsändning ⇨ **retransmission**

omvandla ⇨ **convert, transform**

omvandlare ⇨ **converter**

omvandlingskontakt ⇨ **changer**

omvandlingsprogram ⇨ **interface**

omvänd ⇨ **inverse, reverse**

omärkbara avbrott ⇨ **transparent**

on-board [ˈɒnˈbɔːd] *adj.* (feature *or* circuit) which is contained on a motherboard *or* main PCB *på (moder)kortet*

QUOTE the electronic page is converted to a printer-readable video image by the on-board raster image processor
QUOTE the key intelligence features of these laser printers are emulation modes and on-board memory
                                                                    Byte

on chip [ˈɒnˈtʃɪp] *subst.* circuit constructed on a chip *integrerad krets*

on-chip [ˈɒnˈtʃɪp] *adj.* (circuit) constructed on a chip *integrerad i kretsen;* **the processor uses on-chip bootstrap software to allow programs to be loaded rapidly**

one address computer [ˈwʌnəˈdres kəmˈpjuːtə] *subst.* computer structure whose machine code only uses one address at a time *enadressdator;* **one address instruction =** instruction made up of an operator and one address *enadressinstruktion*

one element [ˈwʌnˈelɪmənt] *subst.* logical function that produces a true output if any input is true *ett-element*

one for one [ˈwʌnfəˈwʌn] *subst.* programming language, usually assembler, that produces one machine code instruction for each instruction *or* command word in the language *ett-till-ett-språk*

COMMENT: compilers and interpreters are usually used for translating high-level languages which use more than one machine code instruction for each high-level instruction

one-level address [ˈwʌnˌlevl əˈdres] *subst.* storage address that directly, without any modification, accesses a location *or* device *absolutadress;* **one-level code =** binary code which directly operates the CPU, using only absolute addresses and values (this is the final form of a program after a compiler *or* assembler pass) *absolutkod;* **one-level store =** organization of storage in which each different type of storage device is treated as if it were the same *enlagersminne, virtuellt minne;* **one-level subroutine =** subroutine which does not call another subroutine during its execution *enkel subrutin*

one-pass assembler ['wʌnpɑːs əˈsemblə] *subst.* assembler program that translates the source code in one action *enstegsassemblerare;* **this new one-pass assembler is very quick in operation**

one-plus-one address ['wʌnplʌsˈwʌn əˈdres] *subst.* address format that provides the location of one register and the location of the next instruction *en-plus-ettadress*

one's complement ['wʌnz ˈkɒmplɪmənt] *subst.* inverse of a binary number *ettkomplement;* **the one's complement of 10011 is 01100;** *see also* COMPLEMENT; TWO'S COMPLEMENT

one-time pad ['wʌntaɪm 'pæd] *subst.* coding system that uses a unique cipher key each time it is used *engångsnyckelkryptering*

COMMENT: two identical pieces of paper with an encrypted alphabet printed on each one are used, one by the sender, one by the receiver; this is one of the most secure cipher systems

one to zero ratio ['wʌntəˈzɪərəʊ ˈreɪʃɪəʊ] *subst.* ratio between the amplitude of a binary one and zero output *ett-till-noll-förhållande*

on hook ['ɒnˈhʊk] *adv.* state of a telephone unit indicating that it is not busy and can receive incoming calls *öppen*

onion skin architecture ['ʌnjənskɪn ˈɑːkɪtektʃə] *subst.* design of a computer system in layers, according to function *or* priority *flerlagersarkitektur;* **the onion skin architecture of this computer is made up of a kernel at the centre, an operating system, a low-level language and then the user's program**

onion skin language ['ʌnjənskɪn ˈlæŋgwɪdʒ] *subst.* database manipulation language that can process hierarchical data structures *flerlagerspråk*

on-line ['ɒnlaɪn] *adv. & adj.* (terminal *or* device) connected to and under the control of a central processor *direktansluten;* **the terminal is on-line to the mainframe; on-line database =** interactive search, retrieve and update of database records, with a terminal that is on-line *direktansluten databas;* **on-line information retrieval =** system that allows an operator of an on-line terminal to access, search and display data held in a main computer *direktansluten informationsåtersökning;* **on-line processing =** processing by devices connected to and under the control of the central computer (the user remains in contact with the central computer while

processing) *direktansluten databehandling;* **on-line storage =** data storage equipment that is directly controlled by a computer *direktansluten datalagring;* **on-line system =** computer system that allows users who are on-line to transmit and receive information *direktanslutet system;* **on-line transaction processing =** interactive processing in which a user enters commands and data on a terminal which is linked to a central computer, with results being displayed on the screen *direktansluten transaktionsbehandling*

on-screen ['ɒnˈskriːn] *adj.* (information) that is displayed on a computer screen rather than printed out *på skärmen*

on-site ['ɒnsaɪt] *adj.* at the place where something is *på plats;* **the new model has an on-site upgrade facility**

on the fly ['ɒnðəˈflaɪ] *adv.* (to examine and modify data) during a program run without stopping the run *under drift*

O/P ['aʊtpʊt] *or* **o/p** = OUTPUT

opacity [ə(ʊ)ˈpæsətɪ] *subst.* measure of how opaque an optical lens is *opacitet* NOTE: opposite is **transmittance**

op amp ['ɒp 'æmp] = OPERATIONAL AMPLIFIER term for a versatile electronic component that provides amplification, integration, addition, subtraction and many other functions on signals depending on external components added *operationsförstärkare*

COMMENT: usually in the form of an 8 pin IC package with 2 inputs (inverting and non-inverting), output, power supply and other control functions

opaque [ə(ʊ)ˈpeɪk] *adj.* will not allow light to pass through it *ogenomskinlig, mjölkvit, opak;* **the screen is opaque - you cannot see through it; opaque projector =** device that is able to project an image of an opaque object *episkop, balloptikon(apparat)*

op code ['ɒpˈkəʊd] = OPERATION CODE part of the machine code instruction that defines the action to be performed *operationskod*

QUOTE the subroutine at 3300 is used to find the op code corresponding to the byte whose hex value is in B
Computing Today

open ['əʊp(ə)n] **1** *adj.* **(a)** command to prepare a file before reading *or* writing actions can occur *öppen;* **you cannot access the data unless the file is open (b)** not closed *öppen;* **open access =** system where many workstations are available for anyone to use *fri åtkomst;* **open code =** extra instructions required in a program that

mainly uses macroinstructions *öppen kod;*
open-ended program = program designed
to allow future expansion and easy
modification *öppet program;* **open loop** =
control system whose input is free of
feedback *öppen slinga; see also* FEEDBACK;
open reel = magnetic tape on a reel that is
not enclosed in a cartridge *or* cassette
rullband; **open routine** = routine which can
be inserted into a larger routine *or* program
without using a call instruction
inbyggnadsrutin; **open subroutine** = code
for a subroutine which is copied into
memory whenever a call instruction is
found, rather than executing a jump to the
subroutine's address *öppen subrutin;* **open
system** = system which is constructed in
such a way that different operating systems
can work together *öppet system;* **Open
System Interconnection (OSI)** =
standardized ISO network which is
constructed in layered form, with each
layer having a specific task, allowing
different systems to communicate if they
conform to the standard *OSI-nät; see also*
ISO/OSI LAYERS, INTERNATIONAL **2** *vb.* **(a)**
to take the cover off *or* to make a door open
öppna; **open the disk drive door; open the
top of the computer by lifting here (b)** to
prepare a file before accessing *or* editing *or*
carrying out other transactions on stored
records *öppna;* **you cannot access the data
unless the file has been opened**

operand ['ɒpərænd] *subst.* data (in a
computer instruction) which is to be
operated on by the operator *operand;* **in the
instruction ADD 74, the operator ADD will
add the operand 74 to the accumulator;
immediate operand** = within an immediate
addressing operation, the operand is
fetched at the same time as the instruction
direktoperand; **literal operand** = actual
number *or* address to be used rather than a
label *or* its location *verklig operand;*
numeric operand = operand that only
contains numerals *numerisk operand;*
operand field = space allocated for an
operand in a program instruction
adressfält, operandfält; see also
ARGUMENT, MACHINE-CODE
INSTRUCTION

operandfält ⇨ **field**

operate ['ɒpəreɪt] *vb.* to work *or* to make a
machine work *köra, använda, hålla i drift;
do you know how to operate the telephone
switchboard?; disk operating system (DOS)**
= section of the operating system software
that controls disk and file management
*operativsystem för fil- och
skivminneshantering (mest känt är
Microsofts version);* **operating code (op
code)** = part of the machine code
instruction that defines the action to be
performed *operationskod;* **operating
console** = terminal in an interactive system

which sends and receives information
bildskärmsterminal; **operating instructions**
= commands and instructions used to
operate a computer *driftsanvisningar,
körinstruktioner;* **operating system (OS)** =
software that controls the basic, low-level
hardware operations, and file
management, without the user having to
operate it (the operating system is usually
supplied with the computer as part of the
bundled software or in ROM)
operativsystem; **operating time** = total time
required to carry out a task *funktionstid*

operation [ˌɒpəˈreɪʃ(ə)n] *subst.* working
(of a machine) *drift, driftsförhållande;*
arithmetic operation = mathematical
function carried out on data
aritmetikoperation; **binary operation** = (i)
operation on two operands *binär operation;*
(ii) operation on an operand in binary form
binär operation; **block operation** = process
carried out on a block of data
blockbehandling; **Boolean operation** =
logical operation on a number of operands,
conforming to Boolean algebra rules
Booleoperation; **complete operation** =
operation that retrieves the necessary
operands from memory, performs the
operation and returns the results and
operands to memory, then reads the next
instruction to be processed *fullständig
operation;* **dyadic Boolean operation** =
logical operation that produces an output
from two inputs *dyadisk Booleoperation;*
no-address operation = instruction which
does not require an address within it
adressfri operation; **no-operation
instruction (no-op)** = programming
instruction which does nothing
blindinstruktion; **operation code (op code)** =
part of a machine-code instruction that
defines the action to be performed
operationskod; **operation cycle** = section of
the machine cycle during which the
instruction is executed *instruktionscykel;
see also* FETCH-EXECUTE CYCLE,
MACHINE CYCLE; **operation decoder** =
hardware that converts a machine-code
instruction (in binary form) into actions
instruktionsavkodare; **operation field** =
part of an assembly language statement
that contains the mnemonic or symbol for
the op code *operationsdel;* **operation
priority** = the sequence order in which the
operations within a statement are carried
out *operationsordning, operationsprioritet;*
operation register = register that contains
the op code during its execution
operationsregister; **operation time** = period
of time that an operation requires for its
operation cycle *funktionstid;* **operation trial**
= series of tests to check programs and
data preparation *driftsprov, provkörning;*
operations manual *see* INSTRUCTION
MANUAL

operational [ˌɒpəˈreɪʃ(ə)nl] *adj.* which is working *or* which refers to the way a machine works *som är i drift;* **operational information** = information about the normal operations of a system *driftsinformation*

operational amplifier (op amp) [ˌɒpəˈreɪʃ(ə)nl ˈæmplɪfaɪə (ˈɒp ˈæmp)] *subst.* versatile electronic component that provides amplification, integration, addition, subtraction and many other functions on signals depending on external components added *operationsförstärkare*

COMMENT: usually in the form of an 8 pin IC package with 2 inputs (inverting and non-inverting) output, power supply and other control functions

operationsförstärkare ⇨ **op amp**

operationsprioritet ⇨ **precedence**

operativsystemkommando ⇨ **executive**

operator [ˈɒpəreɪtə] *subst.* **(a)** person who makes a machine *or* process work *(dator)operatör;* **the operator was sitting at his console; computer operator** = person who operates a computer *operatör;* **operator's console** = input and output devices used by an operator to control a computer (usually consisting of a keyboard and VDU) *systemkonsoll, operatörsterminal;* **operator procedure** = set of actions that an operator has to carry out to work a machine *or* process *operatörsrutin* **(b)** character *or* symbol *or* word that defines a function *or* operation *operator;* **x is the multiplication operator; operator precedence** = order in which a number of mathematical operations will be carried out *operationsprioritet, operationsprecedens;* **arithmetic operator** = symbol which indicates an arithmetic function (such as + for addition, x for multiplication) *aritmetisk operator*

op register [ˈɒp ˈredʒɪstə] *subst.* register that contains the operating code for the instruction that is being executed *operationsregister*

optical [ˈɒptɪk(ə)l] *adj.* referring to *or* making use of light *optisk;* **an optical reader uses a light beam to scan characters *or* patterns *or* lines; optical bar reader *or* bar code reader *or* optical wand** = optical device that reads data from a bar code *(optisk) streckkodsläsare;* **optical character reader (OCR)** = device which scans printed *or* written characters, recognizes them, and converts them into machine-readable code for processing in a computer *optisk teckenläsare;* **optical character recognition (OCR)** = process that allows printed *or* written characters to be recognized

optically and converted into machine-readable code that can be input into a computer, using an optical character reader *optisk teckenläsning;* **optical communication system** = communication system using fibre optics *optiskt kommunikationssystem;* **optical data link** = connection between two devices to allow the transmission of data using light signals (either line-of-sight or optic fibre) *optisk ledning, optisk förbindelse;* **optical disk** = disk that contains binary data in the form of small holes in the surface which are read with a laser beam *optiskt skivminne* (NOTE: also called WORM (write once, read many times, for computers) which can be programmed once, or compact disk (CD) and video disk which are programmed at manufacture) **optical fibre** = fine strand of glass *or* plastic protected by a surrounding material, that is used for the convenient transmission of light signals *optisk fiber;* **optical font *or* OCR font** = character design that can be easily read using an OCR reader *OCR-typsnitt, optiskt läsbart typsnitt;* **optical mark reader (OMR)** = device that can recognize marks *or* lines on a special forms (such as on an order form *or* a reply to a questionnaire) and convert them into a form a computer can process *optisk märkesläsare;* **optical mark recognition (OMR)** = process that allows certain marks *or* lines on special forms (such as on an order form *or* a reply to a questionnaire) to be recognized by an optical mark reader, and input into a computer *optisk märkesläsning;* **optical memory** = optical disks *optiskt minne;* **optical scanner** = equipment that converts an image into electrical signals which can be stored in and displayed on a computer *optisk läsare, scanner;* **optical storage** = data storage using mediums such as optical disk, etc. *optiskt minne, optisk datalagring;* **optical transmission** = use of fibre optic cables, laser beams and other light sources to carry data, in the form of pulses of light *optisk (data)överföring;* **optical wand** = OPTICAL BAR READER

optic fibres [ˈɒptɪk ˈfaɪbəz] = OPTICAL FIBRES; **fibre optics** = using optical fibres (fine strands of glass *or* plastic protected by a surrounding material) for the transmission of light signals which can carry data *fiberoptik*

optimalkod ⇨ **RISC**

optimization [ˌɒptɪmaɪˈzeɪʃ(ə)n] *subst.* making something work as efficiently as possible *optimering, anpassning*

optimize [ˈɒptɪmaɪz] *vb.* to make something work as efficiently as possible *optimera, anpassa;* **optimized code** = program that has been passed through an optimizer to remove any inefficient code *or* statements *optimerad kod, anpassad kod*

optimizer ['ɒptɪmaɪzə] *subst.* program which adapts another program to run more efficiently *optimerare*

optimum ['ɒptɪməm] *subst. & adj.* best possible *optimum;* **optimum code** *or* **minimum access code** *or* **minimum delay code** = coding system that provides the fastest access and retrieval time for stored data items *optimal kod*

option ['ɒpʃ(ə)n] *subst.* action which can be chosen *valmöjlighet, menyval;* **there are usually four options along the top of the screen; the options available are described in the main menu**

QUOTE with the colour palette option, remarkable colour effects can be achieved on an RGB colour monitor
Electronics & Wireless World

optional ['ɒpʃ(ə)nl] *adj.* which can be chosen *tillvals-, som tillval;* **the system comes with optional 3.5 or 5.25 disk drives**

optisk bildläsare ⇨ **scanner**

optisk länk ⇨ **data**

optisk skiva ⇨ **CD, disk, laser**

optisk teckenläsare ⇨ **OCR**

optisk transistor ⇨ **transphasor**

optodiskett ⇨ **CD**

optoelectrical [,ɒptəʊɪ'lektrɪk(ə)l] *adj.* which converts light to electrical signals *or* electrical signals into light *optoelektrisk*

optoelectronic [,ɒptəʊɪlek'trɒnɪk] *adj.* (microelectronic component) that has optoelectrical properties *optoelektronisk*

optoelectronics [,ɒptəʊɪlek'trɒnɪks] *subst.* electronic components that can generate *or* detect light, such as phototransistors, light-emitting diodes *optoelektronik*

orbit ['ɔːbɪt] **1** *subst.* path in space that a satellite follows around the earth *omloppsbana;* **the satellite's orbit is 100km from the earth's surface; elliptical orbit** = path of a satellite around the earth that is in the shape of an ellipse *elliptisk omloppsbana;* **geostational orbit** = satellite which moves at the same velocity as the earth, so remains above the same area of the earth's surface, and appears stationary when viewed from earth *geostationär omloppsbana;* **polar orbit** = satellite flight path that goes over the earth's poles *polär omloppsbana* **2** *vb.* to follow a path in space around the earth *gå i omloppsbana;* **the weather satellite orbits the earth every four hours**

ordbehandlare ⇨ **word-processor**

ordbehandling ⇨ **word-processing (WP)**

ordbehandlingsprogram ⇨ **editor**

order ['ɔːdə] **1** *subst.* **(a)** instruction *order, kommando;* **order code** = operation code *kommandokod;* **order code processor (OCP)** = *(in a multiprocessor system)* a processor which decodes and performs the arithmetic and logical operations according to the program code *huvudprocessor, OC-processor* **(b)** sorted according to a key *ordning;* **in alphabetical order; ordered list** = list of data items which has been sorted into an order *sorterad lista* **2** *vb.* to direct *or* instruct *beordra, kommendera*

ordlängd ⇨ **data, word**

ordmellanrum ⇨ **interword spacing**

OR function ['ɔː 'fʌŋ(k)ʃ(ə)n] *subst.* logical function that produces a true output if any input is true *disjunktion;* **OR gate** = electronic implementation of the OR function *(logisk) eller-grind*

COMMENT: the result of the OR function will be 1 if either or both inputs is 1; if both inputs are 0, then the result is 0

organization [,ɔːgənaɪ'zeɪʃ(ə)n] *subst.* **(a)** way of arranging something so that it works efficiently *organisation;* **the chairman handles the organization of the sales force; the organization of the group is too centralized to be efficient; the organization of the head office into departments; organization and methods** = examining how an office works, and suggesting how it can be made more efficient *utredning av ett företags infrastruktur;* **organization chart** = list of people working in various departments, showing how acompany *or* office is organized *organisationsdiagram* **(b)** group of people which is arranged for efficient work *organisation;* **government organization** = official body, run by the government *offentlig myndighet;* **employers' organization** = group of employers with similar interests *arbetsgivarförening*
NOTE: no plural for (a)

organizational [,ɔːgənaɪ'zeɪʃ(ə)nl] *adj.* referring to the way in which something is organized *organisations-*

organize ['ɔːgənaɪz] *vb.* to arrange something so that it works efficiently *organisera*

orientated ['ɔːrɪenteɪtɪd] *adj.* aimed towards *orienterad, inriktad;* **problem-orientated language (POL)** = high-level programming language that allows certain problems to be expressed easily *problemorienterat programmeringsspråk*

orientation [ˌɔːrien'teɪʃ(ə)n] *subst.* direction *or* position of an object *plats, belägenhet, riktning*

origin ['ɒrɪdʒɪn] *subst.* **(a)** position on a display screen to which all coordinates are referenced, usually the top left hand corner of the screen *utgångsläge, skärmorigo* **(b)** location in memory at which the first instruction of a program is stored *utgångsposition, första minnespositionen; see also* INDEXED

original [ə'rɪdʒənl] **1** *adj.* used *or* made first *original-;* **this is the original artwork for the advertisement 2** *subst.* **(a)** first document, from which a copy is made *original;* **did you keep the original of the letter? the original document is too faint to photocopy well (b)** (first) master data disk *or* photographic film *or* sound recording used, from which a copy can be made *original*

originalband ⇨ **tape**

originalband/skiva ⇨ **magnetic**

originaldata ⇨ **data**

original equipment manufacturer (OEM) [ə'rɪdʒənl ɪ'kwɪpmənt ˌmænjʊ'fæktʃ(ə)rə ('ɔʊi:'em)] *subst.* company which produces equipment using basic parts made by other manufacturers, and customizes the product for a particular application *ursprungstillverkare, underleverantör (av färdig utrustning);* **one OEM supplies the disk drive, another the monitor; he started in business as a manufacturer of PCs for the OEM market**

originalkopia ⇨ **generation**

originalpapper ⇨ **baryta paper**

originate [ə'rɪdʒəneɪt] *vb.* to start *or* come from *härröra (komma) från;* **the data originated from the new computer**

origination [əˌrɪdʒə'neɪʃ(ə)n] *subst.* work involved in creating something *upphov, skapande, utförande;* **the origination of the artwork will take several weeks**

orphan ['ɔːf(ə)n] *subst.* **orphan (line)** = last line of a section which falls at the top of a page and seems not to be connected with what goes before it *horunge; see also* WIDOW

ortho ['ɔːθəʊ] *or* **orthochromatic film** ['ɔːθə(ʊ)krə(ʊ)'mætɪk film] *subst.* photographic black and white film that is not sensitive to red light *ortokromatisk film*

orthogonal [ɔː'θɒgənl] *adj.* (instruction) made up of independent parameters *or* parts *rätvinklig, ortogonal*

OS ['ɔʊes] = OPERATING SYSTEM software that controls the basic, low-level hardware operations, and file management, without the user having to operate it (the operating system is usually supplied with the computer as part of the bundled software in ROM) *operativsystem*

oscillator ['ɒsɪleɪtə] *subst.* electronic circuit that produces a pulse *or* signal at a particular frequency *oscillator*

oscilloscope [ɒ'sɪlə(ʊ)skəʊp] *subst.* electronic test equipment that displays on a CRT the size and shape of an electrical signal *oscilloskop*

OSI ['ɔʊes'aɪ] = OPEN SYSTEM INTERCONNECTION *see also* ISO/OSI

osynligt avbrott ⇨ **transparent**

outage ['aʊtɪdʒ] *subst.* time during which a system is not operational *tid ur drift, feltid*

outdent [aʊt'dent] *vb.* to move part of a line of text into the margin *utdrag* NOTE: opposite is **indent**

outlet ['aʊtlet] *subst.* connection *or* point in a circuit *or* network where a signal *or* data can be accessed *terminal, anslutning, kontakt(punkt)*

outline ['aʊtlaɪn] *subst.* the main features of something *skiss, utkast;* **outline flowchart** = flowchart of the main features, steps and decisions in a program *or* system *skissdiagram*

out of band signalling ['aʊtəv'bænd 'sɪgnəlɪŋ] *subst.* transmission of signals outside the frequency limits of a normal voice channel *utombandssignalering*

out of phase ['aʊtəv'feɪz] *adv.* situation where a waveform is delayed in comparison to another *ur fas*

out of range ['aʊtəv'reɪn(d)ʒ] *adj.* (number *or* quantity) that is outside the limits of a system *utom räckhåll (för systemet)*

output (o/p *or* **O/P)** ['aʊtpʊt] **1** *subst.* **(a)** information *or* data that is transferred from a CPU *or* the main memory to another device such as a monitor *or* printer *or* secondary storage device *utdata;* **computer output** = data *or* information produced after processing by a computer *utdata* NOTE: opposite is **input (b)** action of transferring the information *or* data from store to a user *sända, ge utdata;* **output area** *or* **block** = section of memory that contains data to be transferred to an output device *utdataarea;* **output bound** *or* **limited** = processor that cannot function at normal speed because of a slower peripheral *utdatabegränsad;* **output buffer register** = temporary store for data that is waiting to be output *utdatabuffert;* **output device** = device (such as a monitor *or* printer) which

allows information to be displayed *utdataenhet;* **output file** = set of records that have been completely processed according to various parameters *utdatafil;* **output formatter** = (i) software used to format data *or* programs (and output them) so that they are compatible with another sort of storage medium *formateringsprogram;* (ii) part of a word processor program that formats text according to embedded commands *formaterare;* **output mode** = computer mode in which data is moved from internal storage *or* the CPU to external devices *utmatningsläge;* **output register** = register that stores data to be output until the receiver is ready *or* the channel is free *utdataregister;* **output stream** = communications channel carrying data output to a peripheral *utdataflöde;* **output port** = circuit and connector that allow a computer to output *or* transmit data to other devices *or* machines *utdatautgång;* **connect the printer to the printer output port; input/output (I/O)** = (i) receiving *or* transmitting of data between a computer and its peripherals and other points outside the system *sända eller ta emot data;* (ii) all data received *or* transmitted by a computer *in- och utdata, in-utdata; see also* INPUT **2** *vb.* to transfer data from a computer to a monitor *or* printer *sända utdata, skriva ut;* **finished documents can be output to the laser printer**
NOTE: **outputting - output**

> QUOTE most CAD users output to a colour plotter
> **PC Business World**

OV [ˈəʊˈviː] = OVERFLOW

overflow [ˈəʊvəfləʊ] *or* **OV** *subst.* **(a)** mathematical result that is greater than the limits of the computer's number storage system *spill;* **overflow bit** *or* **flag** *or* **indicator** = single bit in a word that is set to one (1) if a mathematical overflow has occurred *spillindikator;* **overflow check** = examining an overflow flag to see if an overflow has occurred *spillkontroll* **(b)** situation in a network when the number of transmissions is greater than the line capacity and are transferred by another route *stockning*

overhead [ˈəʊvəhed] *subst.* **(a)** extra code that has to be stored to organize the program *administrationstillägg(skod);* **the line numbers in a BASIC program are an overhead; overhead bit** = single bit used for error detection in a transmission *paritetsbit, kontrollbit;* **polling overhead** = amount of time spent by a computer calling and checking each terminal in a network *avfrågningstid* **(b) overhead projector** = projector which projects an image of transparent artwork onto a screen *stordiaprojektor*

overheat [ˈəʊvəˈhiːt] *vb.* to become too hot *bli för varm (överhettad);* **the system may overheat if the room is not air-conditioned**

overink [ˈəʊvəˈɪŋk] *vb.* to put on too much ink when printing *lägga på (hålla) för mycket färg;* **overinking** *färgsmetning;* **two signatures were spoilt by overinking**

overlap 1 [ˈəʊvəlæp] *subst.* two things where one covers part of the other *or* two sections of data that are placed on top of each other *överlappa;* **multipass overlap** = system of producing higher quality print from a dot matrix printer by repeating the line of characters but shifted slightly, so making the dots less noticeable (used to produce NLQ print) *repititionsöverskrivning (i skönskriftsläge)* **2** [ˌəʊvəˈlæp] *vb.* to cover part of an item with another *delvis täcka, överlappa*

overlay [ˈəʊvəleɪ] *subst.* **(a)** keyboard **overlay** = strip of paper that is placed above keys on a keyboard to indicate their function *tangentbordsmall* **(b)** small section of a program that is larger than the main memory capacity of a computer, and is loaded into memory when required, so that main memory only contains the sections it requires to run a program *överlagringssegment;* **form overlay** = heading *or* other matter held in store and printed out at the same time as the text *formulärmall;* **overlay manager** = system software that manages (during run-time) the loading and execution of sections of a program when they are required *överlagringshanterare, segmenthanterare;* **overlay region** = area of main memory that can be used by the overlay manager to store the current section of the program being run *överlagringsarea;* **overlay segments** = short sections of a long program that can be loaded into memory when required and executed *överlagringssegment*

> COMMENT: contrast with virtual memory management

overlaying [ˈəʊvəˌleɪɪŋ] *subst.* putting an overlay into action *överlagring*

overlay network [ˈəʊvəleɪ ˈnetwɜːk] *subst.* two communications networks that have some common interconnections *nätöverlappning*

overload [ˈəʊvəˈləʊd] *vb.* to demand more than the device is capable of *överlasta;* **the computer is overloaded with that amount of processing; channel overload** = transmission of data at a rate greater than the channel capacity *kanalöverlast*

overmodulation [ˈəʊvəˌmɒdjʊˈleɪʃ(ə)n] *subst.* situation where an amplitude modulated carrier signal is reduced to zero by excessive input signal

overpunching ['əʊvə'pʌn(t)ʃɪŋ] *subst.* altering data on a paper tape by punching additional holes *hålremskorrektion, stansning av extra hål*

overrun ['əʊvə,rʌn] *subst.* data that was missed by a receiver because it was not synchronized with the transmitter *or* because it operates at a slower speed than the transmitter and has no buffer *dataspill*

overscan ['əʊvə,skæn] *subst.* period when the television picture beam is outside the screen limits *översvep*

overstrike ['əʊvə'straɪk] *vb.* to print on top of an existing character to produce a new one *skriva över*

overtones ['əʊvətəʊnz] *subst. see* HARMONICS

over-voltage protection ['əʊvə 'vəʊltɪdʒ prə'tekʃ(ə)n] *subst.* safety device that prevents a power supply voltage exceeding certain specified limits *överspänningsskydd*

overwrite ['əʊvə'raɪt] *vb.* to write data to a location (memory *or* tape *or* disk) and, in doing so, to destroy any data already contained in that location *skriva över;* **the latest data input has overwritten the old information**

ovillkorlig ⇨ **unconditional**

ovillkorligt hopp ⇨ **jump (instruction), unconditional**

oxide ['ɒksaɪd] *subst.* chemical compound of oxygen *oxid;* **ferric oxide =** iron oxide used as a coating for magnetic disks and tapes *järnoxid;* **metal oxide semiconductors (MOS) =** production and design method for a certain family of integrated circuits using patterns of metal conductors and oxide deposited onto a semiconductor *MOS-metoden för kretstillverkning med halvledare; see also* MOSFET, CMOS

oändlig slinga ⇨ **endless, infinite**

Pp

p = PICO-

PA ['piːeɪ] = PUBLIC ADDRESS

PABX ['piːeɪbiːeks] = PRIVATE AUTOMATIC BRANCH EXCHANGE

pack [pæk] **1** *subst.* number of punched cards or magnetic disks *kortpacke;* **disk**

pack = number of magnetic disks on a single spindle, either fixed or removable (from the drive) *skivminnespacke* **2** *vb.* **(a)** to put things into a container for selling *or* sending *packa;* **to pack goods into cartons; the diskettes are packed in plastic wrappers; the computer is packed in expanded polystyrene before being shipped (b)** to store a quantity of data in a reduced form, often by representing several characters of data with one stored character *packa;* **packed decimal =** way of storing decimal digits in a small space, by using only four bits for each digit *binärkodad decimal;* **packed format =** two binary coded decimal digits stored within one computer word *or* byte (usually achieved by removing the check *or* parity bit) *BCD-format*
NOTE: opposite is **padding**

package ['pækɪdʒ] *subst.* **(a)** group of different items joined together in one deal *paket;* **package deal =** agreement where several different items are agreed at the same time *paraplyavtal;* **we are offering a package deal which includes the whole office computer system, staff training and hardware maintenance (b)** applications **package =** set of computer programs and manuals that cover all aspects of a particular task (such as payroll, stock control, invoicing, etc.) *tillämpningspaket;* **packaged** *or* **canned software** *or* **software package =** computer programs and manuals designed for a special purpose *programpaket;* **the computer is sold with accounting and word-processing packages**

packager ['pækɪdʒə] *subst.* person who creates a book for a publisher *person som sammanställer en bok på beställning från ett förlag*

packaging ['pækɪdʒɪŋ] *subst.* **(a)** material used to protect goods which are being packed *emballage;* attractive material used to wrap goods for display *omslagspapper;* **airtight packaging; packaging material (b)** creating books for publishers *sammanställa böcker på beställning från ett förlag* NOTE: no plural

packet ['pækɪt] *subst.* group of bits of uniform size which can be transmitted as a group, using a packet switched network *datapaket;* **packet assembler/disassembler (PAD) =** dedicated computer that converts serial data from asynchronous terminals to a form that can be transmitted along a packet switched (synchronous) network *datapaketerare;* **the remote terminal is connected to a PAD device through which it accesses the host computer; packet switched data service** *or* **packet switched network (PSN) =** service which transmits data in packets of a set length *(data)paketförmedlande nät;* **packet switching =** method of sending messages *or* data in uniform-sized packets, and processing and routing packets rather than bit streams *(data)paketförmedling*

packing ['pækɪŋ] *subst.* **(a)** action of putting goods into boxes and wrapping them for shipping *paketering, emballering;* **what is the cost of the packing? packing is included in the price (b)** putting large amounts of data into a small area of storage *packa;* **packing density** = amount of bits of data which can be stored in a unit area of a disk *or* tape *packningstäthet;* **packing routine** = program which packs data into a small storage area *packningsrutin* **(c)** material used to protect goods *emballage;* **packed in airtight packing; non-returnable packing** = packing which is to be thrown away when it has been used and not returned to the sender *engångsemballage* NOTE: no plural

PAD [pæd] = PACKET ASSEMBLER/DISASSEMBLER

pad [pæd] **1** *subst.* number of keys arranged together *tangentbord, knappsats;* **cursor pad** = group of cursor control keys *piltangenter;* **keypad** = group of special keys used for certain applications *tangentbord, knappsats;* **hex keypad** = set of sixteen keys, with all the figures (0-9, A-F) needed to enter hexadecimal numbers *hexadecimalt tangentbord;* **numerical keypad** = set of ten keys with figures (0-9), included on most computer keyboards as a separate group, used for entering large amounts of data in numeric form *numeriskt tangentbord* **2** *vb.* to *fylla, stoppa;* **pad character** = extra character added to a string *or* packet *or* file until it is a required size *fyllnadsbit*

padding ['pædɪŋ] *subst.* material (characters or digits) added to fill out a string *or* packet until it is the right length *utfyllnadsteknik, fyllning* NOTE: opposite is **packing**

paddle ['pædl] *subst.* computer peripheral consisting of a knob *or* device which is turned to move a cursor *or* pointer on the screen *styrspak;* **games paddle** = device held in the hand to move a cursor *or* graphics in a computer game *styrspak för datorspel*

page [peɪdʒ] *subst.* **(a)** sheet of paper *sida, blad* **(b)** (i) one side of a printed sheet of paper in a book *or* newspaper *or* magazine *or* catalogue, etc. *sida;* (ii) text held on a computer monitor screen (which if printed out will fill a page of paper *or* which fills the screen) *sida;* **page break** = (i) point at which a page ends and a new page starts (in continuous text) *sidbrytning;* (ii) marker used when word-processing to show where a new page should start *sidbrytning;* **page description language**

(PDL) = software that controls a printer's actions to print a page of text to a particular format according to a user's instructions *sidbeskrivningsspråk;* **page display** = showing on the screen a page of text as it will appear when printed out *sidutseende, sidpresentation;* **page length** = length of a page (in word-processing) *sidlängd;* **pages per minute (ppm)** = measurement of the speed of a printer as the number of pages of text printed every minute *sidor per minut;* **page printer** = printer which composes one page of text and then prints it rapidly *sidskrivare, skrivare med arkmatare* **(c)** section of main store, which contains data *or* programs *sida;* **multiple base page** = multi-user system in which each user and the operating system have one page of main memory, which can then call up other pages within main memory *sidbaserat fleranvändarsystem;* **page addressing** = main memory which has been split into blocks, with a unique address allocated to each block of memory which can then be called up and accessed individually, when required *sidadressering;* **page boundary** = point where one page ends and the next starts *sidbrytning;* **page protection** = software controls to ensure that pages are not overwritten by accident or copied into a reserved section of memory *sidskrivskydd;* **page table** = list of all the pages and their locations within main memory, used by the operating system when accessing a page *sidtabell* **(d)** one section of a main program which can be loaded into main memory when required *sida vb.* **(e) to page someone** = to try to find someone in a building (using a PA *or* radiopager) *söka ngn med personsökare; see also* RADIO PAGING **(f)** to make up a text into pages *sidbryta* **(g)** to divide computer backing store into sections to allow long programs to be executed in a small main memory *göra minnesväxling (sidtilldelning)*

pager ['peɪdʒə] *subst.* small device carried by someone, which allows him to be called from a central office, by using a radio signal *personsökare*

pagination [,pædʒɪ'neɪʃ(ə)n] *subst.* putting a text into pages; arrangement of pages in a book *sidbrytning och sidnumrering*

paging ['peɪdʒɪŋ] *subst.* virtual memory technique that splits main memory into small blocks (pages) which are allocated an address and which can be called up when required *sidväxling;* **paging algorithm** = formula by which the memory management allocates memory to pages, also covering the transfer from backing storage to main memory in the most efficient way *sidväxlingsalgoritm*

COMMENT: a virtual memory management system stores data as pages in memory to provide an apparently larger capacity main memory by storing unused pages in backing store, copying them into main memory only when required

paired registers ['peəd 'redʒɪstəz] *subst.* two basic word size registers used together as one large word size register (often used for storing address words) *dubblerat register;* **the 8-bit CPU uses a paired register to provide a 16-bit address register**

paket ⇨ **frame**

paketadministrationsbyte ⇨ **envelope**

paketkanalomvandlare ⇨ **interface**

paketstyrenhet ⇨ **interface**

PAL [pæl] = PHASE ALTERNATING LINE standard that defines television and video formats, using 625 horizontal scan lines and 50 frames per second *PAL-standarden*

COMMENT: mainly used in Western Europe, Australia, some parts of the Middle East and Africa

palette ['pælət] *subst.* range of colours which can be used (on a printer *or* computer display) *palett*

QUOTE the colour palette option offer sixteen colours from a range of over four thousand
Electronics & Wireless World

PAM [pæm] = PULSE AMPLITUDE MODULATION pulse modulation in which the height of the pulse varies with the input signal *pulsamplitudmodulering*

panel ['pænl] *subst.* flat section of a casing with control knobs *or* sockets *panel, instrumentpanel;* **the socket is on the back panel; control panel** = panel with indicators and switches which allows an operator to monitor and control the actions of a computer *or* peripheral *kontrollpanel;* **front panel** = main computer system control switches and status indicators *framsidespanel, frontpanel*

paper ['peɪpə] *subst.* thin material used for making books *or* newspapers *or* stationery items *papper;* **the book is printed on 80gsm paper; glossy paper is used for printing half-tones; bad quality paper gives too much show-through; paper feed** = slot into which paper is introduced (in a printer) *pappersmatning; US* **paper slew** = PAPER THROW; **paper tape** = long strip of paper on which data can be recorded, usually in the form of punched holes *pappersremsa;* **paper tape punch** = device which punches holes in paper tape to carry data *remsstans;* **paper tape reader** = device

which accepts punched paper tape and converts the punched information stored on it into signals which a computer can process *remsläsare;* **paper tape feed** = method by which paper tape is passed into a machine *remsmatning;* **paper throw** = rapid vertical movement of paper in a printer *papperssnabbmatning;* **paper tray** = container used to hold paper to be fed into a printer *pappersbehållare, pappershållare;* **paper weight** = weight of paper used in printing (usually measured in gsm *or* grams per square metre) *pappersvikt*

paperback ['peɪpəbæk] *subst.* book which has a paper cover *pocketbok;* **we are publishing the book as a hardback and as a paperback**

paperbound ['peɪpə,baʊnd] *adj.* (book) bound with a paper cover (as opposed to hardbound) *häftad (bok)*

paper-fed ['peɪpə,fed] *adj.* (device) which is activated when paper is introduced into it *matningsstyrd;* **a paper-fed scanner**

paperless ['peɪpəlɪs] *adj.* without using paper *papperslös;* **paperless office** = electronic office *or* office which uses computers and other electronic devices for office tasks and avoids the use of paper *papperslöst kontor*

papp ⇨ **cardboard**

papper i löpande bana ⇨ **continuous**

papperskopia ⇨ **copy**

pappersmatning ⇨ **feed**

papprets gramvikt ⇨ **weight**

parallel ['pærəlel] *adj.* (i) (computer system) in which two or more processors operate simultaneously on one or more items of data *parallell(dator);* (ii) two or more bits of a word transmitted over separate lines at the same time *parallell(överföring);* **parallel access** = data transfer between two devices with a number of bits (usually one byte wide) being sent simultaneously *parallellåtkomst;* **parallel adder** = number of adders joined together in parallel, allowing several digits to be added at once *parallelladderare;* **parallel computer** = computer with one or more logic *or* arithmetic units, allowing parallel processing *parallelldator;* **parallel connection** = transmission link that handles parallel data *parallellanslutning;* **their average transmission rate is 60,000 bps through parallel connection; parallel data transmission** = transmission of bits of data simultaneously along a number of data lines *parallell dataöverföring;* **parallel input/output (PIO)** = data input *or* output from a computer in a parallel form *parallell*

in- och utmatning; **parallel input/output chip** = dedicated integrated circuit that performs all handshaking, buffering, etc., needed when transferring parallel data to and from a CPU *parallell in- och utkrets;* **parallel input/parallel output (PIPO)** = device that can accept and transmit parallel data *parallell in-utenhet;* **parallel input/serial output (PISO)** = device that can accept parallel data and transmit serial data *parallell till serieomvandlare;* **parallel interface** *or* **port** = circuit and connector that allows parallel data to be received *or* transmitted *parallell anslutning;* **parallel operation** = number of processes carried out simultaneously on a number of inputs *parallell bearbetning;* **parallel port** *see* PARALLEL INTERFACE; **parallel priority system** = number of peripherals connected in parallel to one bus, if they require attention, they send their address and an interrupt signal, which is then processed by the computer according to device priority *parallellt prioritetsstyrt system;* **parallel printer** = printer that accepts character data in parallel form *parallellansluten skrivare;* **parallel processing** = computer operating on several tasks simultaneously *parallell databehandling;* **parallel running** = running an old and a new computer system together to allow the new system to be checked before it becomes the only system used *parallellkörning;* **parallel search storage** = data retrieval from storage that uses part of the data other than an address to locate the data *parallellsökningsminne;* **parallel transfer** = data transfer between two devices with a number of bits (usually one byte wide) being sent simultaneously *parallell överföring;* **parallel transmission** = number of data lines carrying all the bits of a data word simultaneously *parallell överföring*
NOTE: opposite is **serial transmission**

parallell ⇨ **concurrent, parallel**

parallelldataöverföring ⇨ **input/output (I/O)**

parallellgränssnitt ⇨ **Centronics interface, interface**

parallell mellanlagring för överföringssiffra ⇨ **partial carry**

parameter [pə'ræmɪtə] *subst.* information which defines the limits *or* actions of something, such as a variable *or* routine *or* program *parameter;* **the X parameter defines the number of characters displayed across a screen; the size of the array is set with this parameter;** **parameter-driven software** = software whose main functions can be modified and tailored to a user's needs by a number of variables *parameterstyrd programvara;* **parameter testing** = program to examine the parameters and set up the system *or*

program accordingly *parameterkontroll;* **parameter word** = data word that contains information defining the limits *or* actions of a routine or program *parameterord;* **physical parameter** = description of the size, weight, voltage or power of a system *fysisk parameter*

parameterization [pə,ræmɪtəraɪ'zeɪʃ(ə)n] *subst.* action of setting parameters for software *sättning av parametrar*

parametric (subroutine) [ˌprə'metrɪk ('sʌbruː'tiːn)] *subst.* subroutine that uses parameters to define its limits *or* actions *parameterstyrd (subrutin)*

paritet ⇨ **parity**

parity ['pærətɪ] *subst.* being equal *paritet;* **block parity** = parity check on a block of data *blockparitet;* **column parity** = parity check on every punched card *or* tape column *kolumnparitet;* **even parity (check)** = error checking system in which any series of bits transmitted must have an even number of binary ones *jämn paritet(skontroll);* **odd parity (check)** = error checking system in which any series of bits transmitted must have an odd number of binary ones *udda paritet(skontroll);* **parity bit** = extra bit added to a data word as a parity checking device *paritetsbit;* **parity check** = method of checking (odd *or* even parity check) for errors and that transmitted binary data has not been corrupted *paritetskontroll;* **parity flag** = indicator that shows if data has passed a parity check or if data has odd or even parity *paritetsflagga;* **parity interrupt** = interrupt signal from an error checking routine that indicates that received data has failed a parity check and is corrupt *paritetsavbrott;* **parity track** = one track on magnetic *or* paper tape that carries the parity bit *paritetsspår*

parkering av huvudet ⇨ **head**

parsing ['paːzɪŋ] *subst.* operation to break down high-level language code into its element parts when translating into machine code *textanalys, satsanalys*

part [paːt] *subst.* **(a)** section of something *del;* **part page display** = display of only a section of a page, and not the whole page *delsidskärm;* **(b) spare part** = small piece of a machine which is needed to replace a piece which is broken *or* missing *reservdel;* **the printer won't work - we need to get a spare part (c)** one of a series *del, enhet;* **two part stationery** = stationery (invoices, receipts, etc.) with a top sheet and a copy sheet *tvåbladskopieblanketter;* **four-part invoices** = invoices with four sheets (a top sheet and three copies) *fyrdelade fakturablanketter; see also* MULTI-PART

partial carry ['pɑːʃ(ə)l 'kærɪ] *subst.* temporary storage of all carries generated by parallel adders rather than a direct transfer *parallell mellanlagring för överföringssiffra*

partial RAM ['pɑːʃ(ə)l 'ræm] *subst.* RAM chip in which only a certain area of the chip functions correctly, usually in newly released chips (partial RAM's can be used by employing more than one to make up the capacity of one fully functional chip) *delvis fungerande läsminne*

particle ['pɑːtɪkl] *subst.* very small piece of matter *partikel*

partition [pɑːˈtɪʃ(ə)n pəˈt] section of computer memory set aside as foreground *or* background memory

***partvinnad kabel* ⇨ twisted pair cable**

party line ['pɑːtɪ laɪn] *or* **shared line** ['ʃeəd laɪn] *subst.* one telephone line shared by a number of subscribers

PASCAL [ˌpæsˈkæl] high-level structured programming language used both on micros and for teaching programming *programmeringsspråket Pascal*

pass [pɑːs] **1** *subst.* (i) the execution of a loop, once *pass, steg, körning;* (ii) single operation *operation;* **single-pass assembler** = assembler program that translates the source code in one action *enpassassemblerare;* **sorting pass** = single run through a list of items to put them into order *sorteringspass* **2** *vb.* action of moving the whole length of a magnetic tape over the read/write heads *spola*

***passiv* ⇨ idle**

***passiv reserv* ⇨ standby**

***passiv tid* ⇨ idle**

password ['pɑːswɜːd] *subst.* word *or* series of characters which identifies a user so that he can access a system *lösenord;* **the user has to key in the password before he can access the database**

QUOTE the system's security features let you divide the disk into up to 256 password-protected sections
Byte

patch [pætʃ] *subst.* (temporary) correction made to a program *lappning;* small correction made to software by the user, on the instructions of the software publisher *lappning*

patchboard ['pætʃbɔːd] *subst.* board with a number of sockets connected to devices, into which plugs can be inserted to connect other devices *or* functions *kopplingsbord*

patchcord ['pætʃkɔːd] *subst.* cord with a plug at each end, which is used to link sockets in a patchboard *kopplingskabel*

path [pɑːθ] *subst.* possible route or sequence of events *or* instructions within the execution of a program *väg*

***patron* ⇨ cartridge**

pattern ['pætən] *subst.* series of regular lines *or* shapes which are repeated again and again *mönster;* **pattern recognition** = algorithms *or* program functions that can identify a shape from a video camera, etc. *mönsterigenkänning*

patterned ['pætənd] *adj.* with patterns *mönstrad*

PAX [piːeɪˈeks] = PRIVATE AUTOMATIC EXCHANGE

paycable ['peɪˌkeɪbl] *subst.* US form of cable television where the viewer pays an extra fee for extra channels *betal(kabel)-TV*

pay TV ['peɪˌtiːviː] *subst.* form of cable television, where the viewer pays for programs*or* channels watched *betal-TV*

PBX ['piːbiːˈeks] = PRIVATE BRANCH EXCHANGE

PC ['piːˈsiː] **(a)** = PERSONAL COMPUTER low cost microcomputer intended mainly for home and light business use *persondator;* **PC compatible** = computer that is compatible with another common make (usually the IBM PC) *IBM PC-kompatibel (obs. att en PC och en persondator inte är samma sak; PC är ett av IBM inregistrerat varumärke - liksom PC/XT och PC/AT; "persondator" omfattar alla datorer i denna klass - även Macintosh)* **(b)** = PRINTED CIRCUIT (BOARD) **(c)** = PROGRAM COUNTER

QUOTE in the UK, the company is known not for PCs but for PC printers
Which PC?

PCB ['piːsiːˈbiː] = PRINTED CIRCUIT BOARD

p-channel ['piːˈtʃænl] *subst.* section of semiconductor that is p-type *p-dopad halvledare;* **p-channel MOS** = MOS transistor that conducts via a small region of p-type semiconductor *p-dopad MOS-krets; see also* MOS, P-TYPE SEMICONDUCTOR

PCM ['piːsiːˈem] **(a)** = PULSE CODE MODULATION pulse stream that carries data about a signal in binary form *pulskodsmodulering; see also* PULSE AMPLITUDE, PULSE DURATION, PULSE POSITION **(b)** = PLUG-COMPATIBLE MANUFACTURER company that produces add-on boards which are compatible with another manufacturer's computer *pluggkompatibel tillverkare, en som gör direkt anslutningsbar utrustning (främst om tillverkare av kompatibler till IBM:s stordatorer)*

P-code ['piːˈkəʊd] *subst.* intermediate code produced by a compiler that is ready for an interpreter to process, usually from PASCAL programs *p-kod (genom UCSD-Pascal)*

PCU ['piːsiːˈjuː] = PERIPHERAL CONTROL UNIT device that converts input and output signals and instructions to a form that a peripheral device will understand *styrenhet för kringutrustning*

PDL ['piːdiːˈel] = PAGE DESCRIPTION LANGUAGE, PROGRAM DESIGN LANGUAGE

PDM ['piːdiːˈem] = PULSE DURATION MODULATION pulse modulation system where the pulse width varies with the magnitude of the input signal *pulsbreddsmodulering*

PDN ['piːdiːˈen] = PUBLIC DATA NETWORK

peak [piːk] **1** *subst.* highest point *topp;* maximum value of a variable *or* signal *maximalvärde;* **keep the peak power below 60 watts or the amplifier will overheat; the marker on the thermometer shows the peak temperature for today; peaks and troughs =** maximum and minimum points of a waveform *toppar och dalar;* **peak period =** time of the day when most power is being used *toppbelastning;* **time of peak demand =** time when something is being used most *toppbelastning;* **peak output =** highest output *maximalproduktion* **2** *vb.* to reach the highest point *toppa, nå;* **the power peaked at 1,200 volts; sales peaked in January**

peek [piːk] *subst.* BASIC computer instruction that allows the user to read the contents of a memory location *instruktionsord i programmeringsspråket BASIC för att läsa en minnescell;* **you need the instruction PEEK 1452 here to examine the contents of memory location 1452;** *compare* POKE

pegging ['pegɪŋ] *vb.* sudden swing of an analog meter to its maximum readout due to a large signal *slå i taket;* **after he turned up the input level, the signal level meter was pegging on its maximum stop**

pekare ⇨ **data**

pekboll ⇨ **trackball**

pekskiva ⇨ **touch**

pekskärm ⇨ **screen, touch**

pel [pl] *see* PIXEL

pen [pen] *see* LIGHT PEN; **pen recorder =** peripheral which moves a pen over paper according to an input (a value or coordinate) *kurvritare*

per [pɜː] *prep.* **(a) as per =** according to *per, enligt;* **as per sample =** as shown in the sample *enligt prov;* **as per specification =** according to the details given in the specification *enligt specifikation* **(b)** at a rate of *per;* **per hour** *or* **per day** *or* **per week** *or* **per year =** for each hour *or* day *or* week *or* year *per timma (dag, vecka);* **(c)** out of *per;* **the rate of imperfect items is about twenty-five per thousand; the error rate has fallen to twelve per hundred**

per cent [pɜː ˈsent] *adj. & adv.* out of each hundred *or* for each hundred *procent;* **10 per cent =** ten in every hundred *tio procent;* **what is the increase per cent? fifty per cent of nothing is still nothing**

percentage [pəˈsentɪdʒ] *subst.* amount shown as part of one hundred *procentandel;* **percentage increase =** increase calculated on the basis of a rate for one hundred *procentuell ökning;* **percentage point =** one per cent *en procentenhet*

percentile [pəˈsentaɪl] *subst.* one of a series of ninety-nine figures below which a certain percentage of the total falls *procentil*

perfect ['pɜːfɪkt] **1** *adj.* completely correct *or* with no mistakes *perfekt, felfri;* **we check each batch to make sure it is perfect; she did a perfect typing test 2** *vb.* to make something which is completely correct *fullända, förfina;* **he perfected the process for making high grade steel**

perfect binding ['pɜːfɪkt 'baɪndɪŋ] *subst.* method of binding paperback books, where the pages are trimmed at the spine, and glued to the cover *limbindning(smaskin)*

perfect bound ['pɜːfɪkt 'baʊnd] *adj.* (book, usually a paperback) bound without sewing, where the pages are trimmed at the spine and glued to the cover with strong glue *limbunden*

perfectly ['pɜːfɪktlɪ] *adv.* with no mistakes *or* correctly *perfekt, felfritt;* **she typed the letter perfectly**

perfector [pəˈfektə] *subst.* printing machine that prints on both sides of a sheet of paper *dubbelsidig tryckpress, skön- och vidertryckpress, komplettmaskin*

perforated tape ['pɜːfəreɪtɪd 'teɪp] *subst.* paper tape *or* long strip of tape on which data can be recorded in the form of punched holes *hålremsa*

perforations [,pɜːfəˈreɪʃ(ə)nz] *subst.* line of very small holes in a sheet of paper *or* continuous stationery, to help when tearing *perforering*

perforator [ˈpɜːfəreɪtə] *subst.* machine that punches holes in a paper tape *perforerare*

perform [pəˈfɔːm] *vb.* to do well *or* badly *utföra, uträtta*

performance [pəˈfɔːməns] *subst.* way in which someone *or* something acts *uppförande, uppträdande, prestanda;* **as a measure of the system's performance =** as a way of judging if the system is working well *systemprestanda;* **in benchmarking, the performances of several systems** *or* **devices are tested against a standard benchmark; high performance =** high quality *or* high specification equipment *hög prestanda*

periferiavbrottssignal ⇨ **external**

periferienhet ⇨ **external**

perigee [ˈperɪdʒiː] *subst.* point during the orbit of a satellite when it is closest to the earth *perigeum, minsta avstånd (till jorden)*

period [ˈpɪərɪəd] *subst.* **(a)** length of time *tidsperiod;* **for a period of time** *or* **for a period of months** *or* **for a six-year period; sales over a period of three months (b)** *US* full stop *or* printing sign used at the end of a piece of text *punkt*

periodic [,pɪərɪˈɒdɪk] *or* **periodical** [,pɪərɪˈɒdɪk(ə)l] **1** *adj.* **(a)** from time to time *regelbunden;* **a periodic review of the company's performance (b) periodic =** (signal *or* event) that occurs regularly *regelbunden, periodisk;* **the clock signal is periodic 2** *subst.* **periodical =** magazine which comes out regularly *tidskrift*

periodically [,pɪərɪˈɒdɪklɪ] *adv.* from time to time *regelbundet*

peripheral [pəˈrɪfər(ə)l] **1** *adj.* which is not essential *or* which is attached to something else *perifer* **2** *subst.* (i) item of hardware (such as terminals, printers, monitors, etc.) which is attached to a main computer system *kringutrustning;* (ii) any device that allows communication between a system and itself, but is not directly operated by the system *kringutrustning;* **peripherals such as disk drives or printers allow data transfer and are controlled by a system, but contain independent circuits for their operation; fast peripheral =** peripheral that communicates with the computer at very high speeds, limited only by the speed of the electronic circuits *snabb kringutrustning;* **slow peripheral =** peripheral such as a card reader, where mechanical movement determines speed *långsam kringutrustning;* **peripheral**

control unit (PCU) = device that converts the input/output signals and instructions from a computer to a form and protocol which the peripheral will understand *styrenhet för kringutrustning;* **peripheral driver =** program *or* routine used to interface, manage and control an input/output device *or* peripheral *styrprogram för kringutrustning;* **peripheral equipment =** (i) external devices that are used with a computer, such as a printer *or* scanner *kringutrustning;* (ii) (communications) equipment external to a central processor that provides extra features *kringutrustning;* **peripheral interface adapter (PIA) =** circuit that allows a computer to communicate with a peripheral by providing serial and parallel ports and other handshaking signals required to interface the peripheral *anpassnings- gränssnitt mot kringutrustning;* **peripheral limited =** CPU that cannot execute instructions at normal speed because of a slow peripheral *kringutrustningsbegränsad;* **peripheral memory =** storage capacity available in a peripheral *periferiminne;* **peripheral processing units (PPU) =** device used for input, output or storage which is controlled by the CPU *styrdator för kringenhet;* **peripheral software driver =** short section of computer program that allows a user to access and control a peripheral easily *styrrutin (program) för kringenhet; same as* DEVICE DRIVER; **peripheral transfer =** movement of data between a CPU and peripheral *överföring av data till eller från kringutrustning;* **peripheral unit =** (i) item of hardware (such as terminal, printer, monitor, etc.) which is attached to a main computer system *kringutrustning, periferienhet;* (ii) any device that allows communication between a system and itself, but is not operated only by the system *kringutrustning, periferienhet*

permanent [ˈpɜːmənənt] *adj.* which will last for a very long time *or* for ever *permanent;* **permanent dynamic memory =** storage medium which retains data even when power is removed *permanent minne;* **permanent error =** error in a system which cannot be mended *systemfel;* **permanent file =** data file that is stored in a backing storage device such as a disk drive *permanent fil;* **permanent memory =** computer memory that retains data even when power is removed *permanent minne; see also* NON-VOLATILE MEMORY

permanent ⇨ **permanent, resident**

permanent fel ⇨ **error, hard**

permanent formaterad ⇨ **hard-sectoring**

permanently [ˈpɜːmənəntlɪ] *adv.* done in a way which will last for a long time *permanent, ständigt;* **the production number is permanently engraved on the back of the computer casing**

permanentminne ⇨ **nonerasable storage**

permanent minne ⇨ **non-volatile**

permanent sektoriserad ⇨ **hard-sectoring**

permeability [ˌpɜːmjəˈbɪlətɪ] *subst.* measure of the ratio of the magnetic flux in a material to the size of the generating field *permeabilitet*

permutation [ˌpɜːmjʊˈteɪʃ(ə)n] *subst.* number of different ways in which something can be arranged *permutation, variationsmönster;* **the cipher system is very secure since there are so many possible permutations for the key**

persistence [pəˈsɪst(ə)ns] *subst.* length of time that a CRT will continue to display an image after the picture beam has stopped tracing it on the screen *efterlysning;* **slow scan rate monitors need long persistence phosphor to prevent the image flickering**

person ['pɜːsn] *subst.* human being *person;* **person-to-person call** = telephone call placed through an operator, where the caller will only speak to a certain person *personsamtal*

personal ['pɜːsənl] *adj.* referring to one person *personlig;* **personal computer (PC)** = low-cost microcomputer intended mainly for home and light business use *persondator;* **personal identification device (PID)** = device (such as a card) connected *or* inserted into a system to identify *or* provide authorization for a user *personligt identitetskort;* **personal identification number (PIN)** = unique sequence of digits that identifies a user to provide authorization to access a system (often used on automatic cash dispensers *or* with a PID *or* password to enter a system) *personlig kod*

personalize ['pɜːsnəlaɪz] *vb.* to customize *or* to adapt a product specially for a certain user *användaranpassa, personanpassa*

persondator ⇨ **PC**

PERT [pɜːt] = PROGRAM EVALUATION AND REVIEW TECHNIQUE definition of tasks *or* jobs and the time each requires, arranged in order to achieve a goal *PERT, projektplaneringsteknik*

petal printer ['petl 'prɪntə] = DAISY WHEEL PRINTER

pF ['piːkəʊˌfærəd] = PICOFARAD unit of measurement of capacitance equal to one million millionth of a farad *pF*

phantom ROM ['fæntəm 'rɒm] *subst.* duplicate area of read-only memory that is accessed by a special code *dubblerat läsminne*

phase [feɪz] **1** *subst.* **(a)** one part of a larger process *fas;* **run phase** = period of time when a program is run *körfas;* **compile phase** = period of time during which a program is compiled *kompileringsfas* **(b)** delay between two similar waveforms *fasskillnad, fasförskjutning;* **in phase** = two signals that have no time delay between them *i fas;* **out of phase** = one signal that has a time delay when compared to another *ur fas;* **phase alternating line (PAL)** = method of providing colour information in a televisionsignal, used in standard receivers in certain countries *PAL-systemet;* **phase angle** = measurement of the phase difference between two signals, where a phase angle of 0 degrees represents signals that are in phase *fasvinkel;* **phase equalizer** = circuit that introduces delays into signal paths to produce a phase angle of zero degrees *fasriktare, fasutjämnare;* **phase modulation** = modulation method in which the phase of a carrier signal varies with the input *fasmodulering* **2** *vb.* **to phase in** *or* **to phase out** = to introduce something gradually *or* to reduce something gradually *gradvis inkoppling resp. urkoppling;* **phased change-over** = new device that is gradually introduced as the old one is used less and less *gradvis växling (utbyte)*

> COMMENT: when two signals are in phase there is no time delay between them, when one is delayed they are said to be out of phase by a certain phase angle

phon [fɒn] *subst.* measure of sound equal to a one thousand Hertz signal at one decibel *phon, även fon*

phone [fəʊn] **1** *subst.* telephone *or* machine used for speaking to someone over a long distance *telefon;* **we had a new phone system installed last week; house phone** *or* **internal phone** = telephone for calling from one office to another *snabbtelefon, interntelefon;* **by phone** = using the telephone *på telefon;* **to be on the phone** = to be speaking to someone on the telephone *tala i telefon;* **she has been on the phone all morning; he spoke to the manager on the phone; card phone** = public telephone that accepts a phonecard instead of money *korttelefon;* **phone book** = book which lists names of people and companies with their addresses and phone numbers *telefonkatalog;* **look up his address in the phone book; phone call** = speaking to someone on the phone *telefonsamtal;* **to**

make a phone call = to speak to someone on the telephone *ringa (upp);* **to answer the phone** *or* **to take a phone call** = to reply to a call on the phone *svara i telefon;* **phonecard** = special plastic card which allows the user to use a cardphone for a certain length of time *telefonkort;* **phone number** = set of figures for a particular telephone *telefonnummer;* **he keeps a list of phone numbers in a little black book; the phone number is on the company notepaper; can you give me your phone number? 2** *vb.* **to phone someone** = to call someone by telephone *ringa;* **don't phone me, I'll phone you; his secretary phoned to say he would be late; he phoned the order through to the warehouse; to phone for something** = to make a phone call to ask for something *ringa efter något;* **he phoned for a taxi; to phone about something** = to make a phone call to speak about something *ringa i ett ärende;* **he phoned about the order for computer stationery**

phone back [fəʊn 'bæk] *vb.* to reply by phone *ringa tillbaka;* **the chairman is in a meeting, can you phone back in about half an hour? Mr Smith called while you were out and asked if you would phone him back**

phoneme ['fəʊniːm] *subst.* single item of sound used in speech *fonem;* **the phoneme "oo" is present in the words too and zoo**

phonetic [fə(ʊ)'netɪk] *adj.* referring to phonetics *fonetisk;* **the pronunciation is indicated in phonetic script**

phonetics [fə(ʊ)'netɪks] *subst.* written symbols that are used to represent the correct pronunciation of a word *fonetisk skrift*

phosphor ['fɒsfə] *subst.* substance that produces light when excited by some form of energy, usually an electron beam, used for the coating inside a cathode ray tube *fosfor; see* TELEVISION; **phosphor coating** = thin layer of phosphor on the inside of a CRT screen *fosforbeläggning;* **phosphor dots** = individual dots of red, green and blue phosphor on a colour CRT screen *fosforpunkter;* **phosphor efficiency** = measure of the amount of light produced in ratio to the energy received from an electron beam *luminicenseffektivitet;* **long persistence phosphor** = television screen coating that retains the displayed image for a period of time longer than the refresh rate, so reducing flicker effects *fosfor med lång efterlysning*

COMMENT: a thin layer of phosphor is arranged in a pattern of small dots on the inside of a television screen which produces an image when scanned by the picture beam

phosphorescence [,fɒsfə'resns] *subst.* ability of a material to produce light when excited by some form of energy *fosforescens*

photo ['fəʊtəʊ] **1** *prefix* referring to light *foto* **2** *abbreviation of* PHOTOGRAPH

photocell ['fəʊtə(ʊ),sel] *subst.* electronic device that produces *or* varies an electrical signal according to the amount of light shining on it *fotocell*

photocomposition [,fəʊtəʊ,kɒmpə'zɪʃ(ə)n] *subst.* composition of typeset text direct onto film *fotosättning*

photoconductivity [,fəʊtəʊ,kɒndʌk'tɪvɪti] *subst.* material which varies its resistance according to the amount of light striking it *fotokonduktivitet*

photoconductor [,fəʊtəʊkən'dʌktə] *subst.* photocell whose resistance varies with the amount of light shining on it *fotocell, fotokonduktiv cell*

photocopier ['fəʊtəʊ,kɒpɪə] *subst.* machine which makes a copy of a document by photographing and printing it *fotokopiator, kopieringsmaskin*

photocopy ['fəʊtə(ʊ),kɒpi] **1** *subst.* copy of a document made by photographing and printing it *fotokopia;* **make six photocopies of the contract 2** *vb.* to make a copy of a document by photographing and printing it *fotokopiera;* **she photocopied the contract**

photocopying ['fəʊtəʊ,kɒpiːŋ] *subst.* making photocopies *fotokopiering;* **photocopying costs are rising each year; photocopying bureau** = office which photocopies documents for companies which do not possess their own photocopiers *fotokopieringsfirma;* **there is a mass of photocopying to be done** = there are many documents waiting to be photocopied *en hel del måste fotokopieras* NOTE: no plural

photodigital memory [,fəʊtəʊ'dɪdʒɪtl 'memərɪ] *subst.* computer memory system that uses a LASER to write data onto a piece of film which can then be read many times but not written to again *optiskt läsminne* NOTE: also called WORM (Write Once Read Many times memory)

photodiode [,fəʊtəʊ'daɪəʊd] *subst.* electronic component displaying the electrical properties of a diode but whose resistance varies with the amount of light that shines on it *fotodiod; see also* AVALANCHE

photoelectric ['fəʊtə(ʊ)ɪ'lektrɪk] *adj.* (material) that generates an electrical signal when light shines on it *fotoelektrisk;* **photoelectric cell** = component which produces *or* varies an electrical signal when a light shines on it *fotoelektrisk cell;* **the**

photoelectric cell detects the amount of light passing through the liquid

photoelectricity ['fəʊtəʊɪlek'trɪsɪtɪ] *subst.* production of an electrical signal from a material that has light shining on it *fotoelektricitet*

photoemission [,fəʊtəʊɪ'mɪʃ(ə)n] *subst.* material that emits electrons when light strikes it *fotoemission*

photograph ['fəʊtəgrɑːf] *subst.* image formed by light striking a light-sensitive surface, usually coated paper *fotografi;* **colour photograph; black and white photograph; it's a photograph of the author; he took six photographs of the set; we will be using a colour photograph of the author on the back of the jacket**

photographic [,fəʊtə'græfɪk] *adj.* referring to photography *or* photographs *fotografisk;* **the copier makes a photographic reproduction of the printed page**

photographically [,fəʊtəʊ'græfɪklɪ] *adv.* using photography *fotografiskt;* **the text film can be reproduced photographically**

photography [f(ə)'tɒgrəfɪ] *subst.* method of creating images by exposing light-sensitive paper to light, using a camera *fotografering*

photogravure [,fəʊtəʊgrə'vjʊə] *subst.* printing method in which the paper is pressed directly onto the etched printing plate *fotogravyr*

photolithography [,fəʊtə(ʊ)lɪ'θɒgrəfɪ] *subst.* printing using a lithographic printing plate formed photographically *fotolitografi*

photomechanical transfer (PMT) [,fəʊtə(ʊ)mə'kænɪk(ə)l 'trænsfə ('piːem'tiː)] *subst.* system for transferring line drawings and text onto film before printing *fotomekanisk litografi*

photometry [fəʊ'tɒmɪtrɪ] *subst.* study and measurement of light *fotometri*

photon ['fəʊtɒn] *subst.* packet of electromagnetic radiation *foton*

photoprint ['fəʊtəʊprɪnt] *subst. (in typesetting)* final proof *slutkorrektur*

photoresist [,fəʊtəʊrɪ'zɪst] *subst.* chemical *or* material that hardens into an etch resistant material when light is shone on it *fotoresist;* **to make the PCB, coat the board with photoresist, place the opaque pattern above, expose, then develop and etch, leaving the conducting tracks; positive photoresist =** method of forming photographic images where exposed areas of photoresist are removed, used in making PCBs *fotoetsning, fotografietsning*

photosensor ['fəʊtəʊ,sensə] *subst.* component *or* circuit that can produce a signal related to the amount of light striking it *fotocell*

photostat ['fəʊtə(ʊ)stæt] **1** *subst.* type of photocopy *fotostatkopia* **2** *vb.* to make a photostat of a document *fotostatkopiera*

phototelegraphy ['fəʊtə(ʊ)tɪ'legrəfɪ] *subst.* transmission of images over a telephone line *telefoto, telefax; see also* FACSIMILE TRANSMISSION

phototext ['fəʊtəʊtekst] *subst.* characters and text that have been produced by a phototypesetter *text från en fotosättsmaskin*

phototransistor [,fəʊtəʊtræn'zɪstə] *subst.* electronic component that can detect light and amplify the generated signal *or* vary a supply according to light intensity *fototransistor*

phototypesetter [,fəʊtəʊ'taɪp,setə] *subst.* company which specializes in phototypesetting *fotosättare*

phototypesetting [,fəʊtəʊ'taɪp,setɪŋ] *subst.* method of typesetting that creates characters using a computer and exposing a sensitive film in front of a mask containing the required character shape *fotosättning*

> COMMENT: this is the method by which most new publications are typeset, superseding metal type, since it produces a good quality result in a shorter time

photovoltaic [,fəʊtəʊvɒl'teɪk] *adj.* which produces a voltage across a material due to light shining on it *ljusaktiv, ljuskänslig*

physical ['fɪzɪk(ə)l] *adj.* solid *or* which can be touched *fysisk;* **physical database =** organization and structure of a stored database *fysisk databas;* **physical layer =** the ISO/OSI defined network layer that defines rules for bit rate, power and medium for signal transmission *fysiskt skikt; see also* LAYER

physical record ['fɪzɪk(ə)l 'rekɔːd] *subst.* **(a)** maximum unit of data that can be transmitted in a single operation *maximal paketstorlek i dataöverföring* **(b)** all the information, including control data for one record stored in a computer system *fysisk post*

PIA [piːaɪ'eɪ] = PERIPHERAL INTERFACE ADAPTER circuit that allows a computer to communicate with a peripheral by providing serial and parallel ports and other handshaking signals required to interface the peripheral *anpassningsgränssnitt mot kringutrustning*

pica ['paɪkə] *subst.* **(a)** method of measurement used in printing and typesetting (equal to twelve point type) *pica* **(b)** typeface used on a printer, giving ten characters to the inch *typsnittet pica*

pickup ['pɪkʌp] *subst.* arm and cartridge used to playback music from a record *pickup*

pickup reel ['pɪkʌp 'riːl] *subst.* empty reel used to take the tape as it is played from a full reel *tomrulle, uppsamlingsrulle*

pico- (p) ['piːkəʊ] *prefix* representing one million millionth of a unit *pico-;* **picofarad (pF)** = measure of capacitance equal to one million millionth of a farad *pF;* **picosecond (ps)** = one million millionth of a second *ps*

picture ['pɪktʃə] **1** *subst.* printed *or* drawn image of an object or scene *bild;* **this picture shows the new design; picture beam** = moving electron beam in a TV, that produces an image on the screen by illuminating the phosphor coating and by varying its intensity according to the received signal *elektronstråle;* **picture element** *or* **pixel** = smallest single unit *or* point on a display whose colour *or* brightness can be controlled *bildpunkt; see also* PIXEL; **picture phone** = communications system that allows sound and images of the user to be transmitted and received *bildtelefon;* **picture processing** = analysis of information contained in an image, usually by computer *or* electronic methods, providing analysis *or* recognition of objects in the image *bildbehandling;* **picture transmission** = transmission of images over a telephone line *bildöverföring; see also* FACSIMILE TRANSMISSION **2** *vb.* to visualize an object *or* scene *avbilda, visualisera, föreställa sig;* **try to picture the layout before starting to draw it in**

PID [piːaɪˈdiː] = PERSONAL IDENTIFICATION DEVICE device (such as a card) connected *or* inserted into a system to identify or provide authorization for a user *personligt identitetskort*

piece accent ['piːsˌæks(ə)nt] *subst.* floating accent *flytande accent*

piece fraction ['piːsˌfrækʃ(ə)n] *subst.* printed fraction contained in one character space *komplett bråktecken*

pie chart ['paɪtʃɑːt] *subst.* diagram where ratios are shown as slices of a circle *tårtdiagram*

piezoelectric [pɪˈetsəʊɪˌlektrɪk] *adj.* (of certain crystals) being able to change their electrical properties when a force is applied *or* to change their physical dimensions when an electrical signal is applied *piezoelektrisk*

piggyback ['pɪgɪbæk] *vb.* to connect two integrated circuits in parallel, one top of the other to save space *stapelkoppla;* **piggyback those two memory chips to boost the memory capacity; piggyback entry** = to gain unauthorized access to a computer system by using an authorized user's password *or* terminal *aliasinloggning*

piggybacking ['pɪgɪˌbækɪŋ] *subst.* using transmitted messages to carry acknowledgements from a message which has been received earlier *stapelkoppling*

PILOT ['paɪlət] computer programming language that uses a text-based format and is mainly used in computer-aided learning *programmeringsspråket Pilot*

pilot ['paɪlət] **1** *subst.* used as a test, which if successful will then be expanded into a full operation *pilottest;* **the company set up a pilot project to see if the proposed manufacturing system was efficient; the pilot factory has been built to test the new production process; pilot system** = system constructed to see if it can be manufactured, if it works and if the end-user likes it *pilotsystem* **2** *vb.* to test *prova, testa;* **they are piloting the new system**

PIN [pɪn] = PERSONAL IDENTIFICATION NUMBER unique sequence of digits that identifies the user *personlig kod*

COMMENT: the PIN is commonly used in automatic cash machines in banks, along with a card (PID) which allows the user to be identified

pin [pɪn] *subst.* **(a)** one of several short pieces of wire attached to an integrated circuit package that allows the IC to be connected to a circuit board *stift, anslutningsstift* **(b)** short piece of metal, part of a plug which fits into a hole in a socket *kontaktstift;* **use a three-pin plug to connect the printer to the mains; three-pin mains plug** = plug with three pins (one neutral, one live and one earthed) *jordad nätkontakt;* **two-pin mains plug** = plug with two pins (one neutral, one live) *ojordad nätkontakt*

pinchwheel ['pɪn(t)ʃwiːl] *subst.* small rubber wheel in a tape machine that holds the tape in place and prevents flutter *tryckrulle*

pin cushion distortion ['pɪnˌkʊʃ(ə)n dɪsˈtɔːʃ(ə)n] *subst.* optical image distortion in which objects are seen with stretched corners due to lens aberration *kuddförvrängning*

pinfeed ['pɪnfiːd] *subst. see* TRACTOR FEED

pin photodiode ['pɪn ˌfəʊtəʊˈdaɪəʊd] *subst.* electronic photodiode that can detect light, made up of layers of P-type, Intrinsic and N-type semiconductor *P-I-N-fotocell*

PIO [piːaɪˈəʊ] = PARALLEL INPUT/OUTPUT *see also* PIPO, PISO

pipeline (computer) ['paɪplaɪn (kəmˈpjuːtə)] **1** *subst.* CPU or ALU that is constructed in blocks and executes instructions in steps, each block dealing with one part of the instruction, so speeding up program execution *rörledningsdator* **2** *vb.* **(a)** to schedule inputs to arrive at the microprocessor when nothing else is happening, so increasing apparent speed *rörleda logiskt* **(b)** to begin processing of a second instruction while still processing the present one to increase speed of execution of a program *rörleda logiskt*

pipelining ['paɪplaɪnɪŋ] *subst.* **(a)** method of scheduling inputs to arrive at the microprocessor when nothing else is happening, so increasing apparent speed *logisk rörledning* **(b)** beginning the processing of a second instruction while still processing the present one to increase speed of execution of a program *logisk rörledning*

PIPO [piːˈaɪpiːˈəʊ] = PARALLEL INPUT/PARALLEL OUTPUT

piracy ['paɪərəsɪ] *subst.* copying of patented inventions *or* copyright works *intrång i upphovsrätt* NOTE: no plural

pirate ['paɪərɪt] **1** *subst.* person who copies a patented invention *or* a copyright work and sells it *piratkopierare;* **the company is trying to take the software pirates to court; a pirate copy of a computer program 2** *vb.* to manufacture copies of an original copyrighted work illegally *piratkopiera;* **a pirated tape** *or* **a pirated design; the designs for the new system were pirated in the Far East; he used a cheap pirated disk and found the program had bugs in it**

COMMENT: the items most frequently pirated are programs on magnetic disks and tapes which are relatively simple to copy

piratkopia ⇨ **bootleg**

piratkopierare ⇨ **pirate**

PISO [piːˈaɪˈesəʊ] = PARALLEL INPUT/SERIAL OUTPUT

pitch [pɪtʃ] *subst.* **(a)** measurement of the horizontal spacing of typed characters *breddsteg* **(b)** actual frequency of a sound *tonhöjd;* **pitch envelope =** shape that defines how the frequency of a sound will vary with time *frekvensförlopp* **(c)** satellite *or* antenna movement about the horizontal axis *lutning* **(d) sales pitch =** talk by a salesman to persuade someone to buy *säljsnack*

pix [pɪks] *subst.* picture *or* pictures *bild(er), film(klipp)*

pixel ['pɪksl] *or* **picture element** ['pɪktʃərˈelɪmənt] *subst.* smallest single unit *or* point of a display whose colour *or* brightness can be controlled *bildpunkt*

COMMENT: in high resolution display systems the colour or brightness of a single pixel can be controlled; in low resolution systems a group of pixels are controlled at the same time

QUOTE an EGA display and driver give a resolution of 640 x 350 pixels and support sixteen colours
PC Business World
QUOTE adding 40 to each pixel brightens the image and can improve the display's appearance
Byte

pix lock ['pɪkslɒk] *subst.* synchronization of a video playback circuit by an external signal *signalsynkronisering, bildlåsning*

PL1 ['piːelˈwʌn] = PROGRAMMING LANGUAGE/1 high level programming language mainly used in commercial and scientific work on large computers, containing features of ALGOL, COBOL and FORTRAN *programmeringsspråket PL/1*

PLA ['piːelˈeɪ] = PROGRAMMABLE LOGIC ARRAY IC that can be permanently programmed to perform logic operations on data *programmerbar logikmatris*

COMMENT: a PLA consists of a large matrix of paths between input and output pins, with logic gates and a fusible link at each connection point which can be broken or left to conduct when programming to define a function from input to output

place [pleɪs] *subst.* position of a digit within a number *position, plats*

plaintext ['pleɪntekst] *subst.* text *or* information that has not been encrypted *or* coded *klartext;* **the messages were sent as plain text by telephone; enter the plaintext message into the cipher machine**

PLAN [plæn] low-level programming language *programmeringsspråket PLAN*

plan [plæn] **1** *subst.* **(a)** organized way of doing something *plan, schema* **(b)** drawing which shows how something is arranged *or* how something will be built *schema, ritning;* **floor plan =** drawing of a floor in a building, showing where different departments are *planritning;* **street plan** *or* **town plan =** map of a town showing streets and buildings *stadskarta* **2** *vb.* to organize carefully how something should be done *planera, ordna* NOTE: **planning - planned**

planchest ['plæntʃest] *subst.* piece of furniture with wide flat drawers, in which large plans *or* artwork can be kept *ritningsskåp*

planeringsprogram ▷ **planner**

planet ['plænɪt] *subst.* large body in space (such as the earth), moving in orbit round the sun *planet*

planetary camera ['plænɪt(ə)rɪ 'kæm(ə)rə] *subst.* microfilm camera in which the film and article being photographed are stationary *planetkamera*

planner ['plænə] *subst.* (a) software program that allows appointments and important meetings to be recorded and arranged in the most efficient way *planeringsprogram* (b) **desk planner** *or* **wall planner** = book *or* chart which shows days *or* weeks *or* months so that the work of an office can be shown by diagrams *planeringskalender*

planning ['plænɪŋ] *subst.* organizing how something should be done *planering;* **long-term planning** *or* **short-term planning**
NOTE: no plural

plant [plɑːnt] *vb.* to store a result in memory for later use *lagra*

plasma display ['plæzmə dɪs'pleɪ] *or* **gas plasma display** ['gæs ˌplæzmə dɪs'pleɪ] *subst.* display screen using the electroluminescing properties of certain gases to display text *plasmaskärm*

COMMENT: this is a modern thin display usually used in small portable computers

QUOTE the disadvantage of using plasma technology is that it really needs mains power to work for any length of time
QUOTE the plasma panel came out of the extended use test well
Micro Decision

plasmaskärm ▷ **display**

plastic bubble keyboard ['plæstɪk 'bʌbl 'kiːbɔːd] *subst.* keyboard whose keys are small bubbles in a plastic sheet over a contact which when pressed completes a circuit *plant tangentbord, membrantangentbord*

COMMENT: these are very solid and cheap keyboards but are not ideal for rapid typing

plate [pleɪt] *subst.* (a) illustration in a book, usually printed separately and on better quality paper than the text *stick* (b) etched *or* patterned printing surface that carries the ink to the paper *plåt* (c) photographic image using a sheet of glass as the backingmaterial *fotografisk plåt;* **plate**

camera = camera which takes pictures on glass plates *plåtkamera*

COMMENT: photographic plates are now used mainly in high quality, large-format professional cameras while the most popular backing material is still plastic as in a film

platen ['plæt(ə)n] *subst.* (a) roller which supports the paper in a printer *or* typewriter *vals;* **platen press** = printing press where the paper passes under a flat printing plate *digelpress* (b) device that keeps film in a camera in the correct position *rulle*

platsbyte ▷ **transposition**

play back [pleɪ 'bæk] *vb.* to read data *or* a signal from a recording medium *återspela, avlyssna;* **after you have recorded the music, press this button to play back the tape and hear what it sounds like**

playback head ['pleɪbæk 'hed] *subst.* transducer that reads signals recorded on a storage medium and usually converts them to an electrical signal *läshuvud;* **disk playback head; tape playback head**

player missile graphics ['pleɪə 'mɪsaɪl 'græfɪks] *see* SPRITES

PLD ['piːel'diː] = PROGRAMMABLE LOGIC DEVICE

plex database ['pleks'deɪtəbeɪs] *subst.* database structure in which data items can be linked together *plexdatabas*

plex structure ['pleks'strʌktʃə] *subst.* network structure *or* data structure in which each node is connected to all the others *plexdatabas*

PL/M ['piːel'em] = PROGRAMMING LANGUAGE FOR MICROPROCESSORS high level programming language derived from PL/1 for use on microprocessors *programmeringsspråket PL/M*

plot [plɒt] **1** *subst.* graph *or* map *diagram, kurva, graf* **2** *vb.* to draw an image (especially a graph) based on information supplied as a series of coordinates *rita en bild (ett diagram);* **plotting mode** = ability of some word-processors to produce graphs by printing a number of closely spaced characters rather than individual pixels (this results in a broad low-resolution line) *grafikläge*

plotter ['plɒtə] *subst.* computer peripheral that draws straight lines between two coordinates *kurvritare, kurvskrivare;* **plotter driver** = dedicated software that converts simple instructions issued by a user into complex control instructions to direct the plotter *styrprogram för kurvritare;* **plotter pen** = instrument used in a plotter to mark the paper with ink as it moves over the paper *ritpenna;* **digital plotter** = plotter which receives the coordinates to plot to in a digital form *digital kurvritare;* **drum plotter** = computer output device that consists of a movable pen and a piece of paper wrapped around a drum that rotates, creating patterns and text *trumritare;* **incremental plotter** = plotter which receives positional data as increments to its current position rather than separate coordinates *inkrementell kurvritare, stegritare;* **printer-plotter** = high-resolution printer that is able to mimic a plotter and produce low-resolution plots *skrivare med ritfunktion;* **x-y plotter** *or* **graph plotter** = plotter which plots to coordinates supplied, by moving the pen in two planes while the paper remains stationary *X-Y-ritare*

COMMENT: plotters are used for graph and diagram plotting and can plot curved lines as a number of short straight lines

plug [plʌg] **1** *subst.* **(a)** connector with protruding pins that is inserted into a socket to provide an electrical connection *kontakt;* **the printer is supplied with a plug; adapter plug** = plug which allows devices with different plugs (two-pin, three-pin, etc.) to be fitted into the same socket *anpassningskontakt;* **plug-compatible** = equipment manufactured to operate with another system when connected to it by a connector *or* cable *kontaktkompatibel, direkt inkopplingsbar;* **this new plug-compatible board works much faster than any of its rivals, we can install it by simply plugging it into the expansion port (b)** to give a plug to a new product = to publicize a new product *introducera (annonsera) en ny produkt* **2** *vb.* **(a) to plug in** = to make an electrical connection by pushing a plug into a socket *koppla in, plugga in;* **no wonder the computer does nothing, you have not plugged it in at the mains; plug-in unit** = small electronic circuit that can be simply plugged into a system to increase its power *inkopplingsenhet*

NOTE: opposite is **unplug (b)** to publicize *or* to advertise *göra reklam för, annonsera;* **they ran six commercials plugging holidays in Spain**

QUOTE it allows room for up to 40K of RAM via plug-in memory cartridges
Which PC?
QUOTE adding memory is simply a matter of plugging a card into an expansion bus connector
Byte

plugboard ['plʌgbɔːd] *or* **patchboard** ['pætʃbɔːd] *subst.* board with a number of sockets connected to devices into which plugs can be inserted to connect various other devices *kopplingsbord*

plus [plʌs] *or* **plus sign** ['plʌs ˌsaɪn] *subst.* printed *or* written sign (+) showing

that figures are added *or* showing a positive value *plustecken*

pluspol ⇨ **positive**

plus-tre-kod ⇨ **excess**

PMBX ['piːembiːeks] = PRIVATE MANUAL BRANCH EXCHANGE small telephone exchange inside a company where all calls coming in or going out have to be placed through the switchboard *manuell telefonväxel*

PMOS ['piːmɒs] = P-channel METAL OXIDE SEMICONDUCTOR metal oxide semiconductor transistor that conducts via a small region of p-type semiconductor *PMOS-krets*

PMR ['piːem'ɑː] = PRIVATE MOBILE RADIO

PMT ['piːem'tiː] = PHOTOMECHANICAL TRANSFER

pn-junction ['piːen 'dʒʌŋ(k)ʃ(ə)n] *subst.* area where regions of p-type and n-type semiconductor meet, resulting in a diode characteristic *pn-övergång;* **diffused pn-junction** = practical result of doping one section of semiconductor asp-type and an adjacent section as n-type, where the doping concentration drops gradually over a short distance between the two areas *diffunderad pn-övergång;* **step pn-junction** = ideal junction between p-type and n-type areas in a semiconductor where the doping changes occur suddenly *stegvis pn-övergång*

pnp transistor ['piːen'piː træn'zɪstə] *subst.* layout of a bipolar transistor whose collector and emitter are of p-type semiconductor and whose base is n-type semiconductor *pnp-transistor*

pocket ['pɒkɪt] *subst.* **pocket calculator** *or* **pocket diary** = calculator *or* diary which can be carried in the pocket *miniräknare, fickräknare, fickalmanacka*

point [pɔɪnt] **1** *subst.* **(a)** place *or* position *punkt, plats;* **access point** = point on a circuit board *or* in software, allowing an engineer to check signals *or* data *testpunkt;* **breakpoint** = symbol inserted into a program which stops its execution at that point to allow registers, variables and memory locations to be examined (used when debugging a program) *brytpunkt;* **re-entry point** = point in a program *or* routine where it is re-entered *återgångspunkt;* **starting point** = place where something starts *startpunkt* **(b) binary point** = dot which indicates the division between the bits for the numbers' whole units and the fractional part of the binary number *binärpunkt;* **decimal point** = dot (in a decimal number) which indicates the division between a whole unit and its fractional parts (such as 4.25) *decimalkomma;* **percentage point** = 1 per cent *procentenhet* **(c)** measurement system used in typesetting (one point is equal to 0.351 mm) *punkt (i det typografiska måttsystemet);* **the text of the book is set in 9 point Times; if we increase the point size to 10, will the page extent increase?** NOTE: usually written **pt** after figures: **10pt Times Bold 2** *vb.* **to point out** = to show *peka ut, visa*

QUOTE the arrow keys, the spacebar or the mouse are used for pointing, and the enter key or the left mouse button are to pick
PC User
QUOTE pointing with the cursor and pressing the joystick button eliminates use of the keyboard entirely
Soft

pointer ['pɔɪntə] *subst.* **(a)** variable in a computer program that contains the address to a data item *or* instruction *pekare;* **increment the contents of the pointer to the address of the next instruction; pointer file =** file of pointers referring to large amounts of stored data *pekarfil* **(b)** graphical symbol used to indicate the position of a cursor on a computer display *markör, pekare, pil;* **desktop publishing on a PC is greatly helped by the use of a pointer and mouse**

point-of-sale (POS) ['pɔɪntəv'seɪl ('piːəʊ'es)] *subst.* the place where goods in a shop are paid for *(butiks)kassa;* **point-of-sale material =** display material (such as posters, dump bins) to advertise a product where it is being sold *butiksskyltning;* **point-of-sale terminal** *or* **POS terminal =** computer terminal at a point-of-sale, used to provide detailed product information and connected to a central computer to give immediate stock control information *kassaterminal, butiksterminal;* **electronic point-of-sale (EPOS) =** system that uses a computer terminal at a point-of-sale site for electronic funds transfer, as well as for product identification and stock control *elektroniskt kassasystem, kassaterminal, butiksterminal*

point to point ['pɔɪnttə'pɔɪnt] *subst.* communications network where every point is connected to every other *punkt-till-punkt*

COMMENT: this provides rapid reliable transmissions but is very expensive and wasteful in cabling

poke [pəʊk] *subst.* computer instruction that modifies an entry in a memory by writing a number to an address in memory *instruktionsord i programmeringsspråket BASIC för att skriva i en minnescell;* **poke 1423,74 will write the data 74 into location 1423;** *compare with* PEEK

POL [piːæʊ'el] = PROBLEM-ORIENTATED LANGUAGE

polar ['pəʊlə] *adj.* referring to poles *polär;* **polar coordinates =** system of defining positions as an angle and distance from the origin *polära koordinater; compare with* CARTESIAN COORDINATES; **polar diagram** = graphical representation of polar coordinates *polärdiagram;* **polar orbit =** satellite flight path that flies over the earth's poles *polär omloppsbana;* **polar signal =** signal that uses positive and negative voltage levels *polär signal, plus/minus-signal;* **unipolar signal =** signal that uses only positive voltage levels *enpolär signal*

polarity [pə(ʊ)'lærətɪ] *subst.* definition of direction of flow of flux *or* current in an object *polaritet;* **electrical polarity =** definition of whether an electrical signal is positive *or* negative, indicating if a point is a source or collector of electrical current (positive polarity terminals are usually marked red, negative are black) *elektrisk polaritet;* **magnetic polarity =** method of indicating if a point is a source *or* collector of magnetic flux patterns *magnetisk polaritet;* **polarity test =** check to see which electrical terminal is positive and which negative *polaritetstest;* **reverse polarity =** situation where positive and negative terminals have been confused, resulting in the equipment not functioning *omvänd polaritet*

polarized ['pəʊləraɪzd] *adj.* **(a)** broadcast signal waveforms are all aligned in one plane *polariserad;* **vertically polarized =** signal whose waveforms travel horizontally while alternating vertically *vertikalt polariserad* **(b)** polarized plug = plug which has a feature (usually a peg *or* a special shape) so that it can only be inserted into a socket in one way *polariserad kontakt, ej förväxlingsbar kontakt;* **polarized edge connector =** edge connector that has a hole or key to prevent it being plugged in the wrong way round *säkerhetskontakt*

polaroid filter ['pəʊlərɔɪd 'fɪltə] *subst.* photographic filter that only allows light in one plane, vertical *or* horizontal, to be transmitted *polariseringsfilter*

COMMENT: often used to remove glare by placing in front of a camera lens or as glasses in front of a person's eyes

Polish notation ['pəʊlɪʃ nə(ʊ)'teɪʃ(ə)n] *see* REVERSE

poll [pəʊl] *vb. (of computer)* to determine the state of a peripheral in a network *avfråga, rösta;* **polled interrupt =** interrupt signal determined by a polling device *avfrågat avbrott*

polling ['pəʊlɪŋ] *subst.* system of communication between a controlling computer and a number of networked terminals (the computer checks each terminal in turn to see if it is ready to receive *or* transmit data, and takes the required action) *avfrågning;* **polling characters** = special sequence of characters for each terminal to be polled (when a terminal recognises its sequence, it responds) *avfrågningstecken;* **polling interval** = period of time between two polling operations *avfrågningsintervall;* **polling list** = order in which terminals are to be polled by a computer *avfrågningslista;* **polling overhead** = amount of time spent by a computer in calling and checking each terminal in a network *avfrågningstid*

COMMENT: the polling system differs from other communications systems in that the computer asks the terminals to transmit *or* receive, not the other way round

polynomial code [ˌpɒlɪˈnəʊmj(ə)l ˈkəʊd] *subst.* error detection system that uses a set of mathematical rules applied to the message before it is transmitted and again when it is received to reproduce the original message *polynominal kod*

pop [pɒp] *vb.* (instruction to a computer) to read and remove the last piece of data from a stack *poppa, hämta från stack;* **pop-down menu** *or* **pop-up menu** = menu that can be displayed on the screen at any time by pressing the appropriate key, usually displayed over material already on the screen *fönstermeny, rullgardinsmeny;* **to pop off** *or* **pop on** = to remove *or* add suddenly an image *or* section of image from a frame *klippa in, klippa ut;* **this is the last frame of the film so pop on the titles**

QUOTE you can use a mouse to access pop-up menus and a keyboard for word processing
Byte

POP 2 [ˈpɒpˈtuː] high level programming language used for list processing applications *programmeringsspråket POP 2*

pop filter [ˈpɒpˈfɪltə] *subst.* electronic circuit used when recording voices to attenuate signals caused by wind *or* breathing *brusfilter, puffskydd;* **every time you say a 'p' you overload the tape recorder, so put this pop filter in to stop it**

poppa ⇨ pop

porch [pɔːtʃ] *see* FRONT PORCH

port [pɔːt] *subst.* socket *or* physical connection allowing data transfer between a computer's internal communications channel and another external device *utgång, kontakt, port, ingång, anslutning;* **asynchronous port** = connection to a computer allowing asynchronous data communications *asynkron anslutning;*

input port = circuit *or* connector that allows a computer to receive data from other external devices *indataingång;* **joystick port** = socket and interfacing circuit into which a joystick can be plugged *styrspaksingång;* **output port** = circuit *or* connector that allows a computer to output *or* transmit data to another machine *or* device *utdatautgång;* **parallel port** = circuit and connector that allows parallel data to be received *or* transmitted *parallellanslutning;* **printer port** = output port of a computer with a standard connector to which a printer is connected to receive character data (either serial *or* parallel) *skrivarutgång;* **serial port** = circuit that converts parallel data in a computer to and from a serial form, allowing serial data access *seriell anslutning;* **port selector** = switch that allows the user to choose which peripheral a computer (via its o/p port) is connected to *utgångsväljare;* **port sharing** = device that is placed between one I/O port and a number of peripherals, allowing the computer access to all of them *anslutningsfördelare*

QUOTE the 40 Mbyte hard disk model is provided with eight terminal ports
Micro Decision

portability [ˌpɔːtəˈbɪlətɪ] *subst.* extent to which software *or* hardware can be used on several systems *flyttbarhet*

QUOTE although portability between machines is there in theory, in practice it just isn't that simple
Personal Computer World

portable [ˈpɔːtəbl] **1** *subst.* compact self-contained computer that can be carried around and used either with a battery pack *or* mains power supply *bärbar dator* **2** *adj.* (any hardware *or* software *or* data files) that can be used on a range of different computers *flyttbar;* **portable software** *or* **portable programs** = programs that can be run on several different computer systems *flyttbara program*

portföljdator ⇨ **lapheld computer**

POS [ˈpiːəʊˈes] = POINT-OF-SALE place in a shop where goods are paid for *(butiks)kassa;* **EPOS** = ELECTRONIC POINT-OF-SALE system that uses a computer terminal at a point-of-sale site for electronic fund transfer *or* stock control as well as product pricing, etc. *elektroniskt kassasystem, kassaterminal, butiks-terminal*

position [pəˈzɪʃ(ə)n] **1** *subst.* place where something is *position, plats;* **this is the position of that chip on the PCB 2** *vb.* to place something in a special place *placera, positionera;* **the VDU should not be positioned in front of a window; position this photograph at the top right-hand corner of**

the page; **positioning time** = amount of time required to access data stored in a disk drive *or* tape machine, including all mechanical movements of the read head and arm *åtkomsttid*

positional [pə'zɪʃənl] *adj.* referring to position *positions-;* in a certain position *i position*

positive ['pɒzətɪv] *adj.* **(a)** meaning "yes" *positiv;* **positive response** = communication signal that indicates correct reception of a message *positivt svar;* **positive terminal** = connection to a power supply source that is at a higher electrical potential than ground and supplies current to a component *pluspol, positiv anslutning* **(b)** (image) which shows objects as they are seen *positivbild;* **positive display** = (screen) where the text and graphics are shown as black on a white background to imitate a printed page *positivskärm;* **positive presentation** = screen image which is coloured on a white background *positiv presentation; compare* NEGATIVE **(c)** electrical voltage greater than zero *positiv spänning;* **positive logic** = logic system in which a logical one is represented by a positive voltage level, and a logical zero represented by a zero or negative voltage level *positiv logik*

positive feedback ['pɒzətɪv 'fiːdbæk] *subst.* part of an output signal that is added into the input of a device *positiv återkoppling;* **make sure the microphone is not too close to the loudspeaker or positive feedback will occur and you will overload the amplifier**

> COMMENT: positive feedback is often accidental, resulting in a stronger output which provides a bigger positive feedback signal which rapidly overloads the system

positiv återkoppling ⇨ **feedback**

post [pəʊst] **1** *vb.* to enter data into a record in a file *lägga in data* **2** *prefix* action that occurs after another *post-, efter-;* **post-editing** = editing and modifying text after it has been compiled *or* translated by a machine *efterredigering;* **post-formatted** = (text) arranged at printing time rather than on screen *efterformatering;* **post mortem** = examination of a computer program *or* piece of hardware after it has failed to try to find out why the failure took place *haveriundersökning*

post ⇨ **mail, record**

postbyte ['pəʊstbaɪt] *subst.* in a program instruction, the data byte following the op code that defines the register to be used *postbyte*

poster ['pəʊstə] *subst.* large printed sheet, used to advertise something *affisch*

postfix ['pəʊstfiks] *subst.* word *or* letter written after another *postfix;* **postfix notation** = mathematical operations written in a logical way, so that the operator appears after the operands, this removes the need for brackets *postfix notation, omvänd polsk notation;* **normal notation: (x-y) + z, but using postfix notation: xy - z+** NOTE: often referred to as **reverse Polish notation**

posthanterare ⇨ **manager**

postmellanrum ⇨ **gap**

postprocessor ['pəʊst'prəʊsesə] *subst.* **(a)** microprocessor that handles semi-processed data from another device *efterprocessor* **(b)** program that processes data from another program, which has already been processed *efterbehandlingsprogram*

postslutssignal ⇨ **end**

pot [pɒt] = POTENTIOMETER

potential [pə(ʊ)'tenʃ(ə)l] *subst.* ability of energy to carry out work (by transformation) *potential;* **potential difference** = voltage difference between two points in a circuit *potentialskillnad*

potentiometer [pə,tenʃɪ'ɒmɪtə] *subst.* mechanical variable resistance component consisting of a spindle which is turned to move a contact across a resistance track to vary the resistance of the potentiometer *potentiometer; see also* VARIABLE RESISTOR

power ['paʊə] *subst.* **(a)** unit of energy in electronics equal to the product of voltage and current, measured in Watts *(el)kraft;* **automatic power off** = equipment that will switch itself off if it has not been used for a certain time *automatisk avstängning;* **power dump** = to remove all power from a computer *avstängning;* **power failure** = stoppage of the electrical power supply (for a long *or* very short period of time) which will cause electrical equipment to stop working or malfunction, unless they are battery backed *strömavbrott;* **power loss** = amount of power lost (in transmission *or* due to connection equipment) *kraftförlust;* **"power off"** = switching off *or* disconnecting an electrical device from its power supply *slå av, stänga av;* **"power on"** = indication that a voltage is being supplied to a piece of electrical equipment *slå på, sätta på;* **power-on reset** = automatic reset of a CPU to a known initial state immediately after power is applied (some CPUs will not automatically start with clear registers, etc., but might contain garbage) *automatstart, påslagsåterställning;* **power pack** = self-contained box that will provide a voltage and current supply for a circuit *kraftenhet,* *batteripaket, strömförsörjningsenhet;* **power supply** *or* **power supply unit (PSU) =** electrical circuit that provides certain direct current voltage and current levels from an alternating current source for use in other electrical circuits (a PSU will regulate, smooth and reduce the mains voltage level for use in low power electronic circuits) *strömförsörjning;* **power up =** to switch on *or* apply a voltage to a electrical device *slå på strömmen;* **uninterruptable power supply (UPS) =** power supply that can continue to provide a regulated supply to equipment even after mains power failure *enhet för avbrottsfri kraft* **(b)** mathematical term describing the number of times a number is to be multiplied by itself *upphöjd till, potens;* **5 to the power 2 is equal to 25** NOTE: written as small figures in superscript: 10^5 : say: "ten to the power five"

powered ['paʊəd] *adj.* driven by a type of energy *(el)driven, strömförsörjd*

PPM ['piːpiːem] = PULSE POSITION MODULATION pulse modulation method that varies the time between pulses in relation to the magnitude of an input signal *pulslägesmodulering; see also* PULSE MODULATION

ppm ['piːpiːem] = PAGES PER MINUTE

PR ['piːɑː] = PUBLIC RELATIONS; *PR;* a **PR firm is handling all our publicity; he is working in PR; the PR people gave away 100,000 leaflets**

"pratminus" ⇨ **dash**

pre- [prɪ] *prefix* meaning before *pre-, för-;* **pre-agreed =** which has been agreed in advance *överenskommet (avtalat) i förväg;* **pre-allocation =** execution of a process which does not begin until all memory and peripheral requirements are free for use *förtilldelning, förallokering;* **pre-fetch =** instructions read and stored in a short temporary queue with a CPU that contains the next few instructions to be processed, increasing the speed of execution *förhämtning*

pre-amplifier [priːˈæmplɪfaɪə] *subst.* low noise electronic circuit that increases the magnitude of very small signals, used before a power amplifier *förförstärkare*

precede [prɪˈsiːd] *vb.* to come before *föregå;* **instruction which cancels the instruction which precedes it**

precedence [prɪˈsiːd(ə)ns] *subst.* computational rules defining the order in which mathematical operations are calculated (usually multiplications are done first, then divisions, additions, and subtractions last) *precedens, prioritet;* **operator precedence =** order in which a

number of mathematical operations will be carried out *operationsprecedens, operationsprioritet*

precise [prɪˈsaɪs] *adj.* very exact *precis, exakt;* **the atomic clock will give the precise time of starting the process**

precision [prɪˈsɪʒ(ə)n] *subst.* being very accurate *precision, noggrannhet;* **double precision =** using two data words to store a number, providing greater precision *dubbel precision;* **multiple precision =** using more than one byte of data for number storage to increase possible precision *multipel precision;* **precision of a number =** number of digits in a number *antal siffror, noggrannhet;* **single precision =** number stored in one word *enkel precision; compare with* MULTIPLE, DOUBLE

precision ⇨ **accuracy, precision**

precompiled code ['priːkəmˈpaɪld'kəʊd] *subst.* code that is output from a compiler, ready to be executed *förkompilerad kod*

precondition ['priːkənˈdɪʃ(ə)n] *vb.* to condition data before it is processed *förbehandla*

predefined ['priːdɪˈfaɪn] *adj.* which has been defined in advance *fördefinierad*

predesigned ['priːdɪˈzaɪn] *adj.* (graphic material) provided to the customer already designed *förkonstruerad, förhandsutformad;* **a wide selection of predesigned layouts help you automatically format typical business and technical documents**

predetermined ['priːdɪˈtɜːmɪnd] *adj.* which has already been determined *förutbestämd*

predicate ['predɪkət] *subst.* function *or* statement used in rule-based programs such as expert systems *predikat*

> QUOTE we should stick to systems which we know are formally sound, such as predicate logic
> **Personal Computer World**

pre-edit ['priːedɪt] *vb.* to change text before it is run through a machine to make sure it is compatible *förformatering*

pre-emphasise ['priːemfəsaɪz] *vb.* to boost certain frequencies of a signal before transmission *or* processing to minimize noise (signals are de-emphasised on reception) *frekvenskorrigera, sändningskorrigera*

prefix ['priːfɪks] *subst.* **(a)** code *or* instruction *or* character at the beginning of a message *or* instruction *prefix* **(b)** word attached to the beginning of another word to give it a special meaning *prefix*

prefix notation ['priːfɪks nə(ʊ)ˈteɪʃ(ə)n] *subst.* mathematical operations written in a logical way, so that the operator appears before the operands, this removes the need for brackets *prefixnotation, polsk notation*

preformatted ['priː'fɔːmætɪd] *adj.* which has been formatted already *förformaterad;* **a preformatted disk**

premix ['priːmɪks] *subst.* combination of a number of signals before they have been processed in any way *råsignal*

preparation [ˌprepə'reɪʃ(ə)n] *subst.* getting something ready *förberedelse;* **data preparation** = conversion of data into a machine-readable form (usually by keyboarding) before data entry *datapreparering*

preparering ➔ **disk**

preprinted ['priː'prɪntɪd] *adj.* already printed *or* printed in advance *förtryckt;* **preprinted form** = paper used for printing databases *or* applications programs that already contain some information printed *förtryckt blankett;* **preprinted stationery** = computer stationery (such as invoices) which has already been printed with the company's logo and address as well as the blank columns, etc. *förtryckt papper, förtryckta blanketter*

preprocess ['priː'prəʊses] *vb.* to carry out initial organization and simple processing of data *förbehandla*

preprocessor ['priː'prəʊsesə] *subst.* **(a)** software that partly processes *or* prepares data before it is compiled *or* translated *förbehandlingsprogram* **(b)** small computer that carries out some initial processing of raw data before passing it to the main computer *förprocessor*

QUOTE the C preprocessor is in the first stage of converting a written program into machine instructions
QUOTE the preprocessor can be directed to read in another file before completion, perhaps because the same information is needed in each module of the program
Personal Computer World

preproduction ['priː'prə'dʌkʃ(ə)n] *subst.* organization of the filming *or* recording of a video *or* compact disk, taking the form of diagrams and scene descriptions *inspelningsplan, förvisualisering*

preprogrammed ['priː'prəʊgræmd] *adj.* (chip) which has been programmed in the factory to perform one function *förprogrammerad*

prerecord ['priː'rɪ'kɔːd] **1** *vb.* to record something which will be played back later *or* to record sound effects that are added to a film at a later date *förinspela;* **the answerphone plays a prerecorded message 2** *subst.* section of text stored in a word-

processor system which will be used as the basis for a form letter *standardbrev*

presentation layer [ˌprez(ə)n'teɪʃ(ə)n 'leɪə] *subst.* ISO/OSI standard network layer that agrees on formats, codes and requests for start and end of a connection *presentationsskikt; see also* ISO/OSI, LAYER

presentationsenhet ➔ **display**

presentationsskikt ➔ **presentation layer**

preset ['priː'set] *vb.* to set something in advance *förinställa;* **the printer was preset with new page parameters**
NOTE: **presetting - preset**

press [pres] **1** *subst.* **(a)** newspapers and magazines *(tidnings)press;* **the local press** = newspapers which are sold in a small area of the country *lokalpressen;* **the national press** = newspapers which sell in all parts of the country *rikspressen;* **the new car has been advertised in the national press; we plan to give the product a lot of press publicity; there was no mention of the new product in the press; press conference** = meeting where reporters from newspapers are invited to hear news of a new product *or* of a takeover bid, etc. *presskonferens;* **press coverage** = reports about something in the press *pressbevakning;* **we were very disappointed by the press coverage of the new car; press cutting** = piece cut out of a newspaper *or* magazine, which refers to an item which you find interesting *pressklipp;* **we have kept a file of press cuttings about the new software package; press release** = advance publicity material about a new product given out to newspapers and other media *pressrelease;* **the company sent out a press release about the launch of the new scanner** NOTE: no plural **(b)** printing press = machine which prints *tryckpress;* **the book is on the press** = the book is being printed *boken är under tryckning* **2** *vb.* to push with the fingers *trycka (på);* **to end the program press ESCAPE**

pressure pad ['preʃəpæd] *subst.* transducer that converts pressure changes into an electrical signal *tryckplatta;* **the pressure pad under the carpet will set off the burglar alarm if anyone steps on it**

prestandatest ➔ **benchmark**

prestore ['priː'stɔː] *vb.* to store data in memory before it is processed *förlagra*

presumptive address [prɪ'zʌm(p)tɪv ə'dres] *subst.* initial address in a program, used as a reference for others *presumtiv adress, referensadress*

presumptive instruction [prɪ'zʌm(p)tɪv ɪn'strʌkʃ(ə)n] *subst.* unmodified program instruction which is processed to obtain the instruction to be executed *presumtiv instruktion, utgångsinstruktion*

presumtiv instruktion ⇨ **unmodified instruction**

prevent [prɪ'vent] *vb.* to stop something happening *förebygga;* **the police prevented anyone from leaving the building; we have changed the passwords to prevent hackers getting into the database**

prevention [prɪ'venʃ(ə)n] *subst.* preventing something happening *förebyggande åtgärd*

preventive [prɪ'ventɪv] *or* **preventative** [prɪ'ventətɪv] *adj.* which tries to stop something happening *förebyggande;* **preventive maintenance** = regular checks on equipment to correct and repair any small faults before they cause a major problem *förebyggande underhåll;* **we have a preventive maintenance contract for the system**

preview ['pri:vju:] *vb.* to display text *or* graphics on a screen as it will appear when it is printed out *förhandsvisa*

previewer ['pri:vju:ə] *subst.* feature that allows a user to see on screen what a page will look like when printed *förhandsvisning;* **the built-in previewer allows the user to check for mistakes**

previous ['pri:vjəs] *adj.* which happens earlier *föregående, tidigare;* **copy data into the present workspace from the previous file**

previously ['pri:vjəslɪ] *adv.* happening earlier *tidigare, i förväg;* **the data is copied onto previously formatted disks**

primarily ['praɪm(ə)rəlɪ] *adv.* mainly *huvudsakligen*

primary ['praɪmərɪ] *adj.* first *or* basic *or* most important *primär, huvudsaklig;* **primary colours** = colours (red, yellow and blue) from which all other colours can be derived *grundfärger;* **primary group** = number of signals that are merged into one signal (which may be merged with others) prior to transmission *primärgrupp;* **primary key** = unique identifying word that selects one entry from a database *primärnyckel;* **primary memory** *or* **store** *or* **main memory** = (i) small fast-access internal memory of a computer system (whose main memory is slower secondary storage) which stores the program currently being used *primärminne;* (ii) main internal memory of a computer system *internminne;* **primary station** = the single station in a data network that can select a path and transmit the primary station status is temporary and is transferred from one station to another *nätledare, nätstyrmaskin*

prime [praɪm] **1** *adj.* very important *viktig, bäst;* **prime attribute** = most important feature *or* design of a system *viktigaste egenskap;* **prime time** = (i) time when there are the greatest number of TV viewers *bästa sändningstid;* (ii) most expensive advertising time for TV commercials *bästa sändningstid;* **we are putting out a series of prime-time commercials 2** *subst.* number that can only be divided by itself and by one *primtal;* **the number seven is a prime**

primer ['praɪmə] *subst.* manual *or* simple instruction book with instructions and examples to show how a new program *or* system operates *förberedande handbok, grundbok*

primitive ['prɪmɪtɪv] *subst.* basic unit *grundläggande enhet*

primärminne ⇨ **main, memory**

primärt styrprogram ⇨ **master**

print [prɪnt] **1** *subst.* **(a)** image produced using an etched printing plate *tryck, kopparstick, stålstick, litografi, träsnitt;* **he collects 18th century prints; the office is decorated with Japanese prints (b)** positive photographic image in which black is black and white is white *positivbild, foto(kopia);* compare with NEGATIVE; **print contrast ratio** = difference between the brightest and darkest areas of an image *kontrast* **(c)** characters made in ink on paper *tryck, utskrift;* **he was very pleased to see his book in print; the print from the daisy-wheel printer is clearer than that from the line printer; print control character** = special character sent to a printer that directs it to perform an action *or* function (such as change font), rather than print a character *skrivarstyrtecken;* **print format** = way in which text is arranged when printed out, according to embedded codes, etc., used to set the margins, headers, etc. *utskriftsformat;* **print hammer** = moving arm in a daisy-wheel printer that presses the metal character form onto the printer ribbon leaving a mark on the paper *anslagsarm;* **print life** = number of characters a component can print before needing to be replaced *livslängd;* **the printhead has a print life of over 400 million characters; print modifiers** = codes in a document that cause a printer to change mode, i.e. from bold to italic *stilstyrtecken;* **print pause** = temporarily stopping a printer while printing (to change paper, etc.) *uppehåll i utskriften;* **print spooling** = automatic printing of a number of different documents in a queue at the normal speed of the printer, while the computer is doing some other task *sekundärbuffring, skrivarbuffring;* **print style** = typeface used on a certain printer *or* for a certain document *typsnitt, stil* **2** *vb.* **(a)** to put letters *or* figures in ink on paper *skriva, trycka;* **printed agreement; printed regulations; the printer prints at 60 characters per second (b)** to put letters *or* illustrations onto sheets of paper so that they form a book *trycka;* **the book was printed in Hong Kong; the book is printing at the moment, so we will have bound copies at the end of the month (c)** to write in capital letters *skriva med versaler;* **please print your name and address on the top of the form**

printed circuit ['prɪntɪd 'sɜːkɪt] *or* **printed circuit board (PCB)** ['prɪntɪd 'sɜːkɪt 'bɔːd ('piːsiː'biː)] *subst.* flat insulating material that has conducting tracks of metal printed *or* etched onto its surface which complete a circuit when components are mounted on it *tryckt kretskort, ledningskort*

printer ['prɪntə] *subst.* **(a)** device that converts input data in an electrical form into a printed readable form *skrivare;* **computer printer** *or* **line printer** = machine which prints information from a computer, printing one line at a time *radskrivare;* **barrel printer** = type of printer where characters are located around a rotating barrel *trumskrivare;* **bi-directional printer** = printer which is able to print characters from left to right *or* from right to left as the head moves backwards and forwards across the paper *tvåvägsskrivare;* **chain printer** = printer whose characters are located on a continuous belt *kedjeskrivare;* **daisy-wheel printer** = printer with characters arranged on interchangeable daisy-wheels *typhjulsskrivare;* **dot-matrix printer** = printer which forms characters from a series of tiny dots printed close together *matrisskrivare;* **impact printer** = printer that prints text and symbols by striking an inked ribbon onto paper with a metal character *anslagsskrivare;* **ink-jet printer** = printer that produces characters by sending a stream of tiny drops of electrically charged ink onto the paper (the movement of the ink drops is controlled by an electric field) *bläckstråleskrivare;* **laser printer** = high-resolution printer that uses a laser source to print high quality dot-matrix characters *laserskrivare;* **line printer** = printer which prints draft-quality information at high speed (typical output is 200 - 3000 lines per minute) *radskrivare;* **page printer** = printer which composes one page of text, then prints it rapidly *sidskrivare;* **thermal printer** = printer where the character is formed on thermal paper with a printhead containing a matrix of small heating elements *termisk skrivare, termotransferskrivare, värmeöverföringsskrivare;* **printer buffer** = temporary store for character data waiting to be printed (used to free the computer before the printing is completed making the

operation faster) *skrivarbuffert;* **printer control characters** = command characters in a text which transmit printing commands to a printer *skrivarstyrtecken;* **printer driver** = dedicated software that converts and formats users' commands ready for a printer *skrivarstyrprogram;* **printer-plotter** = high resolution printer that is able to operate as a low resolution plotter *skrivare med ritfunktion;* **printer port** = output port of a computer to which a printer is connected to receive character data (either parallel or serial) *skrivarutgång;* **printer quality** = standard of printed text from a particular printer (high resolution dot-matrix printers produce near letter-quality, daisy-wheel printers produce letter-quality text) *utskriftskvalitet;* **printer ribbon** = roll of inked material which passes between a printhead and the paper *färgband* **(b)** company which prints books *or* newspapers *tryckeri;* **the book will be sent to the printer next week; we are using Japanese printers for some of our magazines**

printhead ['prɪnthed] *subst.* (i) row of needles in a dot-matrix printer that produce characters as a series of dots *skrivhuvud;* (ii) metal form of a character that is pressed onto an inked ribbon to print the character on paper *skrivhuvud*

printing ['prɪntɪŋ] *subst.* action of printing *tryckning, utskrivning*

printout ['prɪntaʊt] *subst.* **computer printout** = printed copy of information from a computer *utskrift;* **the sales director asked for a printout of the agents' commissions**

print out [prɪnt 'aʊt] *vb.* to print information stored in a computer with a printer *skriva ut*

printrun ['prɪntrʌn] *subst.* number of copies of a book which are printed at one time *(tryck)upplaga*

print shop ['prɪntʃɒp] *subst.* shop where jobbing printing takes place *(accidens)tryckeri, sätteri*

printwheel ['prɪntwiːl] *subst.* daisy-wheel *or* the wheel made up of a number of arms, with a character shape at the end of each arm, used in a daisy-wheel printer *typhjul*

prior ['praɪə] *adj.* happening before *föregående;* **prior to** = before *före, innan;* **the password has to be keyed in prior to accessing the system**

prioritet ⇨ **precedence**

priority [praɪ'ɒrɪtɪ] *subst.* importance of a device *or* software routine in a computer system *prioritet;* **the operating system has priority over the application when disk**

space is allocated; **the disk drive is more important than the printer, so it has a higher priority; job priority =** importance of a job compared to others *jobbprioritet;* **priority interrupt =** signal to a computer that takes precedence over any other task *prioritetsavbrott; see also* INTERRUPT, NON-MASKABLE INTERRUPT; **priority interrupt table =** list of peripherals and their priority when they send an interrupt signal (used instead of a hardware priority scheduler) *prioritetsavbrottstabell;* **priority sequence =** the order in which various devices that have sent an interrupt signal are processed, according to their importance or urgency (a disk drive will usually come before a printer in a priority sequence) *prioritetsföljd;* **priority scheduler =** system that organizes tasks into correct processing priority (to improve performance) *prioritetsfördelare*

privacy ['prɪvəsɪ] *subst.* the right of an individual to limit the extent of and control the access to the data that is stored about him *personlig integritet;* **privacy of data =** rule that data is secret and must not be accessed by users who have not been authorized *datasäkerhet;* **privacy of information =** rule that unauthorized users cannot obtain data about private individuals from databases *or* that each individual has the right to know what information is being held about him *or* her on a database *personlig integritet;* **privacy transformation =** encryption of messages *or* data to ensure that it remains private *chiffrering (för att säkerställa personlig integritet)*

private ['praɪvət] *adj.* belonging to an individual *or* to a company, not to the public *privat;* **private address space =** memory address range that is reserved for a single user, not for public access *användarens adressutrymme;* **private automatic branch exchange (PABX) =** small telephone exchange in a company that handles all internal and external calls to the main public network *automatisk företagsväxel;* **private automatic exchange (PAX) =** small telephone exchange in a company that only allows internal calls within the company to be made *intern telefonväxel;* **private branch exchange (PBX) =** small manual *or* automatic exchange in a company that can handle internal *or* external calls *företagstelefonväxel;* **private dial port =** unlisted telephone number that connects one user to a packet network system *datexnummer;* **private line =** special telephone line, rented from the telephone company and used only by the user *fast ledning;* **private manual branch exchange (PMBX) =** small telephone exchange inside a company where all telephone calls coming in *or* going out have to be placed

through a switchboard *manuell företagsväxel;* **private mobile radio (PMR)** *see* MOBILE; **private telephone system =** telephone system in a company that cannot be accessed from a public telephone system *interntelefonsystem*

privilege ['prɪvəlɪdʒ] *subst.* status of a user referring to the type of program he can run and the resources he can use *privilegium;* **the systems manager has a privileged status so he can access any file on the system; privileged account =** computer account that allows special programs *or* access to sensitive system data *priviligierat konto;* **the system manager can access anyone else's account from his privileged account; privileged instructions =** computer commands which can only be executed via a privileged account, such as delete another account *or* set up a new user *or* examine passwords *priviligierade instruktioner, systemadministrationsinstruktioner*

problem ['prɒbləm] *subst.* **(a)** question to which it is difficult to find an answer *problem;* **to solve a problem =** to find an answer to a problem *lösa ett problem;* **problem definition =** the clear explanation, in logical steps, of a problem that is to be solved *problemdefinition;* **problem-orientated language (POL) =** high-level programming language that allows certain problems to be expressed easily *problemorienterat språk* **(b)** malfunction *or* fault with hardware *or* software *fel, problem;* **problem diagnosis =** finding the cause and method of repairing a fault *or* error *diagnos, felsökning*

procedural [prə(ʊ)'siːdʒər(ə)l] *adj.* using a procedure (to solve a problem) *procedurorienterad, procedurinriktad;* **procedural language =** high-level programming language in which the programmer enters the actions required to achieve the result wanted *procedur-orienterat språk*

procedure [prə(ʊ)'siːdʒə] *subst.* **(a)** small section of computer instruction code that provides a frequently used function and can be called upon from a main program *procedur, rutin;* **this procedure sorts all the files into alphabetic order, you can call it from the main program by the instruction SORT;** *see also* SUBROUTINE **(b)** method *or* route used when solving a problem *metod;* **you should use this procedure to retrieve lost files; the procedure is given in the manual; procedure-orientated language =** high-level programming language that allows procedures to be programmed easily *procedurorienterat språk*

proceed [prə(ʊ)'siːd] *vb.* to move forward *fortsätta;* **after spellchecking the text, you can proceed to the printing stage**

procent ⇨ **per cent**

procentandel ⇨ **percentage**

procentil ⇨ **percentile**

process ['prəʊses] **1** *subst.* a number of tasks that must be carried out to achieve a goal *process;* **the process of setting up the computer takes a long time; there are five stages in the process; process bound** = program that spends more time executing instructions and using the CPU than in I/O operations *processbegränsad;* **process camera** = camera designed for the stages required in printing, such as tone and colour separation *reprokamera;* **process chart** = diagram that shows each step of the computer procedures needed in a system *processdiagram;* **process control** = automatic control of a process by a computer *processtyrning;* **process control computer** = dedicated computer that controls and manages a process *processtyrningsdator;* **process control system** = complete input, output modules, a CPU with memory and a program (usually stored in ROM) and control and feedback devices such as A/D and D/A converters that completely monitors, manages and regulates a process *processtyrsystem* **2** *vb.* to carry out a number of tasks to produce a result (such as sorting data *or* finding the solution to a problem) *behandla;* **we processed the new data; processing all the information will take a long time**

process ⇨ **coroutine, process, thread**

processing ['prəʊsesɪŋ] *subst.* sorting of information *databehandling;* using a computer to solve a problem *or* organize data *databehandling;* **page processing time depends on the complexity of a given page;** *see also* CPU ; **batch processing** = computer system, where information is collected into batches before being loaded into the computer *satsvis databehandling;* **data processing** *or* **information processing** = selecting and examining data in a computer to produce information in a special form *informationsbehandling;* **image processing** = analysis of information contained in an image (usually by electronic means or by using a computer to provide the analysis or for recognition of objects in the image) *bildbehandling;* **immediate processing** = processing data when it appears, rather than waiting for a certain clock pulse or time *direktbearbetning, realtidsbearbetning;* **off-line processing** = processing by devices not under the control of a central computer *fristående databehandling;* **on-line processing** = processing by devices connected to and under the control of the central computer (the user remains in contact with the central computer while processing)

direktansluten databehandling; **query processing** = processing of queries, either by extracting information from a database *or* translating query commands from a query language *frågebehandling;* **real-time processing** = processing operations that take a time of the same order of magnitude as the problem to be solved *realtidsbearbetning;* **serial processing** = executing one instruction at a time *seriell bearbetning; compare with* PARALLEL PROCESSING; **word-processing** *or* **text processing** = working with words, using a computer to produce, check and change texts, reports, letters, etc. *ordbehandling, textbehandling* NOTE: no plural

COMMENT: the central processing unit is a hardware device that allows a computer to manipulate and modify data; a compiler is a software language processor that translates data and instructions in one language into another form

processor ['prəʊsesə] *subst.* hardware *or* software device that is able to manipulate *or* modify data according to instructions *processor;* **array processor** = computer that can act upon several arrays of data simultaneously for very fast mathematical applications *vektorprocessor;* **associative processor** = processor that uses associative storage *associativ processor;* **attached processor** = separate microprocessor in a system that performs certain functions under the control of a central processor *stödprocessor, tillsatsprocessor;* **auxiliary processor** = extra, specialized processor, such as an array or numerical processor, that can work with a main processor to improve performance *tillsatsprocessor, stödprocessor;* **back-end processor** = special purpose auxiliary processor *stödprocessor;* **bit-slice processor** = construction of a large word size CPU by joining a number of smaller word size blocks *bituppdelad processor;* **distributed processor** = using many small computers at different workstations instead of one central computer *distribuerad processor;* **front-end processor (FEP)** = processor placed between an input source and the central computer, whose function is to preprocess received data to reduce the main computer's workload *frontprocessor;* **input/output processor** = processor that handles data communications, including DMA and error correcting functions *in-utprocessor;* **language processor** = program that translates from one language to machine code (there are three types of translator: (i) assembler *assemblerare;* (ii) compiler *kompilator;* (iii) interpreter *interpreterare, tolk);* **network processor** = signal multiplexer controlled by a microprocessor in a network *nätprocessor; (in a multiprocessor system)* **order code processor** = a processor which decodes and performs the arithmetic and logical operations according to the program code *huvudprocessor, OC-processor;* **processor controlled keying** = data entry by an operator which is prompted and controlled by a computer *datorstyrd datainmatning;* **processor interrupt** = to send an interrupt signal to a processor requesting attention, that will usually cause it to stop what it is doing and attend to the calling device *processorsavbrott;* **processor status word (PSW)** = word which contains a number of status bits, such as carry flag, zero flag and overflow flag *processorstatusord;* **processor-limited** = (operation *or* execution time) that is set by the speed of the processor rather than a peripheral *processorbegränsad;* **dual processor** = computer system with two processors for faster program execution *dubblerad processor;* **image processor** = electronic *or* computer system used for image processing *bildbehandlingsdator;* **word-processor** = small computer which is used for working with words, to produce texts, reports, letters, etc. *ordbehandlare*

QUOTE each chip will contain 128 processors and one million transistors
Computer News

processortid ⇨ **CPU**

produce [prə'dju:s] *vb.* to make *or* manufacture *tillverka*

producer [prə'dju:sə] *subst.* **(a)** person *or* company *or* country which manufactures *tillverkare;* **country which is a producer of high quality computer equipment; the company is a major magnetic tape producer (b)** person who is in charge of a film *or* TV show, who has the idea for the show, and organizes the filming, the actors, etc *producent*

producing [prə'dju:sɪŋ] *adj.* which produces *tillverknings-;* **producing capacity** = capacity to produce *tillverknings-kapacitet*

product ['prɒdʌkt] *subst.* **(a)** item which is made *or* manufactured *produkt;* **basic product** = main product made from a raw material *basprodukt;* **end product** *or* **final product** = product made at the end of a production process *slutprodukt* **(b)** manufactured item for sale *vara;* **product advertising** = advertising a particular named product, not the company which makes it *produktreklam;* **product analysis** = examining each separate product in a company's range to see why it sells *or* who buys it, etc. *produktanalys;* **product design** = design of consumer products *utformning, design, formgivning;* **product development** = improving an existing product line to meet the needs of the market *produktutveckling;* **product engineer** = engineer in charge of

the equipment for making a product *produktingenjör;* **product line** *or* **product range** = series of different products made by the same company which form a group (such as printers in different models *or* different colours, etc.) *produktlinje, produktgrupp;* **product management** = directing the making and selling of a product as an independent item *produktledning;* **product mix** = group of quite different products made by the same company *produktsortiment* **(c)** result after multiplication *produkt*

production [prə'dʌkʃ(ə)n] *subst.* making *or* manufacturing of goods for sale *produktion;* **production will probably be held up by industrial action; we are hoping to speed up production by installing new machinery; batch production** = production in batches *satsvis produktion;* **mass production** = manufacturing of large quantities of goods *massproduktion;* **mass production of monitors** *or* **of calculators; rate of production** *or* **production rate** = speed at which items are made *produktionstakt;* **production control** = control of the manufacturing of a product (using computers) *produktionsstyrning;* **production cost** = cost of making a product *produktionskostnad;* **production department** = section of a company which deals with the making of the company's products *produktionsavdelning;* **production line** = system of making a product, where each item (such as a TVset) moves slowly through the factory with new sections added to it as it goes along *produktionslinje;* **he works on the production line; she is a production lineworker; a typical use of an image processor includes production line control; production manager** = person in charge of the production department *fabrikschef, tillverkningschef;* **production run** = manufacturing a product *or* running a program, as opposed to a test run *produktionskörning;* **production unit** = separate small group of workers producing a certain product *produktionsenhet, produktionslag*
NOTE: no plural

productive [prə'dʌktɪv] *adj.* during *or* in which something useful is produced *produktiv;* **productive time** = period of time during which a computer can run error-free tasks *produktiv tid*

program ['prəʊgræm] **1** *subst.* complete set of instructions which direct a computer to carry out a particular task *program;* **assembly program** = number of assembly code instructions which perform a task *assemblerprogram;* **background program** = computer program with a very low priority *bakgrundsprogram;* **blue-ribbon program** = perfect program that runs first time with no errors *felfritt program;* **control program/monitor** *or* **control program for microcomputers (CP/M)** = popular operating system for microcomputers *äldre operativsystem för mikrodatorer;* **diagnostic program** = software that helps find faults in a computer system *diagnostikprogram, felsökningsprogram;* **executive program** = master program in a computer system that controls the execution of other programs *administrationsprogram, övervakningsprogram;* **foreground program** = high priority program in a multitasking system *förgrundsprogram;* **hardwired program** = computer program built into the hardware (and which cannot be changed) *inbyggt program;* **job control program** = short program of job control instructions loaded before a particular application is run, that sets up the system as required by the application *jobbstyrningsprogram;* **library program** = (i) number of specially written *or* relevant software routines, which a user can insert into his own program, saving time and effort *biblioteksprogram;* (ii) group of functions which a computer needs to refer to often, but which are not stored in main memory *biblioteksprogram;* **linear program** = computer program that contains no loops *or* branches *linjärt program;* **user program** = program written by a user (often in a high-level language) *användarprogram;* **program address counter** = register in a CPU that contains the location of the next instruction to be processed *programadressregister;* **program branch** = one or more paths that can be followed after a conditional statement *programförgrening;* **program cards** = punched cards that contain the instructions that make up a program *programkort;* **program coding sheet** = specially preprinted form on which computer instructions can be written, simplifying program writing *programblankett;* **program compatibility** = ability of two pieces of software to function correctly together *(program)kompatibilitet;* **program compilation** = translation of an encoded source program into machine code *kompilering;* **program counter (PC)** *or* **instruction address register (IAR)** = register in a CPU that contains the location of the next instruction to be processed *instruktionsadressregister; see also* INSTRUCTION ADDRESS REGISTER, SEQUENCE CONTROL REGISTER; **program crash** = unexpected failure of a program due to a programming error *or* a hardware fault *(program)haveri;* **I forgot to insert an important instruction which caused a program to crash, erasing all the files on the disk!; program design language (PDL)** = programming language used to design the structure of a program *programkonstruktionsspråk;* **program**

development = all the operations involved in creating a computer program from first ideas to initial writing, debugging and the final product *programutveckling;* **program development system** = all the hardware and software needed for program development on a system *programutvecklingssystem;* **program documentation** = set of instruction notes, examples and tips on how to use a program *(program)dokumentation; see also* MANUAL; **program editor** = software that allows the user to alter, delete and add instructions to a program file *(fil- el. text)redigeringsprogram, textbehandlare, ordbehandlingsprogram;* **program execution** = instructing a processor to execute in sequence the instructions in a program *körning;* **program file** = file containing a program rather than data *programfil;* **program flowchart** = diagram that graphically describes the various steps in a program *flödesplan;* **program generator** = software that allows users to write complex programs using a few simple instructions *programgenerator;* **program instruction** = single word *or* expression that represents one operation (in a high level program each program instruction can consist of a number of low level machine code instructions) *programinstruktion;* **program library** = collection of useful procedures and programs which can be used for various purposes and included into new software *programbibliotek;* **program line** = one row of commands *or* arguments in a computer program *programrad;* **program line number** = number that refers to a line of program code in a computer program *programradsnummer;* **program listing** = list of the set of instructions that make up a program (program listings are displayed in an ordered manner, BASIC listings by line number, assembly listings by memory location; they do not necessarily represent the order in which the program will be executed, since there could be jumps *or* subroutines) *programutskrift, programlistning;* **program maintenance** = keeping a program free of errors and up to date *programunderhåll;* **program name** = identification name for a stored program file *programnamn;* **program origin** = address at which the first instruction of a program is stored *startadress;* **program relocation** = moving a stored program from one area of memory to another *programförflyttning;* **program register** = register in a CPU that contains an instruction during decoding and execution operations *programregister;* **program report generator** = software that allows users to create reports from files, databases and other stored data *rapportgenerator;* **program run** = executing (in correct order) the instructions in a program *körning;* **program segment** = section of a main program that can be executed in its own right, without the rest of the main program being required *självständig subrutin; see also* OVERLAY; **program specification** = document that contains details on all the functions and abilities of a computer program *programspecifikation;* **program stack** = section of memory reserved for storing temporary system *or* program data *(program)stack;* **program statement** = high level program instruction that is made up of a number of machine code instructions *(program)sats;* **program step** = one operation within a program, usually a single instruction *operation;* **program storage** = section of main memory in which programs (rather than operating system *or* data) can be stored *programminne;* **program structure** = the way in which sections of program code are interlinked and operate *programstruktur;* **program testing** = testing a new program with test data to ensure that it functions correctly *provkörning;* **program verification** = number of tests and checks performed to ensure that a program functions correctly *verifiering, kontroll* **2** *vb.* to write *or* prepare a set of instructions which direct a computer to perform a certain task *programmera;* **programmed halt** = instruction within a program that when executed, halts the processor (to restart the CPU a reset action is required) *programmerat stopp;* **programmed learning** = using educational software which allows a learner to follow a course of instruction *programmerad inlärning* NOTE: **programs - programming - programmed**

QUOTE we've included some useful program tools to make your job easier. Like the symbolic debugger
Personal Computer World
QUOTE the other use for the socket is to program 2, 4, 8 or 16Kbyte EPROMS
Electronics & Wireless World

program ⇨ **program**

programfil ⇨ **file**

programgenomgång ⇨ **trace**

programmable [prəʊ'græməbl] *adj.* & *subst.* (device) that can accept and store instructions then execute them *programmerbar (anordning);* **programmable calculator** = small calculator which can hold certain basic mathematical calculating programs *programmerbar räknare;* **programmable logic array (PLA)** *or* **programmable logic device (PLD)** = integrated circuit that can be permanently programmed to perform logic operations on data using a matrix of links between input and output pins *programmerbar logikmatris;* **programmable interrupt controller** = circuit *or* chip which can be programmed to ignore certain interrupts, accept only high priority interrupts and

select the priority of interrupts *programmerbar avbrottshanterare;* **programmable key** = special key on a computer terminal keyboard that can be programmed with various functions *or* characters *programmerbar nyckel;* **programmable memory (PROM)** = electronic device in which data can be stored *programmerbart läsminne; see also* EAROM; EEPROM; EPROM; ROM; **programmable read only memory (PROM)** = memory integrated circuit that can be programmed with data by a user (some PROMs provide permanent storage, others such as EPROMs are erasable) *programmerbart läsminne;* **hand-held programmable** = very small computer, which can be held in the hand, used for inputting information when a larger terminal is not available (as by a salesman on a call) *handdator*

QUOTE each of the 16 programmable function keys has two modes - normal and shift - giving 32 possible functions
Micro Decision

programme ['prəʊgræm] *or US* **program** ['prəʊgræm] *subst.* TV *or* radio broadcast which is separate from other broadcasts, and has its own producer, director, etc; **they were filming a wild life programme; children's programmes are scheduled for early evening viewing**

programmer ['prəʊgræmə] *subst.* **(a)** person who is capable of designing and writing a working program *programmerare;* **the programmer is still working on the new software; applications programmer** = programmer who writes applications software *tillämpningsprogrammerare;* **systems programmer** = programmer who specializes in writing systems software *systemprogrammerare* **(b)** device that allows data to be written into a programmable read only memory *läsminnesprogrammerare*

programmerat stopp ⇨ **halt**

programmerbar logikmatris ⇨ **PLA, programmable**

programmerbart läsminne ⇨ **electrically, programmable, PROM**

programmeringsmiljö ⇨ **language**

programmeringsspråk ⇨ **computer, language**

programming ['prəʊgræmɪŋ] *subst.* **(a)** writing programs for computers *programmering;* **programming in logic** = PROLOG; **programming language** = software that allows a user to write a series of instructions to define a particular task, which will then be translated to a form that is understood by the computer *programmeringsspråk;* **programming standards** = rules to which programs must conform to produce compatible code *programstandarder* **(b)** writing data into a PROM device *programmering*

> COMMENT: programming languages are grouped into different levels: the high-level languages such as BASIC and PASCAL are easy to understand and use, but offer slow execution time since each instruction is made up of a number of machine code instructions; low-level languages such as assembler are more complex to read and program in but offer faster execution time

programpaket ⇨ **package**

programpekare ⇨ **register**

programreferenstabell ⇨ **table**

programräknare ⇨ **instruction**

programsats ⇨ **statement**

project ['prɒdʒekt] **1** *subst.* planned task *projekt;* **his latest project is computerizing the sales team; the design project was entirely worked out on computer; CAD is essential for accurate project design 2** *vb.* to forecast future figures from a set of data *prognosticera;* **the projected sales of the new PC**

projection [prə(ʊ)'dʒekʃ(ə)n] *subst.* **(a)** forecast of a situation from a set of data *projektion;* **the projection indicates that sales will increase (b)** showing pictures on a screen *projektion;* **projection room** = room in a cinema where the projectors which show the films are housed *projektorrum*

projector [prə(ʊ)'dʒektə] *subst.* **film projector** *or* **slide projector** = mechanical device that displays films *or* slides on a screen *projektor; see also* OVERHEAD

PROLOG ['prəʊlɒg] = PROGRAMMING IN LOGIC high-level programming language using logical operations for artificial intelligence and data retrieval applications *programmeringsspråket PROLOG*

PROM [prɒm] **(a)** = PROGRAMMABLE READ-ONLY MEMORY read-only memory which can be programmed by the user (as opposed to ROM, which is programmed by the manufacturer) *programmerbart läsminne;* **PROM burner** *or* **programmer** = electronic device used to program a PROM *läsminnesprogrammerare; see also* EPROM **(b)** = PROGRAMMABLE MEMORY electronic memory in which data can be stored *programmerbart minne*

prompt [prɒm(p)t] *subst.* message *or* character displayed to remind the user that an input is expected *markör;* **the prompt READY indicates that the system is** available to receive instructions; **command prompt** = symbol displayed to indicate a command is expected *kommandomarkör*

proof [pruːf] **1** *subst.* printed matter from a printer that has to be checked and corrected *korrektur(avdrag);* **galley proofs** = proofs in the form of long pieces of text, not divided into pages, printed on long pieces of paper *spaltkorrektur;* **page proofs** = proofs which are divided into pages, but may not have page numbers or headings inserted *sidkorrektur, ombrutet korrektur* **2** *vb.* to produce proofs of a text *korrekturläsa*

> COMMENT: the stages of full proofing are galley proofs, page on galley (where the pages are indicated, but the proofs are still printed on long pieces of paper), and page proofs. It is usual to miss out some of these stages, and many books are proofed in pages from the start

proofer ['pruːfə] *subst.* printer which produces proofs, as opposed to finished printed pages *korrekturavdragare;* **output devices such as laser proofers and typesetters**

proofing ['pruːfɪŋ] *subst.* producing proofs of text which have to be read and corrected *provtryckning*

proofread ['pruːfriːd] *vb.* to correct spelling and printing errors in a printed text *korrekturläsa;* **has all the text been proofread yet?**

proofreader ['pruːfriːdə] *subst.* person who reads and corrects proofs *korrekturläsare*

propagate ['prɒpəgeɪt] *vb.* to travel *or* spread *fortplanta;* **propagated error** = one error in a process that has affected later operations *fortplantat fel;* **propagating error** = an error that occurs in one place *or* operation and affects another operation *or* process *fel som sprider sig*

propagation delay [ˌprɒpə'geɪʃ(ə)n dɪ'leɪ] *subst.* time taken for a signal to travel through a circuit *överföringfördröjning;* time taken for an output to appear in a logic gate after the input is applied *överföringstid;* **propagation delay in the transmission path causes signal distortion**

proportion [prə'pɔːʃ(ə)n] *subst.* size of something as compared to others *proportion*

proportional spacing [prə'pɔːʃənl 'speɪsɪŋ] *subst.* printing system where each letter takes a space proportional to the character width ('i' taking less space than 'm') *proportionell utskrift; compare* MONOSPACING

protect [prə'tekt] *vb.* to stop something being damaged *skydda;* **protected location** =

memory location that cannot be altered *or* cannot be accessed without authorization *skyddad minnesarea;* **protected storage =** section of memory that cannot be altered *skyddat minne;* **copy protect =** switch used to prevent copies of a disk being made *kopieringsskydd;* **all the disks are copy protected; crash protected =** (disk) which uses a head protection *or* data corruption protection system *haveriskyddad;* **if the disk is crash protected, you will never lose your work**

protection [prə'tekʃ(ə)n] *subst.* action of protecting *skydd;* **protection key =** signal checked to see if a program can access a section of memory *skyddskod;* **protection master =** spare copy of a master film *or* tape *säkerhetskopia;* **copy protection =** preventing copies being made *kopieringsskydd;* **a hard disk may crash because of faulty copy protection; the new product will come without copy protection; data protection =** making sure that data is not copied by an unauthorized user *datasäkerhet;* **Data Protection Act =** act which prevents confidential data about people being copied without authority (also every organization that keeps information subject to the act on a computer, must protect it adequately) *amerikanska motsvarigheten till Datalagen*

protective [prə'tektɪv] *adj.* which protects *skydds-;* **the disks are housed in hard protective cases**

protocol ['prəutəkɒl] *subst.* pre-agreed signals, codes and rules to be used for data exchange between systems *protokoll;* **protocol standards =** standards laid down to allow data exchange between any computer systems conforming to the standard *protokollstandarder*

QUOTE there is a very simple protocol that would exclude hackers from computer networks using the telephone system
Practical Computing

prototype ['prəutə(ʊ)taɪp] *subst.* first working model of a device *or* program, which is then tested and adapted to improve it *prototyp*

prototyping ['prəutə,taɪpɪŋ] *subst.* making a prototype *prototyptillverkning*

prototypkort ⇨ **breadboard**

provbänk ⇨ **test**

provfrekvens ⇨ **sample**

provider [prə'vaɪdə] *subst.* information **provider (ip) =** company *or* user that provides an information source for use in a videotext system (such as the company providing weather information *or* stock exchange reports) *informationslämnare*

provkörning ⇨ **dry run, test**

provtagningsintervall ⇨ **sample**

prägla in ⇨ **implant**

ps ['piːkəu,sekənd] = PICOSECOND

PSA ['piːes'eɪ] *US* = PUBLIC SERVICE ANNOUNCEMENT advertisement for a public service *or* charity, which is shown on TV, but for which the TV company is not paid *allmännyttig information (över TV)*

pseudo- ['sjuːdəu] *prefix* meaning similar to something, but not genuine *pseudo-*

pseudo-code ['sjuːdəu 'kəud] *subst.* English sentence structures, used to describe program instructions which are translated at a later date into machine code *pseudokod*

pseudo-digital ['sjuːdəu 'dɪdʒɪtl] *adj.* (modulated analog signals) produced by a modem and transmitted over telephone lines *pseudodigital*

pseudo-instruction ['sjuːdəu ɪn'strʌkʃ(ə)n] *subst.* label (in an assembly language program) that represents a number of instructions *pseudoinstruktion*

pseudoinstruktion ⇨ **quasi-**

pseudo-operation ['sjuːdəu ,ɒpə'reɪʃ(ə)n] *subst.* command in an assembler program that controls the assembler rather than producing machine code *pseudinstruktion*

pseudo-random ['sjuːdəu 'rændəm] *subst.* generated sequence that appears random but is repeated over a long period *skenbart slumpmässig;* **pseudo-random number generator =** hardware *or* software that produces pseudo-random numbers *pseudoslumptal*

PSN ['piːes'en] = PACKET SWITCHED NETWORK

PSTN ['piːestiː'en] = PUBLIC SWITCHED TELEPHONE NETWORK

PSU ['piːes'juː] = POWER SUPPLY UNIT electrical circuit that provides certain direct current voltage and current levels from an alternating current source to other electrical circuits *nätaggregat, kraftaggregat*

COMMENT: a PSU will regulate, smooth and step down a higher voltage supply for use in small electronic equipment

PSW ['piːes'dʌbljuː] = PROCESSOR STATUS WORD

PTR ['piːtiː'ɑː] = PAPER TAPE READER

p-type semiconductor [piː'taɪp 'semɪkən'dʌktə] *subst.* semiconductor material that has been doped with a chemical to provide extra holes (positive charge carriers), giving it an overall positive potential compared to intrinsic semiconductor *p-dopad halvledare; see also* HOLES, INTRINSIC SEMICONDUCTOR

public ['pʌblɪk] *adj.* open to anyone to use *allmän, öppen;* made for the use of everyone *allmän;* **public address system (PA)** = microphone, amplifier and loudspeaker set up to allow one person to be heard by a group of people *högtalaranläggning;* **public data network** = data transmission service for the public *allmänt datanät;* **public dial port** = port connecting a packet network to a public telephone system *datexnummer;* **public domain (PD)** = documents *or* text *or* program that has no copyright and can be copied by anyone *fri programvara;* **public key cipher system** = cipher that uses a public key to encrypt messages and a secret key to decrypt them (conventional cipher systems use one secret key to encrypt and decrypt messages) *chiffer med öppna nycklar; see also* CIPHER, KEY; **public switched telephone network (PSTN)** = national telephone system *or* country and world-wide exchanges, lines and telephone sets that are all interconnected and can be used by the public *allmänna telenätet*

publication [ˌpʌblɪˈkeɪʃ(ə)n] *subst.* **(a)** making something public *publikation, utgivning;* **the publication of the report on data protection; the publication date of the book is November 15th (b)** printed book *or* leaflet, etc. which is sold to the public *or* which is given away *bok, broschyr, katalog etc.;* **government publications can be bought at special shops; the company specializes in publications for the business reader**

publicity [pʌbˈlɪsəti] *subst.* attracting the attention of the public to products *or* services by mentioning them in the media *or* by advertising them *publicitet, reklam, presskontakter;* **publicity bureau** = office which organizes publicity for companies *reklambyrå;* **publicity campaign** = period when planned publicity takes place *reklamkampanj;* **publicity department** = department in a company which organizes the publicity for the company's products *marknadsavdelning, reklamavdelning;* **publicity matter** = leaflets *or* posters, etc., which publicize a product *or* service *direktreklam, datablad, produktinformation*

publicize ['pʌblɪsaɪz] *vb.* to attract people's attention to a product *or* service *göra reklam (PR) för;* **they are publicizing their low prices for computer stationery; the new PC has been publicized in the press**

publish ['pʌblɪʃ] *vb.* to print a text (such as a book *or* newspaper *or* catalogue) and then sell *or* give it to the public *publicera, offentliggöra;* **the institute has published a list of sales figures for different home computers; the company specializes in publishing reference books**

publisher ['pʌblɪʃə] *subst.* company which prints books *or* newspapers and sells *or* gives them to the public *förläggare*

publishing ['pʌblɪʃɪŋ] *subst.* the business of printing books *or* newspapers and selling them *or* giving them to the public *förlagsverksamhet;* **desktop publishing (DTP)** = design, layout and printing of documents using special software, a small computer and a printer *"desktop publishing", datorstödd typografi, autografi, datoriserat ordredigeringssystem;* **electronic publishing** = (i) use of desktop publishing packages and laser printers to produce printed matter *datoriserad originalproduktion;* (ii) using computers to write and display information (such as viewdata) *datorbaserad informationsverksamhet (t.ex. Videotex);* **professional publishing** = publishing books on law, accountancy, and other professions *förlagsverksamhet inriktad på fackböcker*

QUOTE desktop publishing or the ability to produce high-quality publications using a minicomputer, essentially boils down to combining words and images on pages
Byte

puffskydd ⇨ **pop filter**

pull [pʊl] *vb.* to remove data from a stack *ta bort data från en stack; compare with* PUSH

pull-down ['pʊldaʊn] *or* **pull-up menu** ['pʊlʌp 'menju:] *subst.* menu that can be displayed on screen at any time by pressing an appropriate key, usually displayed over the material already on screen *rullgardinsmeny*

pull up [pʊl 'ʌp] *vb.* **to pull up a line** = to connect *or* set a line to a voltage level *spänningssätta;* **pull up the input line to a logic one by connecting it to 5 volts**

QUOTE by the gated inputs lower the standby current and also eliminate the need for input pull-up or pull-down resistors
Electronics & Power

puls ⇨ **impulse**

pulsbrus ⇨ **impulsive**

pulse [pʌls] **1** *subst.* short rush of electricity *puls;* short period of a voltage level *puls;* **pulse amplitude modulation (PAM)** = pulse modulation where the height of the pulse depends on the input signal *pulsamplitudmodulering;* **pulse code modulation (PCM)** = pulse stream that carries data about a signal in binary form *pulskodsmodulering;* **pulse duration modulation (PDM)** = pulse modulation where the pulse width depends on the input signal *pulsbreddsmodulering;* **pulse generator** = electronic test equipment used to produce different size pulses *pulsgenerator;* **pulse modulation** = use of a series of short pulses which are modified by an input signal, to carry information *pulsmodulering;* **pulse position modulation (PPM)** = pulse modulation where the time between pulses depends on the input signal *pulslägesmodulering;* **pulse stream** = continuous series of similar pulses *pulsflöde;* **pulse width modulation (PWM)** = pulse modulation where the pulse width depends on the input signal *pulsbreddsmodulering* **2** *vb.* to apply a short-duration voltage level to a circuit *pulsa;* **we pulsed the input but it still would not work**

COMMENT: electric pulse can be used to transmit information, as the binary digits 0 and 1 correspond to 'no pulse' and 'pulse' (the voltage level used to distinguish the binary digits 0 and 1, is often zero and 5 or 12 volts, with the pulse width depending on transmission rate)

punch [pʌn(t)ʃ] **1** *subst.* device for making holes in punched cards *stansa* **2** *vb.* to make a hole *stansa;* **punch** *or* **punched card** = small piece of card which contains holes which represent various instructions *or* data *hålkort;* **punched card reader** = device that transforms data on a punched card to a form that can be recognized by a computer *hålkortsläsare;* **punched tag** = card attached to a product in a shop, with punched holes containing data about the product *hålkortsetikett;* **punched (paper) tape** = strip of paper tape that contains holes to represent data *hålremsa*

punctuation mark [ˌpʌŋ(k)tjʊˈeɪʃ(ə)n ˌmɑːk] *subst.* printing symbol, which cannot be spoken, but which helps to understand the text *skiljetecken*

COMMENT: the main punctuation marks are the question mark and exclamation mark; inverted commas (which show the type of text being written); the comma, full stop, colon and semicolon (which show how the words are broken up into sequences); the apostrophe (which shows that a letter or word is missing); the dash and hyphen and brackets (which separate or link words)

punktavbildning ⇨ **bit-map**

punkter per tum ⇨ **d.p.i.**

punktkommando ⇨ **dot**

punktmatris ⇨ **dot**

pure [pjʊə] *adj.* clean *or* not mixed with other things *ren;* **pure code** = code that does not modify itself during execution *ren kod;* **pure semiconductor** = semiconductor material that has not had extra doping substances added *ren halvledare; see also* INTRINSIC; **pure tone** = single frequency containing no harmonics *ren ton*

purge [pɜːdʒ] *vb.* to remove unnecessary *or* out of date data from a file *rena, rensa, radera*

push [pʊʃ] *vb.* to press something *or* to move something by pressing on it *trycka, skjuta;* **push-down list** *or* **stack** = temporary storage queue system where the last item added is at the top of the list *stack; see also* LIFO; **push instruction** *or* **operation** = computer instruction that stores data on a LIFO list *or* stack *(instruktionen) push;* **push-up list** *or* **stack** = temporary storage queue system where the last item added is at the bottom of the list *kö; see also* FIFO

pushbutton [ˈpʊʃˌbʌtn] *adj.* which works by pressing on a button *knapp-;* **pushbutton dialling** = using buttons rather than a dial on a telephone to dial a number *knappning av telefonnummer;* **pushbutton telephone** = telephone operated with buttons rather than a dial *knapptelefon, knappsatstelefon*

put [pʊt] *vb.* to push *or* place data onto a stack *lägga, placera*

PWM [ˈpiːˌdʌbljuːˈem] = PULSE WIDTH MODULATION

pålitlighet ⇨ **hardware**

Qq

QBE [ˈkjuːbiːˈiː] = QUERY BY EXAMPLE

QISAM [kjuːaɪˈeseɪem] = QUEUED INDEXED SEQUENTIAL ACCESS METHOD indexed sequential file that is read item by item into a buffer *standardiserad metod för att läsa en indexerad fil*

QL [ˈkjuːel] = QUERY LANGUAGE

QSAM [kjuːˈesaɪem] = QUEUED SEQUENTIAL ACCESS METHOD queue of blocks that are waiting to be processed, retrieved using a sequential access method *standardiserad metod för att hämta sekvensiella block i en kö*

quad [kwɒd] *subst.* **(a)** sheet of paper four times as large as a basic sheet *kvadrat* **(b)** meaning four times *fyrdubbel-;* **quad density** = four bits of data stored in the usual place of one *fyrdubbel täthet* **(c) em quad** = space printed that is equal in size to an em *mellanrum motsvarande bokstaven "m" i 12 punkters storlek, "trepinnarsblock"*; **en quad** = space that is half the width of an em quad space *mellanrum motsvarande bokstaven "n" i 12 punkters storlek, "tvåpinnars-block"*

QUOTE in this case, interfacing is done by a single quad-wide adapter
Minicomputer News

quadding ['kwɒdɪŋ] *subst.* insertion of spaces into text to fill out a line *fyrdubbling*

quadr- [kwɒdr] *prefix* meaning four *kvadr-*

quadrature ['kwɒdrətʃə] *subst.* video playback error due to the heads being wrongly aligned to the edge of the tape *kvadraturfel, tvärsjusteringsfel*

quadrophonic [,kwɒdrə'fɒnɪk] *adj.* (audio music system) using four speakers *kvadrofonisk, fyrkanals-*

quadruplex ['kwɒdrupleks] *subst.* four signals combined into a single one *kvadruplex, fyrhuvuds videoinspelning*

quadruplicate [kwɒ'druːplɪkət] *subst.* **in quadruplicate** = with the original and three copies *kvadruplikat, fyrdubbelt;* **the statements are printed in quadruplicate** NOTE: no plural

quality ['kwɒlətɪ] *subst.* what something is like *or* how good or bad something is *kvalitet;* **there is a market for good quality secondhand computers; high quality** *or* **top quality** = very best quality *högsta kvalitet;* **the store specializes in high quality imported items; printer quality** = standard of printed text from a particular printer (high-resolution dot-matrix printers produce near-letter quality, daisy-wheel printers produce letter-quality text) *utskriftskvalitet; see also* LETTER, NEAR-LETTER, DRAFT; **quality control** = checking that the quality of a product is good *kvalitetskontroll, kvalitetsstyrning;* **quality controller** = person who checks the quality of a product *kvalitetskontrollant* NOTE: no plural

QUOTE the computer operates at 120cps in draft quality mode and 30cps in near letter-quality mode
Minicomputer News

quantifiable ['kwɒntɪfaɪəbl] *adj.* which can be quantified *kvantifierbar;* **the effect of the change in the pricing structure is not quantifiable**

quantifier ['kwɒntɪfaɪə] *subst.* sign *or* symbol which indicates the quantity *or* range of a predicate *förtecken (t. ex. +/-)*

quantify ['kwɒntɪfaɪ] *vb.* **to quantify the effect of something** = to show the effect of something in figures *kvantifiera effekten av något;* **it is impossible to quantify the effect of the new computer system on our production**

quantity ['kwɒntətɪ] *subst.* **(a)** amount *or* number of items *kvantitet;* **a small quantity of illegal copies of the program have been imported; he bought a large quantity of spare parts (b)** large amount *kvantitet;* **the company offers a discount for quantity purchases**

quantization [,kwɒntaɪ'zeɪʃ(ə)n] *subst.* conversion of an analog signal to a numerical representation *digitalisering, kvantisering;* **quantization error** = error in converting an analog signal into a numerical form due to limited accuracy *or* rapidly changing signal *digitaliseringsfel, kvantiseringsfel; see also* A/D

quantize ['kwɒntaɪz] *vb.* to convert an analog signal into a numerical representation *digitalisera, kvantisera;* **the input signal is quantized by an analog to digital converter; quantizing noise** = noise on a signal due to inaccuracies in the quantizing process *digitaliseringsbrus, kvantiseringsbrus*

quantizer ['kwɒntaɪzə] *subst.* device used to convert an analog input signal to a numerical form, that can be processed by a computer *kvantiserare, digitaliserare, analog-digitalomvandlare*

quantum ['kwɒntəm] *subst.* smallest unit of energy of an electromagnetic radiation at a certain frequency *kvanta*

quartile ['kwɔːˈtaɪl] *subst.* one of three figures below which 25%, 50% *or* 75% of a total falls *kvartil*

quarto ['kwɔːtəʊ] *subst.* paper size, made when a sheet is folded twice to make eight pages *kvartoformat*

quartz (crystal) clock ['kwɔːts ('krɪstl) 'klɒk] *subst.* small slice of quartz crystal which vibrates at a certain frequency when an electrical voltage is supplied, used as a very accurate clock signal for computers and other high precision timing applications *kvartsur, kvartsklocka, kristallklocka*

quasi- ['kweɪzaɪ] *prefix* almost *or* which seems like *kvasi-;* **quasi-instruction** = label (in an assembly program) that represents a number of instructions *pseudoinstruktion, subrutinhopp*

quaternary [kwə'tɜːnərɪ] *adj.* referring to four bits *or* levels *or* objects *som består av fyra delar, fyrtal*

query ['kwıərı] 1 *subst.* question *fråga;* **query by example (QBE)** = way of finding information in a database by stating the items that are to be found *fråga genom exempel;* **query facility** = program (usually a database *or* retrieval system) that allows the user to ask questions and receive answers *or* access certain information according to the query *frågeprogram;* **query language (QL)** = language in a database management system, that allows a database to be searched and queried easily *frågespråk;* **query processing** = processing of queries, either by extracting information from a database *or* by translating query commands from a query language *frågebearbetning* 2 *vb.* to ask a question about something *or* to suggest that something may be wrong *fråga*

question ['kwestʃ(ə)n] 1 *subst.* **(a)** words which need an answer *fråga;* **the managing director refused to answer questions about faulty keyboards; the market research team prepared a series of questions to test the public's reactions to colour and price (b)** problem *fråga, problem;* **he raised the question of moving to less expensive offices; the main question is that of cost; the board discussed the question of launching a new business computer** 2 *vb.* **(a)** to ask questions *fråga;* **the police questioned the accounts staff for four hours; she questioned the chairman on the company's sales in the Far East (b)** to query *or* to suggest that something may be wrong *fråga (sig);* **we all question how accurate the computer printout is**

questionnaire [ˌkwestʃə'neə] *subst.* printed list of questions, especially used in market research *frågeformulär, enkät;* **to send out a questionnaire to test the opinions of users of the system; to answer *or* to fill in a questionnaire about holidays abroad**

queue [kju:] 1 *subst.* **(a)** line of people waiting one behind the other *kö;* **to form a queue *or* to join a queue (b)** list of data *or* tasks that are waiting to be processed *kö;* series of documents (such as orders, application forms) which are dealt with in order *kö;* **channel queue** = (i) queue of requests to use a channel *kanalkö;* (ii) queue of data that has yet to be sent over a channel *kanalkö;* **file queue** = number of files temporarily stored in order before being processed *filkö;* **output devices such as laser printers are connected on-line with an automatic file queue; job queue** = number of tasks arranged in order waiting to be processed in a batch system *jobbkö;* **his order went to the end of the queue** = his order was dealt with last *hans order sattes sist i kön;* **queue discipline** = method used as the queue structure, either LIFO *or* FIFO *kömodell;* **queue management** *or* **queue manager** = software which orders

tasks to be processed *köhanterare;* **this is a new software spooler with a built-in queue management** 2 *vb.* to add more data *or* tasks to the end of a queue *köa;* **queued indexed sequential access method (QISAM)** = indexed sequential file that is read item by item into a buffer *standardiserad metod för att läsa en indexerad fil;* **queued sequential access method (QSAM)** = queue of blocks that are waiting to be processed, retrieved using a sequential access method *standardiserad metod för att hämta sekvensiella block i en kö;* **queuing time** = period of time messages have to wait before they can be processed *or* transmitted *kötid, väntetid, fördröjning*

quick [kwık] *adj.* fast *or* not taking any time *snabb;* **the company made a quick recovery; he is looking for a quick return on his investment; we are hoping for a quick sale**

quickly ['kwıklı] *adv.* without taking much time *snabbt*

quicksort ['kwıksɔːt] *subst.* very rapid file sorting and ordering method *mycket snabb sorteringsalgoritm*

quiescent [kwaı'esnt] *adj.* state of a process *or* circuit *or* device when no input signal is applied *vilande*

quiet ['kwaıət] *adj.* not making very much noise *tyst;* **laser printers are much quieter than dot-matrix**

quintet [kwın'tet] *subst.* byte made up of five bits *kvintett*

quit [kwıt] *vb.* to leave a system *or* a program *avsluta, gå ut;* **do not forget to save your text before you quit the system**
NOTE: quitting - quit

quotation marks [kwə(ʊ)'teıʃ(ə)n,mɑːk] *subst.* inverted commas *or* signs printed at the beginning and end of text to show that it has been quoted from another source *citationstecken*

quote [kwəʊt] 1 *vb.* **(a)** to repeat words used by someone else *citera;* to repeat a reference number *citera;* **he quoted figures from the newspaper report; in reply please quote this number; when making a complaint please quote the batchnumber printed on the computer case; he replied, quoting the number of the account (b)** to estimate *or* to say what costs may be *offerera, beräkna;* **to quote a price for supplying stationery; their prices are always quoted in dollars; he quoted me a price of £1,026; can you quote for supplying 20,000 envelopes?** 2 *subst.* **quotes** = quotation marks *or* inverted commas *citationstecken;* **single quotes** = single inverted commas *enkelt citattecken;* **double quotes** = double inverted commas *dubbelt citattecken;* **the**

name of the company should be put in double quotes

quotient ['kwəʊʃ(ə)nt] *subst.* result of one number divided by another *kvot*

> COMMENT: when two numbers are divided, the answer is made up of a quotient and a remainder (the fractional part), 16 divided by 4 is equal to a quotient of 4 and zero remainder, 16 divided by 5 is equal to a quotient of 3 and a remainder of 1

QWERTY ['kwɜːtɪ] *subst.* **QWERTY keyboard =** English language keyboard for a typewriter *or* computer, where the top line of letters are Q-W-E-R-T-Y *standardiserad anglo-saxisk tangentbordslayout;* **the computer has a normal QWERTY keyboard;** *see also* AZERTY

> QUOTE the keyboard does not have a QWERTY layout but is easy to use
>
>   **Micro Decision**

Rr

race [reɪs] *vb.* error condition in a digital circuit, in which the state *or* output of the circuit is very dependent on the exact timing between the input signals (faulty output is due to unequal propagation delays on the separate input signals at a gate) *rusning*

rack [ræk] *subst.* **(a)** frame to hold items for display *rack, ställning;* **a display rack; a rack for holding mag tapes (b)** metal supporting frame for electronic circuit boards and peripheral devices such as disk drives *rack;* **rack mounted =** system consisting of removable circuit boards in a supporting frame *rackmonterad*

rad ⇨ line, row

radanpassning ⇨ wraparound

radar ['reɪdɑː] *subst.* method of finding the position of objects such as aircraft, by transmitting radio waves which are reflected back if they hit an object and are displayed on a screen *radar (förkortning för Radio Detection And Ranging)*

radbrytning ⇨ wraparound

radera ⇨ delete, erase, kill, wipe

radera buffert ⇨ flush

raderbar ⇨ erasable

raderbart läsminne ⇨ electrically, erasable

raderingskommando ⇨ kill

raderminne ⇨ electrically, erasable

radfall ⇨ body

radial transfer ['reɪdjəl 'trænsfɜː] *subst.* data transfer between two peripherals *or* programs that are on different layers of a structured system (such as an ISO/OSI system) *radiell överföring*

radiant ['reɪdjənt] *adj.* which radiates *strålande;* **radiant energy =** amount of energy radiated by an aerial *utstrålad energi*

radiate ['reɪdɪeɪt] *vb.* **(a)** to go out in all directions from a central point *stråla* **(b)** (i) to send out rays *stråla;* (ii) to convert electrical signals into travelling electromagnetic waves *stråla;* **radiating element =** single basic unit of an antenna that radiates signals *strålningselement*

radiation [ˌreɪdɪ'eɪʃ(ə)n] *subst.* (i) sending out of waves of energy from certain substances *strålning;* (ii) conversion of electrical signals in an antenna into travelling electromagnetic waves *utstrålning*

radiator ['reɪdɪeɪtə] *subst.* single basic unit of an antenna *or* any device that radiates signals *strålare*

radiell överföring ⇨ transfer

radio ['reɪdɪəʊ] *subst.* medium used for the transmission of speech, sound and data over long distances by radio frequency electromagnetic waves *radio;* **radio frequency (RF) =** range of electromagnetic waves used for radiocommunications *radiofrekvens;* **the radio frequency range extends from a few hertz to hundreds of gigahertz; radio microphone =** audio microphone with a small radio transmitter attached allowing the transmission of sound signals without wires *trådlös mikrofon;* **radio pager** *or* **radio paging device =** small pocket receiver that responds to a certain unique transmitted code to alert the user *personsökare;* **you could contact your salesman if he had a radio pager; radio paging =** calling someone by transmitting a code to their radio pager *personsökning;* **radio phone** *or* **radio telephone =** mobile two-way radio communications system that can access the public telephone network *mobiltelefon;* **radio receiver =** device that can receive signals broadcast on one radio frequency and convert them into their original audio form *radiomottagare;* **radio spectrum =** range of radio frequencies *radiospektrum;* **radio telegraphy =** telegraph codes transmitted via radio *radiotelegrafi;* **radio transmission of data =** sending data by radio *datasändning via radio, paketradio;* **radio**

waves = electromagnetic radiation waves *radiovågor*

radio ⇨ radio

radiocommunications
[ˌreɪdɪəʊkəˌmjuːnɪˈkeɪʃ *subst.* transmission and reception of sound and data by radio waves *radiokommunikation*

radiokommunikation ⇨
radiocommunications

radix ['reɪdɪks] *subst.* the value of the base of the number system being used *bas;* **the hexadecimal number has a radix of 16; radix complement** *see* TEN'S, TWO'S COMPLEMENT; **radix notation** = numbers represented to a certain radix *bassystem; see also* BASE NOTATION; **radix point** = dot which indicates the division between a whole unit and its fractional parts *bråkdelsmarkering (t.ex. decimalkomma)*

radjustering ⇨ justification

radredigeringsprogram ⇨ editor

radskrivare ⇨ printer, line printer

ragged ['rægɪd] *adj.* not straight *or* with an uneven edge *ojämn;* **ragged left** = printed text with a flush right-hand margin and uneven left-hand margin *ojämn vänstermarginal;* **ragged right** = printed text with a flush left-hand margin and uneven right-hand margin *ojämn högermarginal;* **ragged text** = unjustified text, text with a ragged right margin *ojämn text*

rak högermarginal ⇨ justify

rak vänstermarginal ⇨ justify

RAM [ræm] = RANDOM ACCESS MEMORY; memory that allows access to any location in any order, without having to access the rest first *direktminne;* compare SEQUENTIAL ACCESS MEMORY; **partial RAM** = RAM chip in which only a certain area of the chip functions correctly, usually in newly released chips (partial RAM's can be used by employing more than one to make up the capacity of one fully functional chip) *partiellt fungerande direktminne;* **RAM chip** = chip which stores data, allowing random access *direktminneskrets;* **RAM disk** = section of RAM that is made to look like and behave as a high-speed disk drive (using special software) *simulerat skivminne;* **RAM loader** = routine that will transfer a program from external backing store into RAM *minnesladdare;* **RAM refresh** = signals used to update the contents of dynamic RAM chips every few thousandths of a second, involving reading and rewriting the contents, needed to retain data *återuppladdningsfrekvens;* **RAM refresh rate** = number of times every

second that the data in a dynamic RAM chip has to be read and rewritten *återuppladdningsfrekvens;* **self-refreshing RAM** = dynamic RAM chip that has built-in circuitry to generate refresh signals, allowing data to be retained when the power is off by using a battery *självuppladdande direktminne;* **dynamic RAM** = most common RAM ICs, which use capacititive charge to retain data but which must be refreshed (read from and rewritten to) every few thousandths of a second *dynamiskt direktminne, dynamiskt RAM;* **static RAM** = RAM ICs that do not have to be refreshed but cannot store as much data per chip as dynamic RAM *statiskt direktminne, statiskt RAM; see also* CHIP, ROM NOTE: there is no plural for RAM, and it often has no article: **512K of RAM** ; the file is stored in RAM

COMMENT: dynamic RAM which uses a capacitor to store a bit of data (as a charge) needs to have each location refreshed from time to time to retain the data, but is very fast and can contain more data per unit area than static RAM which uses a latch to store the state of a bit, and has the advantage of not requiring to be refreshed to retain its data, and will keep data for as long as power is supplied

QUOTE in addition the board features 512K of video RAM, expandable up to a massive 1MB
PC Business World
QUOTE fast memory is RAM that does not have to share bus access with the chip that manages the video display
Byte

ramantenn ⇨ loop

ramsträckning ⇨ banding, elastic banding

random ['rændəm] *adj.* (event) that cannot be anticipated *slumpmässig;* **pseudo-random** = generated sequence that appears random but is repeated over a long period *skenbart slumpmässig;* **random number** = number that cannot be predicted *slumptal;* **random number generator** = program which generates random numbers (used in lotteries, games, etc.) *slumptalsgenerator;* **random process** = system whose output cannot be related to its input *or* internal structure *slumpmässig process*

random access ['rændəm 'ækses] *subst.* direct acces *or* ability to access immediately memory locations in any order *direktåtkomst;* **disk drives are random access, magnetic tape is sequential access memory; random access device** = device whose access time to retrieve data is not dependent on the location or type of data *direktåtkomstenhet;* **random access file** = file in which each item *or* record can be immediately accessed by its address, without searching through the rest of the file, and is not dependent on the previous location *direktåtkomstfil;* **random access storage =** storage medium that allows access to any location in any order *direkt(åtkomst)minne;* **random access memory (RAM) =** memory that allows access to any location in any order, usually in the form of ICs *direkt(åtkomst)minne, RAM*

random processing ['rændəm 'prəʊsesɪŋ] *subst.* processing of data in the order required rather than the order in which it is stored *slumpmässig databehandling*

range [reɪn(d)ʒ] **1** *subst.* **(a)** series of items from which the customer can choose *sortiment, utbud;* **a wide range of products; the catalogue lists a wide range of computer stationery (b)** set of allowed values between a maximum and minimum *område, räckvidd;* **the telephone channel can accept signals in the frequency range 300 - 3400Hz; magnetic tape is stable within a temperature range of 0° to 40°C; number range =** set of allowable values *talområde;* **frequency range =** range of allowable frequencies, between two limits *frekvensområde* **2** *vb.* **(a)** to vary *or* to be different *sträcka sig;* **the company's products range from a cheap lapheld micro to a multistation mainframe (b)** to put text in order to one side *ordna, rätta, justera;* **range left =** move text to align it to the left margin *vänsterställa, vänsterjustera;* to move the contents of a word to the left edge *vänsterjustera, vänsterställa*

rank [ræŋk] *vb.* to sort data into an order, usually according to size *or* importance *klassa, rangordna*

rapid ['ræpɪd] *adj.* fast *hastig, snabb;* **rapid access =** device *or* memory whose access time is very short *snabbåtkomst;* **rapid access memory** *or* **fast access memory (FAM) =** storage locations that can be read from *or* written to very quickly *snabbminne*

rapportbyggnad ⇨ **index**

rapportera ⇨ **call in**

rapportgenerator ⇨ **report generator**

raster ['ræstə] *subst.* system of scanning the whole of a CRT screen with a picture beam by sweeping across it horizontally, moving down one pixel *or* line at a time *raster;* **raster graphics =** graphics where the picture is built up in lines across the screen *or* page *rastergrafik;* **raster image processor =** raster which translates software instructions into an image *or* complete page which is then printed by the printer *rastergrafikprocessor;* **an electronic page can be converted to a printer-readable video**

image by an on-board raster image processor; raster scan = one sweep of the picture beam horizontally across the front of a CRT screen *raster*

rate [reɪt] **1** *subst.* quantity of data *or* tasks that can be processed in a set time *belopp, värde, mått;* **the processor's instruction execution rate is better than the older version; error rate =** number of errors that occur within a certain time *felfrekvens, felförhållande;* **information rate =** amount of information content per character multiplied by the number of characters transmitted per second *informationsmängd* **2** *vb.* to evaluate how good something is *or* how large something is *klassificera, värdera;* **rated throughput =** maximum throughput of a device that will still meet original specifications *nominellt (maximalt) genomlopp, nominell (maximal) kapacitet*

ratings ['reɪtɪŋz] *subst.* calculation of how many people are watching a TV programme *klassificering;* **ratings battle** *or* **war =** fight between two TV companies to increase their share of the market *kampen om tittarsiffrorna*

ratio ['reɪʃɪəʊ] *subst.* proportion of one number to another *förhållande;* **the ratio of 10 to 5 is 2:1; the ratio of corrupt bits per transmitted message is falling with new technology**

rational number ['ræʃənl 'nʌmbə] *subst.* number that can be written as the ratio of two whole numbers *rationellt tal;* **24 over 7 is a rational number; 0.333 can be written as the rational number 1/3**

ratt ⇨ **knob**

raw [rɔː] *adj.* in the original state *or* not processed *rå;* **raw data =** (i) pieces of information that have not yet been input into a computer system *rådata;* (ii) data in a database which has to be processed to provide information to the user *rådata;* **this small computer collects raw data from the sensors, converts it and transmits it to the mainframe**

ray [reɪ] *subst.* one line of light *or* radiation in a beam *or* from a source *stråle;* **the rays of light pass down the optical fibre**

R & D ['ɑːrən'diː] = RESEARCH AND DEVELOPMENT; **R & D department =** department in a company that investigates new products, discoveries and techniques *forsknings- och utvecklingsavdening*

react [rɪˈækt] *vb.* **to react to something =** to act in response to something *reagera på något;* **to react with something =** to change because a substance is present *reagera med något*

reactance [rɪˈæktəns] *subst.* impedance associated with a component (capacitor *or* inductor) *reaktans*

reaction [rɪˈækʃ(ə)n] *subst.* action which takes place because of something which has happened earlier *reaktion*

reactive mode [rɪˈæktɪv ˈməʊd] *subst.* computer operating mode in which each entry by the user causes something to happen but does not provide an immediate response *reaktivt tillstånd; compare with* INTERACTIVE; BATCH

read [riːd] *vb.* **(a)** to look at printed words and understand them *läsa;* **conditions of sale are printed in such small characters that they are difficult to read; can the OCR read typeset characters? (b)** to retrieve data from a storage medium *läsa;* **this instruction reads the first record of a file; access time can be the time taken to read from a record; destructive read =** read operation in which the stored data is erased as it is retrieved *raderande läsning;* **read back check =** system to ensure that data was correctly received, in which the transmitted data is sent back and checked against the original for any errors *återläsningskontroll;* **read cycle =** period of time between address data being sent to a storage device and the data being returned *läscykel;* **read head =** transducer that reads signals stored on a magnetic medium and converts them back to their original electrical form *läshuvud;* **read only =** device *or* circuit whose stored data cannot be changed *läs-;* **read only memory (ROM) =** memory device that has had data written into it at the time of manufacture, and now its contents can only be read *läsminne;* **the manufacturer provided the monitor program in two ROM chips; read rate =** number of bytes *or* bits that a reader can read in a certain time *läshastighet;* **read/write channel =** channel that can carry signals travelling in two directions *läs- och skrivkanal;* **read/write cycle =** sequence of events used to retrieve and store data *läs- och skrivcykel;* **read/write head =** transducer that can read *or* write data from the surface of a magnetic storage medium, such as a floppy disk *läs- och skrivhuvud;* **read/write memory =** storage medium that can be written to and read from *läs- och skrivminne; compare with* READ ONLY

readable [ˈriːdəbl] *adj.* that can be read *or* understood by someone *or* an electronic device *läsbar;* **the electronic page is converted to a printer-readable video image;**

machine readable = (commands *or* data) stored on a medium that can be directly input to the computer *maskinläsbar*

reader [ˈriːdə] *subst.* device that reads data stored on one medium and converts it into another form *läsare;* **card reader =** device that transforms data on a punched card to a form that can be recognized by the computer *kortläsare;* **tape reader =** machine that reads punched holes in paper tape *or* signals on magnetic tape *remsläsare; see also* OPTICAL

read-in [riːd ˈɪn] *or* **read in** *vb.* to transfer data from an external source to main memory *läsa in;* **the computer automatically read-in thirty values from the A/D converter**

reading [ˈriːdɪŋ] *subst.* note taken of figures *or* degrees, especially of degrees on a scale *avläsning, mätvärde*

readout [ˈriːdaʊt] *subst.* display of data *utskrift, indikering, skärmutskrift;* **the readout displayed the time; the clock had a digital readout; destructive readout =** display device that erases previous characters when displaying new ones *överskrivningsskärm, förstörande skrivning på skärm;* **readout device =** device that allows information (numbers *or* characters) to be displayed *utskriftsenhet, skärm*

ready [ˈredɪ] *adj.* fit to be used *or* sold *färdig;* (equipment) that is waiting and able to be used *redo;* **the green light indicates the system is ready for another program; the programming will not be ready until next week; the maintenance people hope that the system will be ready for use in 24 hours; ready state =** communications line *or* device that is waiting to accept data *redotillstånd*

realisera ⇨ **implement**

realisering ⇨ **implementation**

real memory [ˈrɪəl ˈmemərɪ] *subst.* actual physical memory that can be addressed by a CPU *reellt minne, fysiskt minne; compare with* VIRTUAL MEMORY

real number [ˈrɪəl ˈnʌmbə] *subst. (in computing)* number that is represented with a fractional part (sometimes refers to numbers represented in a floating-point form) *reellt tal, flyttal*

realtid ⇨ **real time**

realtidsbearbetning ⇨ **inline, processing**

realtidskörning ⇨ **multitasking**

real time [ˈrɪəl ˈtaɪm] *subst.* actions *or* processing time that is of the same order of magnitude as the problem to be solved (i.e. the processing time is within the same time as the problem to be solved, so that the result can influence the source of the data *realtid;* **a navigation system needs to be able to process the position of a ship in real time and take suitable action before it hits a rock;** *US* **program shown in real time** = TV program which is broadcast live *direktsändning;* **real-time clock** = clock in a computer that provides the correct time of day *realtidsklocka; compare* RELATIVE-TIME CLOCK; **real-time input** = data input to a system as it happens *or* is required *realtidsinmatning;* **real-time multi-tasking** = executing several real-time tasks simultaneously without slowing the execution of any of the processes *fleruppdragskörning i realtid;* **real-time processing** = processing operation that takes a time of the same order of magnitude as the problem to be solved *realtidsbearbetning;* **real-time simulation** = computer model of a process where each process is executed in a similar time to the real process *realtidssimulering*

QUOTE a real-time process is one which interacts with a real external activity and respects deadlines imposed by that activity
.EXE

real-time system [ˈrɪəlˌtaɪm ˈsɪstəm] *subst.* system whose processing time is within that of the problem, so that it can influence the source of the data *realtidssystem;* **in a real-time system, as you move the joystick left, the image on the screen moves left. If there is a pause for processing it is not a true real-time system**

QUOTE define a real-time system as any system which is expected to interact with its environment within certain timing constraints
British Telecom Technology Journal

reboot [ˈriːˈbuːt] *vb.* to reload an operating system during a computing session *starta om;* **we rebooted and the files reappeared;** *see also* BOOT

recall [rɪˈkɔːl] **1** *subst.* bringing back text *or* files from store *återskapande, återhämtning* **2** *vb.* to bring back text *or* files from store for editing *återskapa, återhämta*

QUOTE automatic recall provides the facility to recall the last twenty commands and to edit and re-use them
Practical Computing

receive [rɪˈsiːv] *vb.* to accept data from a communications link *motta;* **the computer received data via the telephone line; receive only** = computer terminal that can only accept and display data (but not transmit) *mottagningsterminal*

receiver [rɪˈsiːvə] *subst.* electronic device that can detect transmitted signals and present them in a suitable form *mottagare;* **radio receiver** = device that detects signals

broadcast on one radio frequency and converts them into their original audio form *radiomottagare;* **the radio receiver picked up your signal very strongly; receiver register** = temporary storage register for data inputs, before processing *mottagarregister*

reception [rɪˈsepʃ(ə)n] *subst.* quality of a radio *or* TV signal received *mottagning;* **signal reception is bad with that aerial**

re-chargeable [ˈriːˈtʃɑːdʒəbl] *adj.* (battery) which can be charged again with electricity when it is flat *uppladdningsbar*

recode [rɪˈkəʊd] *vb.* to code a program which has been coded for one system, so that it will work on another *flytta, koda om*

recognition [ˌrekəgˈnɪʃ(ə)n] *subst.* (i) being able to recognize something *identifiering;* (ii) process that allows something to be recognized, such as letters on a printed text *or* bars on bar codes, etc. *igenkännade;* **recognition logic** = logical software used in OCR, AI, etc. *teckenigenkänningsprogram, mönster-igenkänningsprogram;* **optical character recognition** = process that allows printed *or* written characters to be recognized optically (using an optical character reader), and converted into a form that can be input into a computer *OCR, (optisk) teckenläsning;* **optical mark recognition** = process that allows certain marks *or* lines *or* patterns to be recognized optically (using an optical character reader), and converted into a form that can be input into a computer *optisk teckenläsare*

recognizable [ˈrekəgnaɪzəbl] *adj.* which can be recognized *igenkänningsbar*

recognize [ˈrekəgnaɪz] *vb.* to see something and remember that it has been seen before *känna igen;* **the scanner will recognize most character fonts**

recompile [ˈriːkəmˈpaɪl] *vb.* to compile a source program again, usually after changes *or* debugging *omkompilera*

reconfiguration [ˈriːkənˌfɪɡjʊˈreɪʃ(ə)n] *subst.* altering the structure of data in a system *omkonfigurering;* **I reconfigured the field structure in the file; this program allows us to reconfigure the system to our own requirements;** *see also* CONFIGURE, SET UP

reconfigure [ˈriːkənˈfɪɡə] *vb.* to alter the structure of data in a system *strukturera om*

reconnect [ˈriːkəˈnekt] *vb.* to connect again *koppla in igen;* **the telephone engineers are trying to reconnect the telephone**

reconstitute [ˈriːˈkɒnstɪtjuːt] *vb.* to return a file to a previous state, usually to restore a file after a crash *or* corruption *återskapa*

record [ˈrekɔːd] **1** *subst.* **(a)** set of items of related data *post;* **your record contains several fields that have been grouped together under the one heading; this record contains all their personal details; chained record** = data record in a chained file *länkad post;* **change** *or* **transaction record** = record containing new data which is to be used to update a master record *transaktionspost;* **logical record** = number of items of related data that are held in temporary memory ready to be processed *logisk post;* **physical record** = record and control data combination stored on a backing device *fysisk post;* **record count** = number of records within a stored file *postantal;* **record format** *or* **layout** = organization and length of separate fields in a record *postformat;* **record length** = quantity of data in a record *postlängd;* **records manager** = program which maintains records and can access and process them to provide information *posthanterare;* **records management** = program which maintains records and can access and process them to provide information *posthantering* **(b)** plastic disk on the surface of which music *or* other sounds are recorded *(grammofon)skiva* **2** *vb.* to store data *or* signals on tape *or* on disk *or* in a computer *spela in;* **record the results in this column; this device records signals onto magnetic tape; digitally recorded data are used to generate images; record button** = key pressed on a recorder when ready to record signals onto a medium *inspelningsknapp;* **record gap** *see* BLOCK GAP; **record head** *or* **write head** = transducer that converts an electrical signal into a magnetic field to write the data onto a magnetic medium *skrivhuvud*

QUOTE you can echo the previous record if a lot of replication is involved

QUOTE records may be sorted before the report is created, using up to nine sort fields

Byte

QUOTE file and record-locking procedures have to be implemented to make sure that files cannot be corrupted when two users try to read or write to the same record simultaneously

Micro Decision

recorder [rɪˈkɔːdə] *subst.* equipment able to transfer input signals onto a storage medium *inspelningsapparat;* **magnetic tape recorder** = device with a motor, read/write head and circuitry to allow electrical signals to be recorded onto *or* played back from magnetic tape *bandspelare*

COMMENT: the signal recorded is not always in the same form as the input signal: many recorders record a modulated carrier signal for better quality. A recorder is usually combined with a suitable playback circuit since the read and write heads are often the same physical device

recording [rɪˈkɔːdɪŋ] *subst.* **(a)** action of storing signals *or* data on tape *or* in a computer *inspelning;* **recording density** = number of bits of data that can be stored in a unit area on a magnetic disk *or* tape *inspelningstäthet;* **recording trunk** = telephone line between a local and long distance exchange for operator use *nätadministrationsledning* **(b)** signal (especially music) which has been recorded on tape *or* disk *inspelning;* **a new recording of Beethoven's quartets**

recover [rɪˈkʌvə] *vb.* to get back something which has been lost *återskapa, rädda;* **it is possible to recover the data but it can take a long time**

recoverable error [rɪˈkʌv(ə)rəbl ˈerə] *subst.* error type that allows program execution to be continued after it has occurred *fel efter vilket körningen kan återupptas*

recovery [rɪˈkʌvərɪ] *subst.* **(a)** returning to normal operating after a fault *återhämtning;* **automatic recovery program** = software that is automatically run when a piece of equipment fails, to ensure that the system continues to operate *automatiskt återhämtningsprogram, återstartprogram;* **failure recovery** = resuming a process *or* program after a failure has occurred and has been corrected *återhämtning efter fel;* **fall back recovery** = resuming a program after a fault has been fixed, from a point at which the fall back routines were called *omstart från avbrottspunkten;* **sense recovery time** = time that a RAM device takes to switch from read to write mode *(läs-skriv)omkopplingsbar;* **recovery procedure** = processes required to return a system to normal operation after an error *räddningsprocedur, återstartprocedur* **(b)** getting back something which has been lost *återhämtning;* **the recovery of lost files can be carried out using the recovery procedure**

rectangular waveguide [rekˈtæŋɡjʊlə ˈweɪvɡaɪd] *subst.* microwave channel that is rectangular in cross section *rektangulär vågledare*

rectifier [ˈrektɪfaɪə] *subst.* electronic circuit that converts an alternating current supply into a direct current supply *likriktare*

rectify [ˈrektɪfaɪ] *vb.* **(a)** to correct something *or* to make something right *korrigera, rätta till;* **they had to rectify the error at the printout stage (b)** to remove the positive *or* negative sections of a signal so that it is unipolar *likrikta*

recto ['rektəʊ] *subst.* right hand page of a book (usually given an odd number) *högersida*

recursion [rɪ'kɜ:ʃ(ə)n] *or* **recursive routine** [rɪ'kɜ:sɪv ru:'ti:n] *subst.* subroutine in a program that calls itself during execution *rekursion;* **recursive call =** subroutine that calls itself when it is run *rekursivt anrop*

redaktör ⊳ **editor**

redefinable ['ri:dɪ'faɪnəbl] *adj.* which can be redefined *omdefinierbar*

redefine ['ri:dɪ'faɪn] *vb.* to change the function *or* value assigned to a variable *or* object *omdefiniera;* **we redefined the initial parameters; to redefine a key =** to change the function of a programmable key *definiera om en tangent;* **I have redefined this key to display the figure five when pressed**

QUOTE the idea of the packages is that they enable you to redefine the keyboard
Practical Computing
QUOTE one especially useful command lets you redefine the printer's character-translation table
Byte

red, green, blue (RGB) ['red,gri:n,blu: ('ɑ:dʒi:'bi:)] *subst.* **(a)** high-definition monitor system that uses three separate input signals controlling red, green and blue colour picture beams *RGB-bildskärm, RGB-signal, RGB-kontakt* **(b)** the three colour picture beams used in a colour TV *RGB-signal*

COMMENT: there are three colour guns producing red, green and blue beams acting on groups of three phosphor dots at each pixel location

redigera ⊳ **edit**

redigeringsfönster ⊳ **edit**

redigeringskommandon ⊳ **edit**

redigeringsprogram ⊳ **program, screen**

redigeringstangent ⊳ **edit**

redigeringsterminal ⊳ **ip**

redirect ['ri:dɪ'rekt] *vb.* to send a message to its destination by another route *omdirigera*

redirection ['ri:dɪ'rekʃ(ə)n] *subst.* sending a message to its destination by another route *omdirigering;* **call forwarding is automatic redirection of calls**

redo ['ri:'du:] *vb.* to do something again *göra om;* **redo from start =** start again from the beginning *starta om*

redraw ['ri:'drɔ:] *vb.* to draw again *rita om;* **can the computer redraw the graphics showing the product from the top view?**

reduce [rɪ'dju:s] *vb.* **(a)** to make smaller *förminska* **(b)** to convert raw data into a more compact form which can then be easily processed *reducera*

reduced instruction set computer (RISC) [rɪ'dju:sd ɪn'strʌkʃ(ə)n set kəm'pju:tə (rɪsk)] *subst.* CPU design whose instruction set contains a small number of simple fast-executing instructions, that makes program writing more complex, but increases speed *optimalkodsdator, RISC-processor; compare with* WISC

reduction [rɪ'dʌkʃ(ə)n] *subst.* act of reducing *förminskning;* proportion by which something is made smaller *förminskning;* **we need a 25% reduction to fit the halftone in the space**

redundancy [rɪ'dʌndənsɪ] *subst.* providing extra components in a system in case there is a breakdown *redundans;* **longitudinal redundancy check =** check on received blocks of data to detect any errors *längsgående redundanskontroll;* **network redundancy =** extra links between points allowing continued operation in the event of one failing *nätredundans (genom extra linjer);* **vertical redundancy check =** (odd) parity check on each character of a block received, to detect any errors *tvärsgående redundanskontroll, paritetskontroll (av tecken);* **redundancy checking =** checking of received data for correct redundant codes to detect any errors *redundanskontroll*

redundans ⊳ **redundancy, replication**

redundant [rɪ'dʌndənt] *adj.* **(a)** (data) that can be removed without losing any information *tilläggs-, redundant;* **the parity bits on the received data are redundant and can be removed; redundant character =** character added to a block of characters for error detection *or* protocol purposes, and carries no information *kontrolltecken;* **redundant code =** check bit *or* data added to a block of data for error detection purposes, and carries no information *redundant kod* **(b)** extra piece of equipment kept ready for a task in case of faults *extra, reserv*

reel [ri:l] *subst.* holder round which a tape is rolled *hjul, spole;* **he dropped the reel on the floor and the tape unwound itself; pickup reel =** empty reel used to store tape as it is played from a full reel *tomrulle, uppsamlingsrulle*

reel to reel ['riːltə'riːl] *subst.* copying one tape of data onto another magnetic tape *(band)kopiering;* **reel to reel recorder** = magnetic tape recording machine that uses tape held on one reel and feeds it to a pick-up reel *rullbandspelare*

re-entrant program [riː'entr(ə)nt 'prəʊgræm] *or* **code** [kəʊd] *or* **routine** [ruː'tiːn] *subst.* one program *or* code shared by many users in a multi-user system (it can be interrupted *or* called again by another user before it has finished its previous run, and returns to the point at which it was interrupted when it has finished that run) *relativadresserat fleranvändarprogram, multikörbart program*

re-entry [riː'entrɪ] *subst.* calling a routine from within that routine *återingång;* running a program from within that program *återingång;* **re-entry point** = point in a program *or* routine where it is re-entered *återingångspunkt*

refer [rɪ'fɜː] *vb.* to mention *or* to deal with *or* to write about something *syfta, referera, hänvisa;* **the manual refers to the serial port, but I cannot find it**

reference ['ref(ə)r(ə)ns] **1** *subst.* **(a)** value used as a starting point for other values, often zero *referens;* **reference address** = initial address in a program used as an origin *or* base for others *referensadress;* **reference level** = signal level to which all others are calibrated *referensnivå* **(b)** mentioning *or* dealing with something *referens;* **reference file** = file of data which is kept so that it can be referred to *referensfil;* **reference instruction** = command that provides access to sorted *or* stored data *referensinstruktion;* **reference list** = list of routines *or* instructions and their location within a program *referenslista;* **reference mark** = printed symbol to indicate the presence of a note *or* reference not in the text *referensmarkering;* **reference retrieval system** = index which provides a reference to a document *referensindex;* **reference table** = list of ordered items *referenstabell;* **reference time** = point in time that is used as an origin for further timings *or* measurements *referenstid* **2** *vb.* to access a location in memory *referera, komma åt;* **the access time taken to reference an item in memory is short**

QUOTE a referencing function dynamically links all references throughout a document
Byte

referens ⇨ **reference**

referensadress ⇨ **presumptive address**

referensdata ⇨ **master**

referensfil ⇨ **master**

referenskort ⇨ **flash**

referensspänning ⇨ **bias**

referenstabell ⇨ **table**

referera ⇨ **refer**

reflect [rɪ'flekt] *vb.* to send back (light *or* image) from a surface *reflektera;* **in a reflex camera, the image is reflected by an inbuilt mirror**

reflectance [rɪ'flekt(ə)ns] *subst.* difference between the amount of light *or* signal incident and the amount that is reflected back from a surface *reflektans* NOTE: the opposite is **absorptance**

reflected code [rɪ'flektɪd 'kəʊd] *subst.* coding system in which the binary representation of decimal numbers changes by only one bit at a time from one number to the next *reflekterande kod*

reflection [rɪ'flekʃ(ə)n] *subst.* light *or* image which is reflected *reflektion, återspegling;* **signal reflection** = amount of transmitted signal that is reflected at the receiver due to an impedance mismatch *or* fault *signalreflektion*

reflective disk [rɪ'flektɪv 'dɪsk] *subst.* video disk that uses a reflected laser beam to read the data etched into the surface *optisk (reflekterande) skiva*

reflekterad stråle ⇨ **indirect**

reflex (camera) ['riːfleks ('kæmərə)] *subst.* camera with an optical mirror that allows a scene to be viewed through the camera lens so that the user sees what he is photographing *spegelreflexkamera*

reformat ['riː'fɔːmæt] *vb.* to format a disk that already contains data, and erasing the data by doing so *omformatera;* **do not reformat your hard disk unless you can't do anything else**

reformatting ['riː'fɔːmætɪŋ] *subst.* act of formatting a disk which already contains data *omformatering;* **reformatting destroys all the data on a disk;** *see also* FORMAT

refract [rɪ'frækt] *vb.* to change the direction of light as it passes through a material (such as water *or* glass) *bryta*

refraction [rɪ'frækʃ(ə)n] *subst.* change in direction of light rays as they pass through a material *refraktion, brytning*

refractive index [rɪ'fræktɪv 'ɪndeks] *subst.* measure of the angle that light is refracted by, as it passes through a material *brytningsindex*

refresh [rɪ'freʃ] *vb.* **(a)** to update regularly the contents of dynamic RAM by reading and rewriting stored data to ensure data is retained *uppdatera, återuppladda;* **memory refresh signal; RAM refresh rate** = number of times every second that the data in a dynamic RAM chip has to be read and rewritten *återskrivningssfrekvens (för direktminne);* **self-refreshing RAM** = dynamic RAM chip that has built-in circuitry to generate refresh signals, allowing data to be retained when the power is off, using a battery backup *självåterskrivande direktminne* **(b) screen refresh** = to update regularly the images on a CRT screen by scanning each pixel with a picture beam to make sure the image is still visible *skärmuppdatering;* **refresh rate** = number of times every second that the image on a CRT is redrawn *uppdateringsfrekvens*

regel ⇨ **rule**

regelverk ⇨ **inference**

regenerate [rɪ'dʒenəreɪt] *vb.* (i) to redraw an image on a screen many times a second so that it remains visible *kontinuerligt regenerara (som tevebild);* (ii) to receive distorted signals, process and error check them, then retransmit the same data *mottagningskontrollera och vidaresända*

regeneration [rɪ,dʒenə'reɪʃ(ə)n] *subst.* process of regenerating a signal *återskapande, regenerering*

regenerative memory [rɪ'dʒenərətɪv 'memərɪ] *subst.* storage medium whose contents need to be regularly refreshed to retain its contents *regenererande minne;* **dynamic RAM is regenerative memory - it needs to be refreshed every 250ns; the CRT display can be thought of as regenerative memory, it requires regular refresh picture scans to prevent flicker; regenerative reading** = reading operation that automatically regenerates and rewrites the data back into memory *återskrivande läsning*

region ['riːdʒ(ə)n] *subst.* special *or* reserved area of memory or program *område*

regional breakpoint ['riːdʒənl 'breɪkpɔɪnt] *subst.* breakpoint that can be inserted anywhere within a program that is being debugged *regional brytpunkt (i ett visst område); see also* BREAKPOINT, DEBUGGING

register ['redʒɪstə] **1** *subst.* **(a)** (i) special location within a CPU (usually one or two words wide) that is used to hold data and addresses to be processed in a machine code operation *register;* (ii) reserved memory location used for special storage purposes *register;* **accumulator register** =

most important internal storage register in a CPU, containing the data to be processed *ackumulatorregister;* **address register** = register in a computer that is able to store all the bits of an address which can then be processed as a single unit *adressregister;* **base register** = register in a CPU (not usually in small computers) that contains the address of the start of a program *basregister;* **buffer register** = temporary storage for data being written to *or* read from memory *buffertregister;* **circulating register** = shift register whose output is fed back into its input (to form a closed loop) *shiftregister;* **control register** = storage location for control data *styrregister, flaggregister;* **data register** = area within a CPU used to store data temporarily before it is processed *dataregister;* **external register** = registers which are located outside the main CPU, in locations within main memory, allowing the user to access them easily *externt register;* **index register** = computer address register that is added to a reference address to provide the location to be accessed *indexregister;* **input/output register** = temporary storage for data received from memory before being transferred to an I/O device *or* data from an I/O device waiting to be stored in main memory or to be processed *in-utregister;* **instruction register** = temporary storage for the instruction that is being executed *instruktionsregister;* **instruction address register (IAR)** = register in a CPU that stores the location of the next instruction to be processed *instruktionsadressregister, instruktionspekare;* **memory address register (MAR)** = register within the CPU that contains the address of the next location to be accessed *minnesadressregister, (minnes)pekare;* **next instruction register** = register in the CPU that contains the address of the next instruction to be processed *programpekare;* **program status word register (PSW register)** = register which contains a number of status bits, such as carry flag, zero flag, overflow flag *programstatusregister;* **sequence control register (SCR)** = CPU register that contains the address of the next instruction to be processed *programpekare; see also* NEXT INSTRUCTION ADDRESS REGISTER; **shift register** = temporary storage into which data can be shifted *skiftregister;* **register addressing** = instruction whose address field contains the register in which the operand is stored *registeradressering;* **register file** = number of registers used for temporary storage *registerfil;* **register length** = size (in bits) of a register *registerlängd;* **in this small micro, the data register is eight bits wide, an address register is sixteen bits wide; register map** = display of the contents of all the registers *registerbild* **(b)** superimposing two images correctly *register, passning;* **the two colours are out of register =** the colours are not correctly printed one on top of the other *det är dålig färgpassning, det är misspassning i färgerna* **2** *vb.* **(a)** to react to a stimulus *registrera;* **light-sensitive films register light intensity (b)** to correctly superimpose two images *ställa in passningen;* **register marks =** marks at the corners of a film used to help in lining up two images *passmärken*

register ⇨ register

registerkort ⇨ filing, master

registrerat fel ⇨ detect

reglera ⇨ regulate

regulate ['regjʊleɪt] *vb.* to control a process (usually using sensors and a feedback mechanism) *reglera, stabilisera;* **regulated power supply =** constant, controlled voltage *or* current source whose output will not vary with input supply variation *stabiliserat nätaggregat*

COMMENT: a regulated power supply is required for all computers where components cannot withstand voltage variations

rehyphenation ['riː,haɪfə'neɪʃ(ə)n] *subst.* changing the hyphenation of words in a text after it has been put into a new page format *or* line width *avstavning, radplanering*

reject [rɪ'dʒekt] *vb.* to refuse to accept something *förkasta, kassera;* **the computer rejects all incoming data from incompatible sources**

rejection [rɪ'dʒekʃ(ə)n] *subst.* refusing to accept something *avvisning, kassering;* **rejection error =** error by a scanner which cannot read a character and so leaves a blank *läsfel*

rekursion ⇨ recursion

relation ⇨ relationship

relational database [rɪ'leɪʃ(ə)nl 'deɪtəbeɪs] *subst.* set of data where all the items are related *relationsdatabas;* **relational operator** *or* **logical operator =** symbol that compares two items *relationsoperator, logisk operator;* **relational query =** database query that contains relational operators *relationsfråga;* **the relational query 'find all men under 35 years old' will not work on this system**

relationsdatabas ⇨ relational database

relationship [rɪ'leɪʃ(ə)nʃɪp] *subst.* way in which two similar things are connected *relation, släktskap*

relativadress ⇨ floating

relative ['relətɪv] *adj.* which is compared to something *relativ;* **relative address =** location specified in relation to a reference address *relativadress;* **relative coding =** writing a program using relative address instructions *relativ kodning;* **relative coordinates =** positional information given in relation to a reference point *relativa koordinater;* **relative data =** data that gives new coordinate information relative to previous coordinates *relativa data;* **relative error =** difference between a number and its correct value (caused by rounding off) *relativfel;* **relative-time clock =** regular pulses that allow software in a computer to calculate the real time *relativ systemklocka*

relay ['riːleɪ] **1** *subst.* electromagnetically controlled switch *relä;* **there is a relay in the circuit; it is relay-rated at 5 Amps; microwave relay =** radiocommunications equipment used to receive microwave signals, then boost and retransmit them *mikrovågsrelä* **2** *vb.* to receive data from one source and then retransmit it to another point *vidarebefordra, vidaresända;* **all messages are relayed through this small micro**

release [rɪ'liːs] **1** *subst.* **(a)** version of a product *version;* **the latest software is release 5;** *see also* VERSION **(b)** putting a new product on the market *lansera;* **new releases =** new records put on the market *nyutsläppta skivor;* **on general release =** (i) available to the public *publicerad;* (ii) (film) shown at many cinemas *släppt för offentlig visning* **(c) press release =** sheet giving news about a news item which is sent to newspapers and TV and radio stations so that they can use the information in it *pressrelease* **2** *vb.* to put a new product on the market *publicera, släppa*

relevance ['reləvəns] *subst.* (i) way in which something has a connection with something else *relevans, samband;* (ii) importance of something in a situation *or* process *relevans, tillämplighet*

relevans ⇨ relevance

relevant ['reləvənt] *adj.* which has an important connection *relevant, tillämplig*

reliability [rɪ,laɪə'bɪlətɪ] *subst.* the ability of a device to function as intended, efficiently and without failure *tillförlitlighet;* **it has an excellent reliability record; the product has passed its reliability tests**

reliable [rɪ'laɪəbl] *adj.* which can be trusted to work properly *tillförlitlig;* **the early versions of the software were not completely reliable**

relief printing [rɪ'liːf 'prɪntɪŋ] *subst.* printing process in which the ink is held on a raised image *relieftryck*

reload ['riː'ləʊd] *vb.* to load again *ladda om;* **we reloaded the program after the crash;** *see also* LOAD

relocatable ['riːlə(ʊ)'keɪtəbl] *adj.* which can be moved to another area of memory without affecting its operation *relokerbar;* **relocatable program** = computer program that can be loaded into and executed from any area of memory *relokerbart program;* **the operating system can load and run a relocatable program from any area of memory**

relocate ['riːlə(ʊ)'keɪt] *vb.* to move data from one area of storage to another *relokera;* **the data is relocated during execution; self-relocating program** = program that can be loaded into any part of memory (that will modify its addresses depending on the program origin address) *självrelokerande program*

relocation ['riːlə(ʊ)'keɪʃ(ə)n] *subst.* moving to another area in memory *relokering;* **dynamic relocation** = moving data *or* coding *or* assigning absolute locations during a program execution *dynamisk relokering;* **relocation constant** = quantity added to all addresses to move them to another section of memory, (equal to the new base address) *relokeringskonstant;* **static relocation** = moving data *or* coding *or* assigning absolute locations before a program is run *statisk relokering*

relä ⇨ **relay**

REM [rem] = REMARK statement in a BASIC program that is ignored by the interpreter, allowing the programmer to write explanatory notes *programsatsen REM i programmeringsspråket BASIC*

remainder [rɪ'meɪndə] **1** *subst.* number equal to the dividend minus the product of the quotient and divider *rest;* **7 divided by 3 is equal to 2 remainder 1;** *compare with* QUOTIENT **2** *vb.* to sell products below cost price *sälja ut;* **this computer model is out of date so we have to remainder the rest of the stock**

remedial maintenance [rɪ'miːdjəl 'meɪntənəns] *subst.* maintenance to repair faults which have developed in a system *stödunderhåll, åtgärdande underhåll*

remote [rɪ'məʊt] *adj.* (communications) with a computer at a distance from the systems centre *fjärr-;* **users can print reports on remote printers; remote console** *or* **device** = input/output device located away from the computer (sending data to it by line *or* modem) *fjärrkonsoll;* **remote control** = control of a process *or* machine from a distance *fjärrstyrning;* **the video recorder has a remote control facility ; remote job entry (RJE)** = batch processing system where instructions are transmitted to the computer from a remote terminal *fjärrinmatning av jobb (enligt IBM:s RJE-system);* **remote station** = communications station that can be controlled by a central computer *fjärrstation;* **remote terminal** = computer terminal connected to a distant computer system *fjärrterminal*

removable [rɪ'muːvəbl] *adj.* which can be removed *flyttbar;* **a removable hard disk**

removal [rɪ'muːv(ə)l] *subst.* taking away *flyttning, avlägsnande;* **the removal of this instruction could solve the problem**

remove [rɪ'muːv] *vb.* to take away *or* to move to another place *flytta;* **the file entry was removed from the floppy disk directory**

rename ['riː'neɪm] *vb.* to give a new name to a file *döpa om;* **save the file and rename it CUSTOM**

rengöringsskiva ⇨ **head**

renumber ['riː'nʌmbə] *subst.* feature of some computer languages that allows the programmer to allocate new values to all *or* some of a program's line numbers *omnumrera; see also* LINE NUMBER

reorganize ['riː'ɔːgənaɪz] *vb.* to organize again *omorganisera;* **wait while the spelling checker database is being reorganized**

repaginate ['riː'pædʒɪneɪt] *vb.* to change the lengths of pages of text before they are printed *ompaginera, byta sidnumrering;* **the dtp package allows simple repagination; the text was repaginated with a new line width**

repeat [rɪ'piːt] *vb.* to do an action again *repetera;* **repeat counter** = register that holds the number of times a routine *or* task has been repeated *repetitionsräknare, varvräknare;* **repeat key** = key on a keyboard which repeats the character pressed *repetitionstangent*

repeater [rɪ'piːtə] *subst.* device that receives a signal, amplifies it, then retransmits it (sometimes regenerating the received signal) *relästation, repeater;* **this cheap repeater does not regenerate the signals**

repeating group [rɪ'piːtɪŋ 'gruːp] *subst.* pattern of data that is duplicated in a bit stream *upprepad grupp*

reperforator ['riːpɜːfəreɪtə] *subst.* machine that punches paper tape according to received signals *fjärrstyrd remsstans;* **reperforator transmitter** = reperforator and a punched tape transmitter connected together *fjärrstansningssystem*

repertoire ['repətwɑː] *subst.* the range of functions of a device *or* software *repertoar, uppsättning;* **the manual describes the full repertoire; character repertoire =** list of all the characters that can be displayed *or* printed *teckenuppsättning;* **instruction repertoire =** all the commands that a system can recognise and execute *instruktionsuppsättning;* *see also* RESERVED WORD

QUOTE the only omissions in the editing repertoire are dump, to list variables currently in use, and find
Computing Today

repetera ⇨ repeat

repetitive letter [rɪ'petətɪv 'letə] *subst.* form letter *or* standard letter into which the details of each addressee (such as name and address) are inserted *massbrev*

replace [rɪ'pleɪs] *vb.* **(a)** to put something back where it was before *sätta tillbaka;* to put something in the place of something else *ersätta;* **the printer ribbons need replacing after several thousand characters (b)** instruction to a computer to find a certain item of data and put another in its place *ersätta; see also* SEARCH AND REPLACE

replay ['riːpleɪ] **1** *subst.* **(a)** playback *or* reading back data *or* a signal from a recording *återspelning* **(b)** repeating a short section of filmed action, usually in slow motion *omspelning;* **the replay clearly showed the winner; this video recorder has a replay feature; instant replay =** feature of video recording systems that allows an action that has just been recorded to be viewed immediately *snabbåterspelning* **2** *vb.* to play back (something which has been recorded) *återspela, spela upp;* **he replayed the tape; she recorded the TV programme on video tape and replayed it the next evening**

replenish [rɪ'plenɪʃ] *vb.* to charge a battery with electricity again *förnya, återuppladda*

replicate ['replɪkeɪt] *vb.* to copy *kopiera, duplicera;* **the routine will replicate your results with very little effort**

replication [,replɪ'keɪʃ(ə)n] *subst.* (i) extra components in a system in case there is a breakdown *or* fault in one *redundans;* (ii) copying a record *or* data to another location *kopiering*

report generator [rɪ'pɔːt 'dʒenəreɪtə] *subst.* software that allows data from database files to be merged with a document (in the form of graphs or tables) to provide a complete report *rapportgenerator*

report program generator (RPG) [rɪ'pɔːt 'prəʊgræm 'dʒenəreɪtə] *subst.* programming language used mainly on personal computers for the preparation of business reports, allowing data in files, databases, etc., to be included *IBM:s programspråk RPG för rapportgenerering (huvudsakligen använt i S/3K och AS/400 idag), rapportgenerator*

represent [,reprɪ'zent] *vb.* **(a)** to act as a symbol for something *representera;* **the hash sign is used to represent a number in a series (b)** to act as a salesman for a product *representera, sälja*

representation [,reprɪzen'teɪʃ(ə)n] *subst.* action of representing something *representation;* **character representation =** combination of bits used for each character code *teckenrepresentation*

representative [,reprɪ'zentətɪv] **1** *adj.* typical example of something *representativ* **2** *subst.* salesman who represents a company *säljare;* **the representative called yesterday about the order**

reprint ['riːprɪnt] **1** *vb.* to print more copies of a document *or* book *nytrycka* **2** *subst.* printing of copies of a book after the first printing *nytryck;* **we ordered a 10,000 copy reprint**

repro ['riːprəʊ] *subst. informal* finished artwork *or* camera-ready copy, ready for filming and printing *repro;* **repro proof =** perfect proof ready to be reproduced *reprokorrektur*

reproduce [,riːprə'djuːs] *vb.* to copy data *or* text from one material *or* medium to another similar one *reproducera, återge*

reproduction [,riːprə'dʌkʃ(ə)n] *subst.* action of copying *kopiering*

reprogram ['riːprəʊgræm] *vb.* to alter a program so that it can be run on another type of computer *omprogrammera*

request [rɪ'kwest] **1** *subst.* thing which someone asks for *begära, anhålla;* **request to send signal (RTS) =** signal sent by a transmitter to a receiver asking if the receiver is ready to accept data (used in the RS232C serial connection) *RTS-signal, sändningsbegäran* **2** *vb.* to ask for something *begära*

require [rɪ'kwaɪə] *vb.* to need something *or* to demand something *begära, fordra;* **delicate computer systems require careful handling**

required hyphen [rɪ'kwaɪəd 'haɪf(ə)n] *or* **hard hyphen** [hɑːd 'haɪf(ə)n] *subst.* hyphen which is always in a word, even if the word is not split (as in co-administrator) *hårt bindestreck; see also* SOFT

requirements [rɪ'kwaɪəmənts] *subst.* things which are needed *krav;* **memory requirements depend on the application software in use**

re-route ['riː'ruːt] *vb.* to send by a different route *omdirigera;* **the call diverter re-routes a call**

rerun ['riː'rʌn] *vb.* to run a program *or* a printing job again *omkörning;* **rerun point** = place in the program from where to start a running again after a crash *or* halt *omkörningspunkt*

res [rez] *see* RESOLUTION; **hi-res** = HIGH RESOLUTION; **lo-res** = LOW RESOLUTION

resave ['riː'seɪv] *vb.* to save again *återlagra;* **it automatically resaves the text**

rescue dump ['reskjuː 'dʌmp] *subst.* data saved on disk automatically when a computer fault occurs (it describes the state of the system at that time, used to help in debugging) *reservdump, säkerhetsdump*

research [rɪ'sɜːtʃ] *subst.* scientific investigation to learn new facts about a field of study *forskning;* **research and development (R & D)** = investigation of new products, discoveries and techniques *forskning och utveckling (FoU);* **the company has spent millions of dollars on R**

reserved sector [rɪ'zɜːvd 'sektə] *subst.* area of disk space that is used only for control data storage *reserverad sektor, upptagen sektor;* **reserved word** = word *or* phrase used as an identifier in a programming language (it performs a particular operation *or* instruction and so cannot be used for other uses by the programmer *or* user) *reserverat ord, upptaget ord*

QUOTE sometimes a process will demand cache space when the only free cache space is reserved for higher priority processes
.EXE

reserverad linje ⇨ **dedicated**

reservkopia ⇨ **backup**

reservsystem ⇨ **standby**

reset ['riː'set] *vb.* **(a)** to return a system to its initial state, to allow a program *or* process to be started again *återställa;* **reset button** *or* **key** = switch that allows a program to be terminated and reset manually *återställningsknapp;* **hard reset** = electrical signal that usually returns the system to its initial state when it was switched on, requiring a reboot *kallstart;* **soft reset** = instruction that terminates any program execution and returns the user to the monitor *or* BIOS *varmstart* **(b)** to set a

register *or* counter to its initial state *återställa;* **when it reaches 999 this counter resets to zero (c)** to set data equal to zero *nollställa*

COMMENT: hard reset is similar to soft reset but with a few important differences: it is a switch that directly signals the CPU, while soft reset signals the operating system; hard reset clears all memory contents, a soft reset does not affect memory contents; hard reset should always reset the system, a soft reset does not always work (if for example, you have really upset the operating system, a soft reset will not work)

resident ['rezɪd(ə)nt] *adj.* (data *or* program) that is always in a computer *resident, permanent;* **resident engineer** = engineer who works permanently for one company *ingenjör anställd av ett företag, men permanent placerad hos ett annat;* **resident software** *or* **memory-resident software** = program that is held permanently in memory (whilst the machine is on) *(minnes)resident programvara*

resident ⇨ **resident**

residual [rɪ'zɪdjʊəl] *adj.* which remains behind *överbliven;* **residual error rate** = ratio between incorrect and undetected received data and total data transmitted *kvarvarande felfrekvens*

residue check ['rezɪdjuː 'tʃek] *subst.* error detection check in which the received data is divided by a set number and the remainder is checked against the required remainder *restkontroll*

resist [rɪ'zɪst] **1** *vb.* to fight against something *or* to refuse to do something *motstå* **2** *subst.* substance used to protect a pattern of tracks on a PCB, that is not affected by etching chemicals *motstånd; see also* PHOTORESIST

resistance [rɪ'zɪst(ə)ns] *subst.* measure of the voltage drop across a component with a current flowing through it *resistans, motstånd; see also* OHM'S LAW

resistor [rɪ'zɪstə] *subst.* electronic component that provides a known resistance *motstånd;* **resistor transistor logic (RTL)** = circuit design method using transistors and resistors *RTL-logik, diskret logik;* **variable resistor** = component whose resistance can be changed by turning a knob *variabelt motstånd*

resolution [,rezə'luːʃ(ə)n] *subst.* number of pixels that a screen *or* printer can display per unit area *upplösning;* **the resolution of most personal computer screens is not much more than 70 dpi (dots per inch); graphic display resolution** = number of pixels that a computer is able to display on the screen *grafikupplösning;* **high resolution (hi-res)** = ability to display *or* detect a very large number of pixels per unit area *högupplösning, högupplösande;* **the high resolution screen can display 640 by 450 pixels; limiting resolution** = maximum number of lines that make up an image on a CRT screen *begränsande upplösning;* **low resolution (low-res)** = ability of a display system to control a number of pixels at a time rather than individual pixels *lågupplösning, lågupplösande*

QUOTE the resolution is 300 dots per inch and the throughput is up to eight pages per minute
Practical Computing

---

resolving power [rɪ'zɒlvɪŋ 'pauə] *subst.* measurement of the ability of an optical system to detect fine black lines on a white background (given as the number of lines per millimetre) *upplösningsförmåga*

resonance ['rez(ə)nəns] *subst.* situation where a frequency applied to a body being the same as its natural frequency, causes it to oscillate with a very large amplitude *resonans*

resource [rɪ'sɔːs] *subst.* products *or* programs which are useful *resurs;* **resource allocation** = dividing available resources in a system between jobs *resurstilldelning, resursfördelning;* **resource sharing** = the use of one resource in a network *or* system by several users *resursdelning*

respond [rɪ'spɒnd] *vb.* to reply *or* to react because of something *svara*

response [rɪ'spɒns] *subst.* reaction caused by something *svar;* **response frame** = page in a videotext system that allows a user to enter data *svarsram i videotex;* **response position** = area of a form that is to be used for optical mark reading data *optisk läsyta;* **response time** = (i) time which passes between the user starting an action (by pressing a key) and the result appearing on the screen *svarstid;* (ii) speed with which a system responds to a stimulus *svarstid;* **the response time of this flight simulator is very good**

rest ⇨ **remainder**

restart ['riːˌstɑːt] *vb.* to start again *starta om;* **first try to restart your system**

restore [rɪ'stɔː] *vb.* to put back into an earlier state *återlagra*

QUOTE first you have to restore the directory that contains the list of deleted files
Personal Computer World

---

restrict [rɪ'strɪkt] *vb.* to keep something within a certain limit *begränsa;* to allow only certain people to access information

begränsa; **the document is restricted, and cannot be placed on open access**

restriction [rɪ'strɪkʃ(ə)n] *subst.* something which restricts (data flow *or* access) *begränsning*

result [rɪ'zʌlt] *subst.* answer *or* outcome of an arithmetic *or* logical operation *resultat*

resultat ⇨ **result**

resume [rɪ'zjuːm] *vb.* to restart the program from the point where it was left, without changing any data *återuppta*

resurs ⇨ **resource**

retain [rɪ'teɪn] *vb.* to keep *kvarhålla, hålla kvar*

retention [rɪ'tenʃ(ə)n] *subst.* keeping *bevarande;* **image retention** = time taken for a TV image to disappear after it has been displayed, caused by long persistence phosphor *bildefterlysning*

retouch ['riːˌtʌtʃ] *vb.* to change a print *or* photograph slightly by hand, to make it clearer *or* to remove any blemishes *retuschera;* **I retouched the scratch mark on the last print; the artwork for the line drawings needs retouching in places**

retransmission ['riːtrænsˈmɪʃ(ə)n] *subst.* signal *or* data that has been retransmitted *omsändning*

retransmit ['riːtrænsˈmɪt] *vb.* to transmit again (a received signal) *återsända*

retrieval [rɪ'triːv(ə)l] *subst.* the process of searching, locating and recovering information from a file *or* storage device *återsökning av data;* **information retrieval** = locating quantities of data stored in a database and producing information from the data *informationsåtersökning;* **information retrieval centre** = research system, providing specific information from a database for a user *system för informationsåtersökning;* **text retrieval** = information retrieval system that allows the user to examine complete documents rather than just a reference to a document *textåtersökning*

retrieve [rɪ'triːv] *vb.* to extract information from a file *or* storage device *återvinna, återsöka;* **these are the records retrieved in that search; this command will retrieve all names beginning with S**

retro- ['retrəu] *prefix* meaning going back *åter-;* progress backwards *tillbaka;* **retrofit** = device *or* accessory added to a system to upgrade it *inbyggnads-, tillbyggnads-*

retrospective parallel running [ˌretrə(u)'spektɪv 'pærəlel 'rʌnɪŋ] *subst.* running a new computer system with old data to check if it is accurate *testkörning med gamla data*

retrospective search [ˌretrə(ʊ)'spektɪv 'sɜːtʃ] *subst.* search of documents on a certain subject since a certain date *begränsad återsökning*

return [rɪ'tɜːn] *subst.* **(a)** instruction that causes program execution to return to the main program from a subroutine *retur, återhopp;* **the program is not working because you missed out the return instruction at the end of the subroutine; return address =** address to be returned to after a called routine finishes *returadress* **(b)** key on a keyboard used to indicate that all the required data has been entered *vagnretur;* **you type in your name and code number then press return (c)** indication of an end of line (in printing) *radslut;* **carriage return (CR) =** code *or* key to indicate the end of an input line and to move the cursor to the start of the next line *radslutstecken*

return to zero signal [rɪ'tɜːn tə 'zɪərəʊ 'sɪgn(ə)l] recording reference mark taken as the level of unmagnetized tape *RZ-signal* NOTE: opposite is **non return to zero**

COMMENT: the return address is put on the stack by the call instruction and provides the address of the instruction after the call, which is to be returned to after the called routine has finished

retuschera ⇨ **touch up**

reveal [rɪ'viːl] *vb.* to display previously hidden information once a condition has been met *avslöja, visa*

reverse [rɪ'vɜːs] **1** *adj.* going in the opposite direction *back-, omvänd;* **reverse channel =** low speed control data channel between a receiver and transmitter *backkanal;* **reverse characters =** characters which are displayed in the opposite way to other characters for emphasis (as black on white *or* white on black, when other characters are the opposite) *backsteg(ning)stecken, tecken i negativt video;* **reverse index =** movement of a printer head up half a line to print superscripts *skriva upphöjd text;* **reverse interrupt =** signal sent by a receiver to request the termination of transmissions *mottagaravbrott;* **reverse polarity =** situation where the positive and negative terminals have been confused, resulting in the equipment not functioning *omvänd polaritet;* **reverse Polish notation (RPN) =** mathematical operations written in a logical way, so that the operator appears after the numbers to be acted upon, this removes the need for brackets *omvänd polsk notation;* **three plus four, minus two is written in RPN as 3 4 + 2 - = 5; normal notation: (x-y) + z, but using RPN: xy - z+;**

same as POSTFIX NOTATION; **reverse video =** screen display mode where white and black are reversed (colours are complemented) *inverterad videobild* **2** *vb.* to go *or* travel in the opposite direction *vända om;* to send (control) data from a receiver to a transmitter *kontrollåtersöka (från sändare till mottagare)*

QUOTE the options are listed on the left side of the screen, with active options shown at the top left in reverse video
PC User

revert [rɪ'vɜːt] *vb.* to return to a normal state *återgå;* **after the rush order, we reverted back to our normal speed; revert command =** command (in text) that returns a formatted page to its original state *återställningskommando*

review [rɪ'vjuː] *vb.* to see again *or* replay and check *granska, undersöka;* **the program allows the user to review all wrongly spelled words**

revise [rɪ'vaɪz] *vb.* to update *or* correct a version of a document *or* file *granska, revidera;* **the revised version has no mistakes**

rewind [riː'waɪnd] *vb.* to return a tape *or* film *or* counter to its starting point *återspola, spola tillbaka;* **the tape rewinds onto the spool automatically**

rewrite ['riː'raɪt] **1** *vb.* to write something again *skriva om; see also* REGENERATE **2** *subst.* act of writing something again *omskrivning;* **the program is in its second rewrite**

RF ['ɑː'ref] = RADIO FREQUENCY; **RF modulator** *or* **radio frequency modulator =** electronic circuit that modulates a high frequency carrier signal with a video signal to enable it to be displayed on a domestic TV *radiofrekvens*

RGB ['ɑːdʒiː'biː] = RED, GREEN, BLUE high-definition monitor system that uses three separate input signals controlling red, green and blue colour picture beams *RGB-bildskärm, RGB-signal, RGB-kontakt*

COMMENT: there are three colour guns producing red, green and blue beams acting on groups of three phosphor dots at each pixel location

rheostat ['rɪə(ʊ)stæt] *subst.* resistance with a movable wiper that will provide a variable output voltage *reostat* NOTE: also called **variable potential divider**

RI ['ɑː'raɪ] = RING INDICATOR

ribbon ['rɪbən] *subst.* long thin flat piece of material *band;* **printer ribbon =** roll of inked material which passes between a printhead and the paper *färgband;* **ribbon**

cable = number of insulated conductors arranged next to each other forming a flat cable *bandkabel*

right [raɪt] *adj.* not left *höger;* **right justify** = to align the right margin so that the text is straight *högerjustera;* **right justification** = aligning the text and spacing characters so that the right margin is straight *högerjustering;* **right shift** = to move a section of data one bit to the right *högerskift; see also* LOGICAL SHIFT, ARITHMETIC SHIFT

rigid ['rɪdʒɪd] *adj.* hard *or* which cannot bend *styv*

riksledning ⇨ **trunk**

rikssamtal ⇨ **trunk call**

riksväxel ⇨ **trunk exchange**

riktmärke ⇨ **benchmark**

riktnummer ⇨ **dialling**

ring [rɪŋ] **1** *subst.* data list whose last entry points back to the first entry *cirkulär lista;* **ring (data) network** = type of network where each terminal is connected one after the other in a circle *ringnät; see also* CHAINED LIST **2** *vb.* to telephone *ringa;* **ring back system** = remote computer system in which a user attempting to access it phones once, allows it to ring a number of times, disconnects, waits a moment, then redials (usually in a bulletin board system) *återuppringande system;* **ring down** = to call a number of users in a telephone network *ringa upp flera samtidigt;* **ring indicator (RI)** = signal from a line answering device that it has detected a call to the DTE and has answered by going into an off-hook state *ringsignalsindikering*

ring counter ['rɪŋˌkaʊntə] *subst.* electronic counter in which any overflow from the last digitis fed into the input *ringräknare*

ringnät ⇨ **loop, ring**

ring shift ['rɪŋˌʃɪft] *subst.* data movement to the left *or* right in a word, the bits falling outside the word boundary are discarded, the free positions are filled with zeros *cirkulärt skifte*

ringsignalsundertryckning ⇨ **anti-tinkle suppression**

RIP [rɪp] = REST IN PROPORTION printing instruction to indicate that all the material is to be reduced *or* enlarged in the same proportion *instruktionen "ändra proportionellt"*

ripple ['rɪpl] *subst.* small alternating current voltage apparent on a badly regulated direct current output supply *rippel, brum*

ripple-through carry ['rɪplˌθruː 'kærɪ] *subst.* one operation producing a carry out from a sum and a carry in *serieöverföring (i asynkronräknare)*

RISC [rɪsk] = REDUCED INSTRUCTION SET COMPUTER CPU design whose instruction set contains a small number of simple fast-executing instructions, that makes program writing more complex, but increases speed *optimalkod; see also* WISC

rise time ['raɪztaɪm] *subst.* time taken for a voltage to increase its amplitude (from 10 to 90 per cent or zero to RMS value of its final amplitude) *stigtid;* **the circuit has a fast rise time** = electronic circuit that is able to handle rapidly changing signals such as very high frequency signals *kretsen har en snabb stigtid*

RJE ['aːdʒeiˈiː] = REMOTE JOB ENTRY batch processing system where instructions are transmitted to the computer from a remote terminal *fjärrinmatning av jobb (enligt IBM:s RJE-system)*

RMS ['aːremˈes] = ROOT MEAN SQUARE; **RMS line current** = the root mean square of the electrical current on a line *effektivvärde*

RO ['aːrˈəʊ] = RECEIVE ONLY computer terminal that can only accept and display data, not transmit *visningsterminal*

robot ['rəʊbɒt] *subst.* device which can be programmed to carry out certain manufacturing tasks which are similar to tasks carried out by people *robot*

QUOTE so far no robot sensor has been devised which can operate quickly enough to halt the robot if a human being is in its path of work
IEE News

robotics [rə(ʊ)ˈbɒtɪks] *subst.* study of artificial intelligence, programming and building involved with robot construction *robot(konstruktions)teori*

robust [rə(ʊ)ˈbʌst] *adj.* solid *or* (system) which can resume working after a fault *robust, kraftig, tålig;* **this hard disk is not very robust**

robustness [rə(ʊ)ˈbʌstnɪs] *subst.* **(a)** strength of a system's casing and its ability to be knocked *or* dropped *(slag)tålighet* **(b)** system's ability to continue functioning even with errors *or* faults during a program execution *tålighet*

rogue indicator ['rəʊgˌɪndɪkeɪtə] *subst.* special code used only for control applications such as end of file marker *speciell styrkod*

rogue value ['rəʊgˌvæljuː] *or* **terminator** ['tɜːmɪˌneɪtə] *subst.* item in a list of data, which shows that the list is terminated *slutvärde, slutmarkör*

role indicator ['rəʊl‚ɪndɪkeɪtə] *subst.* symbol used to show the role of an index entry in its particular context *rollindikator*

roll [rəʊl] **1** *subst.* length of film *or* tape wound around itself *filmrulle;* **he put a new roll of film into the camera 2** *vb.* **(a)** to rotate a device about its axis *rulla, snurra* **(b)** to start filming *filma;* **roll in/roll out =** the transfer of one process (in a multiprogramming system) from storage to processor then back once it has had its allocated processing time *flytta in (ut)*

rollback ['rəʊlbæk] *subst.* reloading software after the master software has been corrupted *återladdning (av originalprogram)*

roll-in [rəʊl 'ɪn] *vb.* to transfer data from backing store into main memory *flytta in*

rolling headers ['rəʊlɪŋ 'hedəz] *subst.* titles *or* headers of (teletext) pages displayed as they are received *löpande sidhuvuden*

roll-out [rəʊl 'aʊt] *vb.* to save the contents of main memory onto backing store *flytta ut*

rollover ['rəʊl‚əʊvə] *subst.* keyboard with a small temporary buffer so that it can still transmit correct data when several keys are pressed at once *tangentbordsbuffert;* **key rollover =** use of a buffer between the keyboard and computer to provide rapid keystroke storage for fast typists *tangentbordsbuffert*

roll scroll [rəʊl ‚skrəʊl] *vb.* displayed text that moves up *or* down the computer screen one line at a time *radrullning*

ROM [rɒm] = READ ONLY MEMORY; **CD-ROM** *or* **compact disk-ROM =** compact disk-ROM small plastic disk that is used as a high capacity ROM device, data is stored in binary form as holes etched on the surface which are then read by a laser *läsminne;* **ROM cartridge =** software stored in a ROM mounted in a cartridge that can be easily plugged into a computer *läsminnespatron* NOTE: there is no plural for ROM, and it is often used without the article: **the file is stored in ROM**

roman ['rəʊmən] *subst.* ordinary typeface, neither italic nor bold *typsnittsarten antikva (i grundform);* **the text is set in Times Roman**

Roman numerals ['rəʊmən 'njuːmər(ə)lz] *subst.* figures written I, II, III, IV, etc. (as opposed to Arabic numerals such as 1, 2, 3, 4, etc.) *romerska siffror*

romware ['rɒmweə] *subst.* software which is stored in ROM *program(vara) i läsminne*

root [ruːt] *subst.* **(a)** starting node from which all paths branch in a data tree structure *rot* **(b)** fractional power of a number *rot;* **square root =** number raised to the power one half *kvadratrot;* **the square root of 25 is 5; root mean square (RMS) =** measure of the amplitude of a signal (equal to the squareroot of the mean value of the signal) *effektivvärde;* **the root mean square of the pure sinusoidal signal is 0.7071of its amplitude**

rotary ['rəʊtərɪ] *adj.* which works by turning *roterande;* **rotary camera =** camera able to photograph microfilm as it is moved in front of the lens by moving the film at the same time *roterande kamera;* **rotary press =** printing press whose printing plate is cylindrical *rotationspress*

rotate [rə(ʊ)'teɪt] *vb.* to move data within a storage location in a circular manner *rotera*

rotation [rə(ʊ)'teɪʃ(ə)n] *subst.* amount by which an object has been rotated *rotation;* **bit rotation** *or* **rotate operation =** shifting a pattern of bits in a word to the left or right, the old last bit moving to the new first bit position *rotationsoperation;* **matrix rotation =** swapping the rows with the columns in an array (equal to rotating by 90 degrees) *matrisrotation; see also* SHIFT (CYCLIC)

rotera ⇨ **rotate**

round [raʊnd] **1** *adj.* which goes in a circle *rund;* **round robin =** way of organizing the use of a computer by several users, who each use it for a time and then pass it on the next in turn *"alla-mot-alla"organisation* **2** *vb.* **to round down =** to approximate a number to a slightly lower one of lower precision *avrunda nedåt;* **we can round down 2.651 to 2.65; to round off =** to approximate a number to a slightly larger *or* smaller one of lower precision *avrunda;* **round off 23.456 to 23.46; round off errors =** inaccuracies in numbers due to rounding off *avrundningsfel;* **to round up =** to approximate a number to a slightly larger one of lower precision *avrunda uppåt;* **we can round up 2.647 to 2.65**

rounding ['raʊndɪŋ] *subst.* **(a)** approximation of a number to a slightly larger *or* smaller one of lower precision *avrundning;* **rounding error =** error in a result caused by rounding off the number *avrundningsfel* **(b)** giving graphics a smoother look *kantjämna;* **character rounding =** making a displayed character more pleasant to look at (within the limits of pixel size) by making sharp corners and edges smooth *kantutjämning*

route [ruːt] *subst.* path taken by a message between a transmitter and receiver in a network *väg;* **the route taken was not the most direct since a lot of nodes were busy**

routine [ruːˈtiːn] *subst.* a number of instructions that perform a particular task, but are not a complete program; they are included as part of a program *rutin;* **the routine copies the screen display onto a printer; the RETURN instruction at the end of the routine sends control back to the main program; closed routine** *or* **closed subroutine** = one section of code at a location, that is used by all calls to the routine *sluten rutin;* **fall back routines** = routines that are called *or* processes which are executed by a user when a machine *or* system has failed *reservrutiner, nödfallsrutiner;* **floating-point routines** = set of routines that allow floating-point numbers to be handled and processed *flyttalsrutiner;* **input routine** = short section of code that accepts data from an external device, such as reading an entry from a keyboard *inmatningsrutin;* **open routine** *or* **open subroutine** = set of instructions in a routine, that are copied to whichever part of the program requires them *öppen rutin;* **packing routine** = program which packs data into a small storage area *packningsrutin, arkiveringsrutin; see also* CALL, RETURN

COMMENT: routines are usually called from a main program to perform a task, control is then returned to the part of the main program from which the routine was called once that task is complete

routing [ˈruːtɪŋ] *subst.* determining a suitable route for a message through a network *vägval;* **there is a new way of routing data to the central computer; routing overheads** = actions that have to be taken when routing messages *vägvalsadministration;* **the information transfer rate is very much less once all routing overheads have been accommodated; routing page** = videotext page describing the routes to other pages *vägvisningssida;* **routing table** = list of preferred choices for a route for a message *vägtabell, vägvalstabell*

row [rəʊ] *subst.* **(a)** (i) line of printed *or* displayed characters *rad;* (ii) horizontal line on a punched card *rad;* **the figures are presented in rows, not in columns; each entry is separated by a row of dots (b)** horizontal set of data elements in an array *or* matrix *rad*

RPG [ˈɑːpiːˈdʒiː] = REPORT PROGRAM GENERATOR

RS-232C [ˈɑːrˈesˈtuːˈθriːˈtuːˈsi] EIA approved standard used in serial data transmission, covering voltage and control signals *gränssnittstandard för seriekommunikation (detsamma som V24)*

COMMENT: the RS232C has now been superceeded by the RS423 and RS422 interface standards, similar to the RS232, but allowing higher transmission rates

RSA cipher system [ˈɑːresˈei ˈsaifə ˈsistəm] the Rivest, Shamir and Adleman public key cipher system *kryptosystem med öppna nycklar*

RS-flip-flop [ˈɑːres ˈflipflɒp] = RESET-SET FLIP-FLOP electronic bistable device whose output can be changed according to the Reset and Set inputs *RS-vippa; see also* FLIP-FLOP

RTE [ˈɑːrtiːˈiː] = REAL TIME EXECUTION

RTL [ˈɑːrtiːˈel] = RESISTOR-TRANSISTOR LOGIC

RTS [ˈɑːrtiːˈes] = REQUEST TO SEND SIGNAL

rubber banding [ˈrʌbəˈbændɪŋ] *see* ELASTIC BANDING

rubout [ˈrʌbaʊt] *see* ERASE

rubric [ˈruːbrɪk] *subst.* printed headings of a book chapter *or* section *rubrik*

rubrik ⇨ **heading**

rubrikstilstorlek ⇨ **display**

rule [ruːl] *subst.* **(a)** set of conditions that describe a function *regel;* **the rule states that you wait for the clear signal before transmitting; rule-based system** = software that applies the rules and knowledge defined by experts in a particular field to a user's data to solve a problem *regelbaserat system* **(b)** thin line in printing *linje;* **em rule** = dash as long as an em, used to show that words are separated *tankstreck;* **en rule** = dash as long as an en, used to show that words are joined *bindestreck*

ruler [ˈruːlə] *subst.* graduated line, displaying the horizontal position of text *or* distance *linjal*

rulla ⇨ **roll, scroll**

rullband ⇨ **tape**

rullgardinsmeny ⇨ **pop, pull-down**

run [rʌn] **1** *subst.* execution by a computer of a set of instructions *or* programs *or* procedures *körning, exekvering;* **the next invoice run will be on Friday; program run** = executing (in correct order) the instructions in a program *programkörning, programexekvering;* **run indicator** = indicator bit *or* LED that shows that a computer is currently executing a program *körindikator* **2** *vb.* to make a device work *köra, exekvera;* **the computer has been**

running ten hours a day; do not interrupt the spelling checker while it is running; the new package runs on our PC; parallel running = running old and new computer systems together to allow the new system to be checked before it becomes the only system used *parallellkörning, parallellexekvering;* **run around =** to fit text around an image on a printed page *textsätta;* **run in =** to operate a system at a lower capacity for a time in case of any faults *köra in*

runaway ['rʌnəweɪ] *subst.* uncontrolled operation of a device *or* computer (due to a malfunction *or* error) *skenande operation*

rund ⇨ round

rundstrålande ⇨ omnidirectional

running head ['rʌnɪŋ 'hed] *subst.* title line of each page in a document *kolumntitel*

run on [rʌn 'ɒn] *vb.* **(a)** to make text continue without a break *sätta i följd;* **the line can run on to the next without any space (b)** to print more copies to add to a print run *utöka tryckupplagan;* **we decided to run on 3,000 copies to the first printing; run-on price =** price of extra copies printed after a fixed print run *pris per följande exemplar*

run-time ['rʌntaɪm] *or* **run-duration** ['rʌn djʊ(ə)'reɪʃ(ə)n] **1** *subst.* **(a)** period of a time a program takes to run *körtid, exekveringstid* **(b)** time during which a computer is executing a program *körtid* **2** *adj.* (operation) carried out only when a program is running *kör-, exekverings-;* **run-time error =** fault only detected when a program is run *or* error made while a program is running *körfel, exekveringsfel;* *see also* EXECUTION ERROR; **run-time system =** software that is required in main storage while a program is running (to execute instructions to peripherals, etc.) *laddat (exekverbart) system*

rusning ⇨ race

ruta ⇨ frame ✱

rutin ⇨ routine

rutinuppgifter ⇨ housekeeping

rutraster ⇨ grid

R/W ['ɑ:'dʌblju:] = READ/WRITE

R/W cycle ['ɑ:'dʌblju: 'saɪkl] = READ/WRITE CYCLE sequence of events used to retrieve *or* store data *läs-skrivcykel*

R/W head ['ɑ:'dʌblju: 'hed] = READ/WRITE HEAD electromagnetic device that allows data to be read from *or* written to a storage medium *läs-skrivhuvud*

RX ['ɑ:'reks] = RECEIVE, RECEIVER **the RXed signal needs to be amplified**

rå ⇨ raw

rådataband ⇨ idiot tape

rå kant ⇨ deckle edge

räckvidd ⇨ range

räddningsprogram ⇨ document

räkna ⇨ count

räknare ⇨ calculator, counter

rätt ⇨ correct

rätta till ⇨ rectify

röntgen ⇨ X-ray

rörledningsdator ⇨ pipeline
(computer)

röstavtryck ⇨ voice

röstenhet ⇨ voice unit

röstigenkänning ⇨ voice

röstinmatning ⇨ voice

Ss

S100 bus ['es'wʌn'hʌndrəd bʌs] *or* **S-100 bus** *subst.* IEEE-696 standard bus, a popular 8 and 16 bit microcomputer bus using 100 lines and a 100-pin connector *S-100-bussen, äldre datorbuss för persondator; see also* BUS
NOTE: say "S one hundred bus"

SAFE [seɪf] = SIGNATURE ANALYSIS USING FUNCTIONAL ANALYSIS signature validation technique *teknik för verifiering av underskrifter*

safe area ['seɪf 'eərɪə] *subst.* area of a TV image that will be seen on a standard television set *säkerhetsområde*

safety net ['seɪftɪnet] *subst.* software *or* hardware device that protects the system *or* files from excessive damage in the event of a system crash *skyddsnät;* **if there is a power failure, we have a safety net in the form of a UPS**

salami technique [sə'lɑ:mɪ tek'ni:k] *subst.* computer fraud involving many separate small transactions that are difficult to detect and trace *"öresavrundning" vid datoriserat bedrägeri*

SAM [sæm] = SERIAL ACCESS MEMORY storage where a particular data item can only be accessed by reading through all the previous items in the list (as opposed to random access) *sekventiellt minnne, serieåtkomstminne*

✱ Cor) (EDP) text box (in a dialog box)

COMMENT: magnetic tape is a form of SAM; you have to go through the whole tape to access one item, while disks provide random access to stored data

samband ⊳ relevance

samhälle ⊳ community

samkommunikation ⊳ interactive

samla in ⊳ collect, gather

sammanbindning ⊳ continuity

sammanfläta ⊳ interlace

sammankoppling ⊳ interconnection

sammansatt krets ⊳ composite circuit

sammanställning ⊳ juxtaposition

sample ['sɑːmpl] **1** *subst.* measurement of a signal at a point in time *stickprov;* **the sample at three seconds showed an increase; sample and hold circuit** = circuit that freezes an analog input signal for long enough for an A/D converter to produce a stable output *hållkrets* **2** *vb.* to obtain a number of measurements of a signal that can be used to provide information about the signal *insamla (mätvärden);* **sampling interval** = time period between two consecutive samples *provtagningsintervall;* **sampling rate** = number of measurements of a signal recorded every second *provfrekvens; see also* ANALOG/DIGITAL CONVERSION, QUANTIZE

sampler ['sɑːmplə] *subst.* **(a)** electronic circuit that takes many samples of a signal and stores them for future analysis *stickprovsinsamlare* **(b)** electronic circuit used to record audio signals in digital form and store them to allow future playback *sampler, ljuddigitaliserare*

COMMENT: if the sampling is on a music signal and the sampling frequency is great enough, digitally stored signals sound like the original analog signal. For analog signals, a sampling rate of at least two times the greatest frequency is required to provide adequate detail

samsortering ⊳ merge

samtal ⊳ call

samtalsräknare ⊳ logger

samåtkomst ⊳ integrated

sann ⊳ high, TRUE

sans serif [sæn'serɪf] *subst.* typeface whose letters have no serifs *grotesk (fackterm för typsnitt utan schatteringar)*

sapphire ['sæfaɪə] *subst.* blue-coloured precious stone used as a substrate for certain chips *safir*

SAR ['eseɪɑː] = STORE ADDRESS REGISTER register within the CPU that contains the address of the next location to be accessed *programpekare, nästa-adresspekare*

satellite ['sætəlaɪt] *subst.* **(a)** device that orbits the earth receiving, processing and transmitting signals *or* generating images *or* data to be transmitted back to earth, such as weather pictures *satellit;* **communications satellite** = satellite that relays radio *or* TV signals from one point on the earth's surface to another *kommunikationssatellit;* **direct broadcast satellite (DBS)** = TV and radio signal broadcast over a wide area from an earth station via a satellite to homes (received with a dish aerial) *direktsändande satellit, lågeffektstation;* **weather satellite** = device that orbits the earth, transmitting images of the weather systems above the earth's surface *vädersatellit;* **satellite broadcasting** = sending public radio and TV signals from one part of the earth to another, using a communications satellite *satellitöverföring;* **satellite link** = use of a satellite to allow the transmission of data from one point on earth to another *satellitlänk;* **satellite network** = series of satellites which provide wide coverage of an area *satellitnät* **(b)** small system that is part of a larger system *satellit;* **satellite computer** = computer doing various tasks under the control of another computer *satellitdator;* **satellite terminal** = computer terminal that is outside the main network *satellitterminal*

COMMENT: in a network the floppy disk units are called 'satellites' and the hard disk unit the 'server'. In a star network each satellite is linked individually to a central server

sats ⊳ batch, form

satsvis bearbetning ⊳ batch processor

satsvis databehandling ⊳ processing

saturation [ˌsætʃəˈreɪʃ(ə)n] *subst.* point where a material cannot be further magnetized *mättning;* **saturation noise** = errors due to saturation of a magnetic storage medium *mättningsbrus;* **saturation testing** = testing a communications network, by transmitting large quantities of data and messages over it *mättningsprovning*

save [seɪv] *vb.* to store data *or* a program on an auxiliary storage device *spara, lagra;* this WP saves the text every 15 minutes in case of a fault; don't forget to save the file before switching off; **save area** = temporary storage area of main memory, used for registers and control data *mellanlagringsarea*

sawtooth waveform ['sɔːtuːθ 'weɪvfɔːm] *subst.* waveform that regularly rises to a maximum and drops to a minimum in a linear way *sågtandsvåg*

SBC ['esbiːˈsiː] = SINGLE BOARD COMPUTER computer whose main components such as processor, input/output and memory are all contained on one PCB *enkortsdator*

S-box ['esˈbɒks] *subst.* matrix transformation process used in certain cipher systems *S-box-överföring*

scalar ['skeɪlə] *subst.* variable that has a single value assigned to it *skalär;* **a scalar has a single magnitude value, a vector has two or more positional values**

scale [skeɪl] **1** *subst.* ratio of two values *skala;* **large scale** *or* **small scale** = working with large *or* small amounts of data *stor (liten) skala;* **large scale integration (LSI)** = integrated circuit with 500 - 10,000 components *höggradig kretsintegration;* **medium scale integration (MSI)** = integrated circuit with 10 - 500 components *medelgradig kretsintegration;* **small scale integration (SSI)** = integrated circuit with 1 - 10 components *låggradig kretsintegration;* **very large scale integration (VLSI)** = integrated circuit with 10,000 - 100,000 components *mycket höggradigkretsintegration* **2** *vb.* **to scale down** *or* **scale up** = to lower *or* increase in proportion *förminska, förstora*

scan [skæn] **1** *subst.* examination of an image *or* object *or* list of items to obtain data *avsökning;* **the heat scan of the computer quickly showed which component was overheating; the scan revealed which records were now out of date; raster scan** = one sweep of the picture beam horizontally across the front of the CRT screen *rasteravsökning* **2** *vb.* to examine and produce data from the shape *or* state of an object *or* drawing *or* file *or* list of items *avsöka;* **he scanned the map for Teddington; the facsimile machine scans the picture and converts this to digital form before transmission; the machine scans at up to 300 dpi resolution; scan area** = section of an image read by a scanner *avsökningsyta;* **scan length** = number of items in a file *or* list that are examined in a scan *aktiv söklängd*

scanner ['skænə] *subst.* device that scans *avsökare, bildläsare, dokumentläsare, inläsare;* **a scanner reads the bar-code on the product label using a laser beam and photodiode; scanner memory** = memory area allocated to store images which have been scanned *avsökningsminne;* **image**

scanner = input device that converts documents *or* drawings *or* photographs into digitized machine-readable form *bildläsare, scanner;* **optical scanner** = equipment that converts an image into electrical signals which can be stored in and displayed on a computer *optisk bildläsare*

COMMENT: a scanner can be a device using photoelectric cells as in an image digitizer, or a device that samples data from a process

scanner ⇨ **scanner**

scanning ['skænɪŋ] *subst.* action of examining and producing data from the shape of an object *or* drawing *avsökning, läsning;* **scanning device** = device that allows micrographic images to be selected rapidly from a reel of film *bildläsare (för mikrofilm);* **scanning error** = error introduced while scanning an image *läsfel, avsökningsfel;* **scanning radio receiver** = radio receiver that can check a range of frequencies to find a strong signal *or* a particular station *avsökande radiomottagare;* **scanning line** = path traced on a CRT screen by the picture beam *avsökningslinje;* **scanning rate** = time taken to scan one line of a CRT image *sveptid;* **scanning resolution** = ability of a scanner to distinguish between small points (usual resolution is 300 dpi) *upplösning;* **scanning software** = dedicated program that controls a scanner and allows certain operations (rotate *or* edit *or* store, etc.) to be performed on a scanned image *styrprogramvara för bildläsare;* **scanning speed** = how fast a line *or* image is scanned *avsökningshastighet, inläsningshastighet;* **throughput is 1.3 inches per second scanning speed; its scanning speed is 9.9 seconds for an 8.5inch by 11inch document;** *(of modem)* **auto-baud scanning** *or* **auto-baud sensing** = circuit that can automatically sense and select the correct baud rate for a line *automatisk hastighetsinställning*

COMMENT: a modem with auto-baud scanning can automatically sense which baud rate to operate on and switches automatically to that baud rate

QUOTE scanning time per page ranged from about 30 seconds to three minutes
PC Business World

scanning spot ['skænɪŋspɒt] *subst.* **(a)** small area of an image that is being read by a facsimile machine that moves over the whole image *bildpunkt, avsökningspunkt* **(b)** small area covered by the picture beam on a TV screen that moves to follow a scanning line to write the whole of an image onto the screen *skärmpunkt;* **scanning spot beam** = satellite transmission to a number of areas, as the satellite passes over them *avsökningsstråle*

scatter ['skætə] *subst.* part of a beam that is deflected *or* refracted *spridning;* **scatter graph** = individual points *or* values plotted on a two axis graph *spridningsdiagram;* **scatter proofs** = proofs not arranged in any order prior to PMT *spridda korrektur; see also* BACKSCATTER

scatter load ['skætə'ləʊd] *vb.* to load sequential data into various (non-continuous) locations in memory *spridningslagring;* **scatter read** = to access and read sequential data stored in various (non-continuous) locations *spridnings-läsning*

scavenging ['skævɪn(d)ʒɪŋ] *vb.* to search through and access database material without permission *söka i databaser utan tillstånd*

schablon ⇨ **stencil**

schedule ['ʃedjuːl] **1** order in which tasks are to be done *or* order in which CPU time will be allocated to processes in a multi-user system *(tidsfördelnings)schema* **2** *vb.* to organize the broadcasting of TV *or* radio programmes at certain times *schemalägga*

scheduled circuits ['ʃedjuːld 'sɜːkɪts] *subst.* telephone lines for data communications only *fasta linjer*

scheduler ['ʃedjuːlə] *subst.* program which organizes use of a CPU *or* of peripherals which are shared by several users *tidsfördelningsfunktion*

scheduling ['ʃedjuːlɪŋ] *subst.* **(a)** method of working which allows several users to share the use of a CPU *tidsfördelning;* **job scheduling** = arranging the order in which jobs are to be processed *tidsfördelning av jobb* **(b) programme scheduling** = organizing the broadcasting of radio *or* TV programmes at certain times *schemaläggning av program*

schema ['skiːmə] *subst.* graphical description of a process *or* database structure *strukturdiagram*

schema ⇨ **chart, schedule**

schemadiagram ⇨ **schematic**

schemalägga ⇨ **schedule**

schematic [skɪ'mætɪk] *adj. & subst.* (diagram) showing system components and how they are connected *schematisk, schemadiagram*

schematisk ⇨ **schematic**

scientific [ˌsaɪən'tɪfɪk] *adj.* referring to science *vetenskaplig, vetenskaps-;* **scientific calculator** = specially adapted calculator

which has several scientific functions built into it *teknikräknare, kalkylator med tekniska och vetenskapliga funktioner*

scissor ['sɪzə] *vb.* to remove the areas of text *or* graphics that lie outside a page's limits *skära, putsa*

SCR ['essiɑː] = SEQUENCE CONTROL REGISTER

scramble ['skræmbl] *vb.* to code speech *or* data which is transmitted in such a way that it cannot be understood unless it is decoded *slumpkoda*

scrambler ['skræmblə] *subst.* **(a)** device that codes a data stream into a pseudo random form before transmission to eliminate any series of one's or zero's *or* alternate one's and zero's that would cause synchronization problems at the receiver and produce unwanted harmonics *slumpkodare* **(b)** device that codes speech *or* other signals prior to transmission so that someone who is listening in without authorization cannot understand what is being transmitted (the scrambled signals are de-scrambled on reception to provide the original signals) *slumpkodare, skramlare;* **he called the President on the scrambler telephone**

scratch [skrætʃ] **1** *subst.* mark on a disk *or* on a film *repa* **2** *vb.* to delete *or* move an area of memory to provide room for other data *tömma*

scratch file ['skrætʃfaɪl] *or* **work file** ['wɜːkfaɪl] *subst.* work area which is being used for current work *slaskfil;* **scratch tape** = magnetic tape used for a scratch file *slaskband*

scratchpad ['skrætʃpæd] *subst.* workspace *or* area of high speed memory that is used for temporary storage of data currently in use *anteckningsblock, slaskarea*

screen [skriːn] **1** *subst.* **(a)** display device capable of showing a quantity of information, such as a CRT *or* VDU *skärm, bildskärm; see also* READOUT; **screen border** = margin around text displayed on a screen *skärmkant;* **screen buffer** = temporary storage area for characters *or* graphics before they are displayed *skärmbuffert;* **screen dump** = outputting the text *or* graphics displayed on a screen to a printer *skärmdump;* **screen editor** *or* **text editor** = software that allows the user to edit text on-screen, with one complete screen of information being displayed at a time *redigeringsprogram;* **screen format** = way in which a screen is laid out *skärmformat;* **screen grab** = digitizing a single frame from a display *or* television *skärmbildfångst, lagring i minne;* **screen memory** = in a memory-mapped screen, the area of memory that represents the whole screen, usually with one byte representing one *or* a number of pixels *skärmminne, videominne;* **on-screen =** information displayed on a screen *på skärmen;* **the dtp package offers on-screen font display; text screen =** area of a computer screen that has been set up to display text *textskärm;* **touch screen =** computer display that allows the user to control the cursor position by touching the screen *pekskärm* (b) thing which protects *skydd, avskärmning, skärm;* **magnetic screen =** metal screen to prevent stray magnetic fields affecting electronic components *magnetskärm;* **without the metal screen over the power supply unit, the computer just produced garbage 2** *vb.* (a) to protect something with a screen *avskärma;* **the PSU is screened against interference** (b) to display *or* show information *visa, ta fram, förevisa;* **the film is now being screened** (c) to select *utföra en sökning*

QUOTE the screen memory is, in fact a total of 4K in size, the first 2K hold the character codes, of which 1K is displayed. Scrolling brings the remaining area into view

Computing Today

screenful ['skri:nful] *subst.* complete frame of information displayed on a screen *full skärm*

script [skrɪpt] *subst.* text which will be spoken by actors in a film *or* TV programme *manuskript*

scriptwriter ['skrɪpt,raɪtə] *subst.* person who writes film *or* TV scripts *manusförfattare*

scroll [skrəʊl] *vb.* to move displayed text vertically *or* down the screen, one line *or* pixel at a time *rulla;* **roll scroll =** displayed text that moves up *or* down the screen one line at a time *radrullning;* **smooth scroll =** text that is moved up a screen pixel by pixel rather than line by line, which gives a smoother movement *mjukrullning;* **scroll mode =** terminal mode that transmits every key press and displays what is received *rullningsläge*

scrub [skrʌb] *vb.* to wipe information off a disk *or* remove data from store *radera;* **scrub all files with the .BAK extension**

SCSI ['essi:es'aɪ] = SMALL COMPUTER SYSTEM INTERFACE

QUOTE the system uses SCSI for connecting to the host and ESDI for interconnecting among drives within a multidrive system

Byte

SD ['es'di:] = SINGLE DENSITY (DISK)

SDI ['esdi:'aɪ] = SELECTIVE DISSEMINATION OF INFORMATION

SDLC ['esdi:el'si:] = SYNCHRONOUS DATA LINK CONTROL

SDR ['esdi:'ɑː] = STORE DATA REGISTER register in a CPU which holds data before it is processed *or* moved to memory location *mellanlagringsregister*

seal [si:l] *vb.* to close something tightly so that it cannot be opened *försegla, försluta;* **the hard disk is in a sealed case**

search [sɜːtʃ] **1** *subst.* process of looking for and identifying a character *or* word *or* section of data in a document *or* file *sökning;* **chaining search =** searching a file of elements arranged as a chained list *kedjesökning;* **linear search =** search method which compares each item in a list with the search key until the correct entry is found (starting with the first item and working sequentially towards the end) *linjär sökning;* **retrospective search =** search of documents on a certain subject since a certain date *sökning bakåt (efter visst datum);* **search key =** (i) word *or* phrase that is to be found in a text *söknyckel;* (ii) field and other data used to select various records in a database *söknyckel;* **search memory =** method of data retrieval that uses part of the data rather than an address to locate the data *minnessökning, sökning på innehåll;* **search and replace =** feature on some word processors that allows the user to find certain words *or* phrases, then replace them with another word *or* phrase *sök och ersätt;* **global search and replace =** word-processor search and replace function covering a complete file *or* document *genomgående sökning och ersättning* **2** *vb.* to look for an item of data *söka*

QUOTE a linear search of 1,000 items takes 500 comparisons to find the target, and 1,000 to report that it isn't present. A binary search of the same set of items takes roughly ten divisions either to find or not to find the target

Personal Computer World

searching storage ['sɜːtʃɪŋ 'stɔːrɪdʒ] *subst.* method of data retrieval that uses part of the data rather than an address to locate the data *sökning i minne, minnessökning, sökning på innehåll*

SECAM ['si:,kæm] = SEQUENTIEL A MEMOIRE

COMMENT: standard which defines TV and video formats in France, the USSR and Saudi Arabia. It is similar to PAL, and uses 625 horizontal scan lines and 50 frames per second

second ['sek(ə)nd] *adj.* (thing) which comes after the first *andra;* **we have two computers, the second one being used if the first is being repaired; second generation computers =** computer which used transistors instead of valves *andra generationens datorer;* **second-level addressing** = instruction that contains an address at which the operand is stored *tvånivåadressering;* **second sourcing** = granting a licence to another manufacturer to produce an electronic item *or* component when production capacity is not great enough to meet demand *tvåleverantörspolitik, alternativleverantörssystem;* **second user** *or* **second hand** = (old equipment) that has already been used and is to be sold again *andrahands-, begagnad*

secondary ['sek(ə)nd(ə)rɪ] *adj.* second in importance *or* less important than the first *sekundär;* **secondary channel** = second channel containing control information transmitted at the same time as data *sekundärkanal;* **secondary colour** = colour produced from two primary colours *sekundärfärg;* **secondary station** = temporary status of a station that is receiving data *sekundärstation;* **secondary storage** = any data storage medium (such as magnetic tape *or* floppy disk) that is not the main, high-speed computer storage (RAM) *sekundärminne, externminne*

> COMMENT: this type of storage is usually of a higher capacity, lower cost and slower access time than main memory

section ['sekʃ(ə)n] *subst.* part of a main program that can be executed in its own right, without the rest of the main program being required *avsnitt, självständig programmodul*

sector ['sektə] **1** *subst.* smallest area on a magnetic disk that can be addressed by a computer *sektor* **2** *vb.* to divide a disk into a series of sectors *sektorisera, formatera;* **(disk) sector formatting** = dividing a disk into a series of addressable sectors (a table of their addresses is also formed, allowing each sector to be accessed) *formatera;* **sectoring hole** = hole in the edge of a disk to indicate where the first sector is located *styrhål, indexhål;* **hard-sectored** = disk with sector start locations described by holes *or* other physical marks on the disk, which are set when the disk is manufactured *hårdsektoriserad, fabrikssektoriserad;* **soft-sectored** = disk where sectors are described by an address and start code data written onto it when the disk is formatted *mjuksektoriserad, programsektoriserad; see also* FORMAT

> COMMENT: a disk is divided into many tracks, each of which is then divided into a number of sectors which can hold a certain number of bits

secured [sɪ'kjuəd] *adj.* (file) that is protected against accidental writing *or*

deletion *or* against unauthorized access *säkrad*

secure system [sɪ'kjuə 'sɪstəm] *subst.* system that cannot be accessed without authorization *säkert system*

security [sɪ'kjuərətɪ] *subst.* being protected *or* being secret *säkerhet;* **the system has been designed to assure the security of the stored data;** **security backup** = copy of a disk *or* tape *or* file kept in a safe place in case the working copy is lost *or* damaged *säkerhetskopia;* **security check** = identification of authorized users (by a password) before granting access *säkerhetskontroll*

seek [siːk] *vb.* to try to find *söka;* **seek area** = section of memory that is to be searched for a particular item of data *or* a word *sökarea;* **seek time** = time taken by a read/write head to find the right track on a disk *söktid;* **the new hard disk drive has a seek time of just 35ms**

segment ['segmənt] **1** *subst.* section of a main program that can be executed in its own right, without the rest of the main program being required *segment, självständig programmodul, självständig subrutin* **2** *vb.* to divide a long program into shorter sections which can then be called up when required *segmentera; see also* OVERLAY

> QUOTE you can also write in smaller program segments. This simplifies debugging and testing
> **Personal Computer World**

sektor ⇨ disk, sector

sekundärminne ⇨ memory, secondary

sekventiellt läge ⇨ mode

select [sɪ'lekt] *vb.* to find and retrieve specific information from a database *välja, söka, hämta fram;* **chip select (CS)** = single line on a chip that will enable it to function when a signal is present (often ICs do not function even when power is applied, until a CS signal is provided) *aktiveringssignal, kretsvalssignal*

selectable [sɪ'lektəbl] *adj.* which can be selected *valbar;* **jumper-selectable** = circuit *or* device whose options can be selected by positioning various wire connections *valbar genom bygling;* **selectable attributes** = the function *or* attributes of a device which can be chosen by the user *valbara parametrar;* **user-selectable** = which can be chosen or selected by the user *valbar av användaren;* **this modem has user-selectable baud rates** = the receive and transmit baud rates of the modem can be chosen by the user, and are not preset *valbara sändhastigheter*

selection [sɪ'lekʃ(ə)n] *subst.* action of selecting *urval, hämtning, avsökning, sortering;* **selection of information from a large database may take some time**

selective [sɪ'lektɪv] *adj.* which chooses certain items *selektiv;* **selective calling =** calling a remote station from a main site *selektivt anrop;* **selective dump =** display *or* printout of a selected area of memory *selektiv dumping;* **selective sort =** sorting a section of data items into order *selektiv sortering*

selectivity [sɪlek'tɪvətɪ] *subst.* ability of a radio receiver to distinguish between two nearby carrier frequencies *selektivitet, kanalseparering*

selector [sɪ'lektə] *subst.* mechanical device that allows a user to choose an option *or* function *väljare, omkopplare, ratt;* **the selector knob for the amplification is located there; turn the selector control; selector channel =** communications link that operates with only one transmitter/receiver at a time *selektiv kanal*

selektivt anrop ⇨ **selective**

self- [self] *prefix* referring to oneself *själv-;* **self-adapting system =** system that can adapt itself to various tasks *självanpassande system;* **self-checking system =** system that carries out diagnostic tests on itself usually at switch on *självkontrollerande system;* **self-checking code =** character coding system that can detect an error *or* bad character but not correct it *självkontrollerande kod;* **self-correcting codes =** character coding system that can detect and correct an error *or* bad character *självkorrigerande;* **self-diagnostic =** computer that runs a series of diagnostic programs (usually when it is switched on) to ensure that it is all working correctly, often memory, peripherals and disk drives are tested *självdiagnosticerande;* **self-documenting program =** computer program that provides the user with operating instructions as it runs *självdokumenterande program;* **self-learning =** (expert system) that adds each new piece of information or rule to its database, improving its knowledge, expertise and performance as it is used *program med inlärningsfunktion;* **self-refreshing RAM =** dynamic RAM chip that has built in circuitry to generate refresh signals, allowing data to be retained when the power is off, using battery back-up *självåterskrivande minne;* **self-relocating program =** program that can be loaded into any part of memory (that will modify its addresses depending on the program origin

address) *adressanpassande program;* **self-resetting** *or* **self-restoring loop =** loop that returns any locations *or* registers accessed during its execution to the state they were in *självåterställande slinga*

semantics [sɪ'mæntɪks] *subst.* (i) part of language which deals with the meaning of words, parts of words or combinations of words *semantik;* (ii) (in computing) meanings of words or symbols used in programs *semantik;* **semantic error =** error due to use of an incorrect symbol within a program instruction *semantiskt fel*

semaphore ['seməfɔ:] *subst.* **(a)** coordination of two jobs and appropriate handshaking to prevent lock-outs *or* other problems when both require a peripheral *or* function *semaforering* **(b)** signalling system that uses two flags held in different positions by two mechanical *or* human arms *semaforering*

semi- ['semɪ] *prefix* meaning half *or* partly *semi-, halv-;* **semi-processed data =** raw data which has had some processing carried out, such as sorting, recording, error detection, etc. *halvbearbetade data*

semicolon ['semɪ'kəʊlən] *subst.* printing sign *semikolon (;);* which indicates a separation between parts of a sentence *or* marks the end of a program line *or* statement in some languages (such as C and Pascal) *semikolon*

semicompiled ['semɪkəm'paɪld] *adj.* (object code) program converted from a source code program, but not containing the code for functions from libraries, etc., that were used in the source code *halvkompilerad (kod)*

semiconductor ['semɪkən'dʌktə] *subst.* material that has conductive properties between those of a conductor (such as a metal) and an insulator *halvledare;* **semiconductor device =** electronic component that is constructed on a small piece of semiconductor (the components on the device are constructed using patterns of insulator *or* conductor *or* semiconductor material whose properties have been changed by doping) *halvledarkrets;* **semiconductor memory =** storage using capacitors (dynamic memory) *or* latches and bistables (static memory) constructed as a semiconductor device to store bits of data *halvledarminne;* **semiconductor** *or* **solid-state laser =** piece of semiconductor bar that has a polished end, and a semi-silvered mirror, generating pulses of photons that reflect inside the bar until they have enough power to leave via the semi-silvered end *halvledarlaser*

COMMENT: semiconductor material (such as silicon) is used as a base for manufacturing integrated circuits and other solid-state components, usually by depositing various types of doping substances on or into its surface

sender ['sendə] *subst.* person who sends a message *avsändare*

send-only device ['send 'əʊnlı dı'vaıs] *subst.* device such as a terminal which cannot receive data, only transmit it *sändarterminal*

sense [sens] *vb.* to examine the state of a device or electronic component *känna, känna av, mäta;* **the condition of the switch was sensed by the program; this device senses the holes punched in a paper tape; auto-baud sensing** *see* SCANNING; **sense recovery time** = time that a RAM takes to switch from read to write mode *tillståndsväxlingstid;* **sense switch** = switch on a computer front panel whose state can by examined by the computer *avkänningskontakt, funktionskontakt*

sensitive ['sensətıv] *adj.* which can sense even small changes *känslig;* **the computer is sensitive even to very slight changes in current; light-sensitive film changes when exposed to light**

sensitivity [,sensə'tıvətı] *subst.* being sensitive to something *känslighet;* **the scanner's sensitivity to small objects**

sensor ['sensə] *subst.* electronic device that produces an output dependent upon the condition or physical state of a process *sensor, känselkropp; see also* TRANSDUCER; **the sensor's output varies with temperature; the process is monitored by a bank of sensors; image sensor** = photoelectric device that produces a signal related to the amount of light falling on it *fotocell*

sentinel ['sentınl] *subst.* (i) marker or pointer to a special section of data *signalbit, markör, pekare;* (ii) a flag that reports the status of a register after a mathematical or logical operation *flagga, semafor*

separat datafil ⇨ **external**

separate ['seprət] **1** *adj.* not together *åtskilda, separata;* **separate channel signalling** = use of independent communications channel or bands in a multichannel system to send the control data and messages *signalering över separat kanal* **2** *vb.* to divide *skilja, separera;* **separated graphics** = displayed characters that do not take up the whole of a character matrix, resulting in spaces between them *åtskilda tecken*

separation [,sepə'reıʃ(ə)n] *subst.* act of separating *separering;* **colour separation** = process by which colours are separated into primary colours *färgseparering;* **colour separations** = different artwork or film for the various colours to be used in multicolour printing *färgseparerad film*

separator ['sepəreıtə] *subst.* symbol used to distinguish parts of an instruction line in a program, such as command and argument *avgränsare, avgränsningstecken; see also* DELIMITER

septet [sep'tet] *subst.* word made up of seven bits *septett*

sequence ['siːkwəns] *subst.* number of items or data arranged as a logical, ordered list *följd, lista, sekvens;* **the sequence of names is arranged alphabetically; the program instructions are arranged in sequence according to line numbers; binary sequence** = series of binary digits *binär sekvens;* **control sequence** = (series of) codes containing a control character and various arguments, used to carry out a process or change mode in a device *styrsekvens;* **sequence check** = check to ensure that sorted data is in the correct order *sekvenskontroll;* **sequence control register (SCR)** or **sequence counter** or **sequence register** or **instruction address register** = CPU register that contains the address of the next instruction to be processed *sekvenskontrollregister;* **the logon sequence** = order in which user number, password and other authorization codes are to be entered when attempting to access a system *inloggningssekvens*

sequencer ['siːkwənsə] *subst.* section within a bit-slice microprocessor that contains the next microprogram address *sekventierare*

sequential [sı'kwenʃ(ə)l] *adj.* arranged in an ordered manner *sekventiell;* **queued indexed sequential access method (QISAM)** = indexed sequential file that is read item by item into a buffer *köad indexerad åtkomst, QISA-metoden (för att läsa filer);* **queued sequential access method (QSAM)** = queue of blocks waiting to be processed, retrieved using a sequential access method *köad sekventiell åtkomst, QSA-metoden (för att läsa filer);* **sequential batch processing** = completing one job in a batch before the next can be started *sekventiell satsbearbetning;* **sequential computer** = type of computer, for which each instruction must be completed before the next is started, and so cannot handle parallel processing *sekventiell dator;* **sequential file** or **serial file** = stored file whose records are accessed sequentially *sekventiell fil;* **sequential logic** = logical circuit whose output depends on the logic state of the previous inputs *sekventiell* *logik;* **if the input sequence to the sequential logic circuit is 1101 the output will always be zero (0);** *compare with* COMBINATIONAL CIRCUIT; **sequential mode** = each instruction in a program is stored in consecutive locations *sekventiellt tillstånd;* **sequential operation** = operations executed one after the other *sekventiellt arbetssätt;* **sequential processing** = data *or* instructions processed sequentially, in the same order as they are accessed *sekventiell databehandling; see also* INDEXED; **sequential search** = each item in a list (starting at the beginning) is checked until the required one is found *sekventiell sökning, seriell sökning*

sequential access [sɪˈkwenʃ(ə)l ˈækses] *subst.* method of retrieving data from a storage device by starting at the beginning of the medium (such as tape) and reading each record until the required data is found *sekvenstiell åtkomst;* **sequential access storage** = storage medium in which the data is accessed sequentially *sekventiellt minne, seriellt minne*

COMMENT: a tape storage system uses sequential access, since the tape has to be played through until the section required is found. The access time of sequential access storage is dependent on the position in the file of the data, compared with random access that has the same access time for any piece of data in a list

sequentially [sɪˈkwenʃəlɪ] *adv.* (done) one after the other, in sequence *sekventiellt*

Séquentiel à Mémoire (SECAM) [sekɑ̃sʃlamemˈwa (ˈsiːˌkæm)] standards that define TV and video formats, mainly in France, USSR and Saudi Arabia, using 625 horizontal scan lines and 50 frames per second (similar to PAL) *SECAM-standarden*

serial [ˈsɪərɪəl] *adj.* (data *or* instructions) ordered sequentially (one after the other) and not in parallel *seriell;* **serial access** = one item of the data accessed by reading through all the data in a list until the correct one is found (as on a tape) *seriell åtkomst;* **serial-access memory (SAM)** = storage where a particular data item can only be accessed by reading all the previous items in the list (as opposed to random access) *serieåtkomstminne, seriellt minne;* **serial adder** = addition circuit that acts on one digit at a time from a larger number *serieadderare;* **serial computer** = computer system that has a single ALU and carries out instructions one at a time *seriell dator; see also* SEQUENTIAL COMPUTER; **serial data transmission** = transmission of the separate bits that make up data words, one at a time down a single line *seriell dataöverföring;* **serial file** = stored file

whose records are accessed sequentially *seriell fil;* **serial input/output (SIO)** *see* SERIAL TRANSMISSION; **serial input/parallel output (SIPO)** *or* **serial to parallel converter** = device that can accept serial data and transmit parallel data *serie-till-parallellomvandlare;* **serial input/serial output (SISO)** = *seriell-till-seriell; see* SERIAL TRANSMISSION; **serial interface** *or* **port** = circuit that converts parallel data in a computer to and from a serial form that allows serial data to be transmitted and received from other equipment (the most common form is the RS232C interface) *seriegränssnitt;* **parallel connections are usually less trouble to set up and use than serial interfaces, but are usually limited to 20 feet in length; serial memory** = memory in which data is stored sequentially, only allowing sequential access *seriellt minne;* **serial operation** = device that acts on data in a sequential manner *seriell operation;* **serial printer** = printer that prints characters one at a time *seriell skrivare;* **serial processing** = data *or* instructions processed sequentially, in the same order as they are retrieved *seriell databehandling;* **serial storage** = storage which only allows sequential access *seriell minneslagring;* **serial to parallel converter** = electronic device that converts data from a serial form to a parallel form *serie-till-parallellomvandlare;* **serial transmission** *or* **serial input/output** = data transmitted one bit at a time (this is the normal method of transmission over long distances, since although slower it uses fewer lines and so is cheaper than parallel transmission) *seriella in/utdata;* **word serial** = data words transmitted one after the other, along a parallel bus *ordserie*

serially [ˈsɪərɪəlɪ] *adv.* one after the other *or* in a series *seriellt;* **their transmission rate is 64,000 bits per second through a parallel connection or 19,200 serially**

seriellt dataflöde ⇨ **data**

seriellt gränssnitt ⇨ **interface**

series [ˈsɪəriːz] *subst.* group of related items ordered sequentially *serie;* **series circuit** = circuit in which the components are connected serially *seriekrets, seriekoppling*

COMMENT: in a series circuit the same current flows through each component; in a parallel circuit the current flow is dependent upon the component impedance

serif [ˈserɪf] *subst.* small decorative line attached to parts of characters in certain typefaces *schattering, serif;* **sans serif** = typeface without serifs *grotesk (typsnitt utan schatteringar)*

server ['sɜːvə] *subst.* dedicated computer *or* peripheral that provides a function to a network *nätcentral;* **file server** = small microcomputer and large backing storage device that is used for the management and storage of users' files in a network *nätminne;* **LAN server** = dedicated computer and backing storage used by terminals and operators in a LAN *lokal nätcentral*

COMMENT: in a network the hard disk machine is called the 'server' and the floppy disk units the 'satellites'. In a star network each satellite is linked individually to a central server

service ['sɜːvɪs] *vb.* to check *or* repair *or* maintain a system *reparera, underhålla;* **the disk drives were serviced yesterday and are working well; service bit** = transmitted bit that is used for control rather than data *kontrollbit;* **service contract** = agreement that an engineer will service equipment if it goes wrong *servicekontrakt, underhållsavtal;* **service program** = useful program that is used for routine activities such as file searching, copying, sorting, debugging, etc. *serviceprogram*

servo ['sɜːvəʊ] *or* **servomechanism** ['sɜːvəʊ'mekənɪz(ə)m] *subst.* mechanical device whose position *or* state can be accurately controlled *servomekanism*

session ['seʃ(ə)n] *subst.* period of work *session;* **session key** = cipher key used for a particular session *sessionsnyckel;* **session layer** = layer in the ISO/OSI standard model that makes the connection/disconnection between transmitter and receiver *sessionsskikt*

sessionsskikt ⇨ **session**

set [set] **1** *subst.* **(a)** number of related data items *mängd;* **character set** = all the characters that can be displayed *or* printed *teckenuppsättning;* **set theory** = mathematics related to numerical sets *mängdteori* **(b)** width of a printed typeface *typbredd;* **set size** = measurement of horizontal dimensions in sets (one set equals one point) *typografiskts breddmått;* **set width** = width of the body of a printed character *satsbredd* **(c)** radio *or* television receiver *teve- eller radioapparat;* **set-top converter** = device that converts TV signals from a network *or* satellite into a form that can be displayed *signalomvandlare, dekoder* **(d)** physical layout of a stage *or* filming studio including props and background *scenbild* **2** *vb.* **(a)** (i) to make one variable equal to a value *ställa in, sätta;* (ii) to define a parameter value *ställa in, sätta;* **we set the right-hand margin at 80 characters; set breakpoints** = to define the position of breakpoints within a program

being debugged *sätta brytpunkter* **(b)** to give a bit the value of 1 *sätta en bit (till 1)* **(c)** to compose a text into typeset characters *sätta (text);* **the page is set in 12 point Times Roman;** *see also* TYPESET

setting ['setɪŋ] *subst.* **(a)** action of fixing *or* arranging something *inställning;* **brightness setting** = TV brightness control position *ljusstyrkeinställning;* **contrast setting** = TV contrast control position *kontrastinställning* **(b)** action of composing text into typeset characters *sättning (av text);* **the MS has been sent to the typesetter for setting; setting charges have increased since last year; computer setting** = typesetting using a computerized typesetting machine *datorsättning*

set up [set 'ʌp] *vb.* to initialize *or* define *or* start an application *or* system *installera, sätta upp;* **the new computer worked well as soon as the engineer had set it up; set-up option** = the choices available when setting up a system *installationsmöjligheter, konfigueringsalternativ;* **set-up time** = period of time between a signal to start an operation and the start *uppsättningstid, starttid*

sexadecimal [,seksə'desɪməl] *see* HEXADECIMAL

sextet [seks'tet] *subst.* byte made up of six bits *sextett*

sf signalling ['es'ef'sɪgnəlɪŋ] = SINGLE FREQUENCY SIGNALLING

shade [ʃeɪd] *subst.* (i) variation in a printed colour due to added black *skuggning;* (ii)quantity of black added to a colour to make it darker *skuggning*

shading ['ʃeɪdɪŋ] *subst.* showing darker sections of a line drawing by adding dark colour *or* by drawing criss-cross lines *skuggning, schattering*

shadow ['ʃædəʊ] *subst.* area where broadcast signals cannot be received because of an obstacle that blocks the transmission medium *radioskugga;* **the mountain casts a shadow over those houses, so they cannot receive any radio broadcasts**

shadowmask ['ʃædəʊmɑːsk] *subst.* sheet with holes placed just behind the front of a colour monitor screen to separate the three-colour picture beams *skuggmask*

shadow memory ['ʃædəʊ,memərɪ] *or* **page** [,peɪdʒ] *subst.* duplicate memory locations accessed by a special code *skuggminne;* **shadow page table** = conversion table that lists real memory locations with their equivalent shadow memory locations *skuggminnestabell; see also* VIRTUAL

shadow ROM ['ʃædəʊˌrɒm] *subst.* read-only shadow memory *skuggminne i form av läsminne*

shannon ['ʃænən] *subst.* measure of the information content of a transmission *(enheten) shannon*

Shannon's Law ['ʃænənz'lɔː] *subst.* law defining the maximum information carrying capacity of a transmission line *Shannon's lag*

COMMENT: Shannon's Law is defined as B lg(1 + S/N) where B = Bandwidth, lg is logarithm to the base two and S/N is Signal to Noise ratio

share [ʃeə] *vb.* to own *or* use something together with someone else *dela;* **the facility is shared by several independent companies; shared access** = computer *or* peripheral used by more than one person *or* system *delad åtkomst; see also* TIME-SHARING SYSTEM, MULTI-USER; **shared bus** = one bus used (usually) for address and data transfer between the CPU and a peripheral *delad buss, gemensam buss;* **shared file** = stored file that can be accessed by more than one user *or* system *delad fil, gemensam fil;* **shared line** *or* **party line** = one telephone line shared by a number of subscribers *delad linje, gemensam linje;* **shared logic system** = one computer and backing storage device used by a number of people in a network for an application *gemensam dator;* **shared logic text processor** = word-processing available to a number of users of a shared logic system *gemensam ordbehandlare;* **shared memory** = memory that can be accessed by more than one CPU *gemensamt minne;* **shared resources system** = system where one peripheral *or* backing storage device *or* other resource is used by a number of users *gemensamma resurser;* **time-sharing** = computer system that allows several independent users to use it *or* be on-line at the same time *tidsdelning*

shareware ['ʃeəweə] *subst.* software that is available free to try, but if kept the user is expected to pay a fee to the writer (often confused with public domain software which is completely free) *program till självkostnadspris*

sheet [ʃiːt] *subst.* large piece of paper *ark, blad;* **sheet feed** = paper feed system that puts single sheets of paper into a printer, one at a time *arkmatning;* **sheet feed attachment** = device which can be attached to a printer to allow single sheets of paper to be fed in automatically *arkmatartillsats*

shelf life ['ʃelflaɪf] *subst.* maximum storage time of a product before it is no longer guaranteed good to use *livslängd;* **the developer has a shelf life of one year**

shell sort ['ʃelsɔːt] *subst.* algorithm for sorting data items, in which items can be moved more than one position per sort action *shell-sort-algoritmen*

SHF ['eseɪtʃ'ef] = SUPER HIGH FREQUENCY

shield [ʃiːld] **1** *subst.* metal screen connected to earth, that prevents harmful voltages *or* interference reaching sensitive electronic equipment *skärm* **2** *vb.* to protect a signal *or* device from external interference *or* harmful voltages *skärma;* **shielded cable** = cable made up of a conductive core surrounded by an insulator, then a conductive layer to protect the transmitted signal against interference *skärmad kabel*

shift [ʃɪft] *vb.* **(a)** to move a bit *or* word of data left or right by a certain amount (usually one bit) *flytta, skifta;* **arithmetic shift** = word *or* data moved one bit to the right *or* left inside a register, losing the bit shifted off the end *aritmetiskt skift;* **cyclic shift** = rotation of bits in a word with the previous last bit inserted in the first bit position *(logiskt) rundskift;* **logical shift** = data movement to the left *or* right in a word, the bits falling outside the word boundary are discarded, the free positions are filled with zeros *logiskt skift;* **shift instruction** = computer command to shift the contents of a register to the left or right *skiftinstruktion;* **shift left** = left arithmetic shift of data in a word (the number is doubled for each left shift) *vänsterskift;* **0110 left shifted once is 1100; shift register** = temporary storage into which data can be shifted *skiftregister;* **shift right** = right arithmetic shift of data in a word (the number is halved for each right shift) *högerskift* **(b)** to change from one character set to another, allowing other characters (such as capitals) to be used *byta mellan versaler och gemena, skifta;* **shift character** = transmitted character code that indicates that the following code is to be shifted *skifttecken;* **shift code** = method of increasing total possible bit combinations by using a number of bits to indicate the following code is to be shifted *skiftkod*

shift key ['ʃɪftkiː] *subst.* key on a keyboard that switches secondary functions for keys, such as another character set, by changing the output to upper case *skiftangent*

shoot [ʃuːt] *vb.* to take a film *filma;* **they shot hundreds of feet of film, but none of it was any good; the programme was shot on location in Spain**
NOTE: **shooting - shot**

short [ʃɔːt] *adj.* not long *kort;* **short card** = add-on expansion board that is shorter than a standard size *halvlängdskort, trekvartslängdskort;* **short haul modem** =

modem used to transmit data over short distances (often within a building), usually without using a carrier *korthållsmodem*

short circuit [ˈʃɔːtˈsɜːkɪt] **1** *subst.* electrical connection of very low resistance between two points *kortslutning* **2** *vb.* to connect two points together with a (very low resistance) link *korthållsanslutning;* **short-circuited =** two points that are electrically connected, usually accidentally *kortsluten*

COMMENT: short circuits can be accidental, due to bad circuit design or used as a protective measure

shorten [ˈʃɔːtn] *vb.* to make shorter *korta ned;* **we had to shorten the file to be able to save it on one floppy**

short-run [ˈʃɔːtrʌn] *adj.* with a printrun of only a few hundred copies *liten (tryck)upplaga;* **a printer specializing in short-run printing; the laser printer is good for short-run leaflets**

short wave (SW) [ˈʃɔːtweɪv (ˈesdʌbljuː)] *subst.* radio communications frequency below 60 metres *kortvåg;* **short-wave receiver =** radio receiver able to pick up broadcasts on the short wavebands *kortvågsmottagare*

shotgun microphone [ˈʃɒtɡʌn ˈmaɪkrəfəun] *subst.* long, highly directional microphone *riktad mikrofon, reportagemikrofon*

show-through [ˈʃəuθruː] *subst.* text printed on one side of a piece of paper that can be seen from the other *grad av ogenomskinlighet*

shrink [ʃrɪŋk] *vb.* to become smaller *krympa, minska med;* **the drawing was shrunk to fit the space** NOTE: **shrinks - shrank - has shrunk**

shut down [ʃʌt ˈdaun] *vb.* to switch off and stop the functions of a machine *or* system *slå av, stänga av*

shut-off mechanism [ˈʃʌtɒf ˈmekənɪz(ə)m] *subst.* device which stops a process in case of fault *avstängningsanordning, säkerhetsmekanism*

COMMENT: most hard disks have an automatic shut-off mechanism to pull the head back from the read position when the power is turned off

shutter [ˈʃʌtə] *subst.* device on a camera which opens and shuts rapidly allowing light from an object to fall on the film *slutare*

sibilance [ˈsɪbɪləns] *subst.* excess signal recorded when certain letters such as 's' are spoken *väsande, väsbrus*

sidbeskrivningsspråk ⇨ **page**

sidbrytning ⇨ **format**

sideband [ˈsaɪdbænd] *subst.* frequency band of a modulated signal, a little above or below the carrier frequency *sidband;* **upper sideband; lower sideband; double sideband =** modulation technique whose frequency spectrum contains two modulated signals above and below the unmodulated carrier frequency *dubbelt sidband;* **double sideband suppressed carrier (DSBSC) =** modulation technique that uses two modulated signal sidebands, but no carrier signal *dubbelt sidband med undertryckt bärvåg;* **single sideband =** modulated signal filtered to leave just one sideband, usually the upper (this is very economical on bandwidth but requires more complex circuitry) *enkelt sidband*

side lobe [ˈsaɪdləub] *subst.* side sections of an aerial's response pattern *sidlob*

sideways ROM [ˈsaɪdweɪz ˈrɒm] *subst.* software which allows selection of a particular memory bank *or* ROM device *minneshanterare för läsminne*

sidhuvud ⇨ **head, header, heading**

sidmatning ⇨ **form**

sidminnesbyte ⇨ **exchange**

sidskrivare ⇨ **printer**

sidslutsignal ⇨ **end**

sidväxling ⇨ **paging**

sifferskift ⇨ **figure**

siffra ⇨ **digit, figure, numeral**

siffra, minst signifikanta ⇨ **low-order digit**

siffror i underkant ⇨ **inferior figures**

sign [saɪn] **1** *subst.* polarity of a number *or* signal (whether it is positive *or* negative) *(för)tecken och absolut värde;* **sign and modulus =** way of representing numbers, where one bit shows if the number is positive *or* negative (usually 0 = positive, 1 = negative) *(för)tecken;* **sign bit** *or* **sign indicator =** single bit that indicates if a binary number is positive *or* negative (usually 0 = positive, 1 = negative) *(för)teckenbit, (för)teckenindikator;* **sign digit =** one digit that indicates if a number is positive *or* negative *(för)teckensiffra;* **sign and magnitude** *or* **signed magnitude =** number representation in which the most significant bit indicates the sign of the number, the rest of the bits its value *tecken* *och storlek;* **sign position** = digit *or* bit position that contains the sign bit *or* digit *teckenposition;* **signed field** = storage field which can contain a number and a sign bit *fält med teckenbit* **2** *vb.* to identify oneself to a computer using a personalized signature *logga in, skriva under;* **to sign off** = to logoff a system *logga av, slå av;* **to sign on** = to logon to a system *logga in, slå på*

signal ['sɪgn(ə)l] **1** *subst.* (i) generated analog *or* digital waveform used to carry information *signal;* (ii) short message used to carry control codes *signal;* **the signal received from the computer contained the answer; interrupt signal** = voltage pulse from a peripheral sent to the CPU requesting attention; **signal conditioning** = converting *or* translating a signal into a form that is accepted by a device *signalanpassning;* **signal conversion** = processing, changing or modulating a signal *signalomvandling;* **signal converter** = device that converts signals from one format to another, usually from UHF to VHF for TV signals *signalomvandlare;* **signal distance** = number of bit positions with different contents in two data words *signalavstånd, bitavstånd; see also* HAMMING; **signal element** = smallest basic unit used when transmitting digital data *signalelement;* **the signal element in this system is a short voltage pulse, indicating a binary one; the signal elements for the radio transmission system are 10mS of 40KHz and 10mS of 60KHz for binary 0 and 1 respectively; signal generator** = device that can produce various signals of varying amplitude, frequency and shape *signalgenerator;* **signal to noise ratio (S/N)** = ratio of the amplitude of the transmitted signal to the noise on the received signal *signal/brusförhållande;* **signal processing** = processing of signals to extract the information contained *signalbehandling;* **the system is used by students doing research on signal processing techniques; the message was recovered by carrier signal processing 2** *vb.* to send a radio signal *or* a message to a computer *signalera;* **signal to the network that we are busy**

signalfel ⇨ **hazard**

signalförstärkare ⇨ **launch amplifier**

signalkomprimering ⇨ **compression**

signallaser ⇨ **injection laser**

signalling ['sɪgnəlɪŋ] *subst.* (i) method used by a transmitter to warn a receiver that a message is to be sent *signalering;* (ii) communication to the transmitter about the state of the receiver *signalering;* **in band signalling** = use of a normal voice grade channel for data transmission *dataöverföring på tallinje*

(signal)omvandlare ⇨ **transducer**

signalstyrka ⇨ **magnitude**

signalstyrkevariation ⇨ **fading**

signature ['sɪgnətʃə] *subst.* **(a)** name written in a special way by someone *underskrift;* **do you recognize the signature on the cheque? (b)** series of printed and folded pages in a book (usually 8, 16or 32 pages) *ark* **(c)** special authentication code, such as a password, which a user gives prior to access to a system *or* prior to the execution of a task (to prove identity) *signatur*

COMMENT: in some systems this can be written by the user or determined from the user in some way (such as fingerprint or eyes can: these are very advanced and secure systems)

significance [sɪg'nɪfɪkəns] *subst.* special meaning *signifikans, mening, betydelse*

significant [sɪg'nɪfɪkənt] *adj.* which has a special meaning *signifikant, meningsfull, betydelsefull;* **significant digit codes** *or* **faceted codes** = codes which indicate various details of an item, by assigning each one a value *facettkoder*

signify ['sɪgnɪfaɪ] *vb.* to mean *betyda;* **a carriage return code signifies the end of an input line**

silicon ['sɪlɪkən] *subst.* element with semiconductor properties, used in crystal form as a base for IC manufacture *kisel;* **silicon chip** = small piece of silicon in and on the surface of which a complete circuit *or* logic function has been produced (by depositing other substances *or* by doping) *kiselkrets, kiselchip;* **silicon disk** *or* **RAM disk** = section of RAM that is made to look and behave like a high speed disk drive *simulerat skivminne;* **silicon foundry** = works where pure silicon crystals are grown, sliced into wafers and cleaned ready for use *kiselskivefabrik;* **silicon gate** = type of MOS transistor gate that uses doped silicon regions instead of a metal oxide to provide the function *(kisel)grind; see also* MOS, GATE; **silicon on sapphire (SOS)** = manufacturing technique that allows MOS devices to be constructed onto a sapphire substrate for high speed operation *kisel-på-safir-kretsar;* **Silicon Glen** = area of Scotland where many Scottish IT companies are based *"kiseldalen" i Skottland;* **silicon transistor** = microelectronic transistor manufactured on a silicon semiconductor base *kiselbaserad transistor;* **Silicon Valley** = area in California where many US semiconductor device manufacturers are based *"kiseldalen" i Kalifornien;* **silicon wafer** = thin slice of a pure silicon crystal, usually around 4 inches in diameter on which integrated circuits are produced (these are then cut out of the wafer to produce individual chips) *kiselskiva*

COMMENT: silicon is used in the electronics industry as a base material for integrated circuits. It is grown as a long crystal which is then sliced into wafers before being etched or treated, producing several hundred chips per wafer. Other materials, such as germanium or gallium arsenide, are also used as a base for ICs

silk [sɪlk] *subst.* fine white material used to diffuse light when photographing a subject *silke, gasväv*

SIMD [esaɪemdiː] = SINGLE INSTRUCTION STREAM MULTIPLE DATA STREAM

simple ['sɪmpl] *adj.* not complicated, not difficult *enkel;* **simple to use** = (machine *or* software) easy to use and operate *lättanvänd*

simplex ['sɪmpleks] *subst.* data transmission in only one direction *simplexöverföring, envägsöverföring* NOTE: opposite is **duplex**

simplify ['sɪmplɪfaɪ] *vb.* to make something simpler *förenkla;* **function keys simplify program operation**

simulate ['sɪmjʊleɪt] *vb.* to copy the behaviour of a system *or* device with another *simulera;* **this software simulates the action of an aeroplane**

simulation [ˌsɪmjʊ'leɪʃ(ə)n] *subst.* operation where a computer is made to imitate a real life situation *or* a machine, and shows how something works *or* will work in the future *simulering;* **simulation techniques have reached a high degree of sophistication**

simulator ['sɪmjʊleɪtə] *subst.* device that simulates another system *simulator;* **flight simulator** = computer program which allows a user to pilot a simulated plane, showing a realistic control panel and moving scenes (either as training programme *or* computer game) *flygsimulator*

simultaneity [ˌsɪm(ə)ltə'nɪətɪ] *subst.* in which the CPU and the I/O sections of a computer can handle different data *or* tasks at the same time *simultanfunktion, samtidighet*

simultaneous [ˌsɪm(ə)l'teɪnjəs] *adj.* which takes place at the same time as something else *simultan, samtidig;* **simultaneous processing** = two or more processes executed at the same time *samtidig databehandling;* **simultaneous transmission** = transmission of data *or*

control codes in two directions at the same time *samtidig överföring i duplex* NOTE: same as duplex

COMMENT: true simultaneous processing requires two processors, but can be imitated by switching rapidly between two tasks with a single processor

simultaneously [ˌsɪm(ə)l'teɪnjəslɪ] *adv.* at the same time *samtidigt*

sin [saɪn] *or* **sine** [saɪn] *subst.* mathematical function defined as: the sine of an angle (in a right-angled triangle) is equal to the ratio of opposite to hypotenuse sides *(matematisk) sinusfunktion*

sine wave ['saɪnweɪv] *subst.* waveform that is the sine function with time (classic waveshape, changing between a maximum and minimum with a value of zero at zero time) *sinusvåg*

COMMENT: sine waves are usually the basic carrier waveform shape in modulation systems

single ['sɪŋgl] *adj.* only one *enkel, enstaka;* **single address code** *or* **instruction** = machine code instruction that contains one operator and one address *enadressinstruktion;* **single address message** = message with a single destination *enadressmeddelande;* **single board computer (SBC)** = micro *or* mini computer whose components are all contained on a single printed circuit board *enkortsdator;* **single density disk (SD)** = standard magnetic disk and drive able to store data *diskett med enkel täthet;* **single frequency signalling** *or* **sf signalling** = use of various frequency signals to represent different control codes *frekvenssignalering;* **single function software** = applications program that can only be used for one kind of task *specialprogram;* **single instruction stream multiple data stream (SIMD)** = architecture of a parallel computer that has a number of ALUs and data buses with one control unit *parallelldator, vektorberäkningsdator;* **single instruction stream single data stream (SISD)** = architecture of a serial computer, that has one ALU and data bus, with one control unit *den vanliga datorarkitekturen (von Neumann);* **single key response** = software that requires only one key to be pressed (no CR required) to select an option *tangentvalsprogram;* **single length precision** = number stored in one word; *compare with* DOUBLE, MULTIPLE LENGTH; **single length working** = using numbers that can be stored within a single word *enkel precision, enordsaritmetik;* **single line display** = small screen which displays a single line of characters at a time *enradsskärm, teckenfönster;* **single operand instruction** *see* SINGLE ADDRESS

INSTRUCTION; **single operation** = communications system that allows data to travel in only one direction at a time (controlled by codes S/O = send only, R/O = receive only, S/R = send or receive) *envägssystem; see also* SIMPLEX; **single pass operation** = software that produces the required result *or* carries out a task after one run *enpassoperation;* **single pole** = switch that connects two points *en-polig brytare;* **single precision** = number stored in one word *enkel precision;* **single scan non segmented** = video tape system that allows freeze framing by recording one complete television picture field at a time *enbildsvideo;* **single sheet feed** = device attached to a printer to allow single sheets of paper to be used instead of continuous stationery *(enkel) arkmatning;* **single sideband** = modulated signal filtered to leave just one sideband, usually the upper (this is very economical on bandwidth, but needs more circuitry) *enkelt sidband;* **single-sided disk (SSD)** = floppy disk that can only be used to store data on one side, because of the way it is manufactured *or* formatted; **single step** = to execute a program one instruction at a time *stega (program);* **single-strike ribbon** = printer ribbon which can only be used once *engångskarbon; compare* MULTI-STRIKE; **single-user system** = computer system which can only be used by a single user at a time (as opposed to a multi-user system) *enanvändarsystem*

sink [sɪŋk] *subst.* receiving end of a communications line *mottagare;* **heat sink** = metal device used to conduct heat away from an electronic component to prevent damage *kylfläns;* **sink tree** = description in a routing table of all the paths in a network to a destination *vägträd* NOTE: the opposite of sink is **source**

sinusoidal [ˌsaɪnəˈsɔɪd(ə)l] *adj.* waveform *or* motion that is similar to a sine wave *sinusvågliknande;* **the carrier has a sinusoidal waveform**

SIO [ˈesaɪˈəʊ] = SERIAL INPUT/OUTPUT

siphoning [ˈsaɪfənɪŋ] *subst.* transmission of a direct broadcast TV programme over a cable network *direktsändning över kabelnät*

SIPO [ˈesaɪpiːˈəʊ] = SERIAL INPUT/PARALLEL OUTPUT

SISD [esaɪesˈdiː] = SINGLE INSTRUCTION STREAM SINGLE DATA STREAM

SISO [ˈesaɪesˈəʊ] = SERIAL INPUT/SERIAL OUTPUT

sista tidpunkt ⇨ **deadline**

site [saɪt] *subst.* place where something is based *plats, läge, belägenhet*

site poll [ˈsaɪtpəʊl] *vb.* to poll all the terminals *or* devices in a particular location *or* area *lokal avfrågning; see also* POLLING

SI units [ˈesaɪˈjuːnɪts] = SYSTEME INTERNATIONAL UNITS international measurement units such as candela, lumen, and ampere *SI-enheter; see also* MKS

sixteen-bit [ˈsɪksˈtiːnˈbɪt] *adj.* (microcomputer system *or* CPU) that handles data in sixteen bit words, providing much faster operation than older eight bit systems *16-bits-system*

sixteenmo [sɪksˈtiːnməʊ] *or* **16mo** *subst.* size of a book page, where the sheet of paper has been folded four times to make a signature of 32 pages *sedes(format), sedecimo*

size [saɪz] **1** *subst.* physical dimensions of an image *or* object *or* page *storlek;* **the size of the print has been increased to make it easier to read; page size** = physical dimensions of a printed page *sidstorlek;* **our page sizes vary from 220 x 110 to 360 x 220; screen size** = (i) number of characters a computer display can show horizontally and vertically *skärmstorlek;* (ii) size of a monitor screen based on international paper sizes *skärmstorlek* **2** *vb.* to calculate the resources available, and those required to carry out a particular job *uppskatta, beräkna*

sizing [ˈsaɪzɪŋ] *subst.* reducing *or* enlarging a picture to fit *förminska, förstora;* **photographs can be edited by cropping, sizing, etc**

självanpassande system ⇨ **self-**

självdiagnosticerande ⇨ **self-**

(själv)genererad adress ⇨ **generate**

självgenererat fel ⇨ **generate**

(själv)synkroniserande bildskärm ⇨ **monitor**

självåterskrivande minne ⇨ **self-**

skapa ⇨ **create**

skapa en fil ⇨ **file**

skeletal code [ˈskelɪtl ˈkəʊd] *subst.* program which is not complete, with the basic structure coded *programstomme*

sketch [sketʃ] **1** *subst.* rough drawing made rapidly *skiss* **2** *vb.* to make a rough rapid drawing *skissa*

skew [skjuː] *subst.* image scanned *or* drawn whose horizontal *or* vertical lines are not straight *skevhet, skev bild*

skifta ⇨ **justify, shift**

skifttangent ⇨ **figure, key**

skip [skɪp] *vb.* **(a)** to transmit radio waves over an abnormally long distance due to the reflective properties of the atmosphere *studsa* **(b)** to ignore an instruction in a sequence of instructions *hoppa över;* **the printer skipped the next three lines of text; skip capability** = feature of certain word-processors to allow the user to jump backwards *or* forwards by a quantity of text in a document *hoppmöjlighet;* **skip instruction** = null computer command which directs the CPU to the next instruction *blindinstruktion;* **high-speed skip** = rapid movement of paper in a printer, ignoring the normal line advance *snabbmatning*

skiss ⇨ **outline**

skiva i skivminne ⇨ **magnetic**

skivenhet ⇨ **disk**

skivformatering ⇨ **format**

skivminne ⇨ **memory**

skivminne för säkerhetslagring ⇨ **disk**

skivminnesenhet ⇨ **disk, magnetic**

skivminnesfel ⇨ **disk**

skivminnesformat ⇨ **format**

skivminneskrasch ⇨ **head**

skivminneslagring ⇨ **disk**

skivminnesorienterat operativsystem ⇨ **disk**

skivminnespacke ⇨ **disk, pack**

skivminnesåtkomst ⇨ **access, disk**

skivpacke ⇨ **disk**

skrivarbuffert ⇨ **printer**

skrivare ⇨ **printer**

skrivargränssnitt ⇨ **hard**

skrivarstyrkoder ⇨ **non-printing codes**

skrivarstyrprogram ⇨ **printer**

skrivarstyrtecken ⇨ **print, printer**

skrivarutgång ⇨ **printer**

skrivautomat ⇨ **dedicated**

skrivbart optiskt läsminne ⇨ **write**

skrivbordstest ⇨ **desk**

skrivbyrå ⇨ **bureau, word-processing (WP)**

skrivhuvud ⇨ **head**

skrivmaskin ⇨ **typewriter**

skrivtid ⇨ **write**

skräp ⇨ **junk**

skräpdata ⇨ **garbage**

"skräp in skräp ut" ⇨ **garbage**

skräpminnesinsamling ⇨ **garbage**

skydd ⇨ **protection, screen**

skyddad area ⇨ **field**

skyddat fält ⇨ **field**

skyddsbit ⇨ **guard bit**

skyddsgap ⇨ **guard band**

skyddsnät ⇨ **safety net**

skyddsöverdrag ⇨ **dustcover**

skärm ⇨ **display, monitor, screen, video**

skärmbildfångst ⇨ **screen**

skärmbuffert ⇨ **screen**

skärmbur ⇨ **electrostatic**

skärmdump ⇨ **screen**

skärmformat ⇨ **display, screen**

skärmkant ⇨ **screen**

skärmlinje ⇨ **display**

skärmminne ⇨ **screen**

skärmrullning ⇨ **display**

(skärm)tecken ⇨ **display**

skärmutrymme ⇨ **display**

skärmutskrift ⇨ **readout**

skönskrift ⇨ **correspondence, near letter-quality (NLQ)**

skötsel ⇨ **maintenance**

sladd ⇨ **cable, cord**

slash [slæʃ] *or* **oblique stroke** [ə(ʊ)'bliːk 'strəʊk] *subst.* printing sign (/) like stroke sloping to the right *snedstreck*

slashed zero ['slæʃt 'zɪərəʊ] *subst.* a printed *or* written sign (Ø) to distinguish a zero from the letter O *genomskriven nolla*

slaskfil ⇨ **scratch file**

slaskminne ⇨ **memory**

slave [sleɪv] *subst.* remote secondary computer *or* terminal controlled by a central computer *slav;* **bus slave** = data sink which receives data from a bus master *busslav;* **slave cache** *or* **store** = section of high-speed memory which stores data that the CPU can access quickly *slavminne;* **slave processor** = dedicated processor that is controlled by a master processor *slavprocessor;* **slave terminal** = terminal controlled by a main computer *or* terminal *slavterminal;* **slave tube** = second CRT display connected to another so that it shows exactly the same information *slavskärm*

sleep [sli:p] *subst.* system that is waiting for a signal (log-on) before doing anything *vilande system; see also* WAKE-UP

sleeve [sli:v] *subst.* cover for a magnetic disk *or* for a record *fodral*

slew [slu:] *subst.* rapid movement of paper in a printer, ignoring the normal line advance *snabbmatning*

slice [slaɪs] *subst.* section *or* piece of something *skiva, del;* **bit-slice architecture** = construction of a large word size CPU by joining a number of smaller word size blocks *bituppdelad arkitektur;* **the bit-slice design uses four four-bit word processors to make a sixteen-bit processor; time slice** = period of time allocated for a user *or* program *or* job within a multitasking system *tidsdel;* amount of time allowed for a single task in a time-sharing system *or* in multiprogramming *tidsdel*

slicing ['slaɪsɪŋ] *subst.* cutting thin round wafers from a bar of silicon crystal *skärning (av kiselkristall)*

slide [slaɪd] **1** *subst.* positive transparent photographic image *diabild;* **slide projector** = device that projects slide images onto a screen *diaprojektor;* **slide/sync recorder** = audio tape recorder that can control a slide projector in sync with music *or* commentary *bandspelarstyrd diaprojektor* **2** *vb.* to move smoothly across a surface *glida;* **the disk cover slides on and off easily**

slinga ⇨ **for-next loop, loop**

slip pages ['slɪp,peɪdʒɪz] *or* **slip proofs** ['slɪp,pru:f] *subst.* proofs, where each page of text is printed on a separate piece of paper *sidkorrektur*

slippapper ⇨ **mechanical**

slot [slɒt] **1** *subst.* **(a)** long thin hole *öppning;* **the system disk should be inserted into the left-hand slot on the front of the computer; expansion slot** = expansion connector available on a computer's backplane *or* motherboard, into which an expansion board can be plugged *kortplats;* **there are two free slots in the micro, you only need one for the add-on board (b)** **message slot** = number of bits that can hold a message which circulates round a ring network *meddelandeplats* **2** *vb.* to insert an object into a hole *sticka in, passa in;* **the disk slots into one of the floppy drive apertures**

slow motion ['sləʊ'məʊʃ(ə)n] *subst.* playing back of a video tape *or* disk sequence slower than recorded *slow motion, ultrarapid;* **the film switched to slow motion; play the film again in slow motion**

slow scan television ['sləʊ'skæn 'telɪ,vɪʒ(ə)n] *subst.* television images transmitted line by line over a transmission link at a slow rate *långsam överföring av tevebild*

SLSI ['eselsi:'aɪ] = SUPER LARGE SCALE INTEGRATION

slug [slʌg] *subst.* piece of metal type, with a character at the end *typ, reglett*

slumpkoda ⇨ **scramble**

slumpkodare ⇨ **scrambler**

slumpmässig ⇨ **random**

slumpmässig avrundning ⇨ **noisy mode**

slur [slɜ:] *subst.* (i) printed image which is blurred because of movement during printing *oskärpa;* (ii) distortion of voice during transmission *sludder*

slutbyte ⇨ **trailer**

slutkorrektur ⇨ **master, photoprint**

slutledning ⇨ **inference**

slutmarkör ⇨ **terminator**

slutpost ⇨ **trailer**

slutsats ⇨ **inference**

slutsignal ⇨ **tail**

sluttecken ⇨ **end**

slutvärde ⇨ **terminator**

slå samman filer ⇨ **join**

small [smɔ:l] *adj.* not large *liten;* **small caps** = printing style, with capital letters which are the same size as ordinary letters *kapitäler;* **small scale integration (SSI)** = integrated circuit with 1 to 10 components *låggradig (krets)integration*

smart [smɑ:t] *adj.* intelligent *klipsk, smart;* **smart card** = plastic card with a memory and microprocessor embedded in it, so that it can be used for direct money transfer *or* for identification of the user *aktivt kort; see also* PID; **smart terminal** *or* **intelligent terminal** = computer terminal that is able to process information *intelligent terminal*

smog [smɒg] *subst.* **electronic smog** = excessive stray electromagnetic fields and static electricity generated by large numbers of electronic equipment (this can damage equipment and a person's health) *elektromagnetiskt fält, bildskärmsstrålning*

smoke test ['sməʊktest] *informal* casual test that indicates that the machine must be working if no smoke appears when it is switched on *idiottest, dumtest*

SNA ['esen'eɪ] = SYSTEMS NETWORK ARCHITECTURE

snabb ⇨ fast, quick, rapid

snabbpassning ⇨ first fit

snabbtelefon ⇨ intercom

snabbutskrift ⇨ draft

snabbåtkomstminne ⇨ IAS, fast

snabb(åtkomst)minne ⇨ fast

snapshot ['snæpʃɒt] *subst.* (i) recording of all the states of a computer at a particular instant *ögonblicksbild;* (ii) storing in main memory the contents of a screen full of information at an instant *bildskärmsdump;* **snapshot dump** = printout of all the registers and a section of memory at a particular instant, used when debugging a program *ögonblicksdump*

snedstreck ⇨ slash

SNOBOL ['snəʊbɒl] = STRING ORIENTATED SYMBOLIC LANGUAGE high-level programming language that uses string processing methods *programmeringsspråket SNOBOL*

snow [snəʊ] *subst.* television image distortion in the form of random moving white dots due to a low quality signal *snö (i TV-bild)*

s/n ratio ['es'en 'reɪʃɪəʊ] = SIGNAL TO NOISE RATIO ratio of the amplitude of the transmitted signal to the noise on the received signal *signal/brusförhållande*

soak [səʊk] *vb.* to run a program *or* device continuously for a period of time to make sure it functions correctly *långtidsprov, inkörning;* **the device was soak-tested prior to delivery**

socket ['sɒkɪt] *subst.* device with a set of holes, into which a plug fits *kontakt;* **female socket** = hole into which a pin *or* plug can be inserted to make an electrical connection *honkontakt*

QUOTE the mouse and keyboard sockets are the same, and could lead to the kind of confusion that arose with the early PCs when the keyboard could be connected to the tape socket
PC User

soft [sɒft] *adj.* **(a)** (material) that loses its magnetic effects when removed from a magnetic field *omagnetisk* **(b)** (data) that is not permanently stored in hardware (soft usually refers to data stored on magnetic medium) *programmerbar data (om program och dataprogram lagrade på magnetmedium);* **soft copy** = text listed on screen (as opposed to hard copy on paper) *skärmkopia;* **soft error** = random error caused by software or data errors (this type of error is very difficult to trace and identify since it only appears under certain conditions) *datafel, programfel; compare with* HARD ERROR; **soft-fail** = system that is still partly operational even after a part of the system has failed *delvis felsäkert;* **soft hyphen** = hyphen which is inserted when a word is split at the end of a line, but is not present when the word is written normally *mjukt bindestreck;* **soft keys** = keys which can be changed by means of a program *programstyrda tangenter;* **soft keyboard** = keyboard where the functions of the keys can be changed by programs *programstyrt tangentbord;* **soft-reset** = instruction that terminates any program execution and returns the user to the monitor program *or* BIOS *mjuk återstart, varmstart; compare with* HARD RESET; **soft-sectored disk** = disk where the the sectors are described by an address and start code data written onto it when the disk is formatted *programsektoriserad (mjukformaterad) skiva;* **soft zone** = text area to the left of the right margin in a word-processed document, where if a word does not fit completely, a hyphen is automatically inserted *avstavningszon*

software ['sɒftweə] *subst.* any program *or* group of programs which instructs the hardware on how it should perform, including operating systems, word processors and applications programs *programvara, program;* **applications software** = programs which are used by the user to perform a certain task *tillämpningsprogram;* **bundled software** = software which is included in the price of the system *medföljande program, i priset ingående program;* **common software** = useful routines that can be used by any program *allmänt programbibliotek;* **network software** = software which is used to establish the link between a users' program and a network *nätverksprogram;* **pirate software** = illegal copy of a software package *piratkopia;* **system software** = programs which direct the basic functions, input-output control, etc., of a computer *systemprogram;* **unbundled software** = software which is not included in the price of a system *program som måste köpas separat;* **user-friendly software** = program that is easy for a non-expert to use and interact with *användarvänligt program;* **software compatible** = computer that will load and run programs written for another computer *programkompatibel;* **software development** = processes required to

produce working programs from an initial idea *programutveckling;* **software documentation** = information, notes and diagrams that describe the function, use and operation of a piece of software *programdokumentation;* **software engineer** = person who can write working software to fit an application *programmerare, programkonstruktör;* **software engineering** = field of study covering all software-related subjects *programkonstruktion;* **software house** = company which develops and sells computer programs *programvaruhus;* **software interrupt** = high priority program generated signal, requesting the use of the central processor *programavbrott;* **software library** = number of specially written routines, stored in a library file which can be inserted into a program, saving time and effort *programbibliotek;* **software licence** = agreement between a user and a software house, giving details of the rights of the user to use *or* copy the software *program(varu)licens;* **software life cycle** = period of time when a piece of software exists, from its initial design to the moment when it becomes out of date *programs livslängd;* **software maintenance** = carrying out updates and modifications to a software package to make sure the program is up to date *programunderhåll;* **software package** = complete set of programs (and the manual) that allow a certain task to be performed *programpaket;* **software piracy** = illegal copying of software for sale *piratkopiering;* **software quality assurance (SQA)** = making sure that software will perform as intended *kvalitetssäkring av program(vara);* **software reliability** = ability of a piece of software to perform the task required correctly *programs tillförlitlighet;* **software specification** = detailed information about a piece of software's abilities, functions and methods *programspecifikation;* **software system** = all the programs required for one or more tasks *program(varu)system;* **software tool** = program used in the development of other programs *programverktyg*
NOTE: no plural for **software** ; for the plural say **pieces of software**

solar ['səʊlə] *adj.* referring to the sun *sol-;* **solar cell** = component that converts the light of the sun into electrical energy *solcell;* **solar power** = (electrical) power derived from the sun *solkraft;* **solar-powered calculator** = calculator with a battery powered by light *soldriven räknare*

solder ['sɒldə] **1** *subst.* soft lead which, when melted, forms a solid electrical connection to join wires, pins and metal components *lödtenn* NOTE: no plural **2** *vb.* to join two pieces of metal with molten solder *löda*

solderless ['sɒldəlɪs] *adj.* which does not use solder; (board, such as a breadboard) which does not need solder *lödfri, utan lödning*

solenoid ['səʊlənɔɪd] *subst.* mechanical device operated by an electromagnetic field *elektromagnet*

solid ['sɒlɪd] *adj.* (printed text) with no spaces between the lines *kompakt sats;* **solid error** = error that is always present when certain equipment is used *utrustningsfel;* **solid font printer** = printer which uses a whole character shape to print in one movement, such as a daisy wheel printer *typskrivare*

solid-state ['sɒlɪd'steɪt] *adj.* referring to semiconductor devices *halvledar-;* **solid-state device** = electronic device that operates by using the effects of electrical *or* magnetic signals in a solid semiconductor material *halvledarkrets, halvledaranordning;* **solid-state memory device** = solid-state memory storage device (usually in the form of RAM or ROM chips) *halvledarminne, minneskrets*

solution [sə'luːʃ(ə)n] *subst.* **(a)** answer to a problem *lösning* **(b)** liquid in which certain chemicals have been dissolved *lösning*

solve [sɒlv] *vb.* to find the answer to a problem *lösa*

sonar ['səʊnɑː] *subst.* device that uses sound waves to determine the state and depth of water *ekolod*

son file ['sʌnfaɪl] *subst.* latest working version of a file *senaste version (av fil);* compare with FATHER FILE, GRANDFATHER FILE

sonic ['sɒnɪk] *adj.* referring to sound *ljud-, sonisk;* (sound signals) within the human hearing range (20 - 20,000Hz); **ultrasonic** = (sound pressure waves) at a frequency above the audio band (above 20kHz) *ultraljuds-*

sophisticated [sə'fɪstɪkeɪtɪd] *adj.* technically advanced *avancerad, sofistikerad;* **a sophisticated desktop publishing program**

sophistication [sə,fɪstɪ'keɪʃ(ə)n] *subst.* being technically advanced *förfining, finesser;* **the sophistication of the new package is remarkable** *det nya projektet är påfallande avancerat*

sort [sɔːt] *vb.* to put data into order, according to a system, on the instructions of the user *sortera;* **to sort addresses into alphabetical order; to sort orders according to account numbers; bubble sort** = sorting method which repeatedly exchanges various pairs of data items until they are in order *bubbelsortering;* **shell sort** =

algorithm for sorting data items, in which items can be moved more than one position per sort action *shell-algoritmen;* **sort/merge** = program which allows new files to be sorted and then merged in correct order into existing files *sorterings-sammanslagningsprogram, samsorte-ringsprogram;* **tree selection sort** = rapid form of selection where the information from the first sort pass is used in the second pass to speed up selection *förgrenings-sortering*

sortering av fil ▷ **file**

sortiment ▷ **range**

sortkey ['sɔːtkiː] *or* **sort field** ['sɔːtfiːld] *subst.* field in a stored file that is used to sort the file *sorteringsnyckel;* **the orders were sorted according to dates by assigning the date field as the sortkey**

SOS ['esəʊ'es] = SILICON ON SAPPHIRE

sound [saʊnd] *subst.* noise *or* something which can be heard *ljud;* **sound advance** = distance between a film frame and its sound track on a film due to the difference in position of the sound head and camera aperture *ljudglapp;* **sound chip** = electronic device that can generate sound signals *ljudkrets;* **sound effects** = artificially produced sounds used when recording to give the impression of real sounds *ljudeffekter;* **all the sound effects for the film were produced electronically; sound head** = device that converts to or from a magnetic signal stored on tape *ljudhuvud;* **sound pressure level (SPL)** = measurement of the magnitude of the pressure wave conveying sound *ljudtrycksnivå;* **sound synthesizer** = device able to produce complex real sounds by the combination of various generated signals *ljudgenerator;* **sound track** = track on a film on which the sound is recorded *ljudspår*

soundproof ['saʊndpruːf] *adj.* which does not allow sound to pass through *ljudisolerad, ljudtät;* **the telephone is installed in a soundproof booth**

source [sɔːs] *subst.* **(a)** point where a transmitted signal enters a network *källa* NOTE: opposite is **sink (b)** name of a terminal on an FET device ▷ *APPENDIX källelektrod* **(c)** original *or* initial point *källa, ursprung;* **source code** = set of codes written by the programmer which cannot be directly executed by the computer, but has to be translated into an object code program by a compiler *or* interpreter *källkod, ursprungskod;* **source deck** *or* **pack** = set of punched cards that contain the source code for a program *ursprungspacke;* **source document** = form *or* document from which data is extracted prior to entering it into a

database *källdokument;* **source editor** = software that allows the user to alter, delete or add instructions in a program source file *källkodsediterare, textbehandlare;* **source file** = program written in source language, which is then converted to machine code by a compiler *källfil;* **source language** = programming language in which the source program is written *källspråk;* **source listing** = (i) listing of a text in its original form *utskrift av originalutförande;* (ii) listing of a source program *källkodsutskrift;* **source machine** = computer which can compile source code *källkodsdator; compare with* OBJECT MACHINE; **source program** = program, prior to translation, written in a programming language by a programmer *källkodsprogram*

source language ['sɔːs,læŋgwɪdʒ] *subst.* (i) language in which a program is originally written *källspråk;* (ii) language of a program prior to translation *källspråk* NOTE: opposite is **object** *or* **target language**

SP ['es'piː] = STACK POINTER

space [speɪs] **1** *subst.* **(a)** gap (printed *or* displayed in text) *mellanrum, mellanslag;* **space character** = character code that prints a space *mellanslag;* **space bar** = long bar at the bottom of a keyboard, which inserts a space into the text when pressed *mellanslagstangent* **(b)** transmitted signal representing a binary zero *mellanrum* NOTE: opposite is **mark (c)** region extending out and around from the earth's atmosphere *rymden;* **space craft** = vehicle that travels in space *rymdskepp;* **space station** = space craft which remains in orbit for a long time, and can be visited by other space vehicles *rymdstation* **2** *vb.* to spread out text *spärra, sluta ut;* **the line of characters was evenly spaced out across the page**

spacer ['speɪsə] *subst.* **intelligent spacer** = facility on a word-processing system used to prevent words from being hyphenated *or* separated at the wrong point *avstavningsprogram*

spacing ['speɪsɪŋ] *subst.* way in which spaces are inserted in a printed text *mellanrum, kägel;* **the spacing on some lines is very uneven**

spaltkorrektur ▷ **galley proof** *or* **slip, proof**

span [spæn] *subst.* set of allowed values between a maximum and minimum *bredd, omfång, intervall*

spark printer ['spɑːk,prɪntə] *subst.* thermal printer which produces characters on thermal paper by electric sparks *gnistskrivare*

sparse array ['spɑːs ə'reɪ] *subst.* data matrix structure containing mainly zero *or* null entries *gles vektor*

speaker ['spiːkə] *see* LOUDSPEAKER

speakerröst ▷ **voice-over**

spec [spek] *informal* = SPECIFICATION; **high-spec** = high specification *noggrann specifikation*

special ['speʃ(ə)l] *adj.* which is different *or* not usual *speciell;* **special character** = character which is not a normal one in a certain font (such as a certain accent *or* a symbol) *specialtecken;* **special effects** = way of making strange things happen in films (such as monsters *or* explosions, etc.) *specialeffekter;* **special purpose** = system designed for a specific *or* limited range of applications *speciellt system;* **special sort** = extra printing character not in the standard font range *specialtecken*

specialanpassa ▷ **customize**

specialiserad dator ▷ **fix**

specialiserad terminal ▷ **job**

specialist ['speʃəlɪst] *subst.* expert in a certain field of study *expert, specialist;* **you need a specialist programmer to help devise a new word-processing program**

specialize ['speʃəlaɪz] *vb.* to study and be an expert in a subject *specialisera sig;* **he specializes in the design of CAD systems**

specific address [spə'sɪfɪk ə'dres] *subst.* storage address that directly, without any modification, accesses a location *or* device *specifik adress*

specification [ˌspesɪfɪ'keɪʃ(ə)n] *subst.* detailed information about what is to be supplied *or* about a job to be done *specifikation;* **to work to standard specifications** = to work to specifications which are accepted anywhere in the same industry *följa standarder;* **the work is not up to specification** *or* **does not meet the customer's specifications** = the product was not manufactured in the way which was detailed in the specifications *arbetet följer inte specifikationen;* **high specification** *or* **high spec** = high degree of accuracy *or* large number of features *noggrann specifikation;* **high spec cabling needs to be very carefully handled;** **program specification** = detailed information about a program's abilities, features and methods *programspecifikation*

specific code [spə'sɪfɪk 'kəʊd] *subst.* binary code which directly operates the central processing unit, using only absolute addresses and values *absolut kod;* **specific coding** = program code that has been written so that it only uses absolute addresses and values *absolut program*

specificity [ˌspesɪ'fɪsɪtɪ] *subst.* ratio of non-relevant entries not retrieved to the total number of non-relevant entries contained in a file, database or library *relevansfrekvens*

specify ['spesɪfaɪ] *vb.* to state clearly what is needed *specifiera, ange*

spectrum ['spektrəm] *subst.* range of frequencies *spektrum;* range of colours *färgspektrum, regnbåge;* **spectrum analyzer** = electronic test equipment that displays the amplitudes of a number of frequencies in a signal *spektrumanalysator*

speech [spiːtʃ] *subst.* speaking *or* making words with the voice *tal(språk);* **speech signal** = signal which transmits spoken words *talsignal;* **speech plus** = method of transmitting a bandlimited speech signal and a number of low speed data signals in a voice grade channel *tal-plus-data-överföring;* **speech processor** = device that alters speech, such as a scrambler *ljudförvrängare;* **speech chip** = integrated circuit that generates sounds (usually phonemes) which when played together sound like human speech *talgeneratorkrets;* **speech recognition** = analysing spoken words in such a way that a computer can recognize spoken words and commands *taligenkänning;* **speech synthesis** = production of spoken words by a speech synthesizer *talsyntes;* **speech synthesizer** = device which takes data from a computer and outputs it as spoken words *talgenerator*

QUOTE speech conveys information, and the primary task of computer speech processing is the transmission and reception of that information
Personal Computer World

speed [spiːd] *subst.* **(a)** measure of the sensitivity of a photographic material (film *or* paper) to light *hastighet;* **high speed film is very sensitive to light (b)** time taken for a movement divided by the distance travelled *hastighet, fart;* **speed of loop** = method of benchmarking a computer by measuring the number of loops executed in a certain time *varvhastighet;* **playback speed** = rate at which tape travels past a playback head *avspelningshastighet*

spegelvändning ▷ **lateral reversal**

spela in ▷ **record**

spellcheck ['speltʃek] *vb.* to check the spelling in a text by comparing it with a dictionary held in the computer *kontrollstavning*

spellchecker ['spelˌtʃekə] *or* **spelling checker** ['spelɪŋˌtʃekə] *subst.* dictionary of correctly spelled words, held in a computer, and used to check the spelling of a text *stavningskontrollprogram;* **the**

program will be upgraded with a word-processor and a spelling checker

spherical aberration [ˈsferɪk(ə)l ˌæbəˈreɪʃ(ə)n] *subst.* optical distortion causing lines to appear curved *sfärisk aberration*

spike [spaɪk] *subst.* very short duration voltage pulse *spets, topp, spik*

spill ⇨ **overflow**

spillage [ˈspɪlɪdʒ] *subst.* situation when too much data is being processed and cannot be contained in a buffer *spill, situation där data flödar över bufferten*

spillindikering ⇨ **flag**

spin [spɪn] *vb.* to turn round fast *rotera, snurra;* **the disk was spun by the drive; the disk drive motor spins at a constant velocity** NOTE: spinning - span - spun

spindle [ˈspɪndl] *subst.* object which grips and spins a disk in the centre hole *spindel*

spindling [ˈspɪndlɪŋ] *subst.* turning a disk by hand *vridande skiva för hand*

spine [spaɪn] *subst.* back edge of the book which is covered by the binding *bokrygg;* **the author's name and the title usually are shown on the spine as well as on the front cover**

spiralsökning ⇨ **helical scan**

spirit duplicator [ˈspɪrɪt ˈdjuːplɪkeɪtə] *subst.* short-run printing method using spirit to transfer ink onto the paper *spritkopiator*

SPL [ˈespiːˈel] = SOUND PRESSURE LEVEL

splice [splaɪs] *vb.* to join two lengths of magnetic tape *or* film, forming a continuous length *klippa ihop;* **you can use glue or splicing tape to splice the ends; splicing block =** device used to correctly position the ends of two lengths of tape *or* film that are to be spliced *klippmaskin;* **splicing tape =** non-magnetic tape which is applied to the back of the two ends of tape to be spliced *klipptape*

split screen [ˈsplɪt ˈskriːn] *subst.* system where more than one text file can appear on the screen at the same time (such as the text being worked on and another text from memory for comparison) *delad skärm*

splitter [ˈsplɪtə] *subst.* device which allows a number of other devices to be plugged into one supply *or* line *linjedelare;* **beam splitter =** optical device to redirect part of a light beam *stråldelare*

spole ⇨ **inductor, reel**

spool [spuːl] **1** *subst.* reel on which a tape *or* printer ribbon is wound *bandrulle* **2** *vb.* to transfer data from a disk to a tape *föra över data från skiva till band*

spooler [ˈspuːlə] *or* **spooling device** [ˈspuːlɪŋ ˌdɪvaɪs] *subst.* device which holds a tape and which receives information from a disk for storage *(rull)bandsminne*

spooling [ˈspuːlɪŋ] *subst.* transferring data to a disk from which it can be printed at the normal speed of the printer, leaving the computer available to do something else *utskriftsmellanlagring, kömellanlagring*

sporadic fault [spəˈrædɪk ˈfɔːlt] *subst.* error that occurs occasionally *sporadiskt fel*

spot [spɒt] *subst.* point on a CRT screen that is illuminated by the electron beam *punkt*

spot beam [ˈspɒtbiːm] *subst.* narrow (satellite) antenna coverage of a select region (on earth) *smal stråle*

spreadsheet [ˈspredʃiːt] *subst.* (i) program which allows calculations to be carried out on several columns of numbers *kalkyl(matris)program;* (ii) printout of calculations on wide computer stationary *kalkylmatrisutskrift*

spridningsdiagram ⇨ **scatter**

spridningslagring ⇨ **load**

sprite [spraɪt] *subst.* object which moves round the screen in computer graphics *"docka", objekt som rör sig i datorgrafik*

sprocket [ˈsprɒkɪt] *or* **sprocket wheel** [ˈsprɒkɪtwiːl] *subst.* wheel with teeth round it which fit into holes in continuous stationery *or* punched tape *(traktor)matningshål*

sprocket feed [ˈsprɒkɪtfiːd] *subst.* paper feed, where the printer pulls the paper by turning sprocket wheels which fit into a series of holes along each edge of the sheet *traktormatning; see also* TRACTOR FEED

sprocket holes [ˈsprɒkɪthəʊlz] *subst.* series of small holes on each edge of continuous stationery, which allow the sheet to be pulled through the printer *kantperforering*

språkstruktur ⇨ **language**

spur [spɜː] *subst.* connection point into a network *(nät)ingång*

SPX [ˈespiːˈeks] = SIMPLEX

spår ⇨ **disk, track**

spårgrupp ⇨ **band**

spänning ⇨ **voltage**

spänningssätta ⇨ pull up

spänningstopp ⇨ transient

spänningsutjämnare ⇨ transient

spärra ⇨ interlock

SQA ['eskju:'eɪ] = SOFTWARE QUALITY ASSURANCE

square wave ['skweəweɪv] *subst.* waveform with a square shape *fyrkantsvåg*

SS ['es'es] = SINGLE-SIDED

SSBSC ['eses'bi:es'si:] = SINGLE SIDEBAND SUPPRESSED CARRIER

SSD ['eses'di:] = SINGLE-SIDED DISK

SSI ['eses'aɪ] = SMALL SCALE INTEGRATION

stabilisera ⇨ regulate

stability [stə'bɪlətɪ] *subst.* being stable *stabilitet;* **image stability** = ability of a display screen to provide a flicker-free picture *bildstabilitet*

stable ['steɪbl] *adj.* not moving *or* not changing *stabil;* **stable state** = the state of a system when no external signals are applied *stabilt tillstånd*

stack [stæk] *subst.* temporary storage for data, registers *or* tasks where items are added and retrieved from the same end of the list *stack; see also* LIFO; **pushdown stack** *or* **pushdown list** = method of storing data, where the last item stored is always at the same location, the rest of the list being pushed down by one address *stack;* **virtual memory stack** = temporary store for pages in a virtual memory system *virtuell stack;* **stack address** = location pointed to by the stack pointer *stackadress;* **stack base** = address of the origin *or* base of a stack *basadress, grundadress;* **stack job processor** = storing a number of jobs to be processed in a stack and automatically executing one after the other *köprocessor;* **stack pointer (SP)** = address register containing the location of the most recently stored item of data *or* the location of the next item of data to be retrieved *stackpekare*

stack ⇨ push, list

stafettnät ⇨ token

stage [steɪdʒ] *subst.* one of several points in a process *stadium, steg;* **the text is ready for the printing stage; we are in the first stage of running in the new computer system**

staged [steɪdʒd] *adj.* carried out in stages, one after the other *stegvis, i stadier;* **staged change-over** = change between an old and a new system in a series of stages *gradvist övergång*

stamledning ⇨ trunk

stamlinje ⇨ high

stand-alone ['stændə,ləʊn] *or* **standalone** *adj. & subst.* (device *or* system) which can operate without the need of any other devices *fristående (terminal eller system);* **the workstations have been networked together rather than used as stand-alone systems ;** **stand-alone system** = system that can operate independently *fristående system;* **stand-alone terminal** = computer terminal with a processor and memory which can be directly connected to a modem, without being a member of a network *or* cluster *fristående terminal*

standard ['stændəd] *adj.* normal *or* usual *standard;* **standard document** *or* **standard form** *or* **standard paragraph** *or* **standard text** = normal printed document *or* form *or* paragraph which is used many times (with different names and addresses often inserted - as in a form letter) *standardtext;* **standard function** = special feature included as normal in a computer system *standardfunktion;* **standard interface** = interface between two or more systems that conforms to pre-defined standards *standardgränssnitt;* **standard letter** = letter which is sent without any change to the main text, but being personalised by inserting the names and addresses of different people *standardbrev;* **standard subroutine** = routine which carries out an often used function, such as keyboard input *or* screen display *standardrutin*

standardbrev ⇨ form

standardize ['stændədaɪz] *vb.* to make a series of things conform to a standard *standardisera;* **the standardized control of transmission links**

standards ['stændədz] *subst.* normal quality *or* normal conditions which are used to judge other things *standarder;* **production standards** = quality of production *produktionskvalitet;* **to be up to standard** to be of an acceptable quality *möta standarder (kvalitetskrav);* **this batch of disks is not up to standard; standards converter** = device to convert received signals conforming to one standard into a different standard *standard(signal)omvandlare;* **the standards converter allows us to watch US television broadcasts on our UK standards set; video standards** *see* VIDEO; **modem standards** = rules defining transmitting frequencies, etc., which allow different modems to communicate *modemstandarder*

COMMENT: modem standards are set by the CCITT in the UK, the Commonwealth and most of Europe, while the USA and part of South America use modem standards set by Bell

standby ['stæn(d)baɪ] *subst.* (device *or* program) which is ready for use in case of failure *reserv, beredskap;* **standby equipment** = secondary system identical to the main system, to be used if the main system breaks down *reservsystem;* **cold standby** = backup system that will allow the equipment to continue running but with the loss of any volatile data *passiv reserv, ej ansluten reservanslutning;* **hot standby** = backup equipment that is kept operational at all times in case of system failure *aktiv reserv, direkt insatsberedd reservutrustning*

QUOTE before fault-tolerant systems, users had to rely on the cold standby, that is switching on a second machine when the first developed a fault; the alternative was the hot standby, where a second computer was kept running continuously
Computer News

stansare ⇨ **keyboarder**

stapeldiagram ⇨ **bar chart, histogram**

stapelgrafik ⇨ **bar code**

stapelkoppla ⇨ **piggyback**

star network ['stɑːˌnetwɜːk] *subst.* network of several machines where each terminal *or* floppy disk unit *or* satellite is linked individually to a central hard disk machine *or* server *stjärnnät; compare* BUS NETWORK, RING NETWORK

star program ['stɑːˌprəʊgræm] *subst.* perfect program that runs (first time) with no errors *or* bugs *stjärnprogram*

start [stɑːt] *subst.* beginning *or* first part *start, början;* **cold start** = switching on a computer *or* to run a program from its original start point *kallstart (genom att slå på strömmen);* **start bit** *or* **element** = transmitted bit used (in asynchronous communications) to indicate the start of a character *startbit* NOTE: opposite is **stop bit;** **warm start** = restarting a program which has stopped, without losing any data *varmstart (omstart);* **start of header** = transmitted code indicating the start of header (address *or* destination) information for a following message *adresstart;* **start of text (SOT** *or* **STX)** = transmitted code indicating the end of control *or* address information and the start of the message *textstart*

startadress ⇨ **address, execution**

starta om ⇨ **reboot, restart**

startband ⇨ **trailer**

startblock ⇨ **header**

startetikett ⇨ **header**

startindikering ⇨ **head**

startkommando ⇨ **execute**

startkort ⇨ **header**

startläge ⇨ **float**

startpaket ⇨ **header**

startprocess ⇨ **initialization**

startprogram ⇨ **initial**

startpunkt ⇨ **entry, front-end, load point**

startrutin ⇨ **housekeeping**

start(rutin) ⇨ **interlude**

starttid ⇨ **entry**

startvillkor ⇨ **entry**

startvärde ⇨ **initial**

stat [stæt] *informal* = PHOTOSTAT

state [steɪt] *subst.* the way something is *status, tillstånd, läge;* **active state** = state in which an action can *or* does occur *aktivt tillstånd;* **steady state** = circuit *or* device *or* program state in which no action is occurring but can accept an input *stationärt tillstånd, fast tillstånd*

statement ['steɪtmənt] *subst.* (i) expression used to convey an instruction *or* define a process *påstående, utsaga;* (ii) instruction in a source language which is translated into several machine code instructions *programsats;* **conditional statement** = program instruction that will redirect program control according to the outcome of an event *villkorlig sats;* **control statement** = (i) program instruction that directs a program (to another branch, etc.) *styrsats;* (ii) program instruction that directs a CPU to provide controlling actions *or* controls the actions of the CPU *styrsats;* **directive statement** = program instruction used to control the language translator, compiler, etc. *styrsats;* **input statement** = computer programming command that waits for data entry from a port *or* keyboard *inmatningssats;* **multi-statement line** = line from a computer program that contains more than one instruction *or* statement *flera satser på samma rad;* **narrative statement** = statement which set variables and allocates storage *beskrivande sats;* **statement number** = number assigned (in a sequential way) to a series of instruction statements *satsnummer; see also* LINE NUMBER

state-of-the-art ['steɪt əv ði 'ɑːt] *adj.* very modern *or* technically as advanced as possible *på högsta teknologiska nivå*

QUOTE the main PCB is decidedly non-state-of-the-art
Personal Computer World

static ['stætɪk] **1** *subst.* **(a)** (i) loud background noise *or* interference in a radio broadcast due to atmospheric conditions *atmosfärisk störning;* (ii) background noise in a recorded signal *brus* **(b)** charge that does not flow *statisk laddning* NOTE: no plural **2** *adj.* (i) (data) which does not change with time *statiska data;* (ii) (system) that is not dynamic *statiskt system;* **static dump** = printout of the state of a system when it has finished a process *statisk dump;* **static memory** = non-volatile memory that does not require refreshing *statiskt minne;* **static RAM** = RAM which retains data for as long as the power supply is on, and where the data does not have to be refreshed *statiskt direktminne; compare with* DYNAMIC RAM; **static subroutine** = subroutine that uses no variables apart from the operand addresses *statisk subrutin*

COMMENT: static RAM uses bistable devices such as flip-flops to store data; these take up more space on a chip than the capacititive storage method of dynamic RAM but do not require refreshing

station ['steɪʃ(ə)n] *subst.* **(a)** point in a network *or* communications system that contains devices to control the input and output of messages, allowing it to be used as a sink *or* source *station, nod, enhet;* **secondary station** = temporary status of the station that is receiving data *mottagningsläge;* **workstation** = desk with computer, keyboard, monitor, printers, etc., where a person works *arbetsplats, arbetsstation* **(b) earth station** = dish antenna and circuitry used to communicate with a satellite *markstation;* **radio station** = broadcast signal booster *or* relay point consisting of a receiver and transmitter linked with ancillary equipment *radiostation;* **the signal from this radio station is very weak; we are trying to jam the signals from that station**

stationary ['steɪʃ(ə)nərɪ] *adj.* not moving *stationär;* **geostationary orbit** = orbit of a satellite which keeps it above the same part of the earth *geostationär bana*

stationery ['steɪʃ(ə)nərɪ] *subst.* office supplies for writing, especially paper, envelopes, labels, etc. *kontorsmateriel;* **computer stationery** = paper specially made for use in a computer printer *datorpapper;* **continuous stationery** = printer stationery which takes the form of a single long sheet *papper i löpande bana;* **preprinted stationery** = computer stationery (such as invoices) which is preprinted with the company heading and form layout onto which the details will be printed by the computer *förtryckt brevpapper, förtrycka fakturor* NOTE: no plural

statistical [stə'tɪstɪk(ə)l] *adj.* based on statistics *statistisk;* **statistical time division multiplexing (STDM)** = time division multiplexing system that allocates time slots when they are required, allowing greater flexibility and a greater number of devices to transmit *statistiks-tids(delad) multiplexering, tidsmultiplexering (tidsdelad multiplexering); see also* TIME DIVISION MULTIPLEXING

statistician [ˌstætɪs'tɪʃ(ə)n] *subst.* person who analyses statistics *statistiker*

statistics [stə'tɪstɪks] *subst.* (study of) facts in the form of figures *statistik*

statistisk logik ⇨ **fuzzy**

status ['steɪtəs] *subst.* importance *or* position *status;* **status bit** = single bit in a word used to provide information about the state *or* result of an operation *statusbit;* **status line** = line at the top *or* bottom of a screen which gives information about the task currently being worked on (number of lines, number of columns, filename, time, etc.) *statusrad;* **status poll** = signal from a computer requesting information on the current status of a terminal *statusavfrågning;* **status register** = register containing information on the status of a peripheral device *statusregister;* **program status word (PSW)** = word which contains a number of status bits, such as carry flag, zero flag, overflow bit, etc. *programstatusord*

statusbit ⇨ **device**

statusflagga ⇨ **device**

STD ['esti:'di:] = SUBSCRIBER TRUNK DIALLING

STDM ['esti:di:'em] = STATISTICAL TIME DIVISION MULTIPLEXING

steady state ['stedɪ 'steɪt] *subst.* circuit *or* device *or* program state in which no action is occurring but can accept an input *stationärt tillstånd*

steg ⇨ **increment, step**

stegade data ⇨ **incremental computer**

stega (fram) ⇨ **increment**

stegdator ⇨ **incremental computer**

stegritare ⇨ **incremental computer**

stencil ['stensl] *subst.* material with component shapes and symbols already cut out, allowing designers to draw components and other symbols rapidly *schablon;* **the stencil has all the electronic components on it; the schematic looks much neater if you use a stencil; flowchart stencil** *or* **template** = plastic sheet with template symbols cut out, to allow flowcharts to be quickly and clearly drawn *flödesplanschablon*

step [step] **1** *subst.* a single unit *steg, operation;* **single step** = executing a computer program one instruction at a time, used for debugging *stegning (av program)* **2** *vb.* to move forwards *or* backwards by one unit *stega framåt (bakåt);* **we stepped forward through the file one record at a time; we stepped forward the film one frame at a time**

stepper motor ['stepə 'məʊtə] *or* **stepping motor** ['stepɪŋ 'məʊtə] *subst.* motor which turns in small steps as instructed by a computer (used in printers, disk drives and robots) *stegmotor*

steradian [stə'reɪdɪən] *subst. (enheten) steradian;* unit of solid angle

stereo ['stɪərɪəʊ] *informal* = STEREOPHONIC

stereophonic [ˌstɪərɪə'fɒnɪk] *adj.* using two audio signals recorded from slightly different positions to provide a three-dimensional sound effect when replayed through two separate loudspeakers *stereofonisk, stereo-;* **stereophonic microphone** = one device containing two microphones allowing stereo signals to be recorded *stereomikrofon;* **stereophonic recorder** = tape recorder that records two audio signals onto magnetic tape *stereobandspelare*

stickprov ▷ **sample**

stift ▷ **pin**

stigtid ▷ **rise time**

stil ▷ **type, typeface**

still frame ['stɪl 'freɪm] *subst.* one single video *or* film frame displayed by itself *stillbild*

stjärnnät ▷ **star network**

stochastic model [stɒ'kæstɪk 'mɒdl] *subst.* mathematical representation of a system that includes the effects of random actions *stokastisk modell*

stock control program ['stɒk kən,trəʊl 'prəʊgræm] *subst.* software designed to help manage stock in a business *lagerstyrningsprogram*

stockning ▷ **overflow**

stop [stɒp] *vb.* not doing any action *stoppa, stanna;* **stop and wait protocol** = communications protocol in which the transmitter waits for a signal from the receiver that the message was correctly received before transmitting further data *asynkront protokoll;* **tab stop** = preset point along a line, where the printing head *or* cursor will stop for each tabulation command *tabulatorstopp*

stop bit ['stɒpbɪt] *or* **stop element** ['stɒpˌelɪmənt] *subst.* transmitted bit used in asynchronous communications to indicate the end of a character *stoppbit;* **stop code** = instruction that temporarily stops a process to allow the user to enter data *stoppkod;* **stop instruction** = computer programming instruction that stops program execution *stoppinstruktion;* **stop list** = list of words that are not to be used *or* are not significant for a file *or* library search *stopplista;* **stop time** = time taken for a spinning disk to come to a stop after it is no longer powered *stopptid*

stoppa ▷ **cancel, halt, stop**

stoppinstruktion ▷ **halt**

stoppläge ▷ **halt**

stoppvillkor ▷ **halt**

storage ['stɔːrɪdʒ] *subst.* memory *or* part of the computer system in which data *or* programs are kept for further use *minne, lagring;* **archive storage** = storage of data for a long period of time *arkivlagring;* **auxiliary storage** = any data storage medium (such as magnetic tape *or* disk) that is not the main, high speed memory *externt minne;* **dynamic storage** *or* **memory** = memory that requires its contents to be updated regularly *dynamiskt minne;* **external storage** = storage device which is located outside the main computer system but which can be accessed by the CPU *yttre sekundärminne;* **information storage** = storing data in a form which allows it to be processed at a later date *informationsminne;* **instruction storage** = section of memory that is used to store instructions *instruktionsminne;* **intermediate storage** = temporary area of memory for items that are currently being processed *mellanminne;* **mass storage system** = data storage that can hold more than one million million bits of data *massminne;* **nonerasable storage** = storage medium that cannot be erased and re-used *permanent minne;* **primary storage** = (i) small fast-access internal memory of a system which contains the program currently being executed *primärminne;* (ii) main internal memory of a system *primärminne;* **secondary storage** = any data storage medium (such as magnetic tape *or* floppy disk) that is not the main, high-speed computer storage *sekundärminne;* **static storage** = nonvolatile memory that does not require refreshing *statiskt minne;* **temporary storage** = storage which is not permanent *flyktigt minne;* **volatile storage** = memory *or* storage medium that loses data stored when the power supply is switched off *tillfälligt minne;* **storage allocation** = how memory is allocated for different uses, such as programs, variables, data, etc. *minnestilldelning;* **storage capacity** = amount of space available for storage of data *minneskapacitet;* **storage density** = number of bits that can be recorded per unit area of storage medium *minnestäthet;* **storage device** = any device that can store data and then allow it to be retrieved when required *minnesenhet;* **storage disk** = disk used to store data *skiva, diskett;* **storage dump** = printout of all the contents of an area of storage space *minnesdump;* **storage media** = various materials which are able to store data *lagringsmedium, minnesmedium;* **storage tube** = special CRT used for computer graphics that retains an image on screen without the need for refresh actions *minnesrör; see also* REFRESH

COMMENT: storage devices include hard and floppy disk, RAM, punched paper tape and magnetic tape

storbildsteve ⇨ television (TV)

stordator ⇨ mainframe (computer)

stordia ⇨ transparency

store [stɔː] **1** *subst.* memory *or* part of the computer system in which data *or* programs are kept for further use *lagring;* **store address register (SAR)** = register in a CPU that contains the address of the next location to be accessed *programpekare, nästaadress;* **store data register (SDR)** = register in a CPU which holds data before it is processed *or* moved to a memory location *mellanlagringsregister;* **store location** *or* **cell** = unit in a computer system which can store information *minnescell* **2** *vb.* to save data, which can then be used again as necessary *lagra;* **storing a page of high resolution graphics can require 3Mb;** **store and forward** = communications system that stores a number of messages before retransmitting them *lagra och sända vidare;* **stored program** = computer program that is stored in memory (if it is stored in dynamic RAM it will be lost when the machine is switched off, if stored on disk or tape (backing store) it will be permanently retained) *lagrat program;* **stored program signalling** = system of storing communications control signals on computer in the form of a program *signallagring i programform*

storlek ⇨ dimension, size

storstadstillägg ⇨ weighting

straight-line coding ['streɪt‚laɪn 'kəʊdɪŋ] *subst.* program written to avoid the use of loops and branches, providing a faster execution time *linjär kod*

stray [streɪ] *adj.* lost *or* wandering; (something) which has avoided being stopped *sporadisk, spridd, strö-;* **the metal screen protects the CPU against stray electromagnetic effects from the PSU**

streaking ['striːkɪŋ] *subst.* horizontal television picture distortion *streckning*

stream [striːm] *subst.* long flow of serial data *ström, flöde;* **job stream** = number of tasks arranged in order waiting to be processed in a batch system *jobbflöde*

streamer ['striːmə] *subst.* **tape streamer** *or* **streaming tape drive** = (device containing a) continuous loop of tape, used as backing storage *strömbandsminne*

QUOTE the product has 16Mb of memory, 45Mb of Winchester disk storage and 95Mb streaming tape storage
Minicomputer News

streckkod ⇨ bar code

streckkodsetikett ⇨ kimball tag

streckkodsläsare ⇨ bar code

string [strɪŋ] *subst.* any series of consecutive alphanumeric characters *or* words that are manipulated and treated as a single unit by the computer *sträng;* **alphanumeric** *or* **character string** = storage allocated for a series of alphanumeric characters *alfanumerisk (tecken)sträng;* **numeric string** = string which contains only numbers *talsträng, siffersträng;* **null** *or* **blank string** = string that contains nothing *blindsträng;* **string area** = section of memory in which strings of alphanumeric characters are stored *strängarea;* **string concatenation** = linking a series of strings together *stränglänkning;* **string function** = program operation which can act on strings *strängfunktion;* **string length** = the number of characters in a string *stränglängd;* **string name** = identification label assigned to a string *strängnamn;* **string orientated symbolic language (SNOBOL)** = high-level programming language that uses string processing methods *programmeringsspråket SNOBOL;* **string variable** = variables used in a computer language that can contain alphanumeric characters as well as numbers *strängvariabel*

stringy floppy ['strɪŋɪ 'flɒpɪ] *or* **tape streamer** ['teɪp‚striːmə] *subst.* continuous loop of tape, used for backing storage *strömbandsminne*

strip [strɪp] **1** *subst.* long thin piece of material *remsa;* **strip window** = display which shows a single line of text *teckenrad, radfönster;* **magnetic strip** = layer of magnetic material on the surface of a plastic card, used for recording data *magnetremsa* **2** *vb.* to remove the control data from a received message, leaving only the relevant information *"klä av" (data)*

stripe [straɪp] *subst.* long thin line of colour *rand, linje;* **balance stripe** = thin magnetic strip on a cine film on the opposite side to the sound track, so that the whole film will lie flat when played back *balansspår*

strobe [strəʊb] *vb.* to send a pulse (usually on the selection line) of an electronic circuit *avsöka;* **address strobe** = signal indicating that a valid address is on the address bus *adress;* **data strobe** = signal indicating that valid data is on the data bus *datapuls*

stroboscope ['strəʊbəskəʊp] *or* **strobe** [strəʊb] *subst.* light source which produces flashes of light *stroboskop*

stroke [strəʊk] *subst.* basic curved *or* straight line that makes up a character *streck*

strowger exchange ['straʊgər ɪks'tʃeɪn(d)ʒ] *subst.* telephone exchange worked by electromechanical switches *strowgerväljare*

structure ['strʌktʃə] **1** *subst.* way in which something is organized *or* formed *struktur;* **network structure** = data structure that allows each node to be connected to any of the others *nätstruktur* **2** *vb.* to organize *or* to arrange in a certain way *strukturera, organisera;* **you first structure a document to meet your requirements and then fill in the blanks; structured design** = problem solved by a number of interconnected modules *strukturerad konstruktion;* **structured programming** = well-ordered and logical technique of assembling programs *strukturerad programmering*

strukturbeskrivning ⊳ **database**

strukturdiagram ⊳ **schema**

strukturskog ⊳ **forest**

stråla ⊳ **radiate**

stråle ⊳ **beam, ray**

sträckvarning ⊳ **banding**

sträng ⊳ **string**

strängkonstant ⊳ **literal**

ström ⊳ **current**

strömavbrott ⊳ **blackout, failure, power**

strömbandsenhet ⊳ **tape**

strömbandsminne ⊳ **floppy disk, streamer**

strömförsörjning ⊳ **power**

studio ['stjuːdɪəʊ] *subst.* place where a designer draws; place where recordings takeplace; place where films are made *studio, ateljé*

studsfri krets ⊳ **de-bounce**

STX ['estiˈeks] = START OF TEXT

style sheet ['staɪlʃiːt] *subst.* (i) sheet giving the style which should be followed by an editor *stilark;* (ii) template that can be preformatted to generate automatically the style *or* layout of a document such as a manual, a book, a newsletter, etc. *stilark*

stylus ['staɪləs] *subst.* **(a)** (transducer) needle which converts signals on an audio record into electrical signals *grammofonnål* **(b)** pen-like device that is used in computer graphics systems to dictate cursor position on the screen *ljuspenna;* **use the stylus on the graphics tablet to draw (c)** (transducer) that detects data stored on a video disk *videoskiveläshuvud;* **stylus printer** *see* DOT MATRIX PRINTER

stympat sidband ⊳ **vestigial sideband**

styra ⊳ **control**

styrdator ⊳ **control**

styrd sidväxling ⊳ **demand**

styrenhet ⊳ **control, controller**

styrenhet för diskettenhet ⊳ **floppy disk**

styrenhet för skivminne ⊳ **disk**

styrhål ⊳ **feed, index**

styrinstruktion ⊳ **instruction**

styrkod ⊳ **device**

styrkodsminne ⊳ **memory**

styrkort för fast skivminne ⊳ **hard**

styrkort för skivminne ⊳ **disk**

styrkrets för direktminne ⊳ **DMA**

styrläge ⊳ **mode**

styrmarkering ⊳ **index**

styrprocessor ⊳ **microcontroller**

styrprogram ⊳ **device, driver, executive, handler**

styrprogram för skrivare ⊳ driver

styrsats ⊳ statement

styrsekvens ⊳ sequence

styrspak ⊳ joystick

styrspaksingång ⊳ port

styrspråk ⊳ language

styr(tangent) ⊳ CTR

ställa in ⊳ tune

ställdon ⊳ actuator

ställprogram ⊳ hold

ständig ⊳ continual

stöd ⊳ backup

stödminne ⊳ backing

stödprocessor ⊳ back-end processor

stödraster ⊳ grid

störmarginal ⊳ noise

störning ⊳ distortion, interference

störsäkerhet ⊳ interference, noise

sub- [sʌb] *prefix* meaning less (important) than *or* lower than *sub-, under-;* **subaddress** = peripheral identification code, used to access one peripheral (this is then followed by address data to access a location within the peripheral's memory) *underadress;* **subaudio frequencies** = frequencies below the audio range (below 20Hz) *frekvenser nedanför hörbarhetsområdet, infraljud;* **subclass** = number of data items to do with one item in a master class *undergrupp;* **subbing** *or* **sub-editing** = editing of a manuscript before it is sent for typesetting *manuskriptredigering;* **subrange** = below the normal range *under det normala omfänget*

subdirectory [ˈsʌbdɪˌrekt(ə)rɪ] *subst.* directory of disk *or* tape contents contained within the main directory *underkatalog, underbibliotek*

> QUOTE if you delete a file and then delete the subdirectory where it was located, you cannot restore the file because the directory does not exist
> **Personal Computer World**

subprogram [ˈsʌbˌprəʊɡræm] *subst.* (i) subroutine in a program *subrutin;* (ii) program called up by a main program *underprogram*

subroutine [ˈsʌbruːˌtiːn] *subst.* section of a program which performs a required function and that can be called upon at any time from inside the main program *subrutin;* **subroutine call** = computer

programming instruction that directs control to a subroutine *subrutinanrop;* **closed** *or* **linked subroutine** = number of computer instructions in a program that can be called at any time, with control being returned on completion to the next instruction after the call *länkad subrutin, sluten subrutin;* **open subroutine** = code for a subroutine which is copied into memory whenever a call instruction is found *öppen subrutin;* **static subroutine** = subroutine that uses no variables apart from the operand addresses *statisk subrutin;* **two-level subroutine** = subroutine containing another subroutine *tvånivåsubrutin;* **subroutine call** = computer programming instruction that directs control to a subroutine *subrutinanrop*

> COMMENT: a subroutine is executed by a call instruction which directs the processor to its address; when finished it returns to the instruction after the call instruction in the main program

subrutin ⊳ direct

subscriber [səbˈskraɪbə] *subst.* **subscriber trunk dialling (STD)** = system where a person can dial direct from one telephone to another, without referring to the operator *direktuppringning;* (i) person who has a telephone *(telefon)abonnent;* (ii) person who pays for access to a service such as a BBS *(telefon)abonnent*

subscript [ˈsʌbskrɪpt] *subst.* small character which is printed below the line of other characters *index; see also* SUPERSCRIPT (NOTE: used in chemical formulae: CO_2); **subscripted variable** = element in an array, which is identified by a subscript *index*

subsegment [ˈsʌbˈseɡmənt] *subst.* small section of a segment *undersegment, subsegment*

subset [ˈsʌbset] *subst.* small set of data items which forms part of another larger set *undergrupp*

substance [ˈsʌbst(ə)ns] *subst.* any matter whose properties can be described *substans*

substitute [ˈsʌbstɪtjuːt] *vb.* to put something in the place of something else *ersätta;* **substitute character** = character that is displayed if a received character is not recognized *ersättningstecken* NOTE: you substitute one thing **for** another

substitution [ˌsʌbstɪˈtjuːʃ(ə)n] *subst.* replacing something by something else *ersättning, substitut;* **substitution error** = error made by a scanner which mistakes one character *or* letter for another *läsfel;* **substitution table** = list of characters *or* codes that are to be inserted instead of received codes *ersättningstabell*

substrate ['sʌbstreɪt] *subst.* base material on which an integrated circuit is constructed *substrat; see also* INTEGRATED CIRCUIT

subsystem ['sʌb,sɪstəm] *subst.* one smaller part of a large system *subsystem, undersystem*

subtotal ['sʌb,təʊtl] *subst.* total at the end of a column, which when added to others makes the grand total *kolumnsumma, delsumma*

subtraction [səb'trækʃ(ə)n] *subst.* taking one number away from another *subtraktion*

subtrahend ['sʌbtrəhend] *subst.* in a subtraction operation, the number to be subtracted from the minuend *subtrahend*

subvoice grade channel ['sʌbvɔɪs'greɪd 'tʃænl] *subst.* communications channel using frequencies (240 - 300Hz) below a voice channel, used for low speed data transmission *infrabandskanal*

successive [s(ə)k'sesɪv] *adj.* which follow one after the other *efterföljande, succesiv;* **each successive operation adds further characters to the string**

suffix notation ['sʌfɪks nə(ʊ)'teɪʃ(ə)n] *subst.* mathematical operations written in a logical way, so that the symbol appears after the numbers to be acted upon *suffixnotation; see also* POSTFIX NOTATION

suite of programs ['swiːt əv 'prəʊgræmz] *subst.* (i) group of programs which run one after the other *programgrupp, programföljd;* (ii) number of programs used for a particular task *programuppsättning, programkonfiguration;* **the word-processing system uses a suite of three programs, editor, spelling checker and printing controller**

sum [sʌm] *subst.* total of a number of items added together *summa*

summation check [sʌ'meɪʃ(ə)n 'tʃek] *subst.* error detection check performed by adding together the characters received and comparing with the required total *summakontroll*

***summer* ⇨ buzzer**

sun outage ['sʌn'aʊtɪdʒ] *subst.* length of time during which a satellite does not operate due to the position of the moon *or* earth, causing a shadow over the satellite's solar cells *solskuggeavbrott*

super- ['suːpə] *prefix* meaning very good *or* very powerful *super-, över-;* **supercomputer** = very powerful mainframe computer used for high speed mathematical tasks *superdator;* **supergroup**

= a number (60) of voice channels collected together into five adjacent channels for simultaneous transmission *supergrupp*

superheterodyne **radio** ['suːpə'hetərədaɪn 'reɪdɪəʊ] *subst.* radio receiver that converts a received signal by means of a heterodyne process to an intermediate frequency for easier processing *superheterodyn*

super high frequency (SHF) ['suːpər,haɪ 'friːkwənsɪ ('eseɪtʃ'ef)] *subst.* frequency range between 3 - 30GHz *superhög frekvens*

superimpose ['suːp(ə)rɪm'pəʊz] *vb.* to place something on top of something else *placera ovanpå, överexponera*

superior number [suː'pɪərɪə 'nʌmbə] *subst.* superscript figure *exponent*

super large scale integration (SLSI) ['suːpə 'lɑːdʒ skeɪl ,ɪntɪ'greɪʃ(ə)n] *subst.* integrated circuit with more than 100,000 components *superintegrerad krets*

super master group ['suːpə 'mɑːstə 'gruːp] *subst.* collection of 900 voice channels *superstorgrupp*

superscript ['suːpəskrɪpt] *subst.* small character printed higher than the normal line of characters *exponent; compare with* SUBSCRIPT
NOTE: used often in mathematics: 10^5 (say: ten to the power five)

supersede [,suːpə'siːd] *vb.* to take the place of something which is older *or* less useful *ersätta, överträffa;* **the new program supersedes the earlier one, and is much faster**

superstation ['suːpə,steɪʃ(ə)n] *subst. US* TV system, where a single TV station broadcasts many programmes simultaneously via satellite and cable *tevesystem där en tevestation sänder flera program samtidigt via satellit och kabel*

supervise ['suːpəvaɪz] *vb.* to watch carefully to see if work is well done *övervaka, kontrollera;* **the manufacture of circuit boards is very carefully supervised**

supervision [,suːpə'vɪʒ(ə)n] *subst.* being supervised *övervakning*

supervisor ['suːpəvaɪzə] *subst.* (i) person who makes sure that equipment is always working correctly *övervakare;* (ii) section of a computer operating system that regulates the use of peripherals and the operations undertaken by the CPU *övervaknings-program*

supervisory [,suːpə'vaɪz(ə)rɪ] *adj.* as a supervisor *övervakande;* **supervisory program** *or* **executive program** = master program in a computer system that controls the execution of other programs *övervakningsprogram, styrprogram;* **supervisory sequence** = combination of control codes that perform a controlling function in a data communications network *övervakningssekvens;* **supervisory signal** = (i) signal that indicates if a circuit is busy *upptagetsignal;* (ii) signal that provides an indication of the state of a device *statussignal*

supplier [sə'plaɪə] *subst.* company which supplies *leverantör;* **a supplier of computer parts; a supplier of disk drives** *or* **a disk drive supplier; Japanese suppliers have set up warehouses in the country**

supply [sə'plaɪ] **1** *subst.* providing goods *or* products *or* services *utbud, tillförsel;* **the electricity supply has failed; they signed a contract for the supply of computer stationery 2** *vb.* to provide something which is needed (for which someone will pay) *leverera, sälja, förse (med);* **the computer was supplied by a recognized dealer; they have signed a contract to supply on-line information**

support [sə'pɔːt] *vb.* to give help to *or* to help to run *stödja;* **the main computer supports six workstations; support chip** = dedicated IC that works with a CPU, and carries out an additional function *or* a standard function very rapidly, so speeding up the processing time *tillsatskrets;* **the maths support chip can be plugged in here**

suppress [sə'pres] *vb.* to remove *undertrycka, hämma, dämpa;* **the filter is used to suppress the noise due to static interference; suppressed carrier modulation** = modulated waveform where the carrier signal has been suppressed prior to transmission, leaving only the modulated sidebands *modulering med undertryckbärvåg;* **double sideband suppressed carrier (DSBSC)** = amplitude modulation that has a suppressed carrier, leaving only two sidebands *dubbelt sidband med undertryckt bärvåg;* **single sideband suppressed carrier (SSBSC)** = amplitude modulation that has a suppressed carrier, and only one sideband for data transmission *enkelt sidband med undertryckt bärvåg*

suppression [sə'preʃ(ə)n] *subst.* act of suppressing *undertryckande*

suppressor [sə'presə] *subst.* device which suppresses interference *dämpare, störningsskydd;* **echo suppressor** = device used on long-distance speech lines to prevent echoing effects *ekodämpare*

surge [sɜːdʒ] *subst.* sudden increase in electrical power in a system, due to a fault *or* noise *or* component failure *spänningstopp;* **surge protector** = electronic device that cuts off the power supply to sensitive equipment if it detects a power surge that could cause damage *spänningsutjämnare, överspänningsskydd, nät(av)störningsfilter*

sustain [səs'teɪn] *vb.* to keep a voltage at a certain level for a period of time *hålla (uppe)*

svar ▷ answer, response

svarssignal ▷ answer

svarstid ▷ answer, time

svart-på-vit-(bild)skärm ▷ dark trace tube

svart-vit skärm ▷ monochrome

sveptid ▷ scanning

svärtningskontrollknapp ▷ density

svävande läs- och skrivhuvud ▷ flying head

SW ['es'dʌblju:] = SHORT WAVE

swap [swɒp] **1** *subst.* = SWAPPING **2** *vb.* to stop using one program, put it into store temporarily, run another program, and when that is finished, return to the first one *växla, byta (program)*

swapping ['swɒpɪŋ] *or* **swap** ['swɒp] *subst.* system where a program is moved to backing storage while another program is being used *växling, byte*

sweep [swiːp] *subst.* movement of the electron beam over the area of a television screen in regular horizontal and vertical steps, producing the image *svep*

swim [swɪm] *subst.* computer graphics that move slightly due to a faulty display unit *bild som rör sig (pga fel på skärmen)*

switch [swɪtʃ] **1** *subst.* **(a)** point in a computer program where control can be passed to one of a number of choices *delningspunkt, växel* **(b)** mechanical *or* solid state device that can electrically connect *or* isolate two or more lines *strömbrytare, relä;*

switch train = series of switches between a caller and a receiver in a telephone network *relätåg* **2** *vb.* to connect *or* disconnect two lines by activating a switch *växla, koppla, slå på (av);* **to switch on** = to start to provide power to a system by using a switch to connect the power supply lines to the circuit *slå på;* **to switch off** = to disconnect the power supply to a device *slå av;* **to switch over** = to start using an alternative device when the primary one becomes faulty *slå över;* **switched network backup** = user's choice of a secondary route through a network if the first is busy *reservväg i nät;* **switched star** = cable television distribution system *växelstjärnnät;* **switched virtual call** = connection between two devices in a network that is only made when required, after a request signal *tillfälligt uppkopplad nätförbindelse*

switchboard ['swɪtʃbɔːd] *subst.* central point in a telephone system, where the lines from various telephone handsets meet, where calls can be directed to any other telephone *telefonväxel;* **switchboard operator** = person who works a central telephone switchboard, by connecting incoming and outgoing calls to various lines *växeltelefonist*

switching ['swɪtʃɪŋ] *subst.* constant update of connections between changing sinks and sources in a network *växling, koppling;* **switching centre** = point in a communications network where messages can be switched to and from the various lines and circuits that end there *växlingspunkt, kopplingsnod;* **switching circuit** = electronic circuit that can direct messages from one line *or* circuit to another in a switching centre *växelkrets;* **line switching** = communication line and circuit established on demand and held until no longer required *linjeuppkoppling, linjeväxling*

syfta ⇨ **refer**

symbol ['sɪmb(ə)l] *subst.* sign *or* picture which represents something *symbol, tecken;* **this language uses the symbol ? to represent the print command; logic symbol** = graphical symbol used to represent a type of logic function in a diagram *logisk symbol;* **symbol table** *or* **library** = list of labels *or* names in a compiler *or* assembler, which relate to their addresses in the machine code program *symbolbibliotek*

symbolic [sɪm'bɒlɪk] *adj.* which acts as a symbol *or* which uses a symbol name *or* label *symbolisk;* **symbolic address** = address represented by a symbol *or* name *symbolisk adress;* **symbolic code** *or* **instruction** = instruction that is in mnemonic form rather than a binary number *symbolisk instruktion;* **symbolic debugging** = debugger that allows symbolic

representation of variables *or* locations *symbolisk felsökning;* **symbolic language** = (i) any computer language where locations are represented by names *symboliskt språk;* (ii) any language used to write source code *högnivåspråk;* **symbolic logic** = study of reasoning and thought (formal logic) *symbolisk logik;* **symbolic name** = name used as a label for a variable *or* location *symbolnamn;* **symbolic programming** = writing a program in a source language *symbolisk programmering*

symboltecken ⇨ **icon**

symmetric difference [sɪ'metrɪk 'dɪfr(ə)ns] *subst.* logical function whose output is true if either (of 2) inputs is true, and false if both inputs are the same *symmmetrisk differens*

symmetrisk differens ⇨ **equivalence**

sync [sɪŋk] *subst.* *informal* = SYNCHRONIZATION; **sync bit** = transmitted bit used to synchronize devices *synkroniseringsbit;* **sync character** = transmitted character used to synchronize devices *synkroniseringstecken;* **sync pulses** = transmitted pulses used to make sure that the receiver is synchronized with the transmitter *synkroniseringspuls;* **in sync** = synchronized *synkroniserad;* **the two devices are out of sync** = the two devices are not properly synchronized *de två apparaterna är osynkroniserade*

synchronization [ˌsɪŋkrənaɪ'zeɪʃ(ə)n] *subst.* action of synchronizing two or more devices *synkronisering;* **synchronization pulses** = transmitted pulses used to make sure that the receiver is synchronized with the transmitter *synkroniseringspulser*

synchronize ['sɪŋkrənaɪz] *vb.* to make sure that two or more devices *or* processes are coordinated in time or action *synkronisera*

synchronizer ['sɪŋkrənaɪzə] *subst.* device that will perform a function when it receives a signal from another device *synkroniseringsenhet, synkroniserare*

synchronous ['sɪŋkrənəs] *adj.* which runs in sync with something else (such as a main clock) *synkron;* **synchronous computer** = computer in which each action can only take place when a timing pulse arrives *synkrondator;* **synchronous data link control (SDLC)** = protocol and rules used to define the way in which synchronous data is transmitted *or* received *synkront datalänkprotokoll;* **synchronous data network** = communications network in which all the actions throughout the network are controlled by a single timing signal *synkront datanät;* **synchronous detection** = method of obtaining the signal from an amplitude modulation carrier *synkron demodulering;* **synchronous idle character** = character transmitted by a DTE to ensure correct synchronization when no other character is being transmitted *synkront blindtecken;* **synchronous mode** = system mode in which operations and events are synchronized with a clock signal *synkront tillstånd;* **synchronous network** = network in which all the links are synchronized with a single timing signal *synkront nät;* **synchronous system** = system in which all devices are synchronized to a main clock signal *synkront system;* **synchronous transmission** = transmission of data from one device to another, where both devices are controlled by the same clock, and the transmitted data is synchronized with the clock signal *synkron överföring*

synkronisering ⇨ **framing, interlock**

synkroniseringsbit ⇨ **framing**

synkroniseringskod ⇨ **framing**

synonym ['sɪnənɪm] *subst.* word which means the same thing as another word *synonym*

synonymordlista ⇨ **thesaurus**

synonymous [sɪ'nɒnɪməs] *adj.* meaning the same *synonym;* **the words "error" and "mistake" are synonymous**

syntactic error [sɪn'tæktɪk 'erə] *subst.* programming error in which the program statement does not follow the syntax of the language *syntaxfel*

syntax ['sɪntæks] *subst.* grammatical rules that apply to a programming language *syntax;* **syntax analysis** = stage in compilation where statements are checked to see if they obey the rules of syntax *syntaxanalys;* **syntax error** = programming error in which the program statement does not follow the syntax of the language *syntaxfel*

syntaxfel ⇨ **error**

synthesis ['sɪnθəsɪs] *subst.* producing something artificially (from a number of smaller elements) *syntes*

synthesize ['sɪnθəsaɪz] *vb.* to produce something artificially (from a number of smaller elements) *syntetisera*

synthesizer ['sɪnθəsaɪzə] *subst.* device which generates something (signals *or* sound *or* speech) *ljudgenerator, synthesizer;* **music synthesizer** = device which makes musical notes which are similar to those made by musical instruments *synthesizer,*

synt; **speech synthesizer** = device which generates sounds which are similar to the human voice *talgenerator*

synthetic address [sɪn'θetɪk ə'dres] *subst.* location used by a program that has been produced by instructions within the program *syntetisk adress;* **synthetic language** = programming language in which the source program is written *syntetiskt språk*

sysgen ['sɪsdʒen] = SYSTEM GENERATION

system ['sɪstəm] *subst.* any group of hardware *or* software *or* peripherals, etc., which work together *system;* **adaptive system** = system which is able to alter its responses and processes according to inputs *or* situations *självanpassande system;* **computer system** = central processor with storage and associated peripherals which make up a working computer *datorsystem;* **information system** = computer system which provides information according to a user's requests *informationssystem;* **interactive system** = system which provides an immediate response to the user's commands *or* programs *or* data *interaktivt system;* **operating system (op sys)** = basic software that controls the running of the hardware and the management of data files, without the user having to operate it *operativsystem;* **secure system** = system that cannot be accessed without authorization *säkert system;* **system check** = running diagnostic routines to ensure that there are no problems *systemkontroll;* **system control panel** = main computer system control switches and status indicators *system(styr)panel;* **system crash** = situation where the operating system stops working and has to be restarted *systemkrasch;* **system design** = identifying and investigating possible solutions to a problem, and deciding upon the most appropriate system to solve the problem *systemkonstruktion;* **system diagnostics** = tests, features and messages that help find hardware *or* software faults *systemdiagnostik;* **system disk** = disk which holds the system software *systemskiva;* **system firmware** = basic operating system functions and routines in a ROM device *systemprogram;* **system flowchart** = diagram that shows each step of the computer procedures needed in a system *systemflödesplan;* **system generation** *or* **sysgen** = process of producing an optimum operating system for a particular task *systemgenerering;* **system library** = stored files that hold the various parts of a computer's operating system *systembibliotek;* **system life cycle** = time when a system exists, between its initial design and its becoming out of date *(system) livscykel;* **system log** = record of computer processor operations *systemlogg;* **system security** = measures, such as password, priority protection, authorization codes, etc., designed to stop browsing and hackers *systemsäkerhet;* **system software** = software which makes applications run on hardware *systemprogram;* **system specifications** = details of hardware and software required to perform certain tasks *systemspecifikation;* **system support** = group of people that maintain and operate a system *systemstöd*

QUOTE the core of an expert system is its database of rules

Personal Computer World

(system)administration ⇨ **housekeeping**

systemavbrott ⇨ **dead**

systemband ⇨ **master**

systemdump ⇨ **disaster dump**

systemfel ⇨ **fatal error**

system för informationsåtervinning ⇨ **information**

systemklocka ⇨ **main, master, time**

systemkonsol ⇨ **master**

systemlåsning ⇨ **deadlock**

systemnära program ⇨ **intimate**

systems analysis ['sɪstəmzə,næləsɪs] *subst.* (i) analysing a process *or* system to see if it could be more efficiently carried out by a computer *systemanalys;* (ii) examining an existing system with the aim of improving *or* replacing it *systemanalys;* **systems analyst** = person who undertakes system analysis *systemanalytiker;* **systems program** = program which controls the way in which a computer system works *systemprogram;* **systems programmer** = person who writes system software *systemprogrammerare*

systemskiva ⇨ **master**

systemåterförsäljare ⇨ **value added reseller (VAR)**

säkerhet ⇨ **security**

säkerhetskopia ⇨ **backup** *(copy)*

säkerhetskopiera ⇨ **back up**

säkerhetsmarginal ⇨ **margin**

säkerhetsminne ⇨ **backing**

säkerhetsområde ⇨ **safe area**

säkerhetsplan ⇨ **contingency plan**

säkring ⇨ **fuse**

sända ⇨ **transmit**

sända (indata) ⇨ **input (i/p *or* I/P)**

sändare ⇨ **transmitter (TX), transponder**

sändning ⇨ **dispatch**

sändningsbegäran ⇨ **invitation**

sändningslutssignal ⇨ **end**

sändtagare ⇨ **transceiver**

särtryck ⇨ **offprint**

sätta ⇨ **compose**

sättkoda ⇨ **mark up**

sättning ⇨ **composition**

söka ⇨ **search, seek**

sökare ⇨ **viewfinder**

sökarm ⇨ **access**

sökning ⇨ **search**

söknyckel ⇨ **search**

sök och ersätt ⇨ **search**

sök- och ersättkommando ⇨ **find**

sönderhackning ⇨ **thrashing**

Tt

TAB [tæb] = TABULATE

tab [tæb] *vb.* to tabulate *or* to arrange text in columns with the cursor automatically running from one column to the next in keyboarding *tabulera;* **the list was neatly lined up by tabbing to column 10 at the start of each new line; tab memory** = ability of a editing program (usually a word-processor) to store details about various tab settings *tabulatorminne;* **tab rack** *or* **ruler line** = graduated scale, displayed on the screen, showing the position of tabulation columns *tabulatorlinjal;* **the tab rack shows you the left and right margins; tab stops** = preset points along a line, where the printing head *or* cursor will stop for each tabulation command *tabulatorpositioner*

tabbing ['tæbɪŋ] *subst.* movement of the cursor in a word-processing program from one tab stop to the next *tabuleringsstegring;* **tabbing can be done from inside the program; decimal tabbing** = adjusting a column of numbers so that the decimal points are aligned vertically *decimaltabulering*

tabellreferens ⇨ table

table ['teɪbl] *subst.* list of data in columns and rows on a printed page *or* on the screen *tabell;* **decision table** = list of all possible events *or* states that could happen and the actions taken (sometimes used instead of a flowchart) *beslutstabell;* **lookup table** = collection of stored results that can be accessed very rapidly *(kors)referenstabell;* **this is the value of the key pressed, use a lookup table to find its ASCII value; table lookup** = using one known value to select one entry in a table, providing a secondary value *tabellreferens;* **reference program table** = list produced by a compiler *or* system of the location, size and type of the variables, routines and macros within a program *programreferenstabell;* **symbol table** = list of all the symbols that are accepted by a language *or* compiler and their object code translation *symboltabell;* **table of contents** = list of the contents of a book, usually printed at the beginning *innehållsförteckning*

tablet ['tæblət] *subst.* **graphics tablet** = graphics pad *or* flat device that allows a user to input graphical information into a computer by drawing on its surface *tablett, digitaliseringsbräda;* **it is much easier to draw accurately with a tablet than with a mouse**

tablett ⇨ tablet

tabular ['tæbjʊlə] *adj.* **in tabular form** = arranged in a table *i tabellform*

tabulate ['tæbjʊleɪt] *vb.* to arrange text in columns, with the cursor moving to each new column automatically as the text is keyboarded *tabulera*

tabulating ['tæbjʊleɪtɪŋ] *subst.* processing punched cards, such as a sorting operation *tabulering*

tabulation [ˌtæbjʊ'leɪʃ(ə)n] *subst.* (i) arrangement of a table of figures *tabelluppställning;* (ii) moving a printing head *or* cursor a preset distance along a line *tabulering;* **tabulation markers** = symbols displayed to indicate the position of tabulation stops *tabuleringsmarkörer;* **tabulation stops** = preset points along a line at which a printing head *or* cursor will stop for each tabulation command *tabuleringspositioner*

tabulator ['tæbjʊleɪtə] *subst.* part of a typewriter *or* word-processor which automatically sets words *or* figures into columns *tabulator*

TACS [tiːˈeɪsiːˈes] = TOTAL ACCESS COMMUNICATION SYSTEM UK standard for cellular radio systems *brittiskt mobiltelefonsystem*

tactile ['tæktaɪl] *adj.* using the sense of touch *känsel-;* **tactile feedback** = information provided by using the sense of touch *tryckkänsla, känseläterkoppling;* **tactile keyboard** = keyboard that provides some indication that a key has been pressed, such as a beep *beröringskänsligt tangentbord*

tag [tæg] *subst.* **(a)** one section of a computer instruction *etikett, märke* **(b)** identifying characters attached to a file *or* item (of data) *etikett, märke;* **each file has a three letter tag for rapid identification**

tail [teɪl] *subst.* **(a)** data recognized as the end of a list of data *slutmarkering* **(b)** control code used to signal the end of a message *slutsignal*

takedown ['teɪkdaʊn] *vb.* to remove paper *or* disks *or* tape from a peripheral after one job and prepare it for the next *avsluta, färdigställa, iordningställa;* **takedown time** = amount of time required to takedown a peripheral ready for another job *avslutningstid, iordningsställningstid*

take-up reel ['teɪkʌp'riːl] *subst.* reel onto which magnetic tape is collected *tomrulle, uppsamlingsrulle;* **put the full reel on this spindle, and feed the tape into the take-up reel on the other spindle**

talbandet ⇨ voice

talgenerator ⇨ voice

talk [tɔːk] *vb.* to speak *or* to communicate *tala*

QUOTE a variety of technologies exist which allow computers to talk to one another
Which PC?

talkanal ⇨ voice

talkback ['tɔːkbæk] *subst.* speech communications between a control room and a studio *"talkback", tvåvägskommunikation*

tal med ändligt antal siffror ⇨ finite-precision numbers

talsyntes ⇨ voice

tandem ['tændəm] *subst.* **in tandem** = situation where two things are working together *tillsammans, parallellt;* **tandem switching** = one switch controlling another switch in the same exchange by means of a secondary switch *parallellväxelkoppling*

tangent ⇨ key

tangentbord ⇨ keyboard, keypad

tangentbordsavsökning ⇨ keyboard

tangentbordsbuffert ⇨ key

tangentbordskodare ⇨ keyboard

tangentbordslayout ⇨ **keyboard**

tangentbordsmall ⇨ **key, keyboard, overlay**

tangentbordsmatris ⇨ **matrix**

tangentbordsterminal ⇨ **keyboard**

tangentmatris ⇨ **key**

tangentnummer ⇨ **key**

tankstreck ⇨ **dash**

tape [teɪp] *subst.* long thin flat piece of material *tejp, band, remsa;* **cassette tape =** tape stored on two small reels protected by a solid casing *kassettband;* **cassette tape is mainly used with home computers; (magnetic) tape =** narrow length of thin plastic coated with a magnetic material used to store signals magnetically *magnetband;* **master tape =** magnetic tape which contains all the vital operating system routines, loaded by the initial program loader once when the computer is switched on *or* hard reset *originalband;* **(paper) tape** *or* **punched tape =** strip of paper on which information can be recorded in the form of punched holes *hålremsa;* **(video cassette) tape =** magnetic tape used in a video recorder to store pictures and sound *videoband;* **open reel tape =** tape on a reel which is not enclosed in a cassette *or* cartridge *rullband;* **streaming tape drive =** device containing a continuous loop of tape, used as backing store *strömbandsenhet;* **tape back-up =** to use (usually magnetic) tape as a medium for storing back-ups from faster main *or* secondary storage (such as RAM *or* hard disk) *säkerhetskopia på band;* **tape cable** *or* **ribbon cable =** number of insulated conductors arranged next to each other forming a flat cable *bandkabel;* **tape cartridge =** cassette box containing magnetic tape (on a reel) *bandkassett;* **tape cassette =** small box containing a reel of magnetic tape and a pickup reel *kassettband;* **tape code =** coding system used for punched data representation on paper tape *hålremskod;* **tape counter =** indication (on a tape recorder) of the amount of tape that has been used *bandlägesindikator;* **tape deck =** device which plays back and records data onto magnetic tape *bandstation;* **tape drive =** mechanism which controls magnetic tape movement over the tape heads *banddrivverk, bandstation;* **our new product has a 96Mb streaming tape drive; tape format =** way in which blocks of data, control codes and location data is stored on tape *bandformat;* **tape guide =** method by which the tape is correctly positioned over the tape head *bandstyrning;* **the tape is out of alignment because one of the tape guides has broken; tape head =** transducer that

can read and write signals onto the surface of magnetic tape *läs- och skrivhuvud;* **tape header =** identification information at the beginning of a tape *bandetikett;* **tape label =** tape header and trailer containing information about the contents of a tape *bandetikett;* **tape library =** (i) secure area for the storage of computer data tapes *bandbibliotek;* (ii) series of computer tapes kept in store for reference *bandbibliotek;* **tape loadpoint =** position on a magnetic tape at which reading should commence to load a file *laddläge;* **tape punch =** machine that punches holes into paper tape *remsstans;* **tape reader =** machine that reads punched holes in paper tape *or* signals on magnetic tape *remsläsare;* **tape recorder =** machine that records data and signals onto magnetic tape *bandspelare;* **tape streamer =** continuous loop of tape used for backing storage *strömbandskassett;* **tape timer =** device that displays the total time left *or* amount of playing time used on a reel of magnetic tape *bandklocka;* **tape to card converter =** device that reads data from magnetic tape and stores it on punched cards *band-till-hålkorthanterare;* **tape transmitter =** device that reads data from paper tape and transmits it to another point *(hål)remssändare;* **tape trailer =** identification information at the beginning of a tape *bandetikett;* **tape transport =** method (in a magnetic tape recorder) by which the tape is moved smoothly from reel to reel over the magnetic heads *bandmatning;* **tape unit =** device with tape deck, amplifier, circuitry, etc. for recording and playing back tapes *bandstation*

> COMMENT: cassettes *or* reels of tape are easy to use and cheaper than disks, the cassette casing usually conforms to a standard size. They are less adaptable and only provide sequential access, usually being used for master copies *or* making back-ups

target [ˈtɑːɡɪt] *subst.* goal which you aim to achieve *mål;* **target computer =** computer which software is to be run on (but not necessarily written on, e.g. using a cross-assembler) *måldator;* **target language =** language into which a language will be translated from its source language *målspråk;* **the target language for this PASCAL program is machine code**

> QUOTE the target board is connected to the machine through the in-circuit emulator cable
> **Electronics & Wireless World**

target level [ˈtɑːɡɪt ˈlevl] interpretive processing mode for program execution *målnivå;* **target** *or* **run phase =** period of time during which the target program is run *körfas;* **target program =** object program *or* computer program in object code form, produced by a compiler *målprogram*

tariff ['tærɪf] *subst.* charge incurred by a user of a communications *or* computer system *taxa;* **there is a set tariff for logging on, then a rate for every minute of computer time used**

TASI [tiːaɪesˈeɪ] = TIME ASSIGNED SPEECH INTERPOLATION method of using a voice channel for other signals during the gaps and pauses in a normal conversation *tidsmultiplexering på talkanal*

task [tɑːsk] *subst.* job which is to be carried out by a computer *uppgift, uppdrag;* **multitasking** = ability of a computer system to run two or more programs at the same time *fleruppdragskörning, multikörning;* **this operating system provides a multitasking environment, but not a multi-user one; task management** = system software that controls the use and allocation of resources to programs *uppdragshantering;* **task queue** = temporary storage of jobs waiting to be processed *uppdragskö*

TAT [tiːaɪˈtiː] = TURNAROUND TIME

TDB *(administrativ teknisk databehandling)* ⇨ dp

TDM ['tiːdiːˈem] = TIME DIVISION MULTIPLEXING

TDS ['tiːdiːˈes] = TRANSACTION-DRIVEN SYSTEM computer system that will normally run batch processing tasks until interrupted by a new transaction, at which point it allocates resources to the new transaction *transaktionsstyrt system*

tearing ['teərɪŋ] *subst.* distortion of a television image due to bad sweep synchronization *bildstörning i TV-bild*

technical ['teknɪk(ə)l] *adj.* referring to a particular machine *or* process *teknisk;* **the document gives all the technical details on the new computer**

technician [tekˈnɪʃ(ə)n] *subst.* person who is specialized in industrial work *tekniker;* **the computer technicians installed the new system; laboratory technician** = person who deals with practical work in a laboratory *laboratorieassistent*

technique [tekˈniːk] *subst.* skilled way of doing a job *teknik;* **the company has developed a new technique for processing customers' disks; he has a special technique for answering complaints from users of the software**

technological [ˌteknəˈlɒdʒɪk(ə)l] *adj.* referring to technology *teknologisk;* **the technological revolution** = changing of industrial methods by introducing new technology *den teknologiska revolutionen*

technology [tekˈnɒlədʒɪ] *subst.* applying scientific knowledge to industrial processes *teknologi;* **information technology (IT)** = technology involved in acquiring, storing, processing, and distributing information by electronic means (including radio, TV, telephone and computers) *informationsteknik;* **new technology** = electronic instruments which have recently been developed *ny teknik;* **the introduction of new technology** = putting new electronic equipment into a business *or* industry *införandet av ny teknik*

tecken ⇨ character, sign

teckenbit ⇨ bit

teckenfel ⇨ frame

teckengenerator ⇨ display

teckenkontroll ⇨ keystroke

teckenlängd ⇨ frame

teckenmatris ⇨ matrix

teckentangent ⇨ key

teknik ⇨ technique, technology

teknologi ⇨ technology

teknologisk ⇨ technological

tel ['telɪfəʊn] = TELEPHONE

tele- ['telɪ] *prefix* (i) meaning long distance *tele-, fjärr-;* (ii) referring to television *TV-;* **telebanking** = system by which an account holder can carry out transactions with his bank via a terminal and communications network *hembank;* **telecine** = method of displaying a cine film on television *visning av film på teve;* **telecommunications** = technology of passing and receiving messages over a distance (as in radio, telephone, telegram, satellite broadcast, etc.) *telekommunikationer;* **teleconference** *or* **teleconferencing** = several people in different places using a communications network to talk together *telekonferens;* **telecontrol** = control of a remote device by a telecommunications link *fjärrstyrning över telelinje;* **telegram** = message sent to another country by telegraph *telegram;* **to send an international telegram**

telefonförsäljning ⇨ telesales

telefonkiosk ⇨ call box

telefonlur ⇨ handset

telefonnummer ⇨ phone

telefonsamtal ⇨ phone

telefonsvarare ⇨ **answering, answerphone, voice**

telefonväxel ⇨ **exchange**

telegraph ['telɪɡrɑːf] **1** *subst.* message transmitted using a telegraphy system *telegram;* **telegraph office** = office from which telegrams can be sent *telegrafkontor* **2** *vb.* to send a telegram to another person *sända ett telegram;* to send printed *or*written *or* drawn material by long-distance telegraphy *telegrafera;* **they telegraphed their agreement; the photographs were telegraphed to New York**

telegraphic [,telɪ'græfɪk] *adj.* referring to a telegraph system *telegrafisk;* **telegraphic address** = short address to which a telegram is sent *telegramadress*

telegraphy [tə'legrəfɪ] *subst.* system of sending messages along wires using direct current pulses *telegrafi;* **carrier telegraphy** = system of transmitting telegraph signals via a carrier signal *bärvågstelegrafi*

teleinformatic services ['telɪ,ɪnfə'mætɪk 'sɜːvɪsɪz] *subst.* any data only service, such as telex, facsimile, which uses telecommunications *televerksamhet*

telemarketing ⇨ **telesales**

telematics [,telɪ'mætɪks] *subst.* interaction of all data processing and communications devices (computers, networks, etc.) *telematik*

telemessage ['telɪ,mesɪdʒ] *subst. GB* message sent by telephone, and delivered as a card *telefontelegram*

telemetry [tə'lemətrɪ] *subst.* data from remote measuring devices transmitted over a telecommunications link *telemetri*

teleordering ['telɪ,ɔːd(ə)rɪŋ] *subst.* book ordering system, in which the bookseller's orders are entered into a computer which then puts the order through to the distributor at the end of the day *automatbeställning*

telephone ['telɪfəʊn] **1** *subst.* machine used for speaking to someone over a long distance *telefon;* **we had a new telephone system installed last week; to be on the telephone** = to be speaking to someone using the telephone *tala i telefon;* **the managing director is on the telephone to Hong Kong; she has been on the telephone all day; by telephone** = using the telephone *per telefon;* **to place an order by telephone; to reserve a room by telephone; conference telephone** = telephone specially made to be used in a teleconference *konferenstelefon, högtalartelefon or* **internal telephone** = telephone for calling from one room to another in an office *or* hotel *interntelefon, snabbtelefon;* **telephone**

answering machine = device that answers a telephone, plays a prerecorded message and records any response *telefonsvarare;* **telephone book** *or* **telephone directory** = book which lists people and businesses in alphabetical order with their telephone numbers *telefonkatalog;* **he looked up the number of the company in the telephone book; telephone call** = speaking to someone on the telephone *telefonsamtal;* **to make a telephone call** = to dial a number and speak to someone on the telephone *ringa;* **to answer the telephone** *or* **to take a telephone call** = to speak in reply to a call on the telephone *svara i telefon, ta ett telefonsamtal;* **telephone as a data carrier** = using a modem to send binary data as sound signals over a telephone line *dataöverföring över telefonnätet;* **telephone exchange** = central office where the telephones of a whole district are linked *telefonväxel;* **telephone number** = set of figures for a particular telephone subscriber *telefonnummer;* **can you give me your telephone number?; telephone operator** = person who operates a telephone switchboard *(växel)telefonist;* **telephone orders** = orders received by telephone *telefonorder;* **since we mailed the catalogue we have received a large number of telephone orders; telephone repeater** = receiver, transmitter and associated circuits that boost a telephone signal *överdragsstation;* **telephone subscriber** = person who has a telephone connected to the main network *telefonabonnent;* **telephone switchboard** = central point in a private telephone system where all internal and external lines meet *telefonväxel* **2** *vb.* **to telephone a place** *or* **a person** = to call a place *or* a person by telephone *ringa någonstans (någon);* **his secretary telephoned to say he would be late; he telephoned the order through to the warehouse** = he telephoned the warehouse to place an order *han ringde in ordern till lagret;* **to telephone about something** = to make a telephone call to speak about something *ringa om något;* **he telephoned about the order for computer stationery; to telephone for something** = to make a telephone call to ask for something *ringa efter något;* **he telephoned for a taxi**

telephonist [tə'lefənɪst] *subst.* person who works a telephone switchboard *(växel)telefonist*

telephony [tə'lefənɪ] *subst.* data *or* signal transmission over a telephone using audiofrequencies *telefoni*

teleprinter ['telɪ,prɪntə] *subst.* device that is capable of sending and receiving data from a distant point by means of a telegraphic circuit, and printing out the message on a printer *fjärrskriftsmaskin, teleprinter, telex;* **you can drive a teleprinter**

from this modified serial port; **teleprinter interface =** terminal interface *or* hardware and software combination required to control the functions of a terminal *fjärrskrivargränssnitt;* **teleprinter roll =** roll of paper onto which messages are printed *fjärrskrivarpapper*

teleprocessing (TP) [ˌtelɪˈprəʊsesɪŋ (ˈtiːˈpiː)] *subst.* processing of data at a distance (as on a central computer from outside terminals) *fjärrbearbetning*

telesales [ˈtelɪseɪl] *subst.* sales made by telephone *telefonförsäljning, telemarketing*

teleshopping [ˈtelɪˌʃɒpɪŋ] *subst.* use of a telephone-based data service such as viewdata to order products from a shop *telefonorder*

telesoftware (TSW) [ˌtelɪˈsɒftweə (ˈtiːesˈdʌbljuː)] *subst.* software which is received from a viewdata *or* teletext service *programvara överförd via videotex;* **the telesoftware was downloaded yesterday**

teletext [ˈtelɪtekst] *subst.* method of transmitting text and information with a normal television signal, usually as a serial bit stream that can be displayed using a special decoder *text-TV*

teletypesetting [ˈtelɪˈtaɪpˌsetɪŋ] *subst.* typesetter operated from a punched paper tape *sättning med remsstyrd fotosättare*

teletype (TTY) [ˈtelɪtaɪp (ˈtiːtiːˈwaɪ)] *subst.* term used for teleprinter equipment *fjärrskriftsterminal*

teletypewriter [ˈtelɪˈtaɪpˌraɪtə] *subst.* keyboard and printer attached to a computer system which can input data either direct *or* by making punched paper tape *fjärrskriftsterminal*

televerksamhet ⮞ **teleinformatic services**

television (TV) [ˈtelɪˌvɪʒ(ə)n (ˈtiːˈviː)] *subst.* (i) system for broadcasting pictures and sound using high-frequency radio waves, captured by a receiver and shown on a screen *television, TV;* (ii) device that can receive (modulated) video signals from a computer *or* broadcast signals with an aerial and display images on a CRT screen with sound *teveapparat;* **television camera =** optical lenses in front of an electronic device which can convert images into electronic signals in a form that can be transmitted *or* displayed on a TV *tevekamera;* **television monitor =** device able to display signals from a computer without sound, but not broadcast signals (this is usually because there is no demodulator device which is needed for broadcast signals) *teveskärm;* **television projector =** device that projects a TV image

onto a large screen *storbildsteve;* **television receiver =** device able to display with sound, broadcast signals *or* other modulated signals (such as signals from a video recorder) *tevemottagare;* **television receiver/monitor =** device able to act as a TV receiver *or* monitor *tevemottagare (och skärm);* **television scan =** horizontal movement of the picture beam over the screen, producing one line of an image *bildavsökning;* **television tube =** CRT with electronic devices that provide the line by line horizontal and vertical scanning movement of the picture beam *TV-rör, katodstrålerör; see also* CRT, RGB

> COMMENT: in a colour TV there are three electron guns corresponding to red, green and blue signals. In the UK the TV screen has 625 lines to be scanned; this is normally done in two sweeps of alternate lines, providing a flicker-free image

telex [ˈteleks] **1** *subst.* **(a)** system for sending messages using telephone lines, which are printed out at the receiving end on a special printer *telex;* **to send information by telex; the order came by telex; telex line =** wire linking a telex machine to the telex system *telexledning, telexlinje;* **we cannot communicate with our Nigerian office because of the breakdown of the telex lines; telex operator =** person who operates a telex machine *telexoperatör;* **telex subscriber =** company which has a telex *telexabonnent* **(b) a telex =** (i) a machine for sending and receiving telex messages *en telexapparat;* (ii) a message sent by telex *ett telex;* **he sent a telex to his head office; we received his telex this morning 2** *vb.* to send a message using a teleprinter *sända ett telex;* **can you telex the Canadian office before they open? he telexed the details of the contract to New York**

template [ˈtemplət] *subst.* (i) plastic *or* metal sheet with cut-out symbols to help the drawing of flowcharts and circuit diagrams *mall;* (ii) *(in text processing)* standard text (such as a standard letter *or* invoice) into which specific details (company address *or* prices *or* quantities) can be added *standardbrev, textmall;* **template command =** command that allows functions *or* other commands to be easily set *mallkommando;* **a template paragraph command enables the user to specify the number of spaces each paragraph should be indented;** *see also* STANDARD, FORM LETTER

temporarily [ˈtemp(ə)rərəlɪ] *adv.* for a certain time *or* not permanently *tillfälligt, temporärt*

temporary storage [ˈtemp(ə)rən ˈstɔːrɪdʒ] *subst.* storage which is not permanent *tillfälligt (temporärt) minne;* **temporary**

register = register used for temporary storage for the results of an ALU operation *tillfälligt (temporärt) register*

ten's complement ['tenz 'kɒmplɪmənt] *subst.* formed by adding one to the nine's complement of a decimal number *tiokomplement*

tera- ['terə] *prefix* one million million (ten to the power 12) *tera-;* **terahertz** = *THz;* frequency of one million million hertz

terminal ['tɜːmɪnl] **1** *subst.* **(a)** device usually made up of a display unit and a keyboard which allows entry and display of information when on-line to a central computer system *terminal;* **addressable terminal** = terminal that will only accept data if it has the correct address and identification data in the message header *adresserbar terminal;* **all the messages go to all the terminals since none are addressable terminals; applications terminal** = terminal (such as at a sales desk) which is specifically configured to carry out certain tasks *användarterminal, tillämpningsspecifik terminal;* **dumb terminal** = peripheral that can only receive and transmit data, and is not capable of processing data *dum terminal;* **central terminal** = terminal which controls communications between a central *or* host computer and remote terminals *centralterminal;* **intelligent terminal** *or* **smart terminal** = computer terminal which contains a CPU and memory, allowing basic data processing to be carried out, usually with the facility to allow the user to program it independently of the host computer *intelligent terminal;* **the new intelligent terminal has a built-in text editor; master terminal** = one terminal in a network that has priority over any other, used by the system manager to set-up the system *or* carry out privileged commands *systemkonsol;* **the system manager uses the master terminal to restart the system; remote terminal** = computer terminal connected to a distant computer system *fjärransluten terminal;* **slave terminal** = terminal controlled by a main computer *or* terminal *slavterminal;* **terminal area** = part of a printer circuit board at which edge connectors can be connected *anslutningsyta;* **terminal character set** = range of characters available for a particular type of terminal, these might include graphics *or* customized characters *teckenuppsättning;* **terminal controller** = hardware device *or* IC that controls a terminal including data communications and display *terminalstyrkrets;* **terminal identity** = unique code transmitted by a viewdata terminal to provide identification and authorization of a user *terminalidentitet;* **terminal interface** = hardware and software

combination required to control the functions of a terminal from a computer *terminalgränssnitt;* **the network controller has 16 terminal interfaces;** *(slang)* **terminal junky (TJ)** = person (a hacker) who is obsessed with computers *hacker (i nedsättande betydelse);* **my son has turned into a real terminal junky; terminal keyboard** = standard QWERTY *or* special keyboard allowing input at a terminal *tangentbord* **(b)** an electrical connection point *anslutning;* **terminal block** = strip of insulated connection points for wires *sockerbitskontakt* **(c)** point in a network where a message can be transmitted *or* received *nod, terminal, anslutning; see also* SOURCE, SINK **2** *adj.* fatal *or* which cannot be repaired *slutgiltig, ödesdiger;* **the computer has a terminal fault**

COMMENT: computer terminals can be intelligent, smart or dumb according to the inbuilt processing capabilities

terminal ⇨ **data, terminal**

terminalledning ⇨ **access**

terminalstyrenhet ⇨ **interface**

terminate ['tɜːmɪneɪt] *vb.* to end *avsluta, avbryta, döda*

termination [,tɜːmɪ'neɪʃ(ə)n] *subst.* ending *or* stopping *avslutning, avlivande;* **abnormal termination** = unexpected stoppage of a program which is being run, caused by a fault *or* power failure *onormal avslutning*

terminator ['tɜːmɪ,neɪtə] *or* **rogue value** ['rəʊg,væljuː] *subst.* item in a list of data, which indicates the end of a list *slutmarkör, slutvärde*

termisk skrivare ⇨ **electrothermal printer, thermal**

termotransferskrivare ⇨ **electrothermal printer, thermal**

ternary ['tɜːnərɪ] *adj.* (number system) with three possible states *trevärt, ternär*

test [test] **1** *subst.* action carried out on a device *or* program to establish whether it is working correctly, and if not, which component *or* instruction is not working *prov, test;* **test bed** = (software) environment used to test programs *provbänk;* **test data** = data with known results prepared to allow a new program to be tested *provdata;* **test equipment** = special equipment which tests hardware *or* software *provningsutrustning;* **the engineer has special test equipment for this model; test numeric** = check to ensure that numerical information is numerical *numerisk test;* **test pattern** = graphical pattern displayed on a TV screen to test its colour, balance, horizontal and vertical linearity and contrast *testbild;* **test run** = program run with test data to ensure that the software is working correctly *provkörning;* **a test run will soon show up any errors 2** *vb.* to carry out an examination of a device *or* program to see if it is working correctly *prova, testa;* **saturation testing** = testing a communications network by transmitting large quantities of data and messages over it *mättnadsprov; see also* BENCHMARK

testmodell ⊳ **dummy**

testpunkt ⊳ **access**

teveapparat ⊳ **television (TV)**

tevekamera ⊳ **television (TV)**

teveskärm ⊳ **television (TV)**

text [tekst] *subst.* alphanumeric characters that convey information *text;* **ragged text** = unjustified text, text with a ragged right margin *vänsterställd text, text med ojämn höger;* **start-of-text (SOT** *or* **STX)** = transmitted code indicating the end of control and address information and the start of the message *textbörjan;* **text compression** = reducing the space required by a section of text, by using one code to represent more than one character, by removing spaces and punctuation marks, etc. *textkomprimering;* **text-editing facilities** = word-processing system that allows the user to add, delete, move, insert and correct sections of text *textredigeringsfunktioner;* **text-editing function** = option in a program that provides text-editing facilities *textredigeringsfunktion;* **the program includes a built-in text-editing function; text editor** = piece of software that provides the user with text-editing facilities *redigeringsprogram;* **the text editor will only read files smaller than 64Kbytes long; text file** = stored file on a computer that contains text rather than digits *or* data *textfil;* **text formatter** = program that arranges a text file according to preset rules, such as line width and page size *formateringsfunktion;* **people use the text formatter as a basic desk-top publishing program; text management** = facilities that allow text to be written, stored, retrieved, edited and printed *ord/textbehandling;* **text manipulation** = facilities that allow text editing, changing, inserting and deleting *ord/textbehandlingsfunktioner;* **text processing** = word-processing *or* using a computer to keyboard, edit and output text, in the forms of letters, labels, etc. *ord/textbehandling;* **text register** = temporary computer storage register for text characters only *textminnesregister;* **text retrieval** = information retrieval system that allows the user to examine

complete documents rather than just a reference to one *textåtersökning;* **text screen** = area of computer screen that has been set up to display text *textskärm;* **text-to-speech converter** = electronic device that uses a speech synthesizer to produce the spoken equivalent of a piece of text that has been entered *text-till-talomvandlare*

textanalys ⊳ **parsing**

textbehandlare ⊳ **editor, manager**

textbehandling ⊳ **processing**

textfil ⊳ **file**

textläsare ⊳ **document**

textredigeringsprogram ⊳ **editor**

textslutssignal ⊳ **end**

textteve ⊳ **videotext**

text-till-talomvandlare ⊳ **text**

textual ['tekstjuəl] *adj.* referring to text *text-;* **the editors made several textual changes before the proofs were sent back for correction**

thermal ['θɜːm(ə)l] *adj.* referring to heat *termisk, värme-;* **thermal paper** = special paper whose coating turns black when heated, allowing characters to be printed by using a matrix of small heating elements *värmekänsligt papper;* **thermal printer** = type of printer where the character is formed on thermal paper with a printhead containing a matrix of small heating elements *termisk skrivare, värmeöverföringsskrivare, termotransfer-skrivare*

COMMENT: this type of printer is very quiet in operation since the printing head does not strike the paper

thermal transfer ['θɜːm(ə)l 'træn'sfə] *subst.* method of printing where the ink is attached to the paper by heating *värmeöverföring;* **a thermal transfer printer; colour ink-jet technology and thermal transfer technology compete with each other**

thermistor [θɜː'mɪstə] *subst.* electronic device whose resistance changes with temperature *termistor*

thermo-sensitive [,θɜːmə(ʊ)'sensətɪv] *adj.* which is sensitive to heat *värmekänslig*

thesaurus [θɪ'sɔːrəs] *subst.* collection of words, not in alphabetical order like a dictionary *or* encyclopaedia, but under certain headings *synonymordlista, begreppsordbok*

thick [θɪk] *adj.* with a large distance between two surfaces *tjock;* **thick film** = miniature electronic circuit design in which miniature components are mounted on an insulating base, then connected as required *tjockfilmskonstruktion*

> COMMENT: this provides a package that is larger but cheaper for short runs than chips

thimble printer ['θɪmbl 'prɪntə] *subst.* computer printer using a printing head similar to a daisy wheel but shaped like a thimble *typhjulsskrivare*

thin [θɪn] *adj.* with only a small distance between two surfaces *tunn;* **thin film** = method of constructing integrated circuits by depositing in a vacuum very thin patterns of various materials onto a substrate to form the required interconnected components *tunnfilmskonstruktion; see also* CHIP, SUBSTRATE; **thin film memory** = high-speed access RAM device using a matrix of magnetic cells and a matrix of read/write heads to access them *tunnfilmsminne;* **thin window** = single line display window *radfönster*

third [θɜːd] *adj.* coming after second *tredje;* **third generation computers** = range of computers where integrated circuits were used instead of transistors *tredje generationens datorer;* **third party** = company which supplies items *or* services for a system sold by one party (the seller) to another (the buyer) *tredje part*

> COMMENT: a third party might supply computer maintenance *or* might write programs, etc.

> QUOTE they expect third party developers to enhance the operating systems by adding their own libraries
> **PC Business World**

thirty-two bit system ['θɜːtɪ'tuː,bɪt 'sɪstəm] *subst.* microcomputer system *or* CPU that handles data in thirty-two bit words *32-bitssystem*

thrashing ['θræʃɪŋ] *subst.* computer program design fault that results in the CPU wasting time moving pages of data between main memory and backing store *sönderhackning (av programkörning pga för stor programadministration)*

thread [θred] *subst.* program that consists of many independent smaller sections or beads *tråd, länk, process, modul i modulärt program;* **threaded file** = file in which an entry will contain data and an address to the next entry that has the same data content (allowing rapid retrieval of all identical records) *länkad fil, modulär fil;* **threaded language** = programming language that allows many small sections of code to be written then used by a main program *modulärt språk, länkat språk;*

threaded tree = structure in which each node contains a pointer to other nodes *länkat träd*

three-address instruction ['θriː ə'dres ɪn'strʌkʃ(ə)n] *subst.* instruction which contains the addresses of two operands and the location where the result is to be stored *treadressinstruktion*

three-dimensional ['θriːdɪ'menʃənl] *or* **3D** ['θriː'diː] *adj.* (image) which has three dimensions (width, breadth and depth), and therefore gives the impression of being solid *tredimensionell*

three input adder ['θriː 'ɪnpʊt 'ædə] *see* FULL ADDER

three-pin plug ['θriː'pɪn'plʌg] *subst.* standard plug with three connections, to connect an electric device to the mains electricity supply *trestiftskontakt*

> COMMENT: the three pins are for the live, neutral and earth connections

three state logic ['θriː'steɪt 'lɒdʒɪk] *subst.* logic gate *or* IC that has three possible output states (rather than the usual two): logic high, logic low and high impedance *trenivålogik*

throughput ['θruːpʊt] *subst.* rate of production by a machine *or* system, measured as total useful information processed in a set period of time *genomströmning, dataflöde, kapacitet;* **for this machine throughput is 1.3 inches per second (ips) scanning speed; rated throughput** = maximum throughput of a device that will still meet original specifications *(nominell) kapacitet*

thyristor [θaɪ'rɪstə] *subst.* semiconductor device that will allow the control of an ACvoltage according to an input signal *tyristor*

tidsdel ⇨ **slice**

tidsdelning ⇨ **interleaving, time-sharing**

tidsfel ⇨ **hazard**

tidsfördelning ⇨ **scheduling**

tidsfördelning av jobb ⇨ **scheduling**

tidsfördelningsfunktion ⇨ **scheduler**

(tidsfördelnings)schema ⇨ **schedule**

tidtagarur ⇨ **timer**

tie line ['taɪlaɪn] *or* **tie trunk** ['taɪtrʌŋk] *subst.* communications link between switchboards *or* PBX systems *huvudledning, riksledning, stamledning*

tilde ['tɪldɪ] *subst.* printed accent (∼), commonly used over the letter "n" in

Spanish, vowels in Portuguese, etc. *tilde, muljeringstecken*

tillbehör ⊳ **accessory, ancillary equipment**

tilldela ⊳ **allocate, assign**

tillförlitlighet ⊳ **reliability**

tillsatskort ⊳ **expansion**

tillsatsprocessor ⊳ **processor**

tillstånd ⊳ **condition, mode, state**

tillverka ⊳ **manufacture, produce**

tillåta ⊳ **enable**

tillämpning ⊳ **application**

tillämpningsprogram ⊳ **software**

tillämpningsspecifik terminal ⊳ **terminal**

tilt and swivel ['tıltən'swıvl] *adj.* (monitor) which is mounted on a pivot so that it can be moved to point in the most convenient direction for the operator *vridbar (åt alla håll)*

time [taım] **1** *subst.* period expressed in hours, minutes, seconds, etc. *tid;* **addition time** = time an adder takes to carry out an addition operation *additionstid;* **cycle time** = time between start and stop of an operation, especially between addressing a memory location and receiving the data *cykeltid;* **queuing time** = period of time messages have to wait before they are processed *or* transmitted *väntetid, kötid;* **real time** = actions *or* processing time that is of the same order of magnitude as the problem to be solved (i.e. the processing time is within the same time as the problem to be solved, so that the result can influence the source of the data) *realtid;* **response time** = (i) time which passes between the user starting an action (by pressing a key) and the result appearing on the screen *svarstid;* (ii) speed with which a system responds to a stimulus *svarstid;* **stop time** = time taken for a spinning disk to come to rest after it is no longer powered *bromstid, stopptid;* **time address code** = signal recorded on a video tape to display time elapsed when editing *tidskod;* **time base** = (i) signal used as a basis for timing purposes *tidbas, tidssignal;* (ii) regular sawtooth signal used in an oscilloscope to sweep the beam across the screen *tidbas;* **time coded page** = teletext page that contains additional text which is displayed after a period of time *tidskodad sida;* **time derived channel** = communications channel using time division multiplexing techniques *tidsdelad kanal;* **time display** = digits *or* dial which show the current time *urtavla;* **time division multiple access** = time division

multiplexing system that allocates time slots to various users according to demand *tidstilldelning (till flera användare);* **time division multiplexing (TDM)** = multiplexing system that allows a number of signals to be transmitted down a single line by sending a sample of the first signal for a short period, then the second, and so on *tidsmultiplex, tidsdelad multiplexering;* **time division switching** = moving data from one time slot to another *tidsdelningsväxling;* **time domain analysis** = signal analysis as it varies with time *tids(domän)analys;* **time shift viewing** = use of a video recorder to record programs which are then replayed at a more convenient time *förinspelning;* **time slice** = amount of time allowed for a single task in a time-sharing system *or* in multiprogramming; period of time allocated for a user *or* program *or* job within a multitasking system *tidsdel;* **time slot** = period of time that contains an amount of data about one signal in a time division multiplexing system *tidsdel, paketid* **2** *vb.* to measure the time taken by an operation *ta tid, synkronisera;* **microprocessor timing** = correct selection of system clock frequency to allow for slower peripherals etc. *synkronisering (av processor);* **network timing** = signals that correctly synchronize the transmission of data *nätverkssynkronisering;* **timing loop** = computer program loop that is repeated a number of times to produce a certain time delay *tidsfördröjningsslinga, synkroniseringsslinga;* **timing master** = clock signal that synchronizes all the components in a system *systemklocka*

timeout ['taımaut] *subst.* (i) logoff procedure carried out if no data is entered on an on-line terminal *tidsutlösning (eller viss förbestämd tid), tomgångstid;* (ii) period of time reserved for an operation *reserverad tid*

timer ['taımə] *subst.* device which records the time taken for an operation to be completed *tidtagarur, klockregister*

time-sharing ['taım,ʃeərıŋ] *subst.* computer system that allows several independent users to use it *or* be on-line at the same time *tidsdelning*

COMMENT: in time-sharing, each user appears to be using the computer all the time, when in fact each is using the CPU for a short time slice only; the CPU processing one user for a short time then moving on to the next

tiotalsräknare ⊳ **decade**

title ['taıtl] *subst.* identification name given to a file *or* program *or* disk *titel, etikett;* **title of disk** = identification of a disk, referring to its contents *elektronisk* *etikett;* **title page** = first main page of a book, with the title, the name of the author and the name of the publisher *titelsida*

T junction [ˈtiːˌdʒʌŋ(k)ʃ(ə)n] *subst.* connection at right angles with a main signal *or* power carrying cable *T-koppling*

T-märkning ⇨ **BABT**

T network [ˈtiːˌnetwɜːk] *subst.* simple circuit network with three electronic components connected in the shape of a letter T *T-nät*

toggle [ˈtɒgl] *vb.* to switch between two states *vippa över, växla;* **toggle switch** = electrical switch that has only two positions *(tväläges) vippomkopplare*

> QUOTE the symbols can be toggled on or off the display
> **Micro Decision**

token [ˈtəʊk(ə)n] *subst.* internal code which replaces a reserved word *or* program statement in a high-level language *stafettpinne, pant, paket som cirkuleras runt i ett stafettnät och bär data;* **token ring network** = network in which a device can transmit data by taking one free token which circulates and inserting the message after it *stafettnät;* **control token** = special sequence of bits transmitted over a LAN to provide control actions *styrstafettsignal*

tolk ⇨ **interpreter, language, processor**

tom dataarea ⇨ **empty**

tomgångstid ⇨ **timeout**

tom (ledig) kontakt ⇨ **empty**

tom lista ⇨ **empty, null**

tomo- [ˈtəʊməʊ] *prefix* meaning a cutting *or* section *tomo-*

tomogram [ˈtɒmə(ʊ)græm] *subst.* picture of part of the body taken by tomography *tomogram*

tomography [təˈmɒgrəfɪ] *subst.* scanning of a particular part of the body using X-rays *or ultrasound tomografi;* **computerized axial tomography (CAT)** = X-ray examination where a computer creates a picture of a section of a patient's body *datorstödd tomografi*

tomrulle ⇨ **take-up reel**

tomt medium ⇨ **empty**

tomt paket ⇨ **empty**

tone [təʊn] *subst.* **(a)** sound at one single frequency *ton;* **dialling tone** = sound made by a telephone to show that it is ready for the number to be dialled *kopplingston;* **engaged tone** = sound made by a telephone showing that the number dialled is busy

upptagetton; **tone dialling** = telephone dialling system that uses different frequency tones to represent the dialled number *tonval;* **tone signalling** = tones used in a telephone network to convey control *or* address signals *tonsignalering* **(b)** shade of a colour *ton, nyans;* **the graphics package can give several tones of blue**

toner [ˈtəʊnə] *subst.* liquid put into a photocopier *or* photographic device to develop the image *kolpulver;* **toner cartridge** = sealed cartridge containing toner, which can be easily replaced in a photocopier *kolpulverpatron;* **change toner and toner cartridge according to the manual; the toner cartridge and the imaging drum can be replaced as one unit when the toner runs out**

tonkontroll ⇨ **equalizer**

toolbox [ˈtuːlbɒks] *subst.* box containing instruments needed to repair *or* maintain *or* install equipment *verktygslåda*

toolkit [ˈtuːlkɪt] *subst.* series of functions which help a programmer write *or* debug programs *verktygssats*

tools [tuːlz] *subst.* set of utility programs (backup, format, etc.) in a computer system *verktyg*

top [tɒp] *subst.* part which is the highest point of something *topp, överdel, ovansida;* **top down programming** *or* **structured programming** = method of writing programs where a complete system is divided into simple blocks *or* tasks, each block unit is written and tested before proceeding with the next one *strukturerad programmering;* **top of stack** = the newest data item added to a stack *högst i stacken;* **top space** = number of blank lines left at the top of a printed text *toppmarginal*

topology [təˈpɒlədʒɪ] *subst.* way in which the various elements in a network are interconnected *topologi;* **network topology** = layout of machines in a network (such as a star network *or* a ring network *or* a bus network) which will determine what cabling and interfaces are needed and what possibilities the network can offer *nättopologi*

torn tape [ˈtɔːnˈteɪp] *subst.* communications switching method, in which the received message is punched onto a paper tape which is fed by hand into the appropriate tape reader for transmission to the required destination *remsdataöverföring*

torrkörning (av dator) ⇨ **edit**

total [ˈtəʊtl] *subst.* **hash total** = total of a number of hashed entries, used for error detection *nonsenssumma, kontrollsumma* *totalstopp* ⇨ **halt**

touch [tʌtʃ] *vb.* to make contact with something with the fingers *röra vid, beröra, trycka på;* **touch pad** = flat device that can sense where on its surface and when it is touched, used to control a cursor position *or* switch a device on or off *pekskiva;* **touch screen** = computer display that has a grid of infrared transmitters and receivers, positioned on either side of the screen used to control a cursor position (when a user wants to make a selection *or* move the cursor, he points to the screen, breaking two of the beams, which gives the position of his finger) *pekskärm*

touch up [tʌtʃ 'ʌp] *vb.* to remove scratches *or* other marks from a photograph *or* image *retuschera*

TP ['tiː'piː] = TELEPROCESSING, TRANSACTION PROCESSING

TPI ['tiːpiː'aɪ] = TRACKS PER INCH

trace [treɪs] *subst.* method of verifying that a program is functioning correctly, in which the current status and contents of the registers and variables used are displayed after each instruction step *programgenomgång;* **trace program** = diagnostic program that executes a program that is being debugged, one instruction at a time, displaying the states and registers *(fel)spårningsprogram;* **trace trap** = selective breakpoint where a tracing program stops, allowing registers to be examined *kontrollpunkt, avbrottspunkt*

track [træk] **1** *subst.* one of a series of thin concentric rings on a magnetic disk *or* thin lines on a tape, which the read/write head accesses and along which the data is stored in separate sectors *spår;* **address track** = track on a magnetic disk containing the address of files, etc., stored on the other tracks *adresspår;* **track address** = location of a particular track on a magnetic disk *spåradress;* **tracks per inch (TPI)** = number of concentric data tracks on a disk surface per inch *spår per tum* **2** *vb.* to follow a path *or* track correctly *spåra, följa ett spår;* **the read head is not tracking the recorded track correctly**

COMMENT: the first track on a tape is along the edge and the tape may have up to nine different tracks on it, while a disk has many concentric tracks around the central hub; the track and sector addresses are set-up during formatting

trackball ['trækbɔːl] *subst.* device used to move a cursor on-screen, which is controlled by turning a ball contained in a case *pekboll*

tractor feed ['træktəfiːd] *subst.* method of feeding paper into a printer, where sprocket wheels on the printer connect with the sprocket holes on either edge of the paper to pull the paper through *traktormatning*

QUOTE the printer is fairly standard with both tractor and cut sheet feed system
         Which PC?

traffic ['træfɪk] *subst.* term covering all the messages and other signals processed by a system *trafik;* **traffic analysis** = study of the times, types and quantities of messages and signals being processed by a system *trafikanalys;* **traffic density** = number of messages and data transmitted over a network *or* system in a period of time *trafiktäthet;* **traffic intensity** = ratio of messages entering a queue against those leaving the queue within a certain time *trafikintensitet;* **incoming traffic** = data and messages received *inkommande signaler*
NOTE: no plural

trail [treɪl] *subst.* line followed by something *spår, stig;* **audit trail** = recording details of the use made of a system by noting transactions carried out (used for checking on illegal use *or* malfunction) *logg*

trailer ['treɪlə] *subst.* **(a)** leader *or* piece of non magnetic tape to the start of a reel of magnetic tape to make loading easier *startband, laddningsband* **(b)** final byte of a file containing control *or* file characteristics *slutbyte;* **trailer record** = last record in a file containing control *or* file characteristics *slutpost*

traktormatning ⇨ **feed, sprocket feed**

transaction [træn'zækʃ(ə)n] *subst.* one single action which affects a database (a sale, a change of address, a new customer, etc.) *transaktion;* **transaction-driven system (TDS)** = computer system that will normally run batch processing tasks until interrupted by a new transaction, at which point it allocates resources to the transaction *transaktionsstyrt system;* **transaction file** *or* **change file** *or* **detail file** *or* **movement file** = file containing recent changes *or* transactions to records which is then used to update a master file *uppdateringsfil;* **transaction processing (TP)** = interactive processing in which a user enters commands and data on a terminal which is linked to a central computer, with results being displayed on-screen *transaktionsbehandling;* **transaction record** *or* **change record** = record containing new data which is to be used to update a master record *uppdateringspost*

transaktion ⇨ **data**

transborder data flow [ˌtrænz'bɔːdə 'deɪtə 'fləu] *subst.* passing of data from one country to another using communications links such as satellites *or* land lines *dataöverföring mellan länder*

transceiver [træn'si:və] *subst.* transmitter and receiver *or* device which can both transmit and receive signals (such as a terminal *or* modem) *sändtagare;* **radio transceiver** = radio transmitter and receiver in a single housing *radiosändtagare (t. ex. walkie-talkie)*

transcoder [træns'kəʊdə] *subst.* electronic device used to convert television signal standards *TV-signalkonverterare;* **use the transcoder to convert PAL to SECAM**

transcribe [træns'kraib] *vb.* to copy data from one backing storage unit *or* medium to another *kopiera data, överföra*

transcription [træns'krɪpʃ(ə)n] *subst.* action of transcribing data *kopiering, överföring*

transducer [trænz'dju:sə] *subst.* electronic device which converts signals in one form into signals in another *(signal)omvandlare;* **the pressure transducer converts physical pressure signals into electrical signals**

transfer [træns'fɜː] *vb.* **(a)** to change command *or* control *föra över, överlåta, överföra;* **all processing activities have been transferred to the mainframe; conditional transfer** = programming instruction that provides a jump to a section of a program if a certain condition is met *villkorlig övergång;* **radial transfer** = data transfer between two peripherals *or* programs that are on different layers of a structured system (such as an OSI/ISO system) *radiell överföring;* **transfer check** = check that a data transfer is correct according to a set of rules *överföringskontroll;* **transfer command** = instruction that directs processor control from one part of a program to another *överföringsorder; see also* JUMP, CALL; **transfer control** = when a branch *or* jump instruction within a program is executed, control is transferred to another point in the program *överföringsstyrning* **(b)** to copy a section of memory to another location *föra över, kopiera;* **transfer rate** = speed at which data is transferred from backing store to main memory *överföringshastighet;* **transfer time** = time taken to transfer data between devices *or* locations *överföringstid*

transform [træns'fɔːm] *vb.* to change something from one state to another *omvandla, transformera*

transformation [ˌtrænsfə'meɪʃ(ə)n] *subst.* action of changing *omvandling, transformation*

transformational rules [ˌtrænsfə'meɪʃ(ə)nl 'ruːlz] *subst.* set of rules

that are applied to data that is to be transformed into coded form *transformeringsregler, omvandlingsregler*

transformer [træns'fɔːmə] *subst.* device which changes the voltage *or* current amplitude of an AC signal *transformator*

COMMENT: a transformer consists of two electrically insulated coils of wire; the AC signal in one induces a similar signal in the other which can be a different amplitude according to the ratio of the turns in the coils of wire

---

transient ['trænzɪənt] **1** *adj.* state *or* signal which is present for a short period of time *transient, kraftigt olinjär;* **power transient** = very short duration voltage pulse *or* spike *spänningstopp;* **transient suppressor** = device which suppresses voltage transients *spänningsutjämnare;* **transient area** = section of memory for user programs and data *genomgångsarea;* **transient error** = temporary error which occurs for a short period of time *övergående fel* **2** *subst.* **line transient** *or* **voltage transient** = spike of voltage that is caused by a time delay in two devices switching *or* noise on the line *spänningstopp*

transistor [træn'zɪstə] *subst.* electronic semiconductor device which can control the current flow in a circuit (there are two main types of transistors: bipolar and unipolar) *transistor;* **bipolar (junction) transistor (BJT)** = transistor constructed of three layers of alternating types of doped semiconductor (p-n-p or n-p-n), each layer has a terminal labelled emitter, base and collector, usually the base controls the current flow between emitter and collector *bipolär transistor;* **field effect transistor (FET)** = electronic device that can act as a variable current flow control (an external signal varies the resistance of the device and current flow by changing the width of a conducting channel by means of a field. It has three terminals: source, gate and drain) *fälteffekttransistor;* **transistor-resistor logic (TRL)** = early logic gate design method using bipolar transistors and resistors *transistor-motståndslogik;* **transistor-transistor logic (TTL)** = most common family of logic gates and high-speed transistor circuit design, in which the bipolar transistors are directly connected (usually collector to base) to provide the logic function *transistor-transistorlogik, TTL;* **unipolar transistor** = FIELD EFFECT TRANSISTOR

transition [træn'sɪʒ(ə)n] *subst.* change from one state to another *övergång;* **transition point** = point in a program *or* system where a transition occurs *övergångspunkt*

translate [trænsˈleɪt] *vb.* to convert data from one form into another *översätta*

translation tables [trænsˈleɪʃ(ə)n ˈteɪblz] *or* **conversion tables** [kənˈvɜːzən ˈteɪblz] *subst.* lookup tables *or* collection of stored results that can be accessed very rapidly by a process without the need to calculate each result when needed *översättningstabeller*

translator (program) [trænsˈleɪtə (ˈprəʊɡræm)] *subst.* program that translates a high level language program into another language (usually machine code) *översättningsprogram; see also* INTERPRETER, COMPILER

transmission [trænzˈmɪʃ(ə)n] *subst.* sending of signals from one device to another *överföring;* **neutral transmission =** (transmission) in which a voltage pulse and zero volts represent the binary digits 1 and 0 *neutral överföring;* **parallel transmission =** number of data lines carrying all the bits of a data word simultaneously *parallell överföring;* **serial transmission =** data transmission one bit at a time (this is the normal method of transmission over longer distances, since although slower, it uses fewer lines and so is cheaper than parallel) *seriell överföring;* **synchronous transmission =** transmission of data from one device to another, where both devices are controlled by the same clock, and the transmitted data is synchronized with the clock signal *synkron överföring;* **transmission channel =** physical connection between two points that allows data to be transmitted (such as a link between a CPU and a peripheral) *överföringskanal;* **transmission errors =** errors due to noise on the line *överföringsfel;* **transmission media =** means by which data can be transmitted, such as radio, light, etc. *överföringsmedier;* **transmission rate =** measure of the amount of data transmitted in a certain time *överföringshastighet;* **their average transmission is 64,000 bits per second (bps) through a parallel connection or 19,200 bps through a serial connection; transmission window =** narrow range of wavelengths to which a fibre optic cable is most transparent *passband för ljusledare*

transmissive disk [trænzˈmɪsɪv ˈdɪsk] *subst.* optical data storage disk in which the reading laser beam shines through the disk to a detector below *genomlysningsskiva; compare with* REFLECTIVE DISK

transmit [trænzˈmɪt] *vb.* to send information from one device to another, using any medium, such as radio, cable, wire link, etc. *sända*

QUOTE an X-ray picture can be digitized and transmitted from one hospital to a specialist at another for diagnosis
Electronics & Business World

transmittance [trænzˈmɪt(ə)ns] *subst.* amount of light transmitted through a material in ratio to the total light incident on the surface of the material *genomlysbarhet, transmittans*

transmitter (TX) [trænzˈmɪtə (ˈtiːˈeks)] *subst.* device that will take an input signal, process it (modulate *or* convert to sound, etc.) then transmit it by some medium (radio, light, etc.) *sändare*

QUOTE modern high-power transmitters are much reduced in size and a simple and uncluttered appearance
Electronics & Power

transparency [trænsˈpær(ə)nsɪ] *subst.* transparent positive film, which can be projected onto a screen *or* to make film for printing *stordia*

transparent [trænsˈpær(ə)nt] *subst.* **(a)** computer program which is not obvious to the user *or* which cannot be seen by the user when it is running *osynligt (omärkbart) datorprogram;* **transparent interrupt =** mode in which, if an interrupt occurs, all program and machine states are saved, the interrupt is serviced and then the system is restored to its previous states *osynligt avbrott, omärkbart avbrott, avbrott med återställning;* **transparent paging =** software that allows the user to access any memory location in a paged memory system as if it were not paged *osynlig (omärkbar) sidtilldelning* **(b)** device *or* network that allows signals to pass through it without being altered in any way *genomskinligt (osynligt) nätverk*

transphasor [trænsˈfeɪzə] *subst.* optical transistor, that is constructed from a crystal which is able to switch a main beam of light according to a smaller input signal *optisk transistor, transfasor*

COMMENT: this is used in the latest research for an optical computer which could run at very high speeds, i.e., at the speed of light

transponder [trænsˈpɒndə] *subst.* communications device that receives and retransmits signals *sändare, transponder*

transport [trænsˈpɔːt] *vb.* to carry from one place to another *transportera, flytta;* **transport layer =** layer in the ISO/OSI standard that checks and controls the quality of the connection *transportskikt; see also* LAYER

transportable [trænsˈpɔːtəbl] *adj.* which can be carried *transportabel, flyttbar;* **a**

transportable computer is not as small as a portable or a laptop

transposition [ˌtrænspəˈzɪʃ(ə)n] *subst.* changing the order of a series of characters (as "comupter" for "computer" *or* "1898" for "1988" *platsbyte, omkastning;* **a series of transposition errors caused faulty results**

transputer [trænzˈpjuːtə] *subst.* single large very powerful chip containing a 32-bit microprocessor running at around 10 MIPS, that can be connected together to form a parallel processing system (running OCCAM) *transputer*

transverse mode noise [ˈtrænzvɜːs ˈməʊd ˈnɔɪz] *subst.* interference which is apparent between power supply lines *nätledningsinterferens*

transverse scan [ˈtrænzvɜːs ˈskæn] *subst.* method of reading data from a video tape in which the playback head is at right angles to the tape *transversell (korsande) läsning*

trap [træp] *subst.* device, software or hardware that will catch something, such as a variable, fault or value *fälla;* **trace trap =** selective breakpoint where a tracing program stops, allowing registers to be examined *kontrollpunkt*

trapdoor [ˈtræpdɔː] *subst.* way of getting into a system to change data *or* browse *or* hack *fallucka, bakdörr, sätt att få icke auktoriserad åtkomst till ett system*

treadressinstruktion ⇨ **instruction**

tree [triː] *subst.* **tree (structure) =** data structure system where each item of data is linked to several others by branches (as opposed to a line system where each item leads on to the next) *träd;* **tree and branch network system =** system of networking where data is transmitted along a single output line, from which other lines branch out, forming a tree structure that feeds individual stations *trädnät;* **tree selection sort =** rapid form of selection where the information from the first sort pass is used in the second pass to speed up selection *trädvalssortering;* **binary tree =** data system where each item of data *or* node has only two branches *binärt träd*

trefaskoppling ⇨ **delta**

tremendously high frequency (THF) [trɪˈmendəslɪ ˈhaɪ ˈfriːkwənsɪ (ˈtiːeɪtʃˈef)] *subst.* radio frequency between 300GHz and 3000GHz *kortare än millimetervågor*

triad [ˈtraɪəd] *subst.* (i) three elements *or* characters *or* bits *triad;* (ii) triangular shaped grouping of the red, green and blue colour phosphor spots at each pixel location on the screen of a colour RGB monitor *färgpunktstriangel, triad*

trial [ˈtraɪ(ə)l] *subst.* test for new equipment to see if it works *provkörning, provtid;* **trials engineer =** person who designs, runs and analyses trials of new equipment *testingenjör*

tributary station [ˈtrɪbjʊt(ə)rɪ ˈsteɪʃ(ə)n] *subst.* any station on a multilink network other than the main control station *understation*

trim [trɪm] *vb.* to cut off the edge of something *trimma, klippa, beskära;* **the printed pages are trimmed to 198 x 129mm; you will need to trim the top part of the photograph to make it fit**

TRL [ˈtiːɑːrˈel] = TRANSISTOR-RESISTOR LOGIC

Trojan Horse [ˈtrəʊdʒ(ə)n ˈhɔːs] *subst.* program inserted into a system by a hacker that will perform a harmless function while copying information in a classified file into a file with a low priority, which the hacker can then access without the authorized user knowing *trojansk häst, logisk bomb*

troposphere [ˈtrɒpə(ʊ)sfɪə] *subst.* region of space extending up to six miles above the earth's surface, causing radio wave scatter *troposfär; see also* IONOSPHERE

troubleshoot [ˈtrʌblʃuːt] *vb.* (i) to debug computer software *felsöka;* (ii) to locate and repair faults in hardware *felsöka*

troubleshooter [ˈtrʌblˌʃuːtə] *subst.* person who troubleshoots hardware *or* software *felsökare*

trough [trɒf] *subst.* lowest point in a waveform *dal, vågdal; compare* PEAK

TRUE [truː] *subst.* logical condition (representing binary one) *sann; compare* FALSE

trumkurvskrivare ⇨ **drum**

trumminne ⇨ **magnetic**

trumskrivare ⇨ **barrel printer**

truncate [trʌŋˈkeɪt] *vb.* **(a)** to cut short *hugga av, korta ner* **(b)** to give an approximate value to a number by reducing it to a certain number of digits *trunkera*

truncation [trʌŋˈkeɪʃ(ə)n] *subst.* removal of digits from a number so that it is a certain length *trunkering;* **3.5678 truncated to 3.56; truncation error =** error caused when a number is truncated *trunkeringsfel*

trunk [trʌŋk] *subst.* bus *or* communication link consisting of wires *or* leads, which connect different parts of a hardware system *stamledning, huvudledning, riksledning*

trunk call ['trʌŋkkɔːl] *subst. GB* long-distance telephone call *rikssamtal*

trunkera ⇨ **truncate**

trunkering ⇨ **truncation**

trunkeringsfel ⇨ **truncation**

trunk exchange ['trʌŋkiks,tʃeɪn(d)ʒ] *subst. GB* telephone exchange that only handles trunk calls *riksväxel*

truth table ['truːθ,teɪbl] *subst.* method of defining a logic function as the output state for all possible inputs *sanningstabell;* **truth value** = two values (true *or* false, T *or* F, 1 *or* 0) used in Boolean algebra *sanningsvärde*

tryckbokstäver ⇨ **block**

tryckfel ⇨ **literal, typo**

tryckkänsla ⇨ **tactile**

tryckt kretskort ⇨ **printed circuit**

tråd ⇨ **thread**

trådlös ⇨ **wireless**

TSW ['tiːes'dʌbljuː] = TELESOFTWARE

TTL ['tiːtiːel] = TRANSISTOR-TRANSISTOR LOGIC most common family of logic gates and high-speed transistor circuit design in which the bipolar transistors are directly connected (usually collector to base) *TTL, transistor-transistorlogik;* **TTL compatible** = MOS or other electronic circuits *or* components that can directly connect to and drive TTL circuits *TTL-kompatibel;* **TTL logic** = use of TTL design and components to implement logic circuits and gates *TTL-logik*

TTY ['tiːtiː'waɪ] = TELETYPE

tune [tjuːn] *vb.* **(a)** to set a system at its optimum point by careful adjustment *ställa in, finjustera;* **to fine tune** = to adjust by small amounts the parameters of hardware *or* software to improve performance *finjustera* **(b)** (i) to adjust a radio receiver's frequency until the required station is received clearly *ställa in;* (ii) to adjust a transmitter to the correct frequency *ställa in*

tunnfilmsminne ⇨ **magnetic**

Turing machine ['tjʊərɪŋ məˈʃiːn] *subst.* mathematical model of a device that could read and write data to a controllable tape storage while altering its internal states *Turingmaskin*

Turing test ['tjʊərɪŋ'test] *subst.* test to decide if a computer is "intelligent" *Turingtest, Turings test*

turnaround document ['tɜːnəraʊnd 'dɒkjʊmənt] *subst.* document which is printed out from a computer, sent to a user and returned by the user with new notes *or* information written on it, which can be read by a document reader *ifyllningsblankett*

turnaround time (TAT) ['tɜːnəraʊnd 'taɪm ('tiːeɪ'tiː)] *subst.* **(a)** length of time it takes to switch data flow direction in a half duplex system *växlingstid* **(b)** time taken for a product to be constructed and delivered after an order has been received *leveranstid* **(c)** *US* time taken to activate a program and produce the result which the user has asked for *körtid*

turnkey system ['tɜːnkiː 'sɪstəm] *subst.* complete system which is designed to a customer's needs and is ready to use (to operate it, the user only has to switch it on or turn a key) *nyckelfärdigt system*

turn off [tɜːn 'ɒf] *vb.* to switch off *or* to disconnect the power supply to a machine *slå (stänga) av;* **turn off the power before unplugging the monitor**

turn on [tɜːn 'ɒn] *vb.* to switch on *or* to connect the power supply to a machine *slå (sätta) på*

turtle ['tɜːtl] *subst.* device whose movement and position are controllable, which is used to draw graphics (with instructions in the computer language LOGO), either a device which works on a flat surface (floor turtle) *or* which draws on a VDU screen (screen turtle), used as a teaching aid *"sköldpadda";* **turtle graphics** = graphic images created using a turtle and a series of commands *grafik (i programmeringsspråket logo);* **the charts were prepared using turtle graphics**

TV ['tiː'viː] = TELEVISION

TV-bildruta ⇨ **video**

tvetydighetsfel ⇨ **error**

tvetydigt filnamn ⇨ **ambiguous**

TV-konferens ⇨ **video**

TV-signalkonverterare ⇨ **transcoder**

TV-standarder (för videosignaler) ⇨ **video**

tvåadressinstruktion ⇨ **instruction**

(tvåläges) vippomkopplare ⇨ **toggle**

tvångsbrytning ⇨ **force**

två-plus-ett-instruktion ⇨ **instruction**

tvåportsminne ⇨ **dual**

tvåtonssignalering ⇨ **frequency, multifrequency**

tvåvägsskrivare ⇨ **printer**

tvärstopp ⇨ **halt**

tweeter ['twiːtə] *subst. (informal)* small loudspeaker used for high frequency sounds only *diskanthögtalare;* compare WOOFER

twisted pair cable ['twɪstɪd 'peə 'keɪbl] *subst.* cheap cable for telephones, with two wires twisted round each other (as opposed to co-axial cable), to provide some protection against interference and minimize inductive and capacitive effects of the wires *partvinnad fyrträdskabel, partvinnad kabel*

two-address instruction ['tuː ə'dres ɪn'strʌkʃ(ə)n] *subst.* instruction format containing the location of two operands, the result being stored in one of the operand locations *tvåadressinstruktion;* **two-plus-one instruction =** instruction containing the locations of two operands and an address for the result *två-plus-ett-instruktion*

two-dimensional ['tuːdɪ'menʃənl] *adj.* which has two dimensions (that is, flat, with no depth) *tvådimensionell;* **two-dimensional array =** array which locates items both vertically and horizontally *tvådimensionell vektor*

two input adder ['tuːɪnpʊt 'ædə] *see* HALF ADDER

two-level subroutine ['tuːˌlevl 'sʌbruːˌtiːn] *subst.* subroutine containing another subroutine *tvånivåsubrutin*

two-part ['tuːpɑːt] *subst.* paper (for computers *or* typewriters) with a top sheet for the original and a second sheet for a copy *tvådelad blankett;* **two-part invoices; two-part stationery**

two-pass assembler ['tuːpɑːs ə'semblə] *subst.* assembler that converts an assembly language program into machine code in two passes - the first pass stores symbolic addresses, the second converts them to absolute addresses *tvåstegsassemblerare*

two's complement ['tuːz 'kɒmplɪmənt] *subst.* formed by adding one to the one's complement of a binary number, often used to represent negative binary numbers *tvåkomplement*

two way cable ['tuːweɪ 'keɪbl] *subst. US* system of cable TV, where the viewer can take which programmes he wants by selecting them *or* where the viewer can respond to broadcast questions by sending his response down the cable *dubbelriktad kabel-TV*

two way radio ['tuːweɪ 'reɪdɪəʊ] *subst.* radio transmitter and receiver in a single housing, allowing duplex communication with another user *dubbelriktad radiokommunikation*

two wire circuit ['tuː 'waɪə 'sɜːkɪt] *subst.* two insulated wires used to carry transmitted and received messages independently *dubbelriktad överföring (i parkabel)*

TX ['tiː'eks] = TRANSMITTER

type [taɪp] **1** *subst.* **(a)** metal bars with a raised characters used for printing *typ* **(b)** characters used in printing *or* characters which appear in printed form *typer, stil;* **they switched to italic type for the heading (c)** definition of the processes *or* sorts of data which a variable in a computer can contain (this can be numbers, text only, etc.) *datatyp;* **variable data type =** variable that can contain any sort of data, such as numerical, text, etc. *variabel datatyp;* **string type =** variable that can contain alphanumeric characters only *strängtyp* **2** *vb.* to write with a typewriter *skriva maskin;* **he can type quite fast; all his reports are typed on his portable typewriter**

typeface ['taɪpfeɪs] *or* **typestyle** ['taɪpstaɪl] *or* **font** [fɒnt] *subst.* set of characters designed in a certain style *typsnitt, stil*

typescript ['taɪpskrɪpt] *subst.* copy of a text written by an author on a typewriter *maskinutskrift;* compare MANUSCRIPT

typeset ['taɪpset] *vb.* to set text in type for printing *sätta;* **in desktop publishing, the finished work should look almost as if it had been typeset**

typesetter ['taɪpˌsetə] *subst.* company which typesets *sätteri;* **the text is ready to be sent to the typesetter**

typesetting ['taɪpˌsetɪŋ] *subst.* action of setting text in type *sättning;* **typesetting costs can be reduced by supplying the typesetter with prekeyed disks;** *see also* PHOTOTYPESETTING

typesize ['taɪpsaɪz] *subst.* size of type, calculated in "points" which refer to the height of the character but not its width *(typ)grad*

typewriter ['taɪpˌraɪtə] *subst.* machine which prints letters *or* figures on a piece of paper when a key is pressed by striking an inked ribbon onto the paper with a character type *skrivmaskin;* **she wrote the letter on her portable typewriter; he makes fewer mistakes now he is using an electronic typewriter; typewriter faces =** spacing, size and font of characters available on a typewriter *skrivmaskinstypsnitt*

typewritten ['taɪp,rɪtn] *adj.* written on a typewriter *maskinskriven;* **he sent in a typewritten job application**

(typ)grad ⇨ **typesize**

typhjul ⇨ **daisy-wheel**

typhjulsskrivare ⇨ **printer**

typing ['taɪpɪŋ] *subst.* writing letters with a typewriter *maskinskrivning;* **typing error** = mistake made when using a typewriter *skrivfel;* **the secretary must have made a typing error; typing pool** = group of typists, working together in a company, offering a secretarial service to several departments *skrivcentral, sekreterarpool;* **copy typing** = typing documents from handwritten originals, not from dictation *utskrift (på maskin)* NOTE: no plural

typist ['taɪpɪst] *subst.* person whose job is to write letters using a typewriter *maskinskriverska, maskinskrivare;* **copy typist** = person who types documents from handwritten originals not from dictation *person som gör utskrifter (på maskin);* **shorthand typist** = typist who takes dictation in shorthand and then types it *stenograf och maskinskriverska*

typkula ⇨ **golf-ball**

typo ['taɪpəʊ] *subst. informal* typographical error which is made while typesetting *tryckfel*

typographer [taɪ'pɒgrəfə] *subst.* person who designs a typeface *or* text to be printed *typograf, grafisk formgivare*

typographic [ˌtaɪpə'græfɪk] *or* **typographical** [ˌtaɪpə'græfɪkəl] *adj.* referring to typography *or* to typesetting *typografisk, grafisk;* **no typographical skills are required for this job; a typographical error made while typesetting is called a "typo"; typographical error** = mistake made while typesetting *tryckfel*

typography [taɪ'pɒgrəfɪ] *subst.* art and methods used in working with type *typografi*

typsats ⇨ **composition**

typsnitt ⇨ **font, typeface**

typsnittsdefinition ⇨ **image**

typsnittsdiskett ⇨ **font**

typsnittsfamilj ⇨ **family**

typstångsskrivare ⇨ **bar printer**

tårtdiagram ⇨ **pie chart**

täljare ⇨ **dividend**

tömma ⇨ **scratch**

tömma buffert ⇨ **flush**

Uu

UART ['juː,ɑːt] = UNIVERSAL ASYNCHRONOUS RECEIVER/TRANSMITTER chip which converts asynchronous serial bit streams to a parallel form *or* parallel data to a serial bit stream *serie-parallellomvandlare;* **UART controller** = circuit that uses a UART to convert (serial) data from a terminal into a parallel form, then transmits it over a network *serie-parallellomvandlare; see also* USART

UBC ['juːbiː'siː] = UNIVERSAL BLOCK CHANNEL

UHF ['juːeɪtʃ'ef] = ULTRA HIGH FREQUENCY

ULA ['juːel'eɪ] = UNCOMMITTED LOGIC ARRAY chip containing a number of unconnected logic circuits and gates which can then be connected by a customer to provide a required function *halvfabricerad logikkrets, halvfabrikat*

ultra- ['ʌltrə] *prefix* meaning very large *or* further than *ultra-;* **ultra high frequency (UHF)** = very high frequency range between 300MHz and 3GHz *ultrahög frekvens, UHF-bandet;* **ultrafiche** = microfiche with images that have been reduced by more than ninety times *mikrofiche;* **ultrasonic** = sound pressure waves at a frequency above the audio band, above 20KHz *ultraljuds-;* **ultrasound** = sound emitted at a frequency above the audio band *ultraljud;* **ultraviolet (UV) light** = electromagnetic radiation with wavelength just greater than the visible spectrum, from 200 to 4000 angstroms *ultraviolett ljus;* **ultraviolet erasable PROM** = EPROM whose contents are erased by exposing to UV light *(ultraviolett) raderbart läsminne*

umlaut ['ʊmlaʊt] *subst.* accent consisting of two dots over a German a, o or u *omljud, prickar (över bokstäver)*

un- [ʌn] *prefix* meaning not *o-;* **unallowable digit** = illegal combination of bits in a word, according to predefined rules *otillåten siffra;* **unauthorized** = which has not been authorized *oauktoriserad;* **the use of a password is to prevent unauthorized access to the data; uncut** = (pages of a book) whose edges have not been cut *oskuren*

unary operation ['juːnərɪ ˌɒpə'reɪʃ(ə)n] *subst.* computing operation on only one operand, such as the logical NOT operation *unär operation, envärd operation, enställig operation*

unattended operation [ˌʌnəˈtendɪd ˌɒpəˈreɪʃ(ə)n] *subst.* system that can operate without the need for a person to supervise *oövervakad drift*

unbundled software [ˌʌnˈbʌndld ˈsɒftweə] *subst.* software which is not included in the price of the equipment *icke medföljande program*

unclocked [ˌʌnˈklɒkt] *adj.* electronic circuit *or* flip-flop that changes state as soon as an input changes, not with a clock signal *asynkron*

uncommitted logic array (ULA) [ˌʌnkəˈmɪtɪd ˈlɒdʒɪk əˈreɪ (ˈjuːelˈeɪ)] *subst.* chip containing a number of unconnected logic circuits and gates which can then be connected by a customer to provide a required function *halvfabricerad logikkrets, halvfabrikat;* **uncommitted storage list =** table of the areas of memory in a system that are free *or* have not been allocated *lista över lediga minnesareor*

unconditional [ˌʌnkənˈdɪʃ(ə)nl] *adj.* which does not depend on any condition being met *ovillkorlig;* **unconditional branch** *or* **jump** *or* **transfer =** instruction which transfers control from one point in the program to another, without depending on any condition being met *ovillkorligt hopp*
NOTE: opposite is **CONDITIONAL**

undantagskatalog ⇨ **exception**

underbibliotek ⇨ **subdirectory**

underexposed [ˈʌnd(ə)rɪksˈpəʊzd] *adj.* (photograph) that is too dark because it did not receive a long enough exposure *underexponerad*

underflow [ˈʌndəfləʊ] *subst.* result of a numerical operation that is too small to be represented with the given accuracy of a computer *bottning*

underförstådd adressering ⇨ **implied addressing**

underhåll ⇨ **maintenance**

underhålla ⇨ **maintain**

underkatalog ⇨ **subdirectory**

underline *or* **underscore 1** [ˈʌndəlaɪn ˈʌndəskɔː] *subst.* line drawn *or* printed under a piece of text *understrykning;* **the chapter headings are given a double underline and the paragraphs a single underline 2** [ˌʌndəˈlaɪn ˌʌndəˈskɔː] *vb.* to print *or* write a line under a piece of text *stryka under;* **underlining =** word-processing command which underlines text *understrykning*

underrutin ⇨ **coroutine**

underskrift ⇨ **signature**

understation ⇨ **tributary station**

understrykning ⇨ **underline**

undersöka ⇨ **review**

undertake [ˌʌndəˈteɪk] *vb.* to agree to do something *åta sig;* **he has undertaken to reprogram the whole system**
NOTE: undertaking - undertaken - undertook

undetected [ˌʌndɪˈtektɪd] *adj.* which has not been detected *oupptäckt;* **the programming error was undetected for some time**

unedited [ʌnˈedɪtɪd] *adj.* which has not been edited *oredigerad, obearbetad;* **the unedited text is with the publisher for editing**

unformatted [ʌnˈfɔːmætɪd] *adj.* (disk) which has not been formatted *oformaterad;* **it is impossible to copy to an unformatted disk; the cartridge drive provides 12.7Mbyte of unformatted storage**

uni- [ˈjuːnɪ] *prefix* meaning one *or* single *uni-, en-*

unidirectional microphone [ˈjuːnɪdɪˈrekʃənl ˈmaɪkrəfəʊn] *subst.* microphone that is most sensitive in one direction only *riktmikrofon; compare with* OMNIDIRECTIONAL

uninterruptable power supply (UPS) [ˈʌnˌɪntəˈrʌptɪd ˈpaʊə səˈplaɪ] *subst.* power supply that can continue to provide a regulated supply to equipment even after a mains power failure (using a battery) *avbrottsfri kraft*

union [ˈjuːnjən] *subst.* logical function that produces a true output if any input is true *union*

unipolar [juːnɪˈpəʊlə] *adj.* **(a)** (transistor) that can act as a variable current flow control an external signal varies the resistance of the device *fälteffekttransistor; see also* FET, TRANSISTOR **(b)** (transmission system) in which a positive voltage pulse and zero volts represents the binary bits 1 and 0 *enpolär signalering; compare with* POLAR; **unipolar signal =** signal that uses only positive voltage levels *enpolär signal*

unique [juːˈniːk] *adj.* which is different from everything else *unik;* **each separate memory byte has its own unique address**

unit [ˈjuːnɪt] *subst.* **(a)** smallest element *enhet;* **unit buffer =** buffer that is one character long *enhetsbuffert* (NOTE: usually used to mean that there are no buffering facilities) **unit record =** single record of information *enhetspost* **(b)** single machine (possibly with many different parts) *enhet;* **arithmetic and logic unit (ALU)** = section of the CPU that performs all the mathematical and logical functions *aritmetik- och logikenhet;* **central processing unit (CPU)** = group of circuits which perform the basic functions of a computer, made up of three main parts: the control unit, the arithmetic and logic unit and the input/output unit *(central)processor;* **control unit** = section of the CPU that selects and executes instructions *styrenhet;* **desk top unit** = computer *or* machine that will fit onto a desk *skrivbordsenhet;* **input/output unit** *or* **device** = peripheral (such as a terminal in a workstation) which can be used both for inputting and outputting data to a processor *in-utenhet*

universal [ˌjuːnɪˈvɜːs(ə)l] *adj.* which applies everywhere *or* which can be used everywhere *or* used for a number of tasks *universell;* **universal asynchronous receiver/transmitter (UART)** = chip which converts an asynchronous serial bit stream to a parallel form *or* parallel data to a serial bit stream *serie-parallellomvandlare;* **universal block channel (UBC)** = communications channel allowing high speed transfer of blocks of data to and from high speed peripherals *blocköverföringskanal;* **universal device** = (i) UART *konverteringsenhet;* (ii) USRT; (iii) USART; **universal product code (UPC)** = standard printed bar coding system used to identify products in a shop (using a bar code reader *or* at a EPOS) *streckkodsstandard; see also* EAN; **universal programming** = writing a program that is not specific to one machine, so that it can run on several machines *maskinoberoende programmering;* **universal set** = complete set of elements that conform to a set of rules *universell mängd;* **the universal set of prime numbers less than ten and greater than two is 3,5,7; universal synchronous asynchronous receiver-transmitter (USART)** = chip that can be instructed by a CPU to communicate with asynchronous or synchronous bit streams *or* data lines *parallell-serieomvandlare;* **universal synchronous receiver/transmitter (USRT)** = single integrated circuit that can carry out all the serial to parallel and interfacing operations required between a computer and transmission line *parallell-serieomvandlare*

Unix [ˈjuːnɪks] *subst.* popular operating system for small micros and large mainframes *operativsystemet Unix*

unjustified [ˌʌnˈdʒʌstɪfaɪd] *adj.* (text) which has not been justified *ojusterad;* **unjustified tape** *or* **idiot tape** = tape containing unformatted text, which cannot

be printed until formatting data (such as justification, line width and page size) has been added by a computer *rådataband, band med oformaterad text*

unmodified instruction [ˌʌnˈmɒdɪfaɪd ɪnˈstrʌkʃ(ə)n] *subst.* program instruction which is directly processed without modification to obtain the operation to be performed *presumtiv instruktion, omodifierad instruktion*

unmodulated [ˌʌnˈmɒdjʊleɪtɪd] *adj.* (signal) which has not been modulated *omodulerad; see also* BASE BAND

unpack [ˌʌnˈpæk] *vb.* to remove packed data from storage and expand it to its former state *packa upp, dekompilera;* **this routine unpacks the archived file**

unplug [ˌʌnˈplʌg] *vb.* to take a plug out of a socket *dra ur kontakten;* **do not move the system without unplugging it; simply unplug the old drive and plug-in a new one**

unprotected [ˌʌnprəˈtektɪd] *adj.* (data) that can be modified and is not protected by a security measure *oskyddad;* **unprotected field** = section of a computer display that a user can modify *oskyddat område*

unrecoverable error [ˌʌnrɪˈkʌv(ə)rəbl ˈerə] *subst.* computer hardware *or* software error that causes a program to crash *oåterkalleligt fel*

unsigned [ˌʌnˈsaɪnd] *adj.* (number system) that does not represent negative numbers *naturligt tal (utan förtecken)*

unsorted [ˌʌnˈsɔːtɪd] *adj.* (data) which has not been sorted *osorterad;* **it took four times as long to search the unsorted file**

unwanted [ˌʌnˈwɒntɪd] *adj.* which is not needed *oönskad;* **use the global delete command to remove large areas of unwanted text**

up [ʌp] *adv. (of computer or program)* working *or* running *arbetande, i drift, i gång;* **they must have found the fault - the computer is finally up and running; up time** *or* **uptime** = time during which a device is operational and error free *drifttid*
NOTE: opposite is **down**

up and down propagation time [ˌʌpənˈdaʊn ˌprɒpəˈgeɪʃ(ə)nˌtaɪm] *subst.* total length of time that a transmission takes to travel from earth to a satellite and back to an earth station *tid för överföring via satellit*

UPC [ˈjuːpiːsiː] = UNIVERSAL PRODUCT CODE

update 1 [ˈʌpdeɪt] *subst.* (i) master file which has been made up-to-date by adding new material *uppdaterad (aktualiserad) fil;* (ii) printed information which is an up-to-date revision of earlier information *reviderad version;* (iii) new version of a system which is sent to users of the existing system *ny version;* **update file** *or* **transaction file** = file containing recent changes *or* transactions to records which is used to update the master file *uppdateringsfil* **2** [ʌp'deɪt] *vb.* to change *or* add to specific data in a master file so as to make the information up-to-date *uppdatera, aktualisera;* **he has the original and updated documents on disks**

> QUOTE it means that any item of data stored in the system need be updated only once
> **Which PC?**

up/down counter [ʌp'daʊn 'kaʊntə] *subst.* electronic counter that can increment *or* decrement a counter with each input pulse *upp-ner-räknare*

upgrade [ʌp'greɪd] *vb.* to make (a system) more powerful *or* more up-to-date by adding new equipment *förbättra, uppgradera;* **they can upgrade the printer; the single processor with 2Mbytes of memory can be upgraded to 4Mbytes; all three models have an on-site upgrade facility**

> QUOTE the cost of upgrading a PC to support CAD clearly depends on the peripheral devices added
> **PC Business World**

upkeep ['ʌpkiːp] *subst.* keeping data up-to-date; keeping devices in working order *underhåll;* **the upkeep of the files means reviewing them every six months**

upload ['ʌpləʊd] *vb.* to transfer data files *or* programs from a small computer to a main CPU *föra över till stordator;* **the user can upload PC data to update mainframe applications** NOTE: the opposite is **download**

uploading ['ʌp,ləʊdɪŋ] *subst.* action of transferring files to a main CPU *överföring till stordator;* **the image can be manipulated before uploading to the host computer**

uppdateringsfil ▷ file

uppdateringslista ▷ addition, deletion

uppdrag ▷ job, task

uppdragshantering ▷ task

uppdragskö ▷ task

uppdragsorienterat språk ▷ job

uppdragsprioritet ▷ job

uppdragsstyrning ▷ job

uppehållsmarkering ▷ mark

upper case ['ʌpə 'keɪs] *subst.* series of capital letters and other symbols on a typewriter *or* keyboard, which are accessed by pressing the shift key *versaler (på tangentbord)*

uppgift ▷ job, task

upphovsrätt ▷ copyright

upphävande ▷ cancellation

upphöja ▷ exponentiation

upphöra ▷ cancel

uppladdningsbar ▷ re-chargeable

upplösning ▷ definition, display, resolution

uppringning ▷ dialling

uppräkningsbar datatyp ▷ enumerated type

upprätthålla ▷ maintain

uppsamlingsrulle ▷ take-up reel

uppskatta ▷ calculate

uppskjutning ▷ launch

uppsättning ▷ repertoire

upptagetsignal ▷ howler

upptagettid ▷ hold

upptagetton ▷ tone

UPS ['juːpiːes] = UNINTERRUPTABLE POWER SUPPLY power supply that can continue to provide a regulated supply to equipment even after a mains power failure (using a battery) *avbrottsfri kraftenhet*

uptime ['ʌptaɪm] *subst.* time when a computer is functioning correctly (as opposed to downtime) *drifttid*

upwards compatible ['ʌpwədz kəm'pætəbl] *or US* **upward compatible** ['ʌpwəd kəm'pætəbl] *adj.* (hardware *or* software) designed to be compatible either with earlier models *or* with future models which have not yet been invented *kompatibel med (tidigare och) senare versioner*

ur funktion ▷ dead

urkopplad ▷ off-line, local

ursprungsfil ▷ ancestral file

ursprungsformat ▷ native

ursprungstillverkare ▷ original equipment manufacturer (OEM)

ursprungsversion ▷ grandfather file

urtavla ▷ dial, time

usable ['juːzəbl] *adj.* which can be used *or* which is available for use *användbar, brukbar;* **the PC has 512K of usable memory; maximum usable frequency =** highest signal frequency which can be used in a circuit without distortion *högsta användbara frekvens*

USART ['juːsɑːt] = UNIVERSAL SYNCHRONOUS ASYNCHRONOUS RECEIVER-TRANSMITTER chip that can be instructed by a CPU to communicate with asynchronous *or* synchronous bit streams or parallel data lines *parallell-serieomvandlare*

USASCII ['juːesˈæskɪ] *US* = USA STANDARD CODE FOR INFORMATION INTERCHANGE *see* ASCII

use [juːs] **1** *subst.* **(a)** way in which something can be used *användning, drift;* **the printer has been in use for the last two hours; the use of the that file is restricted; to make use of something =** to use something *använda något* **(b)** value; being useful *värde, användbarhet;* **what use is an extra disk drive? it's no use, I cannot find the error; in use =** already in operation *i drift, i bruk (användning);* **sorry, the printer is already in use 2** *vb.* **(a)** to operate something *använda;* **if you use the computer for processing the labels, it will be much quicker; the computer is used too often by the sales staff (b)** to consume heat, light, etc. *använda, förbruka;* **it's using too much electricity**

used [juːzd] *adj.* which is not new *använd, begagnad;* **special offer on used terminals**

user ['juːzə] *subst.* (i) person who uses a computer *or* machine *or* software *användare;* (ii) especially, a keyboard operator *användare;* **user area =** part of the memory which is available for the user, and does not contain the operating system *användararea;* **user-definable =** feature *or* section of a program that a user can customize as required *definierbar av användaren;* **the style sheet contains 125 user-definable symbols; user-defined characters =** characters which are created by the user and added to the standard character set *användardefinierade tecken;* **user documentation =** documentation provided with a program which helps the user run it *användarhandböcker;* **using the package was easy with the excellent user documentation; user group =** association *or* club of users of a particular system *or* computer *användargrupp;* **I found how to solve the problem by asking people at the user group meeting; user guide =** manual describing how to use a software package *or* system *användarhandledning;* **user ID =** unique identification code that allows a computer to recognize a user

användaridentitet; **if you forget your user ID, you will not be able to logon; user interface =** hardware *or* software designed to make it easier for a user to communicate with the machine *användargränssnitt;* **user-operated language =** high-level programming language that allows certain problems *or* procedures to be easily expressed *användarorienterat programmeringsspråk;* **user port =** socket which allows peripherals to be connected to a computer *utgång;* **user's program =** computer software written by a user rather than a manufacturer *användarprogram;* **user-selectable =** which can be chosen *or* selected by the user *valbar av användaren;* **the video resolution of 640 by 300, 240** *or* **200 pixels is user-selectable**

QUOTE the user's guides are designed for people who have never seen a computer, but some sections have been spoiled by careless checking
PC User

user-friendly ['juːzəˈfrendlɪ] *adj.* (language *or* system *or* program) that is easy to use and interact with *användarvänlig;* **it's such a user-friendly machine; compared with the previous version this one is very user-friendly**

QUOTE the first popular microcomputer to have a user-friendly interface built into its operating system
Micro Decision

USRT ['juːesɑːtiː] = UNIVERSAL SYNCHRONOUS RECEIVER/TRANSMITTER

utbud ⇨ **range**

utbyggbar ⇨ **expandable**

utbyggbart programmeringsspråk ⇨ **extensible**

utbyggnadskort ⇨ **card**

utbytbarhet ⇨ **compatibility**

utbytbart skivminne ⇨ **EDS**

utbytesläge ⇨ **mode**

utbytessortering ⇨ **exchange**

utdata ⇨ **information, output (o/p or O/P)**

utdataarea ⇨ **output (o/p or O/P)**

utdatabegränsad ⇨ **output (o/p or O/P)**

utdatabuffert ⇨ **output (o/p or O/P)**

utdataenhet ⇨ **output (o/p or O/P)**

utdatafil ⇨ **file**

utdatalinje ⇨ **forward**

utdataregister ⇨ **output (o/p or O/P)**

utdatautgång ⇨ **output (o/p or O/P)**

utdrag ⇨ outdent

utenhet ⇨ device

utfyllnadstecken ⇨ fill

utgång ⇨ port

utgångsinstruktion ⇨ presumptive instruction

utgångspunkt ⇨ exit

utgåva ⇨ edition

utility (program) [juːˈtɪlətɪ ˈprəʊɡræm] *subst.* useful program that is concerned with such routine activities as file searching, copying files, file directories, sorting and debugging and various mathematical functions *hjälpprogram;* **a lost file cannot be found without a file-recovery utility; on the disk is a utility for backing up a hard disk**

utjämnat fel ⇨ balance

utkast ⇨ outline

utlandskod ⇨ international

utlandsprefix ⇨ international

utlåsning ⇨ lockout

utropstecken ⇨ exclamation mark

utrustning ⇨ device, equipment

utrustningsoberoende ⇨ device

utskrift ⇨ printout, readout

utskriftsformat ⇨ print

utskriftskvalitet ⇨ printer

utskriftsmellanlagring ⇨ spooling

utslutning ⇨ justification

uttagsautomat ⇨ automatic

uttryck ⇨ expression

utvecklingsdator ⇨ host computer

UV light [ˈjuːˈviːˈlaɪt] = ULTRAVIOLET LIGHT

Vv

V [viː] = VOLTAGE

V & V [ˈviːəndˈviː] = VERIFICATION AND VALIDATION

vacuum [ˈvækjʊ(ə)m] *subst.* state with no air *vakuum;* **there is a vacuum in the sealed CRT; vacuum tube** = electronic current flow control device consisting of a heated cathode and an anode in a sealed glass tube with a vacuum inside it *vakuumrör*

COMMENT: used in the first generation of computers, now replaced by solid state current control devices such as the transistor

vagnretur ⇨ carriage

vagnreturtangent ⇨ enter, key

valbart flerskivminnessystem ⇨ multi-disk

valid [ˈvælɪd] *adj.* correct, according to a set of rules *giltig;* **valid memory address** = signal on control bus indicating that an address is available on the address bus *giltig minnesadress*

validate [ˈvælɪdeɪt] *vb.* to check that an input *or* data is correct according to a set of rules *bekräfta, giltighetskontrollera*

validation [ˌvælɪˈdeɪʃ(ə)n] *subst.* check performed to validate data *validering, giltighetskontroll*

validity [vəˈlɪdətɪ] *subst.* correctness of an instruction *or* password *giltighet;* **validity check** = check that data *or* results are realistic *giltighetskontroll*

valmöjlighet ⇨ option

value [ˈvæljuː] *subst.* what something is worth (either in money *or* as a quantity) *värde;* **absolute value** = value of a number regardless of its sign *absolutvärde;* **the absolute value of -62.34 is 62.34; initial value** = starting point (usually zero) set when initializing variables at the beginning of a program *grundvärde*

value added network (VAN) [ˈvæljuːˌædɪd ˈnetwɜːk (ˈviːeɪˈen)] *subst.* network where the transmission lines are leased from a public utility such as the telephone service, but where the user can add on private equipment *mervärdesnät*

value added reseller (VAR) [ˈvæljuːˌædɪd ˌriːˈselə (ˈviːeɪˈɑː)] *subst.* retailer who sells equipment and systems which are specially tailored to certain types of operation *systemåterförsäljare*

valve [vælv] *subst.* electronic current flow control device consisting of a heated cathode and an anode in a sealed glass vacuum tube *ventil*

COMMENT: used in the first generation of computers, now replaced by solid state current control devices such as a transistor

VAN [ˈviːeɪˈen] = VALUE ADDED NETWORK

vanlig ⇨ common

vapourware ['veɪpəweə] *subst. informal* products which exist in name only *luftprodukt*

VAR ['viːeɪ'ɑː] vɑː] = VALUE ADDED RESELLER

variabelvärde ⇨ **definition**

variable ['veərɪəbl] **1** *adj.* able to change *variabel;* **variable data** = data which can be modified, and is not write-protected *variabla data;* **variable length record** = record which can be of any length *post med variabel längd;* **variable word length computer** = computer in which the number of bits which make up a word is variable, and varies according to the type of data *dator med variabel ordlängd* **2** *subst.* (computer program identifier for a) register *or* storage location which can contain any number *or* characters and which may vary during the program run *variabel;* **global variable** = number that can be accessed by any routine *or* structure in a program *allmän variabel;* **local variable** = number which can only be accessed by certain routines in a certain section of a computer program *lokal variabel*

varken-eller-grind ⇨ **gate, NOR function**

varmstart ⇨ **soft**

vary ['veərɪ] *vb.* to change *variera;* **the clarity of the signal can vary with the power supply**

VCR ['viːsiːˈɑː] = VIDEO CASSETTE RECORDER

VDT *or* **VDU** ['viːdiːˈtiː 'viːdiːˈjuː] = VISUAL DISPLAY TERMINAL, VISUAL DISPLAY UNIT terminal with a screen and a keyboard, on which text *or* graphics can be viewed and information entered *bildskärmsterminal*

> QUOTE it normally consists of a keyboard to input information and either a printing terminal or a VDU screen to display messages and results
> **Practical Computing**
> QUOTE a VDU is a device used with a computer that displays information in the form of characters and drawings on a screen
> **Electronics & Power**

vector ['vektə] *subst.* **(a)** address which directs a computer to a new memory location *vektor* **(b)** coordinate that consists of a magnitude and direction *vektor;* **vector graphics** *or* **vector image** *or* **vector scan** = computer drawing system that uses line length and direction from an origin to plot lines *vektorgrafik;* **vector processor** = coprocessor that operates on one row or column of an array at a time *vektorprocessor*

> QUOTE the great advantage of the vector-scan display is that it requires little memory to store a picture
> **Electronics & Power**

vectored interrupt ['vektəd ˌɪntəˈrʌpt] *subst.* interrupt signal which directs the processor to a routine at a particular address *vektoriserat avbrott*

Veitch diagram ['viːtʃ 'daɪəgræm] *subst.* graphical representation of a truth table *Veitch-diagram*

vektoriserat avbrott ⇨ **interrupt**

vektorprocessor ⇨ **array, processor**

velocity [vəˈlɒsətɪ] *subst.* speed *hastighet;* **the disk drive motor spins at a constant velocity**

Venn diagram ['ven 'daɪəgræm] *subst.* graphical representation of the relationships between the states in a system *or* circuit *Venn-diagram*

verification [ˌverɪfɪˈkeɪʃ(ə)n] *subst.* checking that data has been keyboarded correctly *or* that data transferred from one medium to another has been transferred correctly *giltighetskontroll;* **keystroke verification** = check made on each key pressed to make sure it is valid for a particular application *tangenttrycksvalidering;* **verification and validation (V & V)** = testing a system to check that it is functioning correctly and that it is suitable for the tasks intended *systemkontroll*

verifier ['verɪfaɪə] *subst.* special device for verifying input data *verifierare*

verify ['verɪfaɪ] *vb.* to check that data recorded *or* entered is correct *verifiera, kontrollera*

verklig (behandlings)kapacitet ⇨ **effective**

verklig sökhastighet ⇨ **effective**

verktygslåda ⇨ **toolbox**

verktygssats ⇨ **toolkit**

versaler ⇨ **block, capitals, uppercase**

versaler (på tangentbord) ⇨ **upper case**

version ['vɜːʃ(ə)n] *subst.* copy *or* program *or* statement which is slightly different from others *version;* **the latest version of the software includes an improved graphics routine**

version ⇨ **release**

verso ['vɜːsəu] *subst.* left hand page of a book (usually given an even number) *vänstersida*

vertical ['vɜːtɪk(ə)l] *adj.* at right angles to the horizontal *vertikal;* **vertical blanking interval** *see* RASTER; **vertical format unit (VFU)** = part of the control system of a printer which governs the vertical format of the document to be printed (such as vertical spacing, page length) *vertikalformaterare;* **vertical justification** = adjustment of the spacing between lines of text to fit a section of text into a page *vertikaljustering;* **vertical parity check** = error detection test in which the bits of a word are added and compared with a correct total *vertikal paritetskontroll;* **vertical redundancy check (VRC)** = (odd) parity check on each character of a block received, to detect any errors *vertikal redundanskontroll;* **vertical scrolling** = displayed text that moves up or down the computer screen one line at a time *vertikal rullning;* **vertical tab** = number of lines that should be skipped before printing starts again *vertikal tabulering*

vertically ['vɜːtɪk(ə)lɪ] *adv.* from top to bottom or going up and down at right angles to the horizontal *vertikalt, lodrätt;* **the page has been justified vertically; vertically polarized signal** = signal whose waveforms are all aligned in one vertical plane *vertikalpolariserad signal*

very high frequency (VHF) ['verɪ 'haɪ 'friːkwənsɪ ('viːeɪtʃ'ef)] *subst.* range of radio frequencies between 30-300 MHz *VHF-bandet, ultrakortvåg*

very large scale integration (VLSI) ['verɪ 'lɑːdʒ skeɪl ˌɪntɪ'greɪʃ(ə)n ('viːeles'aɪ)] *subst.* integrated circuit with 10,000 to 100,000 components *VLSI-teknik (höggradig integration)*

very low frequency (VLF) ['verɪ 'ləʊ 'friːkwənsɪ ('viːel'ef)] *subst.* range of radio frequencies between 3-30 kHz *VLF-bandet, mycket låg frekvens*

vestigial sideband [ves'tɪdʒɪəl 'saɪdbænd] *subst.* single sideband transmission with a small part of the other sideband kept to provide synchronization data, often used in TV transmissions *stympat sidband*

vf band ['viːef'bænd] = VOICE FREQUENCY BAND

V format ['viːˌfɔːmæt] *subst.* data organization, in which variable length records are stored with a header which contains their length *V-format*

VFU ['viːefjuː] = VERTICAL FORMAT UNIT

VHD ['viːeɪtʃ'diː] = VERY HIGH DENSITY video disk able to store very large quantities of data *diskett med mycket hög lagringstäthet*

VHF [ˌviːeɪtʃ'ef] = VERY HIGH FREQUENCY radio frequency between 30MHz and 300MHZ (used for broadcasting radio and TV programmes) *VHF-bandet, ultrakortvåg*

via ['vaɪə] *prep.* going through something or using something to get to a destination *via;* **the signals have reached us via satellite; you can download the data to the CPU via a modem**

vidarekoppla ⇨ forward

video ['vɪdɪəʊ] *subst.* text or images or graphics viewed on television or a monitor *video;* **video bandwidth** = frequency range required to carry TV images *videobandbredd, TV-bandbredd;* **video camera** = optical lenses in front of an electronic device that can convert images into electronic signals in a form that can be displayed on a TV *videokamera;* **infrared video camera** = video camera sensitive to infrared light *värmekamera;* **some instructors monitor their trainees with infrared videocameras; video cassette** = cassette with video tape in it (either blank for recording, or with a prerecorded film) *videokassett;* **video cassette recorder (VCR)** = device attached to a TV set, which can be programmed to record TV programmes on videotape and play them back at another time *video(bandspelare);* **video compressor** = device that reduces the bandwidth of a TV signal allowing it to be transmitted over a (telephone), using a video expander at the receiving end *videosignalkomprimerare, videokompressor;* **video conference** = conference system where two or more people can talk to and see each other using satellite TV links *TV-konferens;* **videodisk** = read-only optical disk able to store TV pictures and sound in binary form, also capable of storing large amounts of computer data *videoskiva;* **video display** = device which can display text or graphical information, such as a CRT *bildskärm;* **video expander** = device that stores one frame of a video image as it is slowly received over a voice grade communications link, with a video compressor used at the transmitting end *videosignalsexpanderare, videoexpander;* **video frame** = single image on a video tape or TV *TV-bildruta;* **with an image processor you can freeze a video frame; video game** = game played on a computer, with action shown on a video display *videospel;* **video image** = single frame from a video tape or TV *videobild, TV-bild;* **a printer-readable video image can be sent to a basic laser printer through a video port; video interface chip** = chip that controls a video display allowing information stored in a computer (text, graphics) to be displayed *videogränssnittkrets;* **video memory** or **video RAM (VRAM)** = high speed random access memory used to store computer-generated *or* digitized images *videominne;* **video monitor** = device able to display, without sound, signals from a computer *bildskärm; informal* **video nasties** = horror films available on video cassette *skräckfilmer (på video), "videovåld";* **video phone** = two way voice and image transmission *bildtelefon;* **video player** = device that can play back video recordings but cannot record *videospelare, videobox;* **video port** = connection on a video recorder allowing the data read from the tape to be used in other ways, such as being stored in a computer *videoutgång;* **video recorder** = device for recording TV images and sound onto video tape *videobandspelare;* **video signal** = signal which provides line picture information and synchronization pulses *video-signal, bildsignal;* **video scanner** = device which allows images of objects *or* pictures to be entered into a computer *videoscanner;* **new video scanners are designed to scan three-dimensional objects; video standards** = protocols defining video signal format (there are three main international video standards: NTSC, PAL and SECAM) *TV-standarder (för videosignaler);* **videotape** = magnetic tape used in a video recorder, for storing TVpictures and sound information *videoband;* **videotape recorder** = device that can record and playback TV images and sound on video tape *videobandspelare;* **video terminal** = keyboard with a monitor *bildskärmsterminal*

videobandbredd ⇨ video

videominne ⇨ screen, VRAM

videoregister ⇨ display

videotex ⇨ videotext, viewdata

videotext ['vɪdɪəʊtekst] *or* **videotex** ['vɪdɪəʊteks] *subst.* system for transmitting text and displaying it on a screen *videotex, textteve*

> COMMENT: this covers information transmitted either by TV signals (teletext) *or* by signals sent down telephone lines (viewdata)

view [vjuː] *vb.* to look at something, especially something displayed on a screen *se, betrakta;* **the user has to pay a charge for viewing pages on a bulletin board**

viewdata ['vjuːˌdeɪtə] *subst.* interactive system for transmitting text *or* graphics from a database to a user's terminal by telephone lines, providing facilities for information retrieval, transactions, education, games and recreation *videotex*

> COMMENT: the user calls up the page of information required, using the telephone and a modem, as opposed to teletext, where the pages of information are repeated one after the other automatically

viewer ['vjuːə] *subst.* **(a)** person who watches television *tittare* **(b)** device with an eyepiece through which a person can look at film *or* transparencies *bildbetraktare*

viewfinder ['vjuːˌfaɪndə] *subst.* eyepiece in a camera that allows a user to see what is being filmed *sökare, okular;* **electronic viewfinder** = miniature cathode ray tube in a television *or* video camera, that allows the camera operator to see the images being recorded *elektronisk sökare*

viktad ⇨ weighted

vilande ⇨ idle, inactive, quiescent

villkorat hopp ⇨ jump (instruction)

villkorlig ⇨ conditional

villkorlig sats ⇨ statement

villkorlig slinga ⇨ while-loop

villkorlig övergång ⇨ transfer

villkorsinstruktion ⇨ instruction

viloström ⇨ dark current

vilotid ⇨ idle

vippa ⇨ astable multivibrator

vippomkopplare ⇨ toggle

virgin ['vɜːdʒɪn] *adj.* (tape) that has not been recorded on before *nytt videoband*

virning ⇨ wire

virtual ['vɜːtʃʊəl] *adj.* feature *or* device which does not actually exist but which is simulated by a computer and can be used by a user as if it did exist *virtuell, simulerad;* **virtual address** = an address referring to virtual storage *virtuell adress;* **virtual circuit** = link established between a source and sink (in a packet-switching network) for the duration of the call *virtuell linje;* **virtual disk** = section of RAM used with a short controlling program as if it were a fast disk storage system *virtuellt (simulerat) skivminne;* **virtual machine** = simulated machine and its operations *virtuell (simulerad) dator;* **virtual memory** *or* **virtual storage (VS)** = large imaginary main memory made available by loading smaller pages from a backing store into the available main memory only as and when they are required *virtuellt (simulerat) minne;* **virtual terminal** = ideal terminal specifications used as a model by a real terminal *virtuell (simulerad) terminal*

virus ['vaɪərəs] *subst.* short hidden routine that corrupts all data and files, which spreads from computer to computer when disks are exchanged *datorvirus, datavirus*

visible ['vɪzəbl] *adj.* which can be seen *synlig;* **visible light** = range of light colours that can be seen with the human eye *synligt ljus*

visual ['vɪzjuəl] **1** *adj.* which can be seen *or* which is used by sight *synlig, som kan ses, visuell;* **visual programming** = method of programming a computer by showing it or taking it through the processes of what it has to do rather than writing a series of instructions *visuell programmering* **2** *subst.* **visuals** = graphics *or* photographs *or* illustrations, used as part of a printed output *grafik, bilder*

visual display terminal (VDT) ['vɪzjuəl dɪs'pleɪ ˌtɜːmɪnl (viːdiː'tiː)] *or* **visual display unit (VDU)** ['vɪzjuəl dɪs'pleɪ juːnɪt (viːdiː'juː)] *subst.* terminal with a screen and a keyboard, on which text *or* graphics can be viewed and information entered *bildskärmsterminal*

visualize ['vɪzjuəlaɪz] *vb.* to imagine how something will appear, even before it has been created *visualisera*

VLF [ˌviːel'ef] = VERY LOW FREQUENCY radio frequency between 30Hz and 30KHz *VLF-bandet, mycket låg frekvens*

VLSI [ˌviːeles'aɪ] = VERY LARGE SCALE INTEGRATION system with between 10,000 and 100,000 components on a single IC *höggradig integration (VLSI-teknik)*

voice [vɔɪs] *subst.* sound of human speech *röst, tal;* **voice answer back** = computerized response service using a synthesized voice to answer enquiries *talat datorsvar;* **voice band** = minimum bandwidth required for recognizable transmission of speech (usually 300 - 3400Hz) *talbandet;* **voice data entry** *or* **input** = input of information into a computer using a speech recognition system and the user's voice *röstinmatning;* **voice grade channel** = communications channel (bandwidth usually equal to voiceband), able to carry speech and some data (such as facsimile) *talkanal;* **voice messaging** = device for recording a caller's spoken message if the number he calls does not reply *telefonsvarare;* **voice output** = production of sounds which sound like human speech, made as a result of voice synthesis *talsyntes;* **voice print** = identification of a person by registering tones and signals in that person's speech *röstavtryck;* **voice recognition** = ability of a computer to recognize certain words in a human voice and provide a suitable response *röstigenkänning;* **voice response** =

VOICE OUTPUT; **voice synthesis** = reproduction of sounds similar to those of the human voice *talsyntes;* **voice synthesizer** = device which generates sounds which are similar to the human voice *talgenerator*

> QUOTE the technology of voice output is reasonably difficult, but the technology of voice recognition is much more complex
> **Personal Computer World**

voice-over ['vɔɪsˌəuvə] *subst.* spoken commentary by an actor who does not appear on the screen (as the text of a TV commercial) *speakerröst*

voice unit ['vɔɪsˌjuːnɪt] *subst.* unit of signal measurement equal to a one millivolt signal across a 600 ohm resistance *röstenhet*

volatile memory ['vɒlətaɪl 'meməri] *or* **volatile store** ['vɒlətaɪl 'stɔː] *or* **volatile dynamic storage** ['vɒlətaɪl daɪn'næmɪk 'stɔːrɪdʒ] *subst.* memory *or* storage medium which loses data stored in it when the power supply is switched off *icke-permanent minne, flyktigt minne* NOTE: opposite is **non-volatile memory**

volatility [ˌvɒlə'tɪləti] *subst.* number of records that are added *or* deleted from a computer system compared to the total number in store *obeständighet, flyktighet*

volt [vəult] *subst.* SI unit of electrical potential, defined as voltage across a one ohm resistance when one amp is flowing *enheten Volt (v)*

voltage ['vəultɪdʒ] *subst.* electromotive force expressed in volts *spänning;* **voltage dip** *or* **dip in voltage** = sudden fall in voltage which may last only a very short while, but which can affect the operation of a computer system *spänningsfall;* **voltage regulator** = device which provides a steady output voltage even if the input supply varies *spänningsregulator;* **voltage transient** = spike of voltage that is caused by a time delay in two devices switching *or* by noise on the line *spänningsstopp*

> COMMENT: electricity supply can have peaks and troughs of current, depending on the users in the area. Fluctuations in voltage can affect computers; a voltage regulator will provide a steady supply of electricity

volume ['vɒljuːm] *subst.* **(a)** total space occupied by data in a storage system *volym* **(b)** measure of sound pressure *ljudvolym;* **volume control** = knob which turns to increase the volume from a radio, TV or amplifier *volymkontroll*

VRAM ['viːræm] = VIDEO RANDOM ACCESS MEMORY high speed random access memory used to store computer-generated *or* digitized images *videominne*

VRC ['viːɑːˈsiː] = VERTICAL REDUNDANCY CHECK (odd) parity check on each character of a block received, to detect any errors *vertikal paritetskontroll*

VS ['viːˈes] = VIRTUAL STORAGE

V series ['viːˈsɪəriːz] *subst.* CCITT (UK-European) standards for data transmission using a modem *V-serien av dataöverföringsstandarder*
NOTE: **V.21** = 300 baud transmit and receive, full duplex **V.22** = 1200 baud transmit and receive, half duplex **V.22 BIS** = 1200 baud transmit and receive full duplex **V.23** = 75 baud transmit, 1200 baud receive, half duplex

VTR ['viːtiːˈɑː] = VIDEO TAPE RECORDER

VU ['viːˈjuː] = VOICE UNIT

vågform ⇨ waveform

vågledare ⇨ waveguide

våglängd ⇨ wavelength

väg ⇨ path, route

vägval ⇨ data, message, routing

vägvalskatalog ⇨ directory

vänstersida ⇨ verso

vänsterskift ⇨ end

vänsterställd text ⇨ text

väntande ⇨ idle, inactive

vänteläge ⇨ wait condition, waiting state

vänteslinga ⇨ loop, wait loop

väntetecken ⇨ idle

väntetid ⇨ time, wait time

väntprogram ⇨ hold

väntslinga ⇨ hold

värddator ⇨ host computer

värde ⇨ rate, value

värmekamera ⇨ video

värmekänslig ⇨ thermo-sensitive

värmeöverföring ⇨ thermal transfer

värmeöverföringsskrivare ⇨ electrothermal printer, thermal

växeldrift ⇨ alternate

växelriktare ⇨ inverter

växelstation ⇨ area

växelström ⇨ AC

växeltillstånd ⇨ alternate

växelvis tidsdelad ⇨ interleaved

Ww

wafer ['weɪfə] *subst.* thin round slice of a large single crystal of silicon onto which hundreds of individual integrated circuits are constructed, before being cut into individual chips *kiselskiva*

wafer scale integration ['weɪfə 'skeɪl ˌɪntɪ'greɪʃ(ə)n] *subst.* one large chip, the size of a wafer, made up of smaller integrated circuits connected together (these are still in the research stage) *helskiveintegration*

wait condition ['weɪt kən'dɪʃ(ə)n] *or* **state** ['steɪt] *subst.* state where a processor is not active, but waiting for input from peripherals *vänteläge*

waiting list ['weɪtɪŋlɪst] *subst. see* QUEUE

waiting state ['weɪtɪŋsteɪt] *subst.* computer state, in which a program requires an input *or* signal before continuing execution *vänteläge*

wait loop ['weɪtluːp] *subst.* processor that repeats one loop of program until some action occurs *vänteslinga*

wait time ['weɪttaɪm] *subst.* time delay between the moment when an instruction is given and the execution of the instruction *or* return of a result (such as the delay between a request for data and the data being transferred from memory) *väntetid*

wake up [weɪk 'ʌp] *vb.* to switch on *or* start *or* initiate *starta, aktivera;* **wake up a system** = code entered at a remote terminal to indicate to the central computer that someone is trying to log-on at that location *starta ett system*

walk through [wɔːk 'θruː] *vb.* to examine each step of a piece of software *stega igenom*

WAN ['dʌbljuːeɪ'en] = WIDE AREA NETWORK

wand [wɒnd] *subst.* bar code reader *or* optical device which is held in the hand to read bar codes on products in a store *streckkodsläspenna (med inbyggt minne)*

warm standby ['wɔːm 'stæn(d)baɪ] *subst.* secondary backup device that can be switched into action a short time after the main system fails *aktivt vänteläge; compare with* COLD STANDBY, HOT STANDBY

warm start ['wɔːm 'staːt] *subst.* restarting a programme which has stopped, but without losing any data *varmstart; compare* COLD START

warm up [wɔːm 'ʌp] *vb.* to allow a machine to stand idle for a time after switching on, to reach the optimum operating conditions *värma upp*

QUOTE warm-up time measures how long each printer takes to get ready to begin printing
Byte

warn [wɔːn] *vb.* to say that something dangerous is about to happen *varna;* to say that there is a possible danger *ge förvarning om;* **he warned the keyboarders that the system might become overloaded** NOTE: you warn someone **of** something, or **that** something may happen

warning ['wɔːnɪŋ] *subst.* notice of possible danger *varning;* **to issue a warning; warning notices were put up around the high powered laser; warning light =** (small light) which lights up to show that something dangerous may happen *varningslampa;* **when the warning light on the front panel comes on, switch off the system**

warrant ['wr(ə)nt] *vb.* to guarantee *garantera;* **all the spare parts are warranted**

warrantee [ˌwɒr(ə)n'tiː] *subst.* person who is given a warranty *garantitagare*

warrantor ['wɒr(ə)ntɔː] *subst.* person who gives a warranty *garant*

warranty ['wɒr(ə)ntɪ] *subst.* **(a)** guarantee *or* legal document which promises that a machine will work properly *or* that an item is of good quality *garanti;* **the printer is sold with a twelve-month warranty; the warranty covers spare parts but not labour costs (b)** promise in a contract *garanti, avtal;* **breach of warranty =** failing to do something which is a part of a contract *avtalsbrott*

wash PROM ['wɒʃ 'prom] *vb.* to erase the data from a PROM *radera ett läsminne*

waste instruction ['weɪst ɪn'strʌkʃ(ə)n] *subst.* instruction that does not carry out any action (except increasing the program counter to the location of next instruction) *blindinstruktion*

Watt [wɒt] *subst.* SI unit of measurement of electrical power, defined as power produced when one amp of current flows through a load that has one volt of voltage across it *enheten Watt*

wave [weɪv] *subst.* signal motion that rises and falls periodically as it travels through a medium *våg;* **microwave =** high frequency, short wavelength signals used

for communication links, such as an earth station to satellite link *mikrovåg;* **sound wave =** pressure wave that carries sound *ljudvåg*

waveform ['weɪvfɔːm] *subst.* shape of a wave *vågform;* **waveform digitization =** conversion and storing a waveform in numerical form using an A/D converter *vågformsdigitalisering*

waveguide ['weɪvgaɪd] *subst.* physical system used to direct waves in a particular direction (usually metal tubes for microwave signals *or* optical fibres for light signals) *vågledare*

wavelength ['weɪvleŋθ] *subst.* distance between two corresponding points of adjacent waves in a periodic waveform *våglängd;* defined as the speed of the wave divided by the frequency *våglängd*

WBFM ['dʌbljuːbiːefʼem] = WIDEBAND FREQUENCY MODULATION

weigh [weɪ] *vb.* **(a)** to measure how heavy something is *väga;* **he weighed the packet at the post office (b)** to have a certain weight *väga;* **the packet weighs twenty-five grams**

weighing machine ['weɪɪŋ mǝʃiːn] *subst.* machine which measures how heavy a thing *or* a person is *våg*

weight [weɪt] *subst.* measurement of how heavy something is *vikt;* **gross weight =** weight of both the container and its contents *bruttovikt;* **net weight =** weight of goods after deducting the packing material and container *nettovikt;* **paper weight =** amount which a certain quantity of paper weighs *papprets gramvikt;* **our paper weight is 70 - 90 gsm**

weighted ['weɪtɪd] *adj.* sorted according to importance *or* priority *viktad;* **weighted average =** average calculated taking several factors into account, giving some more value than others *viktat medeltal;* **weighted bit =** each bit having a different value depending on its position in a word *viktad bit*

weighting ['weɪtɪŋ] *subst.* **(a)** sorting of users, programs or data by their importance or priority *viktning, prioritering* **(b)** additional salary *or* wages paid to compensate for living in an expensive part of the country *storstadstillägg;* **salary plus a London weighting**

well-behaved ['welbɪ'heɪvd] *subst.* program that does not make any non-standard system calls, using only the standard BIOS input/output calls rather than directly addressing peripherals *or* memory *väluppfostrat program*

> COMMENT: if well-behaved, the software should work on all machines using the same operating system

wetware ['wetweə] *subst. US informal* the human brain *or* intelligence which writes software to be used with hardware *programmerare, programvaruutvecklare*

What-You-See-Is-All-You-Get (WYSIAYG) [,wɒtjuː'siːɪz,ɔːlju:'('wɪzɪ'eɪg)] *subst.* program where the output on screen cannot be printed out in any other form (that is, it cannot contain hidden print *or* formatting commands) *"vad du ser är allt du får"*

What-You-See-Is-What-You-Get (WYSIWYG) [,wɒtjuː'siːɪz,wɒtjuː'g('wɪzɪ'wɪg)] *subst.* program where the output on the screen is exactly the same as the output on printout, including graphics and special fonts *"vad du ser är vad du får"*

while-loop ['waɪlluːp] *subst.* conditional program instructions that carries out a loop while a condition is true *villkorlig slinga*

white [waɪt] *adj. & subst.* the colour of snow *vit;* **white flag** = signal indicating a new frame on a video disk *vit flagga;* **white level** = maximum TV signal strength corresponding to maximum brightness on the screen *vitnivå;* **white noise** = random noise that is of equal power at all frequencies *vitt brus;* **white writer** = laser printer which directs its laser beam on the points that are not printed *"vit skrivare"* NOTE: the opposite is **black writer**

> COMMENT: with a white writer, the black areas are printed evenly but edges and borders are not so sharp

wide angle lens ['waɪd,æŋgl 'lenz] *subst.* lens which has a large acceptance angle *vidvinkelobjektiv*

wide area network (WAN) ['waɪd 'eərɪə 'netwɜːk ('dʌbljuːeɪ'en)] *subst.* network where the various terminals are far apart and linked by radio, satellite and cable *globalt nät; compare with* LAN

> COMMENT: WANs use modems, radio and other long distance transmission methods; LANs use cables or optical fibre links

wideband ['waɪdbænd] *subst.* transmission with a bandwidth greater than that of a voice channel *bredbandsöverföring;* **wideband frequency modulation (WBFM)** = frequency modulation that uses a large frequency bandwidth and has more than one pair of sidebands *bredbandsfrekvensmodulering*

widow ['wɪdəʊ] *subst.* first line of a paragraph which is printed by itself at the bottom of a column *änka; compare* ORPHAN

width [wɪdθ] *subst.* size of something from edge to edge *bredd;* **page width** *or* **line width** = number of characters across a page *or* line *radbredd*

wild card ['waɪldkɑːd] *subst.* symbol that represents all files *or* names used when searching for data *ersättningstecken;* **a wild card can be used to find all file names beginning DIC**

WIMP [wɪmp] = WINDOW, ICON, MOUSE, POINTERS description of an integrated software system that is entirely operated using windows, icons and a mouse controlled pointer *fönsterorienterat användargränssnitt; see also* ENVIRONMENT

Winchester disk ['wɪn(t)ʃɪstə 'dɪsk] *or* **drive** *subst.* compact high-capacity hard disk which is usually built into a computer system and cannot be removed *winchesterminne, fast skivminne;* **removable Winchester** = small hard disk in a sealed unit, which can be detached from a computer when full *or* when not required *löstagbart skivminne*

window ['wɪndəʊ] **1** *subst.* (i) reserved section of screen used to display special information, that can be selected and looked at at any time and which overwrites information already on the screen *fönster;* (ii) part of a document currently displayed on a screen *fönsterinnehåll;* (iii) area of memory *or* access to a storage device *fönster;* **several remote stations are connected to the network and each has its own window onto the hard disk; the operating system will allow other programs to be displayed on-screen at the same time in different windows; active window** = area of the display screen where the operator is currently working *aktivt fönster, arbetsfönster;* **command window** = area of the screen that always displays the range of commands available *kommandofönster;* **the command window is a single line at the bottom of the screen; edit window** = area of the screen in which the user can display and edit text *or* graphics *redigeringsfönster;* **text window** = window in a graphics system, where the text is held in a small space on the screen before being allocated to a final area *textfönster;* **window, icon, mouse, pointer (WIMP)** = description of an integrated software system that is entirely operated using windows, icons and a mouse controlled pointer *fönsterorienterat användargränssnitt* **2** *vb.* to set up a section of screen by defining the coordinates of its corners, that allows information to be temporarily displayed, overwriting previous information but without altering information in the workspace *arbeta med fönster*

> QUOTE when an output window overlaps another, the interpreter does not save the contents of the obscured window
> **Personal Computer World**
> QUOTE you can connect more satellites to the network, each having its own window onto the hard disk
> **PC Plus**

windowing ['wɪndəʊɪŋ] *subst.* (i) action of setting up a window to show information on the screen *fönsterhantering;* (ii) displaying *or* accessing information via a window *fönsterhantering*

> QUOTE windowing facilities make use of virtual screens as well as physical screens
> **Byte**
> QUOTE the network system uses the latest windowing techniques
> **Desktop Publishing**
> QUOTE the functions are integrated via a windowing system with pull-down menus used to select different operations
> **Byte**

wipe [waɪp] *vb.* to clean data from a disk *radera;* **by reformatting you will wipe the disk clean**

wiper ['waɪpə] *subst.* movable arm in a potentiometer, a variable resistor *or* selector switch that can be turned to select a new resistance *or* function *rörlig kontakt (arm)*

wire ['waɪə] **1** *subst.* thin metal conductor *tråd, kabel;* **wire printer** = dot-matrix printer *matrisskrivare;* **wire wrap** = simple method of electrically connecting component terminals together using thin insulated wire wrapped around each terminal which is then soldered into place, usually used for prototype systems *virning* **2** *vb.* to install wiring *kabla, dra kabel;* **the studio is wired for sound; wired** *or* **hardwired program computer** = computer with a program built into the hardware which cannot be changed *dator med inbyggt program; see also* HARDWIRED

wireless ['waɪələs] **1** *subst. (old use)* device that can receive radio broadcasts *radio(mottagare)* **2** *adj.* communication system that does not require wires to carry signals *trådlös;* **wireless microphone** = audio microphone with a small transmitter attached allowing the transmission of signals without interconnecting wires *trådlös mikrofon*

wire tap ['waɪətæp] *subst.* unauthorized connection to a private communications line in order to listen to conversations *or* obtain private data *inkoppling för avlyssning*

wiring ['waɪərɪŋ] *subst.* series of wires *kabeldragning, kablage;* **the wiring in the system had to be replaced**

WISC [wɪsk] = WRITABLE INSTRUCTION SET COMPUTER CPU design that allows a programmer to add extra machine code instructions using microcode, to customize the instruction set *dator med ändringsbar instruktionsuppsättning*

woofer ['wuːfə] *subst. informal* large loudspeaker used to produce low frequency sounds *bashögtalare*

word [wɜːd] *subst.* **(a)** separate item of language, which is used with others to form speech *or* writing which can be understood *ord;* **words per minute (wpm** *or* **WPM)** = method of measuring the speed of a printer *ord per minut;* **word break** = division of a word at the end of a line, where part of the word is left on one line with a hyphen, and the rest of the word is taken over to begin the next line *avstavning;* **word count** = number of words in a file *or* text *ordräkning;* **word wrap** *or* **wraparound** = system in word processing where the operator does not have to indicate the line endings, but can keyboard continuously, leaving the program to insert word breaks and to continue the text on the next line *automatisk avstavning, radanpassning, radbrytning* **(b)** separate item of data on a computer, formed of a group of bits, stored in a single location in a memory *dataord;* **word length** = length of a computer word, counted as the number of bits *ordlängd;* **word mark** = symbol indicating the start of a word in a variable word length machine *ordmarkering;* **word serial** = data words transmitted along a parallel bus one after the other *ordserie;* **word time** = time taken to transfer a word from one memory area *or* device to another *ordhanteringstid*

word-process ['wɜːd'prəʊsəs] *vb.* to edit, store and manipulate text using a computer *ordbehandla;* **it is quite easy to read word-processed files**

word-processing (WP) ['wɜːd 'prəʊsesɪŋ (dʌbljuːˈpiː)] *subst.* using a computer to keyboard, edit, and output text, in the form of letters, labels, address lists, etc. *ordbehandling;* **load the word-processing program before you start keyboarding; word-processing bureau** = office which specializes in word-processing for other companies *skrivbyrå* NOTE: no plural

word-processor ['wɜːd,prəʊsesə] *subst.* **(a)** small computer *or* typewriter with a computer in it, used for word-processing text and documents *ordbehandlare* **(b)** word-processing package *or* program for a computer which allows the editing and manipulation and output of text, such as letters, labels, address lists, etc. *ordbehandlingsprogram*

work [wɜːk] **1** *subst.* things done using the hands *or* brain *arbete;* **work area** = memory space which is being used by an operator *arbetsarea;* **work disk** = disk on which current work is stored *arbetsskiva;* **work file** *or* **scratch file** temporary work area which is being used for current work *slaskfil;* **working store** *or* **scratch pad** = area of high-speed memory used for temporary storage of data in current use *slaskarea* NOTE: no plural **2** *vb.* to function *fungera, vara i drift;* **the computer system has never worked properly since it was installed**

working ['wɜːkɪŋ] *adj.* (something) which is operating correctly *fungerande*

workload ['wɜːkləʊd] *subst.* amount of work which a person *or* computer has to do *arbetsbörda, belastning, last;* **he has difficulty in dealing with his heavy workload**

workplace ['wɜːkpleɪs] *subst.* place where you work *arbetsplats*

work-sharing ['wɜːkˌʃeərɪŋ] *subst.* system where two part-timers share one job *arbetsdelning*

workspace ['wɜːkspeɪs] *subst.* space in memory, which is available for use *or* is being used currently by an operator *arbetsarea*

workstation ['wɜːkˌsteɪʃn] *subst.* place where a computer user works, with a terminal, printer, modem, etc. *arbetsstation;* **the system includes five workstations linked together in a ring network; the archive storage has a total capacity of 1200 Mb between seven workstations**

QUOTE an image processing workstation must provide three basic facilities: the means to digitize, display and manipulate the image data

Byte

WORM [wɜːm] = WRITE ONCE READ MANY times memory

wow [waʊ] *subst.* fluctuation of the frequency of a recorded signal at playback, (usually caused by uneven tape movement) *(långsam) svajning*

WP ['dʌblju:'pi:] = WORD-PROCESSING

WPM ['dʌblju:pi:'em] *or* **wpm** = WORDS PER MINUTE

wrap [ræp] *subst.* **omega wrap** = system of threading video tape round a video head (the tape passes over most of the circular head and is held in place by two small rollers *omega-matning*

wraparound ['ræpəraʊnd] *or* **word wrap** ['wɜːdˌræp] *subst.* system in word-processing where the operator does not have to indicate the line endings, but can keyboard continuously, leaving the program to insert word breaks and to continue the text on the next line *automatisk avstavning, radanpassning, radbrytning;* **horizontal wraparound** = movement of a cursor on a computer display from the end of one line to the beginning of the next *horisontell radbrytning*

writable instruction set computer (WISC) ['raɪtəbl ɪn'strʌkʃ(ə)n set kəm'pjuːtə (wɪsk)] *subst.* CPU design that allows a programmer to add extra machine code instructions using microcode, to customize the instruction set *dator med ändringsbar instruktionsuppsättning*

write [raɪt] *vb.* **(a)** to put words *or* figures on to paper *skriva, rita;* **she wrote a letter of complaint to the manager; the telephone number is written at the bottom of the notepaper (b)** to put text *or* data onto a disk *or* tape *skriva, lagra;* **access time is the time taken to read from** *or* **write to a location in memory; write head** = transducer that can write data onto a magnetic medium *skrivhuvud;* **write once, read many times memory (WORM)** = optical disk storage system that allows one writing action but many reading actions in its life *skrivbart optiskt läsminne;* **writing pad** = special device which allows a computer to read in handwritten characters which have been written onto a special pad *skrivskiva; see* OCR; **write time** = time between requesting data transfer to a storage location and it being written *skrivtid* NOTE: you write data **to** a file. Note also: **writing - wrote - has written**

write-permit ring ['raɪtˌpəmɪt'rɪŋ] *subst.* ring on a reel of magnetic tape which allows the tape to be overwritten *or* erased *skrivning*

write protect ['raɪt prə'tekt] *vb.* to make it impossible to write to a floppy disk *or* tape by moving a special write-protect tab *skrivskydd;* **write-protect tab** = tab on a floppy disk which if moved, prevents any writing to *or* erasing from the disk *skrivskyddsetikett*

writer ['raɪtə] *subst. see* BLACK, WHITE

writing ['raɪtɪŋ] *subst.* something which has been written *skrift;* **to put the agreement in writing; he has difficulty in reading my writing** NOTE: no plural

WYSIAYG ['wɪzɪ'eɪg] = WHAT YOU SEE IS ALL YOU GET

WYSIWYG ['wɪzɪ'wɪg] = WHAT YOU SEE IS WHAT YOU GET

Xx

paper between given coordinates *x-y*-skrivare, kurvritare

X [eks] = EXTENSION

X-axis ['eks'æksɪs] *subst.* horizontal axis of a graph *x-axel*

X-coordinate ['ekskəʊ'ɔːdnət] *subst.* horizontal axis position coordinate *x-koordinat*

X direction ['eks 'dɪ'rekʃ(ə)n] *subst.* movement horizontally *horisontell rörelse*

X distance ['eks 'dɪst(ə)ns] *subst.* distance along an X-axis from an origin *horisontellt avstånd, sträcka längs x-axeln*

xerographic printer [ˌzɪərə'græfɪk 'prɪntə] printer (such as a photocopier) where charged ink is attracted to areas of a charged picture *xerografisk skrivare, laserskrivare*

xerography [zɪə'rɒgrəfi] *subst.* copying method that relies on ink being attracted to dark regions of a charged picture *xerografi*

Xerox ['zɪərɒks] **1** *subst.* **(a)** trademark for a type of photocopier *varumärke för en typ av kopieringsmaskin, XEROX-;* **to make a xerox copy of a letter; we must order some more xerox paper for the copier; we are having a new xerox machine installed tomorrow (b)** photocopy made with a xerox machine *fotokopia;* **to send the other party a xerox of the contract; we have sent xeroxes to each of the agents 2** *vb.* to make a photocopy with a xerox machine *fotokopiera;* **to xerox a document; she xeroxed all the file**

x punch ['eks'pʌn(t)ʃ] *subst.* card punch for column 11, often used to represent a negative number *kortstans för kolumn 11 på hålkort*

X-ray ['eksreɪ] *subst.* **(a)** ray with a very short length, which is invisible, but can go through soft tissue and register as a photograph on a film *röntgen;* **X-ray imaging =** showing images of the inside of a body using X-rays *röntgenfotografering* **(b)** photograph taken using X-rays *röntgenfotografi;* **the medical text is illustrated with X-ray photographs**

X-series ['eks 'sɪəriːz] *subst.* recommendations for data communications over public data networks *standarder för datakommunikation (X.11, X.25 etc.), CCITT-standard*

X-Y ['eks 'waɪ] *subst.* coordinates for drawing a graph, where X is the vertical and Y the horizontal value *x-y-koordinater;* **X-Y plotter =** device for drawing lines on

Yy

yaw [jɔː] *subst.* rotation of satellite about a vertical axis with the earth *vridning*

Y-axis ['waɪ'æksɪs] *subst.* vertical axis of a graph *y-axel*

Y-coordinate ['waɪkəʊ'ɔːdnət] *subst.* vertical axis position coordinate *y-koordinat*

Y direction ['waɪ dɪ'rekʃ(ə)n] *subst.* vertical movement *vertikal rörelse*

Y distance ['waɪ'dɪst(ə)ns] *subst.* distance along an Y-axis from an origin *vertikalt avstånd, sträcka längs y-axeln*

yoke [jəʊk] *subst.* **deflection yoke =** magnetic coils around a TV tube used to control the position of the picture beam *avlänkningsspole*

y punch ['waɪ'pʌn(t)ʃ] *subst.* card punch for column 12 (often used to indicate a positive number) *kortstans för kolumn 12 på hålkort*

yttre diskettenhet ⇨ **external**

yttre klocka ⇨ **external**

yttre minne ⇨ **external, memory**

yttre register ⇨ **external**

yttre sekundärminne ⇨ **external**

yttre sortering ⇨ **external**

Zz

Z [zed] = IMPEDANCE

zap [zæp] *vb.* to wipe off all data currently in the workspace *skjuta med strålpistol, döda, radera;* **he pressed CONTROL Z and zapped all the text**

z-axis ['zed'æksɪs] *subst.* axis for depth in a three-dimensional graph *or* plot *z-axel*

zero ['zɪərəʊ] **1** *subst.* (i) the digit 0 *nolla;* (ii) equivalent of logical off or false state *falskt tillstånd, logiskt från-tillstånd;* **the code for international calls is zero one zero (010); jump on zero =** conditional jump executed if a flag *or* register is zero *villkorligt hopp om noll gäller;* **zero**

compression *or* **zero suppression** = shortening of a file by the removal of unnecessary zeros *nollundertryckning (grupp III-kodning);* **zero flag** = indicator that the contents of a register or result is zero *nollflagga;* **the jump on zero instruction tests the zero flag; zero-level address** *or* **immediate address** = instruction in which the address is the operand *direktoperand* **2** *vb.* to erase *or* clear a file *radera, nollställa;* **to zero a device** = to erase the contents of a programmable device *nollställa en periferienhet;* **to zero fill** = to fill a section of memory with zero values *fylla med nollor*

zero insertion force (ZIF) ['zɪərəʊ ɪn'sɜːʃ(ə)n 'fɔːs ('zedaɪ'ef)] *subst.* chip socket that has movable connection terminals, allowing the chip to be inserted with no force, then a small lever is turned to grip the legs of the chip *ZIF-kontakt, kretskontakt med hävstängsdragen fjäder*

ZIF ['zedaɪ'ef] = ZERO INSERTION FORCE

zip code ['zɪpkəʊd] *subst.* US letters and numbers used to indicate a town *or* street in an address on an envelope *postnummer*
NOTE: the GB English for this is **post code**

zone [zəʊn'] *subst.* region *or* part of a screen defined for specialized printing *zon;* **hot zone** = text area to the left of the right margin in a word-processed document, if a word does not fit completely into the line, a hyphen is automatically inserted *avstavningszon*

zoom [zuːm] *vb.* (i) to change the focal length of a lens to enlarge the object in the viewfinder *zooma;* (ii) to enlarge an area of text (to make it easier to work on) *zooma*

QUOTE there are many options to allow you to zoom into an area for precision work
Electronics & Wireless World
QUOTE any window can be zoomed to full-screen size by pressing the F-5 function key
Byte

zooming ['zuːmɪŋ] *subst.* enlarging an area of text *or* graphics *zoomning;* **variable zooming from 25% to 400% of actual size**

zoom lens ['zuːmlenz] *subst.* lens whose focal length can be varied to make an object larger in the viewfinder *zoomobjektiv*

Åå

återförsäljare ⇨ dealer

återgå ⇨ revert

återhopp ⇨ return

återhämtning ⇨ recovery

återkommande ⇨ continual, continually

återkoppling ⇨ feedback

återkopplingskontroll ⇨ loop

återkopplingsslinga ⇨ feedback

återlagra ⇨ resave

återspegling ⇨ reflection

återspelning ⇨ replay

återställa ⇨ initialize, reset

återsökning av data ⇨ retrieval

åtkomst ⇨ access

åtkomstbegränsning ⇨ exclusion, fetch

åtkomstkod ⇨ access

åtkomstkontroll ⇨ access control

åtkomsttid ⇨ acceleration time, access time, memory

åttatumsdiskett ⇨ eight-inch disk

Ää

ändra ⇨ alter, change

änka ⇨ widow

äventyrsspel ⇨ adventure game

Öö

överbliven ⇨ residual

överföring ⇨ transcription, transmission

överföring, långsam ⇨ low frequency (LF)

överföringsfel ⇨ transmission

överföringsflagga ⇨ flag

överföringshastighet ⇨ data, transfer, transmission

överföringskanal ⇨ transmission

överföringskontroll ⇨ transfer

överföringsmedier ⇨ transmission

överföringsorder ⇨ transfer

överföringsprogram ⇨ link

överföringsstyrning ⇨ transfer

överföringstid ⇨ transfer

övergående fel ⇨ error, transient

övergående (läs)fel ⇨ error

övergång ⇨ junction, transition

övergångsskikt ⇨ junction

överhörning ⇨ babble, crosstalk

överlagrad ⇨ interleaved

överlagring ⇨ interleaving

överlagringssegment ⇨ overlay

överlappning ⇨ interleaving, lap

överordnad ⇨ master

överslag(sberäkning) ⇨ calculation

översättare ⇨ interpreter, language

översättningsprogram ⇨ language, translator (program)

överton ⇨ harmonic

övervakande dator ⇨ master

övervakningsfunktion ⇨ monitor

övervakningsinstruktion ⇨ instruction

övervakningsprogram ⇨ executive

COMPUTER AND PERIPHERALS

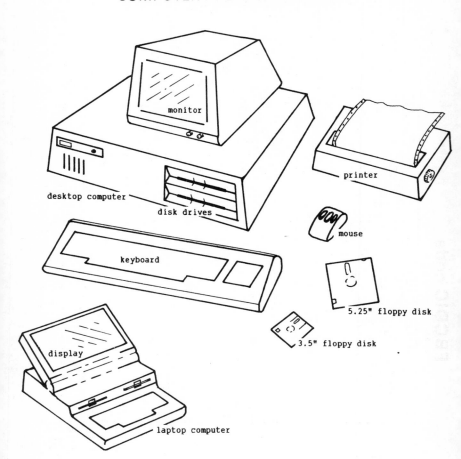

EBCDIC code

bits 0, 1, 2, 3 (columns) — bits 4, 5, 6, 7 (rows)

bits 4,5,6,7 \ bits 0,1,2,3	0	1	2	3	4	5	6	7	8	9	10	11	12	13	14	15
0	NUL	DLE			SP	&	-									0
1	SOH	DC_1					/		a	j			A	J		1
2	STX	DC_2		SYN					b	k	s		B	K	S	2
3	ETX	DC_3							c	l	t		C	L	T	3
4									d	m	u		D	M	U	4
5	HT	NL	LF						e	n	v		E	N	V	5
6	LC	BS	ETB						f	o	w		F	O	W	6
7	DEL		ESC	EOT					g	p	x		G	P	X	7
8									h	q	y		H	Q	Y	8
9									i	r	z		I	R	Z	9
10	RPT				¢	!	¦	:								
11	VT				.	$	,	#								
12	FF	IFS		DC_4	<	*	%	@								
13	CR	IGS	ENQ	NAK	(	)	_	'								
14		IRS	ACK		+	;	>	=								
15			BEL		|	¬	?	"								

SINGLE BUS COMPUTER

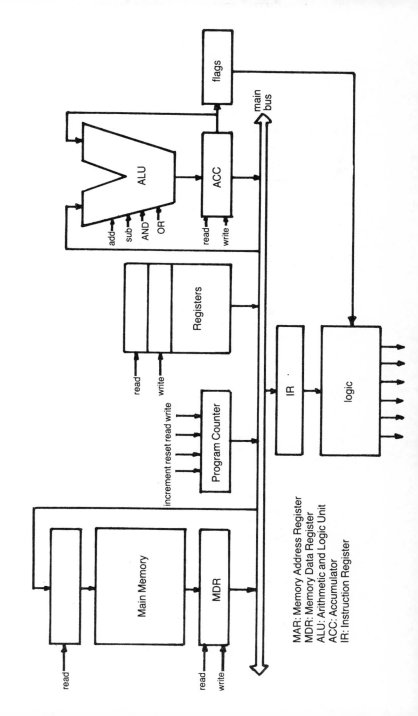

MAR: Memory Address Register
MDR: Memory Data Register
ALU: Arithmetic and Logic Unit
ACC: Accumulator
IR: Instruction Register

RS232 SIGNALS

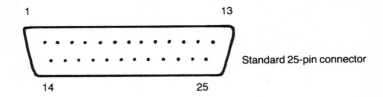

Standard 25-pin connector

Pin	Description	Name
1	frame ground	FG
2	transmit data to equipment	TxD
3	receive data from equipment	RxD
4	request to send	RTS
5	clear to send	CTS
6	data set ready	DSR
7	signal ground	SG
8	data carrier detect	DCD
9	positive DC test voltage	+V
10	negative DC test voltage	−V
11	equalizer mode	QM
12	secondary DCD	(S)DCD
13	secondary clear to send	(S)CTS
14	secondary transmit data	(S)TxD
15	transmitter clock	TxC
16	secondary receive data	(S)RD
17	receiver clock	RxC
18	not used	
19	secondary RTS	(S)RTS
20	data terminal ready	DTR
21	signal quality detect	SQ
22	ring indicator	RI
23	data rate selector	
24	external transmitter clock	(TC)
25	not used	

PROGRAMMING LANGUAGES

The following demonstrates the differences in programming languages for a similar function, an input, n, is requested (the number of entries in the list) then a loop asking for the next entry and comparing it with the current biggest number is repeated n times, the biggest entry is then printed out.

ALGOL

```
begin    integer n,x,q;
         q:=0;
         read n;
         for i:=1 step 1 until n do
         begin
         B:      read x;
                 if x>00 then
                 goto A;
                 if x>q then
                     q:=x;
                 goto B;
         A:      print q;
         end;
end
```

BASIC

```
5 BIG=0
10 INPUT"How many numbers ";N
20 FOR I=1 TO N
30 INPUT X
40 IF X=0 THEN GOTO 100
50 IF X>BIG THEN BIG=X
60 NEXT I
100 PRINT BIG
110 END
```

C

```c
main()
{
        int n,i,x,big;
        scanf(%d,&n);
        (for(i = 0; i < n; i++)
        {
                scanf("%d",&x);
                if (x > big)
                        big=x;
        }
        printf("%d",big);
}
```

FORTRAN

```fortran
        INTEGER BIG
        BIG=0
        READ,N
        DO 2 I=1,N
        READ,X
2       IF (X.GT.BIG)BIG=X
        PRINT,BIG
        STOP
        END
```

PASCAL

```pascal
program bignum(input,output);
var n,i,x,big : integer;
begin
        big := 0;
        read (n);
        for i:=1 to n do;
        begin
                read(x);
                if x > big then big:=x
        end;
        write(big)
end
```

ASCII IN DECIMAL, HEXADECIMAL

dec.	HEX	CHAR	dec.	HEX	CHAR	dec.	HEX	CHAR	dec.	HEX	CHAR
0	00	NUL	32	20	SP	64	40	@	96	60	
1	01	SOH	33	21	!	65	41	A	97	61	a
2	02	STX	34	22	"	66	42	B	98	62	b
3	03	ETX	35	23	#	67	43	C	99	63	c
4	04	EOT	36	24	$	68	44	D	100	64	d
5	05	ENQ	37	25	%	69	45	E	101	65	e
6	06	ACK	38	26	&	70	46	F	102	66	f
7	07	BEL	39	27	'	71	47	G	103	67	g
8	08	BS	40	28	(	72	48	H	104	68	h
9	09	HT	41	29	)	73	49	I	105	69	i
10	0A	LF	42	2A	*	74	4A	J	106	6A	j
11	0B	VT	43	2B	+	75	4B	K	107	6B	k
12	0C	FF	44	2C	,	76	4C	L	108	6C	l
13	0D	CR	45	2D	-	77	4D	M	109	6D	m
14	0E	SO	46	2E	.	78	4E	N	110	6E	n
15	0F	SI	47	2F	/	79	4F	O	111	6F	o
16	10	DLE	48	30	0	80	50	P	112	70	p
17	11	DC1	49	31	1	81	51	Q	113	71	q
18	12	DC2	50	32	2	82	52	R	114	72	r
19	13	DC3	51	33	3	83	53	S	115	73	s
20	14	DC4	52	34	4	84	54	T	116	74	t
21	15	NAK	53	35	5	85	55	U	117	75	u
22	16	SYN	54	36	3	86	56	V	118	76	v
23	17	ETB	55	37	7	87	57	W	119	77	w
24	18	CAN	56	38	8	88	58	X	120	78	x
25	19	EM	57	39	9	89	59	Y	121	79	y
26	1A	SUB	58	3A	:	90	5A	Z	122	7A	z
27	1B	ESC	59	3B	;	91	5B	[	123	7B	{
28	1C	FS	60	3C	<	92	5C	\	124	7C	¦
29	1D	GS	61	3D	=	93	5D	]	125	7D	}
30	1E	RS	62	3E	>	94	5E	↑	126	7E	~
31	1F	US	63	3F	?	95	5F	_	127	7F	DEL

THE ASCII SYMBOLS

NUL	Null	DLE	Data Link Escape
SOH	Start of Heading	DC	Device Control
STX	Start of Text	NAK	Negative Acknowledge
ETX	End of Text	SYN	Synchronous Idle
EOT	End of Transmission	ETB	End of Transmission Block
ENQ	Enquiry	CAN	Cancel
ACK	Acknowledge	EM	End of Medium
BEL	Bell	SUB	Substitute
BS	Backspace	ESC	Escape
HT	Horizontal Tabulation	FS	File Separator
LF	Line Feed	GS	Group Separator
VT	Vertical Tabulation	RS	Record Separator
FF	Form Feed	US	Unit Separator
CR	Carriage Return	SP	Space (Blank)
SO	Shift Out	DEL	Delete
SI	Shift In		

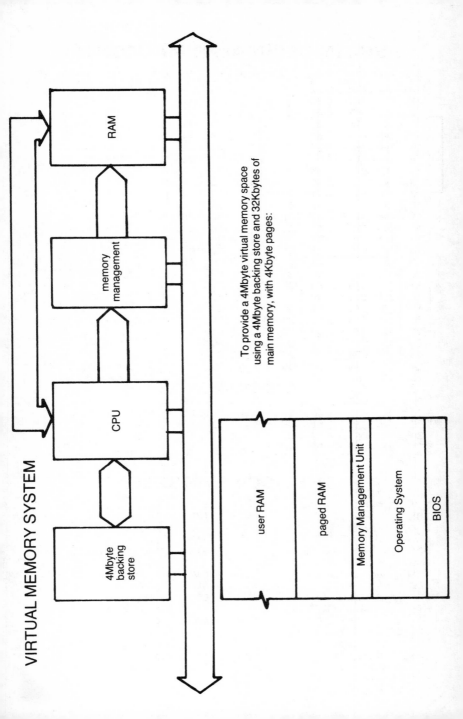

VIRTUAL MEMORY SYSTEM

4Mbyte backing store

CPU

memory management

RAM

To provide a 4Mbyte virtual memory space using a 4Mbyte backing store and 32Kbytes of main memory, with 4Kbyte pages:

user RAM

paged RAM

Memory Management Unit

Operating System

BIOS

HANDSHAKING

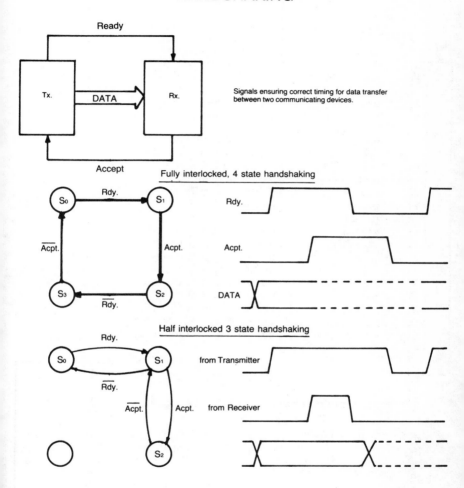

Signals ensuring correct timing for data transfer between two communicating devices.

Fully interlocked, 4 state handshaking

Half interlocked 3 state handshaking

SI UNITS AND ABBREVIATIONS

A	ampere	unit of electrical current
C	coulomb	unit of electrical charge (As)
cd	candela	unit of light intensity
F	farad	unit of capacitance (C/V)
H	henry	unit of inductance (Vs/A)
Hz	hertz	unit of frquency (cycles per second)
J	joule	unit of energy (kg m/s)
K	kelvin	unit of temperature
kg	kilogram	unit of mass
lm	lumen	unit of illumination (cd/sr)
lx	lux	unit of illumination density (lm/m^2)
m	metre	unit of length
mol	mole	unit of amount of substance
N	newton	unit of force (J/m)
Pa	pascal	unit of pressure
rad	radian	unit of plane angle
s	second	unit of time
sr	steradian	unit of solid angle
S	siemens	unit of electrical conductance (1/ohm)
T	tesla	unit of magnetic flux density (WB/m)
V	volt	unit of electrical potential (W/A)
W	watt	unit of power (J/s)
Wb	weber	unit of magnetic flux (Vs)
Ω	ohm	unit of electrical resistance (V/A)
C	degree Celsius	unit of temperature (K+273)

SI PREFIXES

Decimal multiples and submultiples to be used with SI units

prefix	symbol	factor	prefix	symbol	factor
tera-	T	10^{12}	centi-	c	10^{-2}
giga-	G	10^{9}	milli-	m	10^{-3}
mega-	M	10^{6}	micro-	μ	10^{-6}
kilo	k	10^{3}	nano-	n	10^{-9}
hecto-	h	10^{2}	pico-	p	10^{-12}
deda-	da	10^{1}	femto-	f	10^{-15}
deci-	d	10^{-1}	atto-	a	10^{-18}

MOST USED RS232C SIGNALS

pin	description	acronym
1	frame ground	FG
2	trasmit data to equipment	TxD
3	receive data from equipment	RxD
4	request to send	RTS
5	clear to send	CTS
6	data set ready	DSR
7	signal ground	SG
8	data carrier detect	DCD
13	secondary clear to send	(S)CTS
14	secondary transmit data	(S)TxD
15	transmitter clock	TxC
17	receiver clock	RxC
20	data terminal ready	DTR
22	ring indicator	RI
24	external transmitter clock	(TC)

IMPORTANT IEEE-488 BUS SIGNALS

line	name	comments
D101		
D102		
D103		
D104	DATA LINES	data carrying lines
D105		
D106		
D107		
D108		
DAV	DATA VALID	true if data is valid
NRFD	NOT READY FOR DATA	false when all devices are ready
NDAC	NOT DATA ACCEPTED	false when all devices have accepted data
ATN	ATTENTION	data line is carrying an address
IFC	INTERFACE CLEAR	reset signal
SRQ	SERVICE REQUEST	interrupt signal
REN	REMOTE ENABLE	
EOI	END OR IDENTIFY	end of message signal

DECIMAL CONVERSION TABLES

Decimal	BCD	Binary	Octal	Hexadecimal
base 10	2	2	8	16
00	0000 0000	0000	00	0
01	0000 0001	0001	01	1
02	0000 0010	0010	02	2
03	0000 0011	0011	03	3
04	0000 0100	0100	04	4
05	0000 0101	0101	05	5
06	0000 0110	0110	06	6
07	0000 0111	0111	07	7
08	0000 1000	1000	10	8
09	0000 1001	1001	11	9
10	0001 0000	1010	12	A
11	0001 0001	1011	13	B
12	0001 0010	1100	14	C
13	0001 0011	1101	15	D
14	0001 0100	1110	16	E
15	0001 0101	1111	17	F

INTERNATIONAL STANDARD SIZES FOR PAPER

$$A0 = 1189 \times 841 \text{ mm}$$
$$A1 = 841 \times 594 \text{ mm}$$
$$A2 = 594 \times 420 \text{ mm}$$
$$A3 = 420 \times 297 \text{ mm}$$
$$A4 = 297 \times 210 \text{ mm}$$
$$A5 = 210 \times 148 \text{ mm}$$
$$A6 = 148 \times 105 \text{ mm}$$
$$A7 = 105 \times 74 \text{ mm}$$
$$A8 = 74 \times 52 \text{ mm}$$
$$A9 = 52 \times 37 \text{ mm}$$
$$A10 = 37 \times 26 \text{ mm}$$

LOGIC FUNCTION TABLES AND GATES

Written as	Drawn as	logic table

A

A	A
0	0
1	1

A AND B

A	B	A∗B
0	0	0
0	1	0
1	0	0
1	1	1

A OR B

A	B	A+B
0	0	0
0	1	1
1	0	1
1	1	1

A EXOR B

A	B	A exor B
0	0	0
0	1	1
1	0	1
1	1	0

NOT A

A	$\overline{A}$
0	1
1	0

A NAND B

A	B	$\overline{A∗B}$
0	0	1
0	1	1
1	0	1
1	1	0

A NOR B

A	B	$\overline{A+B}$
0	0	1
0	1	0
1	0	0
1	1	0

A EXNOR B

A	B	A exnor B
0	0	1
0	1	0
1	0	0
1	1	1

OTHER CIRCUIT SYMBOLS

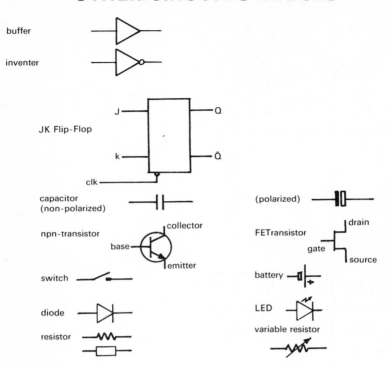

buffer

inverter

JK Flip-Flop

capacitor (non-polarized)

(polarized)

npn-transistor

collector

base

emitter

FETransistor

drain

gate

source

switch

battery

diode

LED

resistor

variable resistor

RESISTOR COLOUR CODING TABLES

colour	band 1 digit 1	band 2 digit 2	band 3 multiplier	band 4 tolerence
black	0	0	×1	
brown	1	1	×10	1%
red	2	2	×100	2%
orange	3	3	×1000	
yellow	4	4	×10000	
green	5	5	×100000	
blue	6	6	×1000000	
violet	7	7		
grey	8	8		
white	9	9		
gold			×0.1	5%
silver			×0.01	10%
none				20%

EXAMPLE:
brown black brown gold = 10 × 10 = 100 Ohms at 5%
red   green red   red = 25 × 100 = 2.5 KOhms at 2%

TYPES OF MODULATION

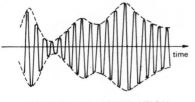

AMPLITUDE MODULATION

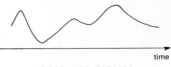

ORIGINAL SIGNAL

FREQUENCY MODULATION

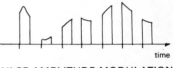

PULSE AMPLITUDE MODULATION

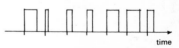

PULSE WIDTH MODULATION

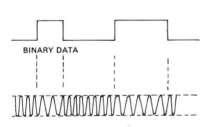

FSK of binary data

PULSE POSITION MODULATION

77

173

180

204

275

308